Criminal Procedure

Criminal Procedure

Joel Samaha

University of Minnesota

WEST PUBLISHING CO.
St. Paul • New York • Los Angeles • San Francisco

Copyeditor: Barbara Bergstrom
Composition: Carlisle Communications
Cover Photo: Courtesy of Wesley Bocxe/Photo Researchers, Inc.

COPYRIGHT © 1990 By WEST PUBLISHING COMPANY
50 W. Kellogg Boulevard
P.O. Box 64526
St. Paul, MN 55164-1003

Printed in the United States of America

97 96 95 94 93 92 91 90   8 7 6 5 4 3 2 1 0

Library of Congress Cataloging-in-Publication Data

Samaha, Joel.
    Criminal procedure / Joel Samaha.
      p.   cm.
    ISBN 0-314-57875-7
    1. Criminal procedure—United States.   I. Title.
KF9616.S26   1990
345.73′05—dc20
[347.3055]

89–36521
CIP

To My Students

Contents

Chapter Six   Other Searches and Seizures   *260*

Chapter Seven   Interrogation and Confessions   *328*

Chapter Eight   Identification Procedures   368

Chapter Nine   The Decision to Charge and the First Appearance   396

Chapter Twelve   Conviction by Trial and Guilty Plea   522

Table of Cases

Preface

Criminal Procedure results from thirty years of interest and more than twenty years of research and teaching in the subject. In 1958, Professors Claude Sowle and Fred Inbau, Northwestern University Law School, introduced me to the fascinating study of government power to enforce the criminal law in a free society. In 1968, I began research for my *Law and Order in Historical Perspective,* a monograph that reconstructed the criminal process in Elizabethan England. Since 1970, both at UCLA and at the University of Minnesota, I have taught undergraduate, graduate, and law students, and criminal justice professionals the history of, and the law of, criminal procedure.

I have loved teaching criminal procedure and its history over these two decades. However, I have *not* enjoyed the teaching materials available to do so. I have had either to use law school casebooks, which are totally unsuited for undergraduates, or textbooks that do not include the stimulating cases so central to teaching the law of criminal procedure. Or, I have collected cases myself, edited them, and reproduced them for students to read. The success of *Criminal Law,* now in its third edition, convinced me to write a criminal procedure book along the general lines of *Criminal Law*—a combined case and textbook specifically designed for undergraduates and other *non*-law students. I have used *Criminal Procedure* now three times in manuscript with great success at the University of Minnesota.

Four themes run through *Criminal Procedure,* recurrent themes in the history of both American and English law, from which our criminal procedure derives. These themes provide the overarching organizational framework of *Criminal Procedure:*

1. **The criminal process constitutes a series of decision points that result both in increasing expenditure of government resources and greater intrusions and deprivations to individuals.**

2. **The Constitution requires that a proper purpose and a sufficient factual foundation, or objective basis, support decisions resulting in government expenditure and deprivation to citizens. The government cannot use its power to enforce the criminal law on whim, hunch, or mere suspicion.**

3. **Formal rules and informal discretion characterize decision making in the criminal process.**

4. **Criminal procedure promotes and balances a range of sometimes conflicting interests: legal, organizational, societal, and political.** These interests include not only the legal interests in obtaining the correct result and procedural regularity, but also the organizational interests in efficiency, economy, and predictability; the ideological interests in individual rights and privacy on the one hand, and crime control on the other; and the democratic interest in community participation in the administration of criminal justice.

Criminal Procedure balances text, cases, and other materials dealing with the constitutional authority—and limits upon it—to enforce the criminal law. Chapters 1 and 2 introduce students to the law of criminal procedure within the context of the themes that run throughout the criminal process, and to the constitutional principles— particularly due process of law and federalism—that govern the whole administration of criminal justice. Chapter 3 surveys the range of procedural and substantive remedies available when the government exceeds its authority to enforce the law, including the exclusionary rule, dismissal, the entrapment defense, reversal of convictions, civil suits for damages and injunctions, and internal disciplinary mechanisms.

Virtually all criminal procedure cases involve either an issue of excluding evidence or some other remedy a criminal defendant seeks. I have found that students fare better in the rest of the course if they understand early on what the specific reason for the appeal in the case involves. Therefore, I thought it best to place the remedies chapter early in the book. However, I have designed the book so that each chapter stands independent of the others. Hence, instructors can teach chapter 3, the remedies chapter, anywhere they wish to fit it into their syllabus. Moreover, I have put all the exclusionary materials first in the chapter. For those who do not have the time, or for other reasons do not wish to teach the other remedies, the exclusionary rule segment stands on its own in the chapter.

The first theme—a series of decision points resulting in greater intrusions and heavier expenditures—has determined the sequence of chapters 4 through 12. These chapters arrange the materials on the law of criminal procedure in a chronology from the earliest encounters between police and citizens on the street prior to arrest, move into the actions that occur in the police station, to the decisions to charge, to prosecute, to try, and finally, to either convict or acquit citizens charged with crimes. The only unusual elements in this arrangement are (1) that stop and frisk precedes arrest and other searches and seizures; (2) the discussion of the right to counsel appears when counsel is appointed in most criminal cases—at the first appearance; and (3) double jeopardy and some other general principles are discussed when these issues usually arise—at the pretrial motion stage in the criminal process. As in the remedies chapter, however, the chapters stand independent of each other. It is possible, and I have done so, to teach chapter 6, "Other Searches and Seizures," or chapter 5, "Seizure of Persons: Arrest," first, and then chapter 4, "Initial Police Citizen Encounters: Stop and Frisk," last as "other searches and seizures."

Sometimes, criminal procedure courses, particularly undergraduate ones, teach only arrest, search, identification, and interrogation. In other words, they focus exclusively on police procedures. *Criminal Procedure* lends itself well to this type of course, since the chapters stand independent of each other. Moreover, the chapters on police practices, in conjunction with the general principles, themes, and remedies chapters, constitute a unified segment that does not require the materials on the period following interrogation and identification procedures. Such courses—and chapters 1 through 7—however, leave a large gap in students' understanding of the criminal process. The remaining chapters should adequately fill that gap. I have written them in such a manner that students can read them independently to fill out their knowledge of criminal procedure.

The text and cases, although they complement each other, also stand independent of each other in the sense that students could read the cases without the text, guided by the **Case Question** that introduces, and the **Case Discussion** that follows every case. The **Case Question** focuses on the major issue in the case, and the **Case Discussion** briefly summarizes the case and asks questions directed at both the specific issue in the case and the general themes, particularly the balance of interests arising in the case. The text also stands independent of the cases. Students can read the text without the cases; the text is self-sufficient.

The best way, and I have found the most effective way, to use the book is as a case-textbook because the text enriches the understanding of the cases, and the cases enhance the understanding of the text. The cases are not intended as mere examples, illustrations, or gimmicks; they are central to showing the elaboration of points of law and broader interests that every case balances and promotes. The text takes a broad view of the law of criminal procedure. The cases, although of course *law* cases, reflect wider sociological and ideological influences. Therefore, the text and cases reinforce this complementary approach—law and society, not simply formal law, or informal law in action.

Criminal procedure, however organized and presented, is a complex subject containing many technical concepts, terms, and phrases. I have tried to help students work through these complexities and technical terms primarily through the prose in the text, and through careful editing of cases. In addition, *Criminal Procedure* includes a variety of special aids to understanding. Each chapter begins with a **Chapter Outline,** and a listing of **Chapter Main Points.** Then follows a list of **Chapter Key Terms** with definitions of those terms. All these terms are bold-faced in the text and appear, along with other terms useful to students, in a **Glossary** at the end of the book. Each chapter ends with a **Summary** of the main points in the chapter, and **Questions for Discussion and Review.** Students have regularly commented that the combination of chapter outline, main points, and key terms at the beginning, and the summary and discussion and review questions at the end, has helped them immensely to understand the materials in the text and cases.

I am grateful to the following reviewers for their thoughtful, provocative, often blunt, and always helpful comments on the various stages of the manuscript of *Criminal Procedure:* Richard E. Givan, Eastern Kentucky University; Robert A. Harvie, Montana State University; Beth Hogan, North Shore Community College; Finn Hornum, LaSalle University; Barton L. Ingraham, University of Maryland; Thomas Lenahan, Herkimer Community College; Kenneth K. Marcus, Sonoma State University; Paul A. Mastriacovo; William F. Michelek, Cochise College; Patrick A. Mueller, Stephen A. Austin University; Charles E. Myers III, Aims Community College; Nancy L. Peterson, Fox Valley Technical College; Robert R. Reinertsen, Western Illinois University; Neil F. Rogers, Northern Arizona University; James D. Stinchcomb, Miami-Dade Community College; John J. Sullivan, Mercy College; Thomas D. Todd, Carl Sandberg College; Donald H. Wallace, Central Missouri State University; and Roger Wright, University of Cincinnati.

University of Minnesota students—undergraduate, graduate, law, and professional criminal justice personnel—enrolled in my criminal procedure course have all enhanced *Criminal Procedure* by their stimulating questions, their lively discussions, and their willingness to tell me frankly, bluntly, and sometimes even irreverently, what they did and did *not* like about the manuscript versions they have used over the past several terms. My past teachers, without even knowing it, have also contributed to *Criminal Procedure.* Professors Claude Sowle and Fred Inbau first aroused my interest in the delicate balancing of interests that make up the law and practice of criminal procedure. Geoffrey R. Elton, Clare College, Cambridge, guided and stimulated my curiosity about the history of criminal procedure. Finally, Lacey B. Smith, Northwestern University, the best teacher I ever had, taught me how to translate my own excitement about criminal procedure to my students, and how to transform my convoluted use of the English language into understandable prose. To all of them I am deeply indebted.

Finally, I want to acknowledge the following hard-working people at West Publishing Company, who have done so much behind the scenes to prod me, to probe into the earlier versions' weaknesses and strengths, and ultimately to improve the final version—*Criminal Procedure*. Terry Casey turned my text into a beautiful finished design; Kristen McCarthy coined the word "textcasebook," capturing *Criminal Procedure*'s essence in doing so; John Och oversaw the art work with great skill. Poh Lin Khoo lived with, overcame, and, surprisingly, got me to pay attention to those details that make the difference between good and excellent books. She did so without ever losing her patience or humor. Mary Schiller encouraged me when I needed it, chided me when I deserved it, cheered me up when I was discouraged, and now, through three books and several editions, always seems to know how to bring out the best in my books. I am happy to give them all credit; they deserve it. Blame me, however, for *Criminal Procedure*'s shortcomings. The reviewers, my teachers and students, and the people at West did their best; the book, however, is mine alone.

Joel Samaha
Professor and Attorney-at-Law
University of Minnesota
Minneapolis, Minnesota
August 19, 1989

Chapter One

Overview of Criminal Procedure

CHAPTER OUTLINE

CHAPTER MAIN POINTS

1. Criminal law defines crimes and prescribes punishment for them; criminal procedure authorizes government intrusions and deprivations to enforce the criminal law.

2. The criminal process is a series of decision points in which responsibility for the decisions lies with different actors: police, prosecutors, defense attorneys, judges, juries, and corrections officers.

3. Each decision to proceed further into the criminal process results in greater cost charged to society and greater deprivations suffered by individual citizens. How these decision points result in greater costs and deprivations represents a major theme throughout this book.

4. Formally, decisions must comport with formal rules; informally, officials decide according to discretion, or outside formal rules. This formal/informal dichotomy represents a second theme in criminal procedure and this textbook.

5. The history of criminal procedure reveals a pendulum swing between emphasis on result and an emphasis on means, between the end of controlling crime and the method of stopping crime by promoting other values.

6. The law of criminal procedure balances several social interests—fact-finding, result, process values, organizational goals, societal values, and democracy. This balancing of interests constitutes a third theme in this book.

7. Each decision to proceed further into the criminal process requires adequate and accurate facts, objectively measured, to support greater costs to society and deprivations to individual citizens. Requiring facts to support decisions constitutes a fourth theme in criminal procedure and this textbook.

CHAPTER KEY TERMS

appellant the party appealing a lower court ruling or decision to a higher court

bench warrant warrant a judicial officer issues directly to a law enforcement officer

certiorari, **or** *cert.* from the Latin "to make sure"; similar to an appeal but court not required to hear it.

collateral attack attacking either errors in the law or facts of a trial court

common law writ court order issued by the ancient English courts of common law

concurring opinion an appellate court opinion in which the justice agrees with the decision, but not necessarily the reasoning, of the majority opinion

defendant a person formally charged with a crime

felony crime punishable by more than one year in prison

habeas corpus writ to challenge lawfulness of imprisonment

indictment formal criminal charge issued by a grand jury

interlocutory appeal an appeal that does not decide the case but involves a matter requiring resolution before decision on the merits

lower criminal court court that manages most pretrial criminal proceedings

majority opinion the law of the case in an appellate court

misdemeanor offense that carries penalties of fines and/or jail terms of one year or less

objective foundation the assumption that decisions to deprive citizens rest on facts that a disinterested third person can assess for sufficiency and accuracy

petitioner the party whose case has come to court by judicial writ

plaintiff-in-error another term for the party appealing a case

plurality opinion a majority of justices favor a decision but do not agree on the reasons for the decision

---

═══ HISTORY OF CRIMINAL PROCEDURE

"Hill Street Blues" fans became indignant a few years ago because they thought their favorite program had revolutionized its philosophy. The viewers had grown used to hearing the sergeant close his station-house briefing with the kindly advice, "Be careful out there." Then, one night the sergeant's replacement said instead, "Let's do it to them before they do it to us." The audience reacted so negatively that the next week the new sergeant elaborated on his admonition: "I'm not saying you should take the law into your own hands." He defended his comment as just another way of saying "Let's have a good shift." In other words, he was not advocating that officers violate citizens' constitutional rights.

The audience's reaction reveals a fundamental tension in criminal procedure between obtaining the right result in individual cases—apprehending and punishing the guilty and protecting the innocent—and achieving these results in a way consistent with other accepted values. In other words, the end does *not* justify the means in American criminal procedure.[1]

This tension between result and process is as old as Western law. The law of criminal procedure reflects this tension. It represents a major theme in this text. Commentators differ on the meaning of result and process. To some, the correct result means simply catching and punishing the guilty. In formal procedure, and in this text, the emphasis on result means *not only* to apprehend, convict, and punish the guilty, *but also* to release and acquit the innocent. In its broadest sense, the emphasis on result means no expenditures of government resources and no deprivations against citizens without adequate and accurate facts to support these expenditures and deprivations whenever they occur in the criminal process. For some, process values mean strictly protecting individual rights in order that citizens may remain free from unwarranted government interference. This text takes a broader view of process interests, including within its scope not only individual rights but also the interest in timely, orderly, and final criminal proceedings.

Roscoe Pound, a leading legal scholar and long-time dean of the Harvard Law School, maintained that the history of criminal procedure is a pendulum swing between the two extremes of this tension. According to Pound, no system has perfectly balanced the government's power to enforce the criminal law and the means to attain that end. Throughout Western history, according to Pound, societies have swung back and forth between first a predominant concern for society's interest in criminal law enforcement and then, in reaction, a predominant concern for society's interest in other values that transcend convicting the guilty.[2]

The early Roman republic established strong safeguards for individuals against government power, in the law of criminal procedure and created a criminal law "that in spite of abundant threats of capital punishment, became in practice the mildest ever known in the history of mankind."A case from the middle of the first century brings into relief this "mildness" or tenderness for individual rights. The Roman praetor seized a notorious violent criminal. Tribune Novius, upon releasing the criminal, said:

> Although I have been wounded by this hanger-on of Clodius and driven from my official duties by armed men distributed in garrisons, and General Pompeius has been besieged by them, yet when appeal is made to me, I will not follow the example of him with whom I find fault, and I will quash this sentence.[3]

In reaction to this mildness, and its attendant emphasis on process, the government of the Roman Empire went to the other extreme. The provincial governors in the era of Imperial Rome were both public prosecutors and judges; the emperor Hadrian noted that merely sending an accused to trial conclusively proved his or her guilt.[4]

This same tension arose several centuries later in medieval England. In the most famous English antecedent to American law and the United States Constitution, the Magna Carta, King John's barons placed several checks on royal power.These checks largely have to do with an emphasis on process at the expense of result. These limitations on royal criminal justice in 1215 led to a reaction expressed in the sixteenth and seventeenth centuries' aggrandizement of royal power. By the reign of King Charles I in the early 1600s, the royal Court of the Star Chamber had abandoned the common law procedural safeguards in favor of royal power to convict the guilty. The expansion of royal power did not stop with creating new royal courts; it extended to kings' political domination of the common law judges. Through intimidation, favor, and other influence, kings brought about decisions favorable to their own and the aristocracy's interests. Although interference in the courts was not new, a middle class increasingly restive for greater political influence regarded royal interference in judicial proceedings as intolerable. The English Revolution—and the founding of the American colonies—was, at least in part, a reaction by the middle-class elite to this expansion of royal power at the expense of the interest in process.

The American Bill of Rights reflects how much the newly dominant middle class suspected—was even hostile to—government power. The middle class had firsthand experience with a royal government and a judiciary impatient with individual interests; the Bill of Rights' demonstrates the people's determination to protect individual interests against government intrusions and deprivations. Throughout the nineteenth century concern for individual rights dominated the law of criminal procedure, if not its practice. A largely rural, widely scattered, sparse population that lived in villages and on farms and shared common values controlled political life. A weak government that allowed individual autonomy to flourish worked in that society.

By the early twentieth century, however, America had changed. The country was increasingly urban, densely populated, industrial, and inhabited by peoples with values different from the dominant nineteenth century Anglo-Saxon Protestant culture. Many people called upon the government to solve the problems that arose in transportation, health, business regulation, employment conditions, consumer protection, and maintenance of public order. Deficiencies in criminal justice led to calls for both an expanded criminal law to regulate behavior and greater government power to enforce the law. These events took place during one of the recurring "crime waves," as the public perceived them to be. This wave, contemporaries imagined, had brought the incidence of crime to epidemic proportions.

Complaints spread that "technicalities" set criminals free, and that constitutional safeguards made it difficult to convict known criminals. The newspapers, the new middle-class magazines, national conventions of criminal justice officials, professors, and lawyers loudly complained about how the criminal justice system favored criminals over innocent citizens. In other words, result was being sacrificed to process.

In the early years of the twentieth century, these complaints provoked open demands to amend the Constitution, sometimes drastically. At the 1910 annual meeting of the American Academy of Political and Social Science, a prestigious New York criminal lawyer, Samuel Untermeyer, told the conference that the Fourth Amendment protection against unreasonable searches and seizures and the Fifth Amendment protection against self-incrimination gave too much protection to criminals. He recommended, in his own words, a "shocking" solution: Abolish the Fourth and Fifth Amendments. Others demanded similar treatment for the jury trial. This "palladium of liberty" and democracy ought to be abolished because sentimental jurors set wanton criminals free to prey on innocent people.[5]

Complaints about the ideal balance between result and process have not subsided appreciably since the turn of the twentieth century. The early twentieth-century complaints fostered a tough law-and-order atmosphere and an accompanying enhanced police power that continued from the 1920s through the 1950s. During the 1960s, this enhanced police power spawned a reaction—the "due process" revolution. Led by the United States Supreme Court—the Warren Court after its then–Chief Justice Earl Warren—this revolution tilted the balance of power toward process, so much so, said its critics, that it favored criminal defendants too much.[6]

The "due process" revolution produced another pendulum swing that led to calls for more attention to result—convicting criminals. Much of the law of criminal procedure in this book reflects the fruits of that revolution and the subsequent reaction to it. During the 1970s and 1980s the United States Supreme Court—first the Burger and now the Rehnquist Courts, after their respective Chief Justices Warren Burger and William Rehnquist—government and federal legislatures, and all criminal justice agencies have adopted sterner measures to protect society against crime and criminals. Some evidence indicates that those measures are presently producing their own reaction—another, perhaps almost imperceptible, shift back toward process.[7]

In part, the 1980s continue this history of efforts to balance process and result, both social interests basic to the quality of life in a free society. Individual freedom is worth little without safety and security from attacks by private citizens. On the other hand, a government that regularly practices unwarranted intrusions and deprivations does not provide citizens with the quality of life associated with free societies. Hence, society has an interest in protecting citizens **both** from attacks by private criminals who prey upon them and their property and privacy, **and** from government intrusions and deprivations that excessively threaten the autonomy associated with life in a free society. This theme of balancing result and process reflects how the law of criminal procedure attempts to provide the government with enough power to enforce the criminal law but not so much to threaten individual autonomy.[8]

FIGURE 1.1   Four Themes in Criminal Procedure

This textbook stresses four major themes in the law and practice of criminal procedure:

1. **The criminal process constitutes a series of decision points that results in both increasing expenditure of government resources and greater intrusions and deprivations to individuals.** Police make the decisions early in the criminal process, until arrest; prosecutors make decisions after arrest; judges and defense attorneys enter the decision-making process following prosecutors' decisions to charge; juries decide the facts presented at trial.
2. **The Constitution requires that both a proper purpose and a sufficient factual foundation support decisions that result in an expenditure by government and deprivation to citizens.** To justify expenditure of public resources and subject citizens to deprivations and intrusions by government, the Constitution requires that agents have both an adequate purpose, such as investigating crime, obtaining evidence, determining guilt, and punishing offenders, and enough facts to assure the correct result.
3. **Formal rules and informal discretion characterize decision making in the criminal process.** Written rules govern formal decision making while discretion, or the freedom to decide outside the formal rules, operates informally.
4. **Criminal procedure promotes and balances legal, organizational, societal, and political interests.** These include not only the legal interests in obtaining the correct result and procedural regularity, but also the organizational interests in efficiency, economy, and predictability, the societal interests in privacy and crime control, and the democratic interest in community participation in criminal justice administration.

These themes recur throughout the cases in criminal procedure and throughout this textbook.

INTERESTS PROMOTED AND BALANCED BY CRIMINAL PROCEDURE

Although the two-dimensional view represented in the outlined brief history of criminal procedure contains considerable merit, it does not adequately describe the reality of American criminal procedure. Since 1900, criminal procedure has come to serve more complex and numerous interests. Close scholarly observation has revealed a host of frequently clashing interests that the criminal process balances and promotes. The principal interests criminal procedure balances include: (1) fact-finding to determine guilt or innocence and obtain the correct result; (2) procedural regularity; (3) organizational interests; (4) societal interests; and (5) democratic interests. The law of criminal procedure and the practices in the criminal process do not always balance all these interests successfully; certainly the law and practices do not do so to satisfy those who are committed to one interest over another.[9]

All the cases, statutes, and rules that appear in the book reflect the balance of conflicting interests in criminal procedure. One of the most famous cases that balanced result and process is the controversial *Miranda v. Arizona.* The United States Supreme Court had to decide whether to admit Miranda's confession to a brutal rape, or to exclude it because the police violated Miranda's right against self-incrimination in obtaining the confession. Excluding the confession might result in setting a confessed rapist free; admitting it might corrupt the criminal process.

Note On Reading Cases

You are about to read your first edited case. Most cases in the textbook involve Supreme Court decisions because the United States Supreme Court is the final arbiter of the meaning of the United States Constitution. However, state cases are also important for two reasons: (1) Virtually every state has a bill of rights nearly identical to the United States Bill of Rights. States apply their own constitutional provisions to decisions in their states. (2) Many criminal procedure cases originate in—and frequently terminate in—state courts. In other words, the day-to-day judicial administration of criminal justice takes place in state courts, not the United States Supreme Court. Hence, including state court decisions gives a fuller picture of the criminal process.

The following provide a guide for reading cases in this textbook.

1. The title in criminal cases always contains at least two names. The first name refers to the party who brought the action. It is always the government at the trial stage because the government initiates all criminal cases in the United States. The "v." is an abbreviation of the Latin *versus*, meaning against. The second name refers to the party against whom the action was brought. In *Miranda v. Arizona,* for example, Miranda appealed his conviction; hence he brought the action against Arizona, the state that convicted him.

2. The citation, the letters, and numbers on the line under the case title, tells what court heard the case, when the court decided the case, and where to find the case reported. For example, in *Miranda v. Arizona,* the citation 384 U.S. 436 (1966) reveals that the United States Supreme Court's 1966 decision in the case appears in Volume 384, page 436 of the United States Reports. The first set of numbers in a citation always refers to a volume in a set of reports, while the second set of numbers refers to the page in that volume.

3. Most cases in this textbook are appellate opinions. This means that a lower court has already taken some action in the case and one of the parties has asked a higher court to review the lower court's action. Parties seek appellate review of what they claim were errors by the trial court or unlawful conduct by police, judges, prosecutors, or defense lawyers. The most familiar appellate review arises when a convicted defendant appeals the conviction. Obviously, only defendants appeal *convictions*; the government can never appeal *acquittals*. However, many appellate reviews arise out of proceedings prior to trial. Sometimes the defendant, sometimes the government seeks review of these pretrial proceedings.

4. Many cases involving alleged police misconduct arise out of what defendants maintain were erroneous rulings on pretrial motions to exclude evidence at proceedings called suppression hearings. *Miranda v. Arizona* demonstrates this. According to Miranda, the police obtained his confession illegally. His lawyer moved to suppress the confession in a hearing prior to the trial in a suppression hearing. The judge ruled against him. Miranda appealed the ruling, first to the Arizona Supreme Court, and then to the United States Supreme Court. Most of the cases in this book will be United States Supreme Court opinions. Some are federal intermediate appeals court opinions from the Circuit Courts of Appeals. (See table 1.2 p. 28 for a list of the federal circuits and districts.) Some are state appellate court opinions.

5. The cases refer variously to parties who seek review of lower court decisions. Most commonly the appellate courts refer to the **appellant**, derived from the word *appeal*. **Petitioners** are defendants whose cases have come to the higher courts by petitions. The principal petitions are *certiorari,* from the Latin "to be sure," and *habeas corpus,* from the Latin "you have the body." *Habeas corpus* requires jailers, prison administrators, and others who have defendants in custody to justify the detention of those defendants who have petitioned the higher court to hear their cases. In *certiorari,* appellate courts are not required to hear the appeals; they do so based on the court's judgment that the case raises important constitutional questions. The United States Supreme Court hears most cases on writs of *certiorari*, literally orders to lower courts to send up their proceedings for certification and review. The Court turns down most of these petitions, but those it accepts often make important law. Older cases refer to the **plaintiff-in-error**, meaning the party who claims the lower courts erred in their rulings.

6. Most of the cases, particularly the United States Supreme Court cases, have two opinions, and sometimes three. The **majority opinion** is the law in the case. The United States Supreme Court has nine members, and each has a right to write his or her own opinion. Hence, if all justices participate, five, a majority, can make the law. Their opinion is called the majority opinion. Sometimes justices agree with the decision in the case but do not agree with the reasoning of, or wish to add some of their own arguments to, the majority opinion. Such **concurring opinions** mean the justice or justices agree with the result in the case, but not necessarily the majority's reasons for its decisions. If a majority of judges does not agree in their reasons but a majority reaches the same result the Court has a **plurality opinion**. If judges do not agree with the majority, they can vote against it and write their own **dissenting opinions** explaining why they do not agree.

   These conflicting arguments in the opinions will challenge you because they are persuasive. First, the majority's arguments will convince you; then the dissent will lead you to the opposite conclusion. This interplay is not only interesting but also important because it teaches you that every case—at least every case that reaches the Supreme Court—has plausible arguments to support both the government's and the defendant's position. Reasonable people do disagree!

7. In reading the cases, try to answer the following questions about each case:

   (a) What exactly were the facts indicating alleged official misconduct or error—the intrusion or deprivation imposed, the mistake made, or the improper, illegal, or unconstitutional conduct in which officials engaged?

   (b) If it was an intrusion or deprivation, what allegedly justified it? First, what was its *purpose*? Second, what was the *factual foundation* upon which it was based? Technically, (a) and (b) refer to the "facts of the case."

   (c) What constitutional provision, statute, or rule was allegedly violated by the police, prosecutor, judge, defense counsel, or other official? Technically, (c) refers to the "issue" in the case.

   (d) What did the court decide with respect to the questions or issues raised? What legal principle can be drawn from the court's opinion? Technically, (d) refers to the "decision" or "holding" in the case.

   (e) What arguments and reasons did the court give to support its decision? What arguments and reasons did the dissent give for not agreeing with the majority? Technically, (e) refers to the court's "opinion."

   (f) What was the disposition in the case? Or, what remedy did the appellate court grant? Several common dispositions in criminal cases include (1) affirmed, meaning the appellate court upholds the lower court's action; (2) reversed, meaning the appellate court set aside, overthrows, or nullifies the lower court's judgment; (3) remanded, meaning the appellate court sends the case back to the court from which it came so that court can conduct further proceedings based on the appellate court's ruling.

At this point, do not expect to answer all these questions fully. Most of the remaining text elaborates upon these points.

CASE

Should a confessed rapist go free?

Miranda v. Arizona

384 U.S. 436, 86 S. Ct. 1602, 16 L.Ed.2d 694 (1966)

FACTS

On March 3, 1963, an 18-year-old girl was kidnapped and forcibly raped near Phoenix, Arizona. Ten days later, on the morning of March 13, petitioner Miranda was arrested and taken to the police station. At this time Miranda was 23 years old, indigent, and educated to the extent of completing half the ninth grade.

He was there identified by the complaining witness. The police then took him to "Interrogation Room No. 2" of the detective bureau. There he was questioned by two police officers. The officers admitted at trial that Miranda was not advised that he had a right to have an attorney present. Two hours later, the officers emerged from the interrogation room with a written confession signed by Miranda. At the top of the statement was a typed paragraph stating that the confession was made voluntarily, without threats or promises of immunity and "with full knowledge of my legal rights, understanding any statement I make may be used against me."

At his trial before a jury, the written confession was admitted into evidence over the objection of defense counsel, and the officers testified to the prior oral confession made by Miranda during the interrogation. Miranda was found guilty of kidnapping and rape. He was sentenced to 20 to 30 years' imprisonment on each count, the sentences to run concurrently. On appeal, the Supreme Court of Arizona held that Miranda's constitutional rights were not violated in obtaining the confession and affirmed the conviction.
[The facts of three other cases decided with Miranda are omitted.]

OPINION

Chief Justice Warren delivered the Court's Opinion.

The cases before us raise questions which go to the roots of our concepts of American criminal jurisprudence: the restraints society must observe consistent with the Federal Constitution in prosecuting individuals for crime. More specifically, we deal with the admissibility of statements obtained from an individual who is subjected to custodial police interrogation and the necessity for procedures which assure that the individual is accorded his privilege under the Fifth Amendment to the Constitution not to be compelled to incriminate himself.

Our holding briefly stated is this: the prosecution may not use statements, whether exculpatory or inculpatory, stemming from custodial interrogation of the defendant unless it demonstrates the use of procedural safeguards effective to secure the privilege against self-incrimination. By custodial interrogation, we mean questioning initiated by law enforcement officers after a person has been taken into custody or otherwise deprived of his freedom of action in any significant way. As for the procedural safeguards to be employed, unless other fully effective means are devised to inform accused persons of their right of silence and to assure a continuous opportunity to exercise it, the following measures are required. Prior to any questioning, the person must be warned that he has a right to remain silent, that any statement he does make may be used as evidence against him, and that he has a right to the presence of an attorney, either retained or appointed. The defendant may waive effectuation of these rights, provided the waiver is made voluntarily, knowingly and intelligently. If, however, he indicates in any manner and at any stage of the process that he wishes to consult with an attorney before speaking there can be no questioning. Likewise, if the individual is alone and indicates in any manner that he does not wish to be interrogated, the police may not question him. The mere fact that he may have answered some questions or volunteered some statements on his own does not deprive him of the right to refrain from answering any further inquiries until he has consulted with an attorney and thereafter consents to be questioned.

In each, the defendant was questioned by police officers, detectives, or a prosecuting attorney in a room in which he was cut off from the outside world. In none of these cases was the defendant given a full and effective warning of his rights at the outset of the interrogation process. In all the cases, the questioning elicited oral admissions, and in three of them, signed statements as well which were admitted at their trials. They all thus share salient features—incommunicado interrogation of individuals in a police-dominated atmosphere, resulting in self-incriminating statements without full warnings of constitutional rights.

It is obvious that such an interrogation environment is created for no purpose other than to subjugate the individual to the will of his examiner. This atmosphere carries its own badge of intimidation. To be sure, this is not physical intimidation, but it is equally destructive of human dignity. The current practice of incommunicado interrogation is at odds with one of our Nation's most cherished principles—that the individual may not be compelled to incriminate himself. Unless adequate protective devices are employed to dispel the compulsion inherent in custodial surroundings, no statement obtained from the defendant can truly be the product of his free choice.

Today, there can be no doubt that the Fifth Amendment privilege is available outside of criminal court proceedings and serves to protect persons in all settings in which their freedom of action is curtailed in any significant way from being compelled to incriminate themselves.

A recurrent argument made in these cases is that society's need for interrogation outweighs the privilege. The whole thrust of our foregoing discussion demonstrates that the Constitution has prescribed the rights of the individual when confronted with the power of government when it provided in the Fifth Amendment that an individual cannot be compelled to be a witness against himself. That right cannot be abridged. As Mr. Justice Brandeis once observed:

"Decency, security and liberty alike demand that government officials shall be subjected to the same rules of conduct that are commands to the citizen. In a government of laws, existence of the government will be imperiled if it fails to observe the law scrupulously. Our Government is the potent, the omnipresent teacher. For good or for ill, it teaches the whole people by its example. Crime is contagious. If the Government becomes a lawbreaker, it breeds contempt for law; it invites every man to become a law unto himself; it invites anarchy. To declare that in the administration of the criminal law the end justifies the means . . . would bring terrible retribution. Against that pernicious doctrine this Court should resolutely set its face."

In this connection, one of our country's distinguished jurists has pointed out: "The quality of a nation's civilization can be largely measured by the methods it uses in the enforcement of its criminal law."
Reversed.

DISSENT

Mr. Justice White, with whom Mr. Justice Harlan and Mr. Justice Stewart join, dissenting.

The proposition that the privilege against self-incrimination forbids in-custody interrogation without the warnings specified in the majority opinion and without a clear waiver of counsel has no significant support in the history of the privilege or in the language of the Fifth Amendment. As for the English authorities and the common-law history, the privilege, firmly established in the second half of the seventeenth century, was never applied except to prohibit compelled judicial interrogations.

The Fifth Amendment deals with compelling the accused himself. It is his free will that is involved. Confessions and incriminating admissions, as such, are not forbidden evidence; only those which are compelled are banned. I doubt that the Court observes these distinctions today.

Criticism of the Court's opinion, however, cannot stop with a demonstration that the factual and textual bases for the rule it propounds are, at best, less than compelling. Equally relevant is an assessment of the rule's consequences measured against community values. The Court's duty to assess the consequences of its action is not satisfied by the utterance of the truth that a value of our system of criminal justice is "to respect the inviolability of the human personality" and to require government to produce the evidence against the accused by its own independent labors. More than the human dignity of the accused is involved; the human personality of others in the society must also be preserved. Thus the values reflected by the privilege are not the sole desideratum; society's interest in the general security is of equal weight.

The obvious underpinning of the Court's decision is a deep-seated distrust of all confessions. This is the not so subtle overtone of the opinion—that it is inherently wrong for the police to gather evidence from the accused himself. And this is precisely the nub of this dissent. I see nothing wrong or immoral, and certainly nothing unconstitutional, in the police's asking a suspect whom they have reasonable cause to arrest whether or not he killed his wife or in confronting him with the evidence on which the arrest was based. There is, in my view, every reason to believe that a good many criminal defendants who otherwise would have been convicted on what this Court has previously thought to be the most satisfactory kind of evidence will now, under this new version of the Fifth Amendment, either not be tried at all or will be acquitted if the State's evidence, minus the confession, is put to the test of litigation.

I have no desire whatsoever to share the responsibility for any such impact on the present criminal process.

In some unknown number of cases the Court's rule will return a killer, a rapist or other criminal to the streets and to the environment which produced him, to repeat his crime whenever it pleases him. As a consequence, there will not be a gain, but a loss, in human dignity. The real concern is not the unfortunate consequences of this new decision on the criminal law as an abstract, disembodied series of authoritative proscriptions, but the impact on those who rely on the public authority for protection and who without it can only engage in violent self-help with guns, knives and the help of their neighbors similarly inclined.

CASE DISCUSSION

Miranda was charged with rape and kidnapping. Over his attorney's objection, Miranda's written confession was admitted into evidence. He was convicted and sentenced to 20 to 30 years imprisonment. On appeal, the Arizona Supreme Court ruled that admitting the confession did not violate Miranda's rights and affirmed his conviction. Miranda appealed to the United States Supreme Court, which reversed the Arizona Supreme Court's decision.

Should the historical meaning of self-incrimination, limiting it to judicial proceedings, affect twentieth-century law? Why should it matter what the term meant in the seventeenth century? Is the result—convicting confessed rapist Ernesto Miranda—more important that the manner in which the police obtained the confession that convicted him? Defend your answer. Should the United States Supreme Court prescribe specific rules governing police conduct? Why? Why not?

How did the Court balance the interest in result with process? Why did the Court balance the interests the way it did? Should this confessed kidnapper-rapist go free? Why? Should his confession be used against him? Why? Do you agree with the Court that his rights are more important than enforcing the criminal law? What reasons can you give for this? Reconsider this case after reading the rest of this section on interests in criminal procedure.

Fact-Finding to Obtain the Correct Result

The law of criminal procedure emphasizes correct decisions: stopping, arresting, and charging only the reasonably suspect; convicting and punishing only the guilty; and—sometimes overlooked—freeing the innocent. Some say that the criminal process should concentrate solely on the search for truth, that it should be entirely result-oriented. This emphasis on correct result represents a recurring theme in this book.[10]

Facts must support all government intrusions. To lawfully stop citizens on the street without their consent, police must have enough facts—not hunches, whims, or mere suspicion—to lead a reasonable person to suspect that crime is afoot. To take suspicious citizens to the police station for further investigation, police need still more facts—probable cause to believe that a crime has been committed and that the arrested person committed it. Prosecutors need still more facts to charge suspects with crimes. Juries, or judges in trials without juries, cannot convict—the prerequisite to punishment—without proof beyond a reasonable doubt, the highest factual foundation in the criminal process. Hence, the greater the deprivation the decision imposes, the greater the factual foundation required to support it. The emphasis on adequate and accurate facts to support all government intrusions represents still another theme that recurs throughout the book.

Procedural Regularity

Decisions in the criminal process and the law of criminal procedure foster, and ultimately must balance, several other interests that compete with fact-finding in individual cases. Put another way, decisions to subject citizens to deprivations and intrusions are not only result-oriented but also process-directed. The criminal process emphasizes both ends and means; and, the law of criminal procedure makes clear that the ends do not justify the means. In short, the law of criminal procedure prohibits searching for truth at *any price*.

Insuring procedural regularity requires reaching beyond, and sometimes even overriding, the correct result in individual cases. On occasion, the reasonably suspect—and even the clearly guilty—go free to serve this interest in procedural regularity. Criminal law enforcement operates within the bounds of the structure of American government, which allocates power between federal and state governments and among the executive, legislative, and judicial branches of government. In other words, government must exercise its power to enforce the criminal law according to the principles of federalism and the separation of powers.[11]

Furthermore, at least formally, the determination of guilt—presenting facts sufficient to prove guilt beyond a reasonable doubt—must take place according to the adversary process. That process rigidly prescribes what evidence the government may present, how it may present it, and how the defense may respond to the government's case, and how defense may present its own evidence. The government and the defense may tell their sides of the story, but only according to well-defined rules.[12]

Moreover, the Fifth and Fourteenth Amendments require that proceedings take place according to due process of law. One dimension of due process promotes the interest in limited government—controlling the means police, prosecutors, and other agents of the government utilize to enforce the criminal law. Due process also emphasizes order, timeliness, and finality, interests related to, yet distinct from, limiting and controlling government power. This second dimension focuses on the interest in moving decision making in an orderly way, meeting deadlines, and reaching closure—settling matters without unduly reopening them for continued reevaluation. The Fifth and Fourteenth Amendments also guarantee equal protection under the laws. The law must treat citizens impartially: Justice is blind. Defendants' wealth, race, gender, or other characteristics should not affect the outcome in particular cases.

Organizational Interests

In addition to these formal institutional and constitutional interests, less formal social and organizational interests influence decisions in the criminal process. Police departments, prosecutors' and public defenders' offices, and the criminal courts are complex social organizations. As organizations, their hallmarks are predictability, efficiency, economy, and harmony; these organizational interests compete with, and sometimes transcend, formal law and fact-finding according to the adversary process. Negotiation, not conflict; accommodation, not triumph; predictability, not uncertainty; settlement, not continuance often take precedence in organizations. Organizational interests manifest themselves clearly in plea bargaining, where certainty, efficiency, harmony, and economy predominate over adversary proceedings, with their unpredictability, open conflict, and demands on the time of judges, lawyers, and court personnel.[13]

Organizational interests and result-orientation are not necessarily at cross-purposes, at least not in regard to obtaining the correct result in individual cases. Some maintain, for example, that plea bargaining collects facts and reaches conclusions based on them more accurately—as well as more efficiently and economically—than the time-consuming adversary process. (See Chapter 12.)

Societal Interests

Perhaps the most controversial aspect of the criminal process is its promotion of broad social interests. The determination of innocence or guilt in individual cases often gets subordinated to these societal interests. During the 1960s, the Warren Court emphasized such societal interests as racial justice, equal treatment under the law, the control of government power, and the rights of individuals against the state. In the 1970s and 1980s, under the Burger and Rehnquist Courts, the Supreme Court has emphasized such societal interests as the rights of victims, control of crime, and support for law enforcement.

Some support the role of the criminal process in promoting the Warren Court's social agenda for instrumentalist reasons: a humane, dignified, nondiscriminatory, compassionate criminal justice system builds public confidence and support for criminal law enforcement. Others argue that the integrity of the criminal process itself requires commitment to these broad social interests. Decisions ought to demonstrate commitment to the American values of equality, impartiality, and humaneness for their own sake because they are right, and because they transcend the narrow interest of punishing defendants. Supporters of the social agenda of the Burger and Rehnquist Courts point to the serious crime problem in the country and the need both to respond to victims and to support law enforcement officers upon whom crime control so heavily depends. Whether the societal interests promoted emphasize crime control and victims' rights or defendants' rights and the control of government, they to some extent subordinate the interest in determining guilt or innocence in individual cases.[14]

Community Participation

Finally, the criminal process promotes the public interest in democracy: it enlists community participation in law enforcement. Determining law enforcement policies—community influence on priorities in police arrest, prosecution charging, and judicial sentencing—is one dimension to community participation. In a more obvious and clearly more formalized manner, the jury symbolizes community interest in participation in the criminal process. Grand juries screen cases prior to trial; trial juries can acquit, even if their acquittals fly in the face of the law. Not even the Supreme Court can reverse not guilty verdicts; they are final. (See Chapter 12.)

United States Supreme Court opinions frequently consider the importance of police discretion in law enforcement, as we shall see in several cases in chapters 4 through 7. However, the Court has not written in detail about the various functions police perform and how the amount of discretion varies depending upon the function the police are performing. New York's highest court has done such a rarely found analysis in *People v. De Bour*.

CASE

What interests did the court balance?

People v. De Bour

40 N.Y. 2d 210, 386 N.Y.S. 2d 375, 352 N.E. 2d 562 (1976)

[Wachtler, J.]

FACTS

. . . At 12:15 a.m. on . . . October 15, 1972, Kenneth Steck, a police officer assigned to the Tactical Patrol Force of the New York Police Department, was working the 6:00 p.m. to 2:00 a.m. tour of duty, assigned to patrol by foot a certain section of Brooklyn. While walking his beat on a street illuminated by ordinary street lamps and devoid of pedestrian traffic, he and his partner noticed someone walking on the same side of the street in their direction. When the solitary figure of the defendant, Louis De Bour, was within 30 or 40 feet of the uniformed officers he crossed the street. The two policemen followed suit and when De Bour reached them Officer Steck inquired as to what he was doing in the neighborhood. De Bour, clearly but nervously, answered that he had just parked his car and was going to a friend's house.

The patrolman then asked De Bour for identification. As he was answering that he had none, Officer Steck noticed a slight waist-high bulge in defendant's jacket. At this point the policeman asked De Bour to unzipper [sic] his coat. When De Bour complied with this request Officer Steck observed a revolver protruding from his waistband. The loaded weapon was removed from behind his waistband and he was arrested for possession of the gun. . . . At [a hearing on a pretrial motion to suppress the admission of the gun into evidence] Officer Steck testified . . . that the encounter lasted "a few minutes." On cross-examination, Officer Steck stated that at the time he believed defendant might have been involved with narcotics and crossed the street to avoid apprehension. . . .

. . . Subsequently, De Bour pleaded guilty to felonious attempted possession of a weapon and was sentenced to a conditional discharge. The Appellate Division unanimously affirmed, without opinion.

OPINION

The role of the police in our society is a multifaceted one. On the one hand the police are mandated to enforce the law; yet the extent to which this authorizes the police to investigate or to prevent crime is ambiguous at best. On the other hand, and more important, we must recognize the multiplicity and complexity of tasks assumed by the police. As public servants, the police perform the lion's share of services expected of local government. Among other functions, the police in a democratic society are charged with the protection of constitutional rights, the maintenance of order, the control of pedestrian and vehicular traffic, the mediation of domestic and other noncriminal conflicts and supplying emergency help and assistance. . . .

Generally, in the performance of their public service functions, not related to criminal law enforcement, the police should be given a wide latitude to approach individuals and request information. . . . However, when police officers are engaged in their criminal law enforcement function their ability to approach people involves other considerations and will be viewed and measured by an entirely different standard of reasonableness. . . .

Due to the tendency to submit to the badge and our belief that the right to be left alone is "too precious to entrust to the discretion of those whose job is the detection of crime" a policeman's right to request information while discharging his law enforcement duties will hinge on the manner and intensity of the interference, the gravity of the crime involved and the circumstances attending the encounter. . . .

Applying these principles to the instant case, we believe that the police officers legitimately approached De Bour to inquire as to his identity. The encounter here was devoid of harassment or intimidation. It was brief lasting only a few minutes and the questions were circumscribed in scope to the officers' task as foot patrolmen. Significantly, the encounter did not subject De Bour to a loss of dignity, for where the police degrade and humiliate their behavior is to be condemned. In addition, the crime sought to be prevented involved narcotics and the Legislature has declared that to be a serious crime. Moreover, the attendant circumstances were sufficient to arouse the officers' interest. The encounter here occurred after midnight in an area known for its high incidence of drug activity and only after De Bour had conspicuously crossed the street to avoid walking past the uniformed officers. In evaluating the police action in light of the combined effect of these factors we conclude that rather than being whimsical it was reasonable. Hence the police officers were authorized to make the brief limited inquiry that they did. . . .

Having concluded that the initial encounter was lawful in its inception and that the subsequent intrusion was reasonably limited in scope and intensity we agree that there should have been no suppression and the order of the Appellate Division should be affirmed and the conviction of De Bour sustained.

DISSENT

Fuschburg, J. (dissenting).

. . . *De Bour* should . . . be reversed, our court being called upon, to act as "the instrument by which a free society imposes on itself the seldom welcome, sometimes dangerous, always indispensable restraints that keep it free" . . . .

Generally, for the fulfillment of that function, a balance needs to be, and long ago was, struck, a balance between society's interest in encouraging law enforcement and society's interest in fostering individual privacy and personal inviolability.

. . . Libertarians have argued that no police-citizen encounter should ever be permitted (including a brief investigative street encounter) in the absence of traditional probable cause, while law enforcement officials urge that the limited intrusion created by a brief investigative encounter justifies removing it from all constitutional constraints, thus authorizing unlimited street "stops" by the police. Again, we have accepted neither extreme. Instead, while the Supreme Court approved the concept of investigative street encounters, . . . it insisted that such an encounter be proceeded by activity which gives rise to an "articulable suspicion" that criminal activity has, in fact, occurred. . . .

[T]here was no reason for the police to confront De Bour. They lacked . . . any cause for his detention as he walked along the street, so to speak, minding his own business. They lacked any, that is unless a person's act in choosing to cross a street when in sight of a uniformed police officer in and of itself may be said to give rise to an "articulable suspicion" of criminal activity.

CASE DISCUSSION

De Bour attracted Police Officer Steck's attention, was stopped, arrested, and charged with illegal possession of a gun. In a pretrial motion, De Bour moved to suppress the gun as evidence because the police stopped and frisked him illegally. The judge denied the motion. De Bour appealed the judge's denial of his motion to suppress. The intermediate appellate court upheld the trial court judge's decision on the motion. The defendant appealed to New York's highest court, the Court of Appeals.

What exactly constituted informal police decision making in this case? Was this decision within the proper scope of informal discretion? What deprivation did De Bour experience? What, if anything, justified stopping and frisking De Bour? (See chapter 4 for a full discussion of stop and frisk.) Specifically, what interests did the court balance in its decision? Which did it promote? Was result more important than the other interests involved? Do you agree with the dissent or the majority? Which interests do you consider paramount?

LAWFUL INTRUSIONS AND DEPRIVATIONS

The criminal process consists of a series of government intrusions on private citizens. To enforce the criminal law the government itself infringes on the lives, liberty, privacy, and property of citizens. The following hypothetical pairs demonstrate the similar losses citizens suffer both from offenders and from law enforcement.

1a. Allen wants Elaine's new stereo. When he knows she is out, he enters her apartment and takes the stereo.
1b. Officer McKenzie gets a search warrant to search Donald's apartment for a stolen stereo. He breaks into Donald's apartment, enters, finds the stereo, and takes it to the police station.
2a. Knowing that Tania's father is very rich, Brian takes Tania to a cabin in the woods against her will. He holds her there until her father pays him $1,000,000 ransom.
2b. Officer Shapiro sees Ann grab Steve and forcibly take his wallet. The police officer chases Ann and catches her. He arrests her, takes her to the police station, books her, and then takes her to the jail where she is locked up against her will. The court sets bail for Ann at $50,000.
3a. Michael approaches Jessica in a singles' bar. He feels very attracted to her and makes advances to her. Jessica tells him to ''get lost,'' but he persists and, against her will, feels her breasts.
3b. Corrections Officer Gonzales sees John hold up a bank. The officer arrests John and conducts a full-body search.
4a. Katrina was jealous of Sandy for always getting better grades than she. Enraged because Sandy received an A in a Criminal Procedure class while Katrina received only a C, Katrina stabbed Sandy to death. The state in which Katrina killed Sandy has a statute authorizing the death penalty. Katrina is tried, convicted, and sentenced to death for murdering Sandy. After waiting on death row for two years, Katrina was electrocuted. She screamed as the electric currents spread through her body; it took about five minutes to actually kill her.

4b. Tony has just shot Lisa. As he is running away with the gun in his hand, the police arrive. They order Tony to "halt." Tony stops, turns toward the officers, lifts the gun, and begins to squeeze the trigger. The officers shoot and kill him.

These simple examples illustrate the difference between criminal law and criminal procedure. The criminal law prohibits *private* citizens from hurting other citizens. It defines specific harms as crimes and prescribes punishments for those who are convicted of committing them. The law of criminal procedure empowers the *state* to engage in deprivations and intrusions against private citizens to enforce the criminal law. Notice, however, what is often overlooked—citizens suffer harms from *both* private criminals *and* the state. What distinguishes harms by private criminals and harms by the state is that the state can legally impose harms.

Justifications Based on Proper Purposes and Sufficient Foundation

PROPER PURPOSES OF INTRUSIONS AND DEPRIVATIONS. Two types of criteria authorize government intrusions and deprivations: (1) the purposes for which they are made; and (2) the factual foundation upon which they are based. Proper purposes include detecting and investigating crime; apprehending suspects; gathering evidence; charging, prosecuting, and trying defendants; and punishing convicted offenders. Using state power to achieve illegitimate purposes is not justified. Police who harass citizens they do not "like," prosecutors who vindictively charge suspects, judges who discriminate according to race, gender, class, or age when they sentence offenders, and corrections administrators and officers who cruelly abuse prisoners are all examples of individuals using state power to achieve illegitimate purposes.

CASE

Did the police harass him?

Kolender v. Lawson

461 U. S. 352, 103 S.Ct. 1855, 75 L.Ed.2d 903 (1983)

[Justice O'Connor delivered the Court's opinion. Burger, Brennan, Marshall, Blackmun, Powell, and Stevens joined.]

FACTS

Appellee Edward Lawson was detained or arrested on approximately 15 occasions between March 1976 and January 1977 pursuant to Cal. Penal Code Ann. § 647(e) (West 1970). Lawson was prosecuted only twice, and was convicted once. The second charge was dismissed.

Lawson then brought a civil action in the District Court for the Southern District of California seeking a declaratory judgment that § 647(e) is unconstitutional, a mandatory injunction to restrain enforcement of the statute, and compensatory and punitive damages against the various officers who detained him. The District Court found that § 647(e) was overbroad because "a person who is stopped on less than probable cause cannot be punished for failing to identify himself." The District Court enjoined enforcement of the statute, but held that Lawson could not recover damages because the officers involved acted in the good-faith belief that each detention or arrest was lawful. . . . The Court of Appeals affirmed the District Court determination as to the unconstitutionality of § 647(e). The appellate court determined that the statute was unconstitutional in that it violates the Fourth Amendment's proscription against unreasonable searches and seizures, it contains a vague enforcement statute that is susceptible to arbitrary enforcement, and it fails to give fair and adequate notice of the type of conduct prohibited. . . .

The officers appealed to this Court from that portion of the judgment of the Court of Appeals which declared § 647(e) unconstitutional and which enjoined its enforcement. . . .

. . . [T]he trial transcript contains numerous descriptions of the stops given both by Lawson and by the police officers who detained him. For example, one police officer testified that he stopped Lawson while walking on an otherwise vacant street because it was late at night, the area was isolated, and the area was located close to a high crime area. Another officer testified that he detained Lawson, who was walking at a late hour in a business area where some businesses were still open, and asked for identification because burglaries had been committed by unknown persons in the general area. . . .

OPINION

In the courts below, Lawson mounted an attack on the facial validity of § 647(e). . . . § 647(e) requires that an individual provide "credible and reliable" identification when requested by a police officer who has reasonable suspicion of criminal activity. . . .

"Credible and reliable" identification is defined by the State Court of Appeals as identification "carrying reasonable assurance that the identification is authentic and providing means for later getting in touch with the person who has identified himself." In addition, a suspect may be required to "account for his presence. . . to the extent that it assists in producing credible and reliable identification. . . . "Under the terms of the statute, failure of the individual to provide "credible and reliable" identification permits the arrest.

Our Constitution is designed to maximize individual freedoms within a framework of ordered liberty. Statutory limitations on those freedoms are examined for substantive authority and content as well as for definiteness or certainty of expression.

. . . Section 647(e), as presently drafted and as construed by the state courts, contains no standard for determining what a suspect has to do in order to satisfy the requirement to provide a "credible and reliable" identification. As such, the statute vests virtually complete discretion in the hands of the police to determine whether the suspect has satisfied the statute and must be permitted to go on his way in the absence of probable cause to arrest. An individual, who police may think is suspicious but [who they] do not have probable cause to believe has committed a crime, is entitled to continue to walk the public streets "only at the whim of any police officer" who happens to stop that individual under § 647(e). . . .

Appellants stress the need for strengthened law enforcement tools to combat the epidemic of crime that plagues our Nation. The concern of our citizens with curbing criminal activity is certainly a matter requiring the attention of all branches of government. As weighty as this concern is, however, it cannot justify legislation that would otherwise fail to meet constitutional standards for definiteness and clarity. Section 647(e), as presently construed, requires that "suspicious" persons satisfy some undefined identification requirement, or face criminal punishment. Although due process does not require "impossible standards" of clarity, this is not a case where further precision in the statutory language is either impossible or impractical.

We conclude § 647(e) is unconstitutionally vague on its face because it encourages arbitrary enforcement by failing to describe with sufficient particularity what a suspect must do in order to satisfy the statute. Accordingly, the judgment of the Court of Appeals is affirmed, and the case is remanded for further proceedings consistent with this opinion.
It is so ordered.

DISSENT

[Justice White, with Justice Rehnquist joining, dissents.]

The majority finds that the statute "contains no standard for determining what a suspect has to do in order to satisfy the requirement to provide a 'credible and reliable' identification." At the same time, the majority concedes that "credible and reliable" has been defined by the state court to mean identification that carries reasonable assurance that the identification is authentic and that provides means for later getting in touch with the person. The narrowing construction given this statute by the state court cannot be likened to the "standardless" statutes involved in a statute that made it a crime to be a "vagrant." The statute provided:

"Rogues and vagabonds, or dissolute persons who go about begging, common gamblers, . . . common drunkards, common night walkers, . . . lewd, wanton and lascivious persons, . . . common railers and brawlers, persons wandering or strolling around from place to place without any lawful purpose or object, habitual loafers, . . . shall be deemed vagrants."

. . . The present statute, as construed by the state courts, does not fall in the same category.

CASE DISCUSSION

This is not a criminal case. Lawson brought a civil action called seeking declaratory judgment. Declaratory judgment actions arise in situations where plaintiffs are not sure of their rights, and they seek the court's decision on the matter. Furthermore, Lawson wanted damages and an injunction, or court order, to restrain the police from making further arrests under the statute he challenged. The lower court issued the injunction, the intermediate court affirmed, and Kolender, the San Diego Chief of Police, appealed the case to the United States Supreme Court. The Supreme Court held the statute unconstitutional. A "street person" recently told the author that the police regularly stop him, but as long as he has "i.d." and some "money in his pocket," they "don't hassle me." Is this "harassment"?

Lawson is widely known as the "California Walkman" because he spends most of his free time walking, sometimes in odd places at unusual times. He is a large, imposing figure who wears his hair in dreadlocks. Why did the police arrest Lawson? Were they preventing crime? investigating crime? or harassing Lawson? What foundation did they have? Do you agree with the majority or the dissent's opinion? Explain.

OBJECTIVE FOUNDATION FOR INTRUSIONS AND DEPRIVATIONS. In addition to serving proper purposes, government intrusions and deprivations must rest on adequate objective foundations, or a demonstrable quantum of proof (see table 1.1). **Objective foundation** means that officers must have facts that a disinterested third person—usually a judge—can review and weigh for accuracy and sufficiency. Nearly everyone is familiar with the objective foundation or quantum of proof required to support conviction—the proof beyond a reasonable doubt. Two other quanta of proof arise in criminal procedure: reasonable suspicion and probable cause.

TABLE 1.1

Quantum of Proof	Intrusion or Deprivation
reasonable grounds to *suspect* crime is afoot	stop
reasonable grounds to *suspect* person stopped is armed	frisk
probable cause to *believe* crime has been committed and suspect has committed it	arrest
probable cause to *believe* person or items will be found in place searched	search
proof beyond *reasonable* doubt that defendant is guilty	conviction

Probable cause arises in three principal situations, including (1) arrest; (2) search; and (3) requiring defendants to answer criminal charges. These and other evidentiary standards allow for considerable room in their application to specific cases. Still, standards reflect the idea that officials may not engage in deprivations and intrusions simply because they "feel," "guess," or "have a hunch" that their actions serve legitimate criminal law enforcement ends. Chapters 4, 5, 6, 9, and 12, fully discuss reasonable grounds to stop and frisk, probable cause to arrest, search, and detain for trial, and proof beyond a reasonable doubt to convict. *Brinegar v. United States,* the most widely cited case on probable cause to search, introduces the basic theme that intrusions and deprivations require an objective foundation to justify them.

CASE

Did the police have a sufficient foundation?

Brinegar v. United States

338 U.S. 160, 69 S.Ct. 1302, 93 L.Ed. 1879 (1949)

[Mr. Justice Rutledge delivered the opinion of the court. . . .]

FACTS

At about six o'clock on the evening of March 3, 1947, Malsed, an investigator of the Alcohol Tax Unit, and Creehan, a special investigator, were parked in a car beside a highway near the Quapaw Bridge in northeastern Oklahoma. The point was about five miles west of the Missouri-Oklahoma line. Brinegar drove past headed west in his Ford coupe. Malsed had arrested him about five months earlier for illegally transporting liquor; had seen him loading liquor into a car or truck in Joplin, Missouri, on at least two occasions during the preceding six months; and knew him to have a reputation for hauling liquor. As Brinegar passed, Malsed recognized both him and the Ford. He told Creehan, who was driving the officers' car, that Brinegar was the driver of the passing car. Both agents later testified that the car, but not especially its rear end, appeared to be "heavily" loaded and "weighted with something." Brinegar increased his speed as he passed the officers. They gave chase. After pursuing him for about a mile at top speed, they gained on him as his car skidded on a curve, sounded their siren, overtook him, and crowded his car to the side of the road by pulling across in front of it. The highway was one leading from Joplin, Missouri, toward Vinita, Oklahoma, Brinegar's home. As the agents got out of their car and walked back toward petitioner, Malsed said, "Hello Brinegar, how much liquor have you got in the car?" Or, "How much liquor have you got in the car this time?" Petitioner replied, "Not too much," or, "Not so much." After further questioning he admitted that he had twelve cases in the car. Malsed testified that one case, which was on the front seat, was visible from outside the car, but petitioner testified that it was covered by a lap robe. Twelve more cases were found under and behind the front seat. The agents then placed Brinegar under arrest and seized the liquor.

The district judge, after a hearing on the motion to suppress at which the facts stated above appeared in evidence, was of the opinion that "the mere fact that the agents knew that this defendant was engaged in hauling whiskey, even coupled with the statement that the car appeared to be weighted, would not be probable cause for the search of this car.'' Therefore, he thought, there was no probable cause when the agents began the chase. . . .

The Court of Appeals, one judge dissenting, took essentially the view held by the District Court. . . . The crucial question is whether there was probable cause for Brinegar's arrest.

OPINION

. . . [T]he record shows that Brinegar had used Joplin, Missouri, to Malsed's personal knowledge derived from direct observation, not merely from hearsay . . . as a source of supply on other occasions within the preceding six months. It also discloses that Brinegar's home was in Vinita, Oklahoma, and that Brinegar when apprehended was traveling in a direction leading from Joplin to Vinita. . . .

Joplin. . . was a ready source of supply. But. . . it was not an illegal source. So far as appears, Brinegar's purchases there were entirely legal. And so, we may assume for present purposes, was his transportation of the liquor in Missouri, until he reached and crossed the state line into Oklahoma. . . . the important thing here is not whether Joplin was a ready, convenient and probable one for persons disposed to violate the Oklahoma and federal statutes. That fact was demonstrated fully, not only by the geographic facts, but by Malsed's direct and undisputed testimony of his personal observation of Brinegar's use of liquor-dispensing establishments in Joplin for procuring his whiskey. . . .

The situation relating to the probable place of market, as bearing on the probability of unlawful importation, is somewhat different. Broadly on the facts this may well have been taken to be the State of Oklahoma as a whole or its populous northeastern region. From the facts of record we know, as the agents knew, that Oklahoma was a ''dry'' state. At the time of the search, its law forbade the importation of intoxicating liquors from other states, . . . This fact, taken in connection with the known ''wet'' status of Missouri and the location of Joplin close to the Oklahoma line, affords a very natural situation for persons inclined to violate the Oklahoma and federal statutes to ply their trade. The proof therefore concerning the source of supply, the place of probable destination and illegal market, and hence the probability that Brinegar was using the highway for the forbidden transportation, was strong. . . .

Finally, . . . concerning the primary and ultimate fact that the petitioner was engaging in liquor running, Malsed's personal observation of Brinegar's recent activities established that he was so engaged . . . He saw Brinegar loading liquor, in larger quantities than would be normal for personal consumption, into a car or truck in Joplin on other occasions during the six months prior to the search. He saw the car Brinegar was using in this case in use by him at least once in Joplin within that period and followed it. And several months prior to the search he had arrested Brinegar for unlawful transportation of liquor and this arrest had resulted in an indictment which was pending at the time of this trial. Moreover Malsed instantly recognized Brinegar's Ford coupe and Brinegar as the driver when he passed the parked police car. And at that time Brinegar was moving in a direction from Joplin toward Vinita only a short distance inside Oklahoma from the state line. . . .

The evidence here is undisputed, is admissible on the issue of probable cause, and clearly establishes that the agent had good ground for believing that Brinegar was engaged regularly throughout the period in illicit liquor running and dealing. . . .

For a variety of reasons relating not only to probative value and trust-worthiness, but also to possible prejudicial effect upon a trial jury and the absence of opportunity for cross-examination, the generally accepted rules of evidence throw many exclusionary protections about one who is charged with and standing trial for crime. Much evidence of real and substantial probative value goes out on considerations irrelevant to its probative weight but relevant to possible misunderstanding or misuse by the jury.

Thus, in this case, the trial court properly excluded from the record at the trial, . . . Malsed's testimony that he had arrested Brinegar several months earlier for illegal transportation of liquor and that the resulting indictment was pending in another court at the time of the trial of this case. . . . Yet the same court admitted the testimony at the hearing on the motion to suppress the evidence seized in the search, where the issue was not guilt but probable cause and was determined by the court without a jury.

The court's rulings, one admitting, the other excluding the identical testimony, were neither inconsistent nor improper. They illustrate the difference in standards and latitude allowed in passing upon the distinct issues of probable cause and guilt. Guilt in a criminal case must be proved beyond a reasonable doubt and by evidence confined to that which long experience in the common-law tradition, to some extent embodied in the Constitution, has crystallized into rules of evidence consistent with that standard. . . .

However, if those standards were to be made applicable in determining probable cause for an arrest or for search and seizure, more especially in cases such as this involving moving vehicles used in the commission of crime, few indeed would be the situations in which an officer, charged with protecting the public interest by enforcing the law, could take effective action toward that end. . . .

In dealing with probable cause, however, as the very name implies, we deal with probabilities. These are not technical; they are the factual and practical considerations of everyday life on which reasonable and prudent men, not legal technicians, act. The standard of proof is accordingly correlative to what must be proved.

"The substance of all the definitions" of probable cause "is a reasonable ground for belief of guilt." . . . And this "means less than evidence which would justify condemnation" or conviction, . . . Probable cause exists where "the facts and circumstances within their [the officers'] knowledge and of which they had reasonably trustworthy information [are] sufficient in them-selves to warrant a man of reasonable caution in the belief that" an offense has been or is being committed. . . .

These long-prevailing standards seek to safeguard citizens from rash and unreasonable interferences with privacy and from unfounded charges of crime. They also seek to give fair leeway for enforcing the law in the community's protection. Because many situations which confront officers in the course of executing their duties are more or less ambiguous, room must be allowed for some mistakes on their part. But the mistakes must be those of reasonable men, acting on facts leading sensibly to their conclusions of probability. The rule of probable cause is a practical, nontechnical conception affording the best compromise that has been found for accommodating these often opposing interests. Requiring more would unduly hamper law enforcement. To allow less would be to leave law-abiding citizens at the mercy of the officers' whim or caprice. . . .

DISSENT

Mr. Justice Jackson, dissenting. . . .

Among deprivation of rights, none is so effective in cowing a population, crushing the spirit of the individual and putting terror in every heart. Uncontrolled search and seizure is one of the first and most effective weapons in the arsenal of every arbitrary government. And one need only briefly to have dwelt and worked among a people possessed of many admirable qualities but deprived of these rights to know that the human personality deteriorates and dignity and self-reliance disappear where homes, persons and possessions are subject at any hour to unheralded search and seizure by the police.

But the right to be secure against searches and seizures is one of the most difficult to protect. Since the officers are themselves the chief invaders, there is no enforcement outside of court.

. . . We must remember that the extent of any privilege of search and seizure without warrant which we sustain, the officers interpret and apply themselves and will push to the limit. . . . And we must remember that the authority which we concede to conduct searches and seizures without warrant may be exercised by the most unfit and ruthless officers as well as by the fit and responsible, and resorted to in case of petty misdemeanors as well as in the case of the gravest felonies. . . .

The proof that Brinegar was trafficking in illegal liquor rests in inferences from two circumstances, neither one of which would be allowed to be proved at a trial: One, it appears that the same officers previously had arrested Brinegar on the same charge. But there had been no conviction and it does not appear whether the circumstances of the former arrest indicated any strong probability of it. In any event, this evidence of a prior arrest of the accused would not even be admissible in a trial to prove his guilt on this occasion.

As a second basis for inference, the officers also say that Brinegar had the reputation of being a liquor runner. The officers' testimony of reputation would not be admissible in a trial of defendant unless he was unwise enough to open the subject himself by offering character testimony. . . .

I do not say that no evidence which would be inadmissible to prove guilt at a trial may be considered in weighing probable cause, but I am surprised that the Court is ready to rule that inadmissible evidence alone, as to vital facts give little indication of guilt, establish probable cause as matter of law. The only other fact is that officer Malsed stated that twice, on September 23 and on September 30, about six months before this arrest, he saw Brinegar in a Missouri town, loading liquor into a truck, not the car in this case. That is all.

Mr. Justice Frankfurter and Mr. Justice Murphy join his opinion.

CASE DISCUSSION

The police arrested Brinegar for illegal possession of alcohol and seized the alcohol found in his car. Charged with illegal possession, Brinegar moved to suppress the admission of the alcohol into evidence. The trial court judge granted the motion and suppressed the evidence. The intermediate court upheld the trial court's decision. The Supreme Court reversed and ruled the evidence admissible and sufficient to establish probable cause.

What precisely were the facts the police had to arrest Brinegar? (See chapter 5 for a full discussion of probable cause to arrest.) Why did they arrest him? Do you think the police did the "right" thing when they arrested Brinegar? Explain. Were the police more interested in result or in other values? Did the Court promote the "right" values when it ruled that the police lawfully arrested Brinegar? Does the dissent have a point that the decision in this case might endanger freedom? Explain. Justice Jackson, in his dissent, expresses the fear that too much power to search in the hands of the police can lead to totalitarianism. Justice Jackson was the judge in the Nuremberg trials of Nazi war criminals following World War II. This case arose in 1949 amid the fear of another totalitarian state. Do you think his dissent reflects an unwarranted fear?

Increasing Intrusions and Deprivations in the Criminal Process

A citizen stopped for brief questioning on the street suffers a deprivation, but not one so great as an arrested citizen detained in jail for several hours. The arrested suspect in jail does not suffer so great a deprivation as a convicted murderer serving a life sentence, or facing the ultimate deprivation, death. Hence, investigating crime entails less deprivation than apprehending and holding suspects, and much less than punishing convicted offenders. Individuals who proceed beyond investigation suffer greater deprivations and intrusions; however, more people suffer the lesser deprivations associated with investigating crime. Hence, the critical policy question: Which are more serious—superficial intrusions and deprivations that touch many citizens, or greater deprivations and deeper intrusions that affect fewer people?

Throughout the criminal process, law enforcement personnel weigh facts to determine whether to subject citizens to greater deprivations and to devote more governmental resources to these deprivations. Some decisions such as stops, frisks, arrests, searches, pretrial detention, and conviction result in obvious deprivations to citizens suspected of crimes. Other decisions, filing pretrial motions, pretrial hearings on these motions, preliminary hearings, and grand jury screening bring to the fore other interests, such as accuracy in fact-finding and procedural regularity. Nevertheless, even these latter decisions have the capacity both to prolong hardships on defendants and to increase expenditures of public resources (See Figure 1.2).

FIGURE 1.2 The Prosecution of Felony Arrests, 1981

A GENERAL VIEW OF THE CRIMINAL JUSTICE SYSTEM

This chart seeks to present a simple yet comprehensive view of the movement of cases through the criminal justice system. Procedures in individual jurisdictions may vary from the pattern shown here. The differing weights of the line indicate the relative volumes of cases disposed of at various points in the system, but this is only suggestive since no nationwide data of this sort exists.

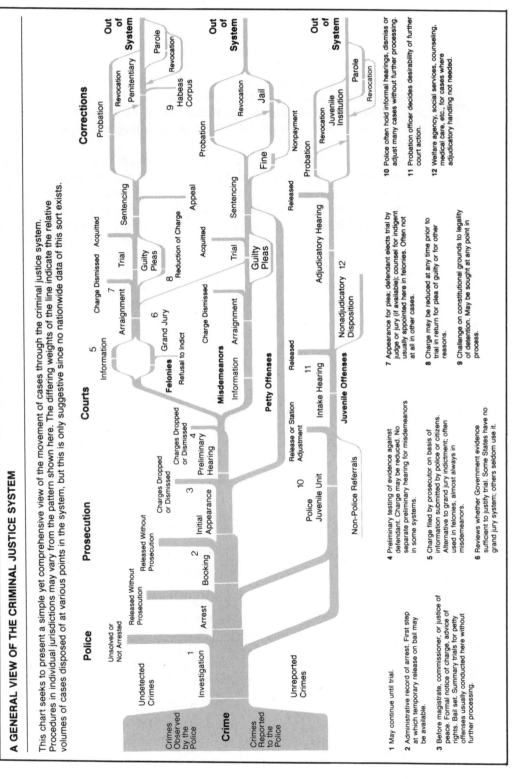

1 May continue until trial.

2 Administrative record of arrest. First step at which temporary release on bail may be available.

3 Before magistrate, commissioner, or justice of peace. Formal notice of charge, advice of rights. Bail set. Summary trials for petty offenses usually conducted here without further processing.

4 Preliminary testing of evidence against defendant. Charge may be reduced. No separate preliminary hearing for misdemeanors in some systems.

5 Charge filed by prosecutor on basis of information submitted by police or citizens. Alternative to grand jury indictment; often used in felonies, almost always in misdemeanors.

6 Reviews whether Government evidence sufficient to justify trial. Some States have no grand jury system; others seldom use it.

7 Appearance for plea; defendant elects trial by judge or jury (if available); counsel for indigent usually appointed here in felonies. Often not at all in other cases.

8 Charge may be reduced at any time prior to trial in return for plea of guilty or for other reasons.

9 Challenge on constitutional grounds to legality of detention. May be sought at any point in process.

10 Police often hold informal hearings, dismiss or adjust many cases without further processing.

11 Probation officer decides desirability of further court action.

12 Welfare agency, social services, counseling, medical care, etc., for cases where adjudicatory handling not needed.

source: Adapted from *The challenge of crime in a free society,* President's Commission on Law Enforcement and Administration of Justice, 1967.

≡ THE AMERICAN CRIMINAL JUSTICE SYSTEM

The American criminal justice system is three tiered, with federal, state, and local criminal justice systems. A loose confederation of agencies at the federal, state, county, and municipal level provides the structure within which criminal law enforcement takes place. Hence, there is no single criminal justice system in the United States; there are many possessing considerable variety. All are similar, however, in that they conform to basic constitutional standards governing the steps in the criminal process.

Most criminal law enforcement takes place at state and local levels. The principal criminal justice agencies are (1) police departments; (2) prosecutors' offices; (3) **lower criminal courts,** or courts of limited jurisdiction—alternatively called municipal, justice of the peace, or magistrate's courts—where most pretrial proceedings take place; (4) **trial courts**—sometimes called superior or district courts—where criminal trials take place; (5) probation departments, often associated with trial courts; (6) jails; (7) **appellate courts** that hear criminal appeals and collateral attacks from criminal trial proceedings; (8) prisons; and (9) parole departments. Police departments are city and town agencies; trial courts and jails, district and county institutions; and appellate courts, prisons, and parole departments, statewide agencies. Local agencies employ more than three-fifths of all justice personnel, most of whom are police.[15]

The federal criminal justice system resembles the state and local systems. The federal police includes not only the well-known Federal Bureau of Investigation (FBI), but also the Drug Enforcement Agency (DEA) and others. There are federal prosecutors—United States attorneys and their assistants—for all the regions in the country. Federal magistrates issue warrants and perform other preliminary proceedings. The United States District Courts try cases and hear challenges to local and state jurisdiction, such as habeas corpus petitions. The Courts of Appeals are the intermediate federal court of appeals; they hear appeals both from federal District Court and often from state courts involving constitutional questions. The United States Supreme Court, the court of last resort in the nation, finally resolves constitutional questions; no appeals remain from its interpretations.

TABLE 1.2   Federal Circuits and Districts

District of Columbia Circuit

District of Columbia

First Circuit

Maine, Massachusetts, New Hampshire, Puerto Rico, Rhode Island

Second Circuit

Connecticut, Eastern District New York, Southern District New York, Western District of New York, Vermont

Third Circuit

Delaware, New Jersey, Eastern District Pennsylvania, Middle District Pennsylvania, Western District Pennsylvania, Virgin Islands

Fourth Circuit

Maryland, Eastern District North Carolina, Middle District North Carolina, Western District North Carolina, South Carolina, Eastern District Virginia, Western District Virginia, Southern District West Virginia

Fifth Circuit

Eastern District Louisiana, Middle District Louisiana, Western District Louisiana, Northern District Mississippi, Southern District Mississippi, Eastern District Texas, Northern District Texas, Southern District Texas, Western District Texas

Sixth Circuit

Eastern District Kentucky, Western District Kentucky, Eastern District Michigan, Western District Michigan, Northern District Ohio, Southern District Ohio, Eastern District Tennessee, Middle District Tennessee, Western District Tennessee

Seventh Circuit

Central District Illinois, Northern District Illinois, Southern District Illinois, Northern District Indiana, Southern District Indiana, Eastern District Wisconsin, Western District Wisconsin

Eighth Circuit

Eastern District Arkansas, Western District Arkansas, Northern District Iowa, Southern District Iowa, Minnesota, Eastern District Missouri, Western District Missouri, Nebraska, North Dakota, South Dakota

Ninth Circuit

Alaska, Arizona, Central District California, Eastern District California, Northern District California, Southern District California, Guam, Hawaii, Idaho, Montana, Nevada, Oregon, Eastern District Western District Washington

Tenth Circuit

Colorado, Kansas, Eastern District Oklahoma, Western District Oklahoma, Utah, Wyoming

Eleventh Circuit

Middle District Alabama, Northern District Alabama, Southern District Alabama, Middle District Florida, Southern District Florida, Middle District Georgia, Northern District Georgia, Southern District Georgia

Federal Circuit

Washington, D.C.

SOURCE: Table 1.1 lists the federal circuits and districts. The circuits are subdivided into districts, sometimes but not always along state lines.

≡ THE STEPS IN THE CRIMINAL PROCESS

In all jurisdictions, the general stages in the criminal process are (1) detection and investigation, largely a police responsibility; (2) formally charging and prosecuting, the duty of prosecutors; (3) adjudication, presided over by judges, with prosecutors and defense attorneys participating; (4) sentencing, the responsibility of trial court judges; (5) appeal and collateral attack, an appellate court function; and (6) punishment, the duty of corrections administrators and officers, with supervisory powers in the judiciary. (See Figure 1.3.) These general stages divide into the specific steps that vary from state to state and between states and the federal government. Furthermore, procedure differs for felony cases and misdemeanor cases. **Felonies** are serious crimes, punishable by more than one year or more in prison. **Misdemeanors** are less-serious offenses, punishable by a fine and/or up to one year in jail. Sometimes, procedural differences depend solely upon whether offenders can be sentenced to prison or jail. Finally, informal practice does not always conform to formal rule. The following outline of the steps in the criminal process, needs therefore, some modification to suit specific jurisdictions' rules and practice.[16]

Detection and Investigation

Citizens and the police primarily control the detection and investigative stage of the criminal process.Crimes come to official attention—and therefore criminal cases enter the criminal justice system—only if either police discover or citizens report them. The police discover some crimes on their own, either by witnessing them in progress or by questioning people behaving in suspicious ways under suspicious circumstances. Most crimes, however, come to official attention because citizens report them to the police. Hence, the investigation process begins, in the vast majority of instances, when the police respond to citizen calls. If it appears to the police that a crime has occurred, they file a report, and the crime becomes officially an offense "known to the police."[17]

PRE-ARREST INVESTIGATION. Pre-arrest investigation is general in that it does not focus on a particular suspect. It is designed to determine whether in fact a crime was committed and who might have committed it, and to collect information that answers those questions, information that later might also be used to prove guilt against a particular person. When the investigation shifts so that it focuses on a specific suspect, the process enters the **accusatory stage.**

Where officers observe a crime in progress, the pre-arrest investigation consists of what they observed at the scene. The police arrest the suspect immediately, and the accusatory stage begins. Quite different is pre-arrest investigation where the police do not witness crimes, as when they either observe merely suspicious behavior or learn of citizens' reports of crimes. In these cases, the police attempt to collect more information. They question suspicious people, commonly asking, "Do you have identification?" "Why are you here?"; they interview possible witnesses; and, they examine the crime scene for possible physical evidence.

The police rarely use other techniques, although they may prove important in some cases. Electronic surveillance, for example, occurs in a tiny proportion of cases. In 1985, only 784 wiretapping or other electronic surveillance operations received authorized approval. Occasionally, police also aggressively "sweep" high-crime

FIGURE 1.3   Differences in how prosecutors handle felony cases can be seen in 4 jurisdictions

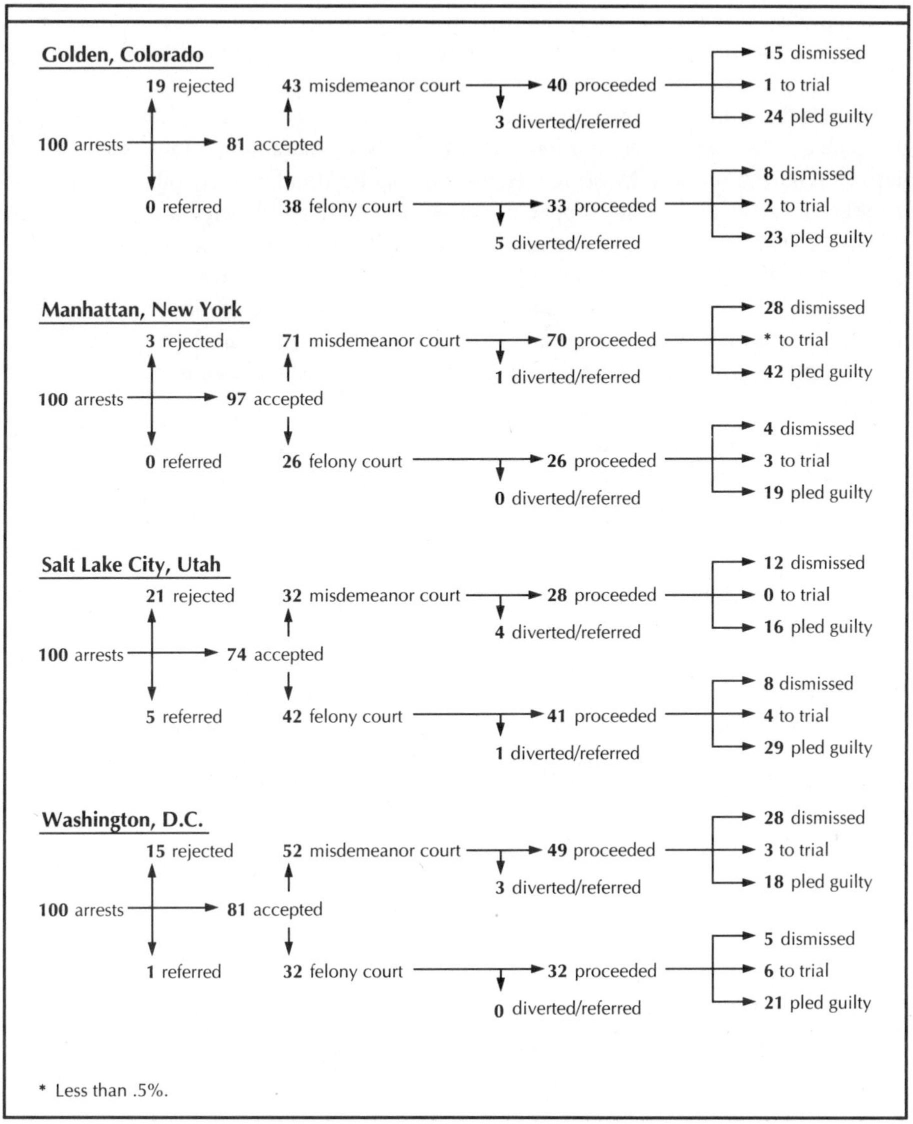

Golden, Colorado

- 19 rejected
- 100 arrests → 81 accepted
- 0 referred
- 43 misdemeanor court → 40 proceeded
  - 3 diverted/referred
  - 15 dismissed
  - 1 to trial
  - 24 pled guilty
- 38 felony court → 33 proceeded
  - 5 diverted/referred
  - 8 dismissed
  - 2 to trial
  - 23 pled guilty

Manhattan, New York

- 3 rejected
- 100 arrests → 97 accepted
- 0 referred
- 71 misdemeanor court → 70 proceeded
  - 1 diverted/referred
  - 28 dismissed
  - * to trial
  - 42 pled guilty
- 26 felony court → 26 proceeded
  - 0 diverted/referred
  - 4 dismissed
  - 3 to trial
  - 19 pled guilty

Salt Lake City, Utah

- 21 rejected
- 100 arrests → 74 accepted
- 5 referred
- 32 misdemeanor court → 28 proceeded
  - 4 diverted/referred
  - 12 dismissed
  - 0 to trial
  - 16 pled guilty
- 42 felony court → 41 proceeded
  - 1 diverted/referred
  - 8 dismissed
  - 4 to trial
  - 29 pled guilty

Washington, D.C.

- 15 rejected
- 100 arrests → 81 accepted
- 1 referred
- 52 misdemeanor court → 49 proceeded
  - 3 diverted/referred
  - 28 dismissed
  - 3 to trial
  - 18 pled guilty
- 32 felony court → 32 proceeded
  - 0 diverted/referred
  - 5 dismissed
  - 6 to trial
  - 21 pled guilty

* Less than .5%.

SOURCE: Barbara Boland with Ronald Sones, INSLAW, Inc., *The prosecution of felony arrests, 1981*, BJS, 1986.

areas, a highly visible investigative tactic. One dramatic example of this occurred in Los Angeles. Following the shooting of a four-year-old boy who was hit in a spray of automatic rifle fire during a gang shoot-out, Police Chief Daryl Gates "vowed to make 'war' on 'rotten little cowards' " who shoot down little children. He dispatched 1,000 officers into "gang-ridden" neighborhoods both specifically to investigate and apprehend the shooters and generally to prevent further gang violence.[18]

ARREST. Once the police are satisfied that they have sufficient evidence that a crime has been committed and that a specific suspect has committed it, they can take the next step in the criminal process—arrest the suspect. There is great controversy over just what constitutes an arrest, but the common formal definition found in many statutes is "taking suspects into custody in order to charge them with crimes." Sometimes, arrests are based on pre-authorized warrants approved by disinterested magistrates; most take place on officers' own initiative without prior judicial approval.

Crimes that officers observe firsthand lead to arrests more often than those that come to police attention either through police-observed mere suspicious behavior or citizen-reported crimes. Most arrests involve public drunkenness, other disorderly-conduct misdemeanors, and property offenses. Less than 10 percent are for serious felonies:—aggravated assault and robbery, about 2 percent; forcible rape and murder, less than 0.005 percent; the remainder spread among arson, nonviolent sex offenses, possession of weapons, and others. A substantial number of arrested persons— between one-fifth and one-third—are juveniles. Most of them will go no further in the adult criminal process; instead they enter the juvenile justice system.

SEARCH INCIDENT TO ARREST. Immediately following arrest, officers search arrested persons for weapons, contraband, and evidence. This is the search incident to a lawful arrest. Other searches accompany other stages in the criminal process.

BOOKING. Shortly following arrest and the search incident to it, the police take suspects to the police station, the jail, or some other short-term "holding facility." Here the police usher suspects through the step in the criminal process called "booking." An officer records in the police "log" or "blotter" suspects' names, times of arrival at the facility, and the offenses for which they were arrested. Next, suspects are fingerprinted and photographed, told what they were booked for, and given permission to make a phone call.

If arrested for a minor offense, suspects might obtain immediate release on "stationhouse bail"—either a small cash security or a promise to appear before a magistrate at an appointed time. If they were arrested for a serious crime or are unable to post adequate security for a minor-offense arrest, they are put in a "lockup" until they appear before a magistrate. Before entering the lockup, suspects undergo a more extensive search than the search incident to the arrest. The inventory search is designed to list suspects' personal belongings and to take any contraband, weapons, and evidence not found at the time of the arrest.

FOLLOW-UP INVESTIGATION. After booking, ordinarily a special investigative unit within the police department called the detective unit conducts more thorough, although not necessarily more productive, investigation. If suspects were caught "red-handed" little or no follow-up may be necessary. Most follow-up investigation utilizes the basic techniques that patrol officers use—interviewing witnesses, including victims and suspects; searching suspects' homes; and examining crime scenes. Follow-up also includes tactics not available to arresting officers. Detectives conduct lineups or "show-ups" where witnesses identify suspects. The detectives may arrange for handwriting samples, take hair samples, and interrogate suspects. Police rarely use these intrusive techniques in misdemeanors, reserving them instead for serious felonies.[19]

The police department reviews the results of most police investigations. If the review discloses insufficient evidence to forward cases for further processing, the department closes them. If the review leads to the conclusion that investigators have gathered sufficient evidence to take the criminal process another step, the department will transfer the case to the prosecutor's office. Police may also make alternative dispositions if they believe a non-criminal-justice response is more appropriate. For example, most police departments do not further process fights among acquaintances but "settle" them within the police department by warning, counsel, or referral to social service agencies. Recently, at least in domestic assault cases, the practice of "settling" has changed in growing numbers of departments.[20]

Instituting Formal Proceedings

If the police decide to take cases to prosecutors, they do so shortly following booking. At that point, the criminal process enters another stage—prosecution. The major responsibility for carrying the criminal process forward now shifts from the police to prosecutors. The police transfer to the prosecutors' office the results of their investigation, including incident reports written by patrol officers at the time of arrest, "rap sheets," and other materials gathered by detectives.

The Decision To Charge

Between booking and suspects' first appearance before lower criminal-court magistrates, prosecutors review the police files. In the initial screening, prosecutors decide whether to charge suspects with any crime at all and, if so, what crime; to dismiss cases outright; or to "divert" them into some non-criminal-justice agency, such as drug and alcohol treatment, family counseling, and juvenile court. In some jurisdictions prosecutors review cases thoroughly before they charge suspects; in other jurisdictions the prosecutors' initial reviews are superficial. For example, some prosecutors glance at the police reports and do nothing more prior to charging; others review the written record extensively, as well as interview police officers and victims. Local practice varies, but prosecutors reject between 30 and 60 percent of all felony arrests in the initial screening. Most decisions to prosecute, divert, or dismiss depend on the facts of the case. The law requires that to charge prosecutors have more than probable cause to detain, but not proof beyond a reasonable doubt. However, in practice most prosecutors do not charge unless they are confident they can convict, either at a trial or in a negotiated plea. The quantum of proof or factual foundation for conviction is proof beyond a reasonable doubt, a considerable higher standard than probable cause.[21]

FILING THE COMPLAINT. If prosecutors decide to charge suspects, they file the **complaint** (the charging document) in a magistrate's court. At the point of filing charges, suspects officially cease to be suspects and become **defendants**, legally innocent citizens formally charged with crimes. In misdemeanor cases, the complaint serves as the only charging document. It will be used throughout criminal proceedings to final disposition in the case. In felony cases, the complaint is only the first charging document. If the criminal process continues, informations and indictments eventually replace complaints after further review by judges and/or grand juries.

Adjudication

Following the decision to charge, the criminal process enters the stage that requires judicial and defense counsels' participation. Adjudication means formal proceedings in court. As soon as prosecutors file charges, every step in the formal criminal justice process demands judicial approval. Adjudication includes all the steps from defendants' first appearance in court, through final disposition by guilty plea, jury verdict, or appeal.

The law requires prosecutors to test their decision to charge before the government can require defendants to answer criminal charges. Prosecutors, on behalf of the government, must satisfy a disinterested third party that they have probable cause that a crime was committed and that the defendant committed it. The probable cause at this point is more than that required to arrest, but considerably short of the quantum of proof required for conviction. Two major mechanisms test the probable cause needed to require defendants to answer criminal charges: (1) the grand jury review, and (2) the preliminary hearing.

If the government satisfies the grand jury, it issues the formal charging instrument, the indictment. If the government satisfies the judge presiding at the preliminary hearing, he or she then issues an order to bind the defendant over for trial. In both cases, the government's establishing the required quantum of proof requires defendants to answer the criminal charges against them; until this point defendants need not answer. Answer in this sense does not literally mean to speak an answer because, of course, this would violate the right against self-incrimination. To ''answer''here means to defend against the charges.

THE FIRST APPEARANCE. The preliminary hearing and grand jury review to test the sufficiency of evidence to prosecute should not be confused with another proceeding, the first appearance. At the first appearance, among other actions, magistrates may determine whether there is probable cause to *detain* arrested suspects in custody. Sometimes, magistrates have already done so by issuing an arrest warrant. However, police arrest most defendants in custody without warrants. In these cases, magistrates either determine probable cause to detain outside court or they do so during defendants' first appearance before the lower criminal courts.[22]

Most states require that officials holding defendants in custody bring them before magistrates without unnecessary delay—usually within hours, but sometimes longer if they were taken into custody at night or on weekends. For defendants not in custody, several days or weeks may lapse between charge and first appearance.

The first appearance takes only a few minutes. Magistrates perform several functions at first appearances. They determine probable cause to detain arrested defendants in custody, if a judicial officer has not already done so. They make certain that the persons before them are those named in the complaint. They, or their clerks, read the charges against defendants and advise them of their rights to remain silent, to an attorney, and to assigned counsel if they cannot afford to hire one. Magistrates determine if defendants are too poor to hire their own lawyers and appoint counsel for these **indigent defendants**.

Magistrates inform felony defendants that the next step in the process will be either the preliminary hearing or grand jury review and will set dates for preliminary hearings. In misdemeanor cases, where defendants do not have a right to a preliminary hearing, magistrates explain available pleas and ask defendants to plead. Most defendants —about 90 percent—eventually plead guilty, although some do not do so at the first appearance because they have not had an opportunity to consult with family, friends, or lawyers.

Finally, magistrates set bail. If defendants have already posted stationhouse bail, magistrates review that decision. They make initial bail decisions for felony defendants, most of whom remain in custody from arrest to first appearance. Magistrates then set the conditions under which defendants can obtain their release from custody. Sometimes, the condition is a mere promise to appear (**release on recognizance** or ROR); sometimes it is a money bond; occasionally, it restricts movement and associations and requires released persons to report there whereabouts periodically.[23]

THE PRELIMINARY HEARING. Preliminary hearings follow the first appearance, usually within a few weeks. During that interval, prosecutors may dispose of cases by plea bargaining or further review before the scheduled preliminary hearing. In thirty states, defendants have a right to preliminary hearings. In states where grand juries have the power to indict, the preliminary hearing status varies. In most of the indictment jurisdictions, prosecutors can bypass the preliminary hearing and take cases directly to the grand jury.

Preliminary hearings permit neutral magistrates to screen prosecutors' decisions to charge, in order to avoid when possible, or justify if necessary, further intrusions against defendants and expenditures of government resources. In preliminary hearings, magistrates address the probable cause to charge defendants with crimes in an adversary setting. Preliminary hearings are public proceedings. At them, lawyers represent defendants, the prosecution presents evidence—usually the government's main witnesses—and the defense counsel cross-examines the witnesses. Magistrates dismiss charges where the government has not satisfied the quantum of proof needed to bind defendants over to answer the charges against them. In cases where the facts do not satisfy the evidentiary standard for binding over for felony, presiding judges usually permit prosecutors to substitute misdemeanor charges for felony charges. If magistrates find probable cause, they **bind over** defendants, that is, they send the case forward for trial, requiring defendants to answer criminal charges formally.[24]

GRAND JURY REVIEW. About half the states require that grand juries **indict**, or formally charge defendants for at least some felonies before the courts may try them. The grand jury comprises up to twenty-three private citizens. Unlike the trial jury that in most jurisdictions, requires a unanimous vote to convict or acquit, the grand jury needs only a majority vote to indict. The grand jury, like the judge in preliminary hearings, screens cases in order to determine if probable cause exists to require defendants to answer. Unlike the preliminary hearing, grand jury proceedings are secret, only the prosecution presents evidence, and neither defendants nor their counsel attend.

If a majority of the grand jury agrees that the prosecution has the required quantum of proof, it issues the indictment. Indictments—formal charging instruments requiring defendants to answer—briefly describe the offense and approve the prosecutor's charge by marking it with the ancient notation, **true bill**. If grand juries reject the prosecutor's case, charges are dismissed. Grand jury rejections are rare—about 3 to 8 percent of the cases. This low rejection rate has led many to conclude that grand juries are prosecutors' rubber stamps. In many instances they are. Most prosecutors, however, avoid presenting cases to grand juries unless they believe they have sufficient evidence to convict. Former United States Attorney General Elliott Richardson said he never asked for an indictment unless he believed he had proof beyond a reasonable doubt to convict the defendant. Hence, the standard in practice is much higher than the legally required **prima facie case**—enough evidence to convict if the evidence the defense presents does not later rebut it.[25]

FILING THE INDICTMENT OR INFORMATION. When prosecutors file indictments in the trial courts after the grand jury issues them, indictments replace complaints as the principal accusatory document. In jurisdictions not requiring grand jury review, prosecutors file a document called the **information**, a substitute for the grand jury indictment. Although grand juries do not screen informations, preliminary hearing bind-overs must support them.

ARRAIGNMENT. Once the government has passed the evidentiary test, and assuming prosecutors file the indictments or informations, courts arraign defendants. **Arraignment** means to bring defendants before trial courts, to inform them of the specific charges against them, and to ask them to plead to those charges. The pleas to the charges include guilty, not guilty, or **nolo contendere** (no contest, which does not admit guilt but simply agrees not to fight the case). Defendants who refuse to plead have pleas of not guilty entered for them. Up to 90 percent of all felony defendants will plead guilty, either because they have negotiated a plea with the government in return for reducing charges or lesser sentences, or because they believe the case against them is so strong that it is futile to contest it.[26]

PRETRIAL MOTIONS. Most jurisdictions require that if defendants have objections, they enter most of them by pretrial motions. Most common motions either challenge the court's jurisdiction or authority to hear the case, or request **discovery**, that is, the government and defendants reveal to the other side information in their possession. Motions to suppress evidence and confessions obtained illegally generate the most litigation. Also included are motions claiming double jeopardy and speedy trial violations.[27] Despite the wide publicity given to excluding evidence and attempts to "get off on technicalities," in less than 10 percent of all cases do defendants file pretrial motions.

TRIAL. In popular conception, the trial is the high point of the criminal process, even though trials dispose of only about 2 percent of all criminal cases. Most trials are brief affairs; misdemeanor trials frequently consume less than a day. Although some felony cases take longer, most are decided in only a few days. Complicated cases might last three weeks or longer. Such cases attract public attention, but they are rare.

Defendants have the right to a jury in all felony cases and in misdemeanors punishable by more than 6 months incarceration. Juries traditionally had twelve members but the required number of jurors is decreasing, with some jurisdictions requiring only six. Although defendants can waive jury trial, most do not. In nearly all cases jury verdicts, either for acquittal or conviction, must be unanimous. Juries that cannot agree on a verdict are called **hung juries**.

The basic ingredients in criminal trials are (1) **the presumption of innocence**, that is, defendants are deemed innocent until the government proves them guilty; (2) the requirement that the government must prove defendants' **guilt beyond a reasonable doubt;** (3) the right of defendants under the Fifth Amendment to the United States Constitution not to take the stand; (4) presentation of evidence; (5) arguments about law

Chapter 1 *Overview of Criminal Procedure*   **37**

and fact; (6) opening and closing statements; (7) instructions to the jury; and (8) jury deliberations. Most trials end in conviction, probably because prosecutors do not go to trial unless they are fairly convinced they can get convictions. Notably excepted from this tendency to convict are cases involving rape and robbery, in which defendants' chances for acquittal rate better than the overall average of 30 percent acquittal and 70 percent conviction.[28]

Sentencing

If defendants are convicted, judges enter a judgment of conviction and schedule a time for sentencing. Statutes prescribe sentences, but to varying degrees, judges have discretion to set alternative sentences. In misdemeanor cases, judges can choose among probation, suspended sentences, fines, and short jail terms. In felonies, judges have less discretion, particularly under recent statutes that both prescribe mandatory sentences and narrow the maximum and minimum limits within which judges may sentence. Still, judges have considerable leeway to sentence in most jurisdictions.

Review Proceedings

Three principal mechanisms exist to review proceedings after sentencing: (1) new trial; (2) appeal; and (3) collateral attack.

NEW TRIAL. Rule 33, *Federal Rules of Criminal Procedure*, the rules governing procedure in federal courts and followed by most state courts, provides:

> The court on motion of a defendant may grant a new trial to him if required in the interest of justice.[29]

Parties base their motion for new trial on such things as the discovery of new evidence. Motions based on the discovery of new evidence must show that the party discovered the evidence after trial, that the parties' lack of diligence led to the failure to discover the evidence, that the evidence is material, and that an acquittal would probably follow trial with the newly discovered evidence available. A motion for new trial will also be granted if prosecutors (1) knowingly use perjured testimony, or even unknowingly use a material witness's perjured testimony, if such testimony could have affected the jury's verdict; or (2) fail to disclose, at defendant's request, evidence that could reasonably affect the outcome of the case; or (3) interfere with communications between defense counsel and defendants. Defendants may move for a new trial because the proof beyond a reasonable doubt did not support the jury's verdict.[30]

APPEALS.   Felony appeals are taken to an intermediate appeals court first, if there is one, and then to the supreme court. Some states and the federal court systems have intermediate appeals courts. In states without intermediate appeals courts, felony appeals are taken directly to the Supreme Court. In misdemeanor cases, appeals go to the trial court. In some decisions, cases are tried over in a proceeding called **trial de novo**. Although all criminal cases can be appealed, in practice most appeals are limited to cases in which defendants have been sentenced to prison.

The American Bar Association Project on Standards for Criminal Justice, produced by some of the nation's leading authorities on criminal procedure, provides the following standard for appellate review:

> Section 5.3 Appellate court disposition; scope of appellate review.
> (a) Appellate courts should exercise a broad scope of review on matters of fact and law consistent with the fundamental rights subject to litigation in post-conviction proceedings.
> (b) A statement of the basis or bases for decision in a reasoned opinion ought to accompany dispositions of appeals.[31]

Most courts comply with subsection (b). Appellate court opinions form the basis of much legal thinking and decision making, as well as instructional materials for law students, students of constitutional law, and students of criminal justice.

The government can appeal adverse rulings in criminal cases only when statutes authorize such appeals, and the Constitution does not bar it. Perhaps the most important constitutional limitation on state appeals is the Fifth Amendment bar to double jeopardy. An appeal of a trial court's dismissal would put the defendant in jeopardy twice if the trial court decided the defendant was innocent. Similarly, the double jeopardy clause prohibits the state from appealing an acquittal. The clause does not bar appeals of guilty verdicts because reversal would result simply in reinstating the guilty verdict. Prosecutors may also appeal sentences without violating the double jeopardy clause.[32]

Contrary to popular belief, most appeals do not result in reversal and freedom for defendants. Particularly in serious crimes where the evidence clearly indicates guilt, appellate courts rarely reverse. Most reversals occur in misdemeanors, less serious felonies, or cases in which doubts exist about the proof of guilt. Although they make sensational journalism, the clearly guilty violent criminal rarely goes free in the real world. In fact, one researcher contends who studied a major appellate court in the San Francisco area concluded that the problem is at the other end—that courts do not afford enough protection to defendants in criminal cases.[33]

COLLATERAL ATTACK. After all appeals are taken and offenders are imprisoned, they may still challenge their convictions in postconviction proceedings on limited grounds called **collateral attack**, or **collateral review**. All jurisdictions have special collateral review proceedings. In addition, convicted defendants can challenge state convictions in federal courts through **habeas corpus**, an order to challenge the lawfulness of imprisonment. All modern collateral attacks derive from the **common law** writs—orders incorporated into American law from the ancient courts of England—of habeas corpus and **coram nobis**, a writ that permitted higher courts to correct trial court errors of fact. Hence, the writ of habeas corpus was used to challenge errors of law and coram nobis to correct errors of fact. Today, statutes govern most collateral review; but common law writs and the United States Constitution influence the content of those statutes.

═══ SUMMARY

The history of criminal procedure demonstrates a tension between ends and means. The primary end in criminal procedure is the interest in the search for truth—apprehending, convicting, and punishing the guilty and protecting the innocent. The interest in means places primary emphasis on the process by which the government enforces the criminal law. Process interests include protecting the rights of the individual, due process of law, timeliness, and finality. Criminal procedure also promotes other interests, including the structural interest in separation of powers and checks and balances; the societal interest in fairness, equality, and human dignity; organizational interest in economy, efficiency, harmony, and effectiveness; and democratic interest in community participation in law enforcement. Because criminal procedure balances these interests, it is both result oriented and means directed. American criminal procedure does not permit the search for truth at any price; means sometimes take precedence over ends.

The criminal process constitutes a series of government intrusions and deprivations beginning with brief street contacts to investigate crime prior to formal criminal proceedings and extending to life imprisonment and capital punishment after conviction. To justify these intrusions and deprivations requires both a proper purpose (investigation of crime, apprehension, prosecution, and punishment of criminals) and sufficient objective factual foundations (reasonable suspicion, probable cause, proof beyond a reasonable doubt). The greater the intrusion or deprivation, the greater the factual foundation required to support it—reasonable suspicion to stop; probable cause to arrest; proof beyond a reasonable doubt to convict.

The structure of the American criminal justice system consists of both federal, state, and local agencies and executive, judicial, and legislative branches. The United States and state constitutions, statutes, and administrative rules allocate the power to enforce the criminal law among these agencies and branches that manage each step in the criminal process. The principal steps include investigation managed mainly by police; institution of formal charges managed by prosecutors; adjudication or formal court proceedings; sentencing; and review proceedings, including appeals and collateral attack.

≡ QUESTIONS FOR REVIEW AND DISCUSSION

1. What are the principal differences between criminal law and criminal procedure?
2. Describe the pendulum swing in the history of criminal procedure and discuss its importance.
3. Identify and explain the interests that criminal procedure promotes and balances.
4. Explain how criminal procedure is both result and process oriented. Which, in your opinion, is more important? Why?
5. What are the main legitimate purposes of the intrusions and deprivations in the criminal process? What are some illegitimate purposes?
6. Explain how the law of criminal procedure justifies the series of greater deprivations and deeper intrusions?
7. Describe the main stages in the criminal process and the agencies and officials responsible for them.
8. Describe the principal steps in the criminal process and the agencies and officials responsible for them.
9. Explain the principal parts of the structure of American criminal justice.

===== **NOTES**

1. See Justice Shirley Abrahamson, Wisconsin Supreme Court, "Criminal Law and State Constitutions: The Emergence of State Constitutional Law," *Texas Law Review* 63(1985): 1141, at 1152–53.

2. Roscoe Pound, "The Future of the Criminal Law," *Columbia Law Review* 21 (1921): 1–16.

3. Strachan-Davidson, *Problems of the Roman Criminal Law* (1912), 114, 168.

4. Pound, "The Future of the Criminal Law," 9.

5. American Academy of Political and Social Science, Annals 46 (1910).

6. Samuel Walker, *Popular Justice* (New York: Oxford University Press, 1980), 161–221, (for the period 1920–1960; Thomas E. Cronin et al., *U.S. v. Crime in the Streets* (Bloomington: Indiana University Press, 1981), for the 1960s and 1970s.

7. Francis T. Cullen and Karen E. Gilbert, *Rethinking Rehabilitation* (Cincinnati: Anderson Publishing Company, 1982); Elliot Currie, *Confronting Crime* (New York: Pantheon, 1985).

8. The classic modern work that discusses balancing the social interest in crime control and individual autonomy is Herbert Packer, *The Limits of the Criminal Sanction* (Stanford: Stanford University Press, 1968).

9. Peter Arenella, "Rethinking the Functions of Criminal Procedure: The Warren and Burger Courts' Competing Ideologies," *The Georgetown Law Journal* 72(1983):185–248.

10. Louis Michael Seidman, "Factual Guilt and the Burger Court: An Examination of Continuity and Change in Criminal Procedure," *Columbia Law Review* 80(1980):436–503.

11. Aranella, "Rethinking the Functions of Criminal Procedure, 199ff.

12. Joseph Goldstein, "Reflections on Two Models: Inquisitorial Themes in American Criminal Procedure," *Stanford Law Review* 26(1974):1099.

13. James Eisenstein and Herbert Jacob, *Felony Justice* (Boston: Little Brown,1977) 24–27.

14. Seidman, "Factual Guilt and the Burger Court" 437–503.

15. *Report to the Nation on Crime and Justice* (Washington, D.C.: National Institute of Justice, 1983), 45.

16. The steps in the criminal process are discussed in many works and generally adhere to the outline included in the discussion that follows. For a recent, authoritative, and more detailed analysis than is possible here, see Wayne R. LaFave and Jerold H. Israel, *Criminal Procedure*, vol.1 (St. Paul: West Publishing Company, 1984), 11–32.

17. This conclusion has been widely confirmed in the literature on policing. For a few discussions and studies, see John A. Webster, "Police Task and Time Study," *Journal of Criminal Law, Criminology, and Police Science* 61(1970): 94–100; Donald J. Black, *The Manners and Customs of the Police* (New York: Academic Press, 1980); Eric J. Scott, *Calls for Service: Citizen Demand and Initial Police Response* (Washington, D.C.: National Institute of Justice, July, 1981); James Q. Wilson, *Thinking About Crime* (New York: Vintage Press, 1985), chap. 4; Jerome H. Skolnick and David H. Bayley, *The New Blue Line* (New York: Free Press, 1986).

18. Katherine M. Jamieson and Timothy J. Flanagan, *Sourcebook of Criminal Justice Statistics* (Washington, D.C.: Bureau of Justice Statistics, 1987), table 5.2 335; "Police Deployed to Curb Gangs in Los Angeles," *The New York Times*, April 9, 1988, p. 7.

19. Peter W. Greenwood and Joan Petersilia, *The Criminal Investigation Process* (Santa Monica: The Rand Corporation, 1975) discusses the follow-up step thoroughly. Using empirical data, the authors conclude that the follow-up investigation rarely yields significant evidence beyond what patrol officers already obtained.

20. Lawrence W. Sherman and Richard A. Berk, "The Specific Deterrent Effects of Arrest for Domestic Assault," *The American Sociological Review* 49(1984):261–72; *Police Report on Domestic Violence: A National Survey* (Washington, D.C.: The Crime Control Institute, 1986).

21. Bureau of Justice Statistics, *The Prosecution of Felony Arrests*, 1981 (Washington, D.C.: July 1986); Brian Forst, Judith Lucianovic, and Sarah J. Cox, *What Happens After Arrest* (Washington, D.C.: National Institute of Law Enforcement and Criminal Justice, 1977); Vera Institute of Justice, *Felony Arrests: Their Prosecution and Disposition in New York City's Courts* (New York: Vera Institute of Justice, 1977).

22. LaFave and Israel, *Criminal Procedure*, 21.

23. Andy Hall et al., *Pretrial Release Program Options* (Washington, D.C.: National Institute of Justice, 1984).

24. LaFave and Israel, *Criminal Procedure*, 23–25.

25. Elliot Richardson's comments appeared on television and radio several times during the week when the special prosecutor announced that he would not seek to indict President Reagan's Attorney General Edwin Meese and reporters wanted to know the significance of the special prosecutor's decision.

26. Arthur Rossett and Donald Cressey, *Justice by Consent: Plea Bargains in American Courthouses* (Philadelphia: J. B. Lippincott Company 1976); William F. McDonald and James A. Cramer, eds., *Plea Bargaining* (Cambridge, Mass.: Lexington Books, 1980); Albert Alschuler, "Plea Bargaining and Its History," *Columbia Law Review* 79 (1979), 1–43.

27. LaFave and Israel, *Criminal Procedure*, 27.

28. LaFave and Israel, *Criminal Procedure*, 28.

29. *Federal Criminal Code and Rules*, 1988 ed. (St. Paul: West Publishing, 1988).

30. "Sixteenth Annual Review of Criminal Procedure," *The Georgetown Law Journal* 75(1987):1219–24.

31. American Bar Association Project on Standards for Criminal Justice, *Standards Relating to Post-Conviction Remedies* (Chicago: American Bar Association, 1967), 19.

32. Ibid., 1225–32.

33. Thomas Y. Davies, "Affirmed: A Study of Criminal Appeals and Decision-Making Norms in a California Court of Appeal," *American Bar Foundation Research Journal* (1982):548–52.

Chapter Two

Formal and Informal Dimensions In Criminal Procedure

CHAPTER OUTLINE

CHAPTER MAIN POINTS

1. There is both a formal and informal dimension to criminal procedure.

2. The United States Constitution, state constitutions, statutes, court decisions, and rules control the formal law of criminal procedure.

3. Discretion determines informal practice in the criminal process.

4. The United States Supreme Court supervises local criminal justice administration by using the due process clause of the Fourteenth Amendment to the United States Constitution to apply the federal Bill of Rights to local criminal procedure.

5. The Supreme Court has an extremely limited power to infuse local criminal practice with the federal Bill of Rights.

6. Discretionary power to control daily practice greatly influences the criminal process.

7. Both formal criminal procedure law and informal discretion promote the result, process, organizational, societal, and democratic interests of the criminal process.

CHAPTER KEY TERMS

accusatory system the government bears the burden of proof

adversary system defense and government are opponents with impartial judge to monitor proceedings

bills of attainder statutes making specifically named individuals criminals

discretion the power to decide without formal rules

due process clause the Fourteenth Amendment to the United States Constitution prohibiting states from depriving citizens of life, liberty, or property without due process of law

due process revolution the 1960s series of Supreme Court decisions applying the federal Bill of Rights to the states through the due process clause

ex post facto laws retroactive statutes

fundamental fairness doctrine leaves to states most criminal practice except that which offends fundamental principles of justice

incorporation doctrine applying the federal Bill of Rights to state criminal procedure

presumption of innocence defendants in criminal cases are presumed innocent unless and until the government proves them guilty beyond a reasonable doubt

selective incorporation only some federal rights are incorporated by the due process clause

total incorporation all federal rights are incorporated by the due process clause.

≡ LAW AND DISCRETION

Rule of law, due process of law, and innocence until proven guilty represent the basic principles underlying the law of criminal procedure, the *formal* dimension in the criminal process. Less visible **discretion,** the power to act without written rules, governs the *informal* side of the criminal process. The public knows the informal side of criminal procedure mainly through criticisms of its agents—police who exercise discretion not to arrest, prosecutors who do not charge suspects or participate in plea bargaining, and judges who release defendants on bail or penalize convicted offenders with "lenient" sentences. The public perceives the failure to abide by the strict prescriptions in the law as being "soft on crime," or "coddling criminals."

To be sure, discretion carries the risk of abuse; but injustice also follows from mechanically applying written rules to all cases. For example, Sandra Keller had lived an exemplary life, working as a hairdresser in New York City. She had never used or sold drugs but knew someone who did. She agreed to set up a small heroin sale for another friend, but when asked to plan a second purchase, she refused. The police arrested her for participating in the first sale. She was convicted of sale of a controlled substance in the first degree and, under New York's mandatory minimum-sentence drug law, received fifteen years to life! The judge, district attorney, and defense counsel agreed that the law was too harsh, but its provisions gave them no choice. Keller was an exemplary prisoner. Governor Cuomo granted her executive clemency after she had served seven years in prison. In the interim, however, she lost almost everything she had, including her hairdressing license and her boyfriend.[1]

Justice, fairness, efficiency, effectiveness, and economy all require both the certainty and the protection against abuses that written rules provide. The same goals also require an equally important flexibility of discretion to soften the rigidity of written rules. The tension between formal law and informal discretion—a recurring theme in this textbook—is as old as law; arguments raged over it in Western civilization as early as the Middle Ages. The expense of full enforcement—maximum arrests, charges, sentences, and punishments—exceeds what the public will willingly pay. Despite the strains inherent in the relationship between formal law and informal discretion, the criminal process requires both.[2]

Decision Point

An ordinance prohibits drinking in city parks; the penalty is a fine of up to $100 and/or a sentence of up to ten days in jail. Consider the following hypotheticals. Should the police arrest? the prosecutor charge? If so, based on the possible penalties above, what penalties would you impose? Reconsider your answers after reading the remainder of the chapter.

1. A gourmet club has a brunch in a city park. It serves salmon mousse, French bread, and white wine.
2. An alcoholic sprawls out in the park, washing down a tuna fish sandwich with a cheap red wine.
3. Twenty-five rowdy youths gather in the park to have a party; they bring six kegs of beer, shout at passersby, and generally make nuisances of themselves.

Formally, all three examples constitute violations of the ordinance. In practice, police exercised discretion not to arrest the gourmet club members, they did arrest the alcoholic, and they would at least disperse, and perhaps arrest, some of the rowdy youths.

THE FORMAL DIMENSION: LAWS REGULATING THE CRIMINAL PROCESS

The Formal Sources of the Law of Criminal Procedure

Criminal justice administration is predominantly a state and local affair. As much as 95 percent of all criminal investigation, prosecution, adjudication, and punishment occurs at the state or municipal level. Nevertheless, both federal and state sources give rise to the formal law of criminal procedure. The law of criminal procedure ultimately derives from the United States Constitution—the ''supreme law of the land'' (Art. VI, U.S.

Const.)—and the constitutions of the individual states. A hierarchy of sources interpret, amplify, and apply constitutional provisions in individual cases. At the top of the hierarchy, the United States Supreme Court defines *minimum* national standards that govern federal and state criminal procedure. However, for a number of reasons, the Supreme Court only addresses some criminal procedure issues, and it depends on local courts and police to apply its decisions.[3]

Lower federal courts and state courts resolve fundamental issues that the Supreme Court has not yet addressed, and perhaps never will. (See chap. 3.) Furthermore, the arguments advanced, and the decisions rendered in these courts, *suggest,* if they do not *compel,* results that extend beyond their own borders. In addition, state court decisions interpreting state constitutional provisions can differ from United States Supreme Court decisions interpreting parallel federal constitutional provisions. The United States Constitution sets *minimum* standards; states may raise these standards. States have increasingly done so recently when federal constitutional procedure law is in flux. A major trend in criminal procedure law in the 1980s is the revival of state constitutional law.[4]

> The United States Supreme Court is not, however, the only supreme court that exercises the power of judicial review. The state supreme courts also exercise this power. They do so not only in cases arising under the Federal Constitution but also in cases arising under their own state constitutions. When they interpret the Federal Constitution, their decisions are not supreme but are subject to review by the United States Supreme Court. When they interpret their own state constitutional provisions, their decisions are supreme, unless their interpretation conflicts with a provision of the Federal Constitution.[5]

Court decisions, whether federal or state, do not cover all the major issues in the law of criminal procedure. Rules of criminal procedure, both federal and state, govern most practices throughout the criminal process, from arrest through appeal following conviction. The federal rules, which most states follow, grew out of the deep dissatisfaction with the administration of justice during the early decades of the twentieth century. In 1940, Congress authorized the Supreme Court to adopt rules of criminal procedure for the federal courts. Pursuant to this authorization, the Court appointed ''a group of eminent practitioners and scholars'' to research and draft rules that would effectively put the ideals of the Constitution into daily practice.

> In three and one half years of hard labor the group produced the Federal Rules of Criminal Procedure. For the first time in history the premises of procedure had been assembled in a body, neatly organized, expressed tersely and concisely.[6]

The federal rules—and the state rules fashioned after them—do not address the pre-arrest stages of the criminal process, particularly the encounters between citizens and the police on the street. (See chap. 4.) The American Law Institute, made up of a group of distinguished practitioners and scholars drafted a *Model Code of Pre-Arraignment Procedure* that fills this gap in existing rules. Although not law, courts frequently cite both the code and the authoritative commentary that accompanies it in decisions interpreting Fourth Amendment stop-and-frisk law. (See chap. 4.) In addition, the code and its commentaries address the basic issues in the criminal process that arise in the interval between citizens' first contacts with police and arraignment (formal charge in court). (See chap. 5–8.) The Model Code provisions provide both a possible resolution to issues that arise during this critical period and stimulating arguments to support their proposals. This textbook presents *what* resolutions the Supreme Court adopts in particular cases. However, it also emphasizes the *continuing* legal and public policy issues in criminal procedure, the *way* the courts resolve them, and the *arguments* that underlie the resolution.

The focus on continuing legal and public policy problems, and the reasoning that underlies decisions, will help you to understand better and, it is hoped, develop a method of resolving general issues as they arise in specific cases. Figure 2.1 sets out the major formal sources found in criminal procedure and in this text that address these issues. In other words, the Supreme Court, lower federal court, and state court opinions, the federal and state rules, and the model rules address *both* the current rule in particular cases *and* the manner of resolving continuing constitutional and policy questions.

FIGURE 2.1   Formal Sources of Criminal Procedure Law Used in the Text

---

United States Constitution

The supreme law of the land, the ultimate source of authority in criminal procedure.

State Constitutions

Parallel provisions to United States Constitution.

United States Supreme Court Decisions

Interpret, amplify, and apply federal constitutional standards to specific cases. Decisions are the law of the land.

United States Courts of Appeals and District Courts

Decisions are the law only in the territory covered by their jurisdiction, and only unless and until the United States Supreme Court rules on the question, at which point the Supreme Court decision takes precedence. Although not law beyond their own jurisdictions, decisions address important issues and suggest results that other jurisdictions may follow.

State Court Opinions

State can *raise* standards under provisions in state constitutions parallel to federal constitutional provisions, but they cannot *reduce* those standards below the minimum set by the United States Constitution as interpreted by the United States Supreme Court.

Federal Rules of Criminal Procedure

The rules established by the United States Supreme Court that govern practice in all federal courts from the time of the filing of a criminal complaint to appeals from, and other challenges to, convictions in federal courts. Most states have adopted rules similar to the Federal Rules of Criminal Procedure.

Model Code of Pre-Arraignment Procedure

The American Law Institute's Model Code to govern practice in police-citizen encounters on the street not covered by the federal rules, but sometimes found in state "stop-and-frisk" statutes. The code and commentary embody the arguments and recommendations of distinguished criminal justice professionals and scholars. The code is not law, but courts often cite both its model provisions and the authoritative commentary accompanying the provisions.

The starting point in the relationship between federal and state law is the United States Constitution. Article I, section 9, guarantees habeas corpus and prohibits **bills of attainder** (laws that make specifically named individuals criminals) and **ex post facto** laws (retroactive criminal statutes). Article III, section 2, guarantees trial by jury and that trials shall take place in the state where they were committed. The supremacy clause in Article VI declares the United States Constitution the supreme law of the land. No laws, federal or state, can contravene the provisions in the United States Constitution. In the landmark case *Marbury v. Madison,* Chief Justice John Marshall declared that the United States Supreme Court had the power to review statutes and determine whether they contravened the Constitution. Hence, the Supreme Court established the principle of **judicial review,** the power of courts to rule on the constitutionality of statutes and, by implication, all government action.[7]

Alexander Hamilton defended judicial review in the *Federalist Papers:*

> The interpretation of laws is the proper and peculiar province of the courts. A constitution is, in fact, and must be regarded by the judges, as a fundamental law. It therefore belongs to them to ascertain its meaning, as well as the meaning of any particular act proceeding from the legislative body. If there should happen to be an irreconcilable variance between the two, that which has the superior obligation and validity ought, of course, to be preferred; or, in other words, the Constitution ought to be preferred to the statute, the intention of the people to the intention of their agents.[8]

The Fourth, Fifth, Sixth, Eighth, and Fourteenth Amendments provide the constitutional framework of criminal procedure, as the attention given to them in the cases and throughout the text makes clear. Table 2.1 summarizes the protections of the Bill of Rights. The Fourth, Fifth, Sixth, and Eighth Amendments guarantee *federal* rights, that is, rights possessed by defendants against the United States government. The Fourteenth Amendment extends a variety of protections to defendants in *state proceedings.* The Fourteenth Amendment guarantees to all citizens the **privileges and immunities** of citizens of the United States and prohibits states from denying any person **equal protection of the laws** and from depriving any person of life, liberty, or property without **due process of law.** The Supreme Court has interpreted the due process clause to require states to grant most of the rights included in the Bill of Rights to persons in state proceedings. Courts interpret and apply the Constitution by means of the **supervisory power,** sometimes called the **police power.**

TABLE 2.1   The Protections of the Bill of Rights

Fourth Amendment
(1) guarantee against unreasonable searches and seizures The right of the people to be secure in their persons, houses, papers, and effects, against unreasonable searches and seizures, shall not be violated, and no warrants shall issue, but upon probable cause, supported by oath or affirmation, and particularly describing the place to be searched, and the persons or things to be seized.

Fifth Amendment

guarantees regarding:
(2) grand jury indictment
(3) double jeopardy
(4) due process
(5) self-incrimination

No person shall be held to answer for a capital, or otherwise infamous crime, unless on a presentment or indictment of a Grand Jury, except in cases arising in the land or naval forces, or in the militia, when in actual service in time of war or public danger; nor shall any person be subject for the same offence to be twice put in jeopardy of life or limb; nor shall be compelled in any criminal case to be a witness against himself, nor be deprived of life, liberty, or property, without due process of law. . . .

Sixth Amendment

rights to:
(6) public and speedy trial
(7) impartial jury
(8) notice of the nature and cause of accusation
(9) confrontation of opposing witnesses
(10) compulsory process
(11) assistance counsel

In all criminal prosecutions, the accused shall enjoy the right to a speedy and public trial, by an impartial jury of the State and district wherein the crime shall have been committed, which district shall have been previously ascertained by law, and to be informed of the nature and cause of the accusation; to be confronted with the witnesses against him; to have compulsory process for obtaining witnesses in his favor, and to have the assistance of counsel for his defense.

Eighth Amendment

prohibitions against:
(12) excessive bail
(13) cruel and unusual punishment

Excessive bail shall not be required, nor excessive fines imposed, nor cruel and usual punishment inflicted.

Someone once said that it does not pay a law much of a compliment to declare it constitutional. What the commentator meant was that the United States Constitution sets a *minimum* standard for criminal justice administration. Hence, Congress, the courts, the states, local government, and other criminal justice agencies cannot abolish or reduce constitutional guarantees, but they can supplement them, fill in the blanks, amplify them, as it were. They often do. Most important, state and local governments can *raise* the standards above the constitutionally required minimum. The text frequently refers to cases where states have raised the constitutional minimum, including (1) search and seizure; (2) self-incrimination; (3) double jeopardy; (4) the right to counsel; (5) trial by jury; (6) bail; and (7) cruel and unusual punishment. The two cases excerpted here, *United States v. Robinson* and *People v. Brisendine,* provide an introduction to this problem of the constitutional minimum in the case of searches accompanying traffic arrests. (See chapter 5 for a full discussion of searches incident to arrest.)[9]

CASE

Should traffic violators be searched?
THE FEDERAL STANDARD

United States v. Robinson

414 U.S. 218, 94 S.Ct. 467, 38 L.Ed.2d 427 (1973)

[Justice Rehnquist delivered the court's opinion.]

FACTS

On April 23, 1968, at approximately 11 p.m., Officer Richard Jenks, a 15-year veteran of the District of Columbia Metropolitan Police Department, observed the respondent driving a 1965 Cadillac near the intersection of 8th and C Streets, N.E., in the District of Columbia. Jenks, as a result of previous investigation following a check of respondent's operator's permit four days earlier, determined there was reason to believe that respondent was operating a motor vehicle after the revocation of his operator's permit. This is an offense defined by statute in the District of Columbia which carries a mandatory minimum jail term, a mandatory minimum fine, or both.

Jenks signaled respondent to stop the automobile, which respondent did, and all three of the occupants emerged from the car. At that point Jenks informed respondent that he was under arrest for "operating after revocation and obtaining a permit by misrepresentation." It was assumed by the Court of Appeals, and is conceded by the respondent here, that Jenks had probable cause to arrest respondent, and that he effected a full-custody arrest.

In accordance with procedures prescribed in police department instructions, Jenks then began to search respondent. He explained at a subsequent hearing that he was "face-to-face" with the respondent, and "placed [his] hands on [the respondent], my right hand to his left breast like this (demonstrating) and proceeded to pat him down thus [with the right hand]." During this patdown, Jenks felt an object in the left breast pocket of the heavy coat respondent was wearing, but testified that he "couldn't tell what it was" and also that he "couldn't actually tell the size of it." Jenks then reached into the pocket and pulled out the object, which turned out to be a "crumpled cigarette package." Jenks testified that at this point he still did not know what was in the package:

> "As I felt the package I could feel objects in the package but I couldn't tell what they were. . . . I knew they weren't cigarettes."

The officer then opened the cigarette pack and found 14 gelatin capsules of white powder which he thought to be, and which later analysis proved to be, heroin. Jenks then continued his search of respondent to completion, feeling around his waist and trouser legs, and examining the remaining pockets. The heroin seized from the respondent was admitted into evidence at the trial which resulted in his conviction in the District Court. . . .

OPINION

. . . A police officer's determination as to how and where to search the person of a suspect whom he has arrested is necessarily a quick *ad hoc* judgment which the Fourth Amendment does not require to be broken down in each instance into an analysis of each step in the search. . . . A custodial arrest of a person based on probable cause is a reasonable intrusion under the Fourth Amendment; that intrusion being lawful, a search incident to the arrest requires no additional justification. It is the fact of the lawful arrest which establishes the authority to search, and we hold that in the case of a lawful custodial arrest a full search of the person is not only an exception to the warrant requirement of the Fourth Amendment, but is also a "reasonable" search under that Amendment. . . .

. . . Since it is the fact of custodial arrest which gives rise to the authority to search, it is of no moment that Jenks did not indicate any subjective fear of the respondent or that he did not himself suspect that respondent was armed. Having in the course of a lawful search come upon the crumpled package of cigarettes, he was entitled to inspect it; and when his inspection revealed the heroin capsules, he was entitled to seize them as "fruits, instrumentalities, or contraband" probative of criminal conduct. . . .

DISSENT

Mr. Justice Marshall, with whom Mr. Justice Douglas and Mr. Justice Brennan join, dissenting.

. . . "There is no formula for the determination of reasonableness. Each case is to be decided on its own facts and circumstances." . . . "The constitutional validity of a warrantless search is preeminently the sort of question which can only be decided in the concrete factual context of the individual case." And the intensive, at times painstaking, case-by-case analysis characteristic of our Fourth Amendment decisions bespeaks our "jealous regard for maintaining the integrity of individual rights."

In the present case, however, the majority turns its back on these principles, holding that "the fact of the lawful arrest" always established the authority to conduct a full search of the arrestee's person, regardless of whether in a particular case "there was present one of the reasons supporting the authority for a search of the person incident to a lawful arrest."

. . . The majority's attempt to avoid case-by-case adjudication of Fourth Amendment issues is not only misguided as a matter of principle, but is also doomed to fail as a practical application. . . . Although, in this particular case Officer Jenks was required by police department regulations to make an in-custody arrest rather than to issue a citation, in most jurisdictions and for most traffic offenses the determination of whether to issue a citation or effect a full arrest is discretionary with the officer. There is always the possibility that a police officer, lacking probable cause to obtain a search warrant, will use a traffic arrest as a pretext to conduct a search. . . . I suggest this possibility not to impugn the integrity of our police, but merely to point out that case-by-case adjudication will always be necessary to determine whether a full arrest was effected for purely legitimate reasons or, rather, as a pretext for searching the arrestee. ''An arrest may not be used as a pretext to search for evidence.'' . . .

THE CALIFORNIA STANDARD

People v. Brisendine

13 Cal.3d 528, 119 Cal.Rptr. 315, 531 P.2d 1099 (1975)

[Mosk, Justice.]

FACTS

On the night of June 3, 1970, two deputy sheriffs . . . were inspecting for county code violations in the Deep Creek area of the San Bernardino National Forest. The locale had been designated a ''high fire hazard area'' in which both open campfires and overnight camping were prohibited.

Upon finding two vehicles parked on the road the deputies proceeded into the forest on foot, where they came upon . . . Marlow Bartels, a lone camper whom they arrested for possession of marijuana. Bartels informed the officers there were other campers downstream who were also in possession of marijuana. . . .

Approximately half a mile from the place where they left Bartels the officers observed another campfire. Nearby were four young men in sleeping bags, one of whom was this defendant. Officer Norman placed the four under arrest for having an open campfire. . . .

Prior to starting back, the officers conducted a thorough search of the persons and effects of all four youths. Denney picked up defendant's knapsack, squeezed it, determined that the outer layer was too solid to ascertain whether it contained weapons, and began a search of its compartments. The contraband was found in a side pocket of the pack: the marijuana was contained in a frosted plastic bottle with a cap on it, and the tablets of restricted dangerous drugs were wrapped in tinfoil and enclosed in envelopes.

OPINION

Defendant contends that the search of his knapsack exceeded the legitimate purpose for which a search was authorized. . . . [W]e see no difference between traffic cases and the instant matter in terms of requiring the officer to point to the specific reasons why he believes weapons may be present. Defendant was arrested for one of the most minor of nontraffic violations—a mere citation offense. In such a case the fact of the arrest does not justify a search of the belongings of the person cited: there can be no instrumentalities and there can be no fruits, and absent some showing on the part of the officer that he has good cause to fear for his safety, there can be no weapons search. . . .

Since the contraband was illegally seized in violation of Article I, section 13, of the California Constitution, [which is identical to the Fourth Amendment search and seizure clause in the Fourth Amendment], we hold that it was erroneously received in evidence. . . .

The People . . . contend that notwithstanding the invalidity of the search under California law, the recent United States Supreme Court case of United States v. Robinson "should be dispositive of any question regarding the permissible scope of the search herein." We disagree. [That] case [was] decided under the Supreme Court's view of the *minimum* standards required in order to satisfy the Fourth Amendment's proscription of unreasonable searches. Our holding today is based exclusively on Article I, section 13, of the California Constitution, which requires a more exacting standard for cases arising in this state. . . .

CASE DISCUSSION

Robinson was convicted in the United States District Court for the District of Columbia of possession and facilitation of concealing heroin. The Court of Appeals reversed the conviction. The United States Supreme Court reversed the Court of Appeals. Brisendine was convicted in the Superior Court of San Bernadino County of possession of marijuana and possession of a restricted dangerous drug and was placed on probation. Brisendine appealed. The California Supreme Court reversed.

Compare the federal and the California interpretation of searches incident to arrests for minor offenses. Do you agree with the reasoning in United States Supreme Court? with that of the California court? Why? Do you agree with the federal or the California standard in these cases? Do you think it is a good idea, in general, to permit states to raise constitutional standards, or should all the states in the nation operate according to one standard? Defend your answer. Does Justice Marshall have a point that these searches are "pretextual," that is, that the traffic arrest provided a pretext to search for drugs? If so, does it matter what the officers' *motive* for the search was? Should the Supreme Court—or any reviewing court—look at these cases individually or prescribe a "bright-line" rule granting the police blanket authority to conduct searches incident to traffic arrests? Would such a bright line further the organizational interests of efficiency and predictability? the legal interest in result? Would it help to catch criminals?[10]

The Features of the Law of Criminal Procedure

THE ADVERSARY SYSTEM. The **adversary system** operates like a contest. The protagonists are the government and the person charged with crime. The police prior to arrest and the prosecutor thereafter represent the government in the contest. Their duty is to marshal all the evidence they can against suspects and defendants, and to present the case against defendants in the light most favorable to the government. Defense counsel represent defendants; they present defendants' cases in the light most favorable to their clients.

Judges decide the law and apply it to the case at hand. They act like umpires who make sure both sides play by the rules of the contest. Juries weigh and decide the facts in the case. They determine whether witnesses are telling the truth, whether the evidence proves defendants guilty, and issue their verdict (from the Latin *veredicto,* meaning to tell the truth).

The adversary system is a basic feature of American criminal justice. Its essence lies in the notion that through adversary proceedings the truth will come out. The confidence that the adversary system reveals the truth arises from the competitive spirit, the "sporting theory of justice." Everyone wants to "win," according to the "sporting theory." Hence, prosecutors will do their best to prove defendants guilty. Defendants do not want to be punished and defense attorneys do not want to lose cases. Hence, both do their best to make sure prosecutors do not prove defendants guilty. Since the criminal trial—and the criminal process in general—operates on proof based on facts, the ruthless search for facts will result in the triumph of truth.

The competitive spirit can lead to excesses—the desire to win at any cost. So, neutral decision makers assure that neither side gains an unfair advantage. In theory, this may be so. But in reality, the truth does not always produce victory: superior persuasive ability, emotional appeals, and superior resources might put truth in jeopardy and allow lies to triumph. Furthermore, the adversary system does not operate in pure form; it shares its importance in the criminal justice system with other goals. For example, prosecutors are not only supposed to win cases for the government, but they are also responsible for doing "justice." Doing justice might mean *not* charging defendants, diverting them into social service agencies for help, or even supplying their counsel with evidence helpful to their case (called discovery). In addition, organizational interests may dictate that prosecutors' offices distribute resources more economically, efficiently, and effectively.[11]

THE ACCUSATORY SYSTEM. Closely related to, and sometimes confused with, the adversary process, the **accusatory system** puts the burden of proof on the government, as summed up in the phrase "innocent until proven guilty." Defendants do not need to prove their innocence, the government must prove their guilt. All legal intrusions and deprivations from police detection and investigation through conviction and punishment rest upon facts secured by the government according to the law.

The accusatory system is based on the ideal of the supremacy of the individual in a free society, on suspicion of the corruptibility of government power and the abuses to which it can be put, and on the reality that in criminal prosecutions the government possesses enormous resources that individuals cannot match. Even wealthy and powerful defendants—and most are neither—can never acquire even a fraction of the investigative power that prosecutors have at their disposal. The best-known characteristics of the accusatory system are the **presumption of innocence**— defendants are presumed innocent unless and until they are proven guilty—and the right of criminal defendants to remain silent and not to answer questions that might incriminate them.

INSURING THE TRUTH. Both the adversary and accusatory systems promote the interest in accurate fact-finding. Wrongful intrusions and deprivations are so offensive to formal criminal justice that safeguards against them exist throughout the criminal process, and ample sanctions support the safeguards. The requirements of a factual foundation to support intrusions and deprivations, rules that exclude illegally obtained evidence, and the rights of appeal and collateral attack reflect this commitment to truth. "Better a hundred guilty persons go free than one innocent person be punished" summarizes the commitment to truth.

SUPREMACY OF THE INDIVIDUAL. All the above features of criminal procedure indicate to more or less degree the central importance of the individual in the criminal justice system. The individual's dignity, autonomy, and equality with others *vis à vis* the government are all dimensions to the supremacy of the individual. Born in a revolution that glorified individual rights and deprecated government power, the American criminal justice system reflects the concerns that brought it into being. Naturally, the general welfare, domestic tranquillity, and social order and safety are also features of the Constitution. In fact, the strong belief that individual liberty is worth little or nothing without basic security and safety has never met serious challenge in America. The American dispute is over how to balance order and liberty, the general welfare and individual rights, government power and individual autonomy.

Hence, we return to the notion that the government must have sufficient power to enforce the criminal law, but in doing so, it must not violate individual dignity by wrongful, excessive, false, or cruel and abusive intrusions and deprivations.

THE IMPORTANCE OF THE DUE PROCESS REQUIREMENT

History of the Due Process Clause

Throughout American history, criminal justice has remained a predominantly local matter. The protections listed in the federal Bill of Rights do not apply directly to the states. As early as 1833, the Supreme court, in an opinion written by Chief Justice John Marshall, noted that the question whether the Bill of Rights extended to the states was "of great importance, but not of much difficulty." The Court reasonsed that

> Had Congress [which proposed the Bill of Rights] engaged in the extraordinary occupation of improving the constitutions of the several states by affording the people additional protection from the exercise of power by their own governments in matters which concerned themselves alone, they would have declared this purpose in plain and intelligible language.[12]

The Fourteenth Amendment, adopted following the Civil War, suggests that the United States Constitution does apply to the states:

> All persons born or naturalized in the United States, and subject to the jurisdiction thereof, are citizens of the United States and of the State wherein they reside. No State shall make or enforce any law which shall abridge the privileges and immunities of citizens of the United States; nor shall any State deprive any person of life, liberty, or property, without due process of law; nor deny to any person within its jurisdiction the equal protection of the laws.

Despite the Fourteenth Amendment, the courts did not extend its protection to state criminal justice until the twentieth century. Up to that time, criminal procedure remained a state and local matter. The Supreme Court made this clear in a series of cases beginning in 1884, with *Hurtado v. California.*

The German war machine of the First World War, and the rise of fascism in its aftermath, revived the historical suspicions that Americans had of arbitrary government. The constitutional history of criminal procedure reflects this suspicion. Perhaps it is no coincidence that the Supreme Court decided the first case applying the Fourteenth Amendment due process clause to state criminal procedure at the time that Hitler was rising to power in Nazi Germany. The Supreme Court decided the landmark "Scottsboro case," *Powell v. Alabama,* in 1932.[13]

CASE

Did the trial court deny them "due process" of law?

Powell v. Alabama

287 U.S. 45, 53 S.Ct. 55, 77 L.Ed. 158 (1932)

[Justice Sutherland delivered the opinion of the Court. Justice Butler dissented.]

FACTS

. . . [O]n the day when the offense is said to have been committed, these defendants, together with a number of other negroes, were upon a freight train on its way through Alabama. On the same train were seven white boys and two white girls. A fight took place between the negroes and the white boys, in the course of which the white boys, with the exception of one named Gilley, were thrown off the train. A message was sent ahead, reporting the fight and asking that every negro be gotten off the train. The participants in the fight, and the two girls, were in an open gondola car. The two girls testified that each of them was assaulted by six different negroes in turn, and they identified the seven defendants as having been among the number. None of the white boys was called to testify, with the exception of Gilley, who was called in rebuttal.

Before the train reached Scottsboro, Alabama, a sheriff's posse seized the defendants and two other negroes. Both girls and the negroes then were taken to Scottsboro, the county seat. Word of their coming and of the alleged assault had preceded them, and they were met in Scottsboro by a large crowd. It does not sufficiently appear that the defendants were seriously threatened with, or that they were actually in danger of, mob violence; but it does appear that the attitude of the community was one of great hostility. The sheriff thought it necessary to call for the militia to assist in safeguarding the prisoners. Chief Justice Anderson [of the Alabama Supreme Court] pointed out in his opinion that every step that was taken from the arrest and arraignment to the sentence was accompanied by the military. Soldiers took the defendants to Gadsden for safekeeping, brought them back to Scottsboro for arraignment, returned them to Gadsden for safekeeping while awaiting trial, escorted them to Scottsboro for trial a few days later, and guarded the court house and grounds at every stage of the proceedings. It is perfectly apparent that the proceedings, from beginning to end, took place in an atmosphere of tense, hostile and excited public sentiment. During the entire time, the defendants were closely confined or were under military guard. The record does not disclose their ages, except that one of them was nineteen; but the record clearly indicates that most, if not all, of them were youthful, and they are constantly referred to as "the boys." They were ignorant and illiterate. All of them were residents of other states, where alone members of their families or friends resided.

. . . [I]mmediately upon the return of the indictment, defendants were arraigned and pleaded not guilty. Apparently they were not asked whether they had, or were able to employ, counsel, or wished to have counsel appointed; or whether they had friends or relatives who might assist in that regard if communicated with. That it would not have been an idle ceremony to have given the defendants reasonable opportunity to communicate with their families and endeavor to obtain counsel is demonstrated by the fact that, very soon after conviction, able counsel appeared in their behalf . . .

[U]ntil the very morning of the trial no lawyer had been named or definitely designated to represent the defendants. Prior to that time, the judge had "appointed all the members of the bar" for the limited "purpose of arraigning the defendants."

OPINION

However guilty defendants, upon due inquiry, might prove to have been, they were, until convicted, presumed to be innocent. It was the duty of the court having their cases in charge to see that they were denied no necessary incident of a fair trial. With any error of the state court involving alleged contravention of the state statutes or constitution we, of course, have nothing to do. The sole inquiry which we are permitted to make is whether the federal Constitution was contravened . . . [A]s to that, we confine ourselves . . . to the inquiry whether the defendants were in substance denied the right of counsel, and if so, whether such denial infringes the due process clause of the Fourteenth Amendment.

[The casual appointment of counsel] in our opinion, [falls] far short of meeting, in any proper sense, a requirement for the appointment of counsel. How many lawyers were members of the bar does not appear; but, in the very nature of things, whether many or few, they would not, thus collectively named, have been given that clear appreciation of responsibility or impressed with that individual sense of duty which should and naturally would accompany the appointment of a selected member of the bar, specifically named and assigned.

Nor do we think the situation was helped by what occurred on the morning of the trial. At that time . . . Mr. Roddy stated to the court that he did not appear as counsel, but that he would like to appear along with counsel that the court might appoint; that he had not been given an opportunity to prepare the case; that he was not familiar with the procedure in Alabama, but merely came down [from Tennessee] as a friend of the people who were interested; that he thought the boys would be better off if he should step entirely out of the case. Mr. Moody, a member of the local bar, expressed a willingness to help Mr. Roddy in anything he could do under the circumstances. To this the court responded, ''All right, all the lawyers that will; of course I would not require a lawyer to appear if—.'' And Mr. Moody continued, ''I am willing to do that for him as a member of the bar; I will go ahead and help him do anything I can do.'' With this dubious understanding, the trials immediately proceeded. The defendants, young, ignorant, illiterate, surrounded by hostile sentiment, haled back and forth under guard of soldiers, charged with an atrocious crime regarded with especial horror in the community where they were to be tried, were thus put in peril of their lives [rape was a capital offense] within a few moments after counsel for the first time charged with any degree of responsibility began to represent them.

It is not enough to assume that counsel thus precipitated into the case thought there was no defense, and exercised their best judgment in proceeding to trial without preparation. Neither they nor the court could say what a prompt and thorough-going investigation might disclose as to the facts. No attempt was made to investigate. No opportunity to do so was given. Defendants were immediately hurried to trial. . . . Under the circumstances disclosed, we hold that defendants were not accorded the right of counsel in any substantial sense. To decide otherwise, would simply be to ignore actualities . . .

It is true that great and inexcusable delay in the enforcement of our criminal law is one of the grave evils of our time. Continuances are frequently granted for unnecessarily long periods of time, and delays incident to the disposition of motions for new trial and hearings upon appeal have come in many cases to be a distinct reproach to the administration of justice. The prompt disposition of criminal cases is to be commended and encouraged. But in reaching that result a defendant, charged with a serious crime, must not be stripped of his right to have sufficient time to advise with counsel and prepare his defense. To do that is not to proceed promptly in the calm spirit of regulated justice but to go forward with the haste of the mob. . . .

The Constitution of Alabama (Const. 1901, s 6) provides that in all criminal prosecutions the accused shall enjoy the right to have the assistance of counsel; and a state statute (Code 1923, s 5567) requires the court in a capital case, where the defendant is unable to employ counsel, to appoint counsel for him. The state Supreme Court held that these provisions had not been infringed, and with that holding we are powerless to interfere. The question, however, which it is our duty, and within our power, to decide, is whether the denial of the assistance of counsel contravenes the due process clause of the Fourteenth Amendment to the Federal Constitution. . . .

We do not overlook the case of *Hurtado v. California*, 110 U.S. 516, 4 S.Ct. 111, 292, 28 L.Ed. 232, where this court determined that due process of law does not require an indictment by a grand jury as a prerequisite to prosecution by a state for murder . . . But the *Hurtado* Case does not stand alone. In the later case of *Chicago, Burlington & Q.R. Co. v. Chicago*, 166 U.S. 226, 241, 17 S.Ct. 581, 41 L.Ed. 979, this court held that a judgment of a state court, even though authorized by statute, by which private property was taken for public use without just compensation, was in violation of the due proces of law required by the Fourteenth Amendment. . . .

Likewise, this court has considered that freedom of speech and of the press are rights protected by the due process clause of the Fourteenth Amendment, Although in the First Amendment, Congress is prohibited in specific terms from abridging the right . . . These later cases establish that notwithstanding the sweeping character of the language in the Hurtado Case, the rule laid down is not without exceptions. . . . The fact that the right involved is of such a character that it cannot be denied without violating those 'fundamental principles of liberty and justice which lie at the base of all our civil and political institutions' (*Hebert v. State of Louisiana*, 272 U.S. 312, 316, 47 S.Ct. 103, 104, 71 L.Ed. 270, 48 A.L.R. 1120), is obviously one of those compelling considerations which must prevail in determining whether it is embraced within the due process clause of the Fourteenth Amendment, although it be specifically dealt with in another part of the Federal Constitution. Evidently this court, in the later cases enumerated, regarded the rights there under the consideraton as of this fundamental character. That some such distinction must be observed is foreshadowed in *Twining v. New Jersey*, 211 U.S. 78, 99, 29 S.Ct. 14, 19, 53 L.Ed. 97, where Mr. Justice Moody, speaking for the court, said that: '***It is possible that some of the personal rights safeguarded by the first eight Amendments against national action may also be safeguarded against state action, because a denial of them would be a denial of due process of law. If this is so, it is not because those rights are enumerated in the first eight Amendments, but because they are of such a nature that they are included in the conception of due process of law.' While the question has never been categorically determined by this court, a consideration of the nature of the right and a review of the expressions of this and other courts makes it clear that the right to the aid of counsel is of this fundamental character.

It never has been doubted by this court, or any other so far as we know, that notice and hearing are preliminary steps essential to the passing of an enforceable judgement, and that they, together with a legally competent tribunal having jurisdiction of the case, constitute basic elements of the constitutional requirement of due process of law. The words of Webster, so often quoted, that by 'the law of the land' is intended 'a law which hears before it condemns,' have been repeated in various forms of expression in a multitude of decisions. In *Holden v. Hardy*, 169 U.S. 366, 389, 18 S. Ct. 383, 387, 42 L.Ed. 780, the necessity of due notice and an opportunity of being heard is described as among the 'immutable principles of justice which inhere the very idea of free government which no member of the Union may disregard.' And Mr. Justice Field, in an earlier case, *Galpin v. Page*, 18 Wall. 350, 368, 369, 21 L.Ed. 959, said that the rule that no one shall be personally bound until he has had his day in court was as old as the law, and it meant that he must be cited to appear and afforded an opportunity to be heard. 'Judgment without such citation and opportunity wants all the attributes of a judicial determination; it is judicial usurpation and oppression, and never can be upheld where justice is justly administered.' . . .

What, then, does a hearing include? Historically and in practice, in our own country at least, it has always included the right to aid counsel. . . . The right to be heard would be, in many cases, of little avail if it did not comprehend the right to be heard by counsel. Even the intelligent and educated layman has small and sometimes no skill in the science of law. If charged with crime, he is incapable, generally, of determining for himself whether the indictment is good or bad. He is unfamiliar with the rules of evidence. Left without the aid of counsel he may be put on trial without a proper charge, and convicted upon incompetent evidence, or evidence irrelevent to the issue or otherwise inadmissible. He lacks both the skill and knowledge adequately to prepare his defense, even though he have a perfect one. He requires the guiding hand of counsel at every step in the proceedings against him. Without it, though he be not guilty, he faces the danger of conviction because he does not know how to establish his innocence. If that be true of men of intelligence, how much more true is it of the ignorant and illiterate, or those of feeble intellect. If in any case, civil or criminal, a state or federal court were arbitrarily to refuse to hear a party by counsel, employed by and appearing for him, it reasonably may not be doubted that such a refusal would be a denial of a hearing, and, therefore, of due process in the constitutional sense. . . .

In the light of the facts outlined in the forepart of this opinion—the ignorance and illiteracy of the defendants, their youth, the circumstances of public hostility, the imprisonment and the close surveillance of the defendants by the military forces, the fact that their friends and family were all in other states and communication with them necessarily difficult, and above all that they stood in deadly peril of their lives—we think the failure of the trial court to give them reasonable time and opportunity to secure counsel was a clear denial of due process. . . .

[T]he necessity of counsel was so vital and imperative that the failure of the trial court to make an effective appointment of counsel was likewise a denial of due process within the meaning of the Fourteenth Amendment. Whether this would be so in other criminal prosecutions, or under other circumstances, we need not determine. All that is necessary now to decide, as we do decide, is that in a capital case, where the defendant is unable to employ counsel, and is incapable adequately of making his own defense because of ignorance, feeble-mindedness, illiteracy, or the like, it is the duty of the court, whether requested or not, to assign counsel for him as a necessary requisite of due process of law; and that duty is not discharged by an assignment at such a time or under such circumstances as to preclude the giving of effective aid in the preparation and trial of the case. To hold otherwise would be to ignore the fundamental postulate, already adverted to, 'that there are certain immutable principles of justice which inhere in the very idea of free government which no member of the Union may disregard.' . . .

The judgments must be reversed and the causes remanded for further proceedings not inconsistent with this opinion. Judgments reversed.

[Justice Butler's dissent is omitted]

CASE DISCISSION

Defendents were convicted of rape in a state court. They appealed on the ground that the state court denied them due process of law. On writ of *certiorari,* the United States Supreme Court reversed the judgment of conviction and remanded the case for further proceedings.

In precisely what way did the trial court deny Powell due process of law? How did the court formulate the fundamental fairness doctrine? What were the precise circumstances of this case that required the advice of counsel? Does this decision promote prcedural regularity over obtaining the correct result, or does it attempt to do both? Explain how the right to counsel may not only assure procedural regularity but also aid in obtaining the correct result in this case?

In 1936, the Supreme Court applied the fundamental fairness doctrine to a case involving a forced confession. In *Brown v. Mississippi*, a sheriff hung Brown from a tree and brutally beat and whipped him until he confessed to murdering a white man. The trial court convicted Brown; the confession was the only evidence against him. Both the trial court and the Mississippi Supreme Court acknowledged that the confession was forced but let the conviction stand. Brown appealed to the United States Supreme Court. Mississippi argued that the United States Constitution did not prohibit the states from practicing compulsory self-incrimination. Chief Justice Hughes wrote for the Court:

> The freedom of the State in establishing its policy is the freedom of constitutional government and is limited by the requirement of due process of law. . . . The rack and the torture chamber may not be substituted for the witness stand. . . . It would be difficult to conceive of methods more revolting to the sense of justice than those taken to procure the confession of [Brown], and the use of the confessions thus obtained as the basis for conviction and sentence was clear denial of due process.[14]

Excepting cases such as *Brown*, which involved extreme physical brutality, the Court left criminal procedure to the states, rejecting the idea that the Bill of Rights applied to the states. At that time, the Supreme Court did not adopt the **incorporation doctrine**—that ''due process'' of law under the Fourteenth Amendment requires that state criminal procedure must guarantee criminal defendants the protections included in the federal Bill of Rights.

It was not until the 1960s that the United States Supreme Court fully applied the Fourteenth Amendment due process clause to state criminal procedure. Led by Chief Justice Earl Warren, a former California prosecutor, the Court so actively pursued this ''constitutionalization'' of state criminal procedure that it was called the **due process revolution.** The Court ''policed'' state criminal procedure by applying the due process clause to progressively earlier stages in the criminal process. As a result, police action came under careful, close, and critical scrutiny.[15]

First, the Court intervened between suspects and the police in the police station— extending the right to counsel and demanding that the police give the now-famous ''Miranda warnings'' to arrested suspects in police custody. (See excerpt in chapter 1 and discussion in chapter 7.) Then, the court extended its policing powers to encounters between citizens and the police on the street before they were arrested or taken into custody. The Supreme Court also scrutinized brief detentions and weapons patdown practices traditionally left to police discretion. As a result, the Supreme Court actively reviewed the day-to-day activities of local police departments.[16]

The Fundamental Fairness and Incorporation Doctrines

The Court used a variety of mechanisms to apply federal constitutional standards to state criminal proceedings, but the principal two were the **fundamental fairness** and the **incorporation** doctrines. Both doctrines promoted process interests in controlling government, particularly the police, and the societal interest in equality for all races and classes, even if it meant sacrificing conviction in specific cases. The process-oriented Warren Court adopted the incorporation doctrine.

The fundamental fairness and incorporation doctrines differed in several respects. First, they defined due process differently. According to the fundamental fairness doctrine, the substantive concept of due process embodied the development of Anglo-American law from the time of Magna Carta.

> The concept of due process dated back to the Magna Carta, and English and American commentators had discussed it at length. The proponents of fundamental fairness viewed those authorities as having established a flexible standard of justice that focused on the essence of fairness rather than the familiarity of form. Due process, under this view, was "a concept less rigid and more fluid than those envisaged in other specific and particular provisions of the Bill of Rights." Indeed, Justice Frankfurter described it as "perhaps, the least frozen concept of our law—the least confined to history and the most absorptive of powerful social standards of a progressive society." Its basic objective was to provide "respect enforced by law" for that feeling of just treatment which has evolved through centuries of Anglo-American constitutional history and civilization. Thus, it had a "natural law" background, which extended beyond procedural fairness and imposed limits as well on the substance of state regulation.[17]

Under the fundamental fairness doctrine, due process might include some rights in the Bill of Rights totally, some partially, and some not at all.

According to the incorporation doctrine definition, due process is simply a procedural guarantee; it insures procedural regularity, namely, that guaranteed in the Bill of Rights. Justice Black, the incorporation doctrine's staunchest proponent, maintained that due process granted only a "right to be tried by an independent and unprejudiced courts using established procedures and applying valid pre-existing laws." According to Justice Black, due process absorbs all rights under the Bill of Rights; others maintain that it encompasses only some of those rights.[18]

The fundamental fairness doctrine derives its meaning independent of the Bill of Rights. In other words, the due process clause is not the equivalent of the rights guaranteed in the Fourth, Fifth, Sixth, and Eighth Amendments. The fundamental fairness doctrine applies the due process clause on a case-by-case basis. It does not restrict its inquiry to the Bill of Rights. Under it, the Supreme Court weighs all the circumstances and decides whether they violate the fundamental norms of American civilized society at a particular time and place. Not all the rights guaranteed in the Bill of Rights violate these fundamental norms; some other actions not included in the Bill of Rights, on the other hand, may do so.

If a defendant contended that a state had denied him due process of law by failing to recognize a right protected by the Bill of Rights, the issue presented was not whether that right, viewed in the abstract, was "implicit in the concept of ordered liberty." Rather, the issue was whether the state's action had resulted in a denial of fundamental fairness in the context of the particular case. . . . Due process under this approach was to be defined on a case-by-case basis, with its "full meaning . . . gradually ascertained by the process of inclusion and exclusion in the course of the decisions of cases as they arise."[19]

The incorporation doctrine applies a uniform standard to a whole category of cases; it focuses on the total guarantee, not on a particular aspect that arises in a specific case. For example, in *Palko v. Connecticut,* the Court applying the fundamental fairness doctrine asked whether the particular double jeopardy denied the individual defendant Palko fundamental fairness; incorporation would have asked whether the prohibition against double jeopardy is "fundamental to the American scheme of justice."[20]

Fundamental fairness and incorporation also differ over the extent and specificity to which they require uniform treatment. Under the fundamental fairness doctrine, state and local criminal justice could define most of their own criminal procedure law. Justice Benjamin Cardozo stated the doctrine in 1937 this way:

Does it [a state's or local agency's criminal procedure] violate those "fundamental principles of liberty and justice which lie at the base of our civil and political institutions?"[21]

Justice Felix Frankfurter used a variety of phrases to capture the fundamental fairness doctrine's essential meaning. They included procedures that "offend the community's sense of fair play and decency," and conduct that "shocks the conscience." The Supreme Court applied the fundamental fairness doctrine in *Rochin v. California.*[22]

CASE

Did the police actions "shock your conscience"?

Rochin v. California

342 U.S. 165, 72 S.Ct. 205, 96 L.Ed. 183 (1952)

FACTS

Having "some information that [the petitioner here] was selling narcotics," three deputy sheriffs of the County of Los Angeles, on the morning of July 1, 1949, made for the two-story dwelling house in which Rochin lived with his mother, common-law wife, brothers and sisters. Finding the outside door open, they entered and then forced open the door to Rochin's room on the second floor. Inside they found petitioner sitting partly dressed on the side of the bed, upon which his wife was lying. On a "night stand" beside the bed the deputies spied two capsules. When asked "Whose stuff is this?" Rochin seized the capsules and put them in his mouth. A struggle ensued, in the course of which the three officers "jumped upon him" and attempted to extract the capsules. The force they applied proved unavailing against Rochin's resistance. He was handcuffed and taken to a hospital. At the direction of one of the officers a doctor forced an emetic solution through a tube into Rochin's stomach against his will. This "stomach pumping" produced vomiting. In the vomited matter were found two capsules which proved to contain morphine.

Rochin was brought to trial before a California Superior Court, sitting without a jury, on the charge of possessing "a preparation of morphine" in violation of the California Health and Safety Code. Rochin was convicted and sentenced to sixty days' imprisonment. The chief evidence against him was the two capsules. They were admitted over petitioner's objection, although the means of obtaining them was frankly set forth in the testimony by one of the deputies, substantially as here narrated.

On appeal, the District Court of Appeal affirmed the conviction, despite the finding that the officers "were guilty of unlawfully breaking into and entering defendant's room and were guilty of unlawfully assaulting and battering defendant while in the room," and "were guilty of unlawfully assaulting, battering, torturing and falsely imprisoning the defendant at the alleged hospital."

OPINION

This Court granted certiorari because a serious question is raised as to the limitations which the Due Process Clause of the Fourteenth Amendment imposes on the conduct of criminal proceedings by the States. . . .

These limitations, in the main, concern not restrictions upon the powers of the States to define crime, except in the restricted area where federal authority has preempted the field, but restrictions upon the manner in which the States may enforce their penal codes. Accordingly, in reviewing a State criminal conviction under a claim of right guaranteed by the Due Process Clause of the Fourteenth Amendment, from which is derived the most far-reaching and most frequent federal basis of challenging State criminal justice, "we must be deeply mindful of the responsibilities of the States for the enforcement of criminal laws, and exercise with due humility our merely negative function in subjecting convictions from state courts to the very narrow scrutiny which the Due Process Clause of the Fourteenth Amendment authorizes."

However, this Court too has its responsibility. Regard for the requirements of the Due Process Clause "inescapably imposes upon this Court an exercise of judgment upon the whole course of the proceedings [resulting in a conviction] in order to ascertain whether they offend those canons of decency and fairness which express the notions of justice of English-speaking peoples even toward those charged with the most heinous offenses."

The faculties of the Due Process Clause may be indefinite and vague, but the mode of their ascertainment is not self-willed. In each case "due process of law" requires an evaluation based on a disinterested inquiry pursued in the spirit of science, on a balanced order of facts exactly and fairly stated, on the detached consideration of conflicting claims, on a judgment not ad hoc and episodic but duly mindful of reconciling the needs both of continuity and of change in a progressive society.

Applying these general considerations to the circumstances of the present case, we are compelled to conclude that the proceedings by which this conviction was obtained do more than offend some fastidious squeamishness or private sentimentalism about combatting crime too energetically. This is conduct that shocks the conscience. Illegally breaking into the privacy of the petitioner, the struggle to open his mouth and remove what was there, the forcible extraction of his stomach's contents—this course of proceeding by agents of government to obtain evidence is bound to offend even hardened sensibilities. They are methods too close to the rack and the screw to permit of constitutional differentiation.

Reversed.

CASE DISCUSSION

A California Superior Court convicted Rochin of possessing morphine in violation of California law. Rochin was sentenced to sixty days in jail. Over Rochin's objection, the government introduced heroin capsules in evidence against him. Rochin appealed on the ground that the capsules were seized illegally. The District Court of Appeal affirmed the conviction. The Supreme Court granted a writ of certiorari to determine whether police violated the due process clause of the Fourteenth Amendment. The Supreme Court ruled that it did and reversed Rochin's conviction.

Why did the Court apply the Fourteenth Amendment to *Rochin* and not to *Palko v. Connecticut?* What is different about the cases? Does the police conduct in this case ''shock your conscience''? Explain. Does the test mean that only physical brutality brings the due process clause to bear on state criminal procedure? Is this a good rule? Defend your answer.

The more-specific incorporation doctrine left the states less free to determine their own criminal procedure than the fundamental fairness doctrine. Supporters of the incorporation doctrine contended that due process meant that the specific provisions in the federal Bill of Rights applied to the states. Prior to the adoption of the Fourteenth Amendment, the Supreme Court had ruled that the Bill of Rights did not apply to the states. After the adoption of the Fourteenth Amendment, the Court continued to reject the incorporation doctrine. When the Court finally adopted the incorporation doctrine, justices continued to disagree strongly over which provisions the Fourteenth Amendment incorporated. Some justices called for **total incorporation,** meaning that all the provisions were incorporated under the due process clause. Others called for **selective incorporation,** meaning some rights were incorporated and others were not.[23]

During the 1960s, the Supreme Court opted for the selective incorporation doctrine in applying the United States Constitution to state criminal proceedings. By the end of that decade, the selective incorporation doctrine had changed the ''face of the law,'' according to Supreme Court Justice William Brennan. The decisions of that decade had incorporated all but four of the Bill of Rights guarantees relating to criminal justice—public trial, notice of charges, prohibition of excessive bail, and prosecution by indictment. Table 2.2 presents a list of cases that brought about the incorporation of specific rights. In cases decided since the 1960s, the Court has suggested that Fourteenth Amendment due process incorporates all but indictment by grand jury. Once a right is incorporated, it applies to the states to the same extent that it applies in federal proceedings, ''jot-for-jot and case for case,'' as its critic Justice Harlan put it.[24]

TABLE 2.2 Cases Incorporating Specific Rights during the 1960s

Right Incorporated	Case Incorporating Right
Right against unreasonable searches and seizures and exclusionary rule applied to state searches and seizures	Mapp v. Ohio, 367 U.S. 643, 81 S.Ct. 1684, 6 L.Ed.2d 1081 (1961)
Self-incrimination	Malloy v. Hogan, 378 U.S. 1, 84 S.Ct. 1489, 12 L.Ed.2d 653 (1964)
Assistance of counsel	Gideon v. Wainright, 372 U.S. 335, 83 S.Ct. 792, 9 L.Ed.2d 799 (1963)
Confront opposing witnesses	Pointer v. Texas, 380 U.S. 400, 85 S.Ct. 1065, 13 L.Ed.2d 923 (1965)
Compulsory process to obtain witnesses	Washington v. Texas, 388 U.S. 14, 87 S.Ct. 1920, 18 L.Ed.2d 1019
Right to a speedy trial	Klopfer v. North Carolina, 386 U.S. 213, 87 S.Ct. 988, 18 L.Ed.2d 1 (1967)
Prohibition against cruel and unusual punishment	Robinson v. California, 370 U.S. 660, 82 S.Ct. 1417, 8 L.Ed.2d 758 (1962)

CASE

Why should the right to counsel be "incorporated"?

Gideon v. Wainright

372 U.S. 335, 83 S.Ct. 792, 9 L.Ed.2d 799 (1963)

[Justice Black delivered the court's opinion.]

FACTS

Petitioner was charged in a Florida state court with having broken and entered a poolroom with intent to commit a misdemeanor. This offense is a felony under Florida law. Appearing in court without funds and without a lawyer, petitioner asked the court to appoint counsel for him, whereupon the following colloquy took place:

"The COURT: Mr. Gideon, I am sorry, but I cannot appoint Counsel to represent you in this case. Under the laws of the State of Florida, the only time the Court can appoint Counsel to represent a Defendant is when that person is charged with a capital offense. I am sorry, but I will have to deny your request to appoint Counsel to defend you in this case."

"The DEFENDANT: The United States Supreme Court says I am entitled to be represented by Counsel."

Put to trial before a jury, Gideon conducted his defense about as well as could be expected from a layman. The jury returned a verdict of guilty, and petitioner was sentenced to serve five years in the state prison. Later, petitioner filed in the Florida Supreme Court this habeas corpus petition attacking his conviction and sentence on the ground that the trial court's refusal to appoint counsel for him denied him rights "guaranteed by the Constitution and the Bill of Rights by the United States government." The State Supreme Court, "upon consideration thereof" but without an opinion, denied all relief.

OPINION

The Sixth Amendment provides, "In all criminal prosecutions, the accused shall enjoy the right . . . to have the Assistance of Counsel for his defence." We have construed this to mean that in federal courts counsel must be provided for defendants unable to employ counsel unless the right is competently and intelligently waived. While the Sixth Amendment laid down "no rule for the conduct of the States, the question recurs whether the constraint laid by the Amendment upon the national courts expresses a rule so fundamental and essential to a fair trial, and so, to due process of law, that it is made obligatory upon the States by the Fourteenth Amendment."

Those guarantees of the Bill of Rights which are fundamental safeguards of liberty immune from federal abridgment are equally protected against state invasion by the Due Process Clause of the Fourteenth Amendment. This same principle was recognized, explained, and applied in *Powell v. Alabama* (1932), a case upholding the right of counsel, where the Court held that despite sweeping language to the contrary in *Hurtado v. California* (1884), the Fourteenth Amendment "embraced" those "fundamental principles of liberty and justice which lie at the base of all our civil and political institutions," even though they had been "specifically dealt with in another part of the federal Constitution."

A provision of the Bill of Rights which is "fundamental and essential to a fair trial" is made obligatory upon the States by the Fourteenth Amendment. We think that the Sixth Amendment's guarantee of counsel is one of these fundamental rights.

Reversed.
Justice Harlan, Clark, and Douglas wrote concurring opinions.

CASE DISCUSSION

Gideon was charged with breaking and entering a poolroom with intent to commit a misdemeanor, a felony in Florida. Gideon asked for a court-appointed lawyer; the judge refused the request because Florida was not trying Gideon for a capital offense. Gideon defended himself, was convicted, and sentenced to five years in prison. Gideon filed a *habeas corpus* petition that the Florida Supreme Court denied; the United States Supreme Court granted *certiorari* to settle the question of defendants' rights under the federal Constitution in state courts. The Court appointed a lawyer to represent Gideon in the Supreme Court. The Court reversed the Florida Supreme Court's decision.

How does the incorporation doctrine, as set out by the Court, differ from the fundamental fairness doctrine announced in *Palko v. Connecticut,* in the last case excerpt? Is there any real difference? Explain what it is. Does the Court adopt total or selective incorporation in this case? Explain.

The incorporation doctrine's critics—there were and still are many—charged that incorporation destroys federalism, interferes with local criminal justice, and eviscerates the need for both local variety and experiments with different solutions to problems in criminal justice administration. They maintain that the great variety among the states and among federal, state, and local criminal justice demands local control and variation.

Federal criminal justice, critics rightly observe, consists in the main of cases involving fraud, tax evasion, and other complex crimes. Investigation takes place largely in offices, not in the field. Hence, federal law enforcement differs markedly from the hurly-burly street crimes that bring local police in contact with violent individuals or strangers who are difficult to identify, apprehend, and bring to trial. Furthermore, the majority of local police are not highly trained college graduates, as are the federal police, particularly FBI agents. Therefore, the Bill of Rights works well for federal criminal justice, they maintain, but not in local law enforcement where, if anything, the Bill of Rights impedes effective criminal justice administration. The incorporation doctrine imposes federal practice that works effectively for only six-tenths of 1 percent of federal criminal cases on the remaining 99.6 percent of state cases where it is ineffective.

The criticisms target all criminal justice agencies, but perhaps nothing generates more controversy than whether or not uniform standards ought to apply to local police departments. Cries that the United States Supreme Court was "running local police departments" from Washington and "handcuffing" local police by doing so were common during the late 1960s, following the decision in the famous *Miranda* case. (See excerpt in chapter 1 and extended discussion and analysis in chapter 7.)

Contrary to its opponents' fears, the incorporation doctrine has not imposed a straitjacket on state and local criminal justice. The Supreme Court's flexible interpretations of the constitutional protections permit local diversity and experimentation. The Court addressed local variation and experimentation in *Chandler v. Florida*.

CASE

Are the states free to experiment with varying procedures?

Chandler v. Florida

449 U.S. 560, 101 S.Ct. 802, 66 L.Ed.2d 740 (1981)

FACTS

In July 1977, appellants were charged with conspiracy to commit burglary, grand larceny, and possession of burglary tools. The counts covered breaking and entering a well-known Miami Beach restaurant.

At the time of their arrest, appellants were Miami Beach policemen. The State's principal witness was John Sion, an amateur radio operator who, by sheer chance, had overheard and recorded conversations between the appellants over their police walkie-talkie radios during the burglary. Not surprisingly, these novel factors attracted the attention of the media.

After several fruitless attempts by the appellants to prevent electronic coverage of the trial, the jury was selected. At voir dire, the appellants' counsel asked each prospective juror whether he or she would be able to be "fair and impartial" despite the presence of a television camera during some, or all, of the trial. Each juror selected responded that such coverage would not affect his or her consideration in any way. A television camera recorded the voir dire.

A television camera was in place for one entire afternoon, during which the State presented the testimony of Sion, its chief witness. No camera was present for the presentation of any part of the case for the defense. The camera returned to cover closing arguments. Only 2 minutes and 55 seconds of the trial below were broadcast—and those depicted only the prosecution's side of the case.

The jury returned a guilty verdict on all counts. Appellants moved for a new trial, claiming that because of the television coverage, they had been denied a fair and impartial trial.

The Florida District Court of Appeal affirmed the convictions.

The Florida Supreme Court denied review.

OPINION

Burger, C. J., delivered the opinion of the Court, in which Brennan, Marshall, Blackmun, Powell, and Rehnquist, JJ., joined. Stewart, J., filed an opinion concurring in the result. White, J., filed an opinion concurring in the judgment. Stevens, J., took no part in the decision of the case.

Any criminal case that generates a great deal of publicity presents some risks that the publicity may compromise the right of the defendant to a fair trial.

An absolute constitutional ban on broadcast coverage of trials cannot be justified simply because there is a danger that, in some cases, prejudicial broadcast accounts of pretrial and trial events may impair the ability of jurors to decide the issue of guilt or innocence uninfluenced by extraneous matter. The risk of juror prejudice in some cases does not justify an absolute ban on news coverage of trials by the printed media; so also the risk of such prejudice does not warrant an absolute constitutional ban on all broadcast coverage.

The Florida guidelines place on trial judges' positive obligations to be on guard to protect the fundamental right of the accused to a fair trial. Inherent in electronic coverage of a trial is the risk that the very awareness by the accused of the coverage and the contemplated broadcast may adversely affect the conduct of the participants and the fairness of the trial. Given this danger, it is significant that Florida requires that objections of the accused to coverage be heard and considered on the record by the trial court.

Whatever may be the "mischievous potentialities [of broadcast coverage] for intruding upon the detached atmosphere which should always surround the judicial process," at present no one has been able to present empirical data sufficient to establish that the mere presence of the broadcast media inherently has an adverse effect on that process. The appellants have offered nothing to demonstrate that their trial was subtly tainted by broadcast coverage—let alone that all broadcast trials would be so tainted.

Dangers lurk in this, as in most experiments, but unless we were to conclude that television coverage under all conditions is prohibited by the Constitution, the state must be free to experiment. We are not empowered by the Constitution to oversee or harness state procedural experimentation; only when the state action infringes fundamental guarantees are we authorized to intervene. We must assume state courts will be alert to any factors that impair the fundamental rights of the accused.

Absent a showing of prejudice of constitutional dimensions to these defendants, there is no reason for this Court either to endorse or to invalidate Florida's experiment.

Affirmed.

CASE DISCUSSION

Chandler and others were charged with conspiracy to commit burglary, grand larceny, and possession of burglary tools. Over Chandler's objections, the court permitted the trial to be televised. The jury returned a guilty verdict. Chandler moved for a new trial. The Florida District Court of Appeal affirmed the convictions, the Florida Supreme Court denied review, and on appeal to the United States Supreme Court, the Court affirmed the convictions.

What does the Court mean by "experiment"? Should the Constitution await the outcomes of experiments? or even allow them? Why? Why not? What standard does the Court create in order to determine when to approve experiments? What interests does local experimentation promote? Does it hinder any? Explain. Consider whether the following rule protects against unfair televised trials. American Bar Association *Standard* § 8-3 provides:

> A judge should prohibit broadcasting, televising, recording, or photographing in courtrooms and areas immediately adjacent thereto during sessions of court, or recesses between sessions except . . . under rules prescribed by a supervising appellate court or other appropriate authority . . . consistent with a fair trial and subject to express conditions, limitations, and guidelines which allow such coverage in a manner that will be unobtrusive, will not distract or otherwise adversely affect witnesses or other trial participants, and will not otherwise interfere with the administration of justice.[25]

THE INFORMAL DIMENSION IN THE CRIMINAL PROCESS: DISCRETION

Constitutional standards provide a framework within which formal rules function; the same standards also permit informal discretion to operate. The major steps in the criminal process are decision points. Each decision presents a criminal justice professional with the opportunity to decide whether or not to initiate, continue further, or terminate the criminal process. The police can investigate suspects or not, and arrest them or not, hence initiating the formal criminal process or stopping it. Prosecutors can charge suspects and continue the criminal process, divert them into some social service agency, or take no further action, effectively terminating the criminal process. Defendants can plead guilty (usually on their lawyers' advice) and avoid trial. Judges can suspend sentences, or sentence convicted offenders to the maximum allowable penalty, hence either minimizing or maximizing the punishment the criminal law prescribes.

Formally, these decisions depend upon the law. Informally, that is, in daily practice, other influences determine whether the criminal process will continue or terminate.

Decision Point

Should the police arrest or not?
Police discretion

The following incidents actually occurred in Chicago. They represent actions the Chicago police took. Consider whether or not the officers should—or should not—have made arrests. Illinois law, Chicago ordinances, or police department rules formally *require* the police to arrest in all these instances.

1. A 19-year-old standing in the street fired three shots at a woman standing in the doorway of her home but missed. The police apprehended him and knew

that neighbors witnessed the shooting, but they released him when the woman asked them to. The police explained that they do not ordinarily arrest when a victim is able to sign a complaint but does not do so.

2. We asked more than a hundred officers at various levels what they would do in the preceding case, and about two-thirds of them said they would release. One patrolman volunteered that he had witnessed an armed robbery, but that he released the robber because the victim so requested.

3. Even when a police officer witnesses shoplifting, the uniform policy is to release the shoplifter if the merchant so requests.

4. Patrolmen often require a juvenile to make restitution for vandalism or a minor theft, but they usually release the juvenile when the owner is satisfied.

5. A patrolman who finds a juvenile drinking something alcoholic is likely to pour out the beverage but is unlikely to take the juvenile into custody.

6. An ordinance makes it a crime to smoke in an elevator, but I have often ridden in an elevator in the police headquarters building with smokers and police, and I have never witnessed a gesture toward enforcement.

7. A man who patronizes a prostitute is guilty of a crime under an Illinois statute, and he is also guilty under the more easily enforced ordinance about loitering for purposes of prostitution, but even when the evidence is clear and even when officers arrest the woman who is with the man, the officers never arrest the man unless he gives the officers a hard time. In most such cases, the police policy probably cannot be explained in terms of limited police resources.

8. Many officers say they never arrest for attempted bribery, even if witnesses see the attempt and are willing to testify. Some officers believe that a conviction is too improbable; others say the law is too harsh, given the expectations citizens have developed on the basis of past police practices.

9. Patterns of systematically permitting parking in no-parking areas are very common.

10. Almost all motorists know that the police are often lenient about some types of traffic violations.

11. The Chicago police found that jaywalking does not cause accidents and announced that nothing will be done to enforce the ordinance against jaywalking, even though the ordinance remains on the books.

12. Spitting on the sidewalk is punishable by a fine of not less than $1 or more than $5, but officers unanimously say they do not enforce the ordinance.

13. Officers who find a couple having intercourse in a parked car generally do not arrest even though the fornication statute has recently been reenacted.

14. More than nine out of ten patrolmen refuse to arrest for smoking marijuana in public even though the possession of even a tiny quantity of marijuana is a crime. Supervising officers have generally asserted in our interviews that the arrest should be made, but they generally acknowledge that they do not require their subordinates to comply with their views.

15. All patrolmen refrain from full enforcement of curfew laws, but the variations in nonarrest patterns from one officer to another are wide; some are fairly strict and some are quite liberal.

16. Possession of unlabeled pills is a crime, but most officers say they do not arrest for a small number. Each officer follows his own idea of what the minimum should be for an arrest, with no guidance from superiors.

17. Even one caught in the act of burglary may be released by some officers if the burglar is an informer about narcotics dealers. The more usual reward to an informer is nonprosecution instead of nonarrest. No statute or ordinance authorizes special deals between police and informers, but such deals are a mainstay of enforcement of the narcotics laws.[26]

Discussion

The law requires the police to arrest in all the examples. Do you agree? In which cases would you arrest? Which ones would you not arrest? What reasons can you give for not following the formal law which requires arrest in all the cases?

There are several reasons why police do not arrest even when the law requires them to do so. One is economics. Budgets simply do not allow enough money to effect total enforcement; hence the police must manage scarce resources wisely. Another reason for nonarrest is victims' preference. Mainly in misdemeanors, although to a considerable extent in felonies as well, police do not arrest if victims oppose arrest. Police are also less likely to arrest if the victim and suspect are related. Moreover, officers—or their departments—set priorities that informally rank offenses for arrest or discretionary disposition.

Sometimes, legislatures did not intend to cover conduct that technically violates a criminal statute. It is impossible for legislators to foresee all the ramifications of the statutes they enact. For example, it is a misdemeanor to drink in public parks in many cities. In Minneapolis, a gourmet group had a brunch in a city park because they thought the park provided the proper ambience in which to enjoy to the fullest their salmon mousse and imported French white wine. Not only did the police not arrest the group for drinking in the park, but the brunch also received press coverage as a social event of the highest respectability.

A public defender felt some consternation over the nonarrest. He pointed out that the police arrested, and the prosecutor was prepared to prosecute, a native American caught washing down a tuna fish sandwich with cheap red wine in another Minneapolis park. The public defender—a bit of a wag—noted that both the gourmet club and the native American were consuming the same food groups. These incidents display both the strengths and weaknesses of discretion. The legislature obviously did not intend the statute to cover drinking of the type in which the gourmet club engaged. Arresting them would have been foolish and contrary to the legislature's intent. On the other hand, arresting and prosecuting the native American might well have been discriminatory, a wholly unintended and unacceptable result of discretionary selective law enforcement.

Similar reasons of efficiency, fairness, legislative intent, tempering the rigidity of the law with the flexibility of discretion, as well as less acceptable and sometimes offensive motivations, affect the exercise of discretion that underlies prosecutors' decisions to charge, defense attorneys' advice to their clients to plead guilty, and judges' sentencing decisions. The law does not require that the laws be inflexibly enforced against everybody in exactly the same way. It does prohibit differential treatment based on unacceptable criteria, such as race, gender, social status, religion, and age. Differences based on acceptable criteria constitute justified disparities; differences based on unacceptable criteria constitute illegal discrimination. Hence, not prosecuting three white suburban youths caught throwing eggs at cars, because they have never been in trouble with the law before, apologize for what they did, and clean up the cars they hit with the eggs is proper. Prosecuting three urban black youths to "teach them a lesson" for insulting whites is illegal discriminatory law enforcement.

≡ SUPREME COURT RULES AND DISCRETIONARY LOCAL ACTION

The United States Supreme Court's criminal procedure decisions are closely followed and receive wide publicity. Rules pronounced from the highest court in the land, however, do not automatically translate into conduct at the state and local levels. In other words, the Supreme Court's standards are not necessarily equivalent to actual practice. The extent to which those standards are turned into daily practice in state courts, local prosecutors' offices, and police departments is extremely limited.

The restrictions on the Supreme Court's power to supervise criminal justice administration and to infuse local behavior with constitutional norms stem from several sources. The Supreme Court—or any court for that matter—does not enjoy the kind of power over practice that criminal justice administrators possess. The Court can only review procedures when defendants complain formally and then fight their cases through the prosecutors' offices, lower courts, state appellate courts, and finally up through the federal courts to the United Supreme Court. The cases that ultimately reach the Court, therefore, are not representative of the majority of, or even the most important, problems facing local criminal justice agencies. Hence, the Court is left to issue decrees concerning defendants in only a very few, selected cases. In short, courts cannot initiate action; they can only decide cases that the government brings before them.

Virtually all cases that reach the Supreme Court are search-and-seizure cases and other cases that involve obtaining evidence. Defendants hope to avoid conviction due to some illegal police action. Some of them, if they have the means to do so, pursue their objections all the way to the Supreme Court. Other cases never come to judicial attention at any level. For example, the station-house indignities associated with "booking" and "mugging" suspects, taking their belts and shoelaces, and so on, practically never come to judicial attention because these actions do not result in seizing evidence that later becomes a search-and-seizure issue. Most people who believe that police mistreat them are "marginal types" who are happy enough to leave well enough alone once they are released from custody. Hence, most criminal suspects never bring their complaints to judicial attention for judicial supervision. This selection process badly skews the representation of cases.

In those cases in which the Supreme Court establishes a constitutional standard, the decision must filter down through lower courts, magistrates, and police officials before it finally reaches suspects and defendants. By that time informal practice has altered the formal rule announced by the Court. Discretion allows the democratic interest in local values, the organizational interest in distributing scarce resources, and personalities and prejudices to modify, sometimes dramatically, the rules in practice from the rules in Supreme Court opinions.

For example, police almost always measure their success by arrest clearances, not by convictions. Whether or not evidence will be legally admitted in court, or if so will convict defendants, is not of primary importance to most police. Of greater weight is whether they clear the case from their books, either by dropping the case or having the prosecutor take it over. The police will exercise their discretion to arrest in line with these clearance requirements.

> Police work is hard work; it is righteous work; it is combative work, and competitive. Policemen are undereducated, they are scandalously underpaid, and their personal advancement lies in producing results according to the standards of the police ethic. When they go to the commander's office or to court, their conformity to this ethic is almost always vindicated. Neither their superiors nor the judges whom they know nor the public find it necessary to impede the performance of their duties with fettering rules respecting rights of suspects. If the Supreme Court finds this necessary, it must be that the Court is out of step. So its decisions—which are difficult to understand anyway—cannot really be taken seriously.[27]

Similarly, prosecutors, judges, and defense attorneys are committed to the harmonious relationships within their courtroom work group, and that commitment affects the way they fulfill their constitutional responsibilities. Supreme Court rulings about defense attorneys' vigorous defense of their clients' interests, prosecutors' duty to do justice, and the speedy trial requirements imposed on the whole adjudicatory phase of the criminal process are all tempered by the courtroom work group's values and relationships. Discretion permits prosecutors' decisions to charge, defense attorneys' advice to their clients to plead guilty, and judges' accessions to plea bargains to conform to these work group values.

The courtroom work group may emphasize getting along with each other and furthering their own ambitions more than doing justice and the functioning of the adversary system. Negotiation, harmony, and accommodation conflict with, and often take precedence over, the conflict, competition, and rivalry that formal adjudication specifies. The following description of a Chicago courtroom is typical of many criminal court work group relationships.

> In many courtrooms daily sessions were frequently preceded (as well as followed) by "coffee klatches" held in the judge's chambers. The coffee klatches were usually attended by the judge, public defender, the two assistant attorneys and a handful of private defense attorneys, who may or may not have had a case in that courtroom on the day in question. Conversations ranged from the fate of the Blackhawks or the Bulls the night before, the potential impact of some changes in criminal law or procedure, the cases scheduled for the day, to what happened in the annual football game between the state's attorney's office and the public defender's office. . . . In short, these sessions were not unlike those that might take place in any office or shop."[28]

In the final analysis, the formal constitutional rules of criminal procedure are modified, tempered, and ultimately translated into actual practice in the criminal process by informal goals that must be reconciled with formal goals. Getting along with others in the work group, desires for career advancement, satisfying community pressures, and working within the constraints imposed by limited budgets compete with crime control and due process goals. Discretion allows these informal goals to shape decision making throughout the criminal process.

The Supreme Court's decisions—and, for that matter, all formal rules—filter through these discretionary informal influences. Discretion in the filtering modifies, and ultimately dilutes, the rules. Hence, the criminal process in practice is an amalgam of the formal law of criminal procedure and informal influences that enter the process by way of discretion. Discretion and law complement each other in promoting and balancing the interests in criminal procedure.

═══ SUMMARY

The United States Constitution, state constitutions, federal and state court decisions, statutes, and sets of rules constitute the formal side of criminal procedure. Discretion—the freedom to decide allowed to officials—also contributes to the day-to-day operation of the criminal process. Justice, fairness, efficiency, effectiveness, and economy require both the certainty that formal rules provide and the flexibility that discretion allows. A tension between law and discretion has pervaded the history of criminal procedure; despite the strain, both contribute to criminal procedure in practice.

Criminal law enforcement in America is primarily local. Nevertheless, there are federal, state, and local criminal justice agencies. The United States Constitution—the supreme law of the land—is the ultimate source of formal authority in criminal procedure. United States Supreme Court decisions interpreting the United States Constitution are also part of the supreme law of the land—their authority extends throughout the nation. The United States Constitution and decisions interpreting it set a *minimum* standard that states are free to raise; they sometimes do. Individual state constitutions have parallel protections for criminal defendants against unreasonable searches and seizures, self-incrimination, jury trial, double jeopardy, cruel and unusual punishment, and others. In all these protections, individual states have established higher standards under their constitutions than what the United States Supreme Court has defined as federal standards.

The United States Constitution and Supreme Court's authority over state and local criminal procedure stems generally from the supremacy clause and specifically from the Fourteenth Amendment's privileges and immunities, equal protection clause, and most important, due process clause. Under the selective incorporation doctrine most of the Bill of Rights has been extended to the states. The incorporation doctrine permits considerable diversity among the states.

Minimum federal standards permit local variety in criminal justice administration. The Court recognizes the need to allow not only for individual differences among states and between state and federal law enforcement, but also for local experimentation in criminal procedure. The court gives considerable deference to local criminal justice despite the incorporation doctrine. Finally, the Supreme Court has only limited capacity to enforce its decisions on day-to-day local practice. Community norms, organizational values, and individual personalities contribute to a gap between Supreme Court decisions handed down in Washington D.C., and local police, prosecution, and judicial behavior. Discretion allows these local, organizational, and personal norms to operate within the framework of formal criminal procedure law.

═══ QUESTIONS FOR REVIEW AND DISCUSSION

1. What are the major elements in the formal and informal dimensions to criminal procedure?

2. What are the advantages and disadvantages of discretion?

3. What are the strengths and weaknesses of the adversary system?

4. What are the principal justifications for the accusatory system?

5. Compare and contrast the accusatory and adversary system.

6. Do you favor the fundamental fairness doctrine or incorporation? Give reasons.

7. What is the difference between selective and total incorporation?

8. Should the Supreme Court determine local criminal practice? Give reasons.

9. Why is the Supreme Court limited in its capacity to infuse local criminal justice with federal constitutional standards?

═══ NOTES

1. See The Correctional Association of New York, *Do They Belong in Prison?* (New York: The Correctional Association of New York, 1985) for this and many other case histories regarding the New York Mandatory Sentencing Laws.

2. Joel Samaha, "Discretion and Law in the Early Penitential Books," *Social Psychology and Discretionary Law* (New York: W. W. Norton, 1978).

3. Anthony Amsterdam, "The Supreme Court and the Rights of Suspects in Criminal Cases," *New York University Law Review* 45(1970):785.

4. Shirley S. Abrahamson, "Criminal Law and State Constitutions: The Emergence of State Constitutional Law," *Texas Law Review* 63(1985):141; William J. Brennan, Jr., "The Bill of Rights and the States: The Revival of State Constitutions as Guardians of Individual Rights," *New York University Law Review* 61(1986):535.

5. Peter J. Galie, "The Other Supreme Courts: Judicial Activism Among State Supreme Courts," *Syracuse Law Review* 33(1982):731, 732.

6. Gerhard O. W. Mueller, "Foreword" to Lester B. Orfield, *Criminal Procedure Under the Federal Rules* (Rochester: The Lawyers Co-Operative Publishing Company, 1966), vol. 1, xiv.

7. 5 U.S. (1 Cranch) 137, 2 L.Ed. 60 (1803).

8. *The Federalist,* (1888), 485–86.

9. "Developments in the Law: The Interpretation of State Constitutional Rights," *Harvard Law Review* 95(1982):1324, 1370–84; Donald E. Wilkes, Jr., "The New Federalism in Criminal Procedure: State Court Evasion of the Burger Court," *Kentucky Law Journal* 62(1974):420–51.

10. John M. Burkoff, "The Pretext Search Doctrine: Now you See It, Now you Don't," *University of Michigan Journal of Law Reform* 17(1984):523.

11. The writings on the adversary system are legion. For a sample, see Joseph Goldstein, "Reflections on Two Models: Inquisitorial Themes in American Criminal Procedure," *Stanford Law Review* 26(1974):1009; Neef and Nagel, "The Adversary Nature of the

American Legal System from a Historical Perspective," *New York Law Forum* 20(1974):123; Thurman Arnold, *Symbols of Government* (1935); Herbert Packer, *The Limits of the Criminal Sanction* (Palo Alto: Stanford University Press, 1968).

12. *Barron v. Baltimore*, 32 U.S. (7 Pet.) 243 at 250, 8 L.Ed. 672 (1833).

13. Francis A. Allen, "The Law as a Path to the World," *Michigan Law Review* 77(1978):157–58.

14. 297 U.S. 278, 56 S.Ct. 461, 80 L.Ed. 682 (1936).

15. Fred Graham, *The Self-Inflicted Wound* (New York: Macmillan, 1970); Francis Allen, "The Judicial Quest for Penal Justice: The Warren Court and the Criminal Cases," *Illinois Law Forum* (1975):518.

16. *Escobedo v. Illinois*, 378 U.S. 478, 84 S.Ct. 1758, 12 L.Ed.2d 977 (1964) on the right to counsel in police custody; *Miranda v. Arizona*, 384 U.S. 436, 86 S.Ct. 1602, 16 L.Ed.2d 694 (1966) on the warnings to suspects in custody.

17. Jerold H. Israel, "Selective Incorporation: Revisited," *Georgetown Law Journal* 71(1982):274.

18. *Duncan v. Louisiana*, 391 U.S. 145 at 169, 88 S.Ct. 1444 at 1457, 20 L.Ed.2d 491 (1968).

19. Jerold H. Israel, "Selective Incorporation," 278–79.

20. Ibid., 291.

21. *Palko v. Connecticut*, 302 U.S. 319 at 328, 58 S.Ct. 149 at 153, 82 L.Ed. 288 (1937).

22. *Rochin v. California*, 342 U.S. 165 at 172, 72 S.Ct. 205 at 209, 96 L.Ed. 183 (1952).

23. *Barron v. The Mayor and City Council of Baltimore*, 32 U.S. (7 Pet.) 243, 8 L.Ed. 672 (1833) (Bill of Rights does not apply to state criminal proceedings).

24. Justice Harlan, concurring in *Duncan v. Louisiana*, 391 U.S. 145, 88 S.Ct. 1444, 20 L.Ed.2d 491 (1968) (incorporating the right to jury trial); LaFave and Israel, *Criminal Procedure*, 1:97–98.

25. American Bar Association, *Standards Relating to the Administration of Justice*, 2d ed.

26. Kenneth Culp Davis, *Police Discretion* (St. Paul: West Publishing Company, 1975), 3–7.

27. Anthony Amsterdam, "The Supreme Court and the Rights of Suspects in Criminal Cases," *New York University Law Review* 45(1970):785–94.

28. Peter F. Nardulli, *The Courtroom Elite* (Cambridge, Mass.: Ballinger, 1978), 179. These observations are confirmed in a national survey reported in Paul B. Wice, *Chaos in the Courthouse* (New York: Praeger, 1985).

Chapter Three

Remedies For State Law Breaking

CHAPTER OUTLINE

CHAPTER MAIN POINTS

1. Excluding illegally seized evidence is the most widely used remedy against police violations of the Fourth, Fifth, and Sixth Amendments.

2. Other "process" remedies include dismissal, the entrapment defense, reversal, and expunging records.

3. "Victims" of illegal state intrusions and deprivations can sue officials, their agencies, and the government for injuries suffered or secure court orders prohibiting further illegal state action.

4. Some believe informal reward and sanction within criminal justice agencies is the most effective remedy against unlawful government action.

5. These remedies are not mutually exclusive; they may all be pursued to redress the same illegal action.

6. None of the existing remedies are totally satisfactory to enforce constitutional standards.

CHAPTER KEY TERMS

1983 action action brought under Civil Rights Act, U.S. Code § 1983 violation of federal civil rights under color of state law

attenuation doctrine evidence remote from illegal conduct is admissible

compensatory damages monetary award for actual injury suffered by plaintiff

constitutional tort a civil action for violating federal constitutional rights

damages remedy in private law suits in the form of money for injuries

exclusionary rule illegally seized evidence cannot be admitted in criminal trials

expungement criminal records removed from official files

good faith exception evidence not excluded when police rely on good faith in a defective search warrant

harmless error mistake in criminal process that does not affect the outcome of the case

impeach contradict a witness's testimony to undermine his or her credibility

independent source doctrine evidence obtained independently of illegal conduct is admissible

inevitable discovery rule illegally seized evidence that would have been discovered anyway is admissible

injunction court order to stop illegal conduct

remand send a case back to lower court for further proceedings

plaintiff party who brings a civil action

punitive damages monetary award intended to punish and deter malicious injury to plaintiffs

reversible error error in criminal process that affects the outcome of the case

silver platter doctrine illegally seized evidence in state courts can be handed over and used in federal courts

sovereign immunity citizens cannot sue their governments

standing right to challenge state's constitutional violations

tainted fruit of the poisonous tree doctrine evidence derived from illegally obtained sources is not admissible

tort private or civil action

≡ INTRODUCTION

Everyone knows what the consequences are—or at least should be—when private citizens violate the rights of other private citizens by committing crimes. Violators are supposed to be arrested, prosecuted, and punished by fine, imprisonment, or sometimes even death. It is not so clear to most people what are—or should be—the consequences of state lawbreaking. In other words, what recourse does the private citizen have against improper, unlawful, and unconstitutional state intrusions and deprivations that occur in the course of enforcing the criminal law?

The mechanisms to enforce the constitutional standards and the values that underpin the law of criminal procedure range across a broad spectrum. They include the following actions against individual officers who commit criminal intrusions while enforcing the criminal law: (1) criminal prosecution; (2) private law suits initiated by victims of official wrongdoing; and (3) disciplinary action within the officer's agency or department. They also include private law suits for damages and/or court orders **(injunctions)** prohibiting specific conduct, issued against criminal justice agency heads, the agencies themselves, or the governmental unit having jurisdictions over the agency. In addition, a number of possible actions affect criminal proceedings against defendants whom the government has injured, including (1) dismissing cases; (2) reversing convictions; and (3) excluding evidence.[1]

These remedies are not mutually exclusive. For example, the government can prosecute police officers who broke into and entered a house and damaged property while conducting an unlawful search and seizure for burglary. The victim can sue the police for damage to property. The department can dismiss or suspend the officers from duty. Moreover, the victim might sue the chief of police, the police department, and the city with jurisdiction over the police department. Finally, the court may exclude the evidence obtained from the illegal search and, in some instances, even dismiss the case against the victim of government lawbreaking—even if the defendant is clearly guilty! This rarely happens in practice, but it could: the law does not require that injured parties choose one action above others.

≡ THE EXCLUSIONARY RULE

Definition and Purposes of the Exclusionary Rule

The best known, most widely discussed, and certainly the most controversial consequence of illegal government action is the **exclusionary rule**. The exclusionary rule forbids the government to use confessions obtained in violation of defendants' right against self-incrimination that is protected by the Fifth Amendment, and physical evidence gathered through unreasonable searches and seizures that are prohibited by the Fourth Amendment. The rule also excludes evidence obtained in violation of the Sixth amendment right to counsel. Occasionally, the Supreme Court has extended the rule to include statutory violations, such as those involving federal wiretapping legislation.[2]

The Supreme Court has recognized that the exclusionary rule promotes three principal interests. First, the rule inheres in the rights protected in the Fourth, Fifth,Sixth, and Fourteenth Amendments. A right without a remedy is a hollow right. Protections against unreasonable searches and seizures, forced incrimination, and denial of counsel would have no meaning if the government could use evidence obtained in their violation to convict defendants. Second, the integrity of the federal judicial system forbids courts from legitimating unconstitutional conduct by admitting illegally seized evidence into judicial proceedings. The rule of law requires that the government obtain criminal convictions without violating fundamental rights. Third, the rule deters law enforcement officers by making the fruits of their illegal behavior inadmissible. If they cannot use illegally obtained evidence, then, the argument is, they will not obtain it illegally.[3]

The Supreme Court has attributed varied importance to these purposes of the exclusionary rule. In the early cases, judicial integrity and protecting individual rights ranked high. Recently, deterring law enforcement misconduct has taken precedence. The degree to which the exclusionary rule serves these purposes has generated heated controversy between the rule's supporters and its critics. Whatever the controversy surrounding them, these purposes make clear the tension between result, process, and societal interests in criminal procedure. Apprehending and convicting criminals is not the only interest the law of criminal procedure promotes; protecting individual rights and the judicial system's integrity are also important. The Constitution supports criminal law enforcement, but not at any price: violating rights to obtain convictions is too high a price. Put another way, the state must prosecute crimes according to the rules of criminal procedure. Convictions must rest upon guilt proven according to those rules. Otherwise, the public loses confidence in the law. That lost confidence, in turn, breeds contempt and hostility to the law. In the end, both law and order suffer.

History of the Exclusionary Rule

The Constitution itself says nothing about excluding evidence obtained in violation of the Fourth and Fifth Amendments. In 1914, the United States became unique among the world's judicial systems when the Supreme Court created the exclusionary rule for *federal* courts regarding the actions of *federal* officers. In *Weeks v. United States*, referring to the Fourth amendment search and seizure clause, the United States Supreme Court wrote:

> If letters and private documents can [illegally] be seized and held and used in evidence against a citizen accused of an offense, the protection of the Fourth Amendment declaring his right to be secure against such searches and seizures is of no value, and, so far as those thus placed are concerned, might as well be stricken from the Constitution. The efforts of the courts and their officials to bring the guilty to punishment, praiseworthy as they are, are not to be aided by the sacrifice of those great principles established by years of endeavor and suffering which have resulted in their embodiment in the fundamental law of the land.[4]

In 1920, the Court expanded the exclusionary rule in *Silverthorne Lumber Co. v. United States*. Justice Holmes, writing for the Court, held that the federal government could not illegally seize papers, study them, and then use what it had learned from them to order the papers produced. In sweeping language, Holmes wrote that the Fourth Amendment forbade "*any* advantages the Government can gain over the object of its pursuit by doing the forbidden act" (italics added).[5]

In 1949, thirty-five years after *Weeks* created it, the Court was called upon to decide whether the *states* were required to abide by the exclusionary rule. In *Wolf v. Colorado,* the Court declared that "security of one's privacy against arbitrary intrusion by the police" is a fundamental right enforceable against the states through the due process clause of the Fourteenth Amendment. The Court went on to hold, however, that the exclusionary rule was not an essential part of the right; the states are free to adopt other means to enforce constitutional rights. Enforcing rights is the essence, not *how* they are enforced. The *Wolf* decision created what was called the **silver platter doctrine.** Under its double standard, state officers could illegally seize evidence and hand it over to federal officers who could use the evidence because the latter had not participated in the illegal seizure. The possibility of this kind of conclusion, as well as other criticisms, led the Court in 1961 to reconsider, and to overrule, its *Wolf* decision in the landmark case, *Mapp v. Ohio.*[6]

CASE

Does the exclusionary rule apply to the states?

Mapp v. Ohio

367 U.S. 643, 81 S.Ct. 1684, 6 L.Ed.2d 933 (1961)

[Justice Clark delivered the opinion of the Court.]

FACTS

On May 23, 1957, three Cleveland police officers arrived at appellant's residence in that city pursuant to information that "a person [was] hiding out in the home, who was wanted for questioning in connection with a recent bombing, and that there was a large amount of policy paraphernalia being hidden in the home ." Miss Mapp and her daughter by a former marriage lived on the top floor of the two-family dwelling. Upon their arrival at that house, the officers knocked on the door and demanded entrance but appellant, after telephoning her attorney, refused to admit them without a search warrant. They advised their headquarters of the situation and undertook a surveillance of the house.

The officers again sought entrance some three hours later when four or more additional officers arrived on the scene. When Miss Mapp did not come to the door immediately, at least one of the several doors to the house was forcibly opened[a] and the policemen gained admittance. Meanwhile Miss Mapp's attorney arrived, but the officers, having secured their own entry, and continuing in their defiance of the law, would permit him neither to see Miss Mapp nor to enter the house. It happens that Miss Mapp was halfway down the stairs from the upper floor to the front door when the officers, in this high-handed manner, broke into the hall. She demanded to see the search warrant. A paper, claimed to be a warrant, was held up by one of the officers. She grabbed the "warrant" and placed it in her bosom. A struggle ensued in which the officers recovered the piece of paper as a result of which they handcuffed appellant because she had been "belligerent" in resisting their official rescue of the "warrant" from her person. Running roughshod over

---

[a] A police officer testified that "we did pry the screen door to gain entrance"; the attorney on the scene testified that a policeman "tried. . . to kick the door" and then "broke the glass in the door and somebody reached in and opened the door and let them in"; the appellant testified that "The back door was broken."

appellant, a policeman "grabbed" her, "twisted [her] hand," and she "yelled [and] pleaded with him" because "it was hurting." Appellant, in handcuffs, was then forcibly taken upstairs to her bedroom where the officers searched the dresser, a chest of drawers, a closet and some suitcases. They also looked in a photo album and through personal papers belonging to the appellant. The search spread to the rest of the second floor including the child's bedroom, the living room, the kitchen, and a dinette. The basement of the building and a trunk found therein were also searched. The obscene materials for possession of which she was ultimately convicted were discovered in the course of that widespread search.

At the trial no search warrant was produced by the prosecution, nor was the failure to produce one explained or accounted for. At best, "There is, in the record, considerable doubt as to whether there ever was any warrant for the search of defendant's home." The Ohio Supreme Court believed a "reasonable argument" could be made that the conviction should be reversed "because the 'methods' employed to obtain the [evidence]. . . were such as to 'offend "a sense of justice,"'" but the court found determinative the fact that the evidence had not been taken "from defendant's person by the use of brutal or offensive physical force against defendant."

The State says that even if the search were made without authority, or otherwise unreasonably, it is not prevented from using the unconstitutionally seized evidence at trial, citing *Wolf v. Colorado,* 338 U.S. 25, 69 s. Ct. 1359, 93 L.Ed. 1782 (1949), in which the Court did indeed hold "that in a prosecution in a State court for a State crime the Fourteenth Amendment does not forbid the admission of evidence obtained by an unreasonable search and seizure." On this appeal, of which we have noted probable jurisdiction, it is urged once again that we review that holding.

OPINION

. . . In 1949, 35 years after *Weeks* was announced, this Court, in *Wolf v. Colorado,* again for the first time, discussed the effect of the Fourth Amendment upon the States through the operation of the Due Process Clause of the Fourteenth Amendment. . . . [T]he Court decided that the *Weeks* exclusionary rule would not then be imposed upon the States as "an essential ingredient of the right." . . .

The Court in *Wolf* . . . stated that "[t]he contrariety of views of the States" on the adoption of the exclusionary rule of *Weeks* was "particularly impressive;" and . . . that it could not "brush aside the experience of the States which deem the incidence of such conduct by the police too slight to call for a deterrent remedy . . . by overriding the [States'] relevant rules of evidence." While in 1949, prior to the *Wolf* case, almost two-thirds of the States were opposed to the use of the exclusionary rule, now, despite the *Wolf* case, more than half of those since passing upon it, by their own legislative or judicial decision, have wholly or partly adopted or adhered to the *Weeks* rule. Significantly, among those now following the rule is California which, according to its highest court, was "compelled to reach that conclusion because other remedies have completely failed to secure compliance with the constitutional provisions. . . . "

[T]he second basis elaborated in *Wolf* in support of its failure to enforce the exclusionary doctrine against the States was that "other means of protection" have been afforded "the right of privacy." The experience of California that such other remedies have been worthless and futile is buttressed by the experience of other States. The obvious futility of relegating the Fourth Amendment to the protection of other remedies has, moreover, been recognized by this Court since *Wolf*. . . .

Since the Fourth Amendment's right of privacy has been declared enforceable against the States through the Due Process Clause of the Fourteenth, it is enforceable against them by the same sanction of exclusion as is used against the Federal Government. Were it otherwise, then. . . the assurance against unreasonable federal searches and seizures would be "a form of words," valueless and undeserving of mention in a perpetual charter of inestimable human liberties, so too, without that rule the freedom from state invasions of privacy would be so ephemeral and so neatly severed from its conceptual nexus with the freedom from all brutish means of coercing evidence as not to merit this Court's high regard as a freedom "implicit in the concept of ordered liberty." . . .

There are those who say, as did Justice (then Judge) Cardozo, that under our constitutional exclusionary doctrine "[t]he criminal is to go free because the constable has blundered." In some cases this will undoubtedly be the result. But, "there is another consideration—the imperative of judicial integrity." The criminal goes free, if he must, but it is the law that sets him free. Nothing can destroy a government more quickly than its failure to observe its own laws, or worse, its disregard of the charter of its own existence. . . . [Justice Brandeis wrote] "Our Government is the potent, the omnipresent teacher. For good or for ill, it teaches the whole people by its example. . . . If the Government becomes a lawbreaker, it breeds contempt for law; it invites every man to become a law unto himself; it invites anarchy." Nor can it lightly be assumed that, as a practical matter, adoption of the exclusionary rule fetters law enforcement. Only last year this Court expressly considered that contention and found that "pragmatic evidence of a sort" to the contrary was not wanting. The Court noted that

> "The federal courts themselves have operated under the exclusionary rule of *Weeks* for almost half a century; yet it has not been suggested either that the Federal Bureau of Investigation has thereby been rendered ineffective, or that the administration of criminal justice in the federal courts has thereby been disrupted. Moreover, the experience of the states is impressive . . . . The movement towards the rule of exclusion has been halting but seemingly inexorable."

. . . Our decision, founded on reason and truth, gives to the individual no more than that which the Constitution guarantees him, to the police officer no less than that to which honest law enforcement is entitled, and, to the courts, that judicial integrity so necessary in the true administration of justice.

The judgment of the Supreme Court of Ohio is reversed and the cause remanded for further proceedings not inconsistent with this opinion.

Reversed and remanded.

DISSENT

Mr. Justice Harlan, whom Mr. Justice Frankfurter and Mr. Justice Whittaker join, dissenting . . . .

At the heart of the majority's opinion in this case is the following syllogism: (1) the rule excluding in federal criminal trial evidence which is the product of an illegal search and seizure is "part and parcel" of the Fourth Amendment; (2) *Wolf* held that the "privacy" assured against federal action by the Fourth Amendment is also protected against state action by the Fourteenth Amendment; and (3) it is therefore "logically and constitutionally necessary" that the *Weeks* exclusionary rule should also be enforced against the States.

This reasoning ultimately rests on the unsound premise that because *Wolf* carried into the States, as part of "the concept of ordered liberty" embodied in the Fourteenth Amendment, the principle of "privacy" underlying the Fourth Amendment, it must follow that whatever configurations of the Fourth Amendment have been developed in the particularizing federal precedents are likewise to be deemed a part of "ordered liberty," and as such are enforceable against the States. For me, this does not follow at all . . . . Since there is not the slightest suggestion that Ohio's policy is "affirmatively to sanction . . . police incursion into privacy" what the Court is now doing is to impose upon the States not only federal substantive standards of "search and seizure" but also the basic federal remedy for violation of those standards. For I think it entirely clear that the *Weeks* exclusionary rule is but a remedy which, by penalizing past official misconduct, is aimed at deterring such conduct in the future.

I would not impose upon the States this federal exclusionary remedy. . . .
[The memorandum of Justice Stewart and the concurring opinions of Justices Black and Douglas are omitted.]

CASE DISCUSSION

Cleveland police officers seized pornography from Mapp's home. She was tried and convicted of illegal possession of pornography. Over her objection, the trial court admitted the pornography in evidence against her. On appeal the Ohio Supreme Court, although conceding that the police may have seized the evidence illegally, upheld the conviction. Mapp appealed to the United States Supreme Court to ask that the Supreme Court apply the exclusionary rule to the states. The Supreme Court reversed Mapp's conviction.

Does Ms. Mapp have no right if the Court excludes the illegally obtained evidence? What possible other remedies might she have? Which would you recommend? Should Ms. Mapp go free because the police violated her rights? Why? What interests did the Court balance? Which should take precedence? Even if the Court excludes the evidence, is Ms. Mapp really set free? Explain.

Scope of the Exclusionary Rule

The exclusionary rule does not ban all illegally obtained evidence from all criminal proceedings. Prosecutors can use illegally seized evidence to **impeach** defendants' testimony, that is, show testimony to be untruthful. For example, in *Walder v. United States,* Walder was tried for purchasing and possessing heroin. During direct examination, Walder denied that he had ever bought or possessed heroin. The government then introduced heroin capsules seized during an illegal search to prove that Walder was lying. The Court admitted the capsules but cautioned the jury they could not consider the heroin capsules to prove Walder's guilt, only to impeach his testimony. However, in John Hinckley's trial for attempting to murder President Reagan, the District of Columbia Circuit Court refused to allow tainted evidence to rebut Hinckley's insanity defense.[7]

The Supreme Court has also ruled that courts must exclude evidence derived from an illegal search or seizure. This is known as the **tainted fruit of the poisonous tree doctrine.**

Decision Point

In Wong Sun v. United States, six federal narcotics agents illegally broke into Toy's laundry, chased him into the living quarters at the back of his shop, where Toy's wife and child were sleeping, and handcuffed him. Toy told the agents that Yee had been selling narcotics. The agents immediately went to Yee, who surrendered heroin to the agents and implicated Wong Sun. The agents then arrested Wong Sun. After a lawful arraignment, the court released Wong Sun on his own recognizance. Several days later, he returned voluntarily to the police station and confessed to narcotics violations. Was the confession the fruit of the poisonous tree? The Supreme Court ruled that his confession was not the fruit of his illegal arrest because "the connection between his arrest and his statements had become so attenuated as to dissipate the taint."[8]

Four circumstances remove the taint sufficiently to render evidence admissible. The **independent source doctrine** admits evidence initially *discovered* during an illegal search and later *seized* from activities not connected to the initial illegality. For example, in *Segura v. United States*, agents illegally entered Segura's apartment, secured the premises, and remained there for nineteen hours until a search warrant arrived. Evidence seized pursuant to the warrant was admitted and Segura was convicted because the warrant constituted an independent source.[9]

According to the **inevitable discovery rule**, evidence that would have come to light by some lawful, independent means need not be excluded.

Decision Point

Shortly after a ten-year-old girl disappeared from a YMCA in Des Moines, Iowa, over two hundred volunteers began searching the area for the girl.

> Meanwhile, police arrested Nix in Davenport, Iowa, in connection with the girl's disappearance. The police in Davenport told Nix's attorney that they would not question Nix on the way from Davenport to Des Moines. However, during the trip, one of the officers initiated a conversation with Nix regarding the case. The conversation ultimately led to Nix's revealing where he hid the body, which the police recovered. Nix was charged with murder and objected to the admission of the evidence due to the illegal interrogation.
>
> Should the evidence be admitted? The United States Supreme Court ruled that evidence was admissible even though the police violated the defendant's right to counsel in order to obtain the information. The Court concluded that the body would have been discovered during a thorough search conducted independent of the defendant's statements.[10]

The **attenuation doctrine** states that a sufficiently remote connection between the evidence and illegal conduct dissipates the taint on the evidence and renders it admissible. To apply the attenuation doctrine, the Supreme Court requires that the prosecution demonstrate a break in the chain of events between the initial misconduct and eventual acquisition of evidence. The Court considers three factors in determining whether the chain has been broken: (1) the time lapse between misconduct and acquisition; (2) intervening circumstances; and (3) the purpose and flagrancy of the misconduct. In *United States v. Ceccolini*, the Supreme Court ruled admissible testimony from a witness whose identity was discovered during an unlawful search. The Court noted that the witness was not coerced, a substantial time had lapsed between the illegal act and the testimony, the police did not intentionally conduct the illegal search, and they used none of the evidence obtained during the search in questioning the witness.

The **good faith exception** admits evidence if the police reasonably and honestly relied on a defective search warrant to obtain the evidence. The good faith exception to the exclusionary rule has generated tremendous controversy since its adoption by the Supreme Court. Civil libertarians believe that conservatives have strangled the right to privacy secured by the Fourth Amendment; law-and-order supporters claim that finally the Court is removing the handcuffs placed on the police in criminal law enforcement and that a safer society is in the offing. The Court's majority and dissenting opinions in *United States v. Leon* reflect that controversy.[11]

CASE

Did the Court balance the interests correctly?

United States v. Leon et. al.

468 U.S. 897, 104 S. Ct. 3405, 82 L.Ed.2d 677 (1984)

FACTS

In August 1981, a confidential informant of unproven reliability informed an officer of the Burbank Police Department that two persons known to him as "Armando" and "Patsy" were selling large quantities of cocaine and methaqualone from their residence at 620 Price Drive in Burbank, Cal. The informant also indicated that he had witnessed a sale of methaqualone by "Patsy" at the residence approximately five months earlier and had observed at that time a shoebox containing a large amount of cash that belonged to "Patsy." He further declared that "Armando" and "Patsy" generally kept only small quantities of drugs at their residence and stored the remainder at another location in Burbank.

On the basis of this information, the Burbank police initiated an extensive investigation focusing first on the Price Drive residence and later on two other residences as well. Cars parked at the Price Drive residence were determined to belong to respondents Armando Sanchez, who had previously been arrested for possession of marihuana, and Patsy Stewart, who had no criminal record. During the course of the investigation, officers observed an automobile belonging to respondent Ricardo Del Castillo, who had previously been arrested for possession of 50 pounds of marihuana, arrive at the Price Drive residence. The driver of that car entered the house, exited shortly thereafter carrying a small paper sack, and drove away. A check of Del Castillo's probation records led the officers to respondent Alberto Leon, whose telephone number Del Castillo had listed as his employer's. Leon had been arrested in 1980 on drug charges, and a companion had informed the police at that time that Leon was heavily involved in the importation of drugs into this country. Before the current investigation began, the Burbank officers had learned that an informant had told a Glendale police officer that Leon stored a large quantity of methaqualone at his residence in Glendale. During the course of this investigation, the Burbank officers learned that Leon was living at 716 South Sunset Canyon in Burbank.

Subsequently, the officers observed several persons, at least one of whom had prior drug involvement, arriving at the Price Drive residence and leaving with small packages; observed a variety of other material activity at the two residences as well as at a condominium at 7902 Via Magdalena; and witnessed a variety of relevant activity involving respondent's automobiles. The officers also observed respondents Sanchez and Stewart board separate flights for Miami. The pair later returned to Los Angeles together, consented to a search of their luggage that revealed only a small amount of marihuana, and left the airport. Based on these and other observations summarized in the affidavit, Officer Cyril Rombach of the Burbank Police Department, an experienced and well-trained narcotics investigator, prepared an application for a warrant to search 620 Price Drive, 716 South Sunset Canyon, 7902 Via Magdalena, and automobiles registered to each of the respondents for an extensive list of items to believed to be related to respondents' drug-trafficking activities. Officer Rombach's extensive application was reviewed by several Deputy District Attorneys.

A facially valid search warrant was issued in September 1981 by a State Superior Court Judge. The ensuing searches produced large quantities of drugs at the Via Magdalena and Sunset Canyon addresses and a small quantity at the Price Drive residence. Other evidence was discovered at each of the residences and in Stewart's and Del Castillo's automobiles. Respondents were indicted by a grand jury in the District Court for the Central District of California and charged with conspiracy to possess and distribute cocaine and a variety of substantive counts.

The respondents then filed motions to suppress the evidence seized pursuant to the warrant. The District Court held an evidentiary hearing and . . . granted the motions to suppress. . . .

The District Court denied the Government's motion for reconsideration and a divided panel of the Court of Appeals for the Ninth Circuit affirmed. . . .

The Court of Appeals refused the Government's invitation to recognize a good-faith exception to the Fourth Amendment exclusionary rule.

The Government's petition for certiorari . . . presented. . . . the question "[w]hether the Fourth Amendment exclusionary rule should be modified so as not to bar the admission of evidence seized in reasonable, good-faith reliance on a search warrant that is subsequently held to be defective." We granted certiorari to consider the propriety of such a modification. . . .

OPINION

White, J., delivered the opinion of the Court, in which Burger, C. J., and Blackmun, Powell, Rehnquist, and O'Connor, JJ., joined. Blackmun, J., filed a concurring opinion. Brennan, J., filed a dissenting opinion, in which Marshall, J., joined. Stevens, J., filed a dissenting opinion.

We have concluded that, in the Fourth Amendment context, the exclusionary rule can be modified somewhat without jeopardizing its ability to perform its intended functions. Accordingly, we reverse the judgment of the Court of Appeals. . . .

The Fourth Amendment contains no provision expressly precluding the use of evidence obtained in violation of its commands. . . . The rule thus operates as "a judicially operated remedy designed to safeguard Fourth Amendment rights generally through its deterrent effect, rather than a personal constitutional right of the party aggrieved."

Whether the exclusionary sanction is appropriately imposed in a particular case, our decisions make clear, is "an issue separate from the question whether the Fourth Amendment rights of the party seeking to invoke the rule were violated by police conduct." Only the former question is currently before us, and it must be resolved by weighing the costs and benefits of preventing the use in the prosecution's case-in-chief of inherently trustworthy tangible evidence obtained in reliance on a search warrant issued by a detached and neutral magistrate that ultimately is found to be defective.

The substantial social costs exacted by the exclusionary rule for the vindication of Fourth Amendment rights have long been a source of concern. "Our cases have consistently recognized that unbending application of the exclusionary sanction to enforce ideals of governmental rectitude would impede unacceptably the truth-finding functions of judge and jury." An objectionable collateral consequence of this interference with the criminal justice system's truth-finding function is that some guilty defendants may go free or receive reduced sentences as a result of favorable plea bargains. Particularly when law enforcement officers have acted in objective good faith or their transgressions have been minor, the magnitude of the benefit conferred on such guilty defendants offends basic concepts of the criminal justice system. . . .

[T]he balancing approach that has evolved in various contexts . . . "forcefully suggests that the exclusionary rule be more generally modified to permit the introduction of evidence obtained in the reasonable good-faith belief that a search or seizure was in accord with the Fourth Amendment. . . . .

"No empirical researcher, proponent or opponent of the rule, has yet been able to establish with any assurance whether the rule has a deterrent effect. . . . ." But even assuming that the rule effectively deters some police misconduct and provides incentives for the law enforcement profession as a whole to conduct itself in accord with the Fourth Amendment, it cannot be expected, and should not be applied, to deter objectively reasonable law enforcement activity. . . .

We conclude that the marginal or nonexistent benefits produced by suppressing evidence obtained in objectively reasonable reliance on a subsequently invalidated search warrant cannot justify the substantial costs of exclusion. We do not suggest, however, that exclusion is always inappropriate in cases where an officer has obtained a warrant and abided by its terms. . . .

Suppression . . . remains an appropriate remedy if the magistrate or judge in issuing a warrant was misled by information in an affidavit that the affiant knew was false or would have known was false except for his reckless disregard of the truth. The exception we recognize today will also not apply in cases where the issuing magistrate wholly abandoned his judicial role; in such circumstances, no reasonably well trained officer should rely on the warrant. Nor would an officer manifest objective good faith in relying on a warrant based on an affidavit "so lacking in indicia of probable cause as to render official belief in its existence entirely unreasonable." Finally, depending on the circumstances of the particular case, a warrant may be so facially deficient—i.e., in failing to particularize the place to be searched or the things to be seized—that the executing officers cannot reasonably presume it to be valid . . . .

When the principles we have enunciated today are applied to the facts of this case, it is apparent that the judgment of the Court of Appeals cannot stand . . . .

In the absence of an allegation that the magistrate abandoned his detached and neutral role, suppression is appropriate only if the officers were dishonest or reckless in preparing their affidavit or could not have harbored an objectively reasonable belief in the existence of probable cause. . . . Officer Rombach's application for a warrant clearly was supported by much more than a "bare bones" affidavit. The affidavit related the results of an extensive investigation and, as the opinions of the divided panel of the Court of Appeals make clear, provided evidence sufficient to create disagreement among thoughtful and competent judges as to the existence of probable cause. Under these circumstances, the officers' reliance on the magistrate's determination of probable cause was objectively reasonable, and application of the extreme sanction of exclusion is inappropriate.[a]

Accordingly, the judgment of the Court of Appeals is Reversed.

Justice Blackmun, concurring . . . .

I join the Court's opinion in this case, because I believe that the rule announced today advances the legitimate interests of the criminal justice system without sacrificing the individual rights protected by the Fourth Amendment. I write separately, however, to underscore what I regard as the unavoidably provisional nature of today's decisions.

As the Court's opinion in this case makes clear, the Court has narrowed the scope of the exclusionary rule because of an empirical judgment that the rule has little appreciable reliance on search warrants . . . .

What must be stressed, however, is that any empirical judgment about the effect of the exclusionary rule in a particular class of cases necessarily is a provisional one. By their very nature, the assumptions on which we proceed today cannot be cast in stone . . . . If it should emerge from experience that, contrary to our expectations, the good-faith exception to the exclusionary rule results in a material change in police compliance with the Fourth Amendment, we shall have to reconsider what we have undertaken here . . . .

If a single principle may be drawn from this Court's exclusionary rule decisions, it is that the scope of the exclusionary rule is subject to change in light of changing judicial understanding about the effects of the rule outside the confines of the courtroom. It is incumbent on the Nation's law enforce-

---

[a] Researchers have only recently begun to study extensively the effects of the exclusionary rule on the disposition of felony arrests. One study suggests that the rule results in the nonprosecution or nonconviction of between 0.6% and 2.35% of individuals arrested for felonies. Davies, A Hard Look at What We Know (and Still Need to Learn) About the ''Costs''of the Exclusionary Rule: The NIJ Study and Other Studies of ''Lost'' Arrests, 1983 A.B.F. Res. J. 611, 621. The estimates are higher for particular crimes the prosecution of which depends heavily on physical evidence. Thus, the cumulative loss due to nonprosecution or nonconviction of individuals arrested on felony drug charges is probably in the range of 2.8% to 7.1% *Id.*, at 680. Davies' analysis of California data suggests that screening by police and prosecutors results in the release because of illegal searches or seizures of as many as 1.4% of all felony arrestees, *id.*, at 650, that 0.9% of felony arrestees are released, because of illegal searches or seizures, at the preliminary hearing or after trial, *id.*, at 653, and that roughly 0.05% of all felony arrestees benefit from reversals on appeal because of illegal searches. *ID.*, AT 654. See also K. Brosi, A Cross-City Comparison of Felony Case Processing 16, 18–19 (1979); U.S. General Accounting Office, Report of the Comptroller General of the United States, impact of the Exclusionary Rule on Federal Criminal Prosecutions 10-11, 14 (1979); F. Feeny, F. Dill, & A. Weir, Arrests Without Convictions: How Often They Occur and Why 203-206 (National Institute of Justice 1983); National Institute of Justice, The Effects of the Exclusionary Rule:A Study in California 1-2 (1982); Nardulli, The Societal Cost of the Exclusionary Rule: An Empirical Assessment, 1983 A.B.F. Res. J. 585, 600. The exclusionary rule has also been found to affect the plea-bargaining process. S. Schlesinger, Exclusionary Injustice: The Problem of Illegally Obtained Evidence 63 (1977). But see Davies, *supra*, at 668-669; Nardulli, *supra*, at 604-606.

Many of these researchers have concluded that the impact of the exclusionary rule is insubstantial, but the small percentages with which they deal mask a large absolute number of felons who are released because the cases against them were based in part on illegal searches or seizures. ''[A]ny rule of evidence that denies the jury access to clearly probative and reliable evidence must bear a heavy burden of justification, and must be carefully limited to the circumstances in which it will pay its way by deterring official lawlessness.'' *Illinois v. Gates*, 462 U.S.., at 257-258,103 S. Ct., at 2342 (White, J., concurring in judgement). Because we find that the rule can have no substantial deterrent effect in the sorts of situations under consideration in this case, we conclude that it cannot pay its way in those situations.

ment officers, who must continue to observe the Fourth Amendment in the wake of today's decisions, to recognize the double-edged nature of that principle.

DISSENT

Justice Brennan, with whom Justice Marshall joins, dissenting.

Ten years ago, I expressed that the Court's decision "may signal that a majority of my colleagues have positioned themselves to reopen the door [to evidence secured by official lawlessness] still further and abandon altogether the exclusionary rule in search-and-seizure cases." Since then, in case after case, I have witnessed the Court's gradual but determined strangulation of the rule. It now appears that the Court's victory over the Fourth Amendment is complete . . . . [T]oday the Court sanctions the use in the prosecution's case in chief of illegally obtained evidence against the individual whose rights have been violated—a result that had previously been thought to be foreclosed.

The Court seeks to justify this result on the ground that the "costs" of adhering to the exclusionary rule in cases like those before us exceed the "benefits." But the language of deterrence and of cost/benefit analysis, if used indiscriminately, can have a narcotic effect. It creates an illusion of technical precision and ineluctability. It suggests that not only constitutional principle but also empirical data support the majority's result. When the Court's analysis is examined carefully, however, it is clear that we have not been treated to an honest assessment of the merits of the exclusionary rule, but have instead been drawn into a curious world where the "costs" of excluding illegally obtained evidence loom to exaggerated heights and where the "benefits" of such exclusion are made to disappear with a mere wave of the hand . . . .

[S]ince the Fourth Amendment became part of the Nation's fundamental law in 1791, what the Framers understood then remains true today—that the task of combatting crime and convicting the guilty will in every era seem of such critical and pressing concern that we may be lured by the temptations of expediency into forsaking our commitment to protecting individual liberty and privacy. It was for that very reason that the Framers of the Bill of Rights insisted that law enforcement efforts be permanently and unambiguously restricted in order to preserve personal freedoms. In the constitutional scheme they ordained, the sometimes unpopular task of ensuring that the government's enforcement efforts remain within the strict boundaries fixed by the Fourth Amendment was entrusted to the courts . . . .

The Court's decisions over the past decade have made plain that the entire enterprise of attempting to assess the benefits and costs of the exclusionary rule in various contexts is a virtually impossible task for the judiciary to perform honestly or accurately. Although the Court's language in those cases suggests that some specific empirical basis may support its analyses, the reality is that the Court's opinions represent inherently unstable compounds of intuition, hunches, and occasional pieces of partial and often inconclusive data . . . . To the extent empirical data is available regarding the general costs and benefits of the exclusionary rule, it has shown, on the one hand, as the Court acknowledges today, that the costs are not as substantial as critics have asserted in the past, and, on the other hand, that while the exclusionary rule may well have certain deterrent effects, it is extremely difficult to determine with any degree of precision whether the incidence of unlawful conduct by police is now lower than it was prior to *Mapp*. The Court has sought to turn this uncertainty to its advantage by casting the burden of proof upon proponents of the rule. "Obviously," however, "the assignment of the burden of proof on an issue where evidence does not exist and cannot be obtained is outcome determinative. [The] assignment of the burden is merely a way of announcing a predetermined conclusion."

By remaining within its redoubt of empiricism and by basing the rule solely on the deterrence rationale, the Court has robbed the rule of legitimacy. A doctrine that is explained as if it were an empirical proposition but for which there is only limited empirical support is both inherently unstable and an easy mark for critics. The extent of this Court's fidelity to Fourth Amendment requirements, however, should not turn on such statistical uncertainties . . . "[P]ersonal liberties are not rooted in the law of averages." Rather than seeking to give effort to the liberties secured by the Fourth Amendment through guesswork about deterrence, the Court should restore to its proper place the principle framed 70 years age in *Weeks* that an individual whose privacy has been invaded in violation of the Fourth Amendment has a right grounded in that Amendment to prevent the government from subsequently making use of any evidence so obtained.

CASE DISCUSSION

A magistrate issued a search warrant, pursuant to which the police seized drugs. Leon and others were indicted for conspiring to possess and distribute cocaine. Their lawyers filed a motion to suppress the cocaine. The District Court granted the motion to suppress. A divided Court of Appeals affirmed the District Court's denial of a motion to reconsider its granting of the motion to suppress the cocaine. The United States Supreme Court granted the government's petition for *certiorari* to consider whether to modify the exclusionary rule by creating an exception for evidence seized in good-faith reasonable reliance on a search warrant subsequently held defective. The Court decided to create the exception.

What interests does the good faith exception promote? Should Leon go free because the government violated his rights? Why? Why not? Does he really go free, if the evidence is excluded? Explain. What remedy, if any, would you provide for Leon in this case? A number of states have declined to adopt the good faith exception to their own constitutions. In *Stringer v. State*, the Mississippi Supreme Court reasoned that under the Mississippi Constitution,

> the fundamental flaw in *Leon* is that its new "insight"—that in the type of cases we are concerned with it is the issuing magistrate who violates the accused's Fourth Amendment rights, not the officer—suggests a *greater* need for the exclusionary rule, not a lesser one.

The Court concluded that the exclusionary rule is

> our only practicable means of getting the attention of the issuing magistrates who disregard the rights of persons to be free of searches except under warrants issued on probable cause.[12]

Do you agree with the Mississippi Supreme Court?

Consider the statistics cited in footnote a on page 94. Do they indicate that the costs of the exclusionary rule are too high? Defend your answer.

The Fourth Amendment protects against unreasonable searches and seizures by *government* agents. According to the Supreme Court, the Fourth Amendment does *not* protect against private unlawful searches and seizures. Hence, the exclusionary rule does not forbid the admission of evidence that a *private* person seizes and turns over the the government, even though the citizen invaded another's property to obtain the evidence. A problem arises when citizens act as government agents: At what point does cooperation become participation? The Supreme Court has not established a test to determine when a private citizen becomes a government agent. The circuit courts have adopted a two-pronged test to determine when citizens become agents: (1) the government must have prior knowledge of the proposed conduct; and (2) private citizens must intend to further a criminal investigation, not their own ends. The Ninth Circuit Court applied this test in *United States v. Walter.*[13]

CASE

Was he a government agent?

United States v. Walther

652 F.2d 788 (9th Cir. 1981)

FACTS

On August 17, 1979, a women's overnight case arrived at the Western Airlines baggage terminal at Seattle-Tacoma International Airport. The case had been shipped as a "Speed Pak" from San Diego and was addressed to a "Mrs. R. Nelson" of Vashon Island, Washington. Shortly after the case arrived, a Western Airlines employee named Hank Rivard found the case to be somewhat suspicious because it was light-weight, did not rattle when shaken, and was taped shut. He opened the case and found that it contained a white powder substance.

After discovering the white powder, Rivard contacted Special Agent Walt Brehm of the Drug Enforcement Administration. Brehm and several other DEA agents went to the Western terminal, where they observed the open case and white powder. A field test confirmed that the substance was cocaine. The case was then repacked with sugar, and resealed. Later that evening, the defendant Karyn Walter arrived, claimed the case, and was arrested in the airport's parking garage. Walter's arrest led to the seizure of other evidence from her purse and car. Apparently, defendant Barba-Barba was responsible for shipping the case to Seattle.

The disclosure of the contents of Walter's overnight case was not Rivard's first contact with the DEA. The DEA has maintained a confidential informant file on Rivard which relates mainly to his reporting suspicious individuals fitting the "drug profile" while working at the ticket counter. According to that file, Rivard was established as a confidential informant and issued an informant number in October 1973. Between 1973 and 1977, Rivard provided information to the DEA on at least eleven occasions for which he received payments in amounts ranging from $25.00 to $250.00, receiving a total of $800.00 during that period. Rivard's file was closed on October 27, 1977, while he was on leave of absence from Western Airlines. Rivard was never made aware that his file had been closed.

According to Rivard's testimony at the suppression hearing, he had opened approximately ten Speed Paks in the past and had frequently discovered illegal drugs. Though he had never been paid for information supplied in connection with Speed Pak openings, the DEA had never discouraged him from doing so and, according to the testimony of one agent, would have paid him had he ever discovered a significant amount of drugs. Rivard also testified that while he did not expect payment ;for notifying the DEA of the contents of Walter's case, he also had no reason not to expect payment.

Walter was indicted on one count of possession of cocaine with intent to distribute, one count of possession of marijuana with intent to distribute, and one count of conspiring with Barba-Barba to possess cocaine with the intent to distribute. Barba-Barba was indicted on one count of possession of cocaine with intent to distribute, and one count of distribution. Both defendants moved to suppress all evidence seized on August 17 . . . .

OPINION

A wrongful search or seizure by a private party does not violate the Fourth Amendment. However, where a private party acts as an "instrument or agent" of the state in effecting a search or seizure, fourth amendment interests are implicated. This court has recognized that there exists a "gray area" between the extremes of overt governmental participation in a search and the complete absence of such participation. The resolution of cases falling within the "gray area" can best be resolved on a case-by-case basis with the consistent application of certain general principles . . . .

The government must be involved either directly as a participant or indirectly as an encourager of the private citizen's actions before we deem the citizen to be an instrument of the state. The requisite degree of governmental participation involves some degree of knowledge and acquiescence in the search.

It is clear from the foregoing that two of the critical factors in the "instrument or agent" analysis are: (1) the government's knowledge and acquiescence, and (2) the intent of the party performing the search. These are the factors which have generated most of the controversy on this appeal and which now occupy our attention.

We cannot agree with the government's contention that the pertinent findings below were clearly erroneous. Though Rivard testified that he believed that a federal regulation gave the airlines the right to open any piece of luggage consigned to them for shipping, he also testified that the only reason why he opened the case was his suspicion that it contained illegal drugs. Thus, legitimate business considerations such as prevention of fraudulent loss claims were not a factor. The record contained sufficient evidence for the court to conclude also that Rivard opened the case with the expectation of probable reward from the DEA. Rivard acknowledged that there was no reason that he should not expect a reward, and the testimony of a DEA agent established that it would be reasonable for him to have such an expectation. Our review of the record, therefore, indicates that the evidence supports the district court's findings. We are thus satisfied that Rivard opened the package with the requisite mental state of an "instrument or agent."

We are also satisfied that Rivard's prior experience with the DEA provides proof of the government's acquiescence in the search. While the DEA had no prior knowledge that this particular search would be conducted and had not directly encouraged Rivard to search this overnight case, it had certainly encouraged Rivard to engage in this type of search. Rivard had been rewarded for providing drug-related information in the past. He had opened Speed Paks before, and did so with no discouragement from the DEA. The DEA thus had knowledge of a particular pattern of search activity dealing with a specific category of cargo, and had acquiesced in such activity. Affirmed.

CASE DISCUSSION

Walter was indicted for possession of marijuana and possession of cocaine with intent to distribute, and conspiracy to possess cocaine with intent to distribute. She moved to suppress all the evidence seized. The district court granted the motion. The court of appeals affirmed the district court's decision.

Should the test require that the government know about each private search? Or do you agree with the Court that knowing about a pattern is sufficient? What interests does defining the knowledge requirement in terms of a pattern promote? Explain. Did the inspector intend to help law enforcement or his own ends? What might those ends be? Is it easy to separate them? How would you decide this case? What interests would you try to promote in your decision?

Decision Point

Films depicting homosexual activity were addressed to "Leggs, Inc.," a fictitious company. The films were delivered by mistake to "L'Eggs Products, Inc." When L'Eggs employees opened the packages and found suggestive drawings and explicit descriptions of the films' contents, the employees notified the FBI. Federal Bureau of Investigation agents, without a warrant, viewed the films.

Was the viewing legal? According to the Supreme Court it was not. The Court held that the viewing was an "expansion of the private search. The viewing might not have been illegal if the employees had viewed it first."[14]

Federal Express employees opened a torn package to inspect it for damage. The package was in an ordinary box wrapped in plain brown paper. Inside the box, under crumpled newspaper was a tube made from silver tape. When they cut the tape, the employees discovered a white, powdery substance inside plastic bags. The employees notified the Drug Enforcement Administration (DEA), then reclosed the package. When DEA officials arrived, they removed the plastic bags and did a field test on the powder. The test revealed that the substance was cocaine. The DEA officials had no warrant.

Was the DEA action lawful? According to the Supreme Court, it was. The Court ruled that the additional invasions by the government, namely, the field test, "must be tested by the degree to which[it] . . . exceeded the scope of the private search." According to the Court: "The field test . . . could disclose only one fact previously unknown to the agent—whether or not the suspicious substance was cocaine. It could tell him nothing more, not even whether the substance was sugar or talcum powder . . . . A chemical test that merely discloses whether or not a particular substance is cocaine does not compromise any legitimate interest in privacy." Justice Stevens announced the judgment in both cases. Do you think there is a meaningful distinction between these two cases? Did the official search go significantly further in the film viewing than in testing the powder?[15]

Standing

In order to challenge the admissibility of evidence, defendants must have **standing:** They must show that they were the victims of the unconstitutional action that produced the evidence. Hence, government action must violate defendants' own constitutional rights, not somebody else's. Defendants who have possessory —custody or ownership—interest in premises have standing. I have standing to challenge a search of the condo or car I own or the apartment I lease. In some instances, if I leave my personal property in someone else's house I might have standing. For example, in *United States v. Jeffers*, Jeffers stashed his drugs in his aunts' hotel room, a room for which he had a key and permission to enter whenever he wished. The Supreme Court ruled that Jeffreys had a reasonable expectation of privacy in his place for his stash and therefore standing to challenge its admissibility.

The Supreme Court has delineated several factors in determining whether defendants have an expectation of privacy that gives them standing to challenge the admissibility of evidence. They include: (1) whether defendants have a possessory interest in the object searched or seized; (2) whether defendants have taken measures to insure their privacy; (3) whether defendants have exclusive control over the area searched; (4) whether the item is in plain view; (5) whether the area searched is a private dwelling or a yard; (6) whether defendants were legitimately on the premises searched; and (7) whether defendants abandoned the place searched or property seized.

The American Law Institute's Model Code of Pre-Arraignment Procedure provides that defendants have standing when items are obtained from searches or seizures of

(a) the defendant; or
(b) a spouse, parent, child, brother, or sister of the defendant, or any member of his or her household; or
(c) any person with whom the defendant resides or sojourns; or
(d) a co-defendant, co-conspirator . . . or
(e) any person with whom the defendant conducts a business; or
(f) any other person if, from the circumstances, it appears that the search or seizure was intended to avoid the application of [search and seizure rules] to any of the persons described in clauses (a) to (e) inclusive.[16]

The Supreme Court addressed the question of standing in *Rakas v. Illinois*.[17]

CASE

Does he have a privacy interest in his friend's car?

Rakas v. Illinois

439 U.S. 128, 99 S. Ct. 421, 58 L.Ed.2d. 387 (1978)

[Rehnquist, J., delivered the opinion of the Court. Powell, J., and Burger, C.J., filed concurring opinions. White, J., filed a dissenting opinion, which Brennan, Marshall, and Stevens, joined.]

FACTS

. . . A police officer on routine patrol received a radio call notifying him of a robbery of a clothing store in Bourbonnais, Ill., and describing the getaway car. Shortly thereafter, the officer spotted an automobile which he thought might be the getaway car. After following the car for some time and after the arrival of assistance, he and several other officers stopped the vehicle. They discovered a box of rifle shells in the glove compartment, which had been locked, and a sawed-off rifle under the front passenger seat. After discovering the rifle and the shells, the officers took petitioners to the station and placed them under arrest.

Before trial petitioners moved to suppress the rifle and shells seized from the car on the ground that the search violated the Fourth and Fourteenth amendments. They conceded that they did not own the automobile and were simply passengers; the owner of the car had been the driver of the vehicle at the time of the search. Nor did they assert that they owned the rifle or the shells seized. The prosecutor challenged petitioners' standing to object to the lawfulness of the search of the car because neither the car, the shells nor the rifle belonged to them. [The trial court denied the motion to suppress. The Illinois Appellate Court affirmed, and the Illinois Supreme Court denied the petitioners leave to appeal.]

OPINION

Petitioners first urge us to relax or broaden the rule of standing . . . so that any criminal defendant at whom a search was directed would have standing to contest the legality of that search and object to the admission at trial of evidence obtained as a result of the search. Alternatively, petitioners argue that they have standing to object to the search . . . because they were ''legitimately on [the] premises'' at the time of the search.

We decline to extend the rule of standing . . . . There is no reason to think that a party whose rights have been infringed will not, if evidence is used against him, have ample motivation to move to suppress it. Even if such a person is not a defendant in the action, he may be able to recover damages for the violation of his Fourth Amendment rights, or seek redress under state law for invasion of property or trespass . . . .

When we are urged to grant standing to a criminal defendant to assert a violation, not of his constitutional rights but of someone else's, we cannot but give weight to practical difficulties such as those foreseen by Mr. Justice Harlan: . . .

> ''[T]he target rule would entail very substantial administrative difficulties. In the majority of cases, I would imagine that the police plant a bug with the expectation that it may well produce leads to a large number of crimes. A lengthy hearing would, then, appear to be necessary in order to determine whether the police knew of an accused's criminal activity at the time the bug was planted and whether the police decision to plant a bug was motivated by an effort to obtain information against the accused or some other individual. I do not believe that this administrative burden is justified in any substantial degree by the hypothesized marginal increase in Fourth Amendment protection. . . .

Conferring standing to raise vicarious Fourth Amendment claims would necessarily mean a more widespread invocation of the exclusionary rule during criminal trials . . . . Each time the exclusionary rule is applied it exacts a substantial social cost for the vindication of Fourth Amendment rights. Relevant and reliable evidence is kept from the trier of fact and the search for truth at trial is deflected. Since our cases generally have held that one whose Fourth Amendment rights are violated may successfully suppress evidence obtained in the course of an illegal search and seizure, misgivings as to the benefit of enlarging the class of persons who may invoke that rule are properly considered when deciding whether to expand standing to assert Fourth Amendment violations . . .

[W]e believe that the phrase ''legitimately on premises'' . . . creates too broad a gauge for measurement of Fourth Amendment rights. For example, applied literally, this statement would permit a casual visitor who has never seen, or been permitted to visit the basement of another's house to object to a search of the basement if the visitor happened to be in the kitchen of the house at the time of the search. Likewise, a casual visitor who walks into a house one minute before a search of the house commences and leaves one minute after the search ends would be able to contest the legality of the search. The first visitor would have absolutely no interest ot legitimate expectation of privacy in the basement, the second would have none in the house, and it advances no purpose served by the Fourth Amendment to permit either of them to object to the lawfulness of the search . . . .

We would not wish to be understood as saying that legitimate presence on the premises is irrelevant to one's expectation of privacy, but it cannot be deemed controlling.

Judged by the foregoing analysis, petitioners' claims must fail. They asserted neither a property nor a possessory interest in the automobile, nor an interest in the property seized. And as we have previously indicated, the fact that they were "legitimately on [the] premises" in the sense that they were in the car with the permission of its owner is not determinative of whether they had a legitimate expectation of privacy in the particular areas of the automobile searched . . . .

Affirmed.

DISSENT

The Court's holding is contrary . . . to the everyday expectations of privacy that we all share. Because of that, it is unworkable in all the various situations that arise in real life. If the owner of the car had not only invited petitioners to join her but had said to them "I give you a temporary possessory interest in my vehicle so that you will share the right to privacy that the Supreme Court says that I won," then apparently the majority would reverse. But people seldom say such things, though they may mean their invitation to encompass them if only they had thought of the problem. If the nonowner were the spouse or child of the owner, would the Court recognize a sufficient interest? If so, would distant relatives somehow have more of an expectation of privacy than close friends? What if the nonowners were driving with the owner's permission? Would the nonowning drivers have more of an expectation of privacy than mere passengers? What about a passenger in a taxicab? *Katz* [see chap. 6] expressly recognized protection for such passengers. Why should Fourth Amendment rights be present when one pays a cabdriver for a ride but be absent when one is given a ride by a friend?

More importantly, the ruling today undercuts the force of the exclusionary rule in the one area in which its use is most certainly justified—the deterrence of bad-faith violations of the Fourth Amendment. This decision invited police to engage in patently unreasonable searches every time an automobile contains more than one occupant. Should something be found, only the owner of the vehicle, or the item, will have standing to seek suppression, and the evidence will presumably be usable against the other occupants . . . .

Of course, most police officers will decline the Court's invitation and will continue to do their jobs as best they can in accord with the Fourth Amendment. But the very purpose of the Bill of Rights was to answer the justified fear that governmental agents cannot be left totally to their own devices, and the Bill of Rights is enforceable in the courts because human experience teaches that not all such officials will otherwise adhere to the stated precepts. Some policemen simply do act in bad faith, even if for understandable ends, and some deterrent is needed. In the rush to limit the applicability of the exclusionary rule somewhere, anywhere, the Court ignores precedent, logic, and common sense to exclude the rule's operation from situations in which, paradoxically, it is justified and needed.

CASE DISCUSSION

Rakas and others were convicted of armed robbery in the Circuit Court of Kankakee County, Illinois, and their convictions were upheld on appeal. Rakas objected to the introduction of the sawed-off rifle and rifle shells seized by police on the grounds that they were seized during an unlawful search. The Illinois Appellate Court held that Rakas did not have standing to object to the alleged unlawful search. On writ of *certioriari*, the United States Supreme Court affirmed the Illinois Appellate Court's holding.

What reasons does the Court give for declining to broaden the definition of standing, as petitioners argued it should? Are they constitutional arguments? or "practical" arguments? Should the administration of the exclusionary rule depend on whether it is practical or not? Do you agree with the dissent that this will encourage police to engage in illegal searches of cars with several passengers? To what extent does the Court's decision place importance on procedural regularity? obtaining the correct result? controlling government? crime control? efficiency and harmony? How does the dissent weigh these interests differently from the Court?

OTHER PROCESS REMEDIES

Several process remedies in addition to the exclusionary rule enforce criminal defendants' rights. The principal process remedies discussed here include: (1) dismissal; (2) the defense of entrapment; (3) reversible error; and (4) expungement.

Dismissal

Historically, courts retained jurisdiction over—authority to hear and decide cases involving—unlawfully arrested defendants appearing before them. The theory was that courts did not look behind the appearance of defendants, that is, they did not consider *how* they got to court. The courts' duty was to insure that proceedings against them were properly conducted, once defendants appeared. In other words, although the exclusionary rule excluded illegally seized evidence, no parallel rule banned illegally seized persons from court proceedings. The rule generated controversy, hence courts have relaxed it. The United States Supreme Court has not ruled on the point. However, the Second Circuit Court of Appeals has addressed the issue in *United States v. Toscanino*. The case illustarates the relaxation of the earlier rule.

CASE

Should the charges be dismissed?

United States v. Toscanino

500 F.2d 267 2d Cir. (1974)

FACTS

Mansfield, Circuit Judge:

Fransisco Toscanino appeals from a narcotics conviction entered against him in the Eastern District of New York by Chief Judge Jacob Mishler after a jury trial. Toscanino was sentenced to 20 years in prison and fined $20,000. He contends that the court acquired jurisdiction over him unlawfully through the conduct of American agents who kidnapped him in Uruguay, used illegal electronic surveillance, tortured him and abducted him to the United States for the purpose of prosecuting him here. We remand the case to the district court for further proceedings in which the government will be required to respond to his allegations concerning the methods by which he was brought into the Eastern District and the use of electronic surveillance to gather evidence against him.

Toscanino, who is a citizen of Italy, and four others were charged with conspiracy to imiport narcotics into the United States in violation of 21 U.S.C. §§ 173 and 174 in a one count indictment returned by a grand jury sitting in the Eastern District on February 22, 1973.

Toscanino does not question the sufficiency of the evidence or claim any error with respect to the conduct of the trial itself. His principal argument, which he voiced prior to trial and again after the jury verdict was returned, is that the entire proceedings in the district court against him were void because his presence within the territorial jurisdiction of the court has been illegally obtained. He alleged that he had been kidnapped from his home in Montevideo, Uraguay, and brought into the Eastern District only after he had been detained for three weeks of interrogation accopmanied by phuysical torture in Brazil. He offered to prove the following:

"On or about January 6, 1973 Francisco Toscanino was lured from his home in Montevideo, Uruguay by a telephone call. This call had been placed by or at the direction of Hugo Campos Hermedia. Hermedia was at that time and still is member of the police in Montevideo, Uraguay. In this effort, however, and those that will follow in this offer, Hermedia was acting *ultra vires* in that he was the paid agent of the United States government . . . .

". . . . The telephone call ruse succeeded in bringing Toscanino and his wife, seven months pregnant at the time, to an area near a deserted bowling alley in the City of Montevideo. Upon their arrival there Hermedia together with six associates abducted Toscanino. This was accomplished in full view of Toscanino's terrified wife by knocking him unconscious with a gun and throwing him into the rear seat of Hermedia's car. Thereupon Toscanino, bound and bindfolded, was driven to Uruguayan-Brazilian border by a circuitous route.

"At one point during the long trip to the Brazilian border discussion was had among Toscanino's captors as to changing the license plates of the abductor's car in order to avoid detention by the Uruguayan authorities. At another point the abductor's car was abruptly brought to a halt, and Toscanino was ordered to get out. He was brought to an apparently secluded place and told to lie perfectly still or he would be shot then and there. Although his blindfold prevented him from seeing, Toscanino could feel the barrel of the gun agazinst his head and could hear the rumbling noises of what appeared to be an Uruguayan military convoy. A short time after the noise of the convoy had died away, Toscanino was placed in another vehicle and whisked to the border. There by pre-arrangement and again at the connivance of the United States government, the car was met by a group of Brazilians who took custody of the body of Francisco Toscanino.

"At no time had there been any formal or informal request on the part of the United States of the government of Uruguay for the extradition of Francisco Toscanino nor was there any legal basis to justify this rank criminal enterprise. In fact, the Uruguayan government claims that it had no prior knowledge of the kidnapping nor did it consent thereto and had indeed condemned this kind of apprehension as alien to its laws.

"Once in the custody of Brazilians, Toscanino was brought to Porto Allegre where he was held incommunicado for eleven hours. His requests to consult with counsel, the Italian Consulate, and his family were all denied. During this time he was denied all food and water.

"Later that same day Toscanino was brought to Brasilia . . . . For seventeen days Toscanino was incessantly tortured and interrogated. Throughout this entire period the United States government and the United States Attorney for the Eastern District of New York prosecuting this case were aware of the interrogation and did in fact receive reports as to its progress. Furthermore, during this period of torture and interrogation a member of the United States Department of Justice, Bureau of Narcotics and Dangerous Drugs was present at one or more intervals and actually participated in portions of the interrogation . . . . [Toscanino's] captors denied him sleep and all forms of nourishment for days at a time. Nourishment was provided intravenously in a manner precisely equal to an amount necessary to keep him alive. Reminiscent of the horror stories told by our military men who returned from Korea and China, Toscanino was forced to walk up and down a hallway for seven or eight hours at a time. When he could no longer stand he was kicked and beaten but all in a manner contrived to punish without scarring. When he would not answer, his fingers were pinched with metal pliers. Alcohol was flushed into his eyes and nose and other fluids . . . were forced up his anal passage. Incredibly, these agents of the United States government attached electrodes to Toscanino's earlobes, toes, and genitals. Jarring jolts of electricity were shot throughtout his body, rendering him unconscious for indeterminate periods of time but again leaving no physical scars.

"Finally on or about January 25, 1973 Toscanino was brought to Rio de Janeiro where he was drugged by Brazilian-American agents and placed on

Pan American Airways Flight #202 destined for the waiting arms of the United States government. On or about January 26, 1973 he woke in the United States, was arrested on the aircraft, and was brought immediately to Thomas Puccio, Assistant United States Attorney.

"At no time during the government's seizure of Toscanino did it ever attempt to accomplish its goal through any lawful channels whatever. From start to finish the government unlawfully, willingly and deliberately embarked upon a brazenly criminal scheme violating the laws of three separate countries."

Toscanino's motion for an order vacating the verdict, dismissing the indictment and ordering his return to Uraguay was denied by the district court on November 2, 1973, without a hearing. Relying principally on the decision of the Supreme Court in *Ker v. Illinios*, 119 U.S. 436, 7 S. Ct. 225, 30 L.Ed 421 (1886), the court held that the manner in which Toscanino was brought into the territory of the United States was immaterial to the court's power to proceed, provided he was physically present at the time of trial.

OPINION

In an era marked by a sharp increase in kidnapping activities, both here and abroad . . . . we face the question as we must in the state of the pleadings, of whether a federal court must assume jurisdiction over the person of a defendant who is illegally apprehended abroad and forcibly abducted by government agents to the United States for the purpose of facing criminal charges here . . . .

[U]nder the so-called *"Ker-Frisbie"* rule, due process was limited to the guarantee of a constitutionally fair trial, regardless of the method by which jurisdiction was obtained over the defendant. Jurisdiction gained through an indisputably illegal act might still be exercised, even though the effect could be to reward police brutality and lawlessness in some cases.

Since *Frisbie* the Supreme Court, in which one distinguished legal luminary describes as a "constitutional revolution," has expanded the interpretation of "due process." No longer is it limited to the guarantee of "fair" procedure at trial. In an effort to deter police misconduct, the term has been extended to bar the government from realizing directly the fruits of its own deliberate and unnecessary lawlessness in bringing the accused to trial . . . .

Faced with a conflict between the two concepts of due process, the one being the restricted version found in *Ker-Frisbie* and the other the expanded and enlightened interpretation expressed in more recent decisions of the Supreme Court, we are persuaded that to the extent that the two are in conflict, the *Ker-Frisbie* version must yield. Accordingly we view due process as now requiring a court to divest itself of jurisdiction over the person of a defendant where it has been required as the result of the government's deliberate, unnecessary and unreasonable invasion of the accused's constitutional rights. This conclusion represents but an extension of the well-recognized power of federal courts in the civil context to decline to exercise jurisdiction over a defendant whose presence has been secured by force or fraud.
[Remanded for further proceedings.]

CASE DISCUSSION

Toscanino was convicted of a narcotics offense and sentenced to up to twenty years in prison and fined $20,000. He appeals on the ground that the court unlawfully acquired jurisdiction over him. The court of appeals remanded the case to the district court for consideration of the means by which the court acquired jurisdiction over Toscanino. **Remand** for further proceedings means that the appeals court "sent the case back to the trial court." The appeals courts had heard arguments concerning the questions involved in Toscanino's arrest, but appelate courts do not conduct trials. Since the trial court—in this instance, the federal distict court—had not heard arguments about the arrest, believing that the law was settled on the point, the appeals court ruled that the defendant had to have a fair hearing on the arrest.

Should it matter how the defendant got to court? Once there, if the proceedings are fair, should he rely on other remedies? Which ones? Does this case demonstarate too much concern for the interest in fair proceedings and not enough for convicting the clearly guilty? Why? Just how offensive must the government's actions be to require dismissal in your judgment? Explain.

Dismissing cases where courts obtain jurisdiction following illegal arrests does not mean the government must *permanently* drop charges against the illegally seized defendant. If prosecutors wish to start over, and police or other enforement agents secure defendants by lawful arrests, they can do so. Of course, this does not mean that the police can wait outside and arrest defendants as they walk out the courtroom door. However, once the police remove taint from the original arrest, proceedings may continue.

Entrapment

American law did not recognize the entrapment defense until the twentieth century. The New York Supreme Court explained why in 1864:

> Even if inducements to commit crime could be assumed to exist in this case, the allegation of the defendant would be but the repetition of the pleas as ancient as the world, and first interposed in Paradise: "The serpent beguiled me and I did eat." That defense was overruled by the great Lawgiver, and whatever estimate we may form, or whatevber judgment pass upon the character or conduct of the tempter, this plea has never since availed to shield crime or give indemnity to the culprit, and it is safe to say that under any code of civilized, not say Christian ethics, it never will.[18]

In 1904, another court summed up the earlier attitude toward entrapment:

> We are asked to protect the defendant, not because he is innocent, but because a zealous public officer exceeded his powers and held out a bait. The courts do not look to see who held out the bait, but to see who took it.[19]

The earlier attitude had its basis in an indifference to government inducements. After all, "once the crime is committed, why should it matter what particular incentives were involved and who offered them?" From the early twentieth century, attitudes have evolved from indifference to government inducement to commit crime to a "limited sympathy" toward entrapped defendants. Furthermore, the law of entrapment reflects a growing intolerance of government inducements to law-abiding citizens, that is, to those not "predisposed" to commit crimes.[20]

The present law of entrapment attempts to balance criminal predisposition and law enforcement practices—to catch the habitual criminal but not at the expense of the innocent law-abiding citizen. The entrapment defense arises because the police find it particularly difficult to detect consensual crimes or crimes without complaining victims, such as those related to illicit drugs, gambling, pornography, prostitution, and official wrongdoing. John DeLorean's prosecution for cocaine trafficking, the Chicago Greylord investigation of judicial corruption, and "Abscam," the exchange of money and other valuables for favorable legislation from members of the United States Congress, all required government inducements to secure convictions. On the other hand, *agents provocateurs* (government agents who induce innocent people to commit crimes) have traditionally represented government oppression of political opponents. From the days of Henry VIII, to the era of Hitler and Stalin, most of the world's police states have utilized government informers to encourage dissidents to admit their disloyalty.Furthermore, the tactic of inducement creates the risk that otherwise law-abiding citizens will commit crimes. Finally, government enticement flouts the admonition of English Prime Minister Sir William Gladstone that government should make it easy to do right and *difficult* to do wrong, as well as the entreaty of the Lord's Prayer to "*lead* us not into temptation, but *deliver* us from evil."[21]

Law enforcement agencies use a variety of techniques to enforce the laws against unsuspecting participants. In addition to the traditional searches and seizures, police utilize electronic surveillance, informants, and "encouragement." Encouragement means a law enforcement officer who

(a) acts as a victim; (b) who intends, by his actions, to encourage the suspect to commit a crime; (c) who actually communicates this encouragement to the suspect; and (d) who thereby has some influence upon the commission of a crime.[22]

Encouragement reflects the need to simulate reality. Officers present an opportunity to commit a crime at a time when agents are available to gather evidence to prove guilt. The tactics vary, but because individuals about to commit crimes suspect strangers, officers need to do more than simply offer or request the targets to commit a crime. The encouragement tactics include making repeated requests to commit a crime, forming personal relationships with suspects, appealing to personal considerations, promising benefits from committing the crime, supplying contraband, and helping to obtain contraband.[23]

Entrapment deals with cases where law enforcement officers cross the line between acceptable and unacceptable "encouragement." **Entrapment** constitutes a defense to crime; it is *not* constitutionally mandated. The Supreme Court has applied entrapment to federal cases by interpreting congressional intent in enacting criminal statutes. The Court has held that Congress did not intend to permit government agents to lure innocent citizens into committing crimes so that government can punish them. Entrapment is an **affirmative defense** in most jurisdictions: defendants bear the burden of bringing forward some evidence of entrapment. Thereafter, the burden may shift, as it does in federal courts, to the prosecution to prove beyond a reasonable doubt that the defendant was not entrapped. The jury—or judge in trials without juries—decides whether officers in fact entrapped defendants. Until recently in federal scourts, and in some states, defendants who deny committing crimes usually cannot use the entrapment defense. In other words, defendants cannot deny they committed the crime and then inconsistently plead that the government entrapped them into committing it. The United States Supreme Court addressed entrapment in *United States v. Russell.*

CASE

Did the government "manufacture" crime?

United States v. Russell

411 U.S. 423, 93 S. Ct. 1637, 36 L. Ed. 2d 366 (1973)

[Mr. Justice Rehnquist delivered the opinion of the Court.]

FACTS

. . . On December 7, 1969, Joe Shapiro, an undercover agent for the Federal Bureau of Narcotics and Dangerous Drugs, went to respondent's home on Whidbey Island in the State of Washington where he met with respondent and his two codefendants, John and Patrick Connolly. Shapiro's assignment was to locate a laboratory where it was believed that methamphetamine was being manufactured illicitly. He told the respondent and the Connollys that he represented an organization in the Pacific Northwest that was interested in controlling the manufacture and distribution of methamphetamine. He than made an offer to supply the defendants with the chemical phenyl-2-propanone, an essential ingredient in the manufacture of methamphentamine, in return for one-half of the drug produced. This offer was made on the condition that Agent Shapiro be shown a sample of the drug which they were making and the laboratory where it was being produced.

During the conversation Patrick Connolly revealed that he had been making the drug since May 1969 and since then had produced three pounds of it. John Connolly gave the agent a bag containing a quantity of methamphetamine that he represented as being from ''the last batch that we made.'' Shortly thereafter, Shapiro and Patrick Connolly left respondent's house to view the laboratory which was located in the Connolly house on Whidbey Island. At the house Shapiro observed an empty bottle bearing the chemical label phenyl-2-propanone.

By prearrangement Shapiro returned to the Connolly house on December 9, 1969, to supply 100 grams of propanone and observe the chemical reaction. When he arrived he observed Patrick Connolly and the respondent cutting up pieces of aluminum foil and placing them in a large flask. There was testimony that some kind of foil pieces accidentally fell on the floor and were picked up by the respondent and Shapiro and put into the flask.[a] Thereafter

---

[a]Agent Shapiro did not otherwise participate in the manufacture of the drug or direct any of the work.

Patrick Connolly added all of the necessary chemicals, including the pro panone brought by Shapiro, to make two batches of methamphetamine. The manufacturing process having been completed the following morning, Shapiro was given one-half of the drug and respondent kept the remainder. Shapiro offered to buy, and respondent agreed to sell, part of the remainder for $60.

About a month later Shapiro returned to the Connolly house and met with Patrick Connolly to ask if he was still interested in their "business arrangement." Connolly replied that he was interested but that he had recently obtained two additional bottles of phenyl-2-propanone and would not be finished with them for a couple of days. He provided some additional methamphetamine to Shapiro at that time. Three days later Shapiro returned to the Connolly house with a search warrant and, among other items, seized an empty 500-gram bottle of propanone and a 100-gram bottle, not the one he had provided, that was partially filled with the chemical.

There was testimony at the trial of the respondent that phenyl-2-propanone was generally difficult to obtain. At the request of the Bureau of Narcotics and Dangerous Drugs, some chemical supply firms had voluntarily ceased selling the chemical.

At the close of the evidence, and after receiving the District Judge's standard entrapment instruction,[a] the jury found the respondent guilty on all counts charged. On appeal, respondent conceded that the jury could have found him predisposed to commit the offenses, but argued that on the facts presented there was entrapment as a matter of law. The Court of Appeals agreed, although it did not find the District Court had misconstrued or misapplied the traditional standards governing the entrapment defense. Rather, the court in effect expanded the traditional notion of entrapment, which focuses on the predisposition of the defendant, to mandate dismissal of a criminal prosecution whenever the court determines that there has been "an intolerable degree of governmental participation in the criminal enterprise." In this case the court decided that the conduct of the agent in supplying a scarce ingredient essential for the manufacture of a controlled substance established that defense.

This new defense was held to rest on . . . theories [which] "are premised on fundamental concepts of due process and evince the reluctance of the judiciary to countenance 'overzealous law enforcement.'"

OPINION

. . . [T]he respondent asks us to reconsider the theory of the entrapment defense. . . . His principal contention is that the defense should rest on constitutional grounds. He argues that the level of Shapiro's involvement in the manufacture of methamphetamine was so high that a criminal peosecution for the drug's manufacture violates the fundamental principles of due process. The respondent argues that the same factors that led this Court to apply the

---

[a]"Where a person has the willingness and the readiness to break the law, the mere fact that the government agent provides what appears to be a favorable opportunity is not entrapment." He then instructed the jury to acquit respondent if it had a "reasonable doubt whether the defendant had the previous intent or purpose to commit the offense . . . and did so only because he was induced or persuaded by some officer or agent of the government." No exception was taken by respondent to this instruction.

exclusionary rule to illegal searches and seizures and confessions should be considered here. But he would have the Court go further in deterring undesirable official conduct by requiring that any prosecution be absolutely barred because of the police involvement in criminal activity. The analogy is imperfect in any event, for the principal reason behind the exclusionary rule was the government's "failure to observe its own laws." . . . [T]he government's conduct here violated no independent constitutional right of the respondent. Nor did Shapiro violate any federal statute or rule or commit any crime in infiltrating the respondent's drug enterprise. . . .

While we may some day be presented with a situation in which the conduct of law enforcement agents is so outrageous that due process principles would absolutely bar the government from invoking juducial processes to obtain a conviction, the instant case is distinctly not of that breed. Shapiro's contribution of propanone to the criminal enterprise already in process was scarcely objectionable. The chemical is by itself a harmless substance and its possession is legal. While the government may have been seeking to make it more difficult for drug rings, such as that of which respondent was a member, to obtain the chemical, the evidence described above shows that it nonetheless was obtainable. The law enforcement conduct here stops far short of violating that "fundamental fairness, shocking to the universal sense of justice," mandated by the Dur Process Clause of the Fifth Amendment.

The illicit manufacture of drugs is not a sporadic, isolated criminal incident, but a continuing, though illegal, business enterprise. In order to obtain convictions for illegally manufacturing drugs, the gathering of evidence of past unlawful conduct frequently proves to be an all but impossible task. Thus in drug-related offenses law enforcement personnel have turned to one of the only practicable means of detection: then infiltration of drug rings and a limited participation in their unlawfull present practices. Such infiltration is a recognized and permissible means of apprehension; if that be so, then the supply of some item of value that the drug ring requires must, as a general rule, also be permissible.. For an agent will not be taken into the confidence of illegal entrepreneurs unless he has something of value to offer them. Law enforcement tactics such as this can hardly be said to violate "fundamental fairness" or "shocking to the universal sense of justice." . . .

Respondent's concession in the Court of Appeals that the jury finding as to predisposition was supported by the evidence is, therefore, fatal to his claim of entrapment. He was an active participant in an illegal drug manufacturing enterprise which began before the government agent appeared on the scene, and continued after the government agent had left the scene. He was . . . not an "unwary innocent" but an "unwary criminal." The Court of Appeals was wrong, we believe, when it sought to broaden the [predisposition test]. Its judgement is therefore Reversed.

DISSENT

Mr. Justice Douglas, with whom Mr. Justice Brennan concurs, dissenting. [Omitted]
Mr. Justice Stewart, with whom Mr. Justice Brennan and Mr. Justice Marshall join, dissenting.

In *Sorrels v. United States* and *Sherman v. United States*, the Court took what might be called a "subjective" approach to the defense of entrapment. In that view, the defense is predicated on an unexpressed intent of Congress to exclude from its criminal statutes the prosecution and conviction of persons, "otherwise innocent," who have been lured to the commission of the prohibited act through the Government's instigation. The key phrase in this formulation is "otherwise innocent," for the entrapment defense is available under this approach only to those who would not have committed the crime but for the Government's inducements. Thus, the subjective approach focuses on the conduct and propensities of the particular defendant in each individual case: if he is "otherwise innocent," he may avail himself of the defense; but if he had the "predisposition" to commit the crime, or if the "criminal design" originated with him, then—regardless of the nature and extent of the Government's participation—there has been no entrapment. And, in the absence of a conclusive showing one way or the other, the question of the defendant's "predisposition" to the crime is a question of fact for the jury.

The concurring opinion of Mr. Justice Roberts, joined by Justices Brandeis and Stone, in the *Sorells* case, and that of Mr. Justice Frankfurter, joined by Mr. Justice Douglas, Harlan, and Brennan, in the *Sherman* case took a different view of the entrapment defense. In their concept, the defense is not grounded on some unexpressed intent of Congress to exclude from punishment under its statutes those otherwise innocent persons tempted into crime by the Government, but rather on the belief that the "methods employed on behalf of the Government to bring about conviction cannot be countenanced." Thus, the focus of this approach is not on the propensities and predisposition of a specific defendant, but on "whether the police conduct revealed in the particular case falls below standards, to which common feelings respond, for the proper use of governmental power." Phrased another way, the question is whether—regardless of the predisposition to crime of the particular defendant involved—the governmental agents have acted in such a way as is likely to instigate or create a criminal offense. Under this approach, the determination of the lawfulness of the Government must be made—as it is on all questions involving the legality of law enforcement methods—by the trial judge, not the jury.

In my view, this objective approach to entrapment . . . is the only one truly consistent with the underlying rationale of the defense. Indeed, the very basis of the entrapment defense itself demands adherence to an approach that focuses on the conduct of the governmental agents, rather than on whether the defendant was "predisposed" or "otherwise innocent." . . .

The purpose of entrapment defense . . . must be to prohibit unlawful governmental activity in instigating crime. . . . "The prosecution should be stopped, not because some right of [the defendant] has been denied, but in order to protect the government. To protect it from illegal conduct of its officers. To preserve the purity of its courts." If that is so, then whether the particular defendant was "predisposed" or "otherwise innocent" is irrelevant; and the important question becomes whether the Government's conduct in inducing crime was beyond judicial toleration. . . .

This does not mean, of course, that the Government's use of undercover activity, strategy, or deception is necessarily unlawful. Indeed, many crimes, especially so-called victimless crimes, could not otherwise be detected. Thus, government agents may engage in conduct that is likely, when objectively considered, to afford a person ready and willing to commit the crime an opportunity to do so.

But when the agent's involvement in criminal activities goes beyond the mere offering of such an opportunity and when their conduct is of a kind that could induce or instigate the commission of a crime by one not ready and willing to commit it, then—regardless of the character or propensities of the particular person induced—I think entrapment has occurred. For in that situation, the Government has engaged in the impermissible manufacturing of crime, and the federal courts should bar the prosecution in order to preserve the institutional integrity of the system of federal criminal justice. . . .

In this case, the chemical ingredient was available only to licensed persons, and the Government itself had requested suppliers not to sell that ingredient even to people with a license. Yet the Government agent readily offered, and supplied, that ingredient to an unlicensed person and asked him to make a certain illegal drug with it. The Government then prosecuted that person for making the drug produced *with the very ingredient* which its agent had so helpfully supplied. This strikes me as the very pattern of conduct that should be held to constitute entrapment as a matter of law.

It is the Government's duty to prevent crime, not to promote it. Here, the Government's agent asked that the illegal drug be produced for him, solved his quarry's practical problems with the assurance that he could provide the one essential ingredient that was difficult to obtain, furnished that element as he had promised, and bought the finished product from the respondent--all so that the respondent could be prosecuted for producing and selling the very drug for which the agent had asked and for which he had provided the necessary component. Under the objective approach that I would follow, this respondent was entrapped, regardless of his predisposition or "innocence."

CASE DISCUSSION

Russell and his codefendants were convicted of illegally manufacturing a controlled substance. He interposed the defense of entrapment, which the trial court rejected. The jury found him guilty. He appealed to the court of appeals, which reversed the district court's judgement, expanding the entrapment defense to include what the government agent's did. The Supreme Court reversed, holding that Russell was not entrapped

What is the difference between the subjective approach to entrapment adopted by the majority, and the objective approach adopted by the dissent? Why was Shapiro's supplying propanone so important? Does it matter whether it is a legal or illegal substance? Why? What reason does the majority give for adopting the subjective approach? Does the subjective approach focus more on crime control or control of government misconduct? What arguments for the objective approach does the dissent give? Does the dissent's test for entrapment promote control of government at the expense of controlling crime?

The majority and dissenting opinions in *United States v. Russell* and *Hampton v. U.S.* (excerpted next) demonstarate two approaches to the entrapment defense. The majority view focuses on subjective intent—the defendant's predisposition to commit the crime. According to this view, only defendants who had no desire to commit crimes but whom the government induced into criminality can claim entrapment. The crucial question in the subjective test is: Where did criminal intent originate? If it originated with the government, then the government could not have entrapped the defendant. For example, in *Sherman v. United States*, Kalchinian, a government informant and undercover agent, met Sherman in a drug treatment center. He struck up a friendship with Sherman and eventually asked Sherman to get him some heroin. Sherman, an addict, at first refused. Following persistent begging and pleading that extended over several weeks, Sherman finally relented and supplied Kalchinian with the requested heroin. The police promptly arrested Sherman. The Supreme Court ruled that the intent originated with the government: Sherman was in treatment for his addition, hence, hardly predisposed to commit a drug offense, according to the Court.[24]

Once defendants have shown some evidence that the government agent induced the crime, the government can prove disposition by showing (1) prior convictions for similar offenses, (2) defendant's willingness to commit similar offenses, (3) defendant's display of some criminal expertise in carrying out the offense, and ready ability to commit the crime. In short, proving predisposition depends on defendants' character as well as past and present conduct.

Decision Point

A man on trial in federal court for distributing cocaine claimed he was entrapped by an old high school friend—an informer. The informer repeatedly asked the man to get him some cocaine. The man finally agreed to supply the former friend cocaine. The government offered proof that the man, now twenty-five had been convicted of distributing a small amount of cocaine when he was nineteen, that he was able to obtain a quarter-ounce of cocaine quickly and with no difficulty, and that when he transferred the cocaine to the informer he was cool, smooth, relaxed, and confident. The jury rejected the entrapment defense and convicted the defendant.

The minority view rejects the subjective predisposition test and focuses insetead on government inducement. The inducement test is objective in that it measures what government conduct constitutes reasonable encouragement, as opposed to improper inducement. According to the objective inducement test, if the government engages in conduct that would induce an "ordinary law-abiding" citizen to commit the crime, the court should dismiss the case. The objective, or government inducement of an ordinarily law-abiding citizen, test is a prophylactic rule aimed to deter "unsavory police methods." Some jurisdictions have adopted a hybrid approach to entrapment. California, for example, "fus[es] elements of both subjective and objective theories of entrapment."[25]

. . . [A]ttempts to fix the origin of intent or determine the defendant's criminal predisposition divert the court's attention from the only proper subject of focus in the entrapment defense: the dubious police conduct which the court must deter. The success of an entrapment defense should not turn on differences among defendants; we are not concerned with who first conceived or who willingly, reluctantly, acquiesced in a criminal project. What we do care about is how much and what manner of persuasion, pressure, and cajoling are brought to bear by law enforcement officials to induce persons to commit crimes. . . .

. . . [T]he proper test of entrapment in California is the following: was the conduct of the law enforcement agent likely to induce a normally law-abiding person to commit the offense? For the purpose of this test, we presume that such a person would normally resist the temptation to commit a crime presented by the simple opportunity to act unlawfully. Official conduct that does no more than offer the opportunity to the suspect—for example, a decoy program—is therefore permissible; but it is impermissible for the police or their agents to pressure the suspect by overbearing conduct such as badgering, cajoling, importuning, or other affirmative acts likely to induce a normally law-abiding person to commit the crime.

Although the determination of what police conduct is impermissible must to some extent proceed on an ad hoc basis, guidance will generally be found in one of two principles. First, if the actions of the law enforcement agent would generate in a normally law-abiding person a motive for the crome other than ordinary criminal intent, entrapment will be established. An example of such conduct could be an appeal by the police that would induce such a person to commit the act because of friendship or sympathy, instead of a desire for personal gain or other typical criminal purpose. Second, affirmative police conduct that would make commission of the crime unusually attractive to a normally law-abiding person will likely constitute entrapment. Such conduct would include, for example, a guarantee that the act is not illegal, or the offense will go undetected, an offer of exorbitant consideration or any similar enticement.[26]

Government conduct may be so outrageous that it violates due process. In that case, according to Justice Rehnquist in *Hampton v. United States*, the remedy is not to release the defendant predisposed to commit a crime, but to sanction the law enforcement officer's misconduct. Other members of the Court did not accept this view. Justice Powell, in his concurring opinion, argues that defendants should have available the defense of entrapment in cases of severe police "overreaching," despite defendants' predisposition to commit the crime.

CASE

Did the government "overreach"?

Hampton v. United States

425 U.S. 484, 96 S. Ct. 1646, 48 L.Ed.2d 113 (1976)

[Justice Rehnquist announced the Court's judgment, which Chief Justice Burger and Justice White joined.]

FACTS

Hutton and Hampton were shooting pool at the pub when Hampton, after observing "track" (needle) marks on Hutton's arms told Hutton that he needed money and knew where he could get some heroin. Hutton responded that he could find a buyer and Hampton suggested that "he get in touch with these people." [Hampton's version of the events is that Hutton supplied the heroin, but the jury did not believe Hampton.] Hutton then called DEA agent Terry Sawyer and arranged a sale for 10 p.m. on February 25.

At the appointed time, Hutton and Hampton went to the pre-arranged meeting place and were met by Agent Sawyer and DEA agent McDowell posing as narcotics dealers. Hampton produced a tinfoil packet from his cap and turned it over to the agents who tested it, pronounced it "okay," and negotiated a price of $145 which was paid to Hampton. Before they parted, Hampton told Sawyer that he could obtain larger quantities of heroin and gave Sawyer a phone number where he could be reached.

The next day Sawyer called Hampton and arranged for another "buy" that afternoon. Hampton got Hutton to go along and they met the agents again near where they had been the previous night.

They all entered the agents' car, and Hampton again produced a tinfoil packet from his cap. The agents again field-tested it and pronounced it satisfactory. Hampton asked for $500 which Agent Sawyer said he would get from the trunk. Sawyer got out and opened the trunk which was a signal to other agents to move in and arrest Hampton, which they did. . . .

[Hampton requested the judge to give the following instruction to the jury:]

> "If you find that the defendant's sales of narcotics were sales of narcotics supplied to him by an informer in the employ of or acting on behalf of the government, then you must acquit the defendant because the law as a matter of policy forbids his convicton in such a case.
>
> Furthermore, under this particular defense, you need not consider the predisposition of the defendant to commit the offense charged, because if the governmental involvement through its informer reached the point that I have just defined in your own minds, then the predisposition of the defendant would not matter."

The trial court refused the instruction and Hampton was found guilty. He appealed to the United States Court of Appeals for the Eighth Circuit, claiming that if the jury had believed that the drug was supplied by Hutton he should have been acquitted.

OPINION

In *Russell* [an earlier entrapment case] we held that the statutory defense of entrapment was not available where it was conceded that a government agent supplied a necessary ingredient in the manufacture of an illicit drug, [phenyl-2-propoanone, a legal subatance in the manufacture of the illicit drug, methamphetamine]. We ruled out the possibility that the defense of entrapment could ever be based on governmental misconduct in a case, such as this one, where the predisposition of the defendant to commit the crime was established. . . .

In view of this holding, Hampton correctly recognizes that his case does not qualify as one involving "entrapment" at all. He instead relies on the language in *Russell* that "we may someday be presented with a situation in which the conduct of law enforcement agents is so outrageous that due process principles would absolutely bar the government from invoking judicial processes to obtain a conviction. . . . "

In urging that this case involves a violation of his due process rights, petitioner misapprehends the meaning of the quoted language in *Russell* . . . Admittedly petitioner's case is different from Russell's but the difference is one of degree, not of kind. In *Russell* the ingredient supplied by the government informant was a legal drug which the defendants demonstrably could have obtained from other sources besides the Government. Here the drug which the government informant allegedly supplied to petitioner was both illegal and constituted the *corpus delicti* for the sale of which the petitioner was convicted. The Government obviously played a more significant role in enabling petitioner to sell contraband in this case than it did in *Russell*.

But in each case the Government agents were acting in concert with the defendant, and in each case either the jury found or the defendant conceded that he was predisposed to commit the crime for which he was convicted. The remedy of the criminal defendant with respect to Government agents, which, far from being resisted, are encouraged by him, lies solely in the defense of entrapment. But, as noted, the petitioner's conceded predisposition rendered this defense unavailable to him.

The limitations of the Due Process Clause of the Fifth Amendment come into play only when the Government activity in question violates some protected right of the *defendant*. Here, as we have noted, the police, the Government informant, and the defendant acted in concert with one another. If the result of the governmental activity is to "implant in the mind of an innocent person the disposition to commit the alleged offense and induce its commission . . . the defendant is protected by the defense of entrapment. If the police engage in illegal activity in concert with a defendant beyond the scope of their duties the remedy lies, not in freeing the equally culpable defendant, but in prosecuting the police under the applicable provisions of state or federal law. . . . But the police conduct here no more deprived defendant of any right secured to him by the United States Constitution than did the police conduct in *Russell* deprived Russell of any rights.

Affirmed.

CONCURRING OPINION

Justice Powell, with whom Justice Blackmun joins, concurring in the judgment.

> In discussing Hampton's due process contention, [the Court] enunciates a *per se* rule:[In Russell, w]e ruled out the possibility that the defense of entrapment could *ever* be based upon govermental misconduct in a case, such as this one, where the predisposition of the defendant to commit the crime was established. The remedy of the criminal defendant with respect to Government agents, which. . . are encouraged by him, lies *solely* in the defense of entrapment.

The plurality thus says that the concept of fundamental fairness inherent in the guarantee of due process would never prevent the conviction of a predisposed defendant, regardless of the outrageousness of police behavior in light of the surrounding circumstances.

I do not understand *Russell* or earlier cases delineating the predisposition-focused defense of entrapment to have gone so far . . . .

DISSENT

Justice Brennan, with whom Justice Stewart and Justice Marshall concur, dissenting.

. . . "Courts refuse to convict an entrapped defendant, not because his condust falls outside the proscription of the statute, but because, even if his guilt be admitted, the methods employed on behalf of the Government to bring about conviction cannot be countenanced."

In any event, I think that reversal of petitioner's conviction is also compelled for those who follow the "subjective" approach to the defense of entrapment. As Mr. Justice Rehnquist notes, the Government's role in the criminal activity involved in this case was more pervasive than the Government involvement in *Russell*. In addition, I agree with Mr. Justice Powell that *Russell* does not foreclose imposition of a bar to conviction—based on our supervisory power or due process principles—where the conduct of law enforcement authorities is sufficiently offensive, even though the individuals entitled to invoke such a defense might be "predisposed." . . .In my view, the police activity was beyond permissible limits.

CASE DISCUSSION

The trial court convicted Hampton of selling heroin. He was not successful in claiming he was entrapped. He appealed, and the court of appeals affirmed the conviction. On writ of *certiorari*, the United States Supreme Court affirmed, holding that Hampton was not entrapped.

Clearly, the plurality on the one hand, and the concurring and dissenting justices on the other, do not agree in what interests to promote in the entrapment defense. Do you agree with the plurality? the concurring justices, or the dissenters? What facts constituted the "encouragement"? Do you think they constituted "entrapment"? Assume, if you do not agree, that the government acted improperly in this case. Should Hampton go free? Why? Should some action be taken against the agents? What? (See below on civil actions.)

Decision Point

1. An undercover agent for the FBI, with the knowledge of other federal agents, developed a sexual relationship with a target. After developing the relation-

ship, she asked the target to sell drugs to some "friends" who, unknown to the target, were FBI agents. The Ninth Circuit Court of Appeals said that it saw "no principled way to identify a fixed point along the continuum from casual physical contact to intense physical bonding beyond which the relationship becomes 'shocking' when entertained by an informant." The court rejected the due process claim.[27]

2. Narcotics agents offered a five-year-old child $5 to tell where her mommy hid her heroin. The court rejected the due process claim.[28]

3. Defendant's friend and former brother-in-law, an informer, presuaded defendant over a period of time to go in on a drug deal. The informer claimed that he desperately needed money to care for himself and his family. The court denied the defense of entrapment.[29]

4. An undercover agent told defendant that he worked for a dentist whose son was an addict. Due to a change in the law, the dentist could no longer write prescriptions for narcotics to supply his son. The officer said his boss needed to get good heroin off the street because the son "was in pretty bad shape, we didn't think he would live very long." After twenty requests, defendant purchased narcotics and resold them to the undercover agent without a profit. A majority of the court upheld the conviction.[30]

Federal law enforcement agencies usually limit encouragement tactics to consensual crimes. Recently, local law enforcement agencies have begun to rely on encouragement to combat street mugging. For example, a common ploy uses decoys who pretend to be drunk. They lie down with money visibly protruding from their pockets, hence inviting would-be muggers to take the money. The Nevada Supreme Court addressed entrapment in a street mugging case in *Oliver v. State*.[31]

CASE

Was he entrapped?

Oliver v. State
101 Nev. 308, 703 P.2d 869 (1985)

FACTS

On the night of Oliver's arrest, three policemen undertook to conduct a "decoy operation" near the intersection of Main and Ogden in Las Vegas. That corner is in a downtown area frequented by substantial numbers of persons commonly characterized as "street people," "vagrants," and "derelicts." It appears Oliver, a black man, is one of these.

Disguised as a vagrant in an old Marine Corps jacket, the decoy officer slumped against a palm tree, pretending to be intoxicated and asleep. His associates concealed themselves nearby. The decoy prominently displayed a ten-dollar bill, positioning it to protrude from the left breast pocket of his jacket. This was done, the decoy later testified, "to provide an opportunity for a dishonest person to prove himself."

Oliver, who had the misfortune to come walking down the street, saw the decoy and evidently felt moved to assist him. Shaking and nudging the decoy with his foot, Oliver attempted to warn the decoy that the police would arrest him if he did not move on. The decoy did not respond, and Oliver stepped away. Up to this point, Oliver had shown no disposition whatever to commit any criminal act.

Then, Oliver saw the ten-dollar bill protruding from the decoy's pocket. He reached down and took it. "Thanks, home boy," he said. Thereupon, he was arrested by the decoy and the two other officers. Following the trial, a jury convicted Oliver of larceny from the person, and he has been sentenced to ten years imprisonment. This appeal followed.

OPINION

Oliver's counsel contends he was entrapped into committing the offense in question. We agree. . . . [G]overnment agents or officers may not employ extraordinary temptations or inducements. They may not manufacture crime. . . .

> Entrapment is the seduction or improper inducement to commit a crime for the purpose of instituting a criminal prosecution, but if a person in good faith and for the purpose of detecting or discovering a crime or offense, furnishes the opportunity for the commission thereof by one who has the requisite criminal intent, it is not entrapment.

Thus, because we discern several facts which we believe combined create an extraordinary temptation, which was inappropriate to apprehending merely those bent on criminal activity, we feel constrained to reverse Oliver's conviction.

We note, first of all, that the decoy portrayed himself as completely susceptible and vulnerable. He did not respond when Oliver attempted to wake him, urging him to avoid arrest by moving to another location. Moreover, the decoy displayed his ten dollar-bill in a manner calculated to tempt any needy person in the area, whether immediatly disposed to crime or not. In the case of Oliver, the police succeeded in tempting a man who apparently did not approach the decoy with larceny in mind, but rather to help him. Even after being lured into petty theft by the decoy's open display of currency, Oliver did not go on to search the decoy's pockets or to remove his wallet.

On the record, then, we think the activities of the officers, however well intentioned, accomplished an impermissible entrapment. . . .

> There is no evidence of any prior conduct of the defendant that would have shown predisposition. There is no evidence that he was engaging in criminal activity before he took the money from the decoy. No ready acquiescence is

shown; on the contrary, the defendant's acts . . . demonstrate only that he succumbed to temptation. The record, as such, reveals that the decoy did not detect or discover, the type of crime the police were attempting to prevent by the use of the decoy, i.e., robberies or snatchings. Indeed, lifting some money protruding from the pocket of a seemingly unconscious, drunken bum is just not sufficiently similar to either robbery or purse snatchings. Upon these facts, the decoy simply provided the opportunity to commit a crime to anyone who succumbed to the lure of the bait.

CASE DISCUSSION

Oliver was convicted of larceny from the person and sentenced to twenty years in prison. He appealed on the ground that the trial court rejected his defense of entrapment. The Nevada Supreme Court reversed on the grounds that Oliver was entrapped.

What facts indicate entrapment in the case? Did the court focus on the Oliver's disposition or on the conduct of the police? Which is more appropriate? Why? What interests does the defense of entrapment promote? Does focusing on the defendant shift the balance of these interests? Explain. If Oliver took the money, why should he not suffer conviction and punishment? Does entrapment sacrifice result to process? How?

Reversible Error

The process remedies discussed above—the exclusionary rule, dismissal, and entrapment—are all directed, and are available almost exclusively, against police misconduct. But what about prosecutors', judges', and defense attorneys' misconduct? The remedy against them, apart from removal by impeachment or denying them reelection, is generally restricted to reversing convictions based on their errors. Many appeals not based on the exclusionary rule charge errors by judges, prosecutors, and defense counsel. Sometimes, appellate courts reverse or overturn lower courts' decisions. Errors in proceedings that result in reversals are called **reversible errors**.

Reversible errors are those that would have made a difference to the outcome of the case if they had not been made. If, for example, a judge makes a mistake and instructs the jury that murder does not require an intention to kill and the jury convicts a defendant of murder when the defendant was only negligent, the error is reversible because negligently killing another person does not constitute murder. Errors that do not affect the outcome of a case are called **harmless errors** and do not lead to reversal. For example, if the court admitted illegally seized evidence but sufficient additional evidence existed to convict the defendant, admitting the illegal evidence would not affect the outcome of the case; hence, the resulting harmless error does not require reversal. The Supreme Court does not review many cases involving reversible error. The intermediate appellate courts review most of these cases. In *United States v. Wolf* an appellate court reviewed a case involving prejudicial remarks by a prosecutor.

CASE

Were the prosecutor's remarks reversible error?

United States v. Wolf

787 F .2d 1094 (7th Cir. 1986)

FACTS

. . . In 1980 the church in New Albany, Indiana to which Wolf's wife and daughter belonged decided to sponsor a refugee family from Southeast Asia. Wolf, who was 67 years old at the time, installed the family in an apartment above his auto-parts business, but in 1981 the family moved out. Between then and 1984 Wolf made a dozen trips to Bangkok, on one of which his translator was a young woman named Wongsaprome with whom Wolf became smitten. Wolf persuaded her to move from Texas to New Albany and live in the apartment above his business. Once she was there he fondled her in a lecherous manner on one occasion and badgered her incessantly to have sexual intercourse with him, but she refused and eventually moved out of the apartment. Wolf's relationship with Miss Wongsaprome was the basis of Count I of the indictment but the jury hung on this count.

Shortly after she left, Wolf induced a young Cambodian refugee, Chenda Or, to come live in the apartment, by promising to help get her sister (who was languishing in a refugee camp in Thailand) admitted to the United States. Before inviting her to come to New Albany he asked her about her attitude toward sex and whether she had any boyfriends, and tried to embrace her, but his attempt was rebuffed. Miss Or was living in Oklahoma City at the time. She flew to Louisville, Kentucky on a ticket Wolf had given her, and when she arrived he drove her from the airport across the Ohio River to New Albany. He assured her that he would support her. One night she woke up and there was Wolf beside her in the bed, nude, with a leg and arm over her body. Wolf had given her pills which he said were for her tuberculosis but which made her fall asleep, and while she was asleep he entered her locked apartment with his key and took off her clothes as well as his own. She persuaded him to leave, however, and then tried to kill herself by drinking a bottle of alcohol. A few days later Wolf took her to a mental health center where she was seen rubbing her body until a social worker told her to stop. When Miss Or was discharged from the center he had sexual intercourse with her after brandishing a gun and telling her to take off her clothes. For two weeks they had intercouse every night. Wolf then went off on one of his trips to Thailand and Miss Or left the apartment and eventually went back to Oklahoma. Wolf's relationship with Miss Or was the subject of Count II, on which he was convicted.

Within two months of her departure Wolf had installed in the apartment a Laotian refugee family of five, the Viravongs, whom he had brought from

Louisville. Several months after they had arrived Wolf began hugging and kissing Mrs. Viravong and asking her to make love to him. Although she refused, he was able to fondle her breasts and put his fingers into her vagina, and he also made her fondle his genitals. Eventually the Viravongs moved out of the apartment. Wolf's relationship with Mrs. Viravong was the subject of Count III, on which he was also convicted.

OPINION

There is no doubt that Wolf made repeated and improper sexual advances to young oriental women whom he had brought to New Albany. Even if there were some exaggerations in Miss Or's testimony, it is plain that Wolf exploited the vulnerable status of these refugees for immoral ends and that—not to put too fine a point on it—he is a disgusting person. But even disgusting people are entitled to appellate review of their convictions. . . . We must therefore go on and discuss the other alleged errors, beginning with Wolf's cross-examination, to see if there is also reversible error as to Count II. The issue again is plain error because defense counsel failed to object.

After the prosecutor asked Wolf whether he had ever had sex in Thailand, and he said no, she asked him, "When you returned [to Thailand] in October, 1983, did you not get gonorrhea?" He said no, and the matter was not pursued. The government had evidence, consisting of Wolf's medical records, that he had contracted gonorrhea in 1983. The judge excluded that evidence, even though Wolf's counsel did not object to its introduction (more later in this opinion on the passivity of defense counsel). But no one knows where or from whom Wolf contracted gonorrhea.

The question was improper. Although Wolf's sexual activities with oriental women were relevant, no one knows the circumstances in which he contracted gonorrhea, and he contracted it a year after his alleged violations of the Mann Act. The innuendo that Wolf had a venereal disease was calculated to demean him in the eyes of the jury—and there is little doubt that was the purpose for which it was planted.

In cross-examining Wolf about his efforts to bring another refuge family to the United States, which ended with the family's going to Canada instead, the prosecutor asked Wolf whether the reason why the family had not been allowed to come to the United States was that "the American Embassy did not consider you to be an appropriate sponsor?" There was no basis in the record for this question (which Wolf answered no). Again the purpose was to diminish Wolf in the eyes of the jury.

Protracted cross-examination followed about Wolf's relationship with a 14-year-old Thai girl whom Wolf had brought into his home, where she had slept in the same bed with Wolf and his wife (according to Thai custom, Wolf testified). The cross-examination was intended to suggest indecent behavior toward the girl. In the course of this examination the prosecutor asked Wolf, "Did you pay her parents for her?" Wolf answered no and there is no evidence that he bought her, as the question suggested. He had given money to the girl's mother for medical treatment but there is no evidence that the girl was taken in exchange. The entire line of cross-examination was improper; the prosecutor was insinuating Wolf's guilt of another crime, which the government should have been but was not prepared to prove by clear and convincing evidence if it wanted to inject it into the case.

Then the prosecutor tried to get Wolf to admit that he had recommended that Mrs. Viravong have an abortion. Since both Mrs. Viravong and Wolf denied that she had had intercourse with Wolf and there was no probative evidence that she had, this line of questions had no business in the case, as well as being inflammatory. The government's brief discretly omits mention of this part of the cross-examination. But at argument the government's counsel (who had been the prosecutor in the district court) told us that ''courts must have faith in prosecutors.''

Although the improprieties of the cross-examination are clear, it is a separate question whether they were prejudicial with respect to Count II. But we think they were. It is true that if Miss Or was believed, the evidence against Wolf was overwhelming. But she had a history of serious physical and mental illness, and some of her testimony, in particular that Wolf had had sexual intercourse with her every night for two consecutive weeks, was sufficiently improbable to raise doubts about her credibility. This in turn made Wolf's own credibility critical. If the jury had believed his testimony it would have had to acquit him. It might have done so but for the improper destruction of his credibility by the prosecutor.

Any doubt about the prejudicial effect of the improper cross-examination is erased when we consider Wolf's last challenge to his conviction, which is that his trial counsel was totally incompetent. Counsel made no objection to any of the improper cross-examination. The government argues that this was a tactical decision: a tactic of no objections. It is true that lawyers will frequently not object to objectionable questions, believing either that the witness will give an answer helpful to the defnese (or at least not harmful to it) or that too-frequent objecting will irritate the jury or make it think the defendant is trying to hide the truth. But to have a *policy* of never objecting to improper questions is forensic suicide. It shifts the main responsibility for the defense from defense counsel to the judge. It would make no sense in a case like this where the prosecutor was intent on bringing in extraneous and at times unfounded charges in order to blacken the defendant's character. The failure to object to any of the improper cross-examination discussed above is incomprehensible, as is the failure to object to the instruction on intent or to offer a ''dominant purpose'' instruction.

But there is more. On direct examination of Mr. Viravong, this colloquy occurred without objection from defense counsel:

Q. Do you think Mr. Wolf did more to your wife than kissing her?
A. Yes, I think because my wife told me that he asked her to.
THE COURT. Just a minute. Are we going to let this hearsay go in? Just cut it off right there.
Q. Besides what your wife said, what makes you think Mr. Wolf did more than kiss your wife?
A. Yes. As I think, but my wife never admit to him [me?] that she never made love to John Wolf, but I think that would be possible.

This was, so far as appears, pure speculation and defense counsel should have objected. It is true that lawyers rightly mistrust instructions that tell juries to disregard what they have just heard; our memories are independent of our wills. But counsel could and should have objected to the question ("what makes you think Mr. Wolf did more than kiss your wife?") before it was answered; this would have forced the government to explain why it thought Mr. Viravong could give admissible testimony on the point. As the government had no basis for thinking he could, the objection would have been sustained and the question never answered. Defense counsel seems to have been paying no attention to the trial. The answer that Mr. Viravong was allowed to give took on added significance because in her opening statement the prosecutor had said that the evidence would show that "on one occasion, he [Wolf] put his penis in her [Mrs. Viravong's] vagina." No such evidence was ever presented other than Mr. Viravong's reply to the prosecutor's improper question, though apparently Mrs. Viravong had told the government before trial that she would testify to having had intercourse with Wolf.

Other instances of ineffective representation include a remarkably inept attempt to impeach the testimony of Mrs. Viravong by calling as a witness the FBI agent who had taken a statement from her and asking him whether her testimony in court was consistent with the statement. The prosecutor objected before the agent could answer, pointing out that before defense counsel could impeach Mrs. Viravong's testimony with her out-of-court statement he must ask her whether she had made the statement. The judge sustained the objection, defense counsel said, "Pardon?" the judge repeated, "Sustain the objection," and the matter was dropped.

There were other instances of ineffective assistance of counsel, but why go on? It is apparent that the handling of Wolf's defense fell "outside the wide range of professionally competent assistance." Even so, Wolf's conviction cannot be set aside on this ground unless "there is a reasonable probability that, absent the errors, the factfinder would have had a reasonable doubt respecting guilt." But given the doubts the jury might have had concerning Miss Or's testimony (Count II), and the weakness of the evidence that Wolf brought the Viravongs to New Albany for the purpose of making sexual advances to Mrs. Viravong (Count III), this exacting standard is satisfied here. When the ineffectiveness of defense counsel is added to the errors in the cross-examination and in the instruction, it is apparent that Wolf was denied a fair trial and that his conviction on both counts must be reversed and the case remanded for a new trial.

DISSENT

. . . I do not believe the several inappropriate questions asked by the prosecution and seized upon by the majority had the cumulative effect of demeaning Wolf to such an extent they prejudiced the outcome of the trial. Again, I believe the abundant evidence, not these isolated questions, convicted Wolf.

I do not feel compelled to spend much time on the majority's assertion defendant's counsel lacked requisite minimal professional competence. In *Strickland v. Washington*, 466 U.S. 668 (1984), the Supreme Court stated:

> Conflict in interest claims aside, actual ineffectiveness claims alleging a deficiency in attorney performance are subject to a general requirement that the defendant affirmatively prove prejudice. . . . The defendant must show that

there is a reasonable probability that, but for counsel's unprofessional errors, the result of the proceeding would have been different. A reasonable probability is a probability sufficient to undermine confidence in the outcome.

I conclude by saying that after all the high-level hair-splitting analysis of the majority is sifted through, I get the gut feeling the jury heard much more than enough admissible evidence against against Mr. Wolf than needed to convict. More objections by defense counsel and a slightly, immaterially-altered instruction would not have made the difference. I have no problem concluding, as the jury did, that a dominant purpose behind defendant's actions was to have these women have sexual relations with him. I see little evidence defendant did anything positive on any consistent basis for these women. Many of defendant's actions are outright shocking and disgusting and are well-documented. This court has had little problem recently employing the harmless error doctrine to uphold reasonable jury verdicts. In recent years the court has become offended by what it sees as the success of highly technical defense counsel arguments which are used to excite the intellectual juices of the judiciary and secure reversals despite reasonable jury verdicts. This decision, unfortunately in my judgment, represents that problem.

CASE DISCUSSION

Wolf was convicted of criminal sexual conduct. Wolf appealed on the ground that the prosecutor made improper remarks during the trial, and that Wolf's lawyer was incompetent, both of which constituted reversible error. The court ruled that the ineffective defense denied Wolf a fair trial.(See chaps. 9 and 11.)

Should this defendant go free because the prosecutor's remarks were out of line? Do you agree with the dissent's "gut feeling" that the jury had enough evidence to convict? Why is this relevant? What do you think should happen in this case? Can you think of a way to punish the guilty—that is, obtain the correct result—and deal with the government's misconduct? How? Was the error harmless? Explain.

Expunging Arrest Records

A basic principle in American justice is that citizens are innocent until proven guilty. But how many people bother to sort out in their minds what guilty really means? Do they distinguish between conviction, indictment, arrest, or merely brought in for questioning? People often suffer intrusions and deprivations following an arrest, even if no further actions transpire. Employment applications frequently ask if applicants have ever been arrested; police keep arrest records for use in future investigations. These are only two examples of the deprivations and intrusions that can occur after an encounter with the law enforcement system.

These harms have led to the call for removing records from official files, or **expungement.** The Supreme Court has not ruled on expungement, although recently all nine justices joined in a decision that FBI "rap sheets" are never subject to disclosure under the Freedom of Information Act. Lower federal courts have addressed the expungement issue, as did the District of Columbia Circuit Court in *Menard v. Saxbe*.[32]

CASE

Should his arrest records be expunged?

Menard v. Saxbe

498 F.2d 1017 (D.C. Cir. 1974)

FACTS

At the time of his arrest, Dale Menard was a 19-year old college student spending the summer working in Los Angeles. On the evening of August 9, 1965, he visited with friends in the vicinity of Sunland Park, a recreational area in Los Angeles. At approximately 11:30 p.m., Menard walked to the park to wait for a friend who had arranged to pick Menard up and drive him to his room in a Los Angeles suburb. The friend failed to arrive at the agreed time, and in the early hours of August 10th, after dozing on a park bench and then walking across the street to look through the window of a rest home in search of a clock, Menard returned to the bench to wait once more.

At approximately 3:00 a.m., Menard was approached by two Los Angeles police officers who questioned him about a prowler report from the rest home. They also confronted him with a wallet they evidently had found on the ground near the park bench. The wallet contained $10 and bore the name and address of an individual who lived about three miles from Sunland Park. Despite Menard's insistence that he knew nothing of the wallet, and despite the subsequent arrival of Menard's friend, who corroborated his account, Menard was placed under arrest, booked and fingerprinted at the station-house, and held in police custody for over two days. No criminal complaint was ever filed; no evidence was found indicating that the wallet had been stolen; and no information was adduced that tied Menard to any crime. Nevertheless, the Los Angeles police routinely forwarded to the FBI a fingerprint card, containing Menard's fingerprints and the notation that he had been arrested for burglary and two days later "Released—Unable to connect with any felony or misdemeanor at this time." The FBI has retained a record of Menard's arrest.[a]

---

[a]Originally the record read as follows:
Date Arrested or Received—8-10-65
Charge or Offense—459 PC Burglary
Disposition or Sentence—8-12-65—Released-Unable to connect with any felony or misdemeanor at this time.

OPINION

Menard seeks the elimination of his arrest record from the FBI's files and rests his claim on a broad base of legal doctrine. It is claimed that retention of his record violates the Fourth and Fifth Amendments of the Constitution, subjects him to harsh penalties without being accorded due process of law, denies him the equal protection of the laws, and violates his rights to privacy.

Appellant is naturally concerned that the incident in which he was, by happenstance, subject to police detention has led to his becoming the subject of a criminal file. The first legal issue that arises is whether he had merely suffered personal distress, or whether there is legal injury.

Although Menard cannot point with mathematical certainty to the exact consequences of his criminal file, we think it is clear that he has alleged a "cognizable legal injury." . . .

The disabilities flowing from a record of arrest have been well documented: There is an undoubted "social stigma" involved in an arrest record. "[I]t is common knowledge that a man with an arrrest record is much more apt to be subject to police scrutiny—the first to be questioned and the last eliminated as a suspect to an investigation." Existence of a record may burden a decision whether to testify at trial. And records of arrest are used by judges in making decisions as to sentencing, whether to grant bail, or whether to release pending appeal.

The arrest record is used outside the field of criminal justice. Most significant is its use in connection with subsequent inquiries on applications for employment and licenses to engage in certain fields of work. An arrest record often proves to be a sustantial barrier to employment. It appears, *interalia*, that Menard's FBI record was supplied, subsequent to the filing of the complaint in this case, to the Marine Corps and the National Agency Check Center.

The jurisprudence on expungement of arrest records has developed, thus far at least, in actions brought against appropriate officials of the government whose officers had responsibility for making the arrest, initiating the arrest record, maintaining the arrest record, and determining the consequences, as in maintaining prosecutions. There arises for consideration the significance of the circumstances that in the action before us it is the Los Angeles police who made the arrest for a violation of state law, and who initiated the arrest record, while the defendants are officials of a federal agency whose involvement and responsibility turns on the receipt, maintenance and dissemination of the allegedly invalid arrest record.

Ultimate disposition of an action against a records agency based on maintenance and dissemination of unlawful arrest records would require decisions on a number of issues, and the interlacing of a number of stands of law. There would be issues such as whether the preservation of constitutional rights embraces, as a corollary, a strict liability like that which pervades the related field of responsibility of publication of libels, a responsibility based on the extent of knowledge in hand or imputable, or on a duty to make inquiry.

Occupation—Student

Residence of Person Fingerprinted—Saticoy & Canoga, Canoga Park

The record was amended so that the entry "Disposition or Sentence" now reads:

8-12-65—Released - Unable to connect with any felony or misdemeanor - in accordance with 849b(1) - not deemed an arrest but detention only.

We think sound principles of justice and judicial administration dictate that in general actions to vindicate constitutional rights, by expungement of arrest records maintained notwithstanding release of the person and absence of probable cause for arrest, be maintained against the local law enforcement agencies involved. The primary duty of executive inquiry into the facts of distant arrests is a burden assigned more appropriately to the local agency whose officials made the arrest than to the FBI. Further, an official finding that an arrest is tainted by illegality stigmatizes the local enforecemnt agency to some extent—apart from the possibility of damage actions—and should be avoided where an alternate course is available. If the local law enforcement agency is a party to the action, it will have opportunity, in instances where it considers the claim improper, to present effectively its version of events and support its denial of relief.

In general, the role played by the FBI's Identification Division is derivative, and relief granted solely against the FBI in this context may be incomplete. The offending ''arrest record'' remains in the files of the local law enforcement agency, and a question arises whether the person involved would be obligated to advise future employers and others that he had been arrested. With the local enforcement agency as defendant, complete relief can be granted, both to obtain such action on local records as may be needed, and to have local authorities request the return of records. Such requests are always honored by the FBI.

We are also reluctant, in the absence of a need greater than that established by this record, to concentrate in the Department of Justice the burden of overall litigation over maintenance of arrest records. Of the 19 million criminal prints on file with the Identification Division, it is impossible to predict how many would be the subject of dispute. We are concerned with the possible effects of a concentration of burden not only on the FBI and the Department of Justice, but also on this court and the District Court for the District of Columbia.

Our conclusion should not be taken to reflect a judgement of the insubstantiality of Menard's claims. On the contrary, the gravity of those claims underscores the need for their adjudication between the appropriate parties. Conventional doctrines of venue may operate to localize the forum, but will not interfere with a call on cognizant Federal courts in the venue when administrative remedy is unavailing.

CASE DISCUSSION

The police arrested, booked, fingerprinted, and held Menard in custsody for two days. The prosecutor did not file any criminal charges against him. Although the police released him, they forwarded fingerprint information to the FBI. Menard brought a civil act to expunge all records of his arrest. The court of appeals ruled that Menard has a claim but he should bring it against the Los Angeles Police Department, not the Department of Justice.

How would you answer these unanswered question that *Menard v. Saxbe* suggest? What if Menard was arrested on probable cause and the prosecutor decided not to prosecute? Or, what if the prosecutor charged Menard with an offense and then later dismissed the charge? Or, what if Menard was charged, tried, and acquitted? What would you do with all of these records? Should all records be automatically destroyed once a suspect or defendant is cleared? Why? Why not? What reasons can you give for your decisions? Does the recent Supreme Court decision regarding FBI "rap sheets" eliminate, or at least reduce, the need for expungement? Explain.

≡ CIVIL ACTIONS—SUING THE GOVERNMENT AND ITS AGENTS

Citizens--whether criminals or innocent victims--can sue government agents who violate their constitutional rights. Civil actions, or private law suits, involve an allegedly injured citizen who in an individual capacity sues either or both the government itself or named officers. Civil actions provide **plaintiffs**—citizens who bring the suits—with one or both of two private remedies. Most commonly plaintiffs ask for **damages,** or monetary satisfaction for wrongs committed by the government. They can also receive an **injunction,** or court order commanding a government unit to do, or refrain from doing, something. Private law suits against the government derive from several sources: (1) the United States Constitution; (2) state constitutions; (3) common law tort or civil actions; (4) federal statutes; and (5) state statutes. Most government unlawful actions constitute state **torts,** or wrongs. For example, illegal searches and seizures are also civil trespasses, damage to property, and assault. Citizens can sue the federal government and its agents for **constitutional torts.** According to the Supreme Court, violating a person's constitutional rights constitutes a federal tort, and plaintiffs can sue federal agents for the damages they suffer for these violations.

Plaintiffs bring most civil actions in federal courts under the Civil Rights Act of 1871. Known commonly as **"1983 actions"** (from U.S. Code § 1983 where the Civil Rights Act is located), the act provides:

> Every person who, under color of any statute, ordinance, regulation, custom, or usage, of any State or Territory, subjects, or causes to be subjected, any citizen of the United States or other person within the jurisdiction thereof to the deprivation of any rights, privileges, or immunities secured by the Constitutions and laws, shall be liable to the party injured in an action at law, suit in equity, or other proper proceeding for redress.[33]

The principle elements in a 1983 action include (1) a person (2) who acts under color of *state* law (3) and such action *causes* (4) a constitutional violation. The Supreme Court has interpreted all of these elements. Person includes municipalities, and other government units within the states. Under color of state law includes not only state statutes but also city ordinances, regulations, and customs. The action under color of law must cause a constitutional violation. Most actions claim that the government or its agents denied citizens' due process of law. Some suits also maintain that the government or its agents denied the plaintiff equal protection of the laws. The Fourteenth Amendment protects citizens against state action that denies them either or both rights.

Most problematic for the Court has been defining "custom" and "causes" in § 1983. The Supreme Court addressed the definition of both of these terms in *Oklahoma City v. Tuttle*.

CASE

Was his death caused by following a custom?

Oklahoma City v. Tuttle

471 U.S. 808, 105 S. Ct. 2427, 85 L.Ed.2d 791 (1985)

[Rehnquist, J., announced the judgment of the Court, in which Burger, C.J., and Brennan, White, Marshall, Blackmun, and Acinar, J.J.,joined. Brennan, J., filed a concurring opinion, in which Marshall and Blackmun, J.J., joined. Stevens, J., dissented.]

FACTS

On October 4, 1980, Officer Julian Rotramel, a member of the Oklahoma City police force, shot and killed Albert Tuttle outside the We'll Do Club, a bar in Oklahoma City. Officer Rotramel, who had been on the force for 10 months, had responded to an all points bulletin indicating that there was a robbery in progress at the Club. The bulletin, in turn, was the product of an anonymous telephone call. The caller had reported the robbery in progress, and had described the robber and reported that the robber had a gun. The parties stipulated at trial that Tuttle had placed the call.

Rotramel was the first officer to reach the bar, and the testimony concerning what happened thereafter is sharply conflicting. Rotramel's version was that when he entered the bar Tuttle walked toward him, and Rotramel grabbed Tuttle's arm and requested that he stay within the bar. Tuttle matched the description contained in the bulletin. Rotramel proceeded to question the barmaid concerning the reported robbery, but while doing so he once again had to restrain Tuttle from leaving, this time by grabbing Tuttle's arm and holding it. The barmaid testified that she told Rotramel that no robbery had occurred. Rotramel testified that while he was questioning the barmaid Tuttle kept bending towards his booths, and attempting to squirm from the officer's grip Tuttle finally broke away from Rotramel, and, ignoring the officer's commands to "halt," went outside. When Rotramel cleared the threshold to the outside door, he saw Tuttle crouched down on the sidewalk, with his hands in or near his boot. Rotramel again ordered Tuttle to halt, but when Tuttle started to come out of his crouch Rotramel discharged his weapon. Rotramel testified at trial that he believed Tuttle had removed a gun from his boot, and that his life was in danger.

Tuttle died from the gunshot wound. When his boot was removed at the hospital prior to surgery, a toy pistol fell out.

Respondent Rose Marie Tuttle is Albert Tuttles widow. . . . She brought suit under § 1983 in the United States District Court, Western District of Oklahoma, against Rotramel and the city, alleging that their actions had deprived Tuttle of certain of his constitutional rights. . . . [An expert testified at the trial] that Rotramel's training was grossly inadequate. . . . The case was presented to the jury on the theory that Rotramel's act had deprived Tuttle of life without due process of law, or that he had violated Tuttle's rights by using "excessive force in his apprehension." With respect to respondent's suit against Rotramel individually, the jury was charged that Rotramel was entitled to qualified immunity to the extent that he had acted in good faith and with a reasonable belief that his actions were lawful. Respondent also sought to hold the city liable . . . presumably on the theory that a municipal "custom or policy" had led to the constitutional violations. . . . The jury returned a verdict in favor of Rotramel but against the city, and awarded respondent $1,500,000 in damages. The city appealed to the Circuit Court of Appeals . . . claim[ing] it was error to instruct the jury that a municipality could be held liable for a "policy" of "inadequate training" based merely upon evidence of a single incident of unconstitutional activity. The Court of Appeals rejected petitioner's claim.

OPINION

Respondent's lawsuit is brought pursuant to 42 U.S.C. §1983 [see provision quoted above]. . . . By its terms, of course, the statute creates no substantive rights; it merely provides remedies for deprivations of rights established elsewhere. Here respondent's claim is that her husband was deprived of his life "without due process of law," in violation of the Fourteenth Amendment, or that he was deprived of his right to be free from the use of "excessive force in his apprehension"—presumably a right secured by the Fourth and Fourteenth Amendments. [See *Tennessee v. Garner*, excerpted in chap. 5.] Having established a deprivation of a constitutional right, however, respondent still must establish that the city was a "person" who "cause[d] [Tuttle] to be subjected" to the deprivation. *Monell [v. New York City Department of Social Services]* teaches that the city may only be held accountable if the deprivation was a result of municipal "custom or policy."

In *Monell*, the plaintiffs challenged the defendant's policy of compelling pregnant employees to take unpaid sick leave before such leave was necessary for medical reasons, on the ground that the policy violated the Due Process or Equal Protection Clauses of the Fourteenth Amendment. . . . The *Monell* Court found. . .a municipality liable "for *its own* violations of the Fourteenth Amendment."

Having determined that municipalities were suable "persons," the *Monell* Court went on to discuss the circumstances under which municipal liability could be imposed. . . . The Court noted that §1983 only imposes liability for deprivations "cause[d]" by a particular defendant, and that it was hard to find such causation where liability is imposed merely because of an employment relationship [that is on a theory of *respondeat* superior]. . . . [T]he *Monell*

Court held that only deprivations visited pursuant to municipal "custom" or "policy" could lead to municipal liability. This language . . . provides a fault-based analysis for imposing municipal liability. . . . Subsequent decisions of this Court have added little to the *Monell* Court's formulation, beyond reaffirming that the municipal policy must be "the moving force of the constitutional violation."

. . . [R]espondent's theory of liability was that the "policy" in question was the city's policy of training and supervising police officers, and that this "policy" resulted in inadequate training, and the constitutional violations alleged. . . . The District Court apparently accepted this theory of liability, though it charged the jury that the city's "policy makers" could not merely have been "negligent" in establishing training policies, but that they must have been guilty of "gross negligence" or "deliberate indifference" to the "police misconduct" that they could thus engender. . . .

The "policy" of the New York City Department of Social Sevices that was challenged in *Monell* was a policy that by its terms compelled pregnant employees to take mandatory leaves of absence before such leaves were required for medical reasons; this policy in and of itself violated the constitutitional rights of pregnant women. . . Here, however, the "policy" that respondent seeks to rely upon is far more nebulous, and a good deal further removed from the constitutional violation, than was the policy in *Monell*. To establish the constitutional violation in *Monell* no evidence was needed other than a statement of the policy by the municipal corporation, and its exercise; but the type of "policy" upon which respondent relies, and its causal relation to the alleged constitutional violation, are not susceptible to such easy proof. In the first place, the word "policy" generally implies a course of action consciously chosen from among various alternatives; it is therefore difficult in one sense even to accept the submission that someone pursues a "policy" of "inadequate training," unless evidence be adduced which proves that the inadequacies resulted from conscious choice—that is, proof that the policymakers deliberately chose a training program which would prove inadequate. And in the second place, some limitation must be placed on establishing municipal liability through policies that are not themselves unconstitutional. . . .

Here the instructions allowed the jury to infer a thoroughly nebulous "policy" of "inadequate training" on the part of the municipal corporation from the single incident described earlier in this opinion, and at the same time sanctioned the inference that the "policy" was the cause of the incident. . . Proof of a single incident of unconstitutional activity is not sufficient to impose liability [on a municipality] unless proof of the incident includes proof that it was caused by an existing, unconstitutional municipal policy, which policy can be attributed to a municipal policymaker. Otherwise the existence of the unconstitutional policy, and its origin, must be separately proved. But where the policy is itself not unconstitutional, considerably more proof than the single incident will be necessary in every case to establish both the requisite fault on the part of the municipality, and the causal connection between the "policy" and the constitutional deprivation. . . . The decision of the Court of Appeals is accordingly
Reversed.

DISSENT

Justice Stevens, dissenting.

When a police officer is engaged in the performance of his official duties, he is entrusted with civic responsibilities of the highest order. His mission is to protect the life, the liberty, and property of the citizenry. If he violates the Federal Constitution while he is performing that mission, I believe that federal law provides the citizen with a remedy against his employer as well as a remedy against him as an individual. . . .

As we have frequently noted, §1983 came onto the books as §1 of the Ku Klux Klan Act of April 20, 1871. The law was an especially important, remedial measure, drafted in expansive language. . . . At the time the statute was enacted the doctrine of *respondeat superior* was well recognized. . . . An employer could be held liable for the wrongful acts of his agents, even when acting contrary to specific instructions, and the rule had been specifically applied to municipal corporations, and to the wrongful acts of police officers. . . .

In this case, all of the policy considerations that support the doctrine of *respondeat superior* in normal tort litigation against municipal corporations apply with special force because of the special quality of the interests at stake. The interest of providing fair compensation for the victim, the interest in deterrring future violations by formulating sound municipal policy, and the interest in fair treatment for individual officers who are performing difficult and dangerous work, all militate in favor of placing primary responsibility on the municipal corporation.

The Court's contrary conclusion can only be explained by a concern about the danger of bankrupting municipal corporations. That concern is surely legitimate, but it is one that should be addressed by Congress—perhaps by imposing maximum limitations on the size of any potential recovery or by requiring the purchase of appropriate liability insurance—rather than by this Court. . . .

I respectfully dissent.

CASE DISCUSSION

A police officer shot and killed a man. The district court jury found the city responsible under §1983, and the jury awarded the man's wife $1,500,000 in damages. The court of appeals affirmed. On writ of *certiorari*, the United States Supreme Court reversed, holding that a single instance of unconstitutional activity by a police officer was not sufficient to establish that a municipal policy caused the unconstitutional action resulting in the man's death.

Can you trace through the elements required to establish liability uner §1983 in this case? Why does the Court reject the policy as a cause of the man's death? What is the difference between the one act of compelling pregnant women to take maternity leaves and the one instance of shooting in this case? Are the differences meaningful? If you were deciding this case, would you hold the city liable for the death? How much in damages does his widow deserve? What would you take into account in determining the amount?

In *Thurman v. City of Torrington*, the United States District Court for the District of Columbia found a municipality liable for injuries suffered by a wife in a domestic violence case because the police department's arrest in domestic assault cases caused the injuries she suffered.

CASE

Was there a policy of lesser enforcement of domestic assaults?

Thurman v. City of Torrington

595 F. Supp. 1521 (D.Conn. 1984)

FACTS

In October 1982, Charles Thurman attacked plaintiff Tracey Thurman at the home of Judy Bentley and Richard St. Hilaire in the City of Torrington. Mr. St. Hilaire and Ms. Bentley made a formal complaint of the attack to one of the unnamed defendant police officers and requested efforts to keep the plaintiff's husband, Charles Thurman, off their property.

On or about November 5 1982, Charles Thurman returned to the St. Hilaire-Bentley residence and using physical force took the plaintiff Charles J. Thurman, Jr. from said residence. Plaintiff Tracey Thurman and Mr. St. Hilaire went to Torrington police headquarters to make a formal complaint. At that point, unnamed defendant police officers of the City of Torrington refused to accept a complaint from Mr. St. Hilaire even as to trespassing.

On or about November 9, 1982, Charles Thurman screamed threats at Tracey while she was sitting in her car. Defendant police officer Neil Germelli stood on the street watching Charles Thurman scream threats at Tracey until Charles Thurman broke the windshield of plaintiff Tracey Thurman's car while she was inside the vehicle. [Charles was arrested, convicted of breach of peace, and received a suspended sentence.

On December 31, 1982 Charles threatened Tracey again; the police did not respond when Tracey called them to report the threat. She reported numerous similar incidents between January 1 and May 4, 1983. On May 4 and 5, 1983, Tracey Thurman and Ms. Bentley reported that Charles Thurman threatened to shoot the plaintiff. Police took Tracey Thurman's complaint but refused to take Ms. Bentley's. On May 6, Tracey Chapman received a restraining order forbidding Charles Thurman from assaulting, threatening, and harassing her. On May 27, 1983 Tracey requested police protection. She was told she would have to wait until after the Memorial Day holiday week-end. When she appeared on May 31, the police delayed her request further.]

On June 10, 1983, Charles Thurman appeared at the Bentley-St. Hilaire residence in the early afternoon and demanded to speak to Tracey. Tracey, remaining indoors, called the defendant police department asking that Charles be picked up for violation of his probation. After about 15 minutes, Tracey went outside to speak to her husband in an effort to persuade him not to take or hurt Charles Jr. Soon thereafter, Charles began to stab Tracey repeatedly in the chest, neck and throat.

Approximately 25 minutes after Tracey's call to the Torrington Police Department, and after her stabbing, a single police officer, the defendant Petrovits, arrive on the scene. Upon the arrival of Officer Petrovits at the scene of the stabbing, Charles Thurman was holding a bloody knife. Charles then dropped the knife and, in the presence of Petrovits, kicked the plaintiff Tracey Thurman in the head and ran into the Bentley-St Hilaire residence. Charles returned from within the residence holding the plaintiff, Charles Thurman, Jr. and dropped the child on his wounded mother. Charles then kicked Tracey in the head a second time. Soon thereafter, defendants DeAngelo, Nukirk, and Columbia arrived on the scene but still permitted Charles Thurman to wander about the crowd and to continue to threaten Tracey. Finally, upon approaching Tracey once again, this time while she lay on a stretcher, Charles Thurman was arrested and taken into custody.

It is also alleged that at all times mentioned above, except for approximately two weeks following his conviction, Charles Thurman resided in Torrington and worked there as a counterman and short order cook at Skie's Diner. There he served many members of the Torrington Police Department including some of the named and unnamed defendants in the case. In the course of his employment Charles Thorman boasted to the defendant police officer patrons that he intended to "get" his wife and that he intended to kill her.

OPINION

. . . [T]he plaintiffs allege that the defendants use an administrative classification that manifests itself in discriminatory treatment violative of the equal protection clause. Police protection in the City of Torrington, they argue, is fully provided to persons abused by someone with whom the victim has no domestic relationship. But the Torrington police have consistently afforded lesser protection, plaintiffs allege, when the victim is (1) a woman abused or assaulted by a spouse of boyfriend, or (2) a child abused by a father or stepfather. The issue to be decided, then, is whether the plaintiffs have properly alleged a violation of the equal protection clause of the Fourteenth amendment.

Police action is subject to the equal protection clause and section 1983 whether in the form of commission of violative acts or omission to perform required acts pursuant to the police offecer's duty to protect. . . . City officials and police officers are under an affirmative duty to preserve law and order, and to protect the personal safety of persons in the community. This duty applies equally to women whose personal safety is threatened, including women not involved in domestic relationships. . . .

Although the plaintiffs point to no law which on its face discriminates against victims abused by someone with whom they have a domestic relationship, the plaintiffs have alleged that there is an administrative classification used to implement the law in a discriminatory fashion. It is well settled that the equal protection clause is applicable not only to discriminatory legislative action, but also to discriminatory governmental action in administration and enforcement of the law. . . . Here the plaintiffs were threatened with assault under Conneticut law. Over the course of eight months the police failed to afford the plaintiffs protection against such assaults, and failed to take action to arrest the perpetrator in three of these assults. The plaintiffs have alleged that this failure to act was pursuant to a pattern or practice of affording inadequate protection, or no protection at all, to women who have complained of having been abused by their husbands or others with whom they have had close relations. Such a practice is tantamount to an administrative classification used to implement the law in a discriminatory fashion.

If the city wishes to discriminate against women, it must articulate an important governmental interest for doing so. . . [T]he city has failed to put forward any justification for its disparate treatment of women. . . .

A man is not allowed to physically abuse or endanger a woman merely because he is her husband. Concomitantly, a police officer may not knowingly refrain from interference in such violence, and may not "automatically decline to make an arrest simply because the assaulter and his victim are not married to each other." Such inaction on the part of the officer is a denial of equal protection of the laws. . . .

[The court then considered the question of whether the plaintiffs had properly alleged a custom or policy on the part of the City of Torrington.] While a municipality is not liable for the constitutional torts of its employees on a *respondeat superior* theory, a municipality may be sued for damages under section 1983 when "the action that is alleged to be unconstitutional implements or executes a policy statement, ordinance, regulation, or decision officially adopted and promulgated by the body's officers" or is "visited pursuant to governmental 'custom' even though such a custom has not received formal approval through the body's decision-making channels."

Some degree of specificity is required in the pleading of a custom or policy on the part of the municipality. Mere conclusory allegations devoid of factual content will not suffice. . . . [A] plaintiff must typically point to facts outside his own case to support his allegation of a policy on the part of a municipality.

In the instant case, however, the plaintiff Tracey Thurman has specifically alleged . . . a series of acts and omissions on the part of the defendant police officers and police department that took place over the course of eight months. From this particularized pleading a pattern emerges that evidences deliberate indifference on the part of the police department to the complaints of the plaintiff Tracey Thurman and to its duty to protect her. Such an ongoing pattern of deliberate indifference raised an inference of "custom" or "policy" on the part of the municipality. Furthermore, this pattern of inaction climaxed on June 10, 1983 in an incident so brutal that under the law of the Second Circuit that "single brutal incident may be sufficient to suggest a link between a violation of constitutional rights and a pattern of police misconduct. Finally, a complaint of this sort will survive dismissal if it alleges a policy or custom of condoning police misconduct that violates constitutional rights and alleges that "the City's pattern of inaction caused the plaintiffs any compensable injury." . . .

[T]he City's motion to dismiss the complaint for failure to allege the deprivation of a constitutional right is denied . . . the City's motion to dismiss for failure to properly allege a "custom" or "policy" on the part of the City is denied. So ordered.

CASE DISCUSSION

Tracey Thurman and her son brought civil rights actions against the city and police officers of the city of Torrington, alleging that the plaintiff's constitutional rights were violated by the nonperformance or malperformance of official duties by the officers in regard to threats and assaults by the wife's estranged husband. The city moved to dismiss the complaint; the district court denied the motion to dismiss.

What constitutional rights did the city allegedly violate? What facts did the plaintiff allege to demonstrate the unconstitutional acts? What facts demonstrates a "custom" or "policy"? Did they cause injury to the plaintiff? Explain.

The standard for suing municipalities under § 1983 is that a municipal "policy" or "practice" "caused" injury to plaintiffs. Apart from municipal liability, plaintiffs can also sue police officers directly as individuals. In civil rights and tort actions against them, police officers have partial immunity. "[A] policeman's lot is not so unhappy that he must choose between being charged with dereliction of duty if he does not arrest when he has probable cause, and being mulcted in damages if he does." Accordingly, police officers are not liable when they act in good faith and with probable cause. Nor are police officers liable for injuries suffered when officers negligently, but in good faith, seek and obtain search warrants that a reviewing judge later rules unlawful. "Under the prevailing view in the country, a peace officer may not be held liable for making negligent errors of law in seeking or executing a search warrant."

On the other hand a court held liable for "reckless use of excessive force" a police officer who chased a suspect for six blocks and then shot him in the leg. Three degrees of culpability determine police officers' civil liability for injuries they cause to private citizens while performing official duties. Police are liable for intentional and reckless injuries, but not for negligent injuries. Reckless injuries result from consciously creating risks that actions will injure citizens; negligent injuries result from actions that reasonable people *should have known*, but do not in fact know, will create risks of injury.[34]

Anthony Amsterdam, prominent defense attorney and constitutional law professor, points out the practical difficulties of successfully suing police officers for their misconduct.

Where are the lawyers going to come from to handle these cases for the plaintiffs? . . . [W]hat on earth would possess a lawyer to file a claim for damages . . . in an ordinary search-and-seizure case? The prospect of a share in the substantial damages to be expected? The chance to earn a reputation as a police-hating lawyer, so that he can no longer count on straight testimony concerning the length of skid marks in his personal injury cases? The gratitude of his client when his filing of the claim causes the prosecutor to refuse a lesser-included-offense plea or to charge priors or pile on ''cover'' charges? The opportunity to represent his client without fee in these resulting criminal matters?

Police cases are an unadulterated investigative and litigative nightmare. Taking on the police in any tribunal involves a commitment to the most frustrating and thankless legal work I know. And the idea that an unrepresented, inarticulate, prosecution-vulnerable citizen can make a case against a team of professional investigators and testifiers in any tribunal beggers belief. Even in a tribunal having recognized responsibilities and some resources to conduct independent investigations, a plaintiff without assiduous counsel devoted to developing his side of the case would be utterly outmastered by the police. No, I think we shall have airings of police searches and seizures on suppression motions or not at all.[35]

Judges, prosecutors, and defense attorneys are absolutely immune from private law suits. Historically, counties and states are partially immune under the doctrine of **soverign immunity** that protected first monarchs, and later states, from private law suits. Some governmental units have waived their sovereign immunity; others have permitted recovery fro unlawful conduct by government officials. Moreover, in *Monell v. United States*, the Supreme Court held that ''persons'' in the Civil Rights Act includes municipalities. (See discussion in *Oklahoma City v. Tuttle*, excerpted earlier.) However, municipalities are immune from **punitive damages**, or awards based on particularly vicious wrongdoing that exceed actual harm to the plaintiff. Punitive damages, as the name suggests, aim to punish wilful or malicious wrongdoers, and to deter future intentional misconduct.[36]

Plaintiffs bring many civil actions to the lower federal courts. Unlike *Oklahoma City v. Tuttle,* they rarely reach the Supreme Court. In most, plaintiffs do not prevail in their suits against the government. *Hall v. St. Helena Parish Sheriff's Department* represents one of the many § 1983 actions brought in lower federal courts. It illustrates how plaintiffs can sue individual officers, their supervisors, and their departments both under the Civil Rights Act and under state tort law. Furthermore, the case raises the issue of the types and amounts of damages plaintiffs can recover. Ordinary damages include amounts for injuries actually suffered, such as medical bills, wages lost, and perhaps pain and suffering. Punitive damages as the name implies, include amounts, to punish defendants for their malicious and intentional wrongdoing. *Hall v. St. Helena Parish Sheriff's Department* provides an excellent illustration of a lower federal court dealing with all these issues.

CASE

Can they sue the sheriff's department?

Hall v. St. Helena Parish Sheriff's Department

668 F. Supp. 535 (M.D. La. 1987)

FACTS

On Saturday, February 20, 1982, plaintiff, Cleo Hall, and Fabian Scott, a nineteen year old Negro man who resided in or near Greensburg, Louisiana, were returning home from a job hunting trip to Houston, Texas. They were travelling in plaintiff's 1982 Ford autimbile. Both had found employment on a construction job due to start in Houston in about a week. They left Houston fairly early in the morning and alternated driving. On the way, each drank "a couple of beers" and Hall, at least, also drank "some vodka."

Hall and Scott arrived safely in Greensburg in the early afternoon and made a stop at "the malt shop," where they returned a borrowed camera and visited with Mary McCoy and Linda Hurst, neither of whom smelled aclcohol on them or noticed anything unusual about either of them.

Somewhere near the hour of 4:00 p.m., Hall and Scott drove north from Greensburg on Louisiana Highway 43 for the purpose of delivering Scott to his home. Hall was driving and as he attempted to make a left turn into a side road, the vehicle went into the roadside ditch. Neither occupant of the vehicle was injured and the vehicle was not significantly damaged—it was still operable.

A passing motorist reported the accident to the St. Helena Parish sheriff's office. Hall and Scott, with the aid of passers-by, were attempting to get the vehicle out of the ditch when Deputy Alton D. Clark, Jr., Caucasian, arrived to investigate the accident.

Clark testified that he smelled alcohol on the breath of both Hall and Scott and that he, after viewing Hall's driver's license, ordered both to get into and stay in the rear seat of the sheriff's vehicle. Clark testified that he intended to obtain a blood alcohol reading on Hall in order to determine whether he would charge him with operating a vehicle while under the influence of alcohol beverages. Clark was unsure as to his reason for arresting Scott. Neither Hall nor Scott was informed that he was under arrest or why he was being detained. The accident report incicates that Hall was issued a citation for reckless operation of a vehicle in violation of LSA-R.S. 14:99.

In ten or fifteen munutes, Deputy David Lea, Caucasian, arrived to assist Clark at the scene. Both deputies were acquainted with both young men, who were still seated in the rear of Clark's vehicle. Clark and Lea had both heard a report that a short time before the accident, a "white lady" had been almost run off the road by another vehicle on Highway 43. Lea ascertained from Clark that Hall was the driver of the Hall vehicle and then approached the Clark vehicle where approximately the following colloquy took place (all the words are not necessarily exact but I find as a fact that the tone is accurate):

Lea: "Boy, were you driving that car?"
Hall: "Yes, I was."
Lea: "Why did you run that white lady off the road back there?"
Hall: "I didn't run no white lady off the road."
Lea: "Boy, I ought to beat your ass."
Hall: "If you do, I'll take you to court."
Lea: "Get your black ass out of that car."

As Hall opened the door and put one foot on the ground prior to leaving the vehicle, Lea began hitting him with his fists. After several blows, Hall hit Lea back. Lea stumbled back and drew his pistol which he first pointed at Hall and then used to pistol whip him around the head. Lea hit Hall repeatedly with the barrel of the postol and after a number of blows, Hall collapesed on the highway in a bloody heap. Lea then proceeded to kick Hall with his booted foot. Hall apparently lost consciousness and an ambulance was summoned. When it arrived, Lea would not permit the attendants to pick Hall up but insisted that Hall get up without assistance.

Hall was taken to the St. Helena Parish Hospital where five lacerations in the temple area of the left side of his head were noted. The lacerations were cleaned and debrided and three lacerations required sutures, a total of seven stitches. Hall was taken to the parish jail where, shortly thereafter, he fainted and was then returned to the hospital. Hall remained in the hospital until February 23, 1982, primarily for observation and testing. He was administered pain medication during his stay. Hall complained, in addition to the injuries to his head, of pain in the jaw and left ribs where Lea had kicked him. Skull x-rays disclosed that the skull was not fractured and other x-rays established that there were no bones broken. A brain scan established that there was no brain damage. Dr. J. W. Varnado testified that Hall suffered no permanent injury. Hall claims that he still has headaches and that there is a "knot" in his jaw. During Hall's stay in the hospital, several blood samples were taken from him and, according to the testimony of a forensic scientist at Hall's state court trial, (see Exhibit D-2) laboratory testing produced results of ".15" and ".14." No explanation of these results were presented to this court.

Dr Varnado's bill was $100. No evidence was offered as to any other medical expense incurred by Hall.

When Hall was returned to the parish jail from the hospital he found that he was facing a great many charges. Although the evidence offered to this court is sketchy as to precisely what charges were lodged, it seems to be undisputed that they included, simply battery, reckless driving, resisting an officer, and public intimidation. Again, the evidence presented to this court is sketchy but it seems to be undisputed that Hall was placed on trial in state court and that he was convicted of at least public intimidation, although he was apparently found not guilty of DWI. Plaintiff testified that he was convicted of public intimidation "and something else" and that he was sentenced to one year in jail, a fine and to pay the costs of prosecution in the amount of $3,500. Hall further testified that he was later arrested for not paying the costs. No further evidence was offered on this point.

Made defendants in this action are deputies Clark and Lea and Sheriff Duncan Bridges.

This case was held open following the trial in order that plaintiff might obtain the deposition of Sheriff Duncan Bridges. That effort failed, apparently because of the sheriff's health, but the parties have stipulated that if Sheriff Bridges had testified, "he would admit to the following":

(a) Duncan Bridges and the St. Helena Parish Sheriff's Department failed to provide any training to Officer David Lee concerning when to use force and the amount of force to be used on a suspect.

(b) That Officer David Lee had no post recruit training in this area.

(c) After David Lee was found guilty in federal court of violating Mrs. Rena Day's civil rights, Sheriff Bridges failed to discipline, suspend or reprimand Officer Lee or to investigate his actions.

(d) Almost immediately after the plaintiff's arrest, a group of concerned black citizens came to Sheriff Bridges concerning complaints they had about the manner in which the plaintiff was arrested. Sheriff Bridges spoke to the group, but made no further inquires or investigations concerning the incident.

(e) St. Helena Parish Sheriff's Department at the time of this incident, did not have a policy or did not convey a policy to the deputies of how to handle an arrestee if the arrestee resisted.

There is no evidence that Sheriff Bridges participated in or was even aware of the beating which Lea administered to Hall or that the beating was a result of Lea's implementation of any policy established by the sheriff.

Deputies Clark and Lea were both acting under color of state law in the performance of their official duties at the time of Hall's beating on February 20, 1982.

OPINION

This court has jurisdiction under 28 U.S.C. § 1343 (a)(3), since this is an action brought under 42 U.S.C. § 1983 to redress the deprivation, under color of state law, of rights and privileges secured by the Constitution ;of the United States. Plaintiff also asserts pendent state law claims under Louisiana law.

Plaintiff claims that his arrest by Clark was illegal because no probable cause existed. The ultimate outcome of the prosecution of state court charges against plaintiff is basically irrelevant to the existance of probable cause. It is well settled that in § 1983 cases, if an arrest is effected for which the police officer had reasonable cause to arrest on any related statutory provision, an acquittal of the offense charged does not vitiate probable cause for the arrest. Accordingly, if Clark had probable cause to arrest Hall for any charge, prosecuted or not, the initial arrest was lawful.

Deputy Clark had before him a vehicle in the roadside ditch which had left the roadway while the driver was making a left turn in broad daylight in dry weather. Deputy Clark concluded in the accident report that the vehicle was traveling too fast to safely make the turn. The driver smelled of alcohol and there were beer cans and a vodka bottle in the vehicle. These facts are sufficient to justify the initial arrest of Hall for reckless driving, for operation of the vehicle while under the influence of alcohol, or for violation of LSA-R.S. 32:64 which generally prohibits operation of a vehicle at a speed "greater than is reasonable and prudent under the conditions and potential hazards then existing." Thus, Hall's initial arrest by Clark was based upon probable cause and was lawful.

Although the initial arrest be lawful, the Fourteenth Amendment shields the person arrested from post-arrest brutality, "inspired by malice rather than merely careless or unwise excess of zeal so that it amount(s) to an abuse of official power that shocks the conscience."

Here, Lea's deliberate, malicious beating of Hall was completely unwarranted. Hall was seated peacefully in the rear of the vehicle where Clark had instructed him to remain. He was unarmed; he posed no threat of harm to anyone; he posed no threat of imminent threat to escape. To attack a peacefully secured arrested person is unconscionable. To repeatedly strike an unarmed man in the head with the barrel of a pistol is to invite a skull fracture or other serious injury. Lea clearly violated Hall's Fourteenth Amendment right to be secure in his person and Lea is liable to Hall under 42 U.S.C. § 1983. Lea is also liable under general principles of Louisiana tort law for his conduct.

The civil rights claim against Clark is more difficult. Although Clark clearly falsely arrested Scott, the passenger, Scott is not a party to this action and this court has found that Clark's initial arrest of Hall was lawful. Clark has varied his testimony from time to time, both as to what he saw and heard as well as to what happened. There is no evidence, however, that Clark participated in the postol whipping of Hall, that he was unaware of Lea's intentions, or that Clark would have prevented or stopped the beating. Clark's actions (or inactions) simply do not rise to that excess of zeal which shocks the conscience and constitutes a violation of 42 U.S.C. § 1983. Accordingly, there will be no recovery against Clark under § 1983. Moreover, there is no evidence that would support a state law negligence recovery against Clark.

Plaintiff insists that the sheriff must be held liable under § 1983 because of his failure to provide training to Deputy Lea ''concerning when to use force and the amount of force to be used on a suspect'' (see stipulation), and his failure to investigate the incident involving plaintiff's injury (see stipulation).

A state supervisory official cannot be held for the actions of a subordinate under § 1983 solely on the basis of vicarious liability.

This is not a case where a law enforcement officer was guilty of using excessive force in the course of subduing a person that he was attempting to arrest. Here their arrest had already been effected before Lea had arrived at the scene and the person arrested was peacefully seated in the rear of the police vehicle. No adult (and few children) ought to require training that it is wrong to attack without provocation a person already arrested. Lea's egregious conduct in this case was his and his alone. There is no evidence to support a finding that Sheriff Bridges is liable to Hall for failure to train Lea not to attack unarmed arrestees.

There is no evidence in this record that the sheriff ordered the beating of Hall or that it was administered pursuant to any custom, practice or policy instituted by the sheriff. There being no personal or policy involvement of the sheriff, his ''failure to investigate'' Lea following the beating cannot impose § 1983 liability upon him. Liabillity under § 1983 requires personal involvement of the defendant, either by action or preincident approval of a custom or policy.

Thus, the record does not support § 1983 liability of Sheriff Bridges.

The result is different, however, under the pendent state law claims. Under Louisiana law, a parish sheriff is liable in his official, but not personal, capacity as an employer of a deputy, for the deputy's torts in the course and scope of employment. Louisiana Civil Code art. 2320. Although Sheriff Bridges is not liable under § 1983, he is liable under general principles of Louisiana law, in his official capacity, for Lea's tort.

As noted earlier, the medical evidence is that Hill suffered no permnanent injury or disability from Lea's beating. He was rendered unconscious and some blows with the pistol were severe. He was in the hospital for three days, he received medication for pain and he did suffer headaches and soreness for some time after his release from the hospital. Hall has proved $100 as the fee of the attending physician and, while the hospital records were received in evidence, no proof of the cost of the hospital stay was offered to the court. Consequently, Hall has proved special damages only in the amount of $100.

Hall is also entitled to an award to compensatory damages in the amount of $5,000 for his physical and mental pain and suffering and the physical injury inflicted upon him by Lea.

Accordingly, there will be judgment in favor of plaintiff in the amount of $5,100 against Lea under 42 U.S.C. § 1983 and against Sheriff Bridges in his official capacity in solido with Lea under Louisiana law.

Punitive damages are allowed in appropriate cases under 42 U.S.C. § 1983. Punitive damages, as distinct from compensatory damages, are awarded, "with the specific purpose of deterring or punishing violations of constitutional rights."

Lea's unwarranted, deliberate and malicious beating of an unarmed and peaceful arrestee demands both punishment and that an example be made so as to deter other law enforcement officers who might be tempted to deprive people of their constitutional protections.

This is not the first case in which this court has found that Deputy Lea has violated the constitutional rights of a citizen by an unprovoked and armed attack.

Punitive damages will be awarded against Lea in the amount of $100,000. That amount has a sound ring in it and it is sufficient both to punish Lea for his transgression and to attract the atttention of others who might be similarly tempted and perhaps to deter them from similar conduct.

Plaintiff is also entitled to an award for attorney's fee under 42 U.S.C. § 1988 and counsel has submitted an itemization of time spent on the case totalling 115.75 hours, to which no exception has been taken by defendants. Counsel suggests that $85 per hour would be appropriate and that attorney's fees in the amount of $9,838.75 should be awarded in this case.

This case was neither complex nor difficult. The trial was one day. Counsel's post-trial brief was not very helpful to the court. Without detailing all the so-called "factors," suffice it to say that a reasonable fee for counsel in this case is $75 per hour and that a reasonable number of hours productively devoted to this case could no exceed 75. Again, without detailing all the details, the court has noted particularly that counsel's time sheets some 112 "telephone conferences" with co-counsel, or a total of 28 hours conferring with co-counsel about the case. The court considers that to be excessive discussion. This court concludes that a sum of $5,625 is an ample fee for services performed by counsel and that will be the amount awarded against Lea under 42 U.S.C. § 1988. Attorney's fees are not allowed under Louisiana law in tort cases.

In post-trial brief, counsel for plaintiff has invited the court to award plaintiff damages because of the "false charges" lodged against him by Lea in an effort to punish and silence plaintiff as well as for the "additional punitive measures . . . taken in the sentence and fine aspect of plaintiff's criminal case," because a "simple one car accident . . . was escalated by DEPUTY LEA into a major tragedy in plaintiff's life, resulting in plaintiff being physically injured and humiliated to suffer incarceration, trial, conviction of a felony, economic hardship.''Neither plaintiff's pleadings nor the pretrial order in this case contain any attack or challenge to plaintiff's state court conviction and there is no evidence as to what state court remedies, if any, plaintiff has pursued. While the line of jurisprudence exemplified by *Battieste v. City of Baton Rouge*, 732 F.2d 439 (5th Cir. 1984) might permit a challenge to plaintiff's state court conviction via a § 1983 action, there is absolutely no evidence in this record upon which a federal challenge could be mounted. Accordingly, the case is limited to the post arrest personal injuries inflicted upon plaintiff by Deputy Lea.

Judgement will be entered accordingly.

CASE DISCUSSION

Hall sued the local government unit (the parish) for violating his constitutional rights under § 1983, the Civil Rights Act. The court ruled that the officers had violated Hall's constitutional rights and awarded him $5100 in damages ''with the specific purpose of deterrring or punishing violations of constitutional rights.''

Why was the sheriff's department not liable in this case? Why was inadequate training not sufficient ground for liability? Why wasn't Officer Clark liable for damages too? What interests do civil actions against law enforcement officers promote? Do they put process over result? What precisely were Hall's ''damages''? How can you measure the dollar value of the injuries he suffered? How do you think the court arrived at $5100? Does it seem proper? Explain. Why does $100,000 punitive damages have a ''sound ring''? Do you agree with the court's conclusion regarding punitive damages? What standard could you apply to measure punitive damages? What interests would such a standard promote? (See chaps. 5 and 6 on unlawful searches and seizures.)

Decision Point

Some important questions about recovering for damages are not as easily answered if the suit involves injuries less apparent than the clearly brutal treatment that Hall and Scott suffered in the case just presented. Far more common are property damages caused by searches. Should ''victims'' recover for damages in the following cases: a door worth $500 is irreparably damaged when police entered a house with the wrong address on a warrant to search an unoccupied house? The same type of door is damaged when the correct house was entered pursuant to a lawful search warrant that produced evidence sufficient to convict the house's owner? The same type of door is broken pursuant to a lawful entry that produced evidence against the house's owner and involved no further proceedings? The same type of door is broken pursuant to an unlawful entry that the police honestly believed was lawful? The same type of door is broken pursuant to an unlawful search, but the ''victim'' turned out to be guilty of the crime that led the police to search for evidence? If the victims are entitled to recover, who should pay? Individual officers who did the damage? Their superiors? The police department? The municipality under whose jurisdiction the department is located?

Recently, the Senate proposed legislation to answer some of these questions. It provided, in part:

Section 2692. Tort Claims; Illegal Search and Seizure

(a) The United States shall be liable for any damages resulting from a search or seizure conducted by an investigative or law enforcement officer, acting within the scope of his office or employment, in violation of the United States Constitution.

(b) Any person aggrieved by such a violation may recover actual damages and such punitive damages as the court may award under subsection (c).

(c) Punitive damages may be awarded by the court, upon consideration of all the circumstances of the sase, including--

(1) The extent of the investigative of law enforcement officer's deviation from permissible conduct;

(2) The extent to which the violation was willful, reckless, or grossly negligent;

(3) The extent to which the aggrieved person's privacy was invaded;

(4) The extent of the aggrieved person's personal injury, both physical and mental;

(5) The extent of any property damage; and

(6) The effect such an award would have in preventing future violations of the United States Constitution.

(d) Notwithstanding subsections (b) and (c), the recovery of any person who is convicted of any offense for which evidence of such offense was seized in violation of the United States Constitution is limited to actual physical injury and to actual property damage sustained as a result of the unconstitutional search and seizure.

(e) No judgment, award, or compromise, or settlement of any action brought under this section shall exceed the amount of $25,000, including actual and punitive damages.[37]

Practically speaking, plaintiffs who sue government agents are rarely successful. Not often do the juries awarding damages look favorably on "criminals" who want to collect money from police officers who "were only doing their jobs." For that reason, some suggest that the following might improve the chances of recovery: (1) government liability for illegal acts of officers; (2) minimum liquidated damages, meaning paid-up or settled amounts of money for particular wrongs; and (3) restrictions on defenses based on reputation, such as where damage to reputation is difficult to prove when the plaintiff is a "disreputable person."[38]

══ INJUNCTION

Injunctions are court orders directed to police departments and other criminal justice agencies ordering them to cease illegal conduct. Sometimes, they order agencies to desist from actions against specific individuals or groups of individuals. For example, in *Lankford v. Gelston,* police engaged in a mass search-and-arrest action to apprehend two armed robbers who had shot a police officer. The officers broke into houses at all hours without probable cause, ransacked housed, and took residents to police stations in the middle of the night. Plaintiffs asked for an injunction against the particular searches involved on the specific occasion. Sometimes, as in *City of Los Angeles v. Lyons* the injunctions take aim at general police department policies—the Los Angeles Police Department's use of chokeholds—that affect the plaintiff who seeks the injunction.

CASE

Should the court order the police to stop using chokeholds?

City of Los Angeles v. Lyons

461 U.S. 95, 103 S.Ct. 1660, 75 L.Ed.2d 675 (1983)

FACTS

Adolph Lyons is a 24-year-old Negro male who resides in Los Angeles. . . . [A]t about 2 a.m. on October 6, 1976, Lyons was pulled over to the curb by two officers of the Los Angeles Police Department (LAPD) for a traffic infraction because one of his headlights was burned out. The officers greeted him with drawn revolvers as he exited from his car. Lyons was told to face his car and spread his legs. He did so. He was then ordered to clasp his hands and put them on top of his head. He again complied. After one of the officers completed a patdown search, Lyons dropped his hands, but was ordered to place them back above his head and slammed them onto his head. Lyons complained about the pain caused by the ring of keys he was holding in his hand. Within 5 to 10 seconds, the officer began to choke Lyons by applying a forearm against his throat. As Lyons struggled for air, the officer handcuffed him, but continued to apply the chokehold[a]—either the "bar arm control" hold or the "carotid-artery control" hold or both—until he blacked out. When Lyons regained consciousness, he was lying face down on the ground, choking, gasping for air, and spitting up blood and dirt. He had urinated and

---

[a] The police control procedures at issue in this case are referred to as "control holds," "chokeholds," strangleholds," and "neck restraints." All these terms refer to two basic control procedures: the "carotid" hold and the "bar arm" hold. In the "carotid" hold, an officer positioned behind a subject places one arm around the subject's neck and holds the wrist of that arm with his other hand. The officer, by using his lower forearm and bicep muscle, applies pressure concentrating on the carotid arteries located on the sides of the subject's neck. "Bar arm" pressure causes pain, reduces the flow of oxygen to the lungs, and may render the subject unconscious.

defecated. He was issued a traffic citation and released. . . . On February 7, 1977 . . . respondent, Adolph Lyons, filed a complaint for damages, injunction, and declaratory relief [under § 1983 of the United States Code] in the United States District Court for the Central District of California. The defendants were the City of Los Angeles and four of its police officers. . . . Counts I through IV of the complaint sought damages against the officers and the City. Count V, with which we are principally concerned here, sought a preliminary and permanent injunction against the City barring the use of the control holds. The count alleged that the City's police officers, "pursuant to the authorization, instruction and encouragement of Defendant City of Los Angeles, regularly and routinely apply these choke holds in innumerable situations where they are not threatened by the use of any deadly force whatsoever," that numerous persons have been injured as the result of the application of the chokeholds, that Lyons and others similarly situated are threatened with irreparable injury in the form of bodily injury and loss of life, and that Lyons "justifiably fears that any contact he has with Los Angeles Police officers may result in his being choked and strangled to death without provocation, justification or other legal excuse." Lyons alleged the threatened impairment of rights protected by the First, Fourth, Eighth, and Fourteenth Amendments. Injunctive relief was sought against the use of the control holds "except in situations where the proposed victim of said control reasonably appears to be threatening the immediate use of deadly force." Count VI sought declaratory relief against the City, *i.e.*, a judgment that use of the chokeholds absent the threat of immediate use of deadly force is a *per se* violation of various constitutional rights. . . . .

The District Court found that Lyons had been stopped for a traffic infringement and that without provocation or legal justification the officers involved had applied a "Department-authorized chokehold which resulted in injuries to the plaintiff." The court further found that the department authorizes the use of the holds in situations where no one is threatened by death or grievous bodily harm, that officers are insufficiently trained, that the use of the holds involves a high risk of injury or death as then employed, and that their continued use in situations where neither death nor serious injury is threatened "is unconscionable in a civilized society." The court concluded that such use violated Lyons' substantive due process rights under the Fourth Amendment. A preliminary injunction was entered enjoining "the use of both the carotid artery and arm bar holds under circumstances which do not threaten death or serious bodily injury." An improved training program and regular reporting and recordkeeping were also ordered. The Court of Appeals affirmed in a brief *per curiam* opinion stated that the District Court had not abused its discretion in entering a preliminary injunction. We granted certiorari, and now reverse.

OPINION

White, J., delivered the opinion of the Court, in which Burger, C.J., and Powell, Rehnquist, and O'Connor, JJ., joined. Marshall, J., filed a dissenting opinion, in which Brennan, Blackmun, and Stevens, JJ., joined.

Since our grant of certiorari, circumstances pertinent to the case have changed. Originally, Lyons' complaint alleged that at least two deaths had occurred as a result of the applications of chokeholds by the police. His first amended complaint alleged that 10 chokehold-related deaths had occurred. By May 1982, there had been five more such deaths. On May 6, 1982, the Chief of Police in Los Angeles prohibited the use of the bar-arm chokehold in any circumstances. A few days later, on May 12, 1982, the Board of Police Commissioners imposed a 6-month moratorium on the use of the carotid-artery chokehold except under circumstances where deadly force is authorized.

Based on these events, on June 3, 1982, the City filed in this Court a memorandum suggesting a question of mootness, reciting the facts but arguing that the case was not moot. Lyons in turn filed a motion to dismiss the writ of certiorari an improvidently granted. We denied that motion but reserved the question of mootness for later consideration.

In his brief and at oral argument, Lyojns has reasserted his polition in light of changed conditions, an injunction decree is now unnecessary because he is no longer subject to a threat of injury. He urges that the preliminary injunction should be vacated. The City, on the other hand, while acknowledging that subsequent events have significantly changed the posture of this case, again asserts that the case is not moot because the moratorium is not permanent and may be lifted at any time

We agree with the City that the case is not moot, since the moratorium by its terms is not permanent. Intervening events have not ''irrevocably eradicated the effects of the alleged violation.'' We nevertheless hold, for another reason, that the federal courts are without jurisdiction to entertain Lyons' claims for injunction relief.

It goes without saying that those who seek to invoke the jurisdiction of the federal courts must satisfy the threshold requirement imposed by Art.III of the Constitution by alleging an actual case or controversy. Plaintiffs must demonstrate a ''personal stake in the outcome'' in order to ''assure that concrete adverseness which sharpens the presentation of issues'' necessary for the proper resolution of constitution questions. Abstract injury in not enough. The plaintiff must show that he ''has sustained or is immediately in danger of sustaining some direct injury'' as a result of the challenged official conduct and the injury or threat of injury must be both ''real and immediate,'' not ''conjectural'' or ''hypothetical.'' . . .

Lyons has failed to demonstrate a case or controversy with the City that would justify the equitable relief sought. Lyons' standing to seek the injunction requested depended on whether he was likely to suffer future injury from the use of the chokeholds by police officers. Count V of the complaint alleged the traffic stop and choking incident five months before. That Lyons may have been illegally choked by the police on October 6, 1976, while presumably affording Lyons standing to claim damages against the individual officers and perhaps against the City, does nothing to establish a real and immediate threat that he would again be stopped for a traffic violation, or for any other offense, by an officer or officers who would illegally choke him into unconsciousness without any provocation or resistance on his part. The additional allegation in the complaint that the police in Los Angeles routinely apply chokeholds in situations where they are not threatened by the use of deadly force falls far short of the allegations that would be necessary to establish a case or controversy between these parties.

In order to establish an actual controversy in this case, Lyons would have had not only to allege that he would have another encounter with the police but also to make the incredible assertion either (1) that *all* police officers in Los Angeles *always* choke any citizen with whom they happen to have an encounter, whether for the purpose of arrest, issuing a citation, or for questioning, or (2) that the City ordered or authorized police officers to act in such a manner. Although Count V alleged that the City authorized the use of the control holds in situations where deadly force was not threatened, it did not indicate why Lyons might be realistically threatened by police officers who acted within the strictures of the City's policy. If, for example, chokeholds were authorized to be used only to counter resistance to an arrest by a suspect, or to thwart an effort to escape, any future threat to Lyons from the City's policy or from the conduct of police officers would be no more real than the possibility that he would again have an encounter with the police and that either he would illegally resist arrest or detention or the officers would disobey their instructions and again render him unconscious without any provocation. . . .

Absent a sufficient likelihood that he will again be wronged in a similar way, Lyons is no more entitled to an injunction than any other citizen of Los Angeles; and a federal court may not entertain a claim by any or all citizens who no more than assert that certain practices of law enforcement officers are unconstitutional. This is not to suggest that such undifferentiated claims should not be taken seriously by local authorities. Indeed, the interest of an alert and interested citizen is an essential element of an effective and fair government, whether on the local, state, or national level. A federal court, however, is not the proper forum to press such claims unless the requirements for entry and the prerequisites for injunctive relief are satisfied.

We decline the invitation to slight the preconditions for equitable relief; for as we have held, recognition of the need for a proper balance between state and federal authority counsels restraint in the issuance of injunctions against state officers engaged in the administration of the State's criminal laws in the absence of irreparable injury which is both great and immediate . . . . [T]he normal principals of equity, comity, and federalism . . . should imform the judgment of federal courts when asked to oversee state law enforcement authorities. In exercising their equitable powers federal courts must recognize "[t]he special delicacy of the adjustment to be preserved between federal equitable power and State administration of its own law." . . .

[W]ithholding injunctive relief does not mean that the "federal law will exercise no deterrent effect in these circumstances." If Lyons has suffered an injury barred by the Federal Constitution, he has a remedy for damages under § 1983. Furthermore, those who deliberately deprive a citizen of his constitutional rights risk conviction under the federal criminal laws.

Beyond these considerations the state courts need not impose the same standing or remedial requirements that govern federal-court proceedings. The individual States may permit their courts to use injunctions to oversee the conduct of law enfoecement authorities on a continuing basis. But this is not the role of a federal court, absent far more justification than Lyons has proffered in this case.

The judgment of the Court of Appeals is accordingly reversed.

DISSENT

Justice Marshall, with whom Justice Brennan, Justice Blackmun, and Justice Stevens join, dissenting.

The District Court found that the City of Los Angeles authorizes its police officers to apply life-threatening chokeholds to citizens who pose no threat of violence, and that respondent, Adolph Lyons, was subjected to such a chokehold. The Court today holds that a federal court is without power to enjoin the enforcement of the city's policy, no matter how flagrantly unconstitutional it may be. Since no one can show that he will be choked in the future, no one—not even a person who, like Lyons, has almost been choked to death—has standing to challenge the continuation of the policy. The city is free to continue the policy indefinitely as long as it is willing to pay damages for the injuries and deaths that result. I dissent from this unprecedented and unwarranted approach to standing.

There is plainly a "case or controversy" concerning the constitutionality of the city's chokehold policy. The constitutionality of that policy is directly implicated by Lyons' claim for damages against the city. The complaint clearly alleges that the officer who choked Lyons was carrying out an official policy, and a municipality is liable under 42 U.S.C. § 1983 for the conduct of its employees only if they acted pursuant to such a policy. Lyons therefore has standing to challenge the city's chokehold policy and to obtain whatever relief a court may ultimately deem appropriate. None of our prior decisions suggests that his requests for particular forms of relief raise any additional issues concerning his standing. Standing has always depended on whether a plaintiff has a "personal stake in the outcome of the controversy," not on the "precise nature of the relief sought." . . .

Although the city instructs its officers that use of a chokehold does not constitute deadly force, since 1975 no less than 16 persons have died following the use of a chokehold by an LAPD police officer. Twelve had been Negro males.[a] The evidence submitted to the District Court established that for many years it has been the official policy of the city to permit officers to employ chokeholds in a variety of situations where they face no threat of violence. In reported "altercations" between LAPD officers and citizens the chokeholds are used more frequently than any other means of physical restraint. Between February 1975 and July 1980, LAPD officers applied chokeholds on at least 975 occasions, which represented more than three-quarters of the reported altercations.

It is undisputed that chokeholds pose a high and unpredictable risk of serious injury or death. Chokeholds are intended to bring a subject under control by causing pain and rendering him unconscious. Depending on the

---

[a] Thus in a city where Negro males constitute 9% of the population, they have accounted for 75% of the deaths resulting from the use of chokeholds. In addition to his other allegations, Lyons alleged racial discrimination in violation of the Equal Protection Clause of the Fourteenth Amendment.

position of the officer's arm and the force applied, the victim's voluntary or involuntary reaction, and his state of health, an officer may inadvertently crush the victim's larynx, traches, or hyoid. The result may be either cardiac arrest or asphyxiation. An LAPD officer described the reaction of a person to being choked as "do[ing] the chicken," in reference apparently to the reactions of a chicken when its neck is wrung. The victim experiences extreme pain. His face turns blue as he is deprived of oxygen, he goes into spasmodic convulsions, his eyes roll back, his body wriggles, his feet kick up and down, and his arms move about wildly . . . .

The Court errs in suggesting that Lyons' prayer for injunctive relief in Court V of his first amended complaint concerns a policy that was not responsible for his injuries and that therefore could not support an award of damages . . . .

There is no basis for the Court's assertion that Lyons has failed to allege "that the City either orders or authorizes application of the chokeholds where there is no resistance or other provocation." . . .

CASE DISCUSSION

Lyons filed a complaint for damages, injunction, and declaratory relief in the United States District Court against the Los Angeles Police Department for using chokeholds. The district court found that the chokeholds violated Lyons constitutional rights and issued a preliminary injunction. The court of appeals affirmed. The United States Supreme Court reversed.

What interests did the Supreme Court balance in its decision? Does the Court favor law enforcement over individual rights? Result over process? What standards did the Court use to determine whether or not Lyons had a case against the Los Angeles Police Department? Do you think it is fair to require Lyons to show that he may suffer chokeholds again before he can ask for relief in court? What arguments does the dissent present to grant Lyons relief? Do you agree with the arguments? What, if any, remedies would you prescribe in this case? Explain.

INTERNAL AGENCY DISCIPLINE

The remedies for enforcing constitutional standards raise complicated issues. Formally, injured citizens can select from a broad range of means to protect them against injuries from government wrongdoing. Informally, however, the remedies are not so all-encompassing. Practically speaking, the exclusionary rule predominates as a remedy, but it protects only guilty persons. Obviously, innocent people have no need to challenge evidence against them. Plaintiffs have frequently sued the government and its agents for constitutional torts, but they rarely succeed in getting the damages or injunctions they seek. Prosecutors, judges, and defense attorneys are immune from civil suits. Prejudices against "unsavory" victims and hard-working police officers prevent jury awards in civil cases against law enforcement officers.

These shortcomings have led to heavier reliance on internal discipline. This remedy rests upon the confidence that the principles and practice of administrative rule making will reduce government misconduct. This very complex concept relies on the following core ideas. Police departments, prosecutors' offices, public defenders' offices, and even courts should state their policies and formulate written rules to implement those policies. The task of formulating rules should involve the broad participation of department or agency personnel particularly those such as patrol officers, assistant attorneys, and others who are mainly responsible for carrying the rules out day to day.

Once formulated, policy makers should put the rules into writing. To enforce them requires review, reward for compliance, and sanctions for violation. Rewards might include promotion and merit increases. Sanctions might include reprimand, counseling, suspension, and in extreme cases dismissal. Supporters of internal discipline believe that this combination of reward for compliance and sanction for violation can most effectively control government officials and, therefore, protect citizens against improper state intrusions and deprivations.

A recent Senate bill with respect to unlawful searches and seizures put this idea into legislative form. The bill provided:

> Section 2693. Sanctions Against Investigative or Law Enforcement Officers; Illegal Search and Seizure
>
> An investigative or law enforcement officer who conducts a search or seizure in violation of the United States Constitution shall be subject to appropriate discipline in the discretion of the Federal agency employing such officer, if that agency determines, after notice and hearing, that the officer conducted such search and seizure lacking a good faith belief that such search or seizure was constitutional.[39]

None of these altenatives to the exclusionary rule is widely practiced, leaving the rule the principal, though not wholly satisfactory, remedy for unconstitutional intrusions and deprivations.

≡ SUMMARY

Criminal law deals with private citizens who violate the criminal code. One aspect of the law of criminal procedure answers the question: What shall be the recourse of the private citizen when the government breaks the law? Several remedies are availiable to citizens who suffer injury from official misconduct. One group of remedies is directed against the criminal process. These include (1) excluding illegally seized evidence; (2) dismissing criminal cases against the victims of official lawbreaking; and (3) reversing convictions where tha government has made reversible errors.

Citizens injured by official lawwbreaking can slao sue the officer directly, the agency employing the officer, or the government unit with jurisdiction over the officer or agency. These suits might arise directly under the United States Constitution and state constitutions for violating constitutional rights. They might also stem from state tort actions or state statutes. Most are brought under § 1983 of the United States Code, or the Civil Rights Act, that gives citizens a right to sue for damages when states violate citizens' constitutional rights. Plaintiffs in private lawsuits can obtain either money damages or court orders (injunctions) prohibiting specific government action.

The government might also prosecute officers whose illegal conduct constitutes a crime. Illegal searches constitute burglary, breaking and entering, and criminal trespass in some instances. Illegal arrests, depending on the circumstances, constitute kidnapping or assault. Finally, agencies can impose internal disciplinary action including suspension and dismissal, against officers' misconduct.

QUESTIONS FOR REVIEW AND DISCUSSION

1. Define and state the purposes of the exclusionary rule.
2. Describe the major exceptions to the exclusionary rule.
3. Should evidence seized illegally by private citizens be admitted into court? Explain your answer.
4. Should the exclusionary rule be abolished? Give reasons for your answer.
5. What are the major remedies against improper conduct by prosecutors, judges, and defense counsel?
6. Define "person," "custom," and "policy" under the Civil Rights Act.
7. What requirements must plaintiffs in § 1983 actions meet to recover against municipalities? against individual officers?
8. Explain the difference between damages and injunctions.
9. In addition to § 1983 actions, what other sources of civil remedies are available to individuals who suffer injuries as a result of government misconduct?
10. Who should pay for damages the government causes to citizens? the individual officers? the agencies who employ them? the municipality? Why should taxpayers pay for official wrongdoing?
11. What interests do remedies against official wrongdoing promote? Do process remedies promote the same ionterests as damages? as injunctions? Explain.
12. Explain internal discipline. Is it a "better" alternative to official wrongdoing than the exclusionary rule? than tort actions? Why? Why not?

NOTES

1. Jon O. Newman, "Suing the Lawbreakers: Proposals to Strengthen the Section 1983 Damage Remedy for Law Enforcers' Misconduct," *The Yale Law Journal* 87 (1978):447–67.

2. *Mapp v. Ohio*, 367 U. S. 643, 81 S. Ct. 1684, 6 L. Ed. 2d 1081 (1961); *Miranda v. Arizona*, 384 U.S. 436 86 S. Ct. 1602, 16 L. Ed. 2d 694 (1966);*United States v. Wade*, 388 U.S. 218, 87 S. Ct.1926, 18 L. Ed. 2d 1149 (1967); *Gelbard v. United States*, 408 U.S. 41, 92 S. Ct. 2357, 33 L. Ed. 2d 179 (1972); *United States v. Caceres*, 440 U.S. 741, 99 S. Ct. 1465, 59 L. Ed. 2d 733 (1979).

3. Milton A. Loewenthal, "Evaluating the Exclusionary Rule in Search and Seizure," University of Missouri at Knasas City Law Review 49 (1980):24–40.

4. 232 U.S. 383, 34 S. Ct. 341, 58 L. Ed. 652 (1914).

5. 251 U.S. 385, 391, 40 S. Ct. 182, 64 L. Ed. 319 (1920).

6. 338 U.S. 25, 69 S. Ct. 1359, 93 L. Ed. 1782 (1949).

7. *Walder v. United States*, 347 U.S. 62, 74 S. Ct. 354, 98 L. Ed. 503 (1954); also to the same effect, *Harris v. New York*, 401 U.S. 222, 91 S. Ct. 643, 28 L. Ed. 2d 1 (1971); *United States v. Hinckley*, 672 F.2d 115 (D.C. Cir. 1982).

8. 371 U.S. 471, 83 S. Ct. 407, 9 L. Ed. 2d 441 (1963).

9. *Nardone v. United states*, 308 U.S. 338, 60 S. Ct. 266, 84 L. Ed. 307 (1939) and *Wong Sun v. United States*, 371 U.S. 471, 83 S. Ct. 407, 9 L. Ed. 2d 441 (1963) (tainted fruit); *Segura v. United States*, 468 U.S. 796, 104 S. Ct. 3380, 82 L. Ed. 2d 599 (1984).

10. *Nix v. Williams*, 467 U.S. 431, 104 S. Ct. 2501, 81 L. Ed. 2d 377 (1984).

11. See also, Ashdown, "Good Faith, The Exclusionary Remedy, and Rule-Oriented Adjudication in the Criminal Process," *William and Mary Law Review* 24 (1983):335; Ball, "Good Faith and the Fourth Amendment: The 'Reasonable' Exception to the Exclusionary Rule," *Journal of Criminal Law and Criminology* 69(1978):635; Yale Kamisar, "Gates, 'Probable Cause,' 'Good Faith,' and Beyond," *Iowa Law Review* 69(1984):551; Schlag, "Assaults on the Exclusionary Rule: Good Faith, Limitations and Damage Remedies," *Journal of Criminal Law and Criminology* 73(1982):875.

12. *Stringer v. State*, 477 So.2d 1335 (Miss. 1985).

13. *Coolidge v. New Hampshire*, 403 U.S. 443, 91 S. Ct. 2022, 29 L. Ed. 2d 564 (1971) (wife was not an agent of the state, hence evidence she seized and gave to the police not protected by Fourth Amendment, plurality opinion).

14. *Walter v. United States*, 447 U.S. 649, 100 S. Ct. 2395, 65 L. Ed. 2d 410 (1980).

15. *United States v. Jacobsen*, 466 U.S. 109, 104 S. Ct. 1652, 80 L. Ed. 2d 85 (1984).

16. American Law Institute,Model Code of Pre-Arraignment Procedure, Section 290.1(5).

17. *Rakas v. Illinois*, 439 U.S. 128, 99 S. Ct. 421, 58 L. Ed. 2d 387 (1978); *United States v. Jeffers*, 342 U.S. 48, 72 S. Ct. 93, 96 L. Ed. 59 (1951); *Rawlings v. Kentucky*, 448 U.S. 98 , 100 S. Ct. 2556, 65 L. Ed. 2d 633 (1980).

18. *Board of Commissioners v. Backus*, 29 How. Pr. 33, 42 (1864).

19. *People v. Mills*, 178 N.Y. 274, 70 N.E. 786, 791 (1904).

20. Paul Marcus, "The Development of Entrapment Law," *Wayne Law Review* 33 (1986):5.

21. Jonathan C. Carlson, "The Act Requirement and the Foundations of the Entrapment Defense," *Virginia Law Review* 73(1987):1011.

22. *United States v. Jenrette* , 744 F. 2d 817 (D.C.Cir.1984) (one of the Abscam cases); "Gershman, Abscam, the Judiciary and the Ethics of Entrapment," *Yale Law Journal* 1565, 91(1982):1565 (history of Abscam); L. Tiffany et. al., *Detection of Crime* (Boston: Little, Brown, and Co., 1967) (quote defining encouragement).

23. LaFave and Israel, *Criminal* Procedure, 1:412–13.

24. *Sherman v. United States*, 356 U.S. 369, 78 S. Ct. 819, 2 L. Ed. 2d 848 (1958).

25. American Law Institute, *Model Penal Code and Commentaries* (Philadelphia: American Law Institute, 1985) Part I, 1:411–12, 406–7.

26. *People v. Barraza*, 23 Cal. 3d 675, 153 Cal. Rptr. 459, 591 P.2d 947 (1979).

27. *United States v. Simpson*, 813 F. 2d 1462 (9thCir.1987).

28. Noted in ibid.

29. *United States v. Struyf*, 701 F.2d 875 (11th Cir.1983).

30. *People v. Toler*, 26 Ill. 2d 100, 185 N.E.2d 874 (1962).

31. *Cruz v. State*, 465 So.2d 516 (Fla.1985).

32. *New York Times*, "Supreme Court Bars Disclosure of F.B.I. Files," March 23, 1989,p.12.

33. 42 U.S.C. A. § 1983 (1976).

34. *Pierson v. Ray*, 386 U.S. 547, 87 S. Ct. 1213, 18 L. Ed.2d 288 (1967); *Stadium Films, Inc. v. Baillargeon*, 542 F.2d 577 (1st Cir. 1976); *Jenkins v. Averett*, 424 F.2d 1228 (4th Cir. 1970).

35. Anthony Amsterdam, "Perspectives on the Fourth Amendment," *Minnesota Law Review* 58(1974):430.

36. *Imbler v. Pachtman*, 424 U.S. 409, 96 S. Ct. 984, 47 L. Ed.2d 128 (1976); *Scheuer v. Rhodes*, 416 U.S. 232, 94 S. Ct. 1683, 40 L. Ed.2d 90 (1974); *Minns v. Paul*, 542 F.2d 899 (4th Cir. 1976).

37. S.751, 97th Cong., 1st Sess. (1981).

38. Caleb Foote, "Tort Remedies for Police Violations of Individual Rights," *Min.:esota Law Review* 39(1955):493; Jon O. Newman, "Suing the Lawbreakers: Proposals to Strengthen the Section 1983 Damage Remedy for Law Enforcers' Misconduct," *Yale Law Journal* 87(1978):447–67.

39. S.751, 97th Cong., 1st Sess. (1981).

Chapter Four

Initial Police-Citizen Contacts: Stop and Frisk

CHAPTER OUTLINE

CHAPTER MAIN POINTS

1. Police investigative activities range across a broad spectrum from brief street contacts to full-body searches, arrests, and custodial interrogation.

2. Stop-and-frisk law formalizes police-initiated contacts with citizens on the street.

3. The law governing stops balances the interest of effective law enforcement, the rule of law, respect for human dignity, impartial law enforcement, and public confidence in the law.

4. Stops are street detentions for the purpose of investigating suspicious circumstances and preventing, interrupting, or investigating ongoing or past criminal conduct.

5. Stops are seizures within the meaning of the Fourth Amendment.

6. Frisks are outer-clothing patdowns justified solely to protect law enforcement officers investigating crimes.

7. Frisks constitute searches within the meaning of the Fourth Amendment.

8. Reasonable suspicion constitutes the quantum of proof that justifies stops and frisks; hunch or mere suspicion does not suffice.

CHAPTER KEY TERMS

accusatory stage the period when investigation focuses on a particular suspect or suspects

amicus curiae a participant other than the parties to a law suit

articulable facts the few specific facts that constitute the quantum of proof required to support a stop

direct information facts that officers know directly through sight, touch, smell, or hearing

frisk an outer-clothing patdown for weapons

hearsay information derived from third persons; not known firsthand by the person providing it

probable cause facts, apparent facts, or circumstances that would lead a reasonable person to conclude that a crime *has* been, *is* being, or *is* about to be committed

reasonable suspicion facts, apparent facts, or circumstances that would lead a reasonable person to believe that a crime *may* have been, *may* be about to be, or *may* be in the process of being committed

reasonableness stop standard stop defined by whether a reasonable person would believe he or she was not free to leave

stop a brief, on-the-spot detention to freeze a suspicious situation to determine whether to arrest, investigate further, or terminate further action

---

≡ POLICE INVESTIGATIVE ACTIVITIES

Amendment IV, United States Constitution

The right of the people to be secure in their persons, houses, papers, and effects, against unreasonable searches and seizures, shall not be violated, and no warrants shall issue, but upon probable cause, supported by oath or affirmation, and particularly describing the place to be searched, and the persons or things to be seized.

Amendment V, United States Constitution

No person . . . shall be compelled in any criminal case to be a witness against himself, nor be deprived of life, liberty, or property, without due process of law. . . .

Amendment VI, United States Constitution

In all criminal prosecutions, the accused shall . . . have the assistance of counsel for his defense.

The Fourth, Fifth, and Sixth Amendments govern most police investigative activities, from brief contacts with citizens on the street, to full-body searches, arrests, and custodial interrogation. Search and seizure covers a broad rubric of intrusions and deprivations, from brief street stops to detention in jail, from surveillance and protective patdowns to strip and body-cavity searches. Police questioning ranges from engaging citizens on the street in voluntary conversations that have no protection under the Fifth Amendment, to subjecting suspects in station houses to intensive interrogations that may continue for hours. Police investigation also encompasses electronic surveillance and eavesdropping, identification procedures such as lineups, blood alcohol tests, and surgical intrusions into the body in search of evidence. At no other stage of the criminal process are the gradations in degree of intrusion and deprivation and quantum of proof or objective foundations required to support them more refined than in the period from initial investigation to the point when police turn cases over to prosecutors.

This and the following three chapters discuss these gradations in several parts. This chapter looks at stop and frisk, the broad but superficial range of initial contacts between citizens and the police on the street before the police take suspects into custody. Chapter 5 analyzes the greater deprivations that attend on arrest. At arrest, investigation becomes accusation, that is, it focuses on specific suspects. Most activity in the **accusatory stage**—when general investigation shifts to a named suspect or suspects—takes place in police stations, jails, and lawyers' offices. Chapter 6 analyzes the full searches that accompany and follow arrest as well as those that may occur prior to arrest. Chapter 7 focuses on identification and interrogation.

Chronological considerations dictate discussing stop and frisk prior to arrests, searches and seizures, identification, and interrogation. Street encounters are the earliest point when official action to enforce the criminal law takes place. Arrests, searches, seizures of physical evidence, and interrogation do not always follow each other in strict chronological order. Some searches precede arrest while others, such as the searches incident to arrest, follow it. Prolonged interrogation usually follows arrest, but not always; identification may well concur with arrest. In addition, stops and frisks take place on the street before any official documentation that initiates the criminal process: they are the most superficial intrusions and deprivations, and they require the least factual foundation to justify them. Stops and frisks represent the beginning of a progression from less intrusive, informal street contacts requiring a minimal objective foundation, to more intrusive, police-station practices demanding more facts to support them.

═══ HISTORY OF STOP-AND-FRISK LAW

The power to stop and question suspicious persons is as old as the common law of England. Ancient statutes and court decisions empowered constables to detain "suspicious nightwalkers" and hold them until morning in order to investigate their suspicious behavior. Until twenty-five years ago, police-initiated contacts with citizens on the street were not controversial; they were left to the officers' discretion. During the 1960s, the police discretionary power to stop and frisk became a matter of national concern. The due process revolution discussed in chapter 2 led some reformers to call for formally extending constitutional protections to all official-citizen contacts, and subjecting those encounters to review by the courts. This extension caused—and still causes—bitter controversy. The police and their supporters argue that their expertise and professional independence require that discretion, not formal rules, govern their contacts with citizens on the street. Civil libertarians, on the other hand, maintain that citizens need, and a free society requires, that the Constitution follow citizens wherever they go. Minorities and individuals on the "fringes of respectable society" who are most vulnerable to official abuse of power particularly need these protections.[1]

For complex reasons not yet sorted out, the courts, led by the United States Supreme Court, formalized stop and frisk during the 1960s. Despite bitter opposition, and modest modification over the past decade or so, this formalization has remained intact. What happens in the police station—until the 1960s another sanctuary from formal judicial interference—has also come under constitutional protection. The formalization of police investigative activities follows a history that began in the seventeenth century. For example, the privilege against self-incrimination, originally intended to protect defendants from testifying at their trials, was gradually extended to pretrial proceedings, until the 1960s when the Supreme Court guaranteed it in the police stations and other custodial settings. (See chap. 7.) The Fourth Amendment search-and-seizure clause did not apply to street contacts amounting to less than arrests and full-body searches until the Supreme Court adopted a balancing approach to intrusions and deprivations. In 1968, the Supreme Court extended the search-and-seizure clause to protect citizen-police street encounters. (See *Terry v. Ohio,* following.)[2]

THE BALANCING APPROACH TO STOP-AND-FRISK LAW

Although Supreme Court supervision of police practices has placed some restrictions on conduct permitted during street encounters, the Court has neither removed such conduct entirely from the realm of discretion, nor put it exclusively under the formal requirements of the Constitution. The United States Supreme Court has made an effort—always difficult, sometimes unclear, and never satisfactory to conservatives or liberals—to balance the need for discretion and individual police judgment in investigating crime against the requirement that citizens remain free from unreasonable searches and seizures. The Court looks to the totality of the circumstances of individual cases to determine whether specific law enforcement actions have "reasonably" balanced the degree of intrusion and deprivation against citizens' privacy and freedom against society's legitimate interest in preventing and detecting crime.

Stop-and-frisk law brings several formal and informal interests into relief:

1. obtaining accurate and sufficient facts to support criminal investigation on the street;
2. protecting citizens against unwarranted or discriminatory invasions of privacy and other indignities in public places;
3. preserving and extending the rule of law to police encounters with citizens on the street;
4. satisfying organizational interests in efficient, economical, and harmonious police operations; and
5. reducing police frustration with interference in their job, sometimes called "handcuffing the police."[3]

Hence, the Court tries to reconcile the formal constitutional guarantees of privacy and liberty and the informal practical needs to protect society from street criminals, run organizations smoothly, and satisfy personal and professional objectives.[4]

Stop and frisk grew out of the problems police face in preventing and detecting crime in the nation's large cities. Most police contacts with citizens on the street in criminal investigation arise when the police observe, or citizens report, suspicious behavior by people whom they do not know and will probably never see again, unless they approach them. However, most suspicious behavior they see does not constitute

Chapter 4   *Initial Police-Citizen Contacts: Stop and Frisk*   **163**

probable cause to arrest. For example, if officers observe two men peer in a shop window, turn as if to see if anyone is watching them, and continue this activity for about five minutes, the police do not have probable cause, the quantum of proof required to arrest the two men. Should the police do nothing? continue to watch the two men? briefly detain them and pat them down for weapons? arrest them, search them, and take them to police station? The Fourth Amendment lends itself to at least three plausible interpretations concerning this and similar situations: (1) The Fourth Amendment protects only full searches and arrests; hence, police discretion, not the Fourth Amendment, governs brief street contacts. (2) Even brief street contacts and patdowns constitute arrests and searches; therefore, to conduct them requires probable cause. (3) Brief stops and outer clothing "frisks" constitute lesser searches and seizures than full-body searches and arrests; accordingly, they are "reasonable" if, in the particular case, the government interest in law enforcement outweighs the intrusion on individual privacy and liberty.[5]

If the police can take no action without probable cause, as in alternative (2), criminal law enforcement suffers because the police will likely never see the suspects again. If the Constitution does not apply to street encounters, as in alternative (1), then citizens on the street are subject to the will of the police alone. The Supreme Court resolved this dilemma by choosing alternative (3), a balancing approach to searches and seizures. According to this approach, the police have the authority to "freeze" suspicious episodes briefly in order to determine whether criminal activity is afoot, and they must have the power to protect themselves while doing so. However, they cannot intrude into citizens' privacy and freedom on hunch or whim. They need *some* facts—not so many as would add up to probable cause—but enough to permit a disinterested third party to independently assess the foundation for the "freeze" later.[6]

The balancing approach to reasonableness under the Fourth Amendment requires courts to weigh the degree of intrusion against the need to deter and detect crime. It is reasonable to freeze a suspicious situation briefly on the basis of a few **articulable facts** (moving away at the sight of police, loitering, pacing up and down) to determine if crime really is in the offing. It is also reasonable to pat down suspects on articulable facts that the latter might be armed.[7]

Stops and frisks are less intrusive than arrests and full searches; they are nonetheless important because they affect more citizens. Police stop, question, and frisk more people than they arrest, search, and take to the station and detail in jail. Street encounters influence public opinion about the police. Few people see the inside of a police station but many witness citizen encounters with the police on the street, particularly in congested "high street crime" neighborhoods in large cities.[8]

Even in high-street-crime neighborhoods, most citizens obey the law and depend upon and want the police to protect them from crimes. Obviously, citizens in high-street-crime neighborhoods need police protection more than citizens in "respectable" suburbs. Law-abiding citizens in high-street-crime districts form lasting opinions about the police from these street encounters. Stop-and-frisk raises the following critical issues that do not have clear answers:

1. how formalized the early investigative stages of the criminal process ought to be;
2. what unreasonable search and seizure means under the Constitution;
3. how much the Supreme Court ought to supervise the day-to-day activities of police on the street;
4. how much discretion police officers need to protect public safety;
5. the degree of confidence and respect the public has for the police;

6. what constitutes discriminatory law enforcement and harassment;

7. how much freedom and privacy citizens, even suspicious ones, have from government interference;

8. how to maintain police professionalism and morale; and

9. should the power to stop and frisk apply to all crimes or only to dangerous crimes against persons.

The United States Supreme Court had all these questions in mind in 1968, when it rendered its landmark decision, *Terry v. Ohio*.

CASE

Was it reasonable to stop and frisk Terry?

Terry v. Ohio

392 U.S. 1, 88 S.Ct. 1868, 20 L.Ed.2d 889 (1968)

FACTS

. . . Officer McFadden testified that while he was patrolling in plain clothes in downtown Cleveland at approximately 2:30 in the afternoon, . . . his attention was attracted by two men, Chilton and Terry, standing on the corner of Huron Road and Euclid Avenue. He had never seen the two men before, and he was unable to say precisely what first drew his eye to them. However, he testified that he had been a policeman for 39 years and a detective for 35 and that he had been assigned to patrol this vicinity of downtown Cleveland for shoplifters and pickpockets for 30 years. He explained that he had developed routine habits of observation over the years and that he would "stand and watch people or walk and watch people at many intervals of the day." He added: "Now, in this case when I looked over they didn't look right to me at the time."

His interest aroused, Officer McFadden took up a post of observation in the entrance to a store 300 to 400 feet away from the two men. "I get more purpose to watch them when I seen their movements," he testified. He saw one of the men leave the other one and walk southwest on Huron Road, past some stores. The man paused for a moment and looked in a store window, then walked on a short distance, turned around and walked back toward the corner, pausing once again to look in the same store window. He rejoined his companion at the corner, and the two conferred briefly. Then the second man went through the same series of motions, strolling down Huron Road, looking in the same window, walking on a short distance, turning back, peering in the store window again, and returning to confer with the first man at the corner. The two men repeated this ritual alternately between five and six times apiece—in all, roughly a dozen trips. At one point, while the two were standing together on the corner, a third man approached them and engaged them briefly in conversation. This man then left the two others and walked west on Euclid Avenue. Chilton and Terry resumed their measured pacing, peering, and conferring. After this had gone on for 10 to 12 minutes, the two men walked off together, heading west on Euclid Avenue, following the path taken earlier by the third man.

By this time Officer McFadden had become thoroughly suspicious. He testified that after observing their elaborately casual and oft-repeated reconnaissance of the store window on Huron Road, he suspected the two men of "casing a job, a stick-up," and that he considered it his duty as a police officer to investigate further. He added that he feared "they may have a gun." Thus, Officer McFadden followed Chilton and Terry and saw them stop in front of Zucker's store to talk to the same man who had conferred with them earlier on the street corner. Deciding that the situation was ripe for action, Officer McFadden approached the three men, identified himself as a police officer and asked for their names. At this point his knowledge was confined to what he had observed. He was not acquainted with any of the men by name or by sight, and he had received no information concerning them from any other source. When the men "mumbled something" in response to his inquiries, Officer McFadden grabbed petitioner Terry, spun him around so that they were facing the other two, with Terry between McFadden and the others, and patted down the outside of his clothing. In the left breast pocket of Terry's overcoat Officer McFadden felt a piston. . . . Officer McFadden seized [Terry's] gun, asked the proprietor of the store to call a police wagon, and took all three men to the station, where Chilton and Terry were formally charged with carrying concealed weapons. . . .

After the court denied [Terry's] motion to suppress [the gun as evidence], Terry waived jury trial and pleaded not guilty. The court adjudged him guilty, and the Court of Appeals for the Eighth Judicial District, Cuyahoga County, affirmed. The Supreme Court of Ohio dismissed [his] appeal. . . . We granted certiorari. . . . We affirm the conviction.

OPINION

Mr. Chief Justice Warren delivered the opinion of the Court. . . .

It is frequently argued that in dealing with the rapidly unfolding and often dangerous situations on city streets the police are in need of an escalating set of flexible responses, graduated in relation to the amount of information they possess. . . . On the other side the argument is made that the authority of the police must be strictly circumscribed by the law of arrest and search as it has developed to date in the traditional jurisprudence of the Fourth Amendment. . . .

We consider first the nature and extent of the governmental interests involved. One general interest is of course that of effective crime prevention and detection. . . . It was this legitimate investigative function Officer McFadden was discharging when he decided to approach petitioner and his companions. He had observed Terry, Chilton, and Katz go through a series of acts, each of them perhaps innocent in itself, but which taken together warranted further investigation. There is nothing unusual about two men standing together on a street corner, perhaps waiting for someone. Nor is there anything suspicious about people in such circumstances strolling up and down the street, singly or in pairs. Store windows, moreover, are made to be looked in. But the story is quite different where, as here, two men hover about a street corner for an extended period of time, at the end of which it becomes apparent that they are not waiting for anyone or anything; where these men pace alternately along an identical route, pausing to stare in the same store window roughly 24 times; where each completion of this route is followed immediately by a conference between the two men on the corner; where they are joined in one of these conferences by a third man who leaves swiftly; and where the two men finally follow the third man and rejoin him a couple of blocks away. It would have been poor police work indeed for an officer of 30 years' experience in the detection of thievery from stores in this same neighborhood to have failed to investigate this behavior further. . . .

We must still consider, however, the nature and quality of the intrusion on individual rights which must be accepted if police officers are to be conceded the right to search for weapons in situations where probable cause to arrest for crime is lacking. Even a limited search of the outer clothing for weapons constitutes a severe, though brief, intrusion upon cherished personal security, and it must surely be an annoying, frightening, and perhaps humiliating experience. . . .

[T]here must be a narrowly drawn authority to permit a reasonable search for weapons for the protection of the police officer, where he has reason to believe that he is dealing with an armed and dangerous individual, regardless of whether he has probable cause to arrest the individual for a crime. . . .

McFadden had observed Terry, together with Chilton and another man, acting in a manner he took to be preface to a ''stick-up.'' We think on the facts and circumstances Officer McFadden detailed before the trial judge a reasonably prudent man would have been warranted in believing petitioner was armed and thus presented a threat to the officer's safety while he was investigating his suspicious behavior. The actions of Terry and Chilton were consistent with McFadden's hypothesis that these men were contemplating a daylight robbery—which, it is reasonable to assume, would be likely to involve the use of weapons. . . .

We conclude that the revolver seized from Terry was properly admitted in evidence against him. At the time he seized petitioner and searched him for weapons, Officer McFadden had reasonable grounds to believe that petitioner was armed and dangerous, and it was necessary for the protection of himself and others to take swift measures to discover the true facts and neutralize the threat of harm if it materialized. The policeman carefully restricted his search to what was appropriate to the discovery of the particular items which he sought. Each case of this sort will, of course, have to be decided on its own facts. We merely hold today that where a police officer observes unusual conduct which leads him reasonably to conclude in light of his experience that criminal activity may be afoot and that the persons with whom he is dealing may be armed and presently dangerous, where in the course of investigating this behavior he identifies himself as a policeman and makes reasonable inquiries, and where nothing in the initial stages of the encounter serves to dispel his reasonable fear for his own or others' safety, he is entitled for the protection of himself and others in the area to conduct a carefully limited search of the outer clothing of such persons in an attempt to discover weapons which might be used to assault him. Such a search is a reasonable search under the Fourth Amendment, and any weapons seized may be properly introduced in evidence against the person from whom they were taken. Affirmed.

[Justices White, Harlan, and Black's concurring opinions are omitted.]

Mr. Justice Douglas, dissenting.

The infringement on personal liberty of any "seizure" of a person can only be "reasonable" under the Fourth Amendment if we require the police to possess "probable cause" before they seize him. Only that line draws a meaningful distinction between an officer's mere inkling and the presence of facts within the officer's personal knowledge which would convince a reasonable man that the person seized has committed, is committing, or is about to commit a particular crime. . . .

There have been powerful hydraulic pressures throughout our history that bear heavily on the Court to water down constitutional guarantees and give the police the upper hand. That hydraulic pressure has probably never been greater than it is today.

Yet if the individual is no longer to be sovereign, if the police can pick him up whenever they do not like the cut of his jib, if they can "seize" and "search" him in their discretion, we enter a new regime. The decision to enter it should be made only after a full debate by the people of this country.

CASE DISCUSSION

Terry was convicted of carrying a concealed weapon and sentenced to one to three years in prison. Following the denial of a pretrial motion to suppress the gun as evidence, the prosecution introduced two revolvers and bullets seized from Terry and his co-defendant. Terry waived jury trial and pleaded not guilty. The court convicted him, and the court of appeals affirmed. The Supreme Court of Ohio dismissed Terry's appeal on the ground that no "substantial constitutional question" was involved. The United States Supreme Court granted *certiorari* and affirmed the conviction because the stop and frisk did not violate the Fourth Amendment.

Identify the specific intrusions and deprivations to which Officer McFadden subjected Terry and his cohorts. What were the "articulable facts" upon which Officer McFadden based his stop? his frisk? What interests did the Court specifically refer to protecting in reaching its decision to formalize stops and frisks? Do you agree with the Court's evaluation of these interests? Which ones do you consider most important? Why? Consider the following excerpt from the amicus curiae brief filed in *Terry*:

"In the litigation now before the Court—as is usual in cases where police practices are challenged—two parties essentially are represented. Law enforcement officials, legal representatives of their respective States, ask the Court to broaden police powers, and thereby to sustain what has proved to be a 'good pinch.' Criminal defendants caught with the goods through what in retrospect appears to be at least shrewd and successful (albeit constitutionally questionable) police work ask the Court to declare that work illegal and to reverse their convictions. Other parties intimately affected by the issues before the Court are not represented. The many thousands of our citizens who have been or may be stopped and frisked yearly, only to be released when the police find them innocent of any crime, are not represented. The records of their cases are not before the Court and cannot be brought here. Yet it is they, far more than those charged with crime, who will bear the consequences of the rules of constitutional law which this Court establishes. The determination of the quantum of 'belief' or 'suspicion' required to justify the exercise of intrusive police authority is precisely the determination of how far afield from instances of obvious guilt the authority stretches. To lower that quantum is to broaden the police net and, concomitantly, to increase the number (and probably the proportion) of innocent people caught up in it. The innocent are those this Court will never see.'' What interests does this brief consider most important? law enforcement? defendants' rights? accurate results? equality of treatment? control of the police and procedural regularity?

≡ STOP

Definition of Stop

Since *Terry v. Ohio*, the framework for analyzing encounters with citizens has placed such encounters into three categories: *(1) contacts* not falling within the scope of the Fourth Amendment, or ''communication between police and citizens involving no coercion or detention''; (2) *stops,* or brief ''seizures,'' such as that in *Terry,* that require reasonable suspicion to support them; and (3) and full-scale *arrests* that demand probable cause to justify them. There are no bright lines that divide either police-citizen contacts from police-initiated stops or stops from arrests. Nor is there a bright line between frisks or weapons' patdowns and full searches. They are all actions on a continuum between voluntary encounters and significant involuntary intrusions and deprivations. The distinctions are, nonetheless, significant because voluntary encounters are not seizures within the meaning of the Fourth Amendment. Hence, the police need not have, nor need they later demonstrate to a magistrate that they had, ''reasonable grounds''—the quantum of proof required for a stop—to justify approaching the citizen in question.[9]

Decision Point

Consider the following examples. Applying the definitions above, which are contacts? stops? arrests?

1. A citizen approaches a police officer and says, ''I saw a man run out of that building with a knife dripping blood.''

2. Police officers approach a citizen and ask, "Did you see a man with a knife run out of that building?"

3. Police approach a citizen and ask, "Did you just leave that building?"

4. Police see a man run out of a building where they had just heard screams. They shout at the man, "Hey, we want to talk to you!"

5. Police see the same man and say, "Stop where you are! We want to ask you some questions."

6. Police see the same man. As he runs by, the officers grab him and, holding on to him, ask, "What's your name? What are you doing here?" When he shows them his ID and says he was visiting a friend, they say, "We may call you later."

7. Police see the same man and order him to get into the squad car where they ask him for ID and an explanation of why he was in the building.

8. Police see the same man and order him to get in the car where one officer sits with him for about half an hour while another officer checks out the building.

9. Police see the same man six blocks from the building. They stop him, drive him to the building, and ask, "Do you know anyone in that building? Did you just leave that building?"

10. Police see the same man. They approach him and inform him, "We're going to take you down to the station to ask you some questions." They drive him there, ask him for ID and why he was in the building, and release him. The whole episode took forty-five minutes.

11. Police officers hear screams from a building. They see a man running away from the building; when he sees the police officers, he turns and runs in the opposite direction.

12. Police smell marijuana in a hotel hall near a specific room. They enter the room where the smell is even stronger. Several people are in the room, but the officers see no one smoking marijuana.

13. Police see a man walking toward them down a street at 2:00 a.m. in a neighborhood with a high burglary rate. The man is carrying a large laundry bag that appears full. When he sees the police officers, he turns, crosses the street, and walks in the opposite direction.

14. They see the same man do the same thing at 2:00 p.m.

15. Police see two men peering in a jewelry store window at 1:00 p.m. in an area with a high robbery rate. The men walk on when they see the police.

16. An informant who has provided the police with accurate information concerning drug offenses in the past informs the police that a woman has heroin in her left jacket pocket.

17. An anonymous caller tells the police that a young, white male with blond hair and blue eyes, wearing blue jeans, a yellow jacket, and white Reebok shoes is standing on a street corner near a group of children. The caller tells the police that the youth has a gun in his jacket pocket. The police go to the scene; the youth is there but they see neither a gun nor a bulge in his jacket.

Reasonableness Stop Standard

Until recently, the definition of what constitutes a stop was vague. Three approaches are possible. First, if *suspects believe* they are not free to go, then they are "stopped" for Fourth Amendment purposes. Second, if *officers intend* to detain suspects, even if suspects do not know the officers' intentions, then the officers have stopped the suspects. Third, despite the officers' intentions and the suspects' beliefs, if *reasonable persons* under the same circumstances would believe they are not free to leave, then the officers have stopped them. The Supreme Court has adopted this **reasonableness stop standard.** The standard is easier stated than applied. The Supreme Court considers three factors in applying the reasonableness standard: (1) the duration of the stop; (2) the intensity of the intrusion; and (3) whether the officers move the suspect from the scene of investigation. In *Terry v. Ohio,* the Court had no difficulty defining the contact as a stop because Officer McFadden actually grabbed Terry and spun him around. Due to the physical force, it was reasonable for Terry to believe that he was not free to go. Other cases, such as *United States v. Mendenhall,* are not so easily resolved.[10]

CASE

Was it reasonable to believe she was free to leave?

United States v. Mendenhall

446 U.S. 544, 100 S.Ct. 1870, 64 L.Ed.2d 497 (1980)

FACTS

. . . [Mendenhall] arrived at the Detroit Metropolitan Airport on a commercial airline flight from Los Angeles early in the morning on February 10, 1976. As she disembarked from the airplane, she was observed by two agents of the DEA, who were present at the airport for the purpose of detecting unlawful traffic of narcotics. After observing the respondent's conduct, which appeared to the agents to be characteristic of persons unlawfully carrying narcotics,[a] the agents approached her as she was walking through the concourse, identified themselves as federal agents, and asked to see her identification and airline ticket. The respondent produced her driver's license, which was in the name of Sylvia Mendenhall, and, in answer to a question of one of the agents, stated that she resided at the address appearing on the license. The airline ticket was issued in the name of "Annette Ford." When

---

[a]The agent testified that the respondent's behavior fit the so-called "drug courier profile"—an informally compiled abstract of characteristics thought typical of persons carrying illicit drugs. In this case the agents thought it relevant that (1) the respondent was arriving on a flight from Los Angeles, a city believed by the agents to be a place of origin for much of the heroin brought to Detroit; (2) the respondent was the last person to leave the plane, "appeared to be very nervous," and "completely scanned the whole area where [the agents] were standing"; (3) after leaving the plane the respondent proceeded past the baggage area without claiming any luggage; and (4) the respondent changed airlines for her flight out of Detroit.

asked why the ticket bore a name different from her own, the respondent stated that she "just felt like using that name." In response to a further question, the respondent indicated that she had been in California only two days. Agent Anderson then specifically identified himself as a federal narcotics agent and, according to his testimony, the respondent "became quite shaken, extremely nervous. She had a hard time speaking."

After returning the airline ticket and driver's license to her, Agent Anderson asked the respondent if she would accompany him to the airport DEA office for further questions. She did so, although the record does not indicate a verbal response to the request. The office, which was located up one flight of stairs about 50 feet from where the respondent had first been approached, consisted of a reception area adjoined by three other rooms. At the office the agent asked the respondent if she would allow a search of her person and handbag and told her she had the right to decline the search if she desired. She responded: "Go ahead." She then handed Agent Anderson her purse, which contained a receipt for an airline ticket that had been issued to "F. Bush" three days earlier for a flight from Pittsburgh through Chicago to Los Angeles. The agent asked whether this was the ticket she had used for her flight to California, and the respondent stated that it was. . . .

The policewoman explained that the search would require that the respondent remove her clothing. The respondent stated that she had a plane to catch and was assured by the policewoman that if she was carrying no narcotics, there would be no problem. The respondent then began to disrobe without further comment. As the respondent removed her clothing, she took from her undergarments two small packages, one of which appeared to contain heroin, and handed both to the policewoman. The agents then arrested the respondent for possessing heroin.

It was on the basis of this evidence that the District Court denied the respondent's motion to suppress. . . .

OPINION

Mr. Justice Stewart announced the judgment of the Court and delivered an opinion, in which Mr. Justice Rehnquist joined.

The Fourth Amendment provides that "the right of the people to be secure in their persons, houses, papers, and effects, against unreasonable search and seizures, shall not be violated. . . ." There is no question in this case that the respondent possessed this constitutional right of personal security as she walked through the Detroit Airport, for "the Fourth Amendment protects people, not places." . . . Here the government concedes that its agents had neither a warrant nor probable cause to believe that the respondent was carrying narcotics. . . .

We conclude that a person has been "seized" within the meaning of the Fourth Amendment only if, in view of all of the circumstances surrounding the incident, a reasonable person would have believed that he was not free to leave. Examples of circumstances that might indicate a seizure, even where the person did not attempt to leave, would be the threatening presence of several officers, the display of a weapon by an officer, some physical touching of the person of the citizen, or the use of language or tone of voice indicating the compliance with the officer's request might be compelled. . . .

On the facts of this case, no "seizure" of the respondent occurred. The events took place in the public concourse. The agents wore no uniforms and displayed no weapons. They did not summon the respondent to their presence, but instead approached her and identified themselves as federal agents. They requested, but did not demand to see the respondent's identification and ticket. Such conduct, without more, did not amount to an intrusion upon any constitutionally protected interest. . . .

Our conclusion that no seizure occurred is not affected by the fact that the respondent was not expressly told by the agents that she was free to decline to cooperate with their inquiry, for the voluntariness of her responses does not depend upon her having been so informed. . . .

Although we have concluded that the initial encounter between the DEA agents and the respondent on the concourse at the Detroit Airport did not constitute an unlawful seizure, it is still arguable that the respondent's Fourth Amendment protections were violated when she went from the concourse to the DEA office. . . .

The Government's evidence showed that the respondent was not told that she had to go to the office, but was simply asked if she would accompany the officers. There were neither threats nor any show of force. The respondent had been questioned only briefly, and her ticket and identification were returned to her before she was asked to accompany the officers.

On the other hand, it is argued that the incident would reasonably have appeared coercive to the respondent, who was 22 years old and had not been graduated from high school. It is additionally suggested that the respondent, a female and a Negro, may have felt unusually threatened by the officers, who were white males. While these factors were not irrelevant, neither were they decisive, and the totality of the evidence in this case was plainly adequate to support the District Court's finding that the respondent voluntarily consented to accompany the officers to the DEA office.

Because the search of the respondent's person was not preceded by an impermissible seizure of her person, it cannot be contended that her apparent consent to the subsequent search was infected by unlawful detention.

Reversed.

[Powell, J., Burger, C.J., and Blackman concurred in the Court's judgment.]

DISSENT

Mr. Justice White, with whom Mr. Justice Brennan, Mr. Justice Marshall, and Mr. Justice Stevens join, dissenting.

The Court today concludes that agents of the Drug Enforcement Administration (DEA) acted lawfully in stopping a traveler changing planes in an airport terminal and escorting her to a DEA office for a strip-search of her person. . . .

Whatever doubt there may be concerning whether Ms. Mendenhall's Fourth Amendment interests were implicated during the initial stages of her confrontation with the DEA agents, she undoubtedly was "seized" within the meaning of the Fourth Amendment when the agents escorted her from the public area of the terminal to the DEA office for questioning and a strip-search of her person. In *Dunaway v. New York,* 442 U.S. 200 (1979), we held that a person accompanying police officers to a police station for purposes of interrogation undoubtedly "was 'seized' in the Fourth Amendment sense," even though "he was not told he was under arrest." . . . Like the "seizure" in Dunaway, the nature of the intrusion to which Ms. Mendenhall was subjected when she was escorted by DEA agents to their office and was detained there for questioning and a strip-search was so great that it "was in important respects indistinguishable from a traditional arrest." Although Ms. Mendenhall was not told that she was under arrest, she was in fact not free to refuse to go to the DEA office and was not told that she was.[a] Furthermore, once inside the office, Ms. Mendenhall would not have been permitted to leave without submitting to a strip-search.[b] . . .

The Court's suggestion that no Fourth Amendment interest possessed by Ms. Mendenhall was implicated because she consented to go to the DEA office is unsupported in the record.

CASE DISCUSSION

The district court denied Mendenhall's motion to suppress heroin seized following a detention at an airport. The court of appeals reversed, holding that the seizure was the result of illegally detaining Mendenhall. The United Supreme Court reversed, holding that Mendenhall was not seized within the meaning of the Fourth Amendment.

Was it reasonable for Ms. Mendenhall to believe she was "free to go"? Did she remain with the DEA agents voluntarily? Do you believe Ms. Mendenhall was "stopped"? Why were the duration, intensity, and location of the contact not sufficiently intrusive to constitute a "seizure"? Is it reasonable to believe that any citizen would feel free to leave under the circumstances of this case? Explain. Is the reasonableness standard realistic? How would you define stop? Is a drug profile a sufficient foundation to stop a person? Would you set a standard that required police to notify citizens that they are free to go? If the police do not so notify citizens, is it reasonable for citizens to believe they are free to go? One police officer polled my class to find out how many believed they could leave when an officer approached them. Most said they could not. He said, "That is what we want you to believe, but the Constitution gives you the right to walk away."

---

[a]Agent Anderson testified on cross-examination at the suppression hearing:

"Q. All right. Now, when you asked her to accompany you to the DEA office for further questioning, if she had wanted to walk away, would you have stopped her?

"A. Once I asked her to accompany me?

"Q. Yes.

"A. Yes, I would have stopped her.

"Q. She was not free to leave, was she?

"A. Not at that point."

[b]Agent Anderson testified:

"Q. Had she tried to leave that room when she was being accompanied by the female officer, would you have known?

"A. If she had attempted to leave the room?

"Q. Yes.

"A. Well yes, I could say that I would have known.

"Q. And if she had tried to leave prior to being searched by the female officer, would you have stopped her?

"A. Yes."

A police approach to citizens and subsequent requests for information do not constitute a stop. Therefore, citizens may simply walk away from law enforcement officers seeking their cooperation, although ''good citizenship'' may impose a moral obligation on them to cooperate. Of course, citizens may always refuse to answer questions under the Fifth Amendment right against self-incrimination. (See chap. 7.) The Model Code of Pre-Arraignment Procedure provides the following regarding law enforcement officers' approaches to citizens to request cooperation:

Section 110.1 Requests for Cooperation by Law Enforcement Officers
(1) *Authority to Request Cooperation.* A law enforcement officer may . . . request any person to furnish information or otherwise cooperate in the investigation or prevention of crime. The officer may request the person to respond to questions, to appear at a police station, or to comply with any other reasonable request. In making requests . . . no officer shall indicate that a person is legally obliged to furnish information or otherwise to cooperate if no such legal obligation exists. Compliance with a request for information or other cooperation . . . shall not be regarded as involuntary or coerced solely on the ground that such request was made by one known to be a law enforcement officer.[11]

According to *Mendenhall* (see earlier excerpt above), questioning by itself does not constitute a stop. The courts do not consider mere police presence or approaches sufficiently intimidating or coercive to constitute a stop, even though most citizens clearly do not feel free to walk away from such encounters. For example, Immigration and Naturalization Services officers surrounded factories suspected of employing illegal aliens, using their agents presence to insure that no employees ''escaped'' while employees were questioned and asked to show their ''papers.'' The Supreme Court held that the questionings did not constitute seizures, the group of officers surrounding the factories notwithstanding.[12]

On the other hand, if intimidating or coercive measures accompany questioning, a voluntary encounter becomes at least a stop, or even an arrest in some circumstances. Therefore, the courts view differently situations where police officers approach citizens to question them and then forcibly detain them. The forcible detention turns the voluntary encounter into a stop. For example, in *Brown v. Texas,* two officers got out of their squad car in El Paso and asked Brown and his companion to identify themselves and explain why they were in an alley. Brown refused to identify himself and angrily asserted that the officers had no right to stop him. The officers frisked Brown and arrested him for violating a Texas statute making it illegal to refuse to give name and address to police officers. The Supreme Court held that the stop violated the Fourth Amendment because it turned the voluntary approach into a stop without factual foundation.[13]

Courts do not agree on what circumstances in addition to brief questioning turn a contact into either a stop or arrest. Some conclude that anything more than a brief detention at the scene for the purpose of asking a few questions turns a stop into an arrest. In an instance where, for example, officers drew their guns, ordered a fleeing suspect whom they did not have probable cause to arrest to stop, forced him to the ground on his stomach, and handcuffed him, a Michigan court ruled that the police had arrested the suspect. An Illinois court held that an officer who blocked a suspect's car and drew his gun as he approached the suspect's car had lawfully stopped, but had not arrested, the suspect. A California court held that taking a suspect from the crime scene to a residence to check out a burglary was a lawful stop, not an arrest.

Roadblocks

Are roadblocks—stopping vehicles and questioning their occupants—voluntary encounters or Fourth Amendment seizures? Roadblocks to apprehend fleeing felons have a long history, and the courts have confirmed their legality; roadblocks to check compliance with vehicle safety requirements also have a considerable history. Roadblocks to prevent illegal aliens from entering the country, or to apprehend them if they have entered, are also legal. More recently, and much more controversial, roadblocks to deter drunk driving and to apprehend drivers who are driving while intoxicated have become established law enforcement practice in some communities. The Supreme Court has not settled the question of the Fourth Amendment's application to roadblocks to enforce the laws against driving while intoxicated. However, New York's highest court, the New York Court of Appeals, has addressed the issue in *People v. Scott.*

CASE

Is a DWI roadblock an unlawful stop?

People v. Scott

63 N.Y.2d 518, 483 N.Y.S.2d 649, 473 N.E. 2d 1 (1984)

FACTS

About 2:00 a.m. on Saturday, September 25, 1982, defendant, while driving on Route 5 in the town of Leroy, came up to a roadblock established pursuant to a directive of the Sheriff of Genesee County. He was directed to pull to the side and there was requested by Chief Deputy Sheriff Maha to produce his license, registration and insurance card. Observing that the defendant fumbled a bit with his wallet, that his eyes were watery and bloodshot and that there was a strong odor of alcohol, Maha asked whether the defendant had been drinking. After defendant responded that he had just left a bar, he was asked to step out of his car. As he did so he was unstable on his feet and was unable successfully to perform heel-to-toe and finger-to-nose tests. Based on those facts and on alco-sensor breath screening test, which defendant agreed to take, Maha concluded that defendant was intoxicated and placed him under arrest.

The roadblock had been established pursuant to a March 5, 1982 memorandum of the County Sheriff which called attention to the deaths, injuries and losses occasioned by intoxicated drivers and the need "to employ every lawful means to deter and apprehend the drunken driver." It quoted from the October, 1981 Report of the Governor's Alcohol and Highway Safety Task Force the value of "systematic traffic checkpoints at known DWI and high accident locations during peak hours", and the advisability that, "Such checks at specific sites . . . be of short duration, with an ability to move quickly to new sites to insure that the drinking driver will not be able to forecast checkpoint locations,'' and noted that the ''greatest risk is on weekend late evening/early morning hours, when one in every ten vehicles or less contains an intoxicated driver.'' In succeeding detailed paragraphs it established procedures for site selection, lighting and signs; avoidance of discrimination by stopping all vehicles, or every second, third or fourth vehicle; location of screening areas off the highway to which vehicles would be directed; the nature of the inquires to be made, with specific direction that unless the operator's appearance and demeanor gave cause to believe him or her intoxicated sobriety tests not to be given. It listed the factors to be considered and stated that neither the odor of alcohol alone nor any one of the listed factors would suffice as a basis for sobriety tests. It also directed that checkpoint sites be prescreened and that from two to four locations be used during a four-hour period.

Under that procedure roadblocks were established once each month between midnight and 3:00 a.m., at locations selected in advance by senior personnel. Of the predetermined sites, four had been selected for use on September 25, 1982, the roadblock at each location being maintained for some 20 to 30 minutes before moving on to the next. Defendant was stopped at the third location in use that night. At that location warning signs were set upon the shoulders facing traffic from both directions some 300 feet in advance of the checkpoint, two police vehicles exhibiting flashing roof lights were placed so that their headlights illuminated the signs, and flares were placed in the center of the road. The checkpoint was manned by 10 persons, 6 from the Sheriff's office and 4 from the auxiliary police, and all vehicles approaching from either direction were stopped. In addition, two patrol cars were stationed in the area to follow and observe for possible violations any vehicle that avoided the roadblock by making a U-turn.

Defendant moved to suppress the evidence obtained at the roadblock. After a hearing the Town Justice denied the motion, finding that it had been operated in a uniform, nonarbitrary and nondiscriminatory manner. The County Court affirmed, finding that the State's interest in curbing drunken drivers great and the operation of the roadblock sufficient to allay feelings of fright or annoyance and to circumscribe sufficiently the discretion of the personnel engaged in the operation. On appeal to this court defendant argues that deterrence is an improper purpose, that a temporary roadblock is constitutionally impermissible, and that it has not been shown that less intrusive means of enforcement would not be effective. We affirm.

OPINION

. . . The permissibility of a particular practice [governed by the Fourth Amendment] is a function of its ''reasonableness,'' which is determined by balancing its intrusion on the Fourth Amendment interests of the individual involved against its promotion of legitimate governmental interests. . . . The importance of the governmental interest here involved is beyond question. ''The carnage caused by drunk drivers is well documented and needs no detailed recitation here.''

Moreover, in light of the specific procedures devised and promulgated to law enforcement personnel by the head of their department, the Sheriff, and the way in which the particular roadblock was being operated when defendant was stopped, the courts below could properly conclude that it did not intrude to an impermissible degree upon the privacy of motorists approaching the checkpoint, that it was being maintained in accordance with a uniform procedure which afforded little discretion to operating personnel, and that adequate precautions [were taken] as to safety, lighting and fair warning of the existence of the checkpoint. . . .

The value of roadblocks in decreasing drunk driving is attested by both the United States Department of Transportation and the Governor's Alcohol and Highway Safety Task Force. A 1983 paper on Safety Checkpoints For DWI Enforcement issued by the Department of Transportation's National Highway Traffic Safety Administration's Office of Alcohol Countermeasures emphasizes the importance of informing the public about DWI checkpoint operations as the chief means of deterring driving while intoxicated, and the Governor's Task Force found "that the systematic, constitutionally conducted traffic checkpoint is the single most effective action in raising the community's perception of the risk of being detected and apprehended for drunk driving." . . . We conclude, therefore, that deterrence by fear of apprehension is a constitutionally proper means of keeping drunk drivers off the highways, though it may not be with respect to pedestrians. . . .

The Report of the Subcommittee on Drunk Driving of the Assembly Transportation Committee contains findings that . . . alcohol-involved fatal accidents decreased 25% from 1981 to 1983; . . . reported alcohol-involved accidents have fallen at almost ten times [the rate of all accidents]; accidents during bar hours have declined 21.3% since 1980 . . . ; and fatal accidents during bar hours have decreased 33% since 1980. . . . The extent to which those results stem from legislative reforms during that period as distinct from the deterrent effect of roadblocks and other educational and public information programs aimed at combatting the problem is not revealed, but in our view is not of constitutional moment. It is enough that some checkpoints, when their use becomes known, do have a substantial impact on the drunk driving problem. The State is entitled in the interest of public safety to bring all available resources to bear, without having to spell out the exact efficiency coefficient of each component and of the separate effects of any particular component. There being a reasonable basis for concluding that considering both its detection and its deterrence effect, the DWI checkpoint procedure in question is a valuable component of the program to control drunk driving, we conclude that it is a sufficiently productive mechanism to justify the minimal intrusion involved.

For the foregoing reasons, the order of the County Court, Genesee County, should be affirmed.

CASE DISCUSSION

Are roadblocks to prevent drunk driving and to apprehend intoxicated drivers stops? What interests does the court say such roadblocks protect? Do you think the court balanced them properly? Can you make an argument that the Fourth Amendment allows the roadblock in *Scott*? Although we have not discussed it yet, what was the factual foundation that supported the road-block? If Scott was lawfully stopped, would random stops of pedestrians who fit a "mugger profile" during times when muggings are most likely to occur be lawful? Why? Why not? The American Civil Liberties Union (ACLU) commented regarding this DWI checkpoint procedure:

> highly publicized local law enforcement efforts such as random roadblocks have prompted civil libertarians to warn of Orwellian intrusions into individual privacy.

Does the ACLU comment have merit? Explain.

Purposes of Stops

Officers most frequently make stops when they suspect crimes are either in progress or are about to be committed. Since *Terry,* the courts have approved stops made to prevent and intercept crimes in progress. Prevention and detection might be directed at specific individuals, as in *Terry v. Ohio,* where articulable facts support police suspicion that identified individuals are committing crimes or are about to do so. Furthermore, as the roadblocks demonstrate, statistics that show patterns of driving while intoxicated might support random stops of drivers where no articulable facts support the stop.

The Supreme Court has identified two other legitimate purposes for stops. Stops to investigate *completed* crimes are lawful. For example, in *United States v. Hensley,* the police stopped a suspect who had been named in a "wanted flyer" distributed by a neighboring police department. The Court ruled that the stop was justified to investigate the suspect who drove the getaway car. Furthermore, the Supreme Court has held that it is a lawful stop to detain all occupants in a house while police execute a search warrant for contraband.[14]

Decision Point

As Detroit Police officers were about to execute a warrant to search a house for narcotics, they encountered Summers descending the front steps. They requested his assistance in gaining entry and detained him while they searched the premises. After finding narcotics in the basement and ascertaining that Summers owned the house, the police arrested him, searched his person, and found an envelope containing 8.5 grams of heroin in his coat pocket. In *Michigan v. Summers,* the United States Supreme Court held that "some seizures constitute such limited intrusions on the personal security of those detained and are justified by such substantial law enforcement interests that they may be made on less than probable cause, so long as police have an articulable basis for suspecting criminal activity." Since the police had a warrant to search Summers's house for contraband, that Summers owned the house constituted the facts necessary to justify the stop, "admittedly a significant restraint on his liberty."[15]

Proper Scope of Stops

Stops should provide police officers enough—but no more—time and authority to gather information sufficient to decide among three alternatives: to arrest the suspect, to conduct further investigation, or to release the detained citizen. The police may only conduct stops in ways that relate reasonably to the circumstances that justified the stop initially. Two actions widely held lawful during a stop are (1) obtaining the stopped person's identity; and (2) maintaining the status quo or "freezing" a suspicious situation for further investigation. Obtaining identification means getting a suspect's name and address. Police may also question suspects briefly about their presence at the scene of the suspicious circumstances that initiated the stop.

According to the Supreme Court, the proper scope of a lawful stop depends on balancing the need to detect and deter crimes against four elements in the stop: (1) its duration; (2) its intrusiveness; (3) whether suspects were moved from the place where the police stopped them; and (4) the stopped person's freedom to leave or terminate the encounter. The Supreme Court has refused to put a specific time length on lawful stops. In one recent case holding that a forty-five-minute stop was reasonable, the Court wrote, "Much as a 'bright line' rule would be desirable, in evaluating whether an investigative detention is unreasonable, common sense and ordinary experience must govern over rigid criteria." The United States Supreme Court addressed both duration and intrusiveness in *United States v. Montoya de Hernandez*.[16]

CASE

Was her detention reasonable?

United States v. Montoya de Hernandez

473 U.S. 531, 105 S.Ct. 3304, 87 L.Ed.2d 381 (1985)

[Rehnquist, J., delivered the opinion of the court, in which Burger, C.J., and White, Blackmun, Powell, and O'Connor, J.J., joined. Stevens, J., filed an opinion concurring in the judgment, . . . Brennan, J., filed a dissenting opinion, in which Marshall, J., joined, . . .]

FACTS

Respondent arrived at Los Angeles International Airport shortly after midnight, March 5, 1983, on Avianca Flight 080, a direct 10-hour flight from Bogota, Colombia. Her visa was in order so she was passed through Immigration and proceeded to the customs desk. At the customs desk she encountered Customs Inspector Talamantes, who reviewed her documents and noticed from her passport that she had made at least eight recent trips to either Miami or Los Angeles. Talamantes referred respondent to a secondary customs desk for further questioning. At this desk Talamantes and another inspector asked respondant general questions concerning herself and the purpose of her trip. Respondent revealed that she spoke no English and had no family or friends in the United States. She explained in Spanish that she had come to the United States to purchase goods for her husband's store in Bogota. The customs inspectors recognized Bogota as a "source city" for narcotics. Respondent possessed $5,000 in cash, mostly $50 bills, but had no billfold. She indicated to the inspectors that she had no appointments with merchandise vendors, but planned to ride around Los Angeles in taxicabs visiting retail stores such as J. C. Penney and K-Mart in order to buy goods for her husband's store with the $5,000.

Respondent admitted that she had no hotel reservations, but stated that she planned to stay at a Holiday Inn. Respondent could not recall how her airline ticket was purchased. When the inspectors opened respondent's one small valise they found about four changes of "cold weather" clothing. Respondent had no shoes other than the high-heeled pair she was wearing. Although respondent possessed no checks, waybills, credit cards, or letters of credit, she did produce a Colombian business card and a number of old receipts, waybills, and fabric swatches displayed in a photo album.

At this point Talamantes and the other inspector suspected that respondent was a "balloon swallower," one who attempts to smuggle narcotics into this country hidden in her alimentary canal. Over the years Inspector Talamantes had apprehended dozens of alimentary canal smugglers arriving on Avianca Flight 080. . . .

The inspectors requested a female customs inspector to take respondent to a private area and conduct a patdown and strip search. During the search the female inspector felt respondent's abdomen area and noticed a firm fullness, as if respondent were wearing a girdle. The search revealed no contraband, but the inspector noticed that respondent was wearing two pairs of elastic underpants with a paper towel lining the crotch area.

When respondent returned to the customs area and the female inspector reported her discoveries, the inspector in charge told respondent that he suspected she was smuggling drugs in her alimentary canal. . . . The inspector then gave respondent the option of returning to Colombia on the next available flight, agreeing to an x ray, or remaining in detention until she produced a monitored bowel movement that would confirm or rebut the inspectors' suspicions. Respondent chose the first option and was placed in a customs office under observation. She was told that if she went to the toilet she would have to use a wastebasket in the women's restroom, in order that female inspectors could inspect her stool for balloons or capsules carrying narcotics. The inspectors refused respondent's request to place a telephone call. . . .

Respondent sat in the customs office, under observation, for the remainder of the night. . . .She remained detained in the customs office under observation, for most of the time curled up in a chair leaning to one side. She refused all offers of food and drink, and refused to use the toilet facilities. The Court of Appeals noted that she exhibited symptoms of discomfort with "heroic efforts to resist the usual calls of nature." . . .

At the shift change at 4:00 o'clock the next afternoon, almost 16 hours after her flight had landed, respondent still had not defecated or urinated or partaken of food or drink. At that time customs officials sought a court order authorizing . . .[a]n x ray, and a rectal examination. The Federal Magistrate issued an order just before midnight that evening, which authorized a rectal examination and involuntary x ray, . . . [a] physician conducted a rectal examination and removed from respondent's rectum a balloon containing a foreign substance. Respondent was then placed formally under arrest. By 4:10 a.m. respondent had passed 6 similar balloons; over the next four days she passed 88 balloons containing a total of 528 grams of 80% pure cocaine hydrochloride.

After a suppression hearing the District Court admitted the cocaine in evidence against respondent. She was convicted of possession of cocaine with intent to distribute, . . .[a]nd unlawful importation of cocaine. . . .A divided panel of the United States Court of Appeals for the Ninth Circuit reversed respondent's convictions. . . .

OPINION

The Fourth Amendment commands that searches and seizures be reasonable. What is reasonable depends upon all of the circumstances surrounding the search or seizure itself. . . . The permissiblity of a particular law enforcement practice is judged by "balancing its intrusion on the individual's Fourth Amendment interest against its promotion of legitimate governmental interests." . . .

Here the seizure of respondent took place at the international border. Since the founding of our Republic, Congress has granted the Executive plenary authority to conduct routine searches and seizures at the border, without probable cause or a warrant, in order to regulate the collection of duties and to prevent the introduction of contraband into this country. . . .

[T]he Fourth Amendment's balance of reasonableness is qualitatively different at the international border than in the interior. Routine searches of the persons and effects of entrants are not subject to any requirement of reasonable suspicion, probable cause, or warrant, and first-class mail may be opened without a warrant on less than probable cause. . . .

These cases reflect longstanding concern for the protection of the integrity of the border. This concern is, if anything, heightened by the veritable national crisis in law enforcement caused by smuggling of illicit narcotics, . . . [a]nd in particular by the increasing utilization of alimentary canal smuggling. This desperate practice appears to be a relatively recent addition to the smugglers' repertoire of deceptive practices, and it also appears to be exceedingly difficult to detect. . . .

Balanced against the sovereign's interests at the border are the Fourth Amendment rights of respondent. Having presented herself at the border for admission, and having subjected herself to the criminal enforcement powers of the Federal Government, . . . [r]espondent was entitled to be free from unreasonable search and seizure. But not only is this expectation of privacy less at the border than in the interior, . . . [t]he Fourth Amendment balance between the interests of the Government and the privacy right of the individual is also struck much more favorably to the Government at the border. . . .

We have not previously decided what level of suspicion would justify a seizure of an incoming traveler for purposes other than a routine border search. . . . The Court of Appeals viewed ''clear indication'' as an intermediate standard between ''reasonable suspicion'' and ''probable cause.'' . . . No other court, including this one, has ever adopted . . . ''[c]lear indication'' language as a Fourth Amendment standard. . . . We do not think that the Fourth Amendment's emphasis upon reasonableness is consistent with the creation of a third verbal standard in addition to ''reasonable suspicion'' and ''probable cause.'' . . .

We hold that detention of a traveler at the border, beyond the scope of a routine customs search and inspection, is justified at its inception if customs agents, considering all the facts surrounding the traveler and her trip, reasonably suspect that the traveler is smuggling contraband in her alimentary canal. . . . The facts, and their rational inferences, known to customs inspectors in this case clearly supported a reasonable suspicion that respondent was an alimentary canal smuggler. . . . The trained customs inspectors had encountered many alimentary canal smugglers and certainly had more than an ''inchoate and unparticularized suspicion or 'hunch,' '' . . . [t]hat respondent was smuggling narcotics in her alimentary canal.The inspectors' suspicion was a '' 'common-sense conclusio[n] about human behavior' upon which 'practical people,' —including government officials, are entitled to rely.'' . . .

The final issue in this case is whether the detention of respondent was reasonably related in scope to the circumstances which justified it initially. In this regard we have cautioned that courts should not indulge in ''unrealistic second-guessing,'' . . . [a]nd we have noted that ''creative judge[s],engaged in *post hoc* evaluations of police conduct can almost always imagine some alternative means by which the objectives of the police might have been accomplished.'' . . . The rudimentary knowledge of the human body which judges possess in common with the rest of humankind tells us that alimentary canal smuggling cannot be detected in the amount of time in which other illegal activity may be investigated through brief *Terry*-type stops. It presents few, if any external signs; a quick frisk will not do, nor will even a strip search. In the case of respondent the inspectors had available, as an alternative to simply awaiting her bowel movement, an x ray. They offered her the alternative of submitting herself to that procedure. But when she refused that alternative, the customs inspectors were left with only two practical alternatives: detain her for such a time as necessary to confirm their suspicions, a detention which would last much longer than the typical *Terry* stop, or turn her loose into the interior carrying the reasonably suspected contraband drugs. . . . The inspectors in this case followed this former procedure. They no doubt expected that respondent, having recently disembarked from 10-hour direct flight with a full and stiff abdomen, would produce a bowel movement without extended delay. But her visible efforts to resist the call of nature, which the court below labeled ''heroic,'' disappointed this expectation and in turn caused her humiliation and discomfort. Our prior cases have refused to charge police with delays in investigatory detention attributabe to the suspect's evasive actions. . . . Respondent alone was responsible for much of the duration and discomfort of the seizure. Under these circumstances, we conclude that the detention was not unreasonably long. It occurred at the international border, where the Fourth Amendment balance of interests leans heavily to the Government. . . . Respondent's detention was long, uncomfortable indeed, humiliating; but both its length and its discomfort resulted solely from the method by which she chose to smuggle illicit drugs into this country. . . .

Justice Stevens, concurring in the judgement. If a seizure and search of the person of the kind disclosed by this record may be made on the basis of reasonable suspicion, we must assume that a significant number of innocent persons will be required to undergo similar procedures. The rule announced in this case cannot, therefore, be supported on the ground that respondent's prolonged and humiliating detention "resulted solely from the method by which she chose to smuggle illicit drugs into this country.". . . The prolonged detention of respondent was, however, justified by a different choice that respondent made; she withdrew her consent to an x ray examination that would have easily determined whether the reasonable suspicion that she was concealing contraband was justified . . . .

DISSENT

Justice Brennan, with whom Justice Marshall joins, dissenting. We confront a "disgusting and saddening episode" at our Nation's border. . . . "[T]hat the [respondent] so degraded herself as to offend the sensibilities of any decent citizen is not questioned." That is not what we face. For "[i]t is a fair summary of history to say that the safeguards of liberty have frequently been forged in controversies involving not very nice people." . . . The standards we fashion to govern the ferreting out of the guilty apply equally to the detention of the innocent, and "may be exercised by the most unfit and ruthless officers as well as by the fit and reasonable." . . . Nor is the issue whether there is a "veritable national crisis in law enforcement caused by smuggling illicit narcotics." . . . "[I]n our democracy such enforcement presupposes a moral atmosphere and a reliance upon intelligence whereby the effective administration of justice can be achieved with due regard for those civilized standards in the use of the criminal law which are formulated in our Bill of Rights." The issue, instead, is simply this: Does the Fourth Amendment permit an international traveler, citizen or alien, to be subjected to the sort of treatment that occurred in this case without the sanction of a judicial officer and based on nothing more than the "reasonable suspicion" of low ranking investigative officers that something might be amiss? The Court today concludes that the Fourth Amendment grants such sweeping and unmonitored authority to customs officials . . . . I dissent. Indefinite involuntary incommunicado detentions "for investigation" are the hallmark of a police state, not a free society. . . . In my opinion, Government officials may no more confine a person at the border under such circumstances for purposes of criminal investigation than they may within the interior of the country. The nature and duration of the detention here may well have been tolerable for spoiled meat or diseased animals, but not for human beings held on simple suspicion of criminal activity. . . . Finally, I believe that the warrant and probable cause safeguards equally govern Justice Stevens' proffered alternative of exposure to x-irradiation for criminal investigative purposes. . . . [T]he available evidence suggests that the number of highly intrusive border searches of suspicious-looking but ultimately innocent travelers may be very high. One physician who at the request of customs officials conducted many "internal searches"—rectal and vaginal examinations and stomach pumping —estimated that he had found contraband in 15 to 20 percent of the persons he had examined. It has similarly been estimated that only 16 percent of women subjected to body cavity searches at the border were in fact found to be carrying contraband. It is precisely to minimize the risk of harassing so many innocent people that the Fourth Amendment requires the intervention of a judicial officer. . . . The Court argues, however, that the length and "discomfort" of De Hernandez' detention "resulted *solely* from the method by which she chose to smuggle illicit drugs into this country," and it speculates that only her "'heroic'" efforts prevented the detention from being brief and to the point. . . . Although we now know that De Hernandez was indeed guilty of smuggling drugs internally, such *post hoc* rationalizations have no place in our Fourth Amendment jurisprudence, which demands that we "prevent hindsight from coloring the evaluation of the reasonableness of a search or seizure." . . . At the time the authorities simply had, at most, a reasonable suspicion that De Hernandez might be engaged in such smuggling. Neither the law of the land nor the law of nature supports the notion that petty government officials can require people to excrete on command; indeed, the Court relies elsewhere on "[t]he rudimentary knowledge of the human body" in sanctioning the "much longer than . . . typical" duration of detentions such as this. And, with all respect to the Court, it is not "'unrealistic second-guessing,'" to predict that an innocent traveler, locked away in incommunicado detention in unfamiliar surroundings in a foreign land, might well be frightened and exhausted as to be unable so to "cooperate" with the authorites. . . . It is tempting , of course, to look the other way in a case that so graphically illustrates the "veritable national crisis" caused by narcotics trafficking. But if there is one enduring lesson to be learned in the long struggle to balance individual rights against society's need to defend itself against lawlessness, it is that "[i]t is easy to make light of insistence on scrupulous regard for the safeguards of civil liberties when invoked on behalf of the unworthy. It is too easy. History bears testimony that by such disregard are the rights of liberty extinguished, heedlessly at first, then stealthily, and brazenly in the end."

CASE DISCUSSION

Montoya de Hernandez was charged with narcotics violations. She moved to suppress the narcotics: the district court denied the motion, admitted the cocaine in evidence, and Montoya de Hernandez was convicted of possessing cocaine with intent to distribute and unlawful importation of cocaine. A divided court of appeals reversed the conviction. The government appealed to the United States Supreme Court, and it reversed the court of appeals, holding that the detention did not violate the Fourth Amendment and hence, the seizure of the cocaine was lawful.

What interests is the Court balancing in this case? Do you think the majority or the dissent balanced them properly? Can a detention for this length of time ever constitute a lawful stop? Why? Why not? Could you write a rule that gives police and other law enforcement officers adequate guidance for how long they can detain suspects? Are the efforts to produce a bowel movement and the close observation to discover its contents an unwarranted invasion on human dignity? What, if anything, justifies such indignities?

Officers who "freeze" suspicious occurrences to ask suspects "a few pertinent questions" ordinarily must restrict their activities to "on the spot" investigation. The power to stop does not encompass the authority to transport suspects considerable distances from the place where they are stopped. Police may, however, ask suspects to step out of their cars, to sit in a patrol car while they are questioned, or to accompany officers to police call boxes. For example, in *United States v. Alvarez-Sanchez,* agents did not unlawfully stop Alverez-Sanchez by asking him to accompany them to an administrative office fifteen feet from where the agents stopped him.[17]

According to the American Law Institute,

> The authority . . .is essentially an authority to immobilize a person, to keep contact with him, while a situation is sorted out, and a determination is made how further to proceed. This is expressed by the term [in the Model Code's provision] "remain in or near such place in the officer's presence." The concept is intended to be flexible.[18]

If the police detain suspects for an unreasonably long time, or move them to an unreasonable distance from the place they have stopped them, or unreasonably interfere with suspects' freedom to depart or terminate the investigative detention, the stop becomes an arrest. For example, in *Florida v. Royer*, when police escorted Royer to a small room in an airport, took his airline ticket and identification, and retrieved his luggage, he was not free to leave and hence was arrested, not stopped.[19]

CASE

Was he stopped for an "on the spot" investigation?

Hayes v. Florida

470 U.S. 811, 105 S.Ct. 1643, 84 L.Ed.2d 705 (1985)

[White,J., delivered the opinion of the court, in which Burger, C. J., and Rehnquist, Stevens, and O'Conner, JJ., joined. Brennan, J., filed an opinion concurring in the judgment, in which Marshall[J., joined, Blackmun, J., concurred in the judgment. Powell, J., took no part in the consideration or decision of the case. . . .]

FACTS

A series of burglary-rapes occured in Punta Gorda, Florida, in 1980. Police found latent fingerprints on the doorknob of the bedroom of one of the victims, fingerprints they believed belonged to the assailant. The police also found a herringbone pattern tennis shoe print near the victim's front porch. Although they had little specific information to tie petitioner Hayes to the crime, after police interviewed him along with 30 to 40 other men who generally fit the description of the assailant, the investigators came to consider petitioner a principal suspect. They decided to visit petitioner's home to obtain his fingerprints or, if he was uncooperative, to arrest him. They did not seek a warrant authorizing this procedure.

Arriving at the petitioner's house, the officers spoke to petitioner on his front porch. When he expressed reluctance voluntarily to accompany them to the station for fingerprinting, one of the investigators explained that they would therefore arrest him. Petitioner, in the words of the investigator, then "blurted out" that he would rather go with the officers to the station than be arrested. While the officers were on the front porch, they also seized a pair of herringbone pattern tennis shoes in plain view.

Petitioner was taken to the station house, where he was fingerprinted. When police determined that his prints matched those at the scene of the crime, petitioner was placed under formal arrest. Before trial, petitioner moved to suppress the fingerprint evidence, claiming it was the fruit of an illegal detention. The trial court denied the motion and admitted the evidence without expressing a reason. Petitioner was convicted of burglary and sexual battery committed at the scene where the latent fingerprints were found.

The District Court of Appeal of Florida, Second District, affirmed the conviction. . . . The Florida Supreme Court denied review by a four to three decision. . . . We granted certiorari to review this application of *Terry*, 469 U.S. 816 (1984), and we now reverse. . . .

OPINION

[T]here was no probable cause to arrest, no consent to the journey to the police station, and no judicial authorization for such a detention for finger-printing purposes. . . . [T]ransportation to and investigative detention at the station house without probable cause or judicial authorization together violate the Fourth Amendment. . . . There is no doubt that at some point in the investigative process, police procedures can qualitatively and quantitatively be so intrusive with respect to a suspect's freedom of movement and privacy interests as to trigger the full protection of the Fourth and Fourteenth Amendments. . . . [O]ur view [is] that the line is crossed when the police, without probable cause or warrant, forcibly remove a person from his home or other place in which he is entitled to be and transport him to the police station, where he is detained, although briefly, for investigative purposes. We adhere to the view that such seizures, at least where not under judicial supervision, are sufficiently like arrests to invoke the traditional rule that arrests may constitutionally be made only on probable cause.

None of the foregoing implies that a brief detention in the field for the purpose of fingerprinting, where there is only reasonable suspicion not amounting to probable cause, is necessarily impermissible under the Fourth Amendment. . . . There is support in our cases for the view that the Fourth Amendment would permit seizures for the purpose of fingerprinting, if there is reasonable suspicion that the suspect has committed a criminal act, if there is a reasonable basis for believing that fingerprinting will establish or negate the suspect's connection with that crime, and if the procedure is carried out with dispatch. . . .

We also do not abandon the suggestion . . . that under circumscribed procedures, the Fourth Amendment might permit the judiciary to authorize the seizure of a person on less than probable cause and his removal to the police staion for the purpose of fingerprinting. We do not, of course, have such a case before us. We do note, however, that some states, . . . have enacted procedures for judicially authorized seizures for the purpose of fingerprinting. . . .

CONCURRING OPINION

Justice Brennan, with whom Justice Marshall joins concurring in the judgment. . . .

The Court reconizes that . . . the seizure here, . . . violated the Fourth Amendment. . . . [T]he Court holds that a suspect may not be apprehended, detained, and forced to accompany the police to another location to be fingerprinted without a warrant or probable cause. . . . The intrusion on the suspect's freedom of action in such a case is simply too great to be ''reasonable'' under the Fourth Amendment. . . .

[H]owever, the Court today—after tidily disposing of the case before it —returns to its regrettable assault on the Fourth Amendment by reaching beyond any issue properly before us virtually to hold that on-site finger-printing without probable cause or a warrant is constitutionally reasonable. . . . I disagree with the Court's strained effort to reach the question today.

If the police wanted to detain an individual for on-site fingerprinting, the intrusion would have to be measured by the standards of *Terry v. Ohio*, 392 U.S. 1, 88 S.Ct. 1868, 20 L.Ed. 2d 889 (1968), and our other Fourth Amendment cases. Yet the record here contains no information useful in applying *Terry* to this hypothetical police practice. It would seem that on-site fingerprinting (apparently undertaken in full view of any passerby) would involve a singular intrusion on the suspect's privacy, an intrusion that would not be justifiable (as was the patdown in *Terry*) as necessary for the officer's protection. How much time would elapse before the individual would be free to go? Could the police hold the individual until the fingerprints could be compared with others? . . . Ordinarily—outside the Fourth Amendment context, at any rate—we wait for a case to arise before addressing the application of a legal standard to a set of facts. I disagree with the Court's apparent attempt to render an advisory opinion concerning the Fourth Amendment implications of a police practice that, as far as we know, has never been attempted by the police in this or any other case.

CASE DISCUSSION

Police officers took Hayes to the police station and fingerprinted him. When his fingerprints matched those found at the scene of the crime, the police arrested Hayes. Prior to trial, Hayes moved to suppress the fingerprints, claiming they were the fruit of illegal detention. The trial court denied the motion and admitted the evidence. Hayes was convicted of burglary and sexual battery. The District Court of Appeal of Florida affirmed. The Florida Supreme Court denied review. The United States Supreme Court granted *certiorari* and reversed the conviction on the grounds that the fingerprinting was the fruit of an unlawful detention.

Is this stop unlawful because the police moved Hayes from the spot where they arrested him? Would you draw a "bright line" rule that calls any movement from the spot where the police stop citizens an "aggravated stop"? Would such stops always be illegal? Was it the movement alone or the further delays and detentions that made this stop illegal? How would you defend this stop as lawful? Were the fingerprints illegally seized? Would you admit the fingerprints into evidence? What remedy, if any, would you give to Hayes, if the fingerprints were seized illegally?

Foundations for Stops

The factual foundation, or quantum of proof, required for lawful stops is called **reasonable suspicion.** Reasonable suspicion has two important elements. First, there must be objective grounds for the suspicion. Officers' stops must have the support of facts; intuition, hunch, or mere subjective suspicion will not suffice. Second, reasonable suspicion is a quantitative term, with quantity referring to the number and quality of facts upon which the stop rests. Reasonable suspicion contrasts with the standard for arrest, **probable cause,** solely on this quantitative basis. To use Longfellow's metaphor, reasonable suspicion resembles probable cause "as the mist resembles the rain." Probable cause requires more facts than reasonable suspicion because an arrest is a greater deprivation than a stop.[20]

No one has ever tried to state the number of facts necessary to add up to reasonable suspicion, and it would be unwise to require a certain amount even if it were possible. The specific quality and quantity of facts that justify stops must vary with the myriad situations the police encounter on city streets and elsewhere. Police can establish reasonable suspicion on which to base stops from a wide range of facts and circumstances, including (1) information that officers know directly from their senses: what they see, hear, smell, and feel; and (2) information that police know indirectly from others: what someone else told them. This indirect information, called **hearsay,** might come from various sources, including victims, witnesses, other police officers, and anonymous, professional, or paid informants.

The following list suggests the kind of information that forms the building blocks of reasonable suspicion to support stops. These same kinds of facts support probable cause to arrest:

- Direct information
- flight
- furtive movement
- hiding

- resisting officers
- attempting to destroy evidence
- evasive answers
- contradictory explanations
- contraband and/or weapons in plain view
- Hearsay information—victims, witnesses, fellow officers[21]

Taken together, some or all of the types of information in the list amounts to reasonable suspicion if it would lead a reasonable person to *suspect* that the person stopped *may* have committed, *may* be committing, or *may* be about to commit a crime, or that his or her "curious or unusual conduct would naturally trigger a police inquiry." The cases excerpted in this chapter give some idea of the kinds and variety of facts and circumstances that satisfy the reasonable suspicion standard: (1) Officer McFadden's observations of Terry and his companions pacing up and down in front of a store in *Terry v. Ohio;* (2) the informant who told Officer Connolly that Williams was armed and possessed heroin in *Adams v. Williams* and (3) the conversations between Hayes and the police in *Hayes v. Florida.* Recently, the Supreme Court thoroughly reviewed the requirements for reasonable suspicion in *United States v. Sokolow.*[22]

CASE

Did the DEA agents have "reasonable suspicion"?

United States v. Sokolow

___ U.S.___, 109 S.Ct. 1581, 104 L.Ed.2d 1 (1989)

[Rehnquist, C.J., delivered the opinion of the Court, in which White, Blackmun, Stevens, O'Connor, Scalia, and Kennedy joined. Marshall, J., filed a dissenting opinion, in which Brennan, J., joined.]

FACTS

This case involves a typical attempt to smuggle drugs through one of the Nation's airports. On a Sunday in July 1984, respondent went to the United Airlines ticket counter at Honolulu Airport, where he purchased two round-trip tickets for a flight to Miami leaving later that day. The tickets were purchased in the names of "Andrew Kray" and "Janet Norian," and had open return dates. Respondent paid $2,100 for the tickets from a large roll of $20 bills, which appeared to contain a total of $4,000. He also gave the ticket agent his home telephone number. The ticket agent noticed that respondent seemed nervous; he was about 25 years old; he was dressed in a black jumpsuit and wore gold jewelry; and he was accompanied by a woman, who turned out to be Janet Norian. Neither respondent nor his companion checked any of their four pieces of luggage.

After the couple left for their flight, the ticket agent informed Officer John McCarthy of the Honolulu Police Department of respondent's cash purchase of tickets to Miami. Officer McCarthy determined that the telephone number respondent gave to the ticket agent was subscribed to a "Karl Herman," who resided at 348-A Royal Hawaiian Avenue in Honolulu. Unbeknownst to McCarthy (and later to the DEA agents), respondent was Herman's roommate. The ticket agent identified respondent's voice on the answering machine at Herman's number. Officer McCarthy was unable to find any listing under the name "Andrew Kray" in Hawaii. McCarthy subsequently learned that return reservations from Miami to Honolulu had been made in the names of Kray and Norian, with their arrival scheduled for July 25, three days after respondent and his companion had left. He also learned that Kray and Norian were scheduled to make stopovers in Denver and Los Angeles.

On July 25, during the stopover in Los Angeles, DEA agents identified respondent. He "appeared to be very nervous and was looking all around the waiting area." App. 43–44. Later that day, at 6:30 p.m., respondent and Norian arrived in Honolulu. As before, they had not checked their luggage. Respondent was still wearing a black jumpsuit and gold jewelry. The couple proceeded directly to the street and tried to hail a cab, where Agent Richard Kempshall and three other DEA agents approached them. Kempshall displayed his credentials, grabbed respondent by the arm and moved him back onto the sidewalk. Kempshall asked respondent for his airline ticket and identification; respondent said that he had neither. He told the agents that his name was "Sokolow," but that he was traveling under his mother's maiden name, "Kray."

Respondent and Norian were escorted to the DEA office at the airport. There, the couple's luggage was examined by "Donker," a narcotics detector dog, which alerted to respondent's brown shoulder bag. The agents arrested respondent. He was advised of his constitutional rights and declined to make any statements. The agents obtained a warrant to search the shoulder bag. They found no illicit drugs, but the bag did contain several suspicious documents indicating respondent's involvement in drug trafficking. The agents had Donker reexamine the remaining luggage, and this time the dog alerted to a medium sized Louis Vuitton bag. By now, it was 9:30 p.m., too late for the agents to obtain a second warrant. They allowed respondent to leave for the night, but kept his luggage. The next morning, after a second dog confirmed Donker's alert, the agents obtained a warrant and found 1,063 grams of cocaine inside the bag.

Respondent was indicted for possession with the intent to distribute cocaine in violation of 21 U.S.C. s 841(a)(1). The United States District Court for Hawaii denied his motion to suppress the cocaine and other evidence seized from his luggage, finding that the DEA agents had a reasonable suspicion that he was involved in drug trafficking when they stopped him at the airport. Respondent then entered a conditional plea of guilty to the offense charged. The United States Court of Appeals for the Ninth Circuit reversed respondent's conviction by a divided vote, holding that the DEA agents did not have a reasonable suspicion to justify the stop. The majority divided the facts bearing on reasonable suspicion into two categories. In the first category, the majority placed facts describing "ongoing criminal activity," such as the use of an alias or evasive movement through an airport; the majority believed that at least one such factor was always needed to support a finding of reasonable suspicion. In the second category, it placed facts describing "personal characteristics" of drug couriers, such as the cash payment for tickets, a short trip to a major source city for drugs, nervousness, type of attire, and unchecked luggage. The majority believed that such facts, "shared by drug couriers and the public at large," were only relevant if there was evidence of ongoing criminal behavior and the Government offered "(e)mpirical documentation" that the combination of facts at issue did not describe the behavior of "significant numbers of innocent persons." Applying this two-part test to the facts of this case, the majority found that there was no evidence of ongoing criminal behavior, and thus that the agents' stop was impermissible. The dissenting judge took the view that the majority's approach was "overly mechanical" and "contrary to the case-by-case determination of reasonable articulable suspicion based on all the facts." We granted certiorari to review the decision of the Court of Appeals because of its serious implications for the enforcement of the federal narcotics laws. We now reverse.

OPINION

The Court of Appeals held that the DEA agents seized respondent when they grabbed him by the arm and moved him back onto the sidewalk. The Government does not challenge that conclusion, and we assume—without deciding—that a stop occurred here. Our decision, then, turns on whether the agents had a reasonable suspicion that respondent was engaged in wrongdoing when they encountered him on the sidewalk. In *Terry v. Ohio* [excerpted earlier], we held that the police can stop and briefly detain a person for investigative purposes if the officer has a reasonable suspicion supported by articulable facts that criminal activity "may be afoot," even if the officer lacks probable cause. The officer, of course, must be able to articulate something more than an "incohate and unparticularized suspicion or 'hunch'." The Fourth Amendment requires "some minimal level of objective justification" for making the stop. That level of suspicion is considerably less than proof of wrongdoing by a preponderance of the evidence. We have held that probable cause means "a fair probability that contraband or evidence of a crime will be found," *Illinois v. Gates* [see Chap. 6] and the level of suspicion required for a *Terry* stop is obviously less demanding than that for probable cause. See *United States v. Montoya de Hernandez* [excerpted earlier].

The concept of reasonable suspicion, like probable cause, is not "readily, or even usefully, reduced to a neat set of legal rules." We think the Court of Appeals' effort to refine and elaborate the requirements of "reasonable suspicion" in this case creates unnecessary difficulty in dealing with one of the relatively simple concepts embodied in the Fourth Amendment. In evaluating the validity of a stop such as this, we must consider "the totality of the circumstances—the whole picture." . . .

"The process does not deal with hard certainties, but with probabilities. Long before the law of probabilities was articulated as such, practical people formulated certain common-sense conclusions about human behavior; jurors as fact-finders are permitted to do the same—and so are law enforcement officers.''

The rule enunciated by the Court of Appeals, in which evidence available to an officer is divided into evidence of ''ongoing criminal behavior,'' on the one hand, and ''probabilistic'' evidence, on the other, is not in keeping with the quoted statements from our decisions. It also seems to us to draw a sharp line between types of evidence, the probative value of which varies only in degree. The Court of Appeals classified evidence of traveling under an alias, or evidence that the suspect took an evasive or erratic path through an airport, as meeting the test for showing ''ongoing criminal activity.'' . . .

On the other hand, the factors in this case that the Court of Appeals treated as merely ''probabilistic'' also have probative significance. Paying $2,100 in cash for two airplane tickets is out of the ordinary, and it is even more out of the ordinary to pay that sum from a roll of $20 bills containing nearly twice that amount of cash. Most business travelers, we feel confident, purchase airline tickets by credit card or check so as to have a record for tax or business purposes, and few vacationers carry with them thousands of dollars in $20 bills. We also think the agents had a reasonable ground to believe that respondent was traveling under an alias; the evidence was by no means conclusive, but it was sufficient to warrant consideration. While a trip from Honolulu to Miami, standing alone, is not a cause for any sort of suspicion, here there was more: surely few residents of Honolulu travel from that city for 20 hours to spend 48 hours in Miami during the month of July.

Any one of these factors is not by itself proof of any illegal conduct and is quite consistent with innocent travel. But we think taken together they amount to reasonable suspicion. . . .

We do not agree with respondent that our analysis is somehow changed by the agents' belief that his behavior was consistent with one of the DEA's ''drug courier profiles.''[a] A court sitting to determine the existence of reasonable suspicion must require the agent to articulate the factors leading to that conclusion, but the fact that these factors may be set forth in a ''profile'' does not somehow detract from their evidentiary significance as seen by a trained agent.

Reversed and remanded. . . .

DISSENT

Justice Marshall, with whom Justice Brennan joins, dissenting.

Because the strongest advocates of Fourth Amendment rights are frequently criminals, it is easy to forget that our interpretations of such rights apply to the innocent and the guilty alike. Illinois v. Gates [see chap. 6] in the present case, the chain of events set in motion when respondent Andrew Sokolow was stopped by Drug Enforcement Administration (DEA) agents at Honolulu International Airport led to the discovery of cocaine and, ultimately, to Sokolow's conviction for drug trafficking. But in sustaining this conviction on the ground that the agents reasonably suspected Sokolow of ongoing criminal

---

[a]Agent Kempshall testified that respondent's behavior ''had all the classic aspects of a drug courier.'' Since 1974, the DEA has trained narcotics officers to identify drug smugglers on the basis of the sort of circumstantial evidence at issue here.

activity, the Court diminishes the rights of all citizens to ''to be secure in their persons,'' U.S. Const. Amdt. IV, as they traverse the Nation's airports. Finding this result constitutionally impermissible, I dissent. The Fourth Amendment cabins government's authority to intrude on personal privacy and security by requiring that searches and seizures usually be supported by a showing of probable cause. The reasonable-suspicion standard is a derivation of the probable cause command, applicable only to those brief detentions which fall short of being full-scale searches and seizures and which are necessitated by law-enforcement exigencies such as the need to stop ongoing crimes, to prevent imminent crimes, and to protect law-enforcement officers in highly charged situations. Terry v. Ohio [excerpted earlier] By requiring reasonable suspicion as a prerequisite to such seizures, the Fourth Amendment protects innocent persons from being subjected to ''overbearing or harassing'' police conduct carried out solely on the basis of imprecise stereotypes of what criminals look like, or on the basis of irrelevant personal characteristics such as race.

To deter such egregious police behavior, we have held that a suspicion is not reasonable unless officers have based it on ''specific and articulable facts.'' . . . [T]o detain, officers must ''have a reasonable suspicion, based on objective facts, that the individual is involved in criminal activity''. . . . The rationale for permitting brief, warrantless seizures is, after all, that it is impractical to demand strict compliance with the Fourth Amendment's ordinary probable-cause requirement in the face of ongoing or imminent criminal activity demanding ''swift action predicated upon the on-the-spot observations of the officer on the beat.'' . . . Evaluated against this standard, the facts about Andrew Sokolow known to the DEA agents at the time they stopped him fall short of reasonably indicating that he was engaged at the time in criminal activity. It is highly significant that the DEA agents stopped Sokolow because he matched one of the DEA's ''profiles'' of a paradigmatic drug courier. In my view, a law enforcement officer's mechanistic application of a formula of personal and behavioral traits in deciding whom to detain can only dull the officer's ability and determination to make sensitive and fact-specific inferences ''in light of his experience,'' particularly in ambiguous or borderline cases. Reflexive reliance on a profile of drug courier characteristics runs a far greater risk than does ordinary, case-by-case police work, of subjecting innocent individuals to unwarranted police harassment and detention. This risk is enhanced by the profile's ''chameleon-like way of adapting to any particular set of observations.''

CASE DISCUSSION

Defendant was convicted in the United States District Court for the District of Hawaii of possessing cocaine with intent to distribute. Defendant appealed. The Court of Appeals reversed and remanded. Certiorari was granted. The Supreme Court, Chief Justice Rehnquist, held that agents had reasonable suspicion to make an investigative stop of the defendant who was suspected as a drug courier.

What were the facts upon which the DEA agents based the ''stop''? Explain the difference between ''ongoing criminal activity'' and ''personal characteristics.'' Why did the Supreme Court reject dividing evidence into these two categories? Do you agree? Should the drug profile alone constitute ''reasonable suspicion that crime may be afoot''? Explain. Under what conditions, if any, should such ''circumstantial'' evidence as the drug profile provide the basis for stops? Does the Supreme Court's rejection of the two-part test promote the interest in obtaining the correct result? procedural regularity? crime control? control of government? Explain.

Should there be a rule that limits stops to investigating ''serious crime''? If so, what crimes would you put on the list? Would you include suspected public drunkenness? suspected prostitution? suspected marijuana possession? Refer to *Kolendar v. Lawson* (the case of the ''California Walkman'') in chapter 1. Would you include those stops? Explain. What facts did Martin have to make the stop? Do you agree they were sufficient?

A Model Stop Provision

Several states have statutes similar to the New York stop-and-frisk law quoted in *Sibron v. New York. (see below.)* These statutes answer vaguely, if at all, several important questions surrounding stops: (1) Do stops include only *street* detentions? (2) Can officers stop for suspicion of *all* crimes? (3) What constitutes a stop? (4) How long may police detain citizens during a stop? (5) How extensively may police question citizens during a stop? (6) Can officers use force and, if so, how much, to stop citizens? The Model Code of Pre-Arraignment Procedure attempts to answer these questions in the provision quoted here.

Section 110.2 Stopping of Persons

(1) *Cases in Which Stop Is Authorized.* A law enforcement officer, lawfully present in any place, may, in the following circumstances, order a person to remain in the officer's presence near such place for such period as is reasonably necessary for the accomplishment of the purposes authorized in this Subsection, but in no case for more than twenty minutes:

  (a) *Persons in suspicious circumstances relating to certain misdemeanors and felonies.*

     (i) Such person is observed in circumstances such that the officer reasonably suspects that he has just committed, is committing, or is about to commit a misdemeanor or felony, involving danger or forcible injury to persons or of appropriation of or damage to property; and

     (ii) such action is reasonably necessary to obtain or verify the identification of such person, to obtain or verify an account of such person's presence or conduct, or to determine whether to arrest such person.

  (b) *Witnesses near scene of certain misdemeanors and felonies.* . . .

  (c) *Suspects sought for certain previously committed felonies.*

     (i) The officer has reasonable cause to believe that a felony involving danger or forcible injury to persons or of appropriation of or damage to property has been committed, and

     (ii) he reasonably suspects person may have committed it, and

     (iii) such action is reasonably necessary to obtain or verify the identification of such person for the purpose of determining whether to arrest him for such felony. . . .

(3) *Use of Force.* In order to exercise the authority conferred in Subsections (1) and (2) of this Section, a law enforcement officer may use such force, other than deadly force, as is reasonably necessary to stop any person or vehicle or to cause any person to remain in the officer's presence.[23]

The code defines a stop as an order to suspects that they remain in the officer's presence near the place where the encounter takes place; an *order* to stop itself constitutes a stop, and the code limits it to an order to remain near the place where the officer gave it. This allows for some movement, such as stepping out of a car. In addition, the model provision limits stops to twenty minutes; it draws the "bright line" the Supreme Court has up to now declined to draw. Twenty minutes is a maximum; if officers can sort the matter out sooner, they must do so. The model provision adopts the reasonable suspicion standard as the foundation for stops. It also expands investigative authority beyond street encounters by empowering officers to stop citizens wherever officers are lawfully present. Hence, officers in any public place or, presumably, inside citizens' homes, either by invitation or some other lawful means, may detain occupants. This expansion is implicit in the cases, since many of them involve situations in bars, airports, stores, and even private homes.

Finally, the model provision places more significant limits on stops than does existing law. The police may detain citizens only to investigate felonies or misdemeanors that threaten to hurt people or their property. This limitation excludes most minor crimes and, perhaps most important, drug offenses. Stops restricted to the situations outlined in the provision are justified despite their costs:

> There are two different sorts of costs associated with the stop. First, there is the imposition upon innocent persons even when the police stay within the terms of the authority granted. Such imposition is an evil itself, and may lead as well to the further evil of resentment against the police and civil authority in general. Second, there is the danger that the stop is susceptible to abuse. It may be used not for its authorized purpose but to harass persons to whom the police may be hostile or about whom they feel a generalized suspicion or apprehension. . . . And the stop and frisk carry the special potential that they may be used to circumvent the constitutional restrictions on search and seizure by providing a pretext to search for narcotics and gambling slips. The danger of abuse is argued to be particularly serious, since the stop must be predicated on a more permissive standard than arrest thus making it more difficult to confine the authority to proper cases and to ascertain after the act whether an abuse has indeed taken place.[24]

Decision Point

Agent Cooke of the Drug Enforcement Agency (DEA) became suspicious of a pickup truck and car traveling in tandem on a highway near a beach. He followed the two vehicles for twenty miles. He decided to make an "investigative stop" and radioed the state highway patrol for assistance. Officer Thrasher responded to the call. Cooke and Thrasher, each in his own vehicle, followed the truck and car for a time, then motioned them to pull off to the side of the road. The car stopped, but the truck continued on the highway. Cooke approached the stopped car; Thrasher followed the truck. Cooke approached the car, identified himself, and asked for identification from the driver, Sharpe. Then Cooke attempted to radio Thrasher to find out if he had stopped the truck. Unable to reach Thrasher for several minutes, Cooke radioed local police for assistance. They arrived in about ten minutes. Cooke asked them to "maintain the situation" while he left to join Thrasher.

In the meantime, Thrasher had stopped the truck about a half-mile down the road. He approached the truck with his revolver drawn. He ordered the driver, Savage, to get out and assume a "spread eagle" position against the side of the truck, then patted him down. Cooke arrived on the scene about fifteen minutes after Thrasher stopped the truck. Cooke put his nose to the truck and said he smelled marijuana. He then sought permission to look in the truck for marijuana. At this point about twenty minutes had lapsed since the stop. Without Savage's permission, Cooke took the keys from the ignition, opened the rear of the truck, and discovered marijuana.

Cooke returned to the car and arrested Sharpe. Approximately thirty to forty minutes had elapsed between the time Cooke stopped the car and the time he arrested Sharpe.

Were Sharpe's and Savage's stops lawful? The United States Supreme Court ruled that since the officers "diligently pursued a means of investigation that was likely to confirm or dispel their suspicions quickly, during which time it was necessary to detain" him, the twenty-minute stop of Savage was reasonable. Would you apply the model code twenty-minute limit to both stops?

═══ FRISKS

Frisks and stops are intimately linked, yet distinct, law enforcement actions. Stops constitute seizures, frisks, searches within the Fourth Amendment. Frisks require separate justification from stops; officers cannot automatically frisk all citizens they stop. The sole purpose for frisks is to protect officers; their sole object, to disarm armed suspects. Officers may not stop a citizens as a pretext to search for contraband. The actions must occur in reverse order: officers making a stop to investigate suspicious circumstances may frisk for weapons to protect themselves. A lawful stop is a prerequisite for any frisk. In other words, without a precedent, contemporaneous lawful stop, officers cannot conduct a frisk of a citizen.

Furthermore, frisks require facts that will support a reasonable suspicion that a suspect is armed. Facts sufficient to support a stop—reasonable suspicion that crime may be afoot—do not automatically constitute reasonable suspicion that the suspect is armed. It may do so, as in *Terry,* where the suspected crime was armed robbery; in most possessory crimes it may not do so.

Four basic Fourth Amendment issues surround the law regarding frisks: (1) what constitutes a frisk; (2) the proper scope of a frisk; (3) the legitimate purposes of a frisk; and (3) the necessary factual foundation for a frisk.

Definition of Frisk

Frisks constitute one type of search on a continuum of intrusiveness. The most intrusive are searches of body cavities. Perhaps only slightly less intrusive are the strip searches, followed by the full-body searches. A frisk, on the other hand îs a

. . . contact or patting of the outer clothing of a person to detect by the sense of touch, if a concealed weapon is being carried. . . . The sense of exterior touch here involved is not very far different from the sense of sight or hearing upon which police customarily act. . . . [It is] a minor inconvenience and petty indignity.[25]

Clearly, patdowns are the least intrusive of the searches protected by the Fourth Amendment; but even the most superficial unwanted touchings constitute significant intrusions. Police physical contacts magnify the intrusiveness of these contacts. This is a primary reason why the Supreme Court has brought frisks within the scope of the Fourth Amendment. All of the restrictions placed upon the power to frisk are directly related to the importance placed upon the intrusive quality of unwanted body contacts by the police.

Decision Point

Consider the following. Which are frisks? searches? neither?

1. Officers look for bulges that might be weapons but do not touch the suspect.
2. An officer sees a bulge and asks a suspect to open his jacket; upon seeing a knife, the officer asks the suspect to hand over the weapon.
3. An officer asks a suspect to open her jacket so she can see what inside; the officer does not touch the suspect.
4. An officer reaches in to an inside pocket of an open jacket and removes a knife; the officer does not touch the suspect's body.
5. An officer goes over the outer clothing lightly to detect weapons.
6. An officer reaches inside and under a heavy overcoat to feel for bulges.
7. An officer opens the handbag a suspect is carrying and looks inside.
8. An officer opens a suspect's handbag and empties its contents.
9. An officer pats down (goes over the outer clothing of) a suspect's companion.
10. An officer lightly feels a suspect's groin area.
11. An officer orders a suspect to raise his hands and lean up against a wall while she feels his outer clothing, including the groin area.

It is often said that frisk law balances citizens' right to privacy and society's need to enforce the criminal law. In a sense, this is true. In a larger sense, both the right to privacy and criminal law enforcement contribute to the same social interest—a sense of security based on the confidence that government will protect its citizens from both criminals and its own excesses.

The Purpose of Frisks

No one can reasonably expect police officers to risk their lives unduly in order to investigate suspicious persons and circumstances. Hence, the law permits police officers to conduct a superficial search, a "once over the outer part of the body lightly,'' or pat down for weapons, incident to a lawful stop. Only if police lawfully stop citizens can they frisk them. A lawful stop is a necessary, not sufficient, condition to authorize a frisk. The other conditions include (1) that the frisk remain within the limited scope necessary to protect investigative officers; and (2) that sufficient facts support it.

When the Supreme Court decided *Terry v. Ohio,* it was also asked to decide whether frisks for evidence were lawful. In *Sibron v. New York* (excerpted under ''Foundations for Lawful Frisks''), the court emphatically rejected that proposition on the ground that frisks are so intrusive that only saving officers' lives justifies them. However, if officers reasonably suspect that suspects are armed and in the course of a patdown for weapons come upon contraband or evidence, the police may seize it. Critics maintain that the police abuse the frisk power in cases where the object of the stop is to discover contraband, particularly in drug offenses. They assert that the police are looking for drugs under the guise of protective patdowns. To avoid abuse, critics recommend limiting Fourth Amendment seizures on less than probable cause to crimes that directly threaten persons, that is, crimes of violence.

> . . . [I]t is hard to ignore the fact that . . . any power will be abused. The courts have made it quite clear that in the name of police safety, they will always allow a frisk of extensive proportions, and it is difficult to see how this can be avoided. A corollary hard reality is that police will use this power not really to protect themselves but to seize and confiscate weapons and other contraband.[26]

The Supreme Court addressed the pretext problem, and others, in *Adams v. Williams,* the first major stop and frisk case decided after *Terry v. Ohio.*

CASE

Was the stop a pretext to frisk for drugs?

Adams v. Williams

407 U.S. 143, 92 S.Ct. 1921, 32 L.Ed.2d 612 (1972)

[Mr. Justice Rehnquist delivered the opinion of the Court.]

FACTS

Police Sgt. John Connolly was alone early in the morning on car patrol duty in a high-crime area of Bridgeport, Connecticut. At approximately 2:15 a.m. a person known to Sgt. Connolly approached his cruiser and informed him that an individual seated in a nearby vehicle was carrying narcotics and had a gun at his waist. After calling for assistance on his car radio, Sgt. Connolly approached the vehicle to investigate the informant's report. Connolly tapped on the car window and asked the occupant, Robert Williams to open the door. When Williams rolled down the window instead, the sergeant reached into the car and removed a fully loaded revolver from Williams' waistband. The gun had not been visible to Connolly from outside the car, but it was in precisely the place indicated by the informant. Williams was then arrested by Connolly for unlawful possession of the pistol. A search incident to that arrest was conducted after other officers arrived. They found substantial quantities of heroin on Williams' person and in the car, and they found a machete and a second revolver hidden in the automobile.

OPINION

Respondent contends that the initial seizure of his pistol, upon which rested the later search and seizure of other weapons and narcotics, was not justified by the informant's tip to Sgt. Connolly. He claims that absent a more reliable informant, or some corroboration of the tip, the policeman's actions were unreasonable under the standards set forth in Terry v. Ohio [excerpted earlier]. In Terry this Court recognized that 'a police officer may in appropriate circumstances and in an appropriate manner approach a person for purposes of investigating possibly criminal behavior even though there is no probable cause to make an arrest.' The Fourth Amendment does not require a policeman who lacks the precise level of information necessary for probable cause to arrest to simply shrug his shoulders and allow a crime to occur or a criminal to escape. On the contrary, Terry recognizes that it may be the essence of good police work to adopt an intermediate response. A brief stop of a suspicious individual, in order to determine his identity or to maintain the status quo momentarily while obtaining more information, may be most reasonable in light of the facts known to the officer at the time.

The Court recognized in Terry that the policeman making a reasonable investigatory stop should not be denied the opportunity to protect himself from attack by a hostile suspect. 'When an officer is justified in believing that the individual whose suspicious behavior he is investigating at close range is armed and presently dangerous to the officer or to others,' he may conduct a limited protective search for concealed weapons. 392 U.S., at 24, 88 S.Ct., at 1881. The purpose of this limited search is not to discover evidence of crime, but to allow the officer to pursue his investigation without fear of violence, and thus the frisk for weapons might be equally necessary and reasonable, whether or not carrying a concealed weapon violated any applicable state law. So long as the officer is entitled to make a forcible stop[a] and has reason to believe that the suspect is armed and dangerous, he may conduct a weapons search limited in scope to this protective purpose.

Applying these principles to the present case, we believe that Sgt. Connolly acted justifiably in responding to his informant's tip. The informant was known to him personally and had provided him with information in the past. This is a stronger case than obtains in the case of an anonymous telephone tip. The informant here came forward personally to give information that was immediately verifiable at the scene. Indeed, under Connecticut law, the informant might have been subject to immediate arrest for making a false complaint had Sgt. Connolly's investigation proved the tip incorrect. Thus, while the Court's

---

[a]Petitioner does not contend that Williams acted voluntarily in rolling down the window in his car.

decisions indicate that this informant's unverified tip may have been insufficient for a narcotics arrest or search warrant, the information carried enough indicia of reliability to justify the officer's forcible stop of Williams.

In reaching this conclusion, we reject respondent's argument that reasonable cause for a stop and frisk can only be based on the officer's personal observation, rather than on information supplied by another person. Informants' tips, like all other clues and evidence coming to a policeman on the scene, may vary greatly in their value and reliability. One simple rule will not cover every situation. Some tips, completely lacking in indicia of reliability, would either warrant no police response or require further investigation before a forcible stop of a suspect would be authorized. but in some situations—for example, when the victim of a street crime seeks immediate police aid and gives a description of his assailant, or when a credible informant warns of a specific impending crime—the subtleties of the hearsay rule should not thwart an appropriate police response.

While properly investigating the activity of a person who was reported to be carrying narcotics and a concealed weapon and who was sitting alone in a car in a high-crime area at 2:15 in the morning, Sgt. Connolly had ample reason to fear for his safety. When Williams rolled down his window, rather than complying with the policeman's request to step out of the car so that his movements could more easily be seen, the revolver allegedly at Williams' waist became an even greater threat. Under these circumstances the policeman's action in reaching to the spot where the gun was thought to be hidden constituted a limited intrusion designed to insure his safety, and we conclude that it was reasonable. The loaded gun seized as a result of this intrusion was therefore admissible at Williams' trial.

Reversed.

DISSENT

Mr. Justice Brennan, dissenting.
The crucial question on which this case turns, as the court concedes, is whether, there being no contention that Williams acted voluntarily in rolling down the window of his car, the State had shown sufficient cause to justify Sgt. Connolly's 'forcible' stop. I would affirm, believing, for the following reasons stated by Judge, now Chief Judge, Friendly, dissenting, that the State did not make that showing:

'To begin, I have the gravest hesitancy in extending (Terry v. Ohio, 392 U.S. 1, 88 S.Ct. 1868, 20 L.Ed.2d 889 (1968)) to crimes like the possession of narcotics. . . . There is too much danger that, instead of the stop being the object and the protective frisk an incident thereto, the reverse will be true. Against that we have here the added fact of the report that Williams had a gun on his person. . . . (But) Connecticut allows its citizens to carry weapons, concealed or otherwise, at will, provided only they have a permit, and gives its police officers no special authority to stop for the purpose of determining whether the citizen has one. . . .

'If I am wrong in thinking that Terry should not be applied at all to mere possessory offenses, . . . I would not find the combination of Officer Connolly's almost meaningless observation and the tip in this case to be sufficient justification for the intrusion. Terry v. Ohio was intended to free a police officer from the rigidity of a rule that would prevent his doing anything to a man reasonably suspected of being about to commit or having just committed a crime of violence, no matter how grave the problem or impelling the need for swift action, unless the officer had what a court would later determine to be probable cause for arrest. It was meant for the serious cases of imminent danger or of harm recently perpetrated to persons or property, not the conventional ones of possessory offenses. If it is to be extended to the latter at all, this should be only where observation by the officer himself or well authenticated information shows 'that criminal activity may be afoot.' I greatly fear that if the (contrary view) should be followed, Terry will have opened the sluice gates for serious and unintended erosion of the protection of the Fourth Amendment.'

Mr. Justice Marshall, with whom Mr. Justice Douglas joins, dissenting. Four years have passed since we decided Terry v. Ohio, . . . the first case in which this court explicitly recognized the concept of 'stop and frisk' and squarely held that police officers may, under appropriate circumstances, stop and frisk persons suspected of criminal activity even though there is less than probable cause for an arrest. This case marks our first opportunity to give some flesh to the bones of Terry et al. Unfortunately, the flesh provided by today's decision cannot possibly be made to fit on Terry's skeletal framework.

'(T)he most basic constitutional rule in this area is that 'searches conducted outside the judicial process, without prior approval by judge of magistrate, are per se unreasonable under the Fourth Amendment—subject only to a few specifically established and well-delineated exceptions.' The exceptions are 'jealously and carefully drawn. . . .

In today's decision the Court ignores the fact that Terry begrudgingly accepted the necessity for creating an exception from the warrant requirement of the Fourth Amendment and treats this case as if warrantless searches were the rule rather than the 'narrowly drawn' exception. This decision betrays the careful balance that Terry sought to strike between a citizen's right to privacy and his government's responsibility for effective law enforcement and expands the concept of warrantless searches far beyond anything heretofore recognized as legitimate. I dissent. . . .

The Court erroneously attempts to describe the search for the gun as a protective search incident to a reasonable investigatory stop. But, as in Terry, . . . there is no occasion in this case to determine whether or not police officers have a right to seize and to restrain a citizen in order to interrogate him. The facts are clear that the officer intended to make the search as soon as he approached the respondent. He asked no questions; he made no investigation; he simply searched. There was nothing a part from the information supplied by the informant to cause the officer to search. Our inquiry must focus, therefore, as it did in Terry on whether the officer had sufficient facts from which he could reasonably infer that respondent was not only engaging in illegal activity, but also that he was armed and dangerous. The focus falls on the informant.

The only information that the informant had previously given the officer involved homosexual conduct in the local railroad station. The following colloquy took place between respondent's counsel and the officer at the hearing on respondent's motion to suppress the evidence that had been seized from him.

'Q. Now, with respect to the information that was given you about homosexuals in the Bridgeport Police Station (sic), did that lead to an arrest? A. No.

'Q. An arrest was not made. A. No. There was no substantiating evidence.

'Q. There was no substantiating evidence? A. No.

'Q. And what do you mean by that? A. I didn't have occasion to witness these individuals committing any crime of any nature.

'Q. In other words, after this person gave you the information, you checked for corroboration before you made an arrest. Is that right? A. Well, I checked to determine the possibility of homosexual activity.

'Q. And since an arrest was made, I take it you didn't find any substantiating information. A. I'm sorry counselor, you say since an arrest was made.

'Q. Was not made. Since an arrest was not made, I presume you didn't find any substantiating information. A. No.

'Q. So that, you don't recall any other specific information given you about the commission of crimes by this informant. A. No. . . .

'Q. And you still thought this person was reliable. A. Yes.' . . .

We must decide whether or not the information possessed by this officer justified this interference with respondent's liberty. . . . Terry did not hold that whenever a policeman has a hunch that a citizen is engaging in criminal activity, he may engage in a stop and frisk. It held that if police officers want to stop and frisk, they must have specific facts from which they can reasonably infer that an individual is engaged in criminal activity and is armed and dangerous. It was central to our decision in Terry that the police officer acted on the basis of his own personal observations and that he carefully scrutinized the conduct of his suspects before interfering with them in any way. When we legitimated the conduct of the officer in Terry we did so because of the substantial reliability of the information on which the officer based his decision to act.

If the Court does not ignore the care with which we examined the knowledge possessed by the officer in Terry when he acted, then I cannot see how the actions of the officer in this case can be upheld. The Court explains what the officer knew about respondent before accosting him. But what is more significant is what he did not know. With respect to the scene generally, the officer had no idea how long respondent had been in the car, how long the car had been parked, or to whom the car belonged. With respect to the gun, the officer did not know if or when the informant had ever seen the gun, or whether the gun was carried legally, as Connecticut law permitted, or illegally. And with respect to the narcotics, the officer did not know what kind of narcotics respondent allegedly had, whether they were legally or illegally possessed, what the basis of the informant's knowledge was, or even whether the informant was capable of distinguishing narcotics from other substances.

Unable to answer any of these questions, the officer nevertheless determined that it was necessary to intrude on respondent's liberty. I believe that his determination was totally unreasonable. As I read Terry, an officer may act on the basis of reliable information short of probable cause to make a stop, and ultimately a frisk, if necessary; but the officer may not use unreliable, unsubstantiated, conclusory hearsay to justify an invasion of liberty. Terry never meant to approve the kind of knee-jerk police reaction that we have before us in this case. . . .

Mr. Justice Douglas was the sole dissenter in Terry. He warned of the 'powerful hydraulic pressures throughout our history that bear heavily on the Court to water down constitutional guarantees. . . .' While I took the position then that we were not watering down rights, but were hesitantly and cautiously striking a necessary balance between the rights of American citizens to be free from government intrusion into their privacy and their government's urgent need for a narrow exception to the warrant requirement of the Fourth Amendment, today's decision demonstrates just how prescient Mr. Justice Douglas was. It seems that the delicate balance that Terry struck was simply too delicate, too susceptible to the 'hydraulic pressures' of the day. As a result of today's decision, the balance struck in Terry is now heavily weighted in favor of the government. And the Fourth Amendment, which was included in the Bill of Rights to prevent the kind of arbitrary and oppressive police action involved herein, is dealt a serious blow. Today's decision invokes the specter of a society in which innocent citizens may be stopped, searched, and arrested at the whim of police officers who have only the slightest suspicion of improper conduct.

CASE DISCUSSION

Acting on a tip supplied moments earlier by an informant known to him, a police officer asked respondent to open his car door. Respondent lowered the window, and the officer reached into the car and found a loaded handgun (which had not been visible from the outside) in respondent's waistband, precisely where the informant said it would be. Respondent was arrested for unlawful possession of the handgun. A search incident to the arrest disclosed heroin on respondent's person (as the informant had reported), as well as other contraband in the car. Respondent's petition for federal habeas corpus relief was denied by the district court. The court of appeals reversed, holding that the evidence that had been used in the trial resulting in respondent's conviction had been by an unlawful search. On writ of *certiorari,* the Supreme Court reversed, holding that the stop and frisk did not violate the Fourth Amendment.

What fact constituted the foundation for the stop? for the frisk? Was the stop a pretext to find drugs? Did Officer Connolly reasonably suspect that Williams was armed? Explain. Should stop and frisk be limited to crimes threatening immediate violence? What interests would such a rule promote? Does it matter that the dissenters clearly believed that *Terry* involved a violent crime, and that the Court intended to limit its holding to such crimes?

The Scope of Frisks

Already clear from *Adams v. Williams* are two elements in the scope of lawful frisks: they must accompany lawful stops, and their sole purpose must be to protect investigating officers. In addition, officers may use only the amount of bodily contact necessary to protect themselves. In most cases, this means officers may lightly touch suspects' outer clothing to locate and seize concealed weapons. Courts are vague about how much further than these outer-clothing patdowns police officers may lawfully go.

The Model Code of Pre-Arraignment Procedure includes the following circumstances that might justify more extensive contact than a patdown of the outer clothing: (1) feeling a hard object inside a coat pocket that could be a weapon authorizes reaching inside the coat; (2) going under unusually bulky winter clothing; and (3) opening handbags.

Decision Point

Two deputies saw a car swerve into a ditch and stopped to investigate. Long, the only occupant, met the deputies at the rear of the car, showed his driver's license, and started back toward the open door of the car when the deputies asked him for the car registration. The officers saw a large hunting knife on the floorboard, so the one of the deputies frisked Long. The other then entered the vehicle and found an open pouch of marijuana under an armrest.

Was the frisk lawful? The United States Supreme Court held that because "roadside encounters between police and suspects are especially hazardous, and that danger may arise from the possible presence of weapons in the area surrounding a suspect," the "search of the passenger compartment of an automobile, limited to those areas in which a weapon may be placed or hidden, is permissible if the police officer possesses a reasonable belief based on 'specific and articulable facts which, taken together with the rational inferences from those facts, reasonably warrant' the officer in believing that the suspect is dangerous and may gain immediate control of weapons." The Court decided, in *Michigan v. Long,* that these conditions were met.[27]

Is it lawful to conduct a protective search of a truck after finding weapons in a house that the driver had just approached at high speed? In *United States v. Denney,* the Seventh Circuit Court approved such a search.[28]

How lawful is the "automatic companion" rule, adopted by several circuits, in which all companions in the immediate vicinity are subject to patdowns? For example, searching a suspect's companion's handbag was lawful. The Sixth Circuit has rejected the automatic companion rule because, according to the court, the reasonable suspicion in *Terry* "has [not] been eroded to the point that an individual may be frisked based upon nothing more than an unfortunate choice of associates."[29]

Foundation for Lawful Frisks

Officers may frisk citizens who they reasonably suspect are armed. What constitutes this reasonable suspicion is not subject to a rigid formula. No specific list of facts constitutes reasonable suspicion that suspects are armed. Some examples, however, suggest the kind of objective basis that justify particular frisks. In *Terry v. Ohio,* it was the nature of the crime. Officer McFadden reasonably suspected that Terry and his companions were about to commit armed robbery. If it was reasonable to suspect that they were going to commit armed robbery, it was, of course, also reasonable to suspect they would use weapons to do so. Hence, it was reasonable to frisk.

Other observations that may lead officers reasonably to suspect that suspects are armed include a bulge in clothing; sudden movement toward a pocket or other place that might contain a weapon; knowledge that the suspect was armed on a previous occasion. The test requires only that officers reasonably conclude suspects may be armed; hence, if the frisk does not produce a weapon (which in four out of five cases they do not), the frisk remains lawful. That the officer did not turn out to be right does not make the frisk unlawful. Furthermore the test measures what is reasonable to a *police officer,* not an average citizen. Police officers, by their experience, can read more into facts surrounding complex criminal behavior, according to the law, than average citizens can. For example, the average person knows virtually nothing about factual patterns surrounding a drug operation, but experienced narcotics officers quickly grasp them. Using what is reasonable to a police officer as a standard allows latitude to benefit from that experience.[30]

CASE

Did Martin reasonably suspect Sibron was armed?

Sibron v. New York

392 U.S. 40, 88 S.Ct. 1889, 20 L.Ed.2d 917 (1968)

FACTS

. . . Sibron . . . was convicted of the unlawful possession of heroin. He moved before trial to suppress the heroin seized from his person by the arresting officer, Brooklyn Patrolman Anthony Martin. After the trial court denied his motion, Sibron pleaded guilty to the charge, preserving his right to appeal the evidentiary ruling. At the hearing on the motion to suppress, Officer Martin testified that while he was patrolling his beat in uniform on March 9, 1965, he observed Sibron "continually from the hours of 4:00 pm to 12:00, midnight...in the vicinity of 742 Broadway." He stated that during this period of time he saw Sibron in conversation with six or eight persons whom he (Patrolman Martin) knew from past experience to be narcotics addicts. The officer testified that he did not overhear any of these conversations, and that he did not see anything pass between Sibron and any of the others. Late in the evening Sibron entered a restaurant. Patrolman Martin saw Sibron speak with three more known addicts inside the restaurant. Once again, nothing was overhead and nothing was seen to pass between Sibron and the addicts. Sibron sat down and ordered pie and coffee, and, as he was eating, Patrolman Martin approached him and told him to come outside. Once outside, the officer said to Sibron, "You know what I am after." According to the officer, Sibron "mumbled something and reached into his pocket." Simultaneously, Patrolman Martin thrust his hand into the same pocket, discovering several glassine envelopes, which, it turned out, contained heroin.

OPINION

Mr. Chief Justice Warren delivered the opinion of the Court.

[This is a companion case to *Terry v. Ohio,* decided the same day.] . . . [It] present[s] related questions under the Fourth and Fourteenth Amendments, but . . . arise[s] in the context of New York's "stop-and-frisk" law, N.Y. Code Crim. Proc. §180-a. This statute provides:

"1. A police officer may stop any person abroad in a public place who he reasonably suspects is committing, has committed, or is about to commit a felony or any of the offenses specified in section five hundred fifty-two of this chapter, and may demand of him his name, address and an explanation of his actions.

"2. When a police officer has stopped a person for questioning pursuant to this section and reasonably suspects that he is in danger of life or limb, he may search such person for a dangerous weapon. If the police officer finds such a weapon or any other thing the possession of which may constitute a crime, he may take and keep it until the completion of the questioning, at which time he shall either return it, if lawfully possessed, or arrest such person."

. . . Sibron . . . [was] convicted of [a] crime in New York state courts on the basis of evidence seized from [his] person by police officers. The Court of Appeals of New York held that the evidence was properly admitted, on the ground that the searches which uncovered it were authorized by the statute. . . .

It is clear that the heroin was inadmissible in evidence against him. The prosecution has quite properly abandoned the notion that there was probable cause to arrest Sibron for any crime at the time Patrolman Martin accosted him in the restaurant, took him outside and searched him. The officer was not acquainted with Sibron and had no information concerning him. He merely saw Sibron talking to a number of known narcotics addicts over a period of eight hours. It must be emphasized that Patrolman Martin was completely ignorant regarding the content of these conversations, and that he saw nothing pass between Sibron and the addicts. So far as he knew, they might indeed "have been talking about the World Series." The inference that people who talk to narcotics addicts are engaged in the criminal traffic in narcotics is simply not the sort of reasonable inference required to support an intrusion by the police upon an individual's personal security. Nothing resembling probable cause existed until after the search had turned up the envelopes of heroin. It is axiomatic that an incident search may not precede an arrest and serve as part of its justification. Thus the search cannot be justified as incident to a lawful arrest.

. . . The Court of Appeals has . . . justified searches during field interrogation on the ground that "[t]he answer to the question propounded by the policeman may be a bullet; in any case the exposure to danger could be very great.'' But the application of this reasoning to the facts of this case proves too much. The police officer is not entitled to seize and search every person whom he sees on the street or of whom he makes inquires. Before he places a hand on the person of a citizen in search of anything, he must have constitutionally adequate, reasonable grounds for doing so. In the case of the self-protective search for weapons, he must be able to point to particular facts from which he reasonably inferred that the individual was armed and dangerous. Patrolman Martin's testimony reveals no such facts. The suspect's mere act of talking with a number of known narcotics addicts over an eight-hour period no more gives rise to reasonable fear of life or limb on the part of the police officer than it justifies an arrest for committing a crime. Nor did Patrolman urge that when Sibron put his hand in his pocket, he feared that he was going for a weapon and acted in self-defense. His opening statement to Sibron—''You know what I am after''—made it abundantly clear that he sought narcotics, and his testimony at the hearing left no doubt that he thought there were narcotics in Sibron's pocket.

Even assuming *arguendo* that there were adequate grounds to search Sibron for weapons, the nature and scope of the search conducted by Patrolman Martin were so clearly unrelated to that justification as to render the heroin inadmissable. The search for weapons approved in *Terry* consisted solely of a limited patting of the outer clothing of the suspect for concealed objects which might be used as instruments of assault. Only when he discovered such objects did the officer in *Terry* place his hands in the pockets of the men he searched. In this case, with no attempt at an initial limited exploration for arms, Patrolman Martin thrust his hands into Sibron's pocket and took from him envelopes of heroin. His testimony shows that he was looking for narcotics, and he found them. The search was not reasonable limited in scope to the accomplishment of the only goal which might conceivably have justified its inception—the protection of the officer by disarming a potentially dangerous man. Such a search violates the guarantee of the Fourth Amendment, which protects the sanctity of the person against unreasonable intrusions on the part of all government agents.

CONCURRING OPINION

Mr. Justice Douglas, concurring.

Officer Martin testified on the night in question he observed appellant Sibron continually from 4:00 p.m. to 12 midnight and that during that eight-hour period, Sibron conversed with different persons each personally known to Martin as narcotics addicts. When Sibron entered a restaurant, Martin followed him inside where he observed Sibron talking to three other persons also personally known to Martin as narcotics addicts. At that point he approached Sibron and asked him to come outside. When Sibron stepped out, Martin said, ''You know what I am after.'' Sibron then reached inside his pocket, and at the same time Martin reached into the same pocket and discovered several glassine envelopes which were found to contain heroin. Sibron was subsequently convicted of unlawful possession of heroin.

Consorting with criminals may in a particular factual settting may be a basis for believing that a criminal project is underway. Yet talking with addicts without more rises no higher than suspicion. This is all we have here; and if it is sufficient for a "seizure" and a "search," then there is no such thing as privacy for this vast group of "sick" people.

[Justice Fortas's, Harlan's, and Black's concurring opinions are omitted. There were no dissents.]

CASE DISCUSSION

What facts supported the frisk? Why don't they constitute reasonable suspicion, according to the Court? Do you agree? Could Officer Martin have reasonably believed Sibron was reaching for a knife when he put his hand in his pocket? Should police officers have to take that chance by the requirement that they have a foundation to support the frisk? Would you favor a "bright line" rule that permitted police officers to frisk any suspect they lawfully stop?

A Model Frisk Provision

The Model Code of Pre-Arraignment Procedure recommends the following provision to address the issues that stop and frisk raise.

> Section 110.2 (4) *Frisk for Dangerous Weapons.* A law enforcement officer who has stopped any person . . . may, if the officer reasonably believes that his safety or the safety of others present so requires, search for any dangerous weapons by an external patting of such person's outer clothing. If in the course of such search he feels an object which he reasonably believes to be a dangerous weapon, he may take such action as is necessary to examine such object.

The model code provision permits frisks only incident to lawful stops, requires an objective standard as a foundation, and limits frisks to searches for weapons. In most cases, the statute provides only for outer-clothing patdowns. It does, however, permit more intrusive searches if an ambiguous bulge requires further examination.

The model code reporters' explanation for the model frisk provision summarizes the issues in frisks and demonstrates the important interests frisk law attempts to balance.

> The authority to search is included with some reluctance. Quite apart from the opportunities for abuse it presents, it must be recognized that such a search would be offensive and humiliating to many people. Moreover, . . . there is a lack of systematic empirical evidence to show how frequently and in what circumstances the frisk is necessary to the officer's safety, or to what extent it will be used only in circumstances which reasonably justify it. Nevertheless, in this case even more than in that of the power to stop, it is necessary to put great weight on the experience and conviction of law enforcement personnel, since in this case the officer feels that his personal safety is at stake. Police officers should not be asked to risk what they generally believe may be a possibly fatal encounter, unless they are authorized to protect themselves by "frisking" the suspect at the outset.[31]

═══ SUMMARY

Police investigative activities range across a broad spectrum, including brief detentions, questioning, and weapons patdowns in public, to highly intrusive in-custody interrogation and strip and body-cavity searches. According to the Supreme Court, stops are seizures, and frisks, searches under the Fourth Amendment. The Fourth Amendment does not encompass all the deprivations and intrusions associated with police investigation. It excludes voluntary encounters between citizens and police on the street; it does cover brief detentions where citizens reasonably believe they are not free to leave the officer's presence.

Under the Fourth Amendment, police must have facts sufficient to lead a resonable person to believe that a crime *may* have been committed, or *may* be afoot in order to detain citizens. Furthermore, the Constitution limits stops' duration, scope, and location. Police may "freeze" a suspicious situation only long enough to conduct an on-the-spot check for ID and to investigate the reasons for suspicious persons' presence. Lawful stops authorize frisks for weapons. Officers who reasonably suspect the suspects are armed may pat them down—go over their outer clothing lightly—for weapons. The sole purpose for frisks is to protect officers; officers should not have to risk their lives unduly to investigate crime.

Stop-and-frisk law balances several interests: (1) obtaining accurate and sufficient facts to support criminal investigation on the street; (2) protecting citizens against unwarranted or discriminatory invasions of privacy and other indignities in public places; (3) preserving and extending the rule of law to police encounters with citizens on the street; (4) satisfying organizational interests in efficient, economical, and harmonious police operations; and (5) reducing the police frustration with interference in their job that is sometimes called "handcuffing the police."

═══ QUESTIONS FOR REVIEW AND DISCUSSION

1. Describe the history of stop-and-frisk law.
2. What basic issues did the Supreme Court have to address when it decided *Terry v. Ohio*?
3. Define a stop and list its main purposes.
4. What is the proper foundation that justifies a stop? Give at least three examples of what might constitute such a foundation.
5. Should mere questioning be a stop? Give reasons for your answer.
6. What are the major criteria the courts consider in determining the proper scope of lawful stops?
7. Define and state the proper purpose of a frisk.
8. What is the proper foundation for a frisk? List three examples of what might constitute this foundation.
9. How extensive a search might a frisk include?
10. What are the major arguments in favor of allowing frisks? What are the major dangers?

≡ NOTES

1. Loren G. Stern, "Stop and Frisk: An Historical Answer to a Modern Problem," *Journal of Criminal Law, Criminology, and Police Science* 58(1967):532; Frank Remington, "The Law Relating to 'On the Street' Detention, Questioning and Frisking of Suspected Persons and Police Arrest Privileges in General," *Journal of Criminal Law, Criminology, and Police Science* 50(1960):390.

2. Leonard Levy, *The Origins of the Fifth Amendment* (New York: Oxford, 1968), discusses the history of these developments at great length. See also Wayne R. LaFave, "Street Encounters and the Constitution: *Terry, Sibron,* and *Peters,* and Beyond," *Michigan Law Review* 37(1968):39.

3. William J. Mertens, "The Fourth Amendment and the Control of Police Discretion," *Journal of Law Reform* 17(1983):551–625.

4. Frank H. Easterbrook, "Criminal Procedure as a Market System," *The Journal of Legal Studies* 12(1983):289; Peter Aranella, "Rethinking the Functions of Criminal Procedure: The Warren and Burger Courts' Competing Ideologies," *Georgetown Law Journal* 72(1983):185; Craig M. Bradley, "Two Models of the Fourth Amendment," *Michigan Law Review* 83:(1985):1468.

5. George E. Dix, "Nonarrest Investigatory Detentions in Search and Seizure Law," *Duke Law Journal* 1985:849, 853–54.

6. American Law Institute, *Model Code of Pre-Arraignment Procedure: Proposed Official Draft, Complete Text and Commentary* (Philadelphia: American Law Institute, 1975), 270–72.

7. *Adams v. Williams,* 407 U.S. 143, 92 S.Ct. 1921, 32 L.Ed.2d 612 (1972).

8. Wayland D. Pilcher, "The Law and Practice of Field Interrogation," *Journal of Criminal Law, Criminology, and Police Science* 58(1967):465, 490 (between 3 to 4 percent of those stopped are arrested).

9. Edwin J. Butterfoss, "Bright Line Seizures: The Need for Clarity in Determining when Fourth Amendment Activity Begins," *The Journal of Criminal Law and Criminology,* 79(1988):437; *United States v. Berry,* 670 F.2d 583, 591 (5th Cir. Unit B 1982).

10. Wayne R. LaFave, "Seizures' Typology: Classifying Detentions of the Person to Resolve Warrant, Grounds, and Search Issues," *Journal of Law Reform* 17(1984):420–26.

11. American Law Institute, *A Model Code of Pre-Arraignment Procedure.*

12. *Immigration and Naturalization Services v. Delgado, 466 U.S. 210, 104 S.Ct. 1758, 80 L.Ed.2d 247 (1984).*

13. *Brown v. Texas,* 443 U.S. 47, 99 S.Ct. 2637, 61 L.Ed.2d 357 (1979).

14. 469 U.S. 221, 105 S.Ct. 675, 83 L.Ed.2d 604 (1985) (wanted flier).

15. *Michigan v. Summers,* 452 U.S. 692, 101 S.Ct. 2587, 69 L.Ed.2d 340 (1981).

16. *United States v. Sharpe,* 470 U.S. 675, 682, 105 S.Ct. 1568, 84 L.Ed.2d 605 (1985).

17. *Hayes v. Florida,* 470 U.S. 811, 105 S.Ct. 1643, 84 L.Ed.2d 705 (1985); *United States v. Alverez-Sanchez,* 774 F.2d 1036 (11th Cir. 1985)

18. American Law Institute, "Commentary," *A Model Code of Pre-Arraignment Procedure,* 283.

19. *Florida v. Royer,* 460 U.S. 491, 103 S.Ct. 1319, 75 L.Ed.2d 229 (1983).

20. Quoted in J. Shane Craemer, *The Law of Arrest, Search, and Seizure,* 3d ed. (New York: Holt, Rhinehart, and Winston, 1980), 37.

21. Craemer, *Law of Arrest, Search and Seizure,* 15 includes these and a full checklist of the kinds of information that qualify for foundations.

22. See Herman Schwartz, "Stop and Frisk," *Journal of Criminal Law, Criminology, and Police Science* 58(1967):433, 446.

23. American Law Institute, *Model Code of Pre-Arraignment Procedure.*

24. American Law Institute, "Commentary," *Model Code of Pre-Arraignment Procedure*, 273.

25. *People v. Rivera, 14 N.Y.2d 441, 252 N.Y.S.2d 458, 462, 463, 201 N.E.2d 32 (1964).*

26. American Law Institute, *Model Code of Pre-Arraignment Procedure*, discussed above; 26.21; Schwartz, "Stop and Frisk," 433, 461.

27. 463 U.S. 1032, 103 S.Ct. 3469, 77 L.Ed.2d 1201 (1983).

28. American Law Institute, *Model Code of Pre-Arraignment Procedure*, 279; *Michigan v. Long*, 463 U.S. 1032, 103 S.Ct. 3469, 77 L.Ed.2d 1201 (1983); *United States v. Denney*, 771 F.2d 318 (7th Cir. 1985).

29. *United States v. Vigo*, 487 F.2d 295 (2d Cir., 1973).

30. *People v. McGowan*, 69 Ill.2d 73, 12 Ill. Dec. 733, 370 N.E.2d 537 (1977), bulge in clothing; *Commonwealth v. Hawkes*, 362 Mass. 786, 291 N.E.2d 411 (1973), reaching toward pocket; *State v. Giltner*, 56 Hawaii 374, 537 P.2d 14 (1975), armed on previous occasion); see Craemer, *Law of Arrest, Search, and Seizure*, for a discussion of experienced police-officer standard.

31. American Law Institute, *Model Code of Pre-Arraignment Procedure*, 279.

Chapter Five

Seizures of Persons: Arrest

CHAPTER OUTLINE

CHAPTER KEY POINTS

1. Arrests are Fourth Amendment ''seizures.''

2. Probable cause constitutes the quantum of proof required by the Fourth Amendment for arrests.

3. Direct and/or hearsay information can demonstrate probable cause for arrests.

4. The Fourth Amendment protects the *manner* of arrest.

5. Law enforcement officers initially determine the reasonableness of arrests without warrants.

6. Arrests with warrants require that magistrates determine reasonableness prior to arrest.

7. Entry into homes to make arrests requires a warrant except in emergencies.

8. The use of deadly force to arrest constitutes a seizure protected by the Fourth Amendment.

9. The Fourth Amendment protects against the use of unreasonable *non*deadly force in making arrests.

10. High-speed chases to apprehend and arrest suspects may, depending on the circumstances, constitute a Fourth Amendment ''seizure.''

CHAPTER KEY TERMS

affidavit written statement sworn to before a person officially authorized to administer oaths

basis of knowledge prong the means by which an informant acquired information

common law ancient judge-made English law brought to America by the English colonists

direct information information officers know directly through their senses: sight, touch, smell, hearing, tasting

hearsay information officers learn through third persons: victims, witnesses, other officers, and professional informants

hearsay rule hearsay information not admissible in court as evidence

misdemeanor minor offense punishable by fine or less than a year in prison

totality-of-circumstances test flexible test considers all relevant factors to measure trustworthiness of informants' information

veracity prong the honesty and reliability of an informant

probable cause to arrest facts that would lead a reasonable person to *believe* that a crime *has* been, *is* being, or *is* about to be, committed, and that the person arrested has committed it

---

═══ THE INTERESTS ARREST PROMOTES AND BALANCES

Arrests, like stops, are Fourth Amendment seizures, but arrests are more intrusive than stops in several respects. Stops are measured in minutes; arrests last hours, sometimes even a day or two. Stops ordinarily begin and end on the street or a place familiar to citizens; arrests involve a trip to the police station, where citizens feel noticeably less comfortable. Arrests produce written documents that become part of a citizen's record or "rap sheet" stops rarely, if ever, get "written up." Arrests can interrupt suspects' work, produce fear, anxiety, and loss of liberty. They can also embarrass, and arrests can cause stress in families that stops seldom arouse.

The decision to arrest not only has adverse effects on suspects and their families, but it also leads to higher government expenditures and consumes more police time than that required to effect stops. The greater intrusion to suspects and the increased cost to the government demand that a higher factual foundation support arrests than stops. The few articulable facts that constitute reasonable grounds to *suspect* that crime *may* be afoot do not suffice to satisfy the standard for arrest—probable cause to *believe* that a crime *has* been committed, and that the suspect *has* committed it.

The decision to arrest balances several interests. It furthers criminal law enforcement. Just as the stop briefly freezes a street situation so that police officers can

Decision Point

Consider the following hypothetical situations. In which did an arrest take place? Review your answers after reading the rest of the chapter:

1. A police officer phones a citizen and "requests" that she "come down to the station" to "discuss" an incident. The citizen complies with the "request."

2. Police officers stop a car. One officer stations herself at the driver's door; her partner stands at the passenger door. The driver asks, "Are you arresting me?" One officer answers, "No, we're just detaining you until we get answers to some questions we have about your involvement in a burglary."

3. Police approach a citizen on the street saying, "You're under arrest." They have made the approach from behind and cannot see the suspect's face. As soon as he turns to face the officers, they realize they have the wrong person. They release him immediately.

4. Police officers order a woman into their squad car, take her to the police station, where they question her. They write nothing down, nor do they "book," fingerprint, or photograph her. She asks if she is under arrest. They answer, "No, we're just questioning you."

5. Police officers stop a citizen. One officer says, "Come with us." The officers take him first to a crime scene, then to his apartment, during which time they question him about a murder. They write a report and release him; the episode lasts two hours.

6. Police officers take a suspect to the station, book, fingerprint, and photograph her. They ask her questions, write a report, and release her. Neither they nor she mention "arrest."

investigate suspicious circumstances, so arrest allows longer detention so that police may gather more information. Furthermore, arrests provide prosecutors with the time to weigh the evidence for its sufficiency, accuracy, and admissibility to decide whether to charge suspects with crimes. Hence, the decision to arrest furthers the interests of punishing the guilty and setting the innocent free; that is, it contributes to producing the correct result in the individual case in question.

The decision to arrest—or *not* to arrest—points to other interests that the law and practice of arrest promote and balance. Police decisions not to arrest, for example, do not always reflect lack of probable cause. (See the examples from the Chicago Police Department in chap. 2.) Community standards that differ from criminal statutes, victims' wishes that offenders not be prosecuted, scarce resources that require the police to put priorities on "serious" crime can lead the police not to arrest even if they have probable cause. These influences reflect the democratic interest in community participation in law enforcement and the organizational interest in efficient, economical, and harmonious operation.

CASE

What interests did Kail's arrest promote and balance?

People v. Kail

150 Ill. App. 3d 75, 501 N.E.2d 979, (4 Dist. 1986), 501 N.E.2d 979 cert denied ____ U.S. ____, 108 S.Ct 95, 98 L.Ed. 2d 56 (1987)

[Judge Webber delivered the opinion of the court.]

FACTS

Defendant was charged by information in the circuit court of Champaign County with the offense of unlawful possession with intent to deliver more than 30 but not more than 500 grams of a substance containing cannabis in violation in section 705(d) of the Cannabis Control Act. . . . [D]efendant and the State stipulated to the evidence produced at the hearing on the defendant's motion to suppress the evidence and submitted the case for a trial at bench upon the stipulated evidence. At the conclusion of the trial, the court found defendant guilty and sentenced her to a term of 12 months. This appeal follows. . . .

[O]n October 3, 1985, at approximately 10:47 p.m., defendant was riding a bicycle on a business sidewalk in the city of Champaign. According to the testimony of Officer Seeley, the arresting officer, she stopped defendant under a police-department policy requiring strict enforcement of all laws against suspected prostitutes, she suspected defendant to be a prostitute, and she would not have stopped defendant if she did not so suspect. After stopping defendant, Officer Seeley noticed that defendant's bicycle lacked a bell. Riding a bicycle on a business sidewalk and failing to equip the bicycle with a bell are violations of the Champaign city ordinances. Officer Seeley then charged defendant with failing to have a bell on her bicycle but did not charge her with riding a bicycle on a sidewalk. Because defendant lacked both adequate proof of identification and $50 dollars to post bond, Officer Seeley arrested her, performed a "pat-down" search, handcuffed defendant and drove her to the police station where she was to be jailed until she could produce bond or proof of identification. Preliminary to placing her in a cell, defendant was subjected to an inventory search during the course of which police uncovered the cannabis.

OPINION

. . . The State contends that the police department's police of enforcing all ordinances against individuals suspected of being prostitutes, but not against individuals not so suspected, furthers its legitimate goal to eradicate prostitution from the community. . . .

We are here confronted with the constitutionality of an administrative policy order under which an otherwise constitutional ordinance is selectively enforced. This case does not involve a police officer's discretion to determine whether under the circumstances enforcement was warranted. Nor does this case involve the enforcement of a law the purpose of which is to combat prostitution. Rather, the law involved is an obscure minor ordinance the purpose of which is to assure a modicum of safety in warning of the approach of a bicycle.

While the State has broad discretion to enforce its laws, that discretion may not be exercised on the basis of an arbitrary classification. Claims of selective enforcement of the laws are appropriately judged according "to ordinary equal protection standards." . . . [T]he State "may not rely on a classification whose relationship to an asserted goal is so attenuated as to render the distinction arbitrary or irrational." . . . It is the duty of the courts to decide whether classifications bear a rational relationship to the law being enforced. . . .

The record in this case is clear. Officer Seeley testified that she stopped defendant pursuant to a police department policy to strictly enforce all ordinances against suspected prostitutes, that she suspected defendant of being a prostitute, and that she would not have stopped defendant but for her suspicion and the department's policy. Moreover, Officer Seeley acknowledged on cross-examination that she had, during the course of her three years of her employment with the Champaign police department, seen literally hundreds, if not thousands of bicycles without bells around the Champaign university campus, but had not arrested anyone, prior to the arrest of the defendant for that offense.

While we recognize the State's right to legislate and enforce laws designed to combat prostitution, the law before us is of a different character. . . . There is no conceivable set of facts which would establish a rational relationship between the class of suspected prostitutes and the State's legitimate interest in enforcing the ordinance requiring bells on bicycles. . . . To suggest that the requirement of a bell on one's bicycle should be enforced only against suspected prostitutes because it helps combat prostitution is clearly so attenuated as to render the classification arbitrary or irrational.

REVERSED.

DISSENT

Justice Green, dissenting:

. . . A difficult question arises as to whether the rational basis must apply to the relationship between the enforcement policy and the law being enforced as the majority holds or between the enforcement policy and a legitimate governmental policy. . . .

I recognize that . . . little authority exists in support of a theory that the rational relationship need exist only between the offense being selectively prosecuted and legitimate governmental interest. . . . [W]hen the classification upon which the selective policy is not suspect within equal protection concepts and there is a legitimate governmental interest served by the prosecution, I do not deem one prosecuted upon a showing of probable cause to be unduly prejudiced by the prosecution. . . .

The legitimate governmental interest in deterring prostitution justified the instant policy of selective prosecution.

CASE DISCUSSION

Kail was charged with unlawful possession with intent to deliver marijuana. Kail moved to suppress the marijuana prior to trial. The case went to trial, Kail was found guilty, sentenced to twelve-months imprisonment. She appealed on the ground that her arrest was an abuse of discretion. The intermediate court of appeals reversed the conviction on the ground that the ordinance under which Kail was arrested was not constitutional.

What is wrong with arresting Kail for violating the bell ordinance? After all, she committed the offense. What interest, or interests, override the interest in obtaining the correct result? Should it (they)? Why?

Limits surrounding the scope, manner, duration, and conditions of arrest point to still further interests beyond reaching the correct result in the case at hand. Even where probable cause exists, the community supports enforcement, and resources are available to arrest, arrests must also comport both with the human dignity valued in a free society and with broad social interests in state impartiality and neutrality regarding race, gender, status, and power. Restrictions on the manner and scope of arrest protect the integrity of the criminal process and control excesses of state power. These interests run counter to arresting the guilty in some individual cases.

THE ELEMENTS OF ARREST

The three criteria for determining whether police have stopped or arrested are (1) the duration of the seizure; (2) the intensity of the intrusion; and (3) whether the suspect was moved. How long must a seizure be to turn a stop into an arrest? How intrusive may a seizure be until it becomes an arrest? Where must police take suspects to constitute an arrest? There are no bright line rules to illuminate the distinction between stops and arrests. The Supreme Court addressed the general standards that govern what constitutes an arrest in *Florida v. Royer.*

CASE

Was Royer arrested?

Florida v. Royer

460 U.S. 491, 103 S.Ct. 1319, 75 L.Ed.2d 229 (1983)

[White, J. announced the judgment of the Court and delivered an opinion in which Marshall, Powell, and Stevens, J.J., joined. Powell, J., filed a concurring opinion. Brennan, J., filed an opinion concurring in the result. Blackmun, J., filed a dissenting opinion. Rehnquist, J., filed a dissenting opinion, in which Burger, C.J., and O'Connor, J., joined.]

FACTS

On January 3, 1978, Royer was observed at Miami International Airport by two plain-clothes detectives of the Dade County, Florida, Public Safety Department assigned to the County's Organized Crime Bureau, Narcotics Investigation Section. Detectives Johnson and Magdalena believed that Royer's appearance, mannerisms, luggage, and actions fit the so-called "drug courier profile"[a] Royer, apparently unaware of the attention he had attracted, purchased a one-way ticket to New York City and checked his two suitcases, placing on each suitcase an identification tag bearing the name "Holt" and the destination, "LaGuardia." As Royer made his way to the concourse which led to the airline boarding area, the two detectives approached him, identified themselves as policemen working out of the sheriff's office, and asked if Royer had a "moment" to speak with them; Royer said "Yes."

Upon request, but without oral consent, Royer produced for the detectives his airline ticket and his driver's license. The airline ticket, like the baggage identification tags, bore the name "Holt," while the driver's license carried respondent's correct name, "Royer." When the detectives asked about the discrepancy, Royer explained that a friend had made the reservation in the name of "Holt." Royer became noticeably more nervous during this conversation, whereupon the detectives informed Royer that they were in fact narcotics investigators and that they had reason to suspect him of transporting narcotics.

The detectives did not return his airline ticket and identification but asked Royer to accompany them to a room, approximately forty feet away, adjacent to the concourse. Royer said nothing in response but went with the officers as he had been asked to do. The room was later described by Detective Johnson as a "large storage closet," located in the stewardesses' lounge and containing a small desk and two chairs. Without Royer's consent or agreement, Detective Johnson, using Royer's baggage check stubs, retrieved the "Holt" luggage from the airline and brought it to the room where respondent and Detective Magdalena were waiting. Royer was asked if he would consent to a search of the suitcases. Without orally responding to this request, Royer produced a key and unlocked one of the suitcases, which the detective then opened without seeking further assent from Royer. Drugs were found in that suitcase. According to Detective Johnson, Royer stated that he

---

[a]The "drug courier profile" is an abstract of characteristics found to be typical of persons transporting illegal drugs. In Royer's case, the detectives' attention was attracted by the following facts which were considered to be within the profile: a) Royer was carrying American Tourister luggage, which appeared to be heavy, b) he was young, apparently between 25–35, c) he was casually dressed, d) Royer appeared pale and nervous, looking around at other people, e) Royer paid for his ticket in cash with a large number of bills, and f) rather than completing the airline identification tag to be attached to checked luggage, which had space for a name, address, and telephone number, Royer wrote only a name and the destination.

did not know the combination to the lock on the second suitcase. When asked if he objected to the detective opening the second suitcase, Royer said "no, go ahead," and did not object when the detective explained that the suitcase might have to be broken open. The suitcase was pried open by the officers and more marihuana was found. Royer was then told that he was under arrest. Approximately fifteen minutes had elapsed from the time the detectives initially approached respondent until his arrest upon the discovery of the contraband. Prior to his trial for felony possession of marihuana, Royer made a motion to suppress the evidence obtained in the search of the suitcases. The trial court found that Royer's consent to the search was "freely and voluntarily given," and that, regardless of the consent, the warrantless search was reasonable because "the officer doesn't have the time to run out and get a search warrant because the plane is going to take off." . . . The District Court of Appeal reversed Royer's conviction. On appeal, a panel of the District Court of Appeal of Florida found that viewing the totality of the circumstances, the finding of consent by the trial court was supported by clear and convincing evidence. The panel decision was vacated and rehearing en banc granted. It is the decision of the en banc court that is reviewed here. . . . We granted the State's petition for certiorari, and now affirm. . . .

OPINION

The State proffers three reasons for holding that when Royer consented to the search of his luggage he was not being illegally detained. First, it is submitted that the entire encounter was consensual and hence Royer was not being held against his will at all. We find this submission untenable. Asking for and examining Royer's ticket and his driver' license were no doubt permissible in themselves, but when the officers identified themselves as narcotics agents, told Royer that he was suspected of transporting narcotics, and asked him to accompany them to the police room, while retaining his ticket and driver's license and without indicating in any way that he was free to depart, Royer was effectively seized for the purposes of the Fourth Amendment. These circumstances surely amount to a show of official authority such that "a reasonable person would have believed he was not free to leave."

Second, the State submits that if Royer was seized, there existed reasonable, articulable suspicion to justify a temporary detention and that the limits of a *Terry*-type stop were never exceeded. We agree with the State that when the officers discovered that Royer was travelling under an assumed name, this fact, and the facts already known to the officers—paying cash for a one-way ticket, the mode of checking the two bags, and Royer's appearance and conduct in general—were adequate grounds for suspecting Royer of carrying drugs and for temporarily detaining him and his luggage while they attempted to verify or dispel their suspicions in a manner that did not exceed the limits of an investigative detention. We also agree that had Royer voluntarily consented to the search of his luggage while he was justifiably being detained on reasonable suspicion, the products of the search would be admissible against him. We have concluded, however, that at the time Royer produced the key to his suitcase, the detention to which he was then subjected was a more serious intrusion on his personal liberty than is allowable on mere suspicion of criminal activity.

By the time Royer was informed that the officers wished to examine his luggage, he had identified himself when approached by the officers and had attempted to explain the discrepancy between the name shown on his identification and the name under which he had purchased his ticket and identified his luggage. The officers were not satisfied, for they informed him they were narcotics agents and had reason to believe that he was carrying illegal drugs. They requested him to accompany them to the police room. Royer went with them. He found himself in a small room—a large closet—equipped with a desk and two chairs. He was alone with two police officers who again told him that they thought he was carrying narcotics. He also found that the officers, without his consent, had retrieved his checked luggage from the airlines. What had begun as a consensual inquiry in a public place has escalated into an investigatory procedure in a police interrogation room, where the police, unsatisfied with previous explanations, sought to confirm their suspicions. The officers had Royer's ticket, they had his identification, and they had seized his luggage. Royer was never informed that he was free to board his plane if he so chose, and he reasonably believed that he was being detained. At least as of that moment, any consensual aspects of the encounter had evaporated, and . . . *Terry v. Ohio* and the cases following it did not justify the restraint to which Royer was then subjected. As a practical matter, Royer was under arrest. Consistent with this conclusion, the State conceded . . . that Royer would not have been free to leave the interrogation room had he asked to do so. . . .

The case before us differs in important respects [from *Mendenhall*, excerpted in chap. 4]. Here, Royer's ticket and identification remained in the possession of the officers throughout the encounter; the officers also seized and had possession of his luggage. As a practical matter, Royer could not leave the airport without them. In *Mendenhall*, no luggage was involved, the ticket and identification were immediately returned, and the officers were careful to advise that the suspect could decline to be searched. Here, the officers had seized Royer's luggage and made no effort to advise him that he need not consent to the search. . . .

We do not suggest that there is a litmus-paper test for distinguishing a consensual encounter from a seizure or for determining when a seizure exceeds the bounds of an investigative stop. Even in the discrete category of airport encounters, there will be endless variations in the facts and circumstances, so much variation that it is unlikely that the courts can reduce to a sentence or a paragraph a rule that will provide unarguable answers to the question whether there has been an unreasonable search or seizure in violation of the Fourth Amendment. . . .

The State's third and final argument is that Royer was not being illegally held when he gave his consent because there was probable cause to arrest him at that time. . . . The facts are that a nervous young man with two American Tourister bags paid cash for an airline ticket to a "target city." These facts led to inquiry, which in turn revealed that the ticket had been bought under an assumed name. The proferred explanation did not satisfy the officers. We cannot agree with the State, if this is its position, that every nervous young man paying cash for a ticket to New York City under an assumed name and carrying two heavy American Tourister bags may be arrested and held to answer for a serious felony charge. . . .

The judgment of the Florida Court of Appeal is accordingly
Affirmed.

DISSENT

Justice Blackmun, dissenting.

. . . "The public has a compelling interest in detecting those who would
traffic in deadly drugs for personal profit. Few problems affecting the health
and welfare of our population, particularly our young, cause greater concern
than the escalating use of controlled substances. Much of the drug traffic is
highly organized and conducted by sophisticated criminal syndicates. The
profits are enormous. And many drugs . . . may be easily concealed. As a
result, the obstacles to detection of illegal conduct may be unmatched in any
other area of law enforcement." In my view, the police conduct in this case
was minimally intrusive. Given the strength of society's interest in overcoming the extraordinary obstacles to the detection of drug traffickers, such
conduct should not be subjected to a requirement of probable cause. Because
the Court holds otherwise, I dissent. . . .
Justice Rehnquist, with whom the Chief Justice and Justice O'Connor join,
dissenting.

. . . The plurality focuses on the transfer of the place of the interview from
the main concourse of the airport to the room off the concourse. . . . He was
alone with two officers who again told him that they thought he was carrying
narcotics. He also found that the officers, without his consent, had retrieved
his checked luggage from the airline. . . .

The question we must decide is what was *unreasonable* about the steps
which *these* officers took with respect to this suspect in the Miami Airport on
this particular day. . . . The plurality concludes that somewhere between the
beginning of the 40-foot journey and the resumption of conversation in the
room the investigation became so intrusive that [it left Royer] . . . "[a]s a
practical matter . . . under arrest." But if Royer was legally approached in the
first instance and consented to accompany the detectives to the room, it does
not follow that his consent went up in smoke and he was "arrested" upon
entering the room.

CASE DISCUSSION

Royer pleaded not guilty to felony possession of marijuana. Prior to trial,
Royer moved to suppress the evidence obtained in the search of his suitcases.
The trial court found that the search was "freely and voluntarily given," and
that regardless of the consent, the search was reasonable because the "officer
doesn't have the time to run out and get a search warrant because the plane is
going to take off." Following the denial of his motion to suppress, Royer
changed his plea from not guilty, to *nolo contendere* (no contest), reserving
the right to appeal the denial of the suppression motion. The district court of
appeal reversed Royer's conviction because, *inter alia,* "Royer had been
involuntarily confined within the small room without probable cause." Royer
was convicted on a narcotics charge. The United States Supreme Court
granted Florida's petition for writ of *certiorari,* and affirmed the court of
appeals reversal of Royer's conviction.

What elements of Royer's detention are problematic? its duration, intrusiveness, or location? Why? Does Justice Rehnquist have a point in his dissent that all "thoughtful, serious" citizens would find this detention reasonable? Royer is guilty; why set him free?

PROBABLE CAUSE

Probable cause constitutes the objective basis, or quantum of proof, required for arrest. The probable cause requirement serves at least two purposes. Accurate and sufficient facts, not hunch, whim, or mere suspicion, must support government intrusions. Furthermore, when later reviewing intrusions, judges need the *facts*, not simply the *conclusions*, upon which officers based an arrest. Judges independently assess whether the facts amounted to probable cause. In other words, judges'

> conclusions, were required so that the magistrate could evaluate the data for himself and then reach his own conclusions as to what to make of the data.[1]

Despite the formal requirement that judges' conclusions determine probable cause, probable cause is a commonsense rule. Its application mainly rests with officers on the street who must often make snap judgments without the benefit of cool reflection that the leisurely atmosphere of a scholar's study—or even a courtroom—allows. Hence, although officers may not arrest on hunch, whim, or mere suspicion, and albeit judges ultimately determine probable cause, courts tend to favor the facts as police see them.

Probable cause consists of facts or apparent facts that would lead a reasonable person to *believe* that a crime *has* been, *is* being, or *is about* to be committed, and that the person arrested *has* committed it. (Contrast the definition of probable cause with the reasonable grounds to suspect standard for stops discussed in chap. 4.) Stating the general definition is straightforward; applying it to specific cases complicates matters.

The United States Supreme Court addressed the question of what constitutes probable cause to arrest in *Draper v. United States.*

CASE

Did the officers have probable cause to arrest?

Draper v. United States

358 U.S. 307, 79 S.Ct. 329, 3 L.Ed.2d 327 (1959)

[Whitaker, J., delivered the opinion of the Court. Warren, C.J., and Frankfurter, J., took no part in this case.]

FACTS

The evidence offered at the hearing on the motion to suppress was not substantially disputed. It established that one Marsh, a federal narcotic agent with 29 years' experience, was stationed at Denver; that one Hereford had been engaged as a 'special employee' of the Bureau of Narcotics at Denver for about six months, and from time to time gave information to Marsh regarding violations of the narcotics laws, for which Hereford was paid small sums of money, and that Marsh had always found the information given by Hereford to be accurate and reliable. On September 3, 1956, Hereford told Marsh that James Draper (petitioner) recently had taken up abode at a stated address in Denver and 'was peddling narcotics to several addicts' in that city. Four days later, on September 7, Hereford told Marsh 'that Draper had gone to Chicago the day before (September 6) by train (and) that he was going to bring back three ounces of heroin (and) that he would return to Denver either on the morning of the 8th of September or the morning of the 9th of September also by train.' Hereford also gave Marsh a detailed physical description of Draper and of the clothing he was wearing,[a] and said that he would be carrying 'a tan zipper bag,' and that he habitually 'walked real fast.'

On the morning of September 8, Marsh and a Denver police officer went to the Denver Union Station and kept watch over all incoming trains from Chicago, but they did not see anyone fitting the description that Hereford had given. Repeating the process on the morning of September 9, they saw a person, having the exact physical attributes and wearing the precise clothing described by Hereford, alight from an incoming Chicago train and start walking 'fast' toward the exit. He was carrying a tan zipper bag in his right hand and the left was thrust in his raincoat pocket. Marsh, accompanied by the police officer, overtook, stopped and arrested him. They then searched him and found the two 'envelopes containing heroin' clutched in his left hand in his raincoat pocket, and found the syringe in the tan zipper bag. Marsh then took him (petitioner) into custody. Hereford died four days after the arrest and therefore did not testify at the hearing on the motion.

OPINION

The Narcotic Control Act of 1956, 70 Stat. 570, 26 U.S.C.A. s 7607, provides, in pertinent part: 'The Commissioner * * * and agents, of the Bureau of Narcotics * * * may—'(2) make arrests without warrant for violations of any law of the United States relating to narcotic drugs * * * where the violation is committed in the presence of the person making the arrest or where such person has reasonable grounds to believe that the person to be arrested has committed or is committing such violation.'

The crucial question for us then is whether knowledge of the related facts and circumstances gave Marsh 'probable cause' within the meaning of the Fourth Amendment, and 'reasonable grounds' within the meaning of § 104(a), supra, to believe that petitioner had committed or was committing

---

[a]Hereford told Marsh that Draper was a Negro of light brown complexion, 27 years of age, 5 feet 8 inches tall, weighed about 160 pounds, and that he was wearing a light colored raincoat, brown slacks, and black shoes.

a violation of the narcotics laws.[a] If it did, the arrest, though without a warrant, was lawful and the subsequent search of petitioner's person and the seizure of the found heroin were validly made incident to a lawful arrest, and therefore the motion to suppress was properly overruled and the heroin was competently received in evidence at the trial.

Petitioner contends (1) that the information given by Hereford to Marsh was 'hearsay' and, because hearsay is not legally competent evidence in a criminal trial, could not legally have been considered, but should have been put out of mind, by Marsh in assessing whether he had 'probable cause' and 'reasonable grounds' to arrest petitioner without a warrant, and (2) that, even if hearsay could lawfully have been considered, Marsh's information should be held insufficient to show 'probable cause' and 'reasonable grounds' to believe that petitioner had violated or was violating the narcotic laws and to justify his arrest without a warrant.

Considering the first contention, we find petitioner entirely in error. The criterion of admissibility in evidence, to prove the accused's guilt, of the facts relied upon to show probable cause goes much too far in confusing and disregarding the difference between what is required to prove guilt in a criminal case and what is required to show probable cause for arrest or search. It approaches requiring (if it does not in practical effect require) proof sufficient to establish guilt in order to substantiate the existence of probable cause. There is a large difference between the two things to be proved (guilt and probable cause), as well as between the tribunals which determine them, and therefore a like difference in the quanta and modes of proof required to establish them.' . . .

Nor can we agree with petitioner's second contention that Marsh's information was insufficient to show probable cause and reasonable grounds to believe that petitioner had violated or was violating the narcotic laws and to justify his arrest without a warrant. The information given to narcotic agent Marsh by 'special employee' Hereford may have been hearsay to Marsh, but coming from one employed for that purpose and whose information had always been found accurate and reliable, it is clear that Marsh would have been derelict in his duties had he not pursued it. And when, in pursuing that information, he saw a man, having the exact physical attributes and wearing the precise clothing and carrying the tan zipper bag that Hereford had described, alight from one of the very trains from the very place stated by Hereford and start to walk at a 'fast' pace toward the station exit, Marsh had personally verified every facet of the information given him by Hereford except whether petitioner had accomplished his mission and had the three ounces of heroin on his person or in his bag. And surely, with every other bit of Hereford's information being thus personally verified, Marsh had 'reasonable grounds' to believe that the remaining unverified bit of Hereford's information—that Draper would have the heroin with him—was likewise true.

'In dealing with probable cause, * * * as the very name implies, we deal with probabilities. These are not technical; they are the factual and practical considerations of everyday life on which reasonable and prudent men, not

[a]The terms 'probable cause' as used in the Fourth Amendment and 'reasonable grounds' as used in § 104(a) of the Narcotic control Act, 70 Stat. 570, are substantial equivalents of the same meaning.

legal technicians, act.' Probable cause exists where 'the facts and circumstances within their (the arresting officers') knowledge and of which they had reasonably trustworthy information (are) sufficient in themselves to warrant a man of reasonable caution in the belief that' an offense has been or is being committed.

We believe that, under the facts and circumstances here, Marsh had probable cause and reasonable grounds to believe that petitioner was committing a violation of the laws of the United States relating to narcotic drugs at the time he arrested him. The arrest was therefore lawful, and the subsequent search and seizure, having been made incident to that lawful arrest, were likewise valid. It follows that petitioner's motion to suppress was properly denied and that the seized heroin was competent evidence lawfully received at the trial.

Affirmed.

DISSENT

Mr. Justice Douglas, dissenting.

Decisions under the Fourth Amendment, taken in the long view, have not given the protection to the citizen which the letter and spirit of the Amendment would seem to require. One reason, I think, is that wherever a culprit is caught red-handed, as in leading Fourth Amendment cases, it is difficult to adopt and enforce a rule that would turn him loose. A rule protective of law-abiding citizens is not apt to flourish where its advocates are usually criminals. Yet the rule we fashion is for the innocent and guilty alike. If the word of the informer on which the present arrest was made is sufficient to make the arrest legal, his word would also protect the police who, acting on it, hauled the innocent citizen off to jail.

Of course, the education we receive from mystery stories and television shows teaches that what happened in this case is efficient police work. The police are tipped off that a man carrying narcotics will step off the morning train. A man meeting the precise description does alight from the train. No warrant for his arrest has been—or, as I see it, could then be—obtained. Yet he is arrested; and narcotics are found in his pocket and a syringe in the bag he carried. This is the familiar pattern of crime detection which has been dinned into public consciousness as the correct and efficient one. It is, however, a distorted reflection of the constitutional system under which we are supposed to live. . . .

The Court is quite correct in saying that proof of 'reasonable grounds' for believing a crime was being committed need not be proof admissible at the trial. It could be inferences from suspicious acts, e.g., consort with known peddlers, the surreptitious passing of a package, an intercepted message suggesting criminal activities, or any number of such events coming to the knowledge of the officer. But, if he takes the law into his own hands and does not seek the protection of a warrant, he must act on some evidence known to him. The law goes far to protect the citizen. Even suspicious acts observed by the officers may be as consistent with innocence as with guilt. That is not enough, for even the guilty may not be implicated on suspicion alone. The reason is, as I have said, that the standard set by the Constitution and by the statute is one that will protect both the officer and the citizen. For if the officer acts with 'probable cause' or on 'reasonable grounds,' he is protected even though the citizen is innocent. This important requirement should be strictly enforced, lest the whole process of arrest revert once more to whispered accusations by people. When we lower the guards as we do today, we risk making the role of the informer—odious in our history—once more supreme. I think the correct rule was stated in *Poldo v. United States,* 9 Cir., 55 F.2d 866, 869. 'Mere suspicion is not enough; there must be circumstances represented to the officers through the testimony of their senses sufficient to justify them in a good-faith belief that the defendant had violated the law.'

Here the officers had no evidence—apart from the mere word of an informer—that petitioner was committing a crime. The fact that petitioner walked fast and carried a tan zipper bag was not evidence of any crime. The officers knew nothing except what they had been told by the informer. If they went to a magistrate to get a warrant of arrest and relied solely on the report of the informer, it is not conceivable to me that one would be granted. For they could not present to the magistrate any of the facts which the informer may have had. They could swear only to the fact that the informer had made the accusation. They could swear to no evidence that lay in their own knowledge. They could present, on information and belief, no facts which the informer disclosed. No magistrate could issue a warrant on the mere word of an officer, without more. We are not justified in lowering the standard when an arrest is made without a warrant and allowing the officers more leeway than we grant the magistrate.

With all deference I think we break with tradition when we sustain this arrest. We said in *United States v. Di Re,* '* * * a search is not to be made legal by what it turns up. In law it is good or bad when it starts and does not change character from its success.' In this case it was only after the arrest and search were made that there was a shred of evidence known to the officers that a crime was in the process of being committed.

CASE DISCUSSION

Draper was prosecuted for knowingly concealing and transporting narcotic drugs in violation of federal narcotics laws. The United States District Court for the District of Colorado, 146 F.Supp. 689 (1956), denied defendant's motion for suppression of evidence and, after trial, a judgment of conviction was entered, and defendant appealed. The court of appeals affirmed and defendant was granted *certiorari.* Supreme Court Justice Whittaker held that where a government agent received from an informer proven reliable in the past, information concerning a certain defendant, then unknown to agent, who would alight from a certain train on either of two days, wear certain clothing, then walk fast and carry a tan zipper bag, and narcotics; and agent observed defendant who fitted informer's description alighting from one of the named trains, agent had probable cause and reasonable grounds for believing that defendant was committing a violation of the federal laws relating to narcotic drugs. Therefore, heroin discovered in search incident to lawful arrest that agent effected after so observing defendant was competent evidence.

What were the facts that constituted probable cause in this case? Were they firsthand, hearsay, or were they a combination of the two? Why does the majority opinion seem to disturb Justice Douglas? Do you think Justice Douglas is overreacting to the decision in this case? Or does he have a point that the hearsay provided by the informant constitutes nothing of substance that would lead a reasonable person to conclude that a crime was committed or in progress, and that Draper committed it? Does the majority ruling favor crime control at the expense of procedural regularity and controlling government? Does the Court give clear guidelines in regard to what constitutes probable cause to arrest? Explain.

The formal judicial review of probable cause concedes ample room for informal police decision making on the street. Courts do not often second-guess these decisions. In a leading Supreme Court case on the point, *Brinegar v. United States* (excerpted in chap. 1), the Court noted:

In dealing with probable cause, . . . as the very name implies, we deal with probabilities. These are not technical; they are the factual and practical considerations of everyday life on which reasonable and prudent men, not legal technicians, act.[2]

Quantity of Facts Required to Support Probable Cause

Brinegar mentions probabilities, but the term probable cause by itself does not clarify the degree of probability required. Some decisions suggest a **more-probable-than-not test.** Under this test, if suspicious activity is as susceptible to an innocent as a guilty interpretation, then probable cause to arrest does not exist. Hence, two men walking up and down in front of a store might be planning to commit a robbery, or they may be trying to keep warm. Two Supreme Court cases illustrate this. In *Terry v. Ohio,* excerpted in chapter 3, Terry and his cohorts were walking up and down in front of Zucker's clothing store, planning to rob it. In *Papichristou v. City of Jacksonville,* two men were arrested. They were walking up and down in front of a tailor shop, trying to keep warm while they waited for a bus to take them to work.[3]

Sometimes, courts have used the more-probable-than-not test to require that officers have facts that point to one specifically identified person before they can arrest. Hence, where officers smelled burning opium outside a hotel room, they did not have probable cause to arrest because they did not know which of the persons in the room were smoking it. And, where the police had a general description that a ''masked black man'' raped a woman in a basement apartment, they did not have probable cause to arrest any of the three black men fitting the general description who had access to the basement where the rape occurred.[4]

Most courts do not strictly adhere to the more-probable-than-not standard; they adopt a more flexible approach. For example, they accept information that narrows the focus of identification even though it does not point to a specific person. Even under this more flexible approach, however, information that points to ''large numbers of people,'' or ''large segments of the community'' would not satisfy the probable cause requirement.[5]

Decision Point

In July 1982, DEA agents initiated a spot surveillance of Murray, Carter, and several people suspected of drug offenses. In early 1983, the agents received information implicating Murray and Carter in a conspiracy to possess and distribute illegal drugs. This information was corroborated by local law enforcement officials, and by April 6, 1983, the federal agents believed that a drug transaction was imminent. During the early afternoon of April 16, fifteen federal agents closely monitored Murray, Carter, and the others. The officers observed a truck and green camper enter a warehouse in South Boston. The vehicles were driven by Murray and Carter. When Murray and Carter drove the vehicles out of the warehouse about twenty minutes later, the agents saw two individuals and a tractor trailer carrying a long, dark container inside the warehouse. The agents followed both of the vehicles, and, shortly thereafter, Murray and Carter turned over the vehicles to two new drivers. The agents stopped the vehicles and arrested the drivers. The vehicles contained marijuana that the agents seized.

Did the officers have probable cause to arrest Murray and Carter? What facts are sufficient to constitute probable cause? The court ruled that the officers did have probable cause to make the arrest.[6]

The quantity of facts required to support probable cause may vary depending on the kind of crime involved and the degree of danger in the circumstances under which police arrest suspects. The United States Supreme Court has not set a rule for the exact quantity of facts required to constitute probable cause for particular offenses or categories of offenses. The lower federal courts and state courts have addressed this problem and adopted different approaches. Some have adopted a sliding-scale approach to probable cause, requiring less facts under dangerous circumstances than probable cause might otherwise compel. The Seventh Circuit Court of Appeals addressed this question in *Llaguno v. Mingey.*

CASE

Did the police have probable cause to arrest?

Llaguno v. Mingey

763 F. 2d 1560 (7th Cir. 1985)

FACTS

On a night in Chicago in 1980, two young Hispanic men committed two robberies, killed four people and wounded three others (including a policeman), and abducted a young girl. When the getaway car crashed, the police were able to shoot and capture one of the killers (Garcia, who has since been sentenced to death) and recover the girl unharmed, but the other killer escaped on foot. A check of the license-plate number showed that the car was registered to Vilma Llaguno at an address two miles from the crash site and that it had not been reported stolen. The crash occurred at North and Oakley; Vilma Llaguno's address was Wabansia, near North Avenue, but farther west than Oakley. One of the robberies had taken place between the crash site and the Llaguno residence.

Several policemen, led by Sergeant Mingey, drove to their headquarters, picked up a shotgun and a sledgehammer there, and then drove to the Llaguno home, believing that the killer who had fled from the car when it crashed may have been living at Vilma Llaguno's address, and that fleeing felons often go home. (Mingey and several other policemen in the entry party are one group of defendants; the other consists of policemen involved in the protracted detention of David Llaguno, of which more shortly.) Upon arrival Mingey banged on the front door and ordered the woman who came to the door, Gloria Llaguno, to open it. She did so, and the police rushed in with drawn guns, searched the house, rounded up the occupants (the plaintiffs in this action), and herded them into the living room. Those seized included Gloria and her husband, several of their children (including David Llaguno), and several grandchildren—a total of 10 people. (Vilma Llaguno, who is Gloria Llaguno's daughter-in-law, was not at home.) In response to questions from the police, David revealed that it was his car that had crashed, and said he had loaned it to a friend. When the police asked him who the friend was, he gave Garcia's name, according to David's testimony; according to the police, he refused to answer. They arrested him. Some of the plaintiffs testified at trial that the police threatened to shoot them, which the police denied; that the police had later come back to the house to speak to David; and that on these occasions they had entered the house without anyone's consent, which they also denied—while acknowledging having held David in custody for 42 hours after his arrest, during which time they neither charged him with a crime nor brought him before a magistrate.

While the police were at the Llaguno residence, the killer who had fled from the crash at North and Oakley was shot and killed by other policemen. He turned out to be Roger Llaguno, a son of Gloria and brother of David but not a resident of the house that the police had entered. No charges were ever lodged against any of the occupants, including David.

OPINION

Posner, J.

. . . Probable cause—the area between bare suspicion and virtual certainty—describes not a point but a zone, within which the graver the crime the more latitude the police must be allowed. The shooting of seven persons (four fatally) by a team of criminals in the space of two hours is about as grave a crisis as a local police department will encounter. The police must be allowed more leeway in resolving it than when they are investigating the theft of a bicycle. Especially when a multiple murderer is at large in circumstances suggesting that he may be about to kill again, the interest in public safety is paramount. . . .

Given the gravity of the crimes they were investigating, the possibility that there would be more shootings unless the killer was seized immediately, and the information (limited as it was) that made it seem that he might well have fled to the Llaguno home, we cannot say, as a matter of law, that the police did not have probable cause to enter and search the house as they did. And if this is right, we do not think it makes a critical difference that they had no definite suspect in mind. . . . [T]here was a sufficient chain linking the house to the killer whom the police were pursuing to allow a reasonable jury to conclude that the police had probable cause to enter the house.

DISSENT

Harlington Wood, Jr., Circuit Judge, with whom Cummings, Chief Judge, and Cudahy and Flaum, Circuit Judges, join, dissenting in part and concurring in part.

The essence of Judge Posner's opinion, as I read it, is simply that when you are short in probable cause you can make up that shortage by adding exigent circumstances. I cannot accept that dangerous, unnecessary, and undefinable blending of two separate and useful traditional concepts in order to justify a warrantless search of a private home at night. The bad factual circumstances in this case are leading us to a bad law for future cases. . . .

If, as the opinion holds, exigencies can substitute for probable cause, we are in effect sanctioning warrantless nighttime home entries for which no warrant would have been issued if one had been sought from a judicial officer. This is clearly an anomalous and untoward result. It seems to me that you have to concede that probable cause in the traditional sense is lacking in this case, and that a magistrate would not have authorized the search warrant. This is why the majority needs to invent this new blended warrantless search concept.

. . . [T]he jury will now have to be instructed with this new "mix-it-all-up-together" rule invented in this case. We will be headed into trackless legal underbrush. A person should be more secure in his home than that.

CASE DISCUSSION

Llaguno and others sued the Chicago police for violating their civil rights by entering and searching their home and arresting them in violation of the Fourth Amendment. The United States District Court rendered judgment for the defendant police. Llaguno appealed. The court of appeals held that the district court should have directed a verdict for the plaintiffs. On rehearing, the court of appeals held that sufficient evidence existed to constitute probable cause, that detaining Llaguno for forty-two hours was too long, and that Llaguno was entitled to a new trial due to serious errors at the trial.

What specific facts did the police have on which to base their arrest? Why did the court require fewer facts in this case? Would you have reduced the requirements for probable cause due to the seriousness of the offenses in question: two robberies, the killing of four people, the wounding of three others, and the abducting of a young girl? Should "reasonableness" under the Fourth Amendment take into account that these suspects may have done terrible harm had the police not acted on the information they had? In other words, as the dissent says, "when you are short in probable cause you can make up that shortage by adding exigent circumstances." Do you agree? Why? Why not?

Direct and Hearsay Information

Officers might have **direct information**—facts known to them through their own senses, including what they see, hear, feel, taste, and even smell (such as marijuana or opium smoke). These facts need not point directly to guilt; they may include circumstances that reasonably lead to the belief that criminal activity has taken place, is in progress, or is about to occur. Probable cause may arise from a roster of firsthand facts and circumstances such as flight, furtive movements, hiding, attempts to destroy evidence, resisting officers, evasive answers, contradictory explanations, fingerprints, hair samples, blood samples, and DNA information.

In addition to first hand observations, officers often rely on information they receive from third persons. This information derived from third-party sources is called **hearsay.** The main sources of hearsay include victims, witnesses, other police officers, and professional informants. According to the **hearsay rule,** courts do not admit hearsay as evidence at trial to prove guilt. However, the hearsay rule does not bar the use of hearsay in probable cause determinations. Hearsay evidence, if it is reliable and truthful, constitutes sufficient proof—probable cause—to allow officials through arrest the time required to determine whether the criminal process should continue or terminate. In other words, arrests are not trials; they significantly deprive citizens of liberty while the government sorts out whether or not to proceed to prosecution and trial.

Courts also relax the hearsay rule in determining probable cause because the technical nature of evidentiary rules applicable at trials does not suit actions on the street. The courtroom has not only experts in the law on hand to testify but also the time to weigh the evidence. Police officers on the street are not lawyers and are not expected to be; nor do they have the leisure to sort out the evidence they have acquired. They must often act immediately or lose their chance to make arrests. Allowing hearsay to show probable cause reflects the deference courts accord these realities. The Federal Rules of Criminal Procedure illustrate this deference; they allow a finding of probable cause based "upon hearsay evidence in whole or in part" (Rule 4).

Hearsay may constitute probable cause, but not all hearsay carries equal weight: like the sources of direct information, some informants are more trustworthy than others. In determining probable cause, magistrates must weigh both the trustworthiness of the information and its source.[7]

Direct information poses few problems because officers are either present to testify or their veracity can be easily tested. They must submit **affidavits**—sworn statements—to what they observe. Courts also accept with little or no question information derived from victims and witnesses who directly observe an incident and report to law enforcement officers. "[I]f the citizen or victim informant is an eyewitness this will be enough to support probable cause even without specific corroboration of reliability." This trustworthiness may not be assumed, however, if victims or witnesses refuse to identify themselves. Hence, courts rarely accept anonymous tips alone as sufficient to establish probable cause to arrest a citizen.[8]

Victims and witnesses do not supply most hearsay information; professional informants, or individuals who derive their information from being part of the "criminal milieu," establish probable cause in most cases. These informants pose much greater problems of trustworthiness than do victims and witnesses.

> It is notorious that the narcotics informer is often himself involved in the narcotics traffic and is often paid for his information in cash, narcotics, immunity from prosecution, or lenient punishment. . . . The reliability of such persons is obviously suspect. . . . [T]he present informer practice amounts to condoning felonies on condition that the confessed or suspected felon brings about the conviction of others. Under such stimulation it is to be expected that the informer will not infrequently reach for shadowy leads, or even seek to incriminate the innocent. The practice of paying fees to the informer for the cases he makes may also be expected from time to time, to induce him to lure non-users into the drug habit and then entrap them into law violations.[9]

THE TWO-PRONGED *AGUILAR* TEST FOR INFORMANTS' INFORMATION. Until recently, the courts used what was called the **two-pronged test** to determine informants' truthfulness. One prong, the **veracity prong,** points to facts that will answer whether informants are basically honest people. A principal way to demonstrate trustworthiness is to show informants have a "good track record," ordinarily by presenting prior instances when informants provided truthful information. That information need not have produced a conviction; informants' prior correct information satisfies the veracity prong without regard to conviction.

That an honest person supplies information does not guarantee its accuracy. The **basis of knowledge prong** focuses on the information itself, particularly the manner in which the informant acquired it. This prong points to the questions: How do informants know what they know? Do they know it firsthand, or was it a rumor? An informant who reports to a police officer that the informant witnessed a drug sale is, of course, much more reliable than the informant who "heard from a friend" that the suspect sold drugs.

THE NEW TOTALITY-OF-CIRCUMSTANCES TEST. Recently, in *Illinois v. Gates,* the Supreme Court adopted a new test called the **totality-of-circumstances test** for probable cause based on informants' information. Although the case deals with probable cause to issue a search warrant, it has relevance to the question of probable cause to arrest. In fact, probable cause generally means the same in both searches and seizures, whether they be seizures of persons or things. The differences are largely over conclusions the facts must support. In searches, facts must lead to the reasonable belief that specifically named items or specifically identified persons will be found in the place to be searched. In arrests, the facts must support the reasonable belief that a crime has been, is being, or is about to be committed, and that the suspect is the perpetrator.

The same *amounts* of information support findings of probably cause in both searches and arrests, but not necessarily the same information. In search cases, the facts must support probable cause to believe (1) that the items are seizable by virtue of their being connected with criminal activity; and (2) that the items will be found in the place searched. It is *not* necessary that facts implicate a particular person. In arrest cases, facts must show probable cause to believe (1) that a crime has been committed; and (2) that the person arrested committed it. Facts need *not* show that officers will find evidence on the arrested suspect's person or in the area under the suspect's control. For example, an officer may have probable cause to arrest a person for armed robbery, but not probable cause to believe that the person possesses a weapon.[10]

CASE

Did the total circumstances add up to probable cause to arrest the Gateses?

Illinois v. Gates

462 U.S. 213, 103 S.Ct. 2317, 76 L.Ed.2d 527 (1983)

[Rehnquist, J., delivered the opinion of the Court, in which Burger, C.J., and Blackmun, Powell, and O'Connor, JJ., joined. White, J., filed an opinion concurring in the judgment, Brennan, J., filed a dissenting opinion, in which Marshall, J., joined, Stevens, J., filed a dissenting opinion, in which Brennan, J., joined.]

FACTS

. . . On May 3, 1978, the Bloomingdale Police Department received by mail an anonymous handwritten letter which read as follows:

> "This letter is to inform you that you have a couple in your town who strictly make their living on selling drugs. They are Sue and Lance Gates, they live on Greenway, off Bloomingdale Rd. in the condominiums. Most of their buys are done in Florida. Sue his wife drives their car to Florida, where she leaves it to be loaded up with drugs, then Lance flys down and drives it back. Sue flys back after she drops the car off in Florida. May 3 she is driving down there again and Lance will be flying down in a few days to drive it back. At the time Lance drives the car back he has the trunk loaded with over $100,000.00 in drugs. Presently they have over $100,000.00 worth of drugs in their basement.
>
> "They brag about the fact they never have to work, and make their entire living on pushers.
>
> "I guarantee if you watch them carefully you will make a big catch. They are friends with some big drug dealers, who visit their house often.
>
> "Lance & Susan Gates
> "Greenway
> "in Condominiums"

The letter was referred by the Chief of Police of the Bloomingdale Police Department to Detective Mader, who decided to pursue the tip. Mader learned, from the office of the Illinois Secretary of State, that an Illinois driver's license had been issued to one Lance Gates, residing at a stated address in Bloomingdale. He contacted a confidential informant, whose examination of certain financial records revealed a more recent address for the Gateses, and he also learned from a police officer assigned to O'Hare Airport that "L. Gates" had made a reservation on Eastern Airlines Flight 245 to West Palm Beach, Fla., scheduled to depart from Chicago on May 5 at 4:15 p.m.

Mader then made arrangements with an agent of the Drug Enforcement Administration for surveillance of the May 5 Eastern Airlines flight. The agent later reported to Mader that Gates had boarded the flight, and that federal agents in Florida had observed him arrive in West Palm Beach and take a taxi to the nearby Holiday Inn. They also reported that Gates went to a room registered to one Susan Gates and that, at 7 o'clock the next morning, Gates and an unidentified woman left the motel in a Mercury bearing Illinois license plates and drove northbound on an interstate highway frequently used by travelers to the Chicago area. In addition, the DEA agent informed Mader that the license plate number on the Mercury was registered to a Hornet station wagon owned by Gates. The agent also advised Mader that the driving time between West Palm Beach and Bloomingdale was approximately 22 to 24 hours.

Mader signed an affidavit setting forth the foregoing facts, and submitted it to a judge of the Circuit Court of Du Page County, together with a copy of the anonymous letter. The judge of that court thereupon issued a search warrant for the Gateses' residence and for their automobile. The judge, in deciding to issue the warrant, could have determined that the *modus operandi* of the Gateses' had been substantially corroborated. As the anonymous letter predicted, Lance Gates had flown from Chicago to West Palm Beach late in the afternoon of May 5th, had checked into a hotel room registered in the name of his wife, and, at 7 o'clock the following morning, had headed north, accompanied by an unidentified woman, out of West Palm Beach on an interstate highway used by travelers from South Florida to Chicago in an automobile bearing license plate issued to him.

At 5:15 a.m. on March 7, only 36 hours after he had flown out of Chicago, Lance Gates, and his wife, returned to their home in Bloomingdale, driving the car in which they had left West Palm Beach some 22 hours earlier. The Bloomingdale police were awaiting them, searched the trunk of the Mercury, and uncovered approximately 350 pounds of marihuana. A search of the Gateses' home revealed marihuana, weapons, and other contraband. The Illinois Circuit Court ordered suppression of all these items, on the ground that the affidavit submitted to the Circuit Judge failed to support the necessary determination of probable cause to believe that the Gateses' automobile and home contained the contraband in question. This decision was affirmed in turn by the Illinois Appellate Court, and by a divided vote of the Supreme Court of Illinois.

OPINION

. . . We agree with the Illinois Supreme Court that an informant's "veracity," "reliability," and "basis of knowledge" are all highly relevant in determining the value of his report. We do not agree, however, that these elements should be understood as entirely separate and independent requirements to be rigidly exacted in every case, which the opinion of the Supreme Court of Illinois would imply. Rather, they should be understood simply as closely intertwined issues that may usefully illuminate the common-sense, practical question whether there is ''probable cause'' to believe that contraband or evidence is located in a particular place.

This totality-of-the-circumstances approach is far more consistent with our prior treatment of probable cause than is any rigid demand that specific ''tests'' be satisfied by every informant's tip. Perhaps the central teaching of our decisions bearing on the probable-cause standard is that it is a ''practical, nontechnical conception.'' ''In dealing with probable cause, . . . as the very name implies, we deal with probabilities. These are not technical; they are the factual and practical considerations of everyday life on which reasonable and prudent men, not legal technicians, act.'' . . .

As these statements illustrate, probable cause is a fluid concept—turning on the assessment of probabilities in particular factual contexts—not readily, or even usefully, reduced to a neat set of legal rules. Informant's tips doubtless come in many shapes and sizes from many different types of persons. As we said in *Adams v. Williams,* 407 U.S. 143, 147, 92 S.Ct. 1921, 1924, 32 L.Ed.2d 612 (1972): ''Informant's tips, like all other clues and evidence coming to a policeman on the scene, may vary greatly in their value and reliability.'' Rigid legal rules are ill-suited to an area of such diversity. ''One simple rule will not cover every situation.''

Moreover, the ''two-pronged test'' directs analysis into two largely independent channels—the informant's ''veracity'' or ''reliability'' and his ''basis of knowledge.'' There are persuasive arguments against according these two elements such independent status. Indeed, they are better understood as relevant considerations in the totality-of-the-circumstances analysis that traditionally has guided probable-cause determinations: a deficiency in one may be compensated for, in determining the overall reliability of a tip, by a strong showing as to the other, or by some other indicia of reliability.

DISSENT

Justice Brennan, with whom Justice Marshall joins, dissenting. . . .

The Court's current Fourth Amendment jurisprudence, as reflected by today's unfortunate decision, patently disregards Justice Jackson's admonition in *Brinegar v. United States,* 338 U.S. 160 (1949):

> ''[Fourth Amendment rights] are not mere second-class rights but belong in the catalog of indispensable freedoms. Among deprivations of rights, none is so effective in cowing a population, crushing the spirit of the individual and putting terror in every heart. Uncontrolled search and seizure is one of the first and most effective weapons in the arsenal of every arbitrary government. . . .
>
> ''But the right to be secure against searches and seizures is one of the most difficult to protect. Since officers are themselves the chief invaders, there is no enforcement outside of the court.'' (dissenting opinion). . . . I . . . fear that the Court's . . . adoption of a new totality-of-the-circumstances test, ''may foretell an evisceration of the probable-cause standard . . . [quoting from Justice White's concurring opinion].

CASE DISCUSSION

Prior to the Gateses' trial on charges of violating state drug laws, the trial court ordered suppression of all the items seized in a search, and the Illinois Appellate Court affirmed. The Illinois Supreme Court also affirmed, holding that probable cause did not support the affidavit accompanying a search warrant. The United States Supreme Court held that probable cause supported the search and reversed the decision. Define the totality-of-circumstances test the Court adopts. What circumstances constituted probable cause in this case? Does Justice White have a point in the dissent, when he says that the totality-of-circumstances test may "eviscerate" (bluntly, take the "guts" out of) the probable cause standard? Why do you think he makes such a strong statement?

MANNER OF ARREST

Arrests without probable cause are unreasonable seizures according to the Fourth Amendment, but probable cause alone does not make an arrest a reasonable seizure. The courts have read the unreasonable seizure clause to extend not only to the foundation for the arrest, but also to the manner in which officers execute the arrest itself. The probable cause requirement focuses on achieving a correct result in the particular case. The manner of arrest focuses on balancing and promoting other interests—protecting privacy, guarding against inhumane treatment of citizens, controlling the police, and promoting organizational goals such as efficient, economical law enforcement. The law of arrest demonstrates that achieving the correct result is necessary but not sufficient to satisfy the Fourth Amendment. The requirements for properly executing arrests apply to the periods both prior to arrest, in apprehending suspects, and after arrest, in subduing suspects already arrested.

The Warrant Requirement

The Fourth Amendment provides:

> no warrants shall issue but upon probable cause, supported by Oath or affirmation, and particularly describing the place to be searched, and the persons or things to be seized.

The critical elements in arrests pursuant to warrants include: (1) that a judicial officer determine probable cause *prior* to arrest; (2) that someone (nearly always law enforcement officers) swears to the facts supporting probable cause; and (3) that the warrant specifically identify the arrested person. Also, although not explicitly stated in the Fourth Amendment but nevertheless implied: (4) a *neutral* magistrate must determine probable cause.

PRIOR DETERMINATION OF PROBABLE CAUSE. Officers make virtually all arrests without warrants. Practically speaking, law enforcement officers determine probable cause on the spot; judicial officers later review their decisions. Arrest warrants, on the other hand, require that officers supply magistrates with the facts to support probable cause *before* they arrest suspects. Hence, judicial oversight occurs before arrest.

There is dispute over what the framers of the Fourth Amendment intended. Some have argued that the framers in their haste inadvertently separated the warrant cause and the unreasonable search and seizure clause. Others maintain that the framers separated the general statement regarding unreasonable searches and seizures from the warrant requirement by design. According to this interpretation, the Founding Fathers intended to direct the warrant requirement only at the hated general warrants. General warrants authorized customs officials and other Crown officers to enter and search all homes in a colony for an extended period of time on the blanket authority of a single warrant. On the other hand, searches linked to ordinary crimes—what we call "street crimes" today—did not require prior judicial approval because local constables rarely abused the search authority.[11]

Officers have conducted considerable prior investigation in arrests made pursuant to warrants. Most arrest warrants involve "white collar" suspects such as tax evaders, price-fixers, and bribers. On the other hand, most arrests without warrants pertain to "street crimes"—robbery, burglary, narcotics violations, and larceny. This has led some to say that middle-class criminals get prior judicial determination while street criminals are at the mercy of "cops on the beat." It would be wrong, however, to conclude that the system intentionally discriminates according to class. The consequences are due mainly to the types of crime, not the social status of the criminals, involved. Street crimes rarely permit long-term investigations, while tax evasion and other white-collar crimes nearly always require detailed, extensive investigation.[12]

The prior determination of probable cause requirement assumes that magistrates carefully review the information law enforcement officers supply them. However, the cases and social science research indicate that

> there is little reason to be reassured by what we know about magistrates in operation. The magistrate can know there are factual issues to be explored only if he looks behind the particulars presented. Yet it is rare for such initiatives to be taken. Most magistrates devote very little time to appraising the affidavit's sufficiency. They assume that the affiant is being honest. . . . They tend to ask no questions and to issue warrants in routine fashion. Over the years the police have adapted their practice not only to the law's requirements but also to the opportunities presented by the manner in which the law is administered. They have often relied on the magistrate's passivity to insulate from review affidavits that are only apparently sufficient—sometimes purposely presenting them through officers who are "ignorant of the circumstances" and, therefore, less likely to provide awkward details in the unlikely event that questions are asked. . . .[13]

Summarizing the results of a study of probable cause determination, Professor Abraham S. Goldstein wrote:

> Proceedings before magistrates generally lasted only two to three minutes and the magistrate rarely asked any questions to penetrate the boilerplate language or the hearsay in the warrant. Witnesses other than the police applicant were never called. And the police often engaged in "magistrate shopping" for judges who would give only minimal scrutiny to the application.[14]

Decision Point

In *Barnes v. State*, at the hearing held by the trial court [challenging the issuance of a warrant] in the absence of the jury, Justice of the Peace Matthews testified that while he did not read all of the three page, single spaced, affidavit presented him by Officers Blaisdale and Bridges, but only 'touched the high parts,' he did question the officers in detail about its contents, and about the necessity of the issuance of the warrant, and that he was acquainted with the requirements for showing probable cause, and that it was only after satisfying himself that probable cause existed for the search of the premises described that he issued the warrant. Appellant's contention that Judge Matthews was not a 'neutral and detached magistrate' is without merit.[15]

In *Clodfelter v. Commonwealth*, the court considered the defendant's threshold claim of invalidity of a search warrant which resulted in the June 16, 1975 search for and the seizure of contraband drugs from a hotel room rented by Clodfelter. While not challenging the sufficiency of the affidavit to state probable cause for the issuance of a search warrant, Clodfelter argues that the search warrant, and the search made pursuant thereto, were illegal and invalid. This is so, he says, because the affidavit shows that it was subscribed and sworn to before the issuing magistrate at 1:05 A.M. and the search warrant was issued two minutes later, at 1:07 A.M. While citing no authority for his position, Clodfelter argues "it is clear that two minutes is not sufficient time for a magistrate to exercise his constitutional and statutory duties to properly analyze the affidavit, and his failure to do so makes the warrant invalid." In effect, Clodfelter argues for a per se rule which would invalidate any search warrant issued within a few minutes after the supporting affidavit is filed with the issuing magistrate.

We decline to adopt such a rule. The affidavit in question was on a one page printed form. Detective T. A. Collins, who signed the affidavit, testified that he filled in the relevant information showing the place to be searched, the contraband for which the search was to be conducted, and material facts establishing probable cause for issuance of the warrant and the offense in relation to which the search was to be made. He then presented the affidavit to the magistrate and made oath to its contents. Our review of the affidavit convinces us that a finding of probable cause by an experienced magistrate, who is by law presumed to have fully discharged his duties, within two minutes after receiving the affidavit would be neither unreasonable nor unusual. Moreover, the law looks with disfavor upon inflexible mechanical rules as tending to defeat rather than attain the ends of justice.[16]

THE OATH REQUIREMENT. The Fourth Amendment requires that magistrates make their probable cause determination on information sworn to under oath. The pain of perjury—the crime of lying under oath—encourages trustworthy facts. A sworn written statement—an **affidavit**—submitted to an officer qualified to administer oaths and attached to the warrant satisfies the Fourth Amendment oath requirement. If the affidavit established probable cause, the magistrate issues the warrant.

The written statement does not always suffice; sometimes it is purposely vague. Police officers who want to preserve undercover agents' anonymity, for example, make only vague references to the circumstances surrounding the information. In these cases, supplemental oral information satisfies the requirement in some jurisdictions. Other courts, however, require that all information be in writing.[17]

Officers usually appear before magistrates in person with the written affidavit, but not all jurisdictions require that officers appear in person. For example, the Federal Rules of Criminal Procedure authorize officers to phone or radio their information to a federal magistrate. The magistrate records the information verbatim. If the information satisfied the probable cause requirement, the magistrate authorizes the officer to sign the magistrate's name to a warrant.

Rule 41. (c)(2) Warrant upon Oral Testimony.

(A) General Rule.—If the circumstances make it reasonable to dispense with a written affidavit, a Federal magistrate may issue a warrant based upon sworn oral testimony communicated by telephone or other appropriate means.

(B) Application.—The person who is requesting the warrant shall prepare a document to be known as a duplicate original warrant and shall read such duplicate original warrant, verbatim, to the Federal magistrate. The Federal magistrate shall enter, verbatim, what is so read to such magistrate on a document to be known as the original warrant. The Federal magistrate may direct that the warrant be modified.

(C) Issuance.—If the Federal magistrate is satisfied that the circumstances are such as to make it reasonable to dispense with a written affidavit and that grounds for the application exist or that there is probable cause to believe that they exist, the Federal magistrate shall order the issuance of a warrant by directing the person requesting the warrant to sign the Federal magistrate's name on the duplicate original warrant. The Federal magistrate shall immediately sign the original warrant and enter on the face of the original warrant the exact time when the warrant was ordered to be issued. The finding of probable cause for a warrant upon oral testimony may be based on the same kind of evidence as is sufficient for a warrant upon affidavit.

(D) Recording and Certification of Testimony.—When a caller informs the Federal magistrate that the purpose of the call is to request a warrant, the Federal magistrate shall immediately place under oath each person whose testimony forms a basis of the application and each person applying for that warrant. If a voice recording device is available, the Federal magistrate shall record by means of such device all of the call after the caller informs the Federal magistrate that the purpose of the call is to request a warrant. Otherwise a stenographic or longhand verbatim record shall be made. If a voice recording devise is used or a stenographic record made, the Federal magistrate shall have the record transcribed, shall certify the accuracy of the transcription, and shall file a copy of the original record and the transcription with the court. If a longhand verbatim record is made, the Federal magistrate shall file a signed copy with the court.

(E) Contents.—The contents of a warrant upon oral testimony shall be the same as the contents of a warrant upon affidavit.

(F) Additional Rule for Execution.—The person who executes the warrant shall enter the exact time of execution on the face of the duplicate original warrant.

(G) Motion to Suppress Precluded.—Absent a finding of bad faith, evidence obtained pursuant to a warrant issued under this paragraph is not subject to a motion to suppress on the ground that the circumstances were not such as to make it reasonable to dispense with a written affidavit. The officer can execute the warrant pursuant to this electronic communication.[18]

Some argue that modern electronic advances should eliminate the need for most warrantless arrests. According to this argument, officers can obtain advance judicial approval for arrests, except in emergencies, without hindering effective law enforcement. If courts adopted this practice:

> [T]he Supreme Court [c]ould actually enforce the warrant doctrine to which it has paid lip service for so many years. That is, a warrant is *always* required for *every* search and seizure when it is practicable to obtain one. However, in order that this requirement be workable and not be swallowed by its exception, the warrant need not be in writing but rather may be phoned or radioed into a magistrate (where it will be tape recorded and the recording preserved) who will authorize or forbid the search orally. By making the procedure for obtaining a warrant less difficult (while only marginally reducing the safeguards it provides), the number of cases where "emergencies" justify an exception to the warrant requirement should be very small.[19]

THE PARTICULARITY REQUIREMENT. The Federal Rules of Criminal Procedure provide that an arrest warrant

> shall contain the name of the defendant or, if his name is unknown, any name or description by which he can be identified with reasonable certainty.[20]

The Supreme Court mandated in one early case that the description be sufficiently specific that it leaves "nothing . . . to the discretion of the officer issuing the warrant." Although that ruling has never been challenged specifically, most cases in practice demand only that the executing officer identify the person with "reasonable certainty."[21]

THE NEUTRAL MAGISTRATE REQUIREMENT. The Fourth Amendment requires that neutral magistrates issue warrants. A personal interest either in issuing warrants in general or in issuing warrants against specific individuals destroys their neutrality. Therefore, a reviewing court declared a warrant illegally issued because the magistrate received a five-dollar fee for issuing warrants, but no fee for declining to do so. The financial interest in issuing the warrants destroyed the magistrate's neutrality. Also, a state attorney general who had taken over a case in which he had issued a warrant pursuant to a state statute authorizing him to do so was not neutral, according to the reviewing court. As the prosecutor in the case, the attorney general benefitted from the suspect's arrest.[22]

THE TIME TO GET-A-WARRANT REQUIREMENT. The desirability of having a magistrate make the probable cause determination prior to arrest has led some to argue that officers must always secure a warrant except in emergencies. In a leading case, *United States v. Watson,* the Supreme Court declined to make this part of the reasonableness requirement of the Fourth Amendment. Hence, so long as officers have probable cause, in most cases (see next section on arrests in homes) they need not get prior judicial approval to arrest.[23]

Decision Point

On August 17, an informant of proven reliability delivered a stolen credit card to federal postal inspectors, alleging that he had received the card from Henry

Watson, who had instructed the informant to purchase airline tickets with it. Although authorities had probable cause to arrest Watson, they neither arrested him immediately nor applied for an arrest warrant. Instead they arranged for a meeting between the informant and Watson on August 22. The meeting was postponed until August 23, at which time the informant signaled to postal inspectors that Watson had indicated that he presently had additional stolen credit cards in his possession. The inspectors entered the restaurant where the meeting had taken place, arrested Watson without a warrant, and searched his person, finding nothing. Watson, however, consented to a search of his nearby car; that search yielded the stolen credit cards.

Was the arrest illegal because the officers had time to get a warrant but did not do so? The Court of Appeals for the Ninth Circuit ruled that when there is time police must secure a warrant to make an arrest, even in a public place. The United States Supreme Court held that the warrantless arrest did not violate the Fourth Amendment. The Court wrote:

> Law enforcement officers may find it wise to seek arrest warrant where practicable to do so, and their judgments about probable cause may be more readily accepted where backed by a warrant issued by a magistrate. But we decline to transform this judicial preference into a constitutional rule when the judgment of the Nation . . . has for so long been to authorize warrantless public arrests on probable cause rather than to encumber criminal prosecutions with endless litigation with respect to the existence of exigent circumstances, whether it was practicable to get a warrant, whether the suspect was about to flee, and the like.

Justice Marshall, dissenting, observed:

> The Government's assertion that a warrant requirement would impose an intolerable burden stems, in large part, from the specious supposition that procurement of an arrest warrant would be necessary as soon as probable cause ripens. There is no requirement that a search warrant be obtained the moment police have probable cause to search. The same rule should obtain for arrest warrants, where it may even make more sense. . . .
>
> This approach obviates most of the difficulties that have been suggested with an arrest warrant rule. Police would not have to cut their investigation short the moment they obtain probable cause to arrest, nor would undercover agents be forced suddenly to terminate their work and forfeit their covers. Moreover, if in the course of continued police investigation exigent circumstances develop that demand an immediate arrest, the arrest may be made without fear of unconstitutionality, so long as the exigency was unanticipated and not used to avoid the arrest warrant requirement.
>
> . . . the requirement that officers about to arrest a suspect ordinarily obtain a warrant before they do so does not seem unduly burdensome. . . .[24]

ARRESTS IN HOME REQUIRE WARRANTS. The Supreme Court recently ruled that law enforcement officers must secure warrants to enter homes to arrest suspects because of the high-privacy interest attached to the home. Hence, warrantless arrests in homes are unreasonable seizures, except in exigent circumstances, such as chasing a suspect in hot pursuit into a home. The Court addressed the warrant requirement regarding entries into homes to arrest suspects in *Payton v. New York*.

CASE

Did they need a warrant?

Payton v. New York

445 U.S. 573, 100 S.Ct. 1371, 63 L.Ed.2d 639 (1980)

[Stevens, J., delivered the opinion of the Court, in which Brennan, Stewart, Marshall, Blackmun, and Powell, JJ., joined. Blackmun, J., filed a concurring opinion. White, J., filed a dissenting opinion, in which Burger, C.J., and Rehnquist, J., joined. Rehnquist, J., filed a dissenting opinion.]

FACTS

. . . On January 14, 1970, after two days of intensive investigation, New York detectives had assembled evidence sufficient to establish probable cause to believe that Theodore Payton had murdered the manager of a gas station two days earlier. At about 7:30 a.m. on January 15, six officers went to Payton's apartment in the Bronx, intending to arrest him. They had not obtained a warrant. Although light and music emanated from the apartment, there was no response to their knock on the metal door. They summoned emergency assistance and, about 30 minutes later, used crowbars to break open the door and enter the apartment. No one was there. In plain view, however, was a .30-caliber shell casing that was seized and later admitted into evidence at Payton's murder trial.

In due course Payton surrendered to the police, was indicted for murder, and moved to suppress the evidence taken from his apartment. The trial judge held that the warrantless and forcible entry was authorized by the New York Code of Criminal Procedure, and that the evidence in plain view was properly seized. He found that exigent circumstances justified the officers' failure to announce their purpose before entering the apartment as required by the statute. He had no occasion, however, to decide whether those circumstances also would have justified the failure to obtain a warrant, because he concluded that the warrantless entry was adequately supported by the statute without regard to the circumstances. The Appellate Division, First Department, summarily affirmed.

On March 14, 1974, Obie Riddick was arrested for the commission of two armed robberies that had occurred in 1971. He had been identified by the victims in June 1973, and in January 1974 the police had learned his address. They did not obtain a warrant for his arrest. At about noon on March 14, a detective, accompanied by three other officers, knocked on the door of the Queens house where Riddick was living. When his young son opened the door, they could see Riddick sitting in bed covered by a sheet. They entered the house and placed him under arrest. Before permitting him to dress, they opened a chest of drawers two feet from the bed in search of weapons and found narcotics and related paraphernalia. Riddick was subsequently indicted on narcotics charges. At a suppression hearing, the judge held that the warrantless entry into his home was authorized by the revised New York Statute, . . .

The New York Court of appeals affirmed the convictions.

OPINION

. . . The Fourth Amendment protects the individual's privacy in a variety of settings. In none is the zone of privacy more clearly defined than when bounded by the unambiguous physical dimensions of an individual's home—a zone that finds its roots in clear and specific constitutional terms: "The right of the people to be secure in their . . . houses . . . shall not be violated." That language unequivocally establishes the proposition that "[a]t the very core [of the Fourth Amendment] stands the right of a man to retreat into his own home and there be free from unreasonable governmental intrusion." In terms that apply equally to seizures of property and to seizures of persons, the Fourth Amendment has drawn a firm line at the entrance to the house. Absent exigent circumstances, that threshold may not reasonably be crossed without a warrant. . . .

A majority of the States that have taken a position on the question permit warrantless entry into the home to arrest even in the absence of exigent circumstances. . . . But these current figures reflect a significant decline during the last decade in the number of States permitting warrantless entries for arrest. . . . A longstanding, widespread practice is not immune from constitutional scrutiny. But neither is it to be lightly brushed aside. . . . Seven state courts have recently held that warrantless home arrests violate their respective *State* constitutions. . . . That is significant because by invoking a state constitutional provision, a state court immunizes its decision from review by this Court. . . .

The parties have argued at some length about the practical consequences of a warrant requirement as a precondition to a felony arrest in the home. In the absence of any evidence that effective law enforcement has suffered in those States that already have such a requirement . . . we are inclined to view such arguments with skepticism. More fundamentally, however, such arguments of policy must give way to a constitutional command that we consider to be unequivocal. . . .

Thus, for Fourth Amendment purposes, an arrest warrant founded on probable cause implicitly carries with it the limited authority to enter a dwelling in which the suspect lives when there is reason to believe the suspect is within.

Because no arrest warrant was obtained in either of these cases, the judgments must be reversed and the cases remanded to the New York Court of Appeals for further proceedings not inconsistent with this opinion.

It is so ordered.

DISSENT

MR. Justice White, with whom The Chief Justice and Mr. Justice Rehnquist join, dissenting. . . .

These four restrictions on home arrests—felony, knock and announce, daytime, and stringent probable cause—constitute powerful and complementary protections for the privacy of interests associated with the home. The felony requirement guards against abusive or arbitrary enforcement and ensures that invasions of the home occur only in case of the most serious crimes. The knock-and-announce and daytime requirements protect individuals against fear, humiliation, and embarrassment of being roused from the beds in states of partial or complete undress. And these requirements allow the arrestee to surrender at his front door, thereby maintaining his dignity and preventing the officers from entering other rooms of the dwelling. The stringent probable-cause requirement would help ensure against the possibility that the police would enter when the suspect was not home, and, in searching for him, frighten members of the family or ransack parts of the house, seizing items in plain view. In short, these requirements, taken together, permit an individual suspected of a serious crime to surrender at the front door of his dwelling and thereby avoid most of the humiliation and indignity that the Court seems to believe necessarily accompany a house entry. . . .

All of these limitations on warrantless arrest entries are satisfied on the facts of the present cases. The arrests here were for serious felonies—murder and armed robbery—and both occurred during daylight hours. The authorizing statutes required that the police announce their business and demand entry; neither Payton nor Riddick makes any contention that these statutory requirements were not fulfilled. And it is not argued that the police had no probable cause to believe that both Payton and Riddick were in their dwellings at the time of the entries. . . .

While exaggerating the invasion of personal privacy involved in home arrests, the Court fails to account for the danger that its rule will "severely hamper effective law enforcement. . . . The policeman on his beat must now make subtle discriminations that perplex even judges in their chambers. . . . [P]olice will sometimes delay making an arrest, even after probable cause is established, in order to be sure that they have enough evidence of convict. Then, if they suddenly have to arrest, they run the risk that the subsequent exigency will not excuse their prior failure to obtain a warrant. This problem cannot effectively be cured by obtaining a warrant as soon as probable cause is established because of the chance that the warrant will go stale before the arrest is made.

Further, police officers will often face the difficult task of deciding whether the circumstances are sufficiently exigent to justify their entry to arrest without a warrant. This is a decision that must be made quickly in the most trying of circumstances. If the officers mistakenly decide that the exigent circumstances are lacking, they may refrain from making the arrest, thus creating the possibility that a dangerous criminal will escape into the community. The police could reduce the likelihood of escape by staking out all possible exits until the circumstances become clearly exigent or a warrant is obtained. But the costs of such a stakeout seem excessive in an era of rising crime and scarce police resources.

CASE DISCUSSION

Payton and another were convicted on felony charges. The New York trial judge held that the warrantless entry into homes was authorized by New York statutes and refused to suppress evidence that was seized upon the entry. The New York Court of Appeals affirmed the convictions. The Supreme Court reversed, holding that the Fourth Amendment, applicable to the states through the Fourteenth Amendment, prohibits police from making warrantless and nonconsensual entries into suspects' homes in order to make routine felony arrests.

Should there be a bright-line rule that officers may never enter a home to arrest without a warrant? What exigent circumstances (emergencies) justify putting aside the warrant requirement, in your opinion? Is the dissent right in its contention that the four restrictions already imposed on warrantless arrests in homes satisfy the Fourth Amendment reasonableness standard? Explain.

MISDEMEANOR ARRESTS. The **common-law**—judge-made law deriving from medieval English custom, and incorporated in American law when the English colonists first settled here—required warrants for misdemeanor arrests unless committed in the officer's presence. The Fourth Amendment does not require officers to secure a warrant if they do not witness a misdemeanor, despite the common-law "in presence" requirement.[25]

Some states have relaxed the "in presence" requirement for misdemeanor arrests. Nebraska, for example, has enacted a statute permitting officers to arrest suspects without a warrant if they have

reasonable cause to believe that such person has committed . . . [a] misdemeanor, and the officer has reasonable cause to believe that such person either

   (a) will not be apprehended unless immediately arrested;
   (b) may cause injury to himself or others or damage to property unless immediately arrested;
   (c) may destroy or conceal evidence of the commission of such misdemeanor; or
   (d) has committed a misdemeanor in the presence of the officer.[26]

The Nebraska statute removes the in-presence requirement generally. However, most states have relaxed the requirement in domestic assault cases specifically. Several states have revised their laws to allow—even require—police officers to arrest for misdemeanor assaults in domestic cases.

Many domestic assault cases do not constitute felonies. Therefore, under the old rule officers could not arrest a suspect in a typical domestic assault case unless the victim accompanied the officer to a police station to sign a complaint. Many victims were not willing to sign complaints, and many officers were unwilling to take them to the police station. Under the new legislation—or in some cases, police department policy changes—this has improved. Hence, if one spouse with obvious bruises or welts tells an officer that the other spouse caused the injury, police officers can arrest without a warrant or a signed complaint, even if they did not witness the alleged assault.[27]

The Use of Deadly Force to Make Arrests

For centuries, the common law permitted the use of deadly force to apprehend fleeing felons. Most American jurisdictions historically authorized the use of deadly force to make felony arrests. Many individual police departments, however, adopted rules that severely restricted the use of deadly force to make arrests. The gist of most of these rules is that officers may use deadly force only when it does not endanger innocent citizens, and when apprehending "dangerous" suspects requires its use. Deadly force raises two Fourth Amendment questions: (1) is shooting a suspect a seizure? and assuming it is, (2) was deadly force reasonably necessary to effect the arrest under the particular circumstances of the specific case where officers used it? The Supreme Court addressed these questions in the landmark case *Tennessee v. Garner.*

CASE

Did Hymon violate the Constitution when he shot Garner?

Tennessee v. Garner

471 U.S. 1, 105 S.Ct. 1694, 85 L.Ed.2d 1 (1985)

FACTS

At about 10:45 p.m. on October 3, 1974, Memphis Police Officers Elton Hymon and Leslie Wright were dispatched to answer a "prowler inside call." Upon arriving at the scene they saw a woman standing on her porch gesturing toward the adjacent house. She told them she had heard glass breaking and that "they" or "someone" was breaking in next door. While Wright radioed the dispatcher to say that they were on the scene, Hymon went behind the house. He heard a door slam and saw someone run across the back yard. The fleeing suspect, who was appellee-respondent's descendent, Edward Garner, stopped at a 6-feet-high chain link fence at the edge of the yard. With the aid of a flashlight, Hymon was able to see Garner's face and hands. He saw no sign of a weapon, and, though not certain, was "reasonable sure" and "figured" that Garner was unarmed. He thought Garner was 17 or 18 years old and about 5'5" or 5'7" tall. While Garner was crouched at the base of the fence, Hymon called out "police, halt" and took a few steps toward him. Garner began to climb over the fence. Convinced that if Garner made it over the fence he would elude capture, Hymon shot him. The bullet hit Garner in the back of the head. Garner was taken by ambulance to a hospital, where he died on the operating table. Ten dollars and a purse taken from the house were found on his body.

In using deadly force to prevent escape, Hymon was acting under the authority of a Tennessee statute and pursuant to Police Department policy. The statute provides that "[i]f, after notice of the intention to arrest the defendant, he either flee or forcibly resist, the officer may use all the necessary means to effect the arrest." Tenn. Code Ann. § 40-7-108 (1982).

The Department policy was slightly more restrictive than the statute, but still allowed the use of deadly force in cases of burglary. The incident was reviewed by the Memphis Police Firearm's Review Board and presented to a grand jury. Neither took any action.

Garner's father then brought this action in the Federal District Court for the Western District of Tennessee, seeking damages under 42 U.S.C. § 1983 for asserted violations of Garner's constitutional rights. The complaint alleged that the shooting violated the Fourth, Fifth, Sixth, Eighth, and Fourteenth Amendments of the United States Constitution. It named as defendants Officer Hymon, the Police Department, its Director, and the Mayor and City of Memphis. After a 3-day bench trial, the District Court entered judgment for all defendants. It dismissed the claims against the Mayor and the Director for lack of evidence. It then concluded that Hymon's actions were authorized by the Tennessee statute, which in turn was constitutional. Hymon had employed the only reasonable and practicable means of preventing Garner's escape. Garner had "recklessly and heedlessly attempted to vault over the fence to escape, thereby assuming the risk of being fired upon."

The District Court . . . found that the statute, and Hymon's actions, were constitutional. The Court of Appeals reversed and remanded. . . .

OPINION

White, J., delivered the opinion of the Court, in which Brennan, Marshall, Blackmun, Powell, and Stevens, JJ., joined. O'Connor, J., filed a dissenting opinion, in which Burger, C.J., and Rehnquist, J., joined.

. . . Whenever an officer restrains the freedom of a person to walk away, he has seized that person. . . . [T]here can be no question that apprehension by the use of deadly force is a seizure subject to the reasonableness requirement of the Fourth Amendment.

A police officer may arrest a person if he has probable cause to believe that person committed a crime. Petitioners and appellant argue that if this requirement is satisfied the Fourth Amendment has nothing to say about *how* that seizure is made. This submission ignores the many cases in which this Court, by balancing the extent of the intrusion against the need for it, has examined the reasonableness of the manner in which a search or seizure is conducted. . . .

The use of deadly force to prevent the escape of all felony suspects, whatever the circumstances, is constitutionally unreasonable. It is not better that all felony suspects die than that they escape. Where the suspect poses no immediate threat to the officer and no threat to others, the harm resulting from failing to apprehend him does not justify the use of deadly force to do so. It is no doubt unfortunate when a suspect who is in sight escapes, but the fact the police arrive a little late or are a little slower afoot does not always justify killing the suspect. A police officer may not seize an unarmed, nondangerous suspect by shooting him dead. The Tennessee statute is unconstitutional insofar as it authorizes the use of deadly force against such fleeing suspects. . . .

Officer Hymon could not reasonably have believed that Garner—young, slight, and unarmed—posed any threat. Indeed, Hymon never attempted to justify his actions on any basis other than the need to prevent escape. . . . [T]he fact that Garner was a suspected burglar could not, without regard to the other circumstances, automatically justify the use of deadly force. Hymon did not have probable cause to believe that Garner, whom he correctly believed to be unarmed, posed any physical danger to himself or to others.

DISSENT

Justice O'Connor, with whom The Chief Justice and Justice Rehnquist joint, dissenting.

For purposes of Fourth Amendment analysis, I agree with the Court that Officer Hymon "seized" Garner by shooting him. Whether that seizure was reasonable and therefore permitted by the Fourth Amendment requires a careful balancing of the important public interest in crime prevention and detection and the nature and quality of the intrusion upon legitimate interests of the individual. In striking this balance here, it is crucial to acknowledge that police use of deadly force to apprehend a fleeing criminal suspect falls within the "rubric of police conduct . . . necessarily [invoking] swift action predicated upon the on-the-spot observations of the officer on the beat." . . .

The public interest involved in the use of deadly force as a last resort to apprehend a fleeing burglary suspect relates primarily to the serious nature of the crime. Household burglaries represent not only the illegal entry into a person's home, but also "pos[e] a real risk of serious harm to others." According to recent Department of Justice statistics, "[t]hree-fifths of all rapes in the home, three-fifths of all home robberies, and about a third of home aggravated and simple assaults are committed by burglars." . . .

Against the strong public interests justifying the conduct at issue here must be weighed the individual interests implicated in the use of deadly force by police officers. The majority declares that "[t]he suspect's fundamental interest in his own life need not be elaborated upon." This blithe assertion hardly provides an adequate substitute for the majority's failure to acknowledge the distinctive manner in which the suspect's interest in his life is even exposed to risk. For purposes of this case, we must recall that the police officer, in the course of the investigating a nighttime burglary, had reasonable cause to arrest the suspect and ordered him to halt. The officer's use of force resulted because the suspected burglar refused to heed this command and the office reasonably believed that there was no means short of firing his weapon to apprehend the suspect. . . . "[T]he policeman's hands should not be tied merely because of the possibility that the suspect will fail to cooperate with legitimate actions by law enforcement personnel." . . .

CASE DISCUSSION

Acting under authority of Tennessee's fleeing felony suspect statute, a Memphis police officer, after warning Garner to halt, shot and killed Garner. Garner's father sued under U.S.C.A. § 1983 (See chap. 3), the "constitutional tort" statute. The district court held that the officer's actions were constitutional. The court of appeals reversed. The Supreme Court held that the Tennessee fleeing-felon statute violated the Constitution, that apprehension by deadly force is a seizure, and that the Fourth Amendment does not permit using deadly force to apprehend any fleeing felon.

Should the Fourth Amendment apply to the *manner* of arrest? Is shooting a suspect a "seizure"? Professor H. Richard Uviller, a long-time student of police power and the Constitution, commented recently on the decision in *Tennessee v. Garner:*

> It is embarrassing for a law professor to be blindsided in his own territory. But the truth is, I didn't see it coming. It had never occurred to me that a police office shooting to kill a fleeing felon might be engaging in an unconstitutional search and seizure. Of course, I can see the connection now that it has been explained to me, [FN1] but I did not spontaneously equate a deadly shot with an arrest. And I have had some prior acquaintance not only with the fourth amendment, but specifically with the issue of the bullet aimed at the back of a retreating felon.[28]

Would the rule in this case permit an officer to shoot a drunk driver swerving erratically down the road headed toward a town? a person wanted for a series of violent crimes but not presently armed who flees from the police? Will this rule embolden criminals? Has the Court tilted the balance too far toward process and societal interests and too far away from the interest in results? Defend your answer.

Tennessee v. Garner was a civil action brought under § 1983. (See chap. 3.) Garner's father sued because Officer Hymon used deadly force with deadly effect. If Officer Hymon had only wounded Garner, the shooting would have had different effects in a criminal case. For example, if the prosecutors had prosecuted Garner, Garner may not have been able to challenge the jurisdiction of the court. If the use of force was unlawful, courts might exclude the physical evidence seized from his person or incriminating statements made in the absence of the *Miranda* warnings. The *Garner* case makes none of this clear. The new doctrine that encompasses deadly force within the Fourth Amendment search-and-seizure clause awaits clarification, through applications in criminal cases.[29]

The Use of Nondeadly Force to Make Arrests

Although most widely known and discussed, shooting is not the most common means used to forcibly arrest suspects who do not willingly submit to police authority. In practice, police use nondeadly force and other mechanisms to arrest suspects unwilling to submit to authority more frequently than shooting. The alternatives to deadly force have come under close constitutional scrutiny since *Tennessee v. Garner.* The Supreme Court did not address the question whether chokeholds constitute unreasonable seizures in *City of Los Angeles v. Lyons,* excerpted in chapter 3. The Court did take up the problem of high-speed chases, and several lower federal courts have addressed—with varying results—the use of mechanisms to subdue arrested persons. The high-speed chase to apprehend suspects and the use of various mechanisms to subdue arrested persons raise in acute form the question what constitutes a Fourth Amendment seizure. The use of nondeadly force in arrests occurs along a chronological continuum. Some strategies such as high-speed chases to apprehend suspects take place prior to arrest. Others—the chokehold, spraying mace, and other means used to subdue persons already arrested—appear afterwards. In *Justice v. Dennis,* the Fourth Circuit Court of Appeals addressed the use of mace following arrest to subdue an unruly suspect.

CASE

Was the use of mace an unreasonable seizure?

Justice v. Dennis

834 F.2d 380 (4th Cir. 1987)

[Before Winter, Chief Judge, and Russell, Widener, Hall, Phillips, Sprouse, Ervin, Chapman, Wilkinson and Wilkins, Circuit Judges, sitting en banc.]

FACTS

K.K. Hall, Circuit Judge:

Justice was arrested on December 19, 1982, by Trooper W. B. Rose of the North Carolina Highway Patrol, who suspected that he was driving while under the influence of alcohol. Rose transported Justice, first, to the Highway Patrol Office, where a Breathalyzer test, which revealed a high blood alcohol concentration, was administered and, subsequently, to the magistrate's office in the Onslow County Courthouse.

It is undisputed that during this time, Justice engaged in constant verbal abuse of the police officers present as well as active physical resistance. For this reason, Trooper Rose requested that Dennis, a fellow officer, accompany him from the Patrol Headquarters to the magistrate's office to provide additional assistance, if necessary.

After a brief appearance, the magistrate found probable cause for Justice's arrest and set bond at $150.00. When Rose and Dennis then attempted to move Justice to the booking area, he actively resisted, forcing Rose to push him down a hallway.

In the booking area, Justice was placed in a small unlocked visitors' room to await processing. Despite being ordered to remain in that room, Justice emerged and again confronted the officers. Although his hands were handcuffed behind his back, Justice kicked at both Rose and Dennis and spat in Dennis' face. Dennis admitted at the trial that in an effort to regain control, he pushed Justice against the wall of the visitors' room. Justice later claimed that the force of this push drove his face against the wall and cracked his front teeth.

Justice continued to resist when he was brought back into the booking area. Viewing the struggle, Gary Dixon, an officer at the Jacksonville, North

Carolina, Police Department, handed, without request, a can of chemical mace to Trooper Dennis, who sprayed it into Justice's face. The spray ended Justice's resistance and he was placed in a holding cell without further incident. Dennis later conceded that he "could have . . . probably subdued" Justice without mace.

Justice subsequently brought a civil rights action against Dennis pursuant to 42 U.S.C. § 1983, alleging that the officer's "brutal and excessive force" had deprived him of liberty without due process of law. The parties consented to the jurisdiction of the United States magistrate pursuant to 28 U.S.C. § 636(c) and the case came to trial on March 5, 1985. The jury returned a verdict in favor of the defendant and the magistrate denied Justice's motion for JNOV [judgment notwithstanding the verdict]. This appeal followed.

OPINION

At trial, Justice proposed the following instruction as the sole standard for assessing liability:

> The Plaintiff Gary Wayne Justice claims that excessive force was used by Defendant Dennis in connection with his arrest. A person, even if he is being lawfully arrested, has a constitutional right to be free of excessive force. An officer is entitled to use such force as a reasonable person would think is required to take one into custody, and this may include such physical force as is reasonably necessary to subdue a person who is struggling with an officer. However, an officer is not allowed to use any force beyond that reasonably necessary to accomplish his lawful purpose. Thus if you find that Defendant used greater force than was reasonably necessary in the circumstances of this case, you must find that the Defendant is liable for a violation of the Plaintiff's constitutional rights.

The court declined to limit its instruction to the jury in that fashion and instead offered a lengthy instruction that included the following language:

> Members of the jury, you are instructed to use the following standard for determining the amount of force necessary to make the defendant liable.
> The force used by the officer is unconstitutionally excessive if the officer used a means so brutal, demeaning and harmful as literally to shock the conscience of a court. You must determine whether the force applied caused injury so severe, was so disproportionate to the need presented and was so inspired by malice or sadism rather than a merely careless or unwise excess of zeal that it amounted to a brutal or inhumane abuse of official power literally shocking to the conscience. . . .

An instruction . . . that directs the jury to consider whether the force "shocks the conscience" and appears to have been applied "maliciously and sadistically for the purpose of causing harm" is a rational, useful and widely-accepted method of focusing that inquiry. . . .

We reject as meritless Justice's contention that reasonable men could not differ regarding whether the use of mace on a handcuffed prisoner was constitutionally excessive force. . . . The question of liability turns upon the circumstances in which the mace was used.

In this instance, Justice, although handcuffed, was under the influence of alcohol and obviously capable of strenuous physical resistance. We do not believe that a rational jury was precluded from finding that the use of mace in these circumstances amounted to a reasonable effort to regain control over a violent and agitated arrestee.

CASE DISCUSSION

Justice sued Officer Dennis who allegedly used excessive force in arresting Justice. The United States District Court entered judgment on a jury verdict in favor of Dennis. Justice appealed. The court of appeals reversed. On rehearing, the court of appeals held that the trial court's instruction properly informed the jury concerning excessive force, and that the jury must determine not only the need for the application of force but also whether the officer used excessive force.

   Which jury instruction appearing in the court's opinion expresses your view of what the law regarding the period following arrest should be? Apply the instruction to the facts of the case. Was Dennis entitled to win his lawsuit according to your application of the rule? Explain why or why not.

High-Speed Chases to Make Arrests

The high-speed chase is a controversial means to make arrests. Whatever its merits, both supporters and critics agree that pursuing fleeing suspects in cars is life threatening not only to suspects but also to police officers and innocent citizens who may be in their path. The strict constitutional questions are the same as they are in the use of force: (1) Are high-speed chases seizures? (2) Are they reasonable? The Supreme Court recently dealt with police pursuits in *Michigan v. Chesternut.*

CASE

Is police pursuit a "seizure"?

Michigan v. Chesternut

486 U.S. 567, 108 S.Ct. 1975, 100 L.Ed.2d 565 (1988)

[Blackmun, J., delivered the opinion for a unanimous Court. Kennedy, J., filed a concurring opinion, in which Scalia, J., joined.]

FACTS

. . . Early on the afternoon of December 19, 1984, four officers riding in a marked police cruiser were engaged in routine patrol duties in metropolitan

Detroit. As the cruiser came to an intersection, one of the officers observed a car pull over to the curb. A man got out of the car and approached respondent Michael Mose Chesternut, who was standing alone on the corner. When respondent saw the patrol car nearing the corner where he stood, he turned and began to run. As Officer Peltier, one of those in the car, later testified, the patrol car followed respondent around the corner "to see where he was going." The cruiser quickly caught up with respondent and drove alongside him for a short distance. As they drove beside him, the officers observed respondent discard a number of packets he pulled from his right-hand pocket. Officer Peltier got out of the cruiser to examine the packets. He discovered that they contained pills. While Peltier was engaged in this inspection, respondent, who had run only a few paces farther, stopped. Surmising on the basis of his experience as a paramedic that the pills contained codeine, Officer Peltier arrested respondent for the possession of narcotics and took him to the stationhouse. During an ensuing search, the police discovered in respondent's hatband another packet of pills, a packet containing heroin, and a hypodermic needle. Respondent was charged with knowingly and intentionally possessing heroin, tablets containing codeine, and tablets containing diazepam, all in violation of Mich.Comp.Laws § 333.7403(2) (1980).

At a preliminary hearing, at which Officer Peltier was the only witness, respondent moved to dismiss the charges on the ground that he had been unlawfully seized during the police pursuit preceding his disposal of the packets. The presiding magistrate granted the motion and dismissed the complaint.[a] Relying on People v. Terrell, 77 Mich.App. 676, 259 N.W.2d 187 (1977),[b] the magistrate ruled from the bench that a police "chase" like the one involved in this case implicated Fourth Amendment protections and could not be justified by the mere fact that the suspect ran at the sight of the police. Applying a clearly erroneous standard to the magistrate's ruling, the trial court upheld the dismissal order.

The Michigan Court of Appeals "reluctantly" affirmed, noting that "although we find the result unfortunate, we cannot say that the lower court's ruling was clearly erroneous under the present law or the facts presented."

Because "the police saw (respondent) do absolutely nothing illegal nor did they observe other suspicious activity," the court determined that the investigatory pursuit had violated the Fourth Amendment's prohibition against unreasonable seizures. . . .

After the Michigan Supreme Court denied petitioner leave to appeal, petitioner sought review here. We granted a writ of certiorari to consider

---

[a] The magistrate did not independently consider whether the codeine pills, if lawfully seized, established probable cause justifying respondent's arrest. The Fourth Amendment issue before us is therefore limited to the police conduct preceding and including respondent's disposal of the packets.

[b] In Terrell, a police officer got out of his unmarked car and "gave chase" on foot after allegedly observing the defendant stick his hand in his pocket and run at the sight of the officer. According to the officer, the defendant ran into an apartment building where the officer observed him drop a clear envelope containing a brown powdery substance. Having determined that the package might contain heroin, the officer arrested the defendant. At a pretrial hearing, the trial court granted the defendant's motion to suppress the envelope and its contents. The Michigan Court of Appeals affirmed, finding that the police "investigatory pursuit" constituted a seizure that was unjustified by any particularized suspicion that the defendant was engaged in criminal activity.

whether the officers' pursuit of respondent constituted a seizure implicating Fourth Amendment protections, and, if so, whether the act of fleeing, by itself, was sufficient to constitute reasonable suspicion justifying that seizure. Because we conclude that the officers' conduct did not constitute a seizure, we need not reach the second question. . . .

OPINION

Petitioner argues that the Fourth Amendment is never implicated until an individual stops in response to the police's show of authority. Thus, petitioner would have us rule that a lack of objective and particularized suspicion would not poison police conduct, no matter how coercive, as long as the police did not succeed in actually apprehending the individual. Respondent contends, in sharp contrast, that any and all police "chases" are Fourth Amendment seizures. Respondent would have us rule that the police may never pursue an individual absent a particularized and objective basis for suspecting that he is engaged in criminal activity.

Both petitioner and respondent, it seems to us, in their attempts to fashion a bright-line rule applicable to all investigatory pursuits, have failed to heed this Court's clear direction that any assessment as to whether police conduct amounts to a seizure implicating the Fourth Amendment must take into account " 'all the circumstances surrounding the incident' " in each individual case. Rather than adopting either rule proposed by the parties and determining that an investigatory pursuit is or is not necessarily a seizure under the Fourth Amendment, we adhere to our traditional contextual approach, and determine only that, in this particular care, the police conduct in question did not amount to a seizure.

In *Terry v. Ohio* [see chap. 4] the Court noted:

"Obviously, not all personal intercourse between policemen and citizens involves 'seizures' of persons. Only when the officer, by means of physical force or show of authority, has in some way restrained the liberty of a citizen may we conclude that a 'seizure' has occurred."

A decade later in *United States v. Mendenhall* [see chap. 4], Justice Stewart, writing for himself and then Justice Rehnquist, first transposed this analysis into a test to be applied in determining whether "a person has been 'seized' within the meaning of the Fourth Amendment." The test provides that the police can be said to have seized an individual "only if, in view of all of the circumstances surrounding the incident, a reasonable person would have believed that he was not free to leave." The Court has since embraced this test. . . .

The test is necessarily imprecise, because it is designed to assess the coercive effect of police conduct, taken as a whole, rather than to focus on particular details of that conduct in isolation. Moreover, what constitutes a restraint on liberty prompting a person to conclude that he is not free to "leave" will vary, not only with the particular police conduct at issue, but also with the setting in which the conduct occurs. . . .

Applying the Court's test to the facts of this case, we conclude that respondent was not seized by the police before he discarded the packets containing the controlled substance. Although Officer Peltier referred to the police conduct as a "chase," and the magistrate who originally dismissed the complaint was impressed by this description,[a] the characterization is not enough, standing alone, to implicate Fourth Amendment protections. Contrary to respondent's assertion that a chase necessarily communicates that detention is intended and imminent, the police conduct involved here would not have communicated to the reasonable person an attempt to capture or otherwise intrude upon respondent's freedom of movement.[b] The record does not reflect that the police activated a siren or flashers; or that they commanded respondent to halt, or displayed any weapons; or that they operated the car in an aggressive manner to block respondent's course or otherwise control the direction or speed of his movement.[c]

While the very presence of a police car driving parallel to a running pedestrian could be somewhat intimidating, this kind of police presence does not, standing alone, constitute a seizure.[d] Cf. *United States v. Knotts,* 460 U.S. 276, 103 S.Ct. 1081, 75 L.Ed.2d 55 (1983) (holding that continuous surveillance on public thoroughfares by visual observation and electronic "beeper" does not constitute seizure); *Florida v. Royer,* 460 U.S., at 497, 103 S.Ct. at 1323-24 (plurality opinion) (noting that mere approach by law enforcement officers, identified as such, does not constitute seizure). Without more, the police conduct here—a brief acceleration to catch up with respondent, followed by a short drive alongside him—was not "so intimidating" that respondent could reasonably have believed that he was not free to disregard the police presence and go about his business. The police therefore were not required to have "a particularized and objective basis for suspecting (respondent) of criminal activity," in order to pursue him.

Because respondent was not unlawfully seized during the initial police pursuit, we conclude that charges against him were improperly dismissed.

---

[a]At the preliminary hearing, the magistrate interrupted the State's attorney, who was asserting that the police were simply performing routine patrolling duties, with the following: "That would be fine until the Officer said we were chasing him in the car, otherwise I would agree with you. My ears picked up when the Officer said that, you know. He said we went around. I asked him why were you chasing him in the car, why were you chasing and he said because he was running and we wanted to see where he was going."

[b]As Officer Peltier explained, the goal of the "chase" was not to capture respondent, but "to see where he was going." Of course, the subjective intent of the officers is relevant to an assessment of the Fourth Amendment implications of police conduct only to the extent that that intent has been conveyed to the person confronted. United States v. Mendenhall [see chap. 4]. See also 3 W. LaFave, Search and Seizure § 9.2(h), p. 407 (2d ed. 1987) (uncommunicated intent of police irrelevant to determination of whether seizure occurred).

[c]The facts of this case are not identical to the facts involved in both Terrell and Shabaz, upon which the Michigan courts relied in finding a seizure in this case. In both Terrell and Shabaz, a police officer got out of the car to chase the pedestrian suspect on foot, after which the defendant abandoned the inculpatory evidence. People v. Terrell, 77 Mich.App., at 678, 259 N.W.2d, at 188; People v. Shabaz, 424 Mich., at 47–48, 378 N.W.2d, at 453. In Shabaz, the State appears to have stipulated that the chase, whose clear object was to apprehend the defendant, constituted a seizure. Id., at 52, 378 N.W.2d, at 455. While no similar stipulation was entered in Terrell, the goal of that chase appears to have been equally clear. We, of course, intimate no view as to the federal constitutional correctness of either of those Michigan state- court cases.

[d]The United States, which has submitted a brief as amicus curiae, suggests that, in some circumstances, police pursuit "will amount to a stop from the outset or from an early point in the chase, if the police command the person to halt and indicate that he is not free to go." Brief for United States as Amicus Curiae 13. Of course, such circumstances are not before us in this case. We therefore leave to another day the determination of the circumstances in which police pursuit could amount to a seizure under the Fourth Amendment.

Accordingly, we reverse the judgment of the Michigan Court of Appeals, and remand the case to that court for further proceedings not inconsistent with this opinion.

It is so ordered.

CONCURRING OPINION

Justice Kennedy, with whom Justice Scalia joins, concurring.

It is no bold step to conclude, as the Court does, that the evidence should have been admitted, for respondent's unprovoked flight gave the police ample cause to stop him. The Court instead concentrates on the significance of the chase; and as to that it is fair to interpret its opinion as finding no more than an absence of improper conduct. We would do well to add that, barring the need to inquire about hot pursuit, which is not at issue here, neither "chase" nor "investigative pursuit" need be included in the lexicon of the Fourth Amendment.

A Fourth Amendment seizure occurs when an individual remains in the control of law enforcement officials because he reasonably believes, on the basis of their conduct toward him, that he is not free to go. The case before us presented an opportunity to consider whether even an unmistakable show of authority can result in the seizure of a person who attempts to elude apprehension and who discloses contraband or other incriminating evidence before he is ultimately detained. It is at least plausible to say that whether or not the officers' conduct communicates to a person a reasonable belief that they intend to apprehend him, such conduct does not implicate Fourth Amendment protections until it achieves a restraining effect. The Court's opinion does not foreclose this holding, and I concur.

CASE DISCUSSION

The state appealed from a magistrate's order dismissing a charge on the ground that the defendant had been unlawfully seized during a police pursuit. The state trial court upheld the dismissal and the Michigan Court of Appeals affirmed. The United States Supreme Court granted *certiorari*. A unanimous Supreme Court, with Justice Blackmun delivering the opinion, held that no seizure of defendant occurred when police officers in automobile observed defendant start to run upon seeing the automobile, and officers accelerated to catch up to defendant and then drove alongside him before he discarded a pack of pills, which the officers then seized. The Supreme Court reversed and remanded.

Would it be better to adopt one of the "bright-line" rules urged by both the state and the defendant? If so, which would you adopt? What are the advantages of using the Court's case-by-case approach to determine whether officers have "seized" citizens? Would you have come to the same conclusion as the Court, using its own test? What if the state's "bright-line" rule was adopted? or, the defendant's "bright-line" rule? What interests do the three possible rules promote? Which ones favor result over procedural regularity? Explain.

≡ SUMMARY

Arrests are Fourth Amendment seizures. They are more intrusive than stops, discussed in chapter 4. Arrested persons go to police stations where the police may interrogate them intensively, then jail officials search them extensively, and law enforcement personnel make written records of their contact with the criminal justice system. The major elements in an arrest are (1) duration, (2) intensity, and (3) location.

The decision to arrest balances several interests: (1) effective law enforcement; (2) obtaining accurate and sufficient facts to substantiate correct results; (3) the democratic interest in community participation in law enforcement; and (4) the organizational interest in efficient, economical, and effective administration.

The foundation for arrests is probable cause: facts or apparent facts that would lead a reasonable person to believe that a suspect has committed, is committing, or is about to commit a crime. Officers may acquire these facts either firsthand by what they directly see, hear, feel, taste, or smell; or they may learn them indirectly through hearsay—what victims, witnesses, other officers, or professional informants tell them. The probable cause standard is not rigid; although it is a quantitative measure, no set number of facts or apparent facts add up to probable cause. It is a commonsense notion, not a legal technicality, where the law permits individual police officers considerable leeway. Police meet the standard so long as they have enough specific information consistent with accuracy and later judicial assessment to determine its sufficiency.

Not only the foundation but also the *manner* of an arrest bears on its reasonableness. Arrests without warrants are reasonable seizures so long as probable cause supports them. Entering houses to make arrests, however, requires a warrant except in emergencies, such as in "hot pursuit" of a fleeing felon. The manner of arrest encompasses the time prior to, during, and following arrest. Hence, force—deadly and other—to effect arrests and means to subdue persons already arrested, such as chokeholds, stun guns, and mace, fall within the meaning of the term *seizure* under the Fourth Amendment. To date the United States Supreme Court has addressed only the question of the reasonableness of deadly force. Two circuit courts have ruled that high speed chases do not constitute Fourth Amendment seizures.

≡ QUESTIONS FOR REVIEW AND DISCUSSION

1. What are the critical elements in an arrest?
2. Compare an arrest with a stop.
3. Define probable cause and give an example of it.
4. What is the difference between hearsay and direct information? Which is more reliable? Why?
5. How do courts determine the trustworthiness of informants' information? Explain.
6. Is the two-pronged or totality-of-circumstances test better? Explain your answer.
7. Should police officers have to have warrants to enter homes to make arrests? Why? Why not?
8. Do you think spraying mace or using chokeholds to subdue arrested suspects is protected by the Fourth Amendment? by any other amendments? Explain.
9. When can police officers use deadly force to make arrests? If you were writing the law, what provision would you write covering deadly force?

≡ NOTES

1. Charles E. Moylan, Jr., "Hearsay and Probable Cause: An *Aguilar* and *Spinelli* Primer," *Mercer Law Review* 25 (1974):742, 744.

2. 338 U.S. 160, 69 S.Ct. 1302, 93 L.Ed. 1879 (1949).

3. *Papichristou v. City of Jacksonville*, 405 U.S. 156, 92 S.Ct. 839, 31 L.Ed.2d 110 (1972).

4. *Johnson v. United States*, 333 U.S. 10, 68 S.Ct. 367, 92 L.Ed. 436 (1948) (smell of burning opium); *Mallory v. United States*, 354 U.S. 449, 77 S.Ct. 1356, 1 L.Ed.2d 1479 (1957) (masked black man).

5. *Commonwealth v. Jackson*, 459 Pa. 669, 331 A.2d 189 (1975); *Commonwealth v. Richards*, 458 Pa. 455, 327 A.2d 63 (1974).

6. *Murray v. United States*, _____ U.S. _____, 108 S.Ct. 2529, 101 L.Ed.2d 472 (1988).

7. *Federal Criminal Code and Rules*, 1987 Edition (St. Paul: West, 1987), 14.

8. Quote from *Allison v. State*, 62 Wis.2d 14, 214 N.W.2d 437 (1974); *Illinois v. Gates*, excerpted later on anonymous tips.

9. *Jones v. United States*, 266 F.2d 924, at 928 (D.C. Cir. 1959).

10. *Commonwealth v. Kline*, 234 Pa. Super. 12, 335 A.2d 361 (1975).

11. Telford Taylor, *Two Studies in Constitutional Interpretation* (Columbus: Ohio State University Press, 1968), pp. 27–44.

12. Kenneth Mann, *Defending White Collar Crime* (New Haven: Yale University Press, 1985).

13. Abraham S. Goldstein, "The Search Warrant, the Magistrate, and Judicial Review," *New York University Law Review* 62 (1987):1173.

14. Ibid.

15. *Barnes v. State*, 520 S.W.2d 401 (Tex.Crim.App. 1975).

16. *Clodfelter v. Commonwealth*, 218 Va. 98, 235 S.E. 2d 340 (1977).

17. *Frazier v. Roberts*, 441 F.2d 1224 (8th Cir. 1971) (permitting supplementary oral information); *Orr v. State*, 382 So.2d 860 (Fla. App. 1980) requiring all information in writing.

18. Federal Rules of Criminal Procedure, 41(c)(2).

19. Craig M. Bradley, "Two Models of the Fourth Amendment," *Michigan Law Review* 83(1985):1471.

20. Federal Rules of Criminal Procedure, 4(c)(1).

21. *Marron v. United States*, 275 U.S. 192, 48 S.Ct.74, 72 L.Ed. 231 (1927).

22. *Connally v. Georgia*, 429 U.S. 245, 97 S.Ct. 546, 50 L.Ed.2d 444 (1977) (fees for issuing warrants impaired neutrality); *Coolidge v. New Hampshire*, 403 U.S. 443, 91 S.Ct. 2022, 29 L.Ed.2d 564 (1971) attorney general issuing warrants.

23. *United States v. Watson*, 423 U.S. 411, 96 S.Ct. 820, 46 L.Ed.2d 598 (1976).

24. *United States v. Watson*, 423 U.S. 411, 96 S.Ct. 820, 46 L.Ed.2d 598 (1976).

25. *Price v. Tehan*, 84 Conn. 164, 79 A. 68 (1911); 76 A.L.R. 2d 1444 (1961).

26. *Street v. Surdyka*, 492 F.2d 368 (4th Cir. 1974) (warrantless misdemeanor arrests do not violate Fourth Amendment); Neb. Rev. Stat. Sec. 29-404.02.

27. *Crime File: Domestic Violence* (Washington, D.C.: National Institute of Justice, 1985).

28. H. Richard Uviller, "Seizure by Gunshot: The Riddle of the Fleeing Felon," *New York University Review of Law of Social Change*" 14 (1986): 705.

29. Ibid.

Chapter Six

Other Searches and Seizures

CHAPTER OUTLINE

CHAPTER MAIN POINTS

1. The Fourth Amendment protects against physical or other intrusions into *some* areas.

2. The Fourth Amendment does not protect against what the unaided senses of sight, hearing, and smell detect.

3. The Fourth Amendment only protects against intrusions into areas in which society is prepared to recognize a privacy interest.

4. Abandoned property, including trash, does not fall within the Fourth Amendment's protection.

5. Formally, searches without warrants are *per se* unreasonable, except for a few well-defined exceptions; in reality, most searches are conducted without warrants.

6. Searches without warrants are reasonable if exigent circumstances require quick action, if authorized persons consent to searches without warrants, or if warrants would interfere with the public interest in inspecting premises or persons.

7. The Fourth Amendment authorizes warrantless searches of the areas under the immediate control of suspects to protect officers and preserve evidence.

8. The Fourth Amendment does not require a warrant to search automobiles both because there is less an expectation of privacy in them and because they are highly mobile.

9. Citizens may voluntarily and knowingly consent to searches and seizures.

10. In administrative searches, balancing the intrusion against the government interest furthered in the intrusion determines the search's reasonableness.

CHAPTER KEY TERMS

exigent circumstances search delay to obtain a search warrant will endanger officer or destroy evidence

in loco parentis doctrine state stands in the place of parent

"mere" evidence rule evidence that is not contraband, fruit of crime, or a weapon

open fields doctrine intrusions onto open lands are not searches

plain view doctrine what the unaided senses can detect is not a search

privacy doctrine the Fourth Amendment protects persons, not places, from intrusions

return of warrant after search, returning a warrant to the court that issued the warrant

search incident to arrest a search without a warrant contemporaneous with an arrest

sliding scale model the lesser the intrusion, the less the factual foundation needed to justify it

trespass doctrine a search requires a physical trespass onto constitutionally protected areas

voluntariness test search is so long as the total circumstances indicate that consent to search was not coerced

waiver test consent requires voluntarily and knowingly waiving the right against searches without warrants

---

≡ PROTECTED AREAS AND INTERESTS

Consider the following examples. Which do you think are "searches" within the meaning of the Fourth Amendment? Why?

1. Police enter a private home and go through every room looking for illegal drugs.
2. Police look through a window of a private residence in order to see if some college students are smoking marijuana inside.
3. Federal Bureau of Investigation agents use a powerful telescope to observe a man in his apartment and read the documents he has in his hand from a quarter of a mile away from the apartment window.
4. Police wire an informant for sound and listen to conversations between the informant and a friend that take place in the friend's home.
5. Police look through the windows of a car parked in a driveway to a private home, hoping to find marijuana on the seat.
6. Police fly over a private home and use ordinary binoculars to see if marijuana is growing in the garden at the rear of the house. A twelve-foot privacy fence that the owner installed prevents their seeing into the property at ground level.
7. Police officers put their ears to an adjoining motel room to hear what the occupants in the room are saying.

8. Police stop a car on the highway, open the trunk, and look for cocaine.

9. Police administer a breatholizer test to the driver of a stopped car.

10. Police use a specially trained dog to detect drugs in a suitcase that comes off a plane into the luggage claim area.

11. Police go through trash outside a home to find evidence of illegal drug use.

12. A crack dealer arranges to meet a customer at the desolate corner of a park to transact an illegal deal. By chance a patrol officer happens by. Just as the officer's flashlight beam settles on them the dealer and customer exchange money for the crack.

13. Undercover police officers closely surveil a suspected cocaine dealer by following and watching her for two months.

14. Police officers look through a hole in the ceiling to a public restroom hoping to catch homosexual men engaging in illicit sex.

15. An officer on routine patrol sees a drug deal take place in broad daylight on a main city street.

16. A welfare worker on a "home visit" looks around an apartment to see if a man is living there with a welfare recipient illegally.

17. A store detective working surveillance in the lingerie department sees a customer shoplifting stockings.

18. An employer requires all employees to take drug tests.

The examples above—some of them real cases—focus on the important question what constitutes a search? Until the 1960s the Supreme Court defined searches according to the **trespass doctrine.** The trespass doctrine required physical intrusions into a "constitutionally protected area." Constitutionally protected areas included the places named in the Fourth Amendment itself—persons, houses, papers, and effects. The Court elaborated upon what those terms encompassed. Searching persons, for example, included touching their bodies, intrusions into their bloodstream, and rummaging through their pockets. It was not a search, on the other hand, to observe physical circumstances, such as handwriting samples or to listen to voice exemplars, to which courts ordered suspects to submit. Houses included apartments, hotel rooms, garages, business offices, stores, and even warehouses. Papers included a broad range of personal writings, including diaries and letters. Effects included many items of personal property—cars, purses, briefcases, and packages.[1]

The Supreme Court replaced the trespass doctrine with the **privacy doctrine** in the landmark case *Katz v. United States,* decided in 1967. The privacy doctrine balances results, process, societal, and other interests. Some cases concentrate on limiting police power: where the courts exclude evidence that the police have illegally seized even though the evidence proves the defendant's guilt. Others bring into focus individual privacy rights: where agents may not rummage through private papers without specific authorization. Still other cases focus on the need to obtain evidence to convict criminals, such as permitting officers to search arrested persons without warrants when they arrest them so they cannot destroy evidence.

In the final analysis, the privacy test is a value judgment that rests upon

whether, if the particular form of surveillance practiced by the police is permitted to go unregulated by constitutional restraints, the amount of privacy and freedom remaining to citizens would be diminished to a compass inconsistent with the aims of a free and open society.[2]

Decision Point

While in a public bathroom, an officer noticed a man briefly pull up his pant leg and expose a bandage wrapped around his ankle. A white packet was clearly visible through the bandage. The officer arrested the man. Did the man have a reasonable expectation of privacy that society is prepared to recognize? A federal circuit court held that he did *not*. When the officer looked by the floor of the stall where the man was located, and noticed the bandage in the gap between the stall's walls and the floor, the man had no reasonable expectation of privacy. Any patron could have noticed the bandage taped to the man's ankle if he looked in the direction of the stall.[3]

On the matter of controlling the police, courts reluctantly and circumspectly tread on police discretion (see chap. 2 on police discretion). Hence courts rarely question what police do in street encounters with citizens, and when they do, they concede great deference to police discretion. As intrusions grow deeper and deprivations greater, however, courts more readily abandon their reticence to intercede and take a more active role in restraining police power, in order to maximize individual liberty. Dean Erwin Griswold, former solicitor general of the United States, had this "working rule" in deciding whether to appeal adverse search-and-seizure rulings:

If the police officer acted decently, and if he did what you would expect a good, careful, conscientious police officer to do under the circumstances, then he should be supported.[4]

In *Katz v. United States,* the Supreme Court thoroughly analyzed the trespass and privacy doctrines.

CASE

Did he have a right to privacy that society recognizes?

Katz v. United States

389 U.S. 347, 88 S.Ct. 507, 19 L.Ed.2d 576 (1967)

[Justice Stewart delivered the opinion of the Court. Justice Marshall did not participate. Justices Douglas and Brennan concurred. Justice Harlan concurred. Justice Black dissented.]

FACTS

At trial the Government was permitted, over the petitioner's objection, to introduce evidence of the petitioner's telephone conversations, overheard by FBI agents who had attached an electronic listening and recording device to the outside of a public telephone booth from which he had placed calls. The petitioner was convicted of transmitting wagering information by telephone from Los Angeles to Miami and Boston, in violation of a federal statute. We granted certiorari to consider the constitutional questions thus presented.

OPINION

The petitioner has phrased those questions as follows:

> A. Whether a public telephone booth is a constitutionally protected area so that evidence obtained by attaching an electronic listening recording device to the top of such a booth is obtained in violation of the right to privacy of the user of the booth.
> B. Whether physical penetration of a constitutionally protected area is necessary before a search and seizure can be said to be violative of the Fourth Amendment to the United States Constitution.

We decline to adopt this formulation of the issues. In the first place, the correct solution of Fourth Amendment problems is not necessarily promoted by incantation of the phrase "constitutionally protected area." Secondly, the Fourth Amendment cannot be translated into a general constitutional "right to privacy." That Amendment protects individual privacy against certain kinds of governmental intrusion, but its protections go further, and often have nothing to do with privacy at all. Other provisions of the Constitution protect personal privacy from other forms of governmental invasion.[a,b] But the protection of a person's *general* right to privacy—is, like the protection of his property and of his very life, left largely to the laws of the individual States.

Because of the misleading way the issues have been formulated, the parties have attached great significance to the characterization of the telephone booth from which the petitioner placed his calls. The petitioner has strenuously argued that the booth was a "constitutionally protected area." The Government has maintained with equal vigor that it was not. But this effort to decide whether or not a given "area," viewed in the abstract, is "constitutionally protected" deflects attention from the problem presented by this case. For the Fourth Amendment protects people, not places. What a person knowingly exposes to the public, even in his own home or office, is not a subject of Fourth Amendment protection. But what he seeks to preserve as private, even in an area accessible to the public, may be constitutionally protected.

---

[a]"The average man would very likely not have his feelings soothed any more by having his property seized openly than by having it seized privately and by stealth. . . . And a person can be just as much, if not more, irritated, annoyed, and injured by an unceremonious public arrest by a policeman as he is by a seizure in the privacy of his office or home."

[b]The First Amendment, for example, imposes limitations upon governmental abridgement of "freedom to associate and privacy in one's associations. The Third Amendment's prohibition against the unconsented peacetime quartering of soldiers protects another aspect of privacy from governmental intrusion. To some extent, the Fifth Amendment too "reflects the Constitution's concern for" . . . the right of each individual "to a private enclave where he may lead a private life."

The Government stresses the fact that the telephone booth from which the petitioner made his calls was constructed partly of glass, so that he was visible after he entered it as he would have been if he had remained outside. But what he sought to exclude when he entered the booth was not the intruding eye—it was the uninvited ear. He did not shed his right to do so simply because he made his calls from a place where he might be seen. No less than an individual in a business office, in a friend's apartment, or in a taxicab, a person in a telephone booth may rely upon the protection of the Fourth Amendment. One who occupies it, shuts the door behind him, and pays the toll that permits him to place a call is surely entitled to assume that the words he utters into the mouthpiece will not be broadcast to the world. To read the Constitution more narrowly is to ignore the vital role that the public telephone booth has come to play in private conversation.

The Government contends, however, that the activities of its agents in this case should not be tested by the Fourth Amendment requirements, for the surveillance technique they employed involved no physical penetration of the telephone booth from which the petitioner placed his calls. It is true that the absence of such penetration was at one time thought to foreclose further Fourth Amendment inquiry . . . , for that Amendment was thought to limit only searches and seizures of tangible property. . . .

We conclude . . . that the "trespass" doctrine . . . can no longer be regarded as controlling. The Government's activities in electronically listening to and recording the petitioner's words violated the privacy upon which he justifiably relied while using the telephone booth and thus constituted a "search and seizure" within the meaning of the Fourth Amendment. The fact that the electronic device employed to achieve that end did not happen to penetrate the wall of the booth can have no constitutional significance.

[The Court reversed the conviction because the FBI agents, although they had probable cause, did not get a warrant. (See later discussion on search warrants.)]

CONCURRING OPINION

[Justice Harlan's concurring opinion.]

. . . As the Court's opinion states, "the Fourth Amendment protects people, not places." The question, however, is what protection it affords to those people. Generally, as here, the answer to that question requires reference to a "place." My understanding of the rule that has emerged from prior decisions is that there is a twofold requirement, first that a person exhibited an actual (subjective) expectation of privacy and, second, that the expectation be one that society is prepared to recognize as "reasonable." Thus a man's home is, for most purposes, a place where he expects privacy, but objects, activities, or statements that he exposes to "plain view" of outsiders are not "protected" because no intention to keep them to himself has been exhibited. On the other hand, conversations in the open would not be protected against being overhead, for the expectation of privacy under the circumstances would be unreasonable.

The critical fact in the case is that "[o]ne who occupies it [a telephone booth], shuts the door behind him, and pays the toll that permits him to place a call is surely entitled to assume'' that his conversation is not being intercepted. The point is not that the booth is ''accessible to the public at other times,'' but that it is a temporarily private place whose momentary occupants' expectations of freedom from intrusion are recognized as reasonable.

DISSENT

Mr. Justice Black, dissenting.

If I could agree with the Court that eavesdropping carried on by electronic means (equivalent to wiretapping) constitutes a 'search' or 'seizure,' I would be happy to join the Court's opinion. . . . My basic objection is twofold: (1) I do not believe that the words of the Amendment will bear the meaning given them by today's decision, and (2) I do not believe that it is the proper role of this Court to rewrite the Amendment in order 'to bring it into harmony with the times' and thus reach a result that many people believe to be desirable. . . .

Tapping telephone wires, of course, was an unknown possibility at the time the Fourth Amendment was adopted. But eavesdropping (and wiretapping is nothing more than eavesdropping by telephone) was, . . . 'an ancient practice which at common law was condemned as a nuisance. In those days the eavesdropper listened by naked ear under the eaves of houses or their windows, or beyond their walls seeking out private discourse.' There can be no doubt that the Framers were aware of this practice, and if they had desired to outlaw or restrict the use of evidence obtained by eavesdropping, I believe that they would have used the appropriate language to do so in the Fourth Amendment. They certainly would not have left such a task to the ingenuity of language-stretching judges. No one, it seems to me, can read the debates on the Bill of Rights without reaching the conclusion that its Framers and critics well knew the meaning of the words they used, what they would be understood to mean by others, their scope and their limitations. Under these circumstances it strikes me as a charge against their scholarship, their common sense and their candor to give to the Fourth Amendment's language the eavesdropping meaning the Court imputes to it today. . . . The Fourth Amendment was aimed directly at the abhorred practice of breaking in, ransacking and searching homes and other buildings and seizing people's personal belongings without warrants issued by magistrates . . . .

In interpreting the Bill of Rights, I willingly go as far as a liberal construction of the language takes me, but I simply cannot in good conscience give a meaning to words which they have never before been thought to have and which they certainly do not have in common ordinary usage. I will not distort the words of the Amendment in order to 'keep the Constitution up to date' or 'to bring it into harmony with the times.' It was never meant that this Court have such power, which in effect would make us a continuously functioning constitutional convention.

With this decision the Court has completed, I hope, its rewriting of the Fourth Amendment, which started only recently when the Court began referring incessantly to the Fourth Amendment not so much as a law against unreasonable searches and seizures as one to protect an individual's privacy. By clever word juggling the Court finds it plausible to argue that language aimed specifically at searches and seizures of things that can be searched and seized may, to protect privacy, be applied to eavesdropped evidence of conversations that can neither be searched nor seized. Few things happen to an individual that do not affect his privacy in one way or another. Thus, by arbitrarily substituting the Court's language, designed to protect privacy, for the Constitution's language, designed to protect against unreasonable searches and seizures, the Court has made the Fourth Amendment its vehicle for holding all laws violative of the Constitution which offend the Court's broadest concept of privacy. As I said in Griswold v. State of Connecticut, 381 U.S. 479, 85 S.Ct. 1678, 14 L.Ed.2d 510, ''The Court talks about a constitutional 'right of privacy' as though there is some constitutional provision or provisions forbidding any law ever to be passed which might abridge the 'privacy' of individuals. But there is not.'' I made clear in that dissent my fear of the dangers involved when this Court uses the 'broad, abstract and ambiguous concept' of 'privacy' as a 'comprehensive substitute' for the Fourth Amendment's guarantee against 'unreasonable searches and seizures.'

The Fourth Amendment protects privacy only to the extent that it prohibits unreasonable searches and seizures of 'persons, houses, papers, and effects.' No general right is created by the Amendment so as to give this Court the unlimited power to hold unconstitutional everything which affects privacy. Certainly the Framers, well acquainted as they were with the excesses of governmental power, did not intend to grant this Court such omnipotent lawmaking authority as that. The history of governments proves that it is dangerous to freedom to repose such powers in courts.

For these reasons I respectfully dissent.

CASE DISCUSSION

Katz was convicted under a federal statute of transmitting wagering information by telephone across state lines. The court of appeals affirmed the conviction. The Supreme Court granted *certiorari* and reversed on the ground that the conversations overheard and recorded were illegally seized under the Fourth Amendment.

Exactly what intrusions and deprivations took place in this case? Why did the Court reject the trespass doctrine? Was it a good idea? What interests does the privacy doctrine promote? How do the two tests differ in the interests they protect? Which test would you adopt? Should Katz go free because FBI agents acted unlawfully, even when they believed they were acting according to the Constitution? Explain your answer.

Plain View, Scent, Hearing

The shift from trespass to privacy reflects an effort to balance and implement the result-process tension and judicial reticence to second-guess police officers. Difficulties in balancing these interests arise out of the complexities of modern society. In earlier times, physical trespass constituted the major form of intrusion. However, today, high-technology listening devises, cameras, telescopes, and the crowded conditions of modern urban life have made possible new intrusions, ones that both put more powerful tools in the hands of law enforcement and subject privacy to greater risk.

History still influences the interpretation of the Fourth Amendment, despite modern advances. Physical intrusion, for example, still looms large in the well-established **plain view doctrine.** Under this doctrine, eyes cannot conduct searches and seizures, nor can ears and noses. Plain view is an inaccurate term because the doctrine covers smelling, tasting, and hearing as well as seeing. Law enforcement officers may look, listen, and sniff without violating the Fourth Amendment.

Decision Point

"Plain Hearing"
United States v. Jackson
588 F.2d 1046 (5th Cir. 1979)

For several years prior to Jackson's arrest, agents of the Drug Enforcement Administration had suspected him of narcotics laws violations. Despite their suspicions and a three-year investigation involving periodic surveillance of his conduct and activities, DEA agents had never observed Jackson passing heroin nor uncovered any hard evidence that he was trafficking in narcotics. On July 4, 1977, Jackson and a Miss Beverly Pertilla checked into room 312 of the Kahler Plaza Hotel in Birmingham, Alabama. An off-duty Birmingham police officer working security at the hotel spotted Jackson on July 5 and notified the DEA of his presence. On July 6 Agent Hahn of the DEA and Sergeant Trucks of the Birmingham Police Department rented room 314 at the hotel for the purpose of monitoring Jackson's activities. Rooms 312 and 314 adjoin and are connected by a set of double doors. After entering room 314 the officers determined that they could hear conversations in room 312 by lying on the motel room floor and pressing their ears to the ¾ crack at the bottom of their connecting door. Although at times their aural surveillance was impeded by the sounds of television, plumbing, and air conditioning in room 312, the officers had no difficulty in overhearing much of the conversation in the adjoining room. At no time did the officers use any electronic or mechanical device to assist them in their aural surveillance.

Utilizing this eavesdropping technique, the officers on July 6 overhead Jackson make two telephone calls to Buffalo, New York. During these calls Jackson stated, "No, I haven't been able to contact my man yet. (Pause.) It is like gold." and "The stuff is coming from L.A. (Pause.) No problem with my man." On the morning of July 7 Jackson told his room guest, Beverly Pertilla, to call an airline and make flight reservations to Buffalo, New York. Sgt. Trucks immediately dispatched two undercover officers to the airport to set up surveillance. Shortly after Pertilla made the reservations, Jackson received a brief telephone call. He then cursed, seemed excited for several minutes, and

told Pertilla that "the stuff may be in trouble" and "the stuff is worth $40,000."
Within twenty minutes Jackson received another telephone call in which he
stated, "Is the stuff all right? Is the suitcase still at the airport?" Following this
conversation Jackson told Pertilla, "I don't know what went wrong. The police
followed him to the airport. The suitcase is still at the airport. The flight came
in at 9:08 and I don't know what went wrong." [Jackson and Porter were later
arrested, convicted, and sentenced to 12 years in prison and fines of $35,000 and
$25,000 respectively for possession and conspiracy to distribute heroin and
cocaine. They claim that the eavesdropping violated their right to privacy and the
court should suppress the seized heroin and cocaine as evidence against them.]

Employing the privacy interest analysis approved in Katz, we hold that these
appellants had not justifiable expectations of privacy with respect to their motel
room conversations which were audible to the unaided ears of the government
agents lawfully occupying an adjoining room. "It has long been settled that
objects falling in the plain view of an officer who has a right to be in the position
to have that view are subject to seizure and may be introduced into evidence."
Harris v. United States, 390 U.S. 234, 236, 88 S.Ct. 992, 993, 19 L.Ed.2d 1067
(1968) (per curiam). The plain view doctrine defines certain sensory observations as being outside the scope of the Fourth Amendment's protections. This
doctrine is entirely consistent with the Katz expectations standard since an
individual can have no justifiable expectation of privacy as to activities he
exposes to the plain view of others. Katz, supra at 351, 88 S.Ct. 507.[FN8] We
think that conversations in a motel room which are audible to one in an adjoining
room constitute words exposed to the "plain view" of others. . . .

"Plain Touch"

United States v. Portillo
633 F.2d 1313 (9th Cir. 1980)

An officer, while checking the nonfunctioning rear lights during an automobile
stop of bank robbery suspects, placed his hand in the trunk of the car which
happened to fall upon a paper bag. The officer instantly recognized the contents
of the bag to be a gun. The Ninth Circuit found the officer's discovery of the gun
lawful because "the contents of the bag were apparent from the outward feel of
the container" and he was able to identify the contents of the bag by touching
them.

"Plain Smell"

Agents from the DEA stopped a man who had just landed in a small private
plane from South America. He had just placed packages taken from the plane in
a car parked a short distance from the plane. He opened the trunk where he had
put the packages at the request of the agents. When he did, the agents testified
that the packages "reeked of marijuana." The agents seized the marijuana and arrested the man. He moved to dismiss the marijuana on the grounds that the officers
seized it illegally. The court denied the motion because the contents of the packages
were inferable from their odor, a conclusion based on an extension of the plain view
doctrine which includes evidence "that can be perceived by the sense of small."[5]

The courts impose two restrictions on plain view. First, law enforcement officers cannot trespass; they must be where they have a legal right to be, either in public or in private places by consent or invitation. Second, only intrusions of the *naked* eye and the *unaided* ear and nose fall outside the scope of Fourth Amendment "searches."

Sometimes, officers push nature to the limit. In one case, two narcotics agents approached a van parked outside a convenience store. While one officer talked to the van's owner whom the officers suspected was illegally manufacturing methamphetamine, the other officer tried to see into the van. The windows were coated with a darkened substance that made it impossible to see anything but the general outline of what was inside.

> However, notwithstanding the coating material on the windows, it was possible for the officer to view the interior by placing his face against the glass, and cupping his hands around his eyes so as to exclude the glare from the exterior lights. This is the manner in which Agent D'Ulisse looked through the window and into the interior of the van. When he did so, he saw a box marked "L-Ephedrine, [a substance used in producing methamphetamines].[6]

The court concluded that D'Ulisse's looking into the van was not an unreasonable search.

> . . . [T]here was no suggestion that [D'Ulisse] did any act in order to increase visibility . . . [He] did not touch the van or the window, he merely leaned closer to the window, which was darkened, shaded his eyes, and looked into it. He did not touch the van or the window, except to rest his hands as he shaded his eyes. This act alone did not convert his view into a search.[7]

Officers who enhance their normal sensory perceptions with electronic aids run the risk of transforming their conduct into searches. Gathering information by means of standard sensory enhancements, such as flashlights and 35-mm. cameras, does not constitute a search. More sophisticated devices, however, may do so. The use of modern powerful sensory aids create problems for the courts. The Supreme Court dealt with electronic transmission in *United States v. White.*

CASE

Did the agents "search" White?

United States v. White

401 U.S. 745, 91 S.Ct. 1122, 28 L.Ed.2d 453 (1971)

[Mr. Justice White announced the judgement of the Court and an opinion in which The Chief Justice, Mr. Justice Stewart, and Mr. Justice Blackmun join.]

FACTS

. . . James A. White was tried and convicted under two consolidated indictments charging various illegal transactions in narcotics. He was fined and sentenced as a second offender to 25-year concurrent sentences. The issue before us is whether the Fourth Amendment bars from evidence the testimony of governmental agents who related certain conversations which had occurred between defendant White and a government informant, Harvey Jackson, and which the agents overheard by monitoring the frequency of a radio transmitter carried by Jackson and concealed on his person. On four occasions the conversations took place in Jackson's home; each of these conversations was overheard by an agent concealed in a kitchen closet with Jackson's consent and by a second agent outside the house using a radio receiver. Four other conversations—one in respondent's home, one in a restaurant, and two in Jackson's car—were overheard by the use of radio equipment. The prosecution was unable to locate and produce Jackson at the trial and the trial court over-ruled objections to the testimony of the agents who conducted the electronic surveillance. The jury returned a guilty verdict and defendant appealed.

The Court of Appeals . . . interpreted the Fourth Amendment to forbid the introduction of the agents' testimony in the circumstances of this case. Accordingly, the court reversed. . . . In our view, the Court of Appeals misinterpreted . . . the Fourth Amendment. . . .

OPINION

. . . The Court of Appeals understood *Katz* to render inadmissible against White the agents' testimony concerning conversations that Jackson broadcast to them. We cannot agree. *Katz* involved no revelation to the Government by a party to conversations with the defendant nor did the Court indicate in any way that a defendant has a justifiable and constitutionally protected expectation that a person with whom he is conversing will not then or later reveal the conversation to the police. . . .

Our problem is not what the privacy expectations of particular defendants in particular situations may be or the extent to which they may in fact have relied on the discretion of their companions. Very probably, individual defendants neither know nor suspect that their colleagues have gone or will go to the police or are carrying recorders or transmitters. Otherwise, conversation would cease and our problem with these encounters would be nonexistent or far different from those now before us. Our problem, in terms of the principles announced in *Katz*, is what expectations of privacy are constitutionally "justifiable"—what expectations the Fourth Amendment will protect in the absence of a warrant. So far, the law permits the frustration of actual expectations of privacy by permitting authorities to use the testimony of those associates who for one reason or another have determined to turn to the police, as well as by authorizing the use of informants. If the law gives no protection to the wrongdoer whose trusted accomplice is or becomes a police agent, neither should it protect him when that same agent has recorded or transmitted the conversations which are later offered in evidence to prove the State's case.

Inescapably, one contemplating illegal activities must realize and risk that his companions may be reporting to the police. If he sufficiently doubts their trustworthiness, the association will very probably end or never materialize. But if he has no doubts, or allays them, or risks what doubt he has, the risk is his. In terms of what his course will be, what he will or will not do or say, we are unpersuaded that he would distinguish between probable informers with transmitters on the other. Given the possibility or probability that one of his colleagues is cooperating with the police, it is only speculation to assert that the defendant's utterances would be substantially different or his sense of security any less if he also thought it possible that the suspected colleague is wired for sound. At least there is no persuasive evidence that the difference in this respect between the electronically equipped and the unequipped agent is substantial enough to require discrete constitutional recognition, particularly under the Fourth Amendment which is ruled by fluid concepts of ''reasonableness.''

Nor should we be too ready to erect constitutional barriers to relevant and probative evidence which is also accurate and reliable. An electronic recording will many times produce a more reliable rendition of what a defendant has said than will the unaided memory of a police agent. It may also be that with the recording in existence it is less likely that the informant will change his mind, less chance that threat of injury will suppress unfavorable evidence and less chance that cross-examination will confound the testimony. Considerations like these obviously do not favor the defendant, but we are not prepared to hold that a defendant who has no constitutional right to exclude the informer's unaided testimony nevertheless has a Fourth Amendment privilege against a more accurate version of the events in question. . . .

DISSENT

Justice Douglas, dissenting.

. . . The issue in this case is clouded and concealed by the very discussion of it in legalistic terms. What the ancients knew as ''eavesdropping,'' we now call ''electronic surveillance''; but to equate the two is to treat man's first gunpowder on the same level as the nuclear bomb. Electronic surveillance is the greatest leveler of human privacy ever known. How most forms of it can be held ''reasonable'' within the meaning of the Fourth Amendment is a mystery. To be sure, the Constitution and Bill of Rights are not to be read as covering only the technology known in the 18th century. Otherwise its concept of ''commerce'' would be hopeless when it comes to the management of modern affairs. At the same time the concepts of privacy which the Founders enshrined in the Fourth Amendment vanish completely when we slavishly allow an all-powerful government, proclaiming law and order, efficiency, and other benign purposes, to penetrate all the walls and doors which men need to shield them from the pressures of a turbulent life around them and give them the health and strength to carry on. . . .

[According to the Court's decision,] must everyone live in fear that every word he speaks may be transmitted or recorded and later repeated to the entire world? I can imagine nothing that has a more chilling effect on people speaking their minds and expressing their views on important matters. The advocates of that regime should spend some time in totalitarian countries and learn first-hand the kind of regime they are creating here.

[Justice Harlan, dissenting.]

Since it is the task of the law to form and project, as well as mirror and reflect, we should not, as judges, merely recite the expectations and risks without examining the desirability of saddling them upon society. The critical question, therefore, is whether under our system of government, as reflected in the Constitution, we should impose on our citizens the risks of the electronic listener or observer without at least the protection of a warrant requirement. This question must, in my view, be answered by assessing the nature of a particular practice and the likely extent of its impact on the individual's sense of security balanced against the utility of the conduct as a technique of law enforcement. For those more extensive intrusions that significantly jeopardize the sense of security which is the paramount concern of Fourth Amendment liberties, I am of the view that more than self-restraint by law enforcement officials is required and at the least warrants should be necessary.

The impact of the practice of third-party bugging, must, I think, be considered such as to undermine that confidence and sense of security in dealing with one another that is characteristic of individual relationships between citizens in a free society. It goes beyond the impact on privacy occasioned by the ordinary type of 'informer' investigation. . . . The argument of the plurality opinion, to the effect that it is irrelevant whether secrets are revealed by the mere tattletale or the transistor, ignores the differences occasioned by third-party monitoring and recording which insures full and accurate disclosure of all that is said, free of the possibility of error and oversight that inheres in human reporting.

Authority is hardly required to support the proposition that words would be measured a good deal more carefully and communication inhibited if one suspected his conversations were being transmitted and transcribed. Were third-party bugging a prevalent practice, it might well smother that spontaneity—reflected in frivolous, impetuous, sacrilegious, and defiant discourse—that liberates daily life. Much offhand exchange is easily forgotten and one may count on the obscurity of his remarks, protected by the very fact of a limited audience, and the likelihood that the listener will either overlook or forget what is said, as well as the listener's inability to reformulate a conversation without having to contend with a documented record. All these values are sacrificed by a rule of law that permits official monitoring of private discourse limited only by the need to locate a willing assistant.

CASE DISCUSSION

White was convicted of narcotics violations following a trial admitting his incriminating statements overheard by a warrantless electronic eavesdropping by Government agents. The court of appeals reversed the conviction on the ground that the eavesdropping violated the Fourth Amendment. The Supreme Court granted *certiorari* and reversed the court of appeals, holding that the government's use of agents may reveal the contents of conversations with the accused without violating the Fourth Amendment.

Is the court saying that it is reasonable to expect that those in whom we confide may be wired for sound to the police? What interests is the Court balancing in this case? Is listening to White in his home, Jackson's home, in a restaurant, on the street, in the car most intrusive? Or, are they all about the same? Why? Does the dissent have a point that everyone will live in fear that what they say will be reported—or transmitted by radio—to the police? Should the police have been required to get a warrant here?

Abandoned "Effects"

The Fourth Amendment protects not only persons, houses, and papers, but also "effects" or personal property; it does not protect abandoned personal property. The courts have had considerable difficulty determining whether owners of trash abandon it totally, or retain in it a privacy interest to the extent that they do not intend police to rummage through it for incriminating evidence. Recently, the Supreme Court settled the issue in *California v. Greenwood*.

CASE

Does he have a privacy interest in his trash?

California v. Billy Greenwood and Dyanne Van Houten

486 U.S. 35, 108 S.Ct. 1625, 100 L.Ed.2d 30 (1988)

[White, J., delivered the opinion of the Court, in which Rehnquist, C. J., and Blackmun, Stevens, O'Connor, and Scalia, JJ., joined. Brennan, J., filed a dissenting opinion, in which Marshall, J., joined. Kennedy, J., took no part in the consideration or decision of the case. . . .]

FACTS

. . . In early 1984, investigator Jenny Stracner of the Laguna Beach Police Department received information indicating that respondent Greenwood might be engaged in narcotics trafficking. Stracner learned that a criminal suspect had informed a federal drug-enforcement agent in February 1984 that a truck filled with illegal drugs was en route to the Laguna Beach address at which Greenwood resided. In addition, a neighbor complained of heavy vehicular traffic late at night in front of Greenwood's single-family home. The neighbor reported that the vehicles remained at Greenwood's house for only a few minutes.

Stracner sought to investigate this information by conducting a surveillance of Greenwood's home. She observed several vehicles make brief stops at the house during the late-night and early-morning hours, and she followed a truck from the house to a residence that had previously been under investigation as a narcotics trafficking location.

On April 6, 1984, Stracner asked the neighborhood's regular trash collector to pick up the plastic garbage bags that Greenwood had left at the curb in front of his house and to turn the bags over to her without mixing their contents with garbage from other houses. The trash collector cleaned his truck bin of other refuse, collected the garbage bags from the street corner in front of Greenwood's house, and turned the bags over to Stracner. The officer searched through the rubbish and found items indicative of narcotics use. She recited the information that she had gleaned from the trash search in an affidavit in support of a warrant to search Greenwood's home.

Police officers encountered both respondents at the house later that day when they arrived to execute the warrant. The police encountered quantities of cocaine and hashish during their search of the house. Respondents were arrested on felony narcotics charges. They subsequently posted bail.

The police continued to receive reports of many late-night visitors to the Greenwood house. On May 4, investigator Robert Rahaeser obtained Greenwood's garbage from the regular trash collector in the same manner as had Stracner. The garbage again contained evidence of narcotics use.

Rahaeser secured another search warrant for Greenwood's home based on the information from the second trash search. The police found more narcotics and evidence of narcotics trafficking when they executed the warrant. Greenwood was again arrested.

The Supreme Court of California dismissed the charges against respondents. . . . The Court of Appeal affirmed. . . . We granted certiorari, and now reverse.

OPINION

. . . It may be that respondents did not expect that the contents of their garbage bags would become known to the police or other members of the public. An expectation of privacy does not give rise to Fourth Amendment protection, however, unless society is prepared to accept that expectation as objectively reasonable.

Here, we conclude that respondents exposed their garbage to the public sufficiency to defeat their claim to Fourth Amendment protection. It is common knowledge that plastic garbage bags left on or at the side of the public street are readily accessible to animals, children, scavengers, snoops, and other members of the public. Moreover, respondents placed their refuse at the curb for the express purpose of conveying it to a third party, the trash collector, who might himself had sorted through respondent's trash or permitted others, such as the police, to do so. Accordingly, having deposited their garbage ''in an area particularly suited for public inspection and, in a manner of speaking, public consumption, for the express purpose of having strangers take it,'' respondents could have had no reasonable expectation of privacy in the inculpatory items they discarded.

Furthermore, . . . the police cannot reasonably be expected to avert their eyes from evidence of criminal activity that could have been observed by any member of the public. Hence, "[w]hat a person knowingly exposes to the public, even in his own home or office, is not a subject of Fourth Amendment protection." . . .

DISSENT

Justice Brennan, with whom Justice Marshall joins, dissenting.

Every week for two months, and at least once more a month later, the Laguna Beach police clawed through the trash that respondent Greenwood left in opaque, sealed bags on the curb outside his home. Complete strangers minutely scrutinized their bounty, undoubtedly dredging up intimate details of Greenwood's private life and habits. The intrusions proceeded without a warrant, and no court before or since has concluded that the police acted on probable cause to believe Greenwood was engaged in any criminal activity. . . .

Had Greenwood flaunted his intimate activity by strewing his trash all over the curb for all to see, or had some nongovernmental intruder invaded his privacy and done the same, I could accept the Court's conclusion that an expectation of privacy would have been unreasonable. Similarly, had police searching the city dump run across incriminating evidence that, despite commingling with the trash of others, still retained its identity as Greenwood's, we would have a different case. But all that Greenwood "exposed . . . to the public," were the exteriors of several opaque, sealed containers. Until the bags were opened by police, they hid their contents from the public's view. . . .

In holding that the warrantless search of Greenwood's trash was consistent with the Fourth Amendment, the Court paints a grim picture of our society. It depicts a society in which local authorities may command their citizens to dispose of their personal effects in the manner least protective of the "sanctity of [the] home and the privacies of life," and then monitor them arbitrarily and without judicial oversight—a society that is not prepared to recognize as reasonable an individual's expectation of privacy in the most private of personal effects sealed in an opaque container and disposed of in a manner designed to commingle it imminently and inextricably with the trash of others. The American society with which I am familiar "chooses to dwell in reasonable security and freedom from surveillance," and is more dedicated to individual liberty and more sensitive to intrusions on the sanctity of the home than the Court is willing to acknowledge.

I dissent.

CASE DISCUSSION

Greenwood was arrested and charged with felony narcotics possession on the basis of contraband seized under two search warrants. Greenwood moved to set aside the warrants on the ground that they violated the Fourth Amendment. The superior court granted the motion on the ground that warrantless searches of trash violate the Fourth Amendment. The appellate court concluded that without the evidence obtained in the trash searches, the state had no probable cause to issue the search warrants and affirmed the superior court's decision. The California Supreme Court denied the state's petition for review. The Supreme Court granted *certiorari* to determine whether the Fourth Amendment prohibits the warrantless search and seizure of garbage left for collection outside the curtilage of a home. The Court reversed the California Court of Appeals on the ground that Greenwood had no privacy interest in the trash.

What interests did the Court balance in this case? When you throw your trash away, do you abandon it totally, or only for the purpose of having it destroyed? What does the dissent mean when he writes that the Court "paints a grim picture of our society"? Do you agree? Explain your answer. Do you think that this case is important enough to get to the Supreme Court? Explain your answer.[8]

At least one state supreme court, Hawaii's, has declared that the Hawaii constitution does protect trash. This case is an important example of the point made in chapter 2 that state courts are free to raise the minimum standards set by the United States Constitution.[9]

"Mere" Evidence

The seizure part of the search-and-seizure clause raises the question: What may the government seize in the course of a search? Clearly, the government may seize persons. So may it seize weapons, contraband, and the fruits of crime, such as stolen property. **Mere evidence,** evidence that is not weaponry, contraband, or stolen goods, however, creates problems, particularly when it includes private papers such as diaries and letters. Seizing such papers not only may invade privacy but also trench upon First Amendment rights to free speech.

Ever since the eighteenth century, the issue of seizing private papers has been controversial. In those days, the law of seditious libel declared a broad range of criticisms of the royal family a crime. The unpopularity of the Hanoverian kings exposed them to considerable public ridicule, and those who criticized them to criminal prosecution. In the famous case *Entick v. Carrington,* the English court ruled that purely private papers were protected against seizure even by the Crown. American constitutional doctrine followed this case. In *Gouled v. United States,* for example, the Supreme Court ruled that search warrants do not authorize entering houses and seizing private papers for the sole purpose of securing evidence. Hence, the **mere evidence rule** provided that officers could seize papers only if they were the fruits or instrumentalities of crime.[10]

In 1967, the Court rejected the mere evidence rule in *Warden v. Hayden.* While searching the house into which Hayden had fled following a robbery, police seized not only weapons and stolen money, but also clothing that was later used to convict Hayden. The clothing obviously was not contraband, a weapon, nor fruits of the robbery; it was mere evidence. The Court ruled that Hayden's clothing was admissible:

> nothing in the nature of property seized as evidence renders it more private than property seized, for example, as an instrumentality; quite the opposite may be true.

Indeed, the distinction is wholly irrational, since, depending on the circumstances, the same "papers and effects" may be "mere evidence" in one case and "instrumentalities" in another.[11]

Some argue that private papers such as diaries and personal letters deserve special Fourth Amendment protection.

Seizure and disclosure of private letters and diaries is a particularly abrasive infringement of privacy. An area of complete freedom for personal conversation and writing . . . preserves important First Amendment values. The forced protection of private diaries and letters, to obtain admissions or other statements against interest runs perilously close to the ban on self- incrimination.[12]

The Supreme Court has not answered the question whether the Fourth Amendment protects diaries and other highly personal papers.[13]

Open Fields

The **open fields doctrine**—trespasses onto open lands are not searches—is based on two ideas. First, the Fourth Amendment's language,

The special protection accorded by the Fourth Amendment to the people in their "persons, houses, papers, and effects," is not extended to the open fields.[14]

Second, the government is not prepared to recognize any reasonable expectation of privacy in open fields:

[O]pen fields do not provide the setting for those intimate activities that the Amendment is intended to shelter from government interference or surveillance. There is no societal interest in protecting the privacy of those activities, such as the cultivation of crops, that occur in open fields.[15]

Some maintain that if owners give notice that they expect privacy—such as building fences or putting up "No Trespassing" signs—the open fields doctrine should not apply. Despite such suggestions, the Supreme Court has declined to limit the open fields doctrine because of practical difficulties officers would face administering it:

police officers would have to guess before every search whether landowners had erected fences sufficiently high, posted a sufficient number of warning signs, or located contraband in an area sufficiently secluded to establish a right of privacy.[16]

The Supreme Court applied the doctrine in *California v. Ciraolo* where the police saw marijuana growing in a yard below from a plane at 1,000 feet. The police hired the plane because two privacy fences blocked their view from the ground. According to the Court, the naked eye observation was not a search. A similar case involved Dow Chemical Corporation. Dow maintains elaborate security around a 2,000-acre chemical plant that bars ground level observation. When Dow refused the Environmental Protection Agency's request for an on-site inspection, the EPA employed a commercial air photographer to fly over the plant and take photographs to determine whether Dow Chemical was complying with EPA standards. The Supreme Court ruled that such aerial observation and photography was not a search.[17]

Decision Point

Acting on reports that marijuana was being raised on Oliver's farm, two narcotics agents of the Kentucky State Police went to the farm to investigate. Arriving at the farm, they drove past Oliver's house to a locked gate with a ''No Trespassing'' sign. A footpath led around one side of the gate. The agents walked around the gate and along the road for several hundred yards, passing a barn and parked camper. At that point, someone standing in front of the camper shouted: ''No hunting is allowed, come back up here.'' The officers shouted back that they were Kentucky State Police Officers, but found no one when they returned to the camper. The officers resumed their investigation of the farm and found a field of marijuana over a mile from Oliver's home. On the basis of the evidence, they arrested Oliver for manufacturing a controlled substance.

After receiving an anonymous tip that marijuana was being grown in the woods behind Thornton's residence, two police officers entered the woods by a path between Thornton's residence and a neighboring house. They followed a footpath through the woods until they reached two marijuana patches fenced with chicken wire. Later, the officers determined that the patches were on Thornton's property, obtained a warrant to search and seize the marijuana. On the basis of the evidence, the police arrested Thornton.

Were the searches lawful? According to the United States Supreme Court, they were. ''We conclude, from the text of the Fourth Amendment and from the historical and contemporary understanding of its purposes, that an individual has no legitimate expectation that open fields will remain free from warrantless intrusion by government officers.'' In Oliver's case, the trial court had suppressed the evidence, holding that the ''No Trespassing'' sign and the secluded location of the marijuana patches ''evinced a reasonable expectation of privacy,'' and the Maine Supreme Judicial Court affirmed. Which, in your opinion, is the better rule?[18]

≡ SEARCH AND SEIZURE PURSUANT TO WARRANT

. . . and no warrants shall issue, but upon probable cause, supported by oath or affirmation, and particularly describing the place to be searched, and the person of things to be seized.
    Amendment IV, United States Constitution

The courts have long held that searches without warrants are unreasonable searches, barring some well-recognized exceptions. (See chapter 5 for discussions of neutral magistrates and probable cause.)

The Particularity Requirement

The Fourth Amendment calls for search warrants ''particularly describing the place to be searched, and the persons or things to be seized.'' Usually, a single dwelling address is sufficient to meet this requirement, such as a warrant to search "125 Willow Street," or "apartment 8-B in Colonial Terrace Apartments." However, a warrant to search "1135 Stone Street," where the address is a large apartment complex and only one apartment is the object of the search, does not satisfy the particularity requirement. Such a warrant authorizes a general search of all apartments in the building; this clearly violates the particularity requirement.[19]

The warrant must also specifically identify the "things to be seized" and may specify an entire class of items. So, a search warrant that specified "address books, diaries, business records, documents, receipts, warranty books, guns, stereo equipment [and] color television" as evidence in a theft case met the particularity requirement. Catchall categories are also acceptable if the context limits the seizure sufficiently. For example, a search warrant that authorized searching for and seizing "records, notes, documents indicating involvement in and control of prostitution activity" was particular enough because officers were directed to seize only items related to prostitution.[20]

Execution of Search Warrants

TIME. Statutes or court rules in most jurisdictions require that officers execute search warrants within a specified time. The Federal Rules of Criminal Procedure, for example, provide that the warrant

> shall command the officer to search, within a specified period of time not to exceed 10 days, the person or place named for the property or person specified.[21]

The ten-day limit is common in jurisdictions that provide for specific execution times for warrants.

In addition to the length of time given to serve warrants, about half the states require that officers execute search warrants during daytime hours unless the warrant specifically authorizes otherwise. The Federal Rules of Criminal Procedure include such a limitation. Rule 41(c)(1) provides as follows:

> The warrant shall be served in the daytime, unless the issuing authority, by appropriate provision in the warrant, and for reasonable cause shown, authorizes its execution at times other than daytime [daytime means between the hours 6:00 A.M. and 10:00 P.M.].[22]

Nothing requires officers to execute warrants when occupants are present. Despite the objection of one federal district court that a search warrant executed in the absence of the occupant constitutes an unreasonable search because there exists the possibility of a general search and "pilferage by officers of the law,"
the Fifth Circuit Court wrote that

> forcible entry pursuant to a search warrant of unoccupied premises is not per se a violation of the Fourth Amendment. . . . The statutory requirements of judicial supervision based on probable cause, the requisites of specificity in describing the premises and the items to be seized, and the delivery of a written inventory of the items taken to the occupant or other competent person provide adequate safeguards against potential abuse and sufficiently limit police discretion.[23]

EXTENT OF SEARCH. The Supreme Court has not specifically ruled on the exact extent of constitutional searches pursuant to warrants. However, a number of lower courts have upheld searches of entire premises of the place named in the warrant. For example, it was reasonable for officers to search a briefcase found under a desk and seize incriminating evidence inside the case pursuant to a warrant to search "the premises of the Hillside Press." In upholding the search's validity, the First Circuit Court of Appeals noted, however, that

> . . . we do not mean to suggest that anything found on the premises would necessarily fall within the scope of a warrant to search premises. Nor would we imply that the result would be different if, when the officers entered, appellant was physically holding the briefcase. To allow our decision to be interpreted as giving carte blanche to seize any objects reposing within premises covered by a warrant would be a disservice to law enforcement officials, individuals who may find their personal privacy invaded by a premises search warrant, and courts which must rule on suppression motions.[24]

A search warrant to search "the premises" does not automatically authorize searching—or even frisking—persons who are on the premises during the search. For example, a warrant to search a tavern for evidence of narcotics did not authorize frisking the dozen patrons who were present during the search.

> There is no reason to suppose that when the search warrant was issued . . . that the authorities had probable cause to believe that any person found on the premises of the Aurora Tap Tavern, aside from "Greg" [the bartender] would be violating the law. [The police had no probable cause to search Ybarra, a patron, either before or after they entered the tavern.] . . . It is true that the police possessed a warrant based on probable cause to search the tavern in which Ybarra happened to be at the time the warrant was executed. But, a person's mere propinquity to others independently suspected of criminality does not, without more, give rise to probable cause to search that person.[25]

The extent of the search depends on the nature of the items for which the warrant authorizes the search. If the warrant specifies searching for stolen refrigerators, officers would go beyond the warrant's scope by searching in dresser drawers, to give an obvious example. According to the Supreme Court, "the same meticulous investigation which would be appropriate in a search for two small cancelled checks could not be considered reasonable where agents are seeking a stolen automobile."[26]

Entry to Search Pursuant to Search Warrant

Generally, officers executing search warrants must announce their entry. The Model Code of Pre-Arraignment Procedure represents typical legislation concerning entries to search pursuant to warrants. It provides:

> 220.3 Execution of the Warrant
> (2) *Notice of Authority.* Except as provided in Subsection (3), the executing officer shall, before entering the premises, give appropriate notice of his authority and purpose to . . . the person in apparent control of the premises to be searched. . . .[27]

The code also approves "no knock" entries to execute search warrants:

> (3) *Execution Without Notice.* If the executing officer has reasonable cause to believe that the notice required by Subsection (2) would endanger the successful execution of

the warrant with all practicable safety, the officer may execute the warrant without such prior notice.[28]

The "no-knock" provision, followed in several state statutes, permits entries without notice under two conditions. First, a situation where suspects might easily destroy evidence requires no notice. For example, when officers knew that illegal drugs were purposely kept near a toilet so they could be quickly flushed away, the court ruled that the officers did not need to announce their entry to search. Second, if an announced entry would endanger officers' safety, announcement is not required.[29]

Copies and Returns of Warrants, Receipts, and Inventories

In addition to the requirements set out in the preceding sections, most jurisdictions add at least three more for proper search warrant execution. First, officers who execute warrants must display or deliver a copy of the warrant at the place they are searching. Second, executing officers must provide a receipt for items seized. Third, officers must make a prompt **return of warrant,** that is, return the warrant to the court where it was issued, accompanied by an inventory of the items seized during the search.

The Federal Rules of Criminal Procedure provide:

> Rule 41 Search and Seizure
> (d) Execution and Return with inventory. The officer taking property under warrant shall give to the person from whom or from whose premises the property was taken a copy of the warrant and a receipt for the property taken or shall leave the copy and receipt at the place from which the property was taken. The return shall be made promptly and shall be accompanied by a written inventory of any property taken. The inventory shall be made in the presence of the applicant for the warrant and the person from whose possession or premises the property was taken, if they are present, or in the presence of at least one credible person other than the applicant for the warrant or the person from whose possession or premises the property was taken, and shall be verified by the officer. The federal magistrate shall upon request deliver a copy of the inventory to the person from whom or from whose premises the property was taken and to the applicant for the warrant.

≡ SEARCHES WITHOUT WARRANTS

Formally, the courts express a preference for search warrants by ruling that the Fourth Amendment mandates them in the absence of well-defined exceptions. Informally, these exceptions are broad enough to permit law enforcement officers' strong preference for searches without warrants. Since searches without warrants far outnumber searches with warrants, day-to-day practice reflects law enforcement officers' preference more than it does the courts' formal rules.[30]

One former Washington, D.C. assistant United States attorney wrote:

> As anyone who has worked in the criminal justice system knows, searches conducted pursuant to these exceptions, particularly searches incident to arrest, automobile and "stop and frisk" searches, far exceed searches performed pursuant to warrants.

The same attorney gave the reason why:

The reason that all of these exceptions have grown up is simple: the clear rule that warrants are required is unworkable and to enforce it would lead to exclusion of evidence in many cases where the police activity was essentially reasonable.[31]

Law enforcement officers express frustration with the delay that complying with the Fourth Amendment usually involves. One police officer said it typically takes four hours from the time he decides he wants a warrant until the time he has one in his hand. He adds:

> . . . and that's if everything goes right. You find people and girls get'em typed and you can find the judges when they are sitting at the bench—because a lot of judges won't see people in their offices. [If you miss them there,] they leave and go to lunch and you have to wait until they come back for the afternoon dockets, and if they are already into the afternoon dockets, they are not going to interrupt the procedures [for a warrant]. So you sit and wait through three or four docket sessions. . . . It can take all day.[32]

Frequently this frustration with delays in fulfilling the formal warrant requirements leads to "getting around the Fourth Amendment." One detective explained how to "get around" the warrant requirement by "shamming" consent.

> [You] tell the guy, "Let me come in and take a look at your house." And he says, "No, I don't want to." And then you tell him, "Then I'm going to leave Sam here, and he's going to live with you until we come back. Now we can do it either way." And very rarely do the people say, "Go get your search warrant, then. . . ."[33]

The more than twenty exceptions to the warrant requirement fall into three major categories. First, and most numerous, **exigent circumstances searches** are those in which there is not time to get a warrant. Principal searches in this category are searches incident to arrest and vehicle searches. Second, **consent searches** are searches where suspects or other authorized persons agree to permit law enforcement officers to search. Third, **inspection searches** do not require consent, warrants, or probable cause. These include border searches for customs violations and illegal alien entry; inspections of buildings, businesses, mines, and other gathering places to enforce health and safety regulations; and vehicle safety checks

Exigent Circumstances Searches

SEARCHES INCIDENT TO ARREST. Police can search arrested suspects without warrants. The **search incident to arrest,** or search contemporaneous with arrest, requires neither probable cause nor a warrant. According to the courts, searches incident to arrest are reasonable for two reasons: (1) they protect officers whom suspects may injure or kill; and (2) they preserve evidence suspects may destroy.

Searches incident to arrest reflect the Supreme Court's balancing approach to reasonableness. Protecting law enforcement officers, preserving evidence, and assuring individual privacy are all at stake. Officers may search people whom they arrest without warrants to disarm them and to prevent them from destroying evidence. To protect privacy, the Court has restricted the extent of the search; police may search only to the extent necessary to protect officers and preserve evidence. The Supreme Court in *Chimel v. California* considered how extensively law enforcement officers without a warrant can search incident to a lawful arrest.

CASE

Was the search "incident" to the arrest?

Chimel v. California

395 U.S. 752, 89 S.Ct. 2034, 23 L.Ed.2d 685 (1969)

[Mr. Justice Stewart delivered the opinion of the Court.]

FACTS

The relevant facts are essentially undisputed. Late in the afternoon of September 13, 1965, three police officers arrived at the Santa Ana, California, home of the petitioner with a warrant authorizing his arrest for the burglary of a coin shop. The officers knocked on the door, identified themselves to the petitioner's wife, and asked if they might come inside. She ushered them into the house, where they waited 10 or 15 minutes until the petitioner returned home from work. When the petitioner entered the house, one of the officers handed him the arrest warrant and asked for permission to 'look around.' The petitioner objected, but was advised that 'on the basis of the lawful arrest,' the officers would nonetheless conduct a search. No search warrant had been issued.

Accompanied by the petitioner's wife, the officers then looked through the entire three-bedroom house, including the attic, the garage, and a small workshop. In some rooms the search was relatively cursory. In the master bedroom and sewing room, however, the officers directed the petitioner's wife to open drawers and 'to physically move contents of the drawers from side to side so that (they) might view any items that would have come from (the) burglary.' After completing the search, they seized numerous items—primarily coins, but also several medals, tokens, and a few other objects. The entire search took between 45 minutes and an hour.

At the petitioner's subsequent state trial on two charges of burglary, the items taken from his house were admitted into evidence against him, over his objection that they had been unconstitutionally seized. He was convicted, and the judgments of conviction were affirmed by both the California Court of Appeal, and the California Supreme Court. . . . We granted certiorari in order to consider the petitioner's substantial constitutional claims.

OPINION

Without deciding the question, we proceed on the hypothesis that the California courts were correct in holding that the arrest of the petitioner was valid under the Constitution. This brings us directly to the question whether the warrantless search of the petitioner's entire house can be constitutionally justified as incident to that arrest. . . .

When an arrest is made, it is reasonable for the arresting officer to search the person arrested in order to remove any weapons that the latter might seek to use in order to resist arrest or effect his escape. Otherwise, the officer's safety might well be endangered, and the arrest itself frustrated. In addition, it is entirely reasonable for the arresting officer to search for and seize any evidence on the arrestee's person in order to prevent its concealment or destruction. And the area into which an arrestee might reach in order to grab a weapon or evidentiary items must, of course, be governed by a like rule. A gun on a table or in a drawer in front of one who is arrested can be as dangerous to the arresting officer as one concealed in the clothing of the person arrested. There is ample justification, therefore, for a search of the arrestee's person and the area 'within his immediate control'—construing that phrase to mean the area from within which he might gain possession of a weapon or destructible evidence. There is no comparable justification, however, for routinely searching any room other than that in which an arrest occurs—or, for that matter, for searching through all the desk drawers or other closed or concealed areas in that room itself. Such searches, in the absence of well-recognized exceptions, may be made only under the authority of a search warrant. The 'adherence to judicial processes' mandated by the Fourth Amendment requires no less. . . .

It is argued in the present case that it is 'reasonable' to search a man's house when he is arrested in it. But that argument is founded on little more than a subjective view regarding the acceptability of certain sorts of police conduct, and not on consideration relevant to Fourth Amendment interests. Under such an unconfined analysis, Fourth Amendment protection in this area would approach the evaporation point. . . .

After arresting a man in his house, to rummage at will among his papers in search of whatever will convict him, appears to us to be indistinguishable from what might be done under a general warrant; indeed, the warrant would give more protection, for presumably it must be issued by a magistrate. . . . Application of sound Fourth Amendment principles to the facts of this case produces a clear result. The search here went far beyond the petitioner's person and the area from within which he might have obtained either a weapon or something that could have been used as evidence against him. There was no constitutional justification, in the absence of a search warrant, for extending the search beyond that area. The scope of the search was, therefore, 'unreasonable' under the Fourth and Fourteenth Amendments and the petitioner's conviction cannot stand. . . .
Reversed. . . .

CASE DISCUSSION

Chimel was prosecuted for burglary. The Superior Court, Orange County, California, rendered judgment, and defendant appealed. The California Supreme Court, vacating an opinion of the Court of Appeal affirmed, and defendant obtained certiorari. The Supreme Court, Mr. Justice Stewart, held that warrantless search of defendant's entire house, incident to defendant's proper arrest in house on burglary charge, was unreasonable because it extended beyond defendant's person and area from which he might have obtained either weapon or something that could have been used as evidence against him.

What is the Court's definition of area under "control"? Does the Court's definition promote the interest in individual liberty over crime control? Does it impede the search for truth? What, if anything, does it have to do with promoting the interest in procedural regularity? If you were defining the term, would you have included the whole house within the scope of the rule? Explain your answer, including what interests you consider paramount in formulating your definition.

Three main questions arise in balancing the officers' safety, criminal law enforcement needs, and individual privacy in the warrantless searches incident to lawful arrests: (1) How extensive a space is subject to a search incident to arrest? (2) How close in time, either prior to or after arrest, must the search take place? (3) Does the exception cover arrests for all crimes? Generally, the area subject to search is what is commonly called "the grabbable area," or the area under the suspect's immediate control. The Supreme Court in *New York v. Belton* expanded the "grabbable area" concept in applying it to automobiles.

CASE

Was the search necessary to protect officers and preserve evidence?

New York v. Belton

453 U.S. 454, 101 S.Ct. 2860, 69 L.Ed.2d 768 (1981)

FACTS

On April 9, 1978, Trooper Douglas Nicot, a New York State policeman driving an unmarked car on the New York Thruway, was passed by another automobile travelling at an excessive rate of speed. Nicot gave chase, overtook the speeding vehicle, and ordered its driver to pull it over to the side of the road and stop. There were four men in the car, one of whom was Roger Belton, the respondent in this case. The policeman asked to see the driver's license and automobile registration, and discovered that none of the men owned the vehicle or was related to its owner. Meanwhile, the policeman had smelt burnt marihuana and had seen on the floor of the car an envelope marked "Supergold" that he associated with marihuana. He therefore directed the men to get out of the car, and placed them under arrest for unlawful possession of marihuana. He patted down each of the men and "split them up into four different areas of the Thruway at this time so they would not be in physical touching area of each other.'' He then picked up the envelope marked ''Supergold'' and found that it contained marihuana. After giving the arrestees the warnings required by *Miranda v. Arizona,* the state policeman searched each one of them. He then searched the passenger compartment of the car. On the back seat he found a black leather jacket belonging to Belton. He unzipped one of the pockets of the jacket and discovered cocaine. Placing the jacket in his automobile, he drove the four arrestees to a nearby police station.

Belton was subsequently indicted for criminal possession of a controlled substance. In the trial court he moved that the cocaine the trooper had seized from the jacket pocket be suppressed. The court denied the motion. Belton then pleaded guilty to a lesser included offense. . . . The Appellate Division of the New York Supreme Court upheld the constitutionality of the search and seizure. . . . The New York Court of Appeals reversed. . . .

OPINION

Stewart, J., delivered the opinion of the Court, in which Burger, C.J., and Blackmun, Powell, and Rehnquist, JJ., joined. Rehnquist, J., filed a concurring statement. Stevens, J., filed a statement concurring in the judgement, Brennan, J., and White, J., filed dissenting opinions, in which Marshall, J., joined. . . .

It is a first principle of Fourth Amendment jurisprudence that the police may not conduct a search unless they first convince a neutral magistrate that there is probable cause to do so. This Court has recognized, however, that ''the exigencies of the situation'' may sometimes make exemption from the warrant requirement ''imperative.'' Specifically, the Court held in *Chimel v. California,* 395 U.S. 752, 89 S.Ct. 2034, 23 L.Ed.2d 685, that a lawful custodial arrest creates a situation which justifies the contemporaneous search without a warrant of the person arrested and of the immediately surrounding area. Such searches have long been considered valid because of the need ''to remove any weapons that [the arrestee] might seek to use in order to resist arrest or effect his escape'' and the need to prevent the concealment or destruction of evidence. . .

But no straightforward rule has emerged from the litigated cases respecting the question involved here—the question of the proper scope of a search of the interior of an automobile incident to a lawful custodial arrest of its occupants. . . .

When a person cannot know how a court will apply a settled principle to a recurring factual situation, that person cannot know the scope of his constitutional protection, nor can a policeman know the scope of his authority. While the *Chimel* case established that a search incident to an arrest may not stray beyond the area within the immediate control of the arrestee, courts have found no workable definition of ''the area within the immediate control of the arrestee'' when that area arguably includes the interior of an automobile and the arrestee is its recent occupant. Our reading of the cases suggests the generalization that articles inside the relatively narrow compass of the passenger compartment of an automobile are in fact generally, even if not inevitably, within ''the area into which an arrestee might reach in order to grab a weapon or evidentiary ite[m]." . . . Accordingly, we hold that when a policeman has made a lawful custodial arrest of the occupant of an automobile, he may, as a contemporaneous incident of that arrest, search the passenger compartment of that automobile. . . .

It follows from this conclusion that the police may also examine the contents of any containers found within the passenger compartment, for if the passenger compartment is within reach of the arrestee, so also will containers in it be within his reach. . . .

The search of the jacket, therefore, was a search incident to a lawful custodial arrest, and it did not violate the Fourth and Fourteenth Amendments. Accordingly, the judgement is reversed. It is so ordered.

DISSENT

Justice Brennan, with whom Justice Marshall joins, dissenting. . . .

It has long been a fundamental principle of Fourth Amendment analysis that exceptions to the warrant requirement are to be narrowly construed. Predicated on the Fourth Amendment's essential purpose of "shield[ing] the citizen from unwarranted intrusions into his privacy," this principle carries with it two corollaries. First, for a search to be valid under the Fourth Amendment, it must be " 'strictly tied to and justified by' the circumstances which renders its initiation permissible." Second, in determining whether to grant an exemption to the warrant requirement, courts should carefully consider the facts and circumstances of each search and seizure, focusing on the reasons supporting the exception rather than on any bright-line rule of general application. . . .

In its attempt to formulate a " 'single, familiar standard . . . to guide police officers, who have only limited time and expertise to reflect on and balance the social and individual interests involved in the specific circumstances they confront,' " the Court today disregards these principles, and instead adopts a fiction—that the interior of a car is *always* within the immediate control of an arrestee who has recently been in the car. . . .

The Court seeks to justify its departure from the principles underlying *Chimel* by proclaiming the need for a new "bright-line" rule to guide the officer in the field. However, "the mere fact that law enforcement may be made more efficient can never by itself justify disregard of the Fourth Amendment." Moreover, the Court's attempt to forge a "bright-line" rule fails on its own terms. While the "interior/trunk" distinction may provide a workable guide in certain cases—for example, where the officer arrests the driver of a car and then immediately searches the seats and the floor—in the long run, I suspect it will create far more problems than it solves. The Court's new approach leaves open too many questions and, more important, it provides the police and the courts with too few tools with which to find the answers.

CASE DISCUSSION

Belton was indicted for possession of a controlled substance found in, and seized from, his car. After the trial court denied Belton's motion to suppress the cocaine seized, Belton pleaded guilty to a lesser included offense, preserving his claim that the police seized the cocaine in violation of the Fourth and Fourteenth Amendments. The intermediate appeals court upheld the seizure, but the New York Court of Appeals reversed. The United States Supreme Court granted *certiorari* to the state and reversed on the ground that the seizure did not violate the Fourth Amendment.

Does this case extend the concept of "grabbable area" too far? Explain. Do you prefer the "bright-line" rule the Court adopted, or the case-by-case approach the dissent favors? Why? Should the officer be permitted to search not only the interior of the car but also the trunk? and under the hood? Should the officer be restricted to patting down the outer part of the jacket? One commentator on the case noted:

> Ten years ago most state court judges might have welcomed the Supreme Court's . . . decision. The new automobile search rule for arrested motorists [that deems the interior of an automobile always to be within the "grabbing area"] . . . certainly makes it easier for courts to apply the law of searches incident to arrest in such cases. . . . This new rule not only allows police to be more certain about the precise scope of their search powers; it also frees lower courts from the burden of case-by-case adjudication of the frequently disputed factual issue of actual grabbing area.[34]

Do you agree? Do you favor the *per se* rule for that reason? Why not?

The Court has ruled that "incident to arrest" includes the time both prior to and following arrest. For example, in *Cupp v. Murphy,* Portland, Oregon, police scraped Daniel Murphy's fingernails for blood residue that might have been that of his strangled wife. Police searched Murphy *before* they arrested him. The Court ruled that since the police had probable cause to arrest Murphy even though they had not done so, the search was still incident to, or contemporaneous with, the arrest. In *United States v. Edwards,* Edwards was lawfully arrested shortly after 11 P.M. and put in jail. The next morning the police took his clothing and searched it for paint chips that would link Edwards to a burglary. Despite the lapse of ten hours, and over a strong dissent that the police had plenty of time to present their evidence to a neutral magistrate to obtain a search warrant, the Court ruled that the search was incident to the arrest.[35]

Decision Point

A California police officer discovered a pistol and drugs on a hitchiker during a lawful patdown, arrested and handcuffed him, and put him in a police vehicle. Only then did a second officer open an unlocked suitcase that had been sitting on the road next to the suspect at the time of the arrest; inside the suitcase were more drugs. Was the search of the suitcase incident to the arrest? The California Court of Appeals said it was, holding that if a container is close enough that the arrested suspect could have reached it at the moment of arrest, "a search does not become unlawful because the police first separate the arrestee from the reach of the article, or handcuff or otherwise restrain the arrestee, so long as the search is made immediately thereafter, while the arrestee is still nearby at the scene of the arrest and before the arresting officers have turned their attention to tasks unrelated to securing the safety of persons and property involved in the arrest."

Alaska police officers entered a tavern and arrested the bartender for selling drugs moments earlier to an informer. Fifteen minutes later, while the suspect was being held at the other end of the room, an officer searched the jacket from which the suspect had gotten the drugs, which had been hanging on a coat rack some ten to fifteen feet from the bar all along. Was the search of the jacket incident to the arrest? The Alaska Supreme Court ruled that it was not because the jacket was not accessible to the suspect at the moment of the arrest. "[P]hysical proximity at the time of the arrest—with the consequent threat to safety and risk of destruction—is the basic requirement upon which the search incident to arrest exception is predicated." The majority held that the exigencies of the situation at the point of the suspect's arrest did not call for a search of the jacket.[36]

The third issue in searches incident to arrest—what crimes the exception covers—the Supreme Court addressed in *United States v. Robinson,* excerpted in chapter 1. Robinson was stopped and arrested for driving without a license. The arresting officer frisked Robinson. When he felt a lump in Robinson's coat pocket, he reached inside and found a crumpled-up cigarette package. He opened it and found heroin inside. Robinson was charged with illegally possessing narcotics. He moved to suppress the evidence but the court denied his motion and admitted it over his objection. The heroin was the principal evidence that convicted Robinson. The Supreme Court upheld the conviction and, in so doing, ruled that full searches incident to traffic offenses—and presumably all other offenses that authorize taking suspects into custody—are reasonable. The Court first held that officers are not restricted to frisks incident to traffic arrests. Then, the Court went on:

> Nor are we inclined, on the basis of what seems to us to be a rather speculative judgment, to qualify the breadth of the general authority to search incident to a lawful custodial arrest on the assumption that persons arrested for the offense of driving while their license has been revoked are less likely to be possessed of dangerous weapons than are those arrested for other crimes. It is scarcely open to doubt that the danger to an officer is far greater in the case of extended exposure which follows the taking of a suspect into custody and transporting him to the police station than in the case of the fleeting contact resulting from a typical *Terry*-type stop. This is an adequate basis for treating all custodial arrests alike for purposes of search justification.

The Court rejected what it considered a call to review all cases in which police encounter citizens. Instead, Justice Rehnquist writing for the Court, concluded:

> A police officer's determination as to how and where to search the person of a suspect whom he has arrested is necessarily a quick *ad hoc* judgment which the Fourth Amendment does not require to be broken down in each instance into an analysis of each step in the search. The authority to search the person incident to a lawful

custodial arrest, while based upon the need to disarm and to discover evidence, does not depend upon what a court may later decide was the probability in a particular arrest situation that weapons or evidence would in fact be found upon the person of the suspect. A custodial arrest of a suspect based on probable cause is a reasonable intrusion under the Fourth Amendment; that intrusion being lawful, a search incident to the arrest requires no additional justification. It is the fact of the lawful arrest which establishes the authority to search, and we hold that in the case of a lawful custodial arrest a full search of the person is not only an exception to the warrant requirement of the Fourth Amendment, but is also a ''reasonable'' search under that Amendment.[37]

The majority decided that two interests justified the search: (1) the possible danger to police officers taking suspects into custody; and (2) the logical impossibility of the Court reviewing every police decision. Hence, the Court decided to leave to police discretion whether suspects ought to be searched incident to their arrests. The combined decisions in *Murphy, Edwards,* and *Robinson* establish broad police power to search incident to arrest. These decisions again illustrate the Court's reticence in second-guessing police law-enforcement judgments, particularly early in the criminal process.

The states have not been so reticent to ''police the police'' search power. The Alaska Supreme Court, for example, ruled that the Alaska constitution's search-and-seizure clause did not permit such broad power to search incident to traffic arrests.

Absent specific articulable facts justifying the intrusion . . . a warrantless search incident to an arrest, other than for weapons, is unreasonable and therefore violative of the Alaska Constitution if the charge on which the arrest is made is not one, evidence of which could be concealed on the person.[38]

The Alaska decision, and others to the same effect in states such as California, make clear that the federal Constitution sets a minimum standard that states may freely raise by interpreting provisions in their own constitutions more strictly than the United States Supreme Court interprets parallel federal provisions. (See chap. 1 for a discussion of the relationship between state and federal constitutions.)

VEHICLE SEARCHES. The Supreme Court created the vehicle exception to the search warrant requirement during Prohibition in the 1920s, when cars were increasingly used in alcohol-related crimes. In the landmark case *Carroll v. United States,* federal agents stopped a car they had probable cause to believe contained illegal liquor.

CASE

Was the search of the car without a warrant reasonable?

Carroll v. United States

267 U.S. 132, 45 S.Ct. 280, 69 L.Ed. 543 (1925)

[Justice Taft delivered the Court's opinion.]

FACTS

Cronenwett, Scully and Thayer, federal prohibition agents, and one Peterson, a state officer [seized alcohol from Carroll and Kiro] in December 1921, as the car was going westward on highway between Detroit and Grand Rapids at a point 16 miles outside Grand Rapids. On September 29, Cronenwett and Scully were in an apartment in Grand Rapids. Three men came to that apartment, a man named Kruska and the two defendants, Carroll and Kiro. Cronenwett was introduced to them as one Stafford, working in the Michigan Chair Company in Grand Rapids, who wishes to buy three cases of whisky. The price was fixed at $130 a case. The three men said they had to go to the east end of Grand Rapids to get the liquor and that they would be back in half or three-quarters of an hour. They went away and in a short time Kruska came back and said they could not get it that night, that the man who had it was not in, but that they would deliver it the next day. They had come to the apartment in an automobile known as an Oldsmobile Roadster, the number of which Cronenwett then identified, as did Scully. The proposed vendors did not return the next day and the evidence disclosed no explanation of their failure to do so. One may surmise that it was suspicion of the real character of the proposed purchaser, whom Carroll subsequently called by his first name when arrested in December following. Cronenwett and his subordinates were engaged in patrolling the road leading from Detroit to Grand Rapids, looking for violations of the Prohibition Act. This seems to have been their regular tour of duty. On the 6th of October, Carroll and Kiro, going eastward from Grand Rapids in the same Oldsmobile Roadster, passed Cronenwett and Scully some distance out of Grand Rapids. Cronenwett called to Scully, who was taking lunch, that the Carroll boys had passed them going toward Detroit and sought with Scully to catch up with them to see where they were going. The officers followed as far as East Lansing, half way to Detroit, but there was no trace of them. On the 15th of December, some two months later, Scully and Cronenwett, on their regular tour of duty, with Peterson, the state officer, were going from Grand Rapids to Ionia, on the road to Detroit, when Kiro and Carroll met and passed them in the same automobile, coming from the direction of Detroit to Grand Rapids. The government agents turned their car and followed the defendants to a point some sixteen miles east of Grand Rapids, where they stopped them and searched the car. They found behind the upholstering in the seats, the filling of which had been removed, 68 bottles. These had labels on them, part purporting to be certificates of English chemists that the contents were blended Scotch whiskeys, and the rest that the contents were Gordon gin made in London. When an expert witness was called to prove the contents, defendants admitted the nature of them to be whiskey and gin. When the defendants were arrested, Carroll said to Cronenwett, "Take the liquor and give us one more chance and I will make it right with you," and he pulled out a roll of bills, of which one was for $10. Peterson and another took the two defendants and the liquor and the car to Grand Rapids, while Cronenwett, Thayer and Scully remained on the road looking for other cars, of whose coming they had information. The officers were not anticipating that the defendants would be coming through on the highway at that particular time, but when they met them there they believed they were carrying liquor; and hence the search, seizure, and arrest.

OPINION

The constitutional and statutory provisions involved in this case include the Fourth Amendment and the National Prohibition Act. . . . The National Prohibition Act, passed to enforce the Eighteenth Amendment, makes it unlawful to have or possess any liquor intended for use in violating the Act, or which has been so used, and provides that no poperty rights shall exist in such liquor. A search warrant may issue and such liquor, with the containers thereof, may be seized under the warrant and ultimately destroyed. [The Act further provides] When . . . any officer of the law shall discover any person in the act of transporting in violation of law, intoxicating liquors in any wagon, buggy, automobile, water or air craft, or other vehicle, it shall be his duty to seize any and all intoxicating liquors found therein. . . . Whenever intoxicating liquors transported or possessed illegally shall be seized by an officer he shall take possession of the vehicle or automobile, boat, air or water craft, or any other conveyance, and shall arrest any person in charge thereof. . . .

The intent of Congress to make a distinction between the necessity of a search warrant in the searching of private dwellings and in that of automobiles and other road vehicles in the enforcement of the Prohibition Act is . . . clearly established by . . . legislative history. . . . Is such a distinction consistent with the Fourth Amendment? We think it is. The Fourth Amendment does not denounce all searches or seizures, but only unreasonable ones. . . .

On reason and authority the true rule is that if the search and seizure without a warrant are made upon probable cause, that is, upon a belief, reasonably arising out of the circumstances known to the seizing officer, that an automobile or other vehicle contains that which by law is subject to seizure and destruction, the search and seizure are valid. The Fourth Amendment is to be construed in the light of what was deemed an unreasonable search and seizure when it was adopted, and in a manner which will conserve public interests as well as the interests and rights of individual citizens. . . .

The guaranty of freedom from unreasonable searches and seizures by the Fourth Amendment has been construed, practically since the beginning of the Government, as recognizing a necessary difference between a search of a store, dwelling house or other structure in respect of which a proper official warrant readily may be obtained, and a search of a ship, motor boat, wagon or automobile, for contraband goods, where it is not practicable to secure a warrant because the vehicle can be quickly moved out of the locality or jurisdiction in which the warrant must be sought. . . .

CONCURRING OPINION

[Justice McReynolds, with whom Justice Sutherland joined concurring, noted:]

The damnable character of the ''bootlegger's'' business should not close our eyes to the mischief which will surely follow any attempt to destroy it by unwarranted methods. To press forward to a great principle by breaking through every other great principle that stands in the way of its establishment; . . . in short, to procure an eminent good by means that are unlawful, is as little consonant to private morality as to public justice.

While quietly driving an ordinary automobile along a much frequented private road, plaintiffs in error were arrested by Federal officers without a warrant upon mere suspicion—ill founded, as I think. The officers then searched the machine and discovered carefully secreted whiskey, which was seized and thereafter used as evidence against plaintiffs in error when on trial for transporting intoxicating liquor contrary to the Volstead Act. They maintain that both the arrest and seizure were unlawful and that use of the liquor as evidence violated their constitutional rights.

CASE DISCUSSION

Carroll and Kiro were convicted of illegally transporting liquor contrary to the Prohibition Act. Over their objection, the trial court admitted liquor they claimed federal officers unlawfully seized. They appealed, on writ of error, to the United States Supreme Court. The Supreme Court held that the Fourth Amendment permits warrantless searches of automobiles on probable cause.

What reason does the Court give for allowing warrantless searches for automobiles? Do you agree? What interests does the Court balance in reaching this conclusion? Would you balance them in the same manner? Does the concurring opinion sound as if it could be written today? What interests does the concurring opinion address? Do you agree with the Court's decision regarding automobile searches? with the concurring opinion's warning? Explain.

The Court noted as its major rationale for the *Carroll* decision that the mobility of automobiles made warrantless searches of cars reasonable so long as probable cause supported the searches. Later, the Court added a second rationale for making warrantless vehicle searches reasonable—there was no reasonable expectation of privacy in vehicles that required warrants to search them.

The mobility and reasonable expectation of privacy rationales work well for ordinary cars, trucks, and vans. The rationales become more difficult to sustain when the situation involves warrantless searches of vehicles used for both transportation and living. The Court addressed the question of searching these hybrid vehicles in *California v. Carney*.

CASE

Did the police search Carney's "home"?

California v. Carney

471 U.S. 386, 105 S.Ct. 2066, 85 L.Ed.2d 406 (1985)

[Burger, C.J., delivered the opinion of the Court, in which White, Blackmun, Powell, Rehnquist, and O'Connor, JJ., joined. Stevens, J., filed a dissenting opinion, in which Brennan and Marshall, JJ., joined.]

FACTS

On May 31, 1979, Drug Enforcement Agency Agent Robert Williams watched respondent, Charles Carney, approach a youth in downtown San Diego. The youth accompanied Carney to a Dodge Mini Motor Home parked in a nearby lot. Carney and the youth closed the window shades in the motor home, including one across the front window. Agent Williams had previously received uncorroborated information that the same motor home was used by another person who was exchanging marihuana for sex. Williams, with assistance from other agents, kept the motor home under surveillance for the entire one and one-quarter hours that Carney and the youth remained inside. When the youth left the motor home, the agents followed and stopped him. The youth told the agents that he had received marihuana in return for allowing Carney sexual contacts.

At the officers' requests, the youth returned to the motor home and knocked on its door; Carney stepped out. The agents identified themselves as law enforcement officers. Without a warrant or consent, one agent entered the motor home and observed marihuana, plastic bags, and a scale of the kind used in weighing drugs on a table. Agent Williams took Carney into custody and took possession of the motor home. A subsequent search of the motor home at the police station revealed additional marihuana in the cupboards and refrigerator.

Respondent was charged with possession of marihuana for sale. At a preliminary hearing, he moved to suppress the evidence discovered in the motor home. The magistrate denied the motion. . . . Respondent renewed his suppression motion in the Superior Court. The Superior Court also rejected the claim. . . . Respondent then pleaded *nolo contendere* to the charges against him, and was placed on probation for three years. Respondent appealed from the order placing him on probation. The California Court of Appeal affirmed. . . . The California Supreme Court reversed the conviction. . . .

We granted certiorari. We reverse.

OPINION

. . . When a vehicle is being used on the highways, or if it is readily capable of such use and is found stationary in a place not regularly used for residential purposes—temporary or otherwise—the two justifications for the vehicle exception come into play. First, the vehicle is obviously readily mobile by the turn of the ignition key, if not actually moving. Second, there is a reduced expectation of privacy stemming from its use as a licensed motor vehicle subject to a range of police regulation inapplicable to a fixed dwelling. At least in these circumstances, the overriding societal interests in effective law enforcement justify an immediate search before the vehicle and its occupants become unavailable.

While it is true that respondent's vehicle possessed some, if not many of the attributes of a home, it is equally clear that the vehicle falls clearly within the scope of the exception. . . . [R]espondent's motor home was readily mobile. Absent the prompt search and seizure, it could have readily been moved beyond the reach of the police. Furthermore, the vehicle was licensed to ''operate on public streets; [was] serviced in public places; . . . and [was] subject to extensive regulation and inspection.'' And the vehicle was so situated that an objective observer would conclude that it was being used not as a residence but as a vehicle.

Respondent urges us to distinguish his vehicle from other vehicles within the exception because it was *capable of functioning as a home*. In our increasingly mobile society, many vehicles used for transportation can be and are being used not only for transportation but for shelter, i.e., as a ''home'' or ''residence.'' To distinguish between respondent's motor home and an ordinary sedan for purposes of the vehicle exception would require that we apply the exception depending upon the size of the vehicle and the quality of its appointments. Moreover, to fail to apply the exception to vehicles such as a motor home ignores the fact that a motor home lends itself easily to use as an instrument of illegal drug traffic and other illegal activity. . . .

DISSENT

Justice Stevens, with whom Justice Brennan and Justice Marshall join, dissenting.

The character of ''the place to be searched'' plays an important role in Fourth Amendment analysis. In this case, police officers searched a Dodge/Midas Mini Motor Home. The California Supreme Court correctly characterized this vehicle as a ''hybrid'' which combines ''the mobility attribute of an automobile . . . with most of the privacy characteristics of a house.'' . . .

When a motor home is parked in a location that is removed from the public highway, I believe that society is prepared to recognize that the expectations of privacy within it are not unlike the expectations one has in a fixed dwelling. . . .

Unlike a brick bungalow or a frame Victorian, a motor home seldom serves as a permanent lifetime abode. The motor home in this case, however, was designed to accommodate a breadth of ordinary living. Photographs in the record indicate that its height, length, and beam provided substantial living space inside: stuffed chairs surround a table; cupboards provide room for storage of personal effects; bunk beds provide sleeping space; and a refrigerator provides ample storage for food and beverages. Moreover, curtains and large opaque walls inhibit viewing the activities inside from the exterior of the vehicle. The interior configuration of the motor home establishes that the vehicle's size, shape, and mode of construction should have indicated to the officers that it was a vehicle containing mobile living quarters.

The State contends that officers in the field will have an impossible task determining whether or not other vehicles contain mobile living quarters. It is not necessary for the Court to resolve every unanswered question in this area in a single case, but common English usage suggests that we already distinguish between a ''motor home'' which is ''equipped as a self-contained traveling home,'' a ''camper'' which is only equipped for ''casual traveling and camping,'' and an automobile which is ''designed for passenger transportation.'' Surely the exteriors of these vehicles contain clues about their different functions which could alert officers in the field to the necessity of a warrant.

CASE DISCUSSION

After his motion to suppress evidence discovered in his motor home, Carney was convicted in a California Superior court on a plea of *nolo contendere*. The California Appeal Court affirmed. The California Supreme Court reversed, holding that the search of the motor home was unreasonable because expectations of privacy in motor home are more like those of a dwelling. On writ of *certiorari*, the United States Supreme Court reversed and remanded the case for further proceedings consistent with the Court's holding. The Supreme Court held that the warrantless search of Carney's motor home did not violate the Fourth Amendment.

Why did the Court hold that Carney had no more expectation of privacy in his motor home than he would have in an ordinary car? Do you agree? What facts does the dissent stress to demonstrate Carney's expectation of privacy that society should recognize? Do you agree? Reconsider *Carroll*. Do you think that Court's reasoning applies here? What interests does the majority promote in *Carney?* What interests does the dissent promote? Which would you promote? And how would you decide the case?

The authority to search vehicles without warrants does not extend to allow searches of persons in the vehicle. The reporters for the Model Code of Pre-Arraignment Procedure disputed this decision, arguing that it was

> absurd to say that [before the police begin to search the vehicle] the occupants can take the narcotics out of the glove compartment and stuff them in their pockets, and drive happily away after the vehicle has been fruitlessly searched.[39]

To avoid this "absurdity," the model code provides that

> Section 260.3 (2) **Search of the Occupants.** If the officer does not find the things subject to seizure by his search of the vehicle, and if
> (a) the things subject to seizure are of such a size and nature that they could be concealed on the person, and
> (b) the officer has reason to suspect that one or more of the occupants of the vehicle may have the things subject to seizure so concealed,
> the officer may search the suspected occupants. . . .[40]

Consent Searches

Consent searches require neither warrants nor probable cause. Police ordinarily seek consent in three situations: (1) They do not have probable cause and cannot get a warrant through a magistrate. (2) They have probable cause but do not obtain a warrant because it is inconvenient. (3) They have probable cause but do not obtain a warrant because no magistrate is available at the time and any delay might impair their capacity to search successfully. In the first two situations, the police should clearly demonstrate that they had consent because the Constitution prefers warrants. In the third situation, the police could argue that they had an emergency and, hence, waiting for a magistrate could jeopardize effective law enforcement.[41]

Decision Point

The police arrested a man who had delivered a large quantity of drugs to an undercover police officer. The police then conducted a warrantless search of the man's car, in which they found several items. They asked the man if they could search his apartment. The police drew no weapons, they informed him that he could refuse to allow them to search, and they asked him if he realized what he was saying when he consented to the search. He replied, "Yes." Did he consent? A circuit court held that the totality of circumstances showed he consented.[42]

VOLUNTARINESS AND WAIVER TESTS FOR CONSENT SEARCHES. Courts justify the consent exception by two separate theories. Some courts use a strict **voluntariness test,** based on the idea that voluntary consent to a search makes it reasonable. Others adopt a **waiver test,** based on the theory that citizens may waive their Fourth Amendment rights, but only if they do so voluntarily and knowingly. The voluntariness test assumes that citizens do not have a right against searches *per se,* only against *unreasonable* searches and seizures. Hence, consent requires only that they do not agree to searches under coercion or deception. According to the waiver test, however, citizens must not only voluntarily consent, but they must also know that they have a right to refuse their consent.

The waiver test is stricter than the voluntariness test. To satisfy it, officers ordinarily must warn citizens that they have a right to refuse their consent and let them know that if officers find incriminating evidence they will seize it and use it against the person consenting to the search. The voluntariness test looks to the totality-of-circumstances surrounding the consent to determine if it was voluntary. The United States Supreme Court has addressed the question whether the voluntariness test meets the requirements of the Fourth Amendment in *Schneckcloth v. Bustamonte.*

CASE

Did Bustamonte voluntarily consent?

Schneckcloth v. Bustamonte

412 U.S. 218, 93 S.Ct. 2041, 36 L.Ed.2d 854 (1973)

[Stewart, J., delivered the opinion of the Court, in which Burger, C.J., and White, Blackmun, Powell, and Rehnquist, JJ., joined. Blackmun, J., filed a concurring opinion. Powell, J., filed a concurring opinion in which Burger, C.J., and Rehnquist, J., joined. Douglas, J., Brennan, J., and Marshall, J., filed dissenting opinions.]

FACTS

The respondent was brought to trial in a California court upon a charge of possessing a check with intent to defraud. He moved to suppress the introduction of certain material as evidence against him on the ground that the material had been acquired through an unconstitutional search and seizure. In response to the motion, the trial judge conducted an evidentiary hearing where it was established that the material in question had been acquired by the State under the following circumstances:

While on routine patrol in Sunnyvale, California, at approximately 2:40 in the morning, Police Officer James Rand stopped an automobile when he observed that one headlight and its license plate light were burned out. Six men were in the vehicle. Joe Alcala and the respondent, Robert Bustamonte, were in the front seat with Joe Gonzales, the driver. Three older men were seated in the rear. When, in response to the policeman's question, Gonzales could not produce a driver's license, Officer Rand asked if any of the other five had any evidence of identification. Only Alcala produced a license, and he explained that the car was his brother's. After the six occupants had stepped out of the car at the officer's request and after two additional policemen had arrived, Officer Rand asked Alcala if he could search the car. Alcala replied, "Sure, go ahead." Prior to the search no one was threatened with arrest and, according to Officer Rand's uncontradicted testimony, it "was all very congenial at this time." Gonzales testified that Alcala actually helped in the search of the car, by opening the trunk and glove compartment. In Gonzales' words: "[T]he police officer asked Joe [Alcala], he goes 'Does this trunk open?' and Joe said, 'Yes.' He went to the car and got the keys and opened up the trunk." Wadded up under the left rear seat, the police officers found three checks that had previously been stolen from a car wash.

. . . Consent could not be found, the court held, solely from the absence of coercion and a verbal expression of assent. Since the District Court had not determined that Alcala had *known* that his consent could have been withheld and that he could have refused to have his vehicle searched, the Court of Appeals vacated the order denying the writ and remanded the case for further proceedings. We granted certiorari to determine whether the Fourth and Fourteenth Amendments require the showing thought necessary by the Court of Appeals. . . .

OPINION

. . . The question whether a consent to a search was in fact "voluntary" or was the product of duress or coercion, express or implied, is a question of fact to be determined from the totality of all the circumstances. While knowledge of the right to refuse consent is one factor to be taken into account, the government need not establish such knowledge as the *sine qua non* of an effective consent. As with police questioning, two competing concerns must be accommodated in determining the meaning of a "voluntary" consent—the legitimate need for such searches and the equally important requirement of assuring the absence of coercion. . . .

The problem of reconciling the recognized legitimacy of consent searches with the requirement that they be free from any aspect of official coercion cannot be resolved by any infallible touchstone. To approve such searches without the most careful scrutiny would sanction the possibility of official coercion; to place artificial restrictions upon such searches would jeopardize their basic validity. Just as was true with confessions, the requirement of a "voluntary" consent reflects a fair accommodation of the constitutional requirements involved. In examining all the surrounding circumstances to determine if in fact the consent to search was coerced, account must be taken of subtly coerced police questions, as well as the possibly vulnerable subjective state of the person who consents. Those searches that are the product of police coercion can thus be filtered out without undermining the continuing validity of consent searches. In sum, there is no reason for us to depart in the area of consent searches, from the traditional definition of "voluntariness." . . .

In this case, there is no evidence of any inherently coercive tactics—either from the nature of the police questioning or the environment in which it took place. Indeed, since consent searches will normally occur on a person's own familiar territory, the specter of incommunicado police interrogation in some remote station house is simply inapposite. There is no reason to believe, under circumstances such as are present here, that the response to a policeman's question is presumptively coerced; and there is, therefore, no reason to reject the traditional test for determining the voluntariness of a person's response. . . .

Our decision today is a narrow one. We hold only that when the subject of a search is not in custody and the State attempts to justify a search on the basis of his consent, the Fourth and Fourteenth Amendments require that it demonstrate that the consent was in fact voluntarily given, and not the result of duress or coercion, express or implied. Voluntariness is a question of fact to be determined from all the circumstances, and while the subject's knowledge of a right to refuse is a factor to be taken into account, the prosecution is not required to demonstrate such knowledge as a prerequisite to establishing a voluntary consent. Because the California court followed these principles in affirming the respondent's conviction, and because the Court of Appeals for the Ninth Circuit in remanding for an evidentiary hearing required more, its judgement must be reversed.
It is so ordered.

DISSENT

Mr. Justice Marshall, dissenting.

Several years ago, Mr. Justice Stewart reminded us that "[t]he Constitution guarantees . . . a society of free choice. Such a society presupposes the capacity of its members to choose." I would have thought that the capacity to choose necessarily depends upon knowledge that there is a choice to be made. But today the Court reaches the curious result that one can choose to relinquish a constitutional right—the right to be free of unreasonable searches—without knowing that he has the alternative of refusing to accede to a police request to search. I cannot agree, and therefore dissent. . . .

The Court contends that if an officer paused to inform the subject of his rights, the informality of the exchange would be destroyed. I doubt that a simple statement by an officer of an individual's right to refuse consent would do much to alter the informality of the exchange, except to alert the subject to a fact that he surely is entitled to know. It is not without significance that for many years the agents of the Federal Bureau of Investigation have routinely informed subjects of their right to refuse consent, when they request consent to search. . . . The reported cases in which the police have informed subjects of their right to refuse consent show, also, that the information can be given without disrupting the casual flow of events. What evidence there is, then, rather strongly suggests that nothing disastrous would happen if the police, before requesting consent, informed the subject that he had a right to refuse consent and that his refusal would be respected.

I must conclude, with some reluctance, that when the Court speaks of practicality, what it really is talking of is the continued ability of the police to capitalize on the ignorance of citizens so as to accomplish by subterfuge what they could not achieve by relying only on the knowing relinquishment of constitutional rights. Of course it would be "practical" for the police to ignore the commands of the Fourth Amendment, if by practicality we mean that more criminals will be apprehended, even though the constitutional rights of innocent people also go by the board. But such a practical advantage is achieved only at the cost of permitting the police to disregard the limitations that the Constitution places on their behavior, a cost that a constitutional democracy cannot long absorb.

I find nothing in the opinion of the Court to dispel my belief that, in such a case, "[u]nder many circumstances a reasonable person might read an officer's 'May I' as the courteous expression of a demand backed by force of law." [In] [m]ost cases . . . consent is ordinarily given as acquiescence in an implicit claim of authority to search. . . .

CASE DISCUSSION

In a *habeas corpus* proceeding, the court of appeals, reversing the district court, held that the prosecution had failed to prove that Bustamonte consented to the search with the understanding that he could withhold it. The Supreme Court reversed, holding that the government need only show that Bustamonte consented voluntarily, which, according to the Court, he did.

Did Bustamonte voluntarily consent? What specific facts demonstrate whether or not he consented? Do citizens ever consent to police, or are all police requests orders? Would you favor a waiver test? If so, how would this case be decided? Consider the consent form used by the St. Paul, Minnesota, Police Department in figure 6–1. If Bustamonte had signed this form, would his consent have been more creditable? Why?

THIRD-PARTY CONSENT. In some instances, one person may consent for another. Some common relationships giving rise to third-party consent include (1) husbandwife; (2) parent-child; (3) roommates; (4) employer-employee; (5) landlord-tenant; and

FIGURE 6.1 A Sample Waiver and Consent to Search Form

WAIVER AND CONSENT TO SEARCH

The undersigned _____

residing at _____

_____ hereby authorizes

the following named St. Paul Police Officers _____

to search the _____

(insert description of place or auto, lic. number, etc.)

owned by/or in possession of the undersigned.

I do hereby waive any and all objections that may be made by me to said search and declare that this waiver and consent is freely and voluntarily given of my own free will and accord.

Signed _____ day of _____ 19 ____ at _____ PM AM

Signed _____

Witnessed _____

_____

(6) schools, including universities and students' rooms and lockers. Ordinarily, spouses can consent for each other. However, if spite motivates the consent, some courts have ruled that this consent is not effective. Parents can always consent for their minor children and for adult children who live at home.[43]

Employers cannot consent to searches of their employees' desks where employees have a reasonable expectation of privacy. For example, a school administrator could not consent to searching a guidance counselor's desk that was locked, located in the counselor's office, and contained psychological profiles and other confidential student records. However, a factory owner could consent to searching items on top of an employee's workbench. Janitors, clerks, and drivers cannot consent to search their employers' premises but managers can.[44]

Decision Point

Which of the following third-party consents are valid?

1. A lover consents to a search of the room shared with the other lover.
2. One roommate consents to a search of an entire apartment, including the other roommate's separate bedroom.
3. A home owner consents to a search of the room a house guest occupies.
4. One joint user of a duffel bag consents to a search of the shared duffel bag.

5. A high school principal consents to a search of high school students' lockers.
6. A college dean permits a search of students' rooms for marijuana.

Courts have upheld all of the above searches on grounds that the consenting party's consent was valid against the other person.[45]

WITHDRAWING CONSENT. What if I consent to a search of my house, but when the police come close to finding contraband, I say, "Stop the search. I have changed my mind." A compelling argument holds that guilty persons will use consent to a search merely to throw police off the track by consenting and will then withdraw the consent if it looks as if the search will produce incriminating evidence, contraband, or weapons. Despite this argument, the Model Code of Pre-Arraignment Procedure provides:

> Section 24.3(3) *Withdrawal or Limitation of Consent.* A consent . . . may be withdrawn or limited at any time prior to the completion of the search, and if so withdrawn or limited, the search . . . shall cease, or be restricted to the new limits, as the case may be. Things discovered and subject to seizure prior to such withdrawal or limitation of consent shall remain subject to seizure despite such change or termination of the consent.[46]

Case authority on this point is limited and divided. In an old Kentucky case, the court ruled that consent once given could not be withdrawn. In a more recent California case, the court ruled that persons authorized to consent may withdraw the consent at any time.[47]

═══ INSPECTION AND REGULATORY SEARCHES

Inspections and regulatory searches deal with a range of special problems police officers do not ordinarily confront. They include customs inspections; immigration regulation, such as border searches; building inspections for health and safety regulation; safety checks; airport searches; vehicle use; and searches of prisoners, probationers, and parolees, and persons visiting prisons. The great variety of activities such searches cover should not obscure their one common element: although their primary purpose is regulation, they all can result in criminal prosecution and conviction. The courts generally do not require the same high standards, such as probable cause and warrants, associated with other searches. The courts' balancing approach weighs the public interest in regulation, the need for practices not permitted by the usual Fourth Amendment standards, and the ordinarily minor penalties that result from violating the regulations against the invasion of individual privacy that inspections and regulatory searches entail.

Border Searches

According to the Supreme Court in *United States v. Ramsey,*

> searches made at the border, pursuant to the long-standing right of the sovereign to protect itself by stopping and examining persons and property crossing into this country, are reasonable simply by virtue of the fact that they occur at the border.[48]

The courts have found border searches reasonable because the national interest in preventing illegal entry and smuggling balances against the limited invasion of privacy that such searches entail. If the searches go beyond superficial intrusions, then the courts require factual foundations to support them. For example, only articulable facts sufficient to support the reasonable conclusion that individuals are concealing contraband on their persons—illegal substances on their bodies—was held to justify a strip search where individuals were "forced to disrobe to a state which would be offensive to the average person." If the search goes beyond strip to the extremely intrusive body-cavity searches, such as the vagina or rectum, or administering laxatives to determine what is in the stomach, then the factual foundation must be still higher. What the court call "clear indication" lies somewhere between reasonable suspicion and probable cause.[49]

Decision Point

Based on the facts that certain incoming, letter-sized airmail envelopes were from Thailand—a known source of narcotics—and were bulky and much heavier than normal airmail letters, a customs inspector opened the envelopes for inspection at the General Post Office in New York City, considered a "border" for border search purposes. The envelopes contained heroin, which was seized and later used to convict the intended receiver. The customs inspector did not obtain a warrant to search the envelopes, even though there was time to do so.

Was this an illegal search and seizure? The United States Supreme Court held that the Fourth Amendment does not include customs inspectors opening envelopes because border searches without warrants are not "unreasonable." The border search exception rests on the need to control who and what may enter the country. Anything crossing the border falls within the border search exception.[50]

Airport Searches

Due to the problems arising out of airline hijacking, travelers must now pass through metal detectors. If the signal sounds, they must remove items from their persons until the signal no longer sounds. They must also pass their luggage through X ray for examination; or sometimes the baggage is opened and inspected without the X ray. If anything suspicious is discovered, further investigation follows. The courts have declared these inspections searches, and hence the Fourth Amendment protects them. Once again, using the balancing approach, the Supreme Court concluded that airport searches are reasonable. Because the regulatory scheme entails minimal intrusions that apply equally to all passengers, it is neither arbitrary nor discriminatory. Furthermore, all passengers have advanced notice that they must pass through the inspection. They are free not to board the airplane if they do not want to subject their persons and luggage to these intrusions.[51]

Decision Point

On the basis of four prior investigations, federal narcotics officers had reasonable grounds to suspect—but not probable cause to believe—that the luggage of a man named Place contained cocaine. After Place refused to consent to a search of his luggage at LaGuardia Airport, the officers took the suitcases to Kennedy Airport. About ninety minutes after the seizure, the luggage was subjected to a ''sniff test'' by a trained narcotics detection dog. The dog reacted positively to one suitcase. The officers kept the luggage over the weekend because it was late on Friday afternoon. On the following Monday they obtained a warrant for the suitcase, which they searched and found cocaine inside. Place was convicted of possession of cocaine with intent to distribute.

Did the police lawfully seize the luggage? The Supreme Court reversed Place's conviction, holding that the ninety-minute retention of the suitcases without probable cause violated the Fourth Amendment. However, the Court at the same time held that ''when an officer's observations lead him to reasonably believe that a traveler is carrying narcotics, the principles of *Terry v. Ohio,* [excerpted in chap. 4] and its progeny would permit the officer to detain the luggage briefly to investigate the circumstances that aroused his suspicion, provided that the investigative detention is properly limited in scope.''[52]

Searches of Prisoners, Probationers, and Parolees

For a long time, the rule was that prisoners have no Fourth Amendment rights, that, in fact, the Constitution stopped at the prison gate. In *Lanza v. New York,* for example, the Supreme Court ruled that

> a jail shares none of the attributes of privacy of a home, automobile, an office or hotel room, . . . [and] official surveillance has traditionally been the order of the day in prisons.[53]

More recently, the Court has concluded that prisoners have an expectation of privacy that society recognizes, but that it is ''of a diminished scope.'' This privacy of diminished scope does not protect prisoners from ''shakedowns''—routine, unannounced, thorough cell searches for weapons and contraband. These are reasonable because they maintain safety, order, and discipline in prisons, according to the Court. Even where a guard conducted a shakedown maliciously and seized personal items such as photographs and other items that a prisoner possessed, the Supreme Court ruled that the shakedown did not violate the Fourth Amendment. In a strong dissent, Justice Stevens wrote

> Personal letters, snapshots of family members, a souvenir, a deck of cards, a hobby kit, perhaps a diary or a training manual for an apprentice in a new trade, or even a Bible—a variety of inexpensive items may enable a prisoner to maintain contact with some part of his past and an eye to the possibility of a better future. Are all these items subject to unrestrained perusal, confiscation or mutilation at the hands of a possibly hostile guard? Is the Court correct in its perception that ''society'' is not prepared to recognize *any* privacy or possessory interest of the prison inmate—no matter how remote the threat to prison security might be?—By telling prisoners that no aspect of their individuality, from a photo of a child to a letter from a wife, is

entitled to constitutional protection, the Court breaks with the ethical tradition that I had thought was enshrined forever in our jurisprudence.[54]

In addition to cell searches, full-body searches, strip searches, and even body-cavity searches without probable cause do not violate the Fourth Amendment if they follow contact with visitors or others who might transfer weapons or contraband to prisoners. In *Bell v. Wolfish,* for example, pretrial detainees had to expose their body cavities for visual inspection as part of a body search conducted after every visit with a person from outside the jail. The Fourth Amendment does not leave prisoners totally without protection from searches, however. The state's interest in security, safety, and discipline must be balanced against prisoners' privacy to make the search reasonable. Highly intrusive custodial searches where security, safety, and discipline do not require them might well violate prisoners' rights. The Seventh Circuit Court of Appeals addressed this question recently in *Mary Beth G. v. City of Chicago.*[55]

CASE

Was the strip search reasonable?

Mary Beth G. and Sharon N. v. City of Chicago

723 F.2d 1263 (7th Cir. 1983)

FACTS

Although the circumstances surrounding the arrests and detentions of each of the plaintiffs-appellees in these consolidated cases are not identical, the situations involve the following common elements: each woman was arrested for a misdemeanor offense[a] and each was subjected to the strip search policy of the City of Chicago.[b] That policy, as described by the City, required each woman placed in detention facilities of the Chicago Police Department and searched by female personnel to:

> 1) lift her blouse or sweater and unhook and lift her brassiere to allow a visual inspection of the breast area, to replace these articles of clothing and then
> 2) to pull up her skirt or dress or to lower her pants and pull down any undergarments, to squat two or three times facing the detention aide and to bend over at the waist to permit visual inspection of the vaginal and anal area.[c]

---

[a]Mary Beth G. and Sharon N. were stopped for traffic violations; they were arrested and taken to detention centers because there were outstanding parking tickets on their cars. Hinda Hoffman was stopped for making an improper left turn and was arrested and taken to the police station when she failed to produce her driver's license.

[b]The specific facts surrounding the searches of each plaintiff-appellee vary. Each woman, however, was subjected to a strip search that included the admitted procedures of the official City policy.

[c]In the description of the policy given by the City, the City claims that all searches were conducted in a closed room away from the view of all persons except the person conducting the search. Defendant's Brief (Tikalsky) at 14. This portion of the description was variously contradicted by the testimony of plaintiffs-appellees. We need not consider these additional allegations, however, because we believe the policy even as described is unconstitutional for the reasons we explain.

The strip search policy was not applied to males. Male detainees were subject to a strip search only if the arresting officers or detention aides had reason to believe that the detainee was concealing weapons or contraband. Otherwise, men were searched thoroughly by hand. The male detainee would place his hands against the wall and stand normally while the searching officer, with his fingers, would go through the hair, into the ears, down the back, under the armpits, down both arms, down the legs, into the groin area, and up the front. The officer would also search the waistband and require the detainee to remove his shoes and sometimes his socks. Originally, women detainees were also searched in this manner, but in 1952 the City changed its policy and began conducting the strip searches.

OPINION

. . . The City argues that its strip search policy is valid under two recognized exceptions to the warrant requirement. One exception allows warrantless searches incident to custodial arrests. A second exception permits warrantless searches incident to the detention of persons lawfully arrested. . . .

Our starting point is the balancing test announced in [*Bell v.*] *Wolfish,* [441 U.S. 520, 99 S.Ct. 1861, 60 L.Ed.2d 447 (1979)], beginning with the magnitude of the invasion of personal rights. Strip searches involving the visual inspection of the anal and genital areas [are] "demeaning, dehumanizing, undignified, humiliating, terrifying, unpleasant, embarrassing, repulsive, signifying degradation and submission. . . ."

Balanced against this invasion of personal privacy is the governmental interest in conducting the *particular* searches in question. In these cases, the governmental interest alleged by the City to justify these particular strip searches was the need to maintain the security of the City lockups by preventing misdemeanor offenders from bringing in weapons or contraband; the need was apparently felt to be so great that women misdemeanants were strip searched even when there was no reason to believe they were hiding weapons or contraband on their persons.

The evidence the City offered to demonstrate the need for requiring strip searches of women minor offenders to maintain jail security, however, belies its purported concerns. The affidavits of the lockup personnel, which lack specificity, suggest that only a few items have been recovered from the body cavities of women arrested on minor charges over the years. In the only analytical survey submitted by the City, conducted over a thirty-five day period in June and July of 1965, all of the items found in the body orifices of the 1,800 women searched during that period were taken from women charged with either prostitution (7 items), assault (1 item), or a narcotics violation (1 item). These are the kinds of crimes, unlike traffic or other offenses, that might give rise to a reasonable belief that the woman arrestee was concealing an item in a body cavity. Although a detention center may be a place "fraught with serious security dangers," *Bell v. Wolfish,* the evidence does not support the view that those dangers are created by women minor offenders entering the lockups for short periods while awaiting bail. Here, the "need for the *particular* search," a strip search, is hardly substantial enough, in light of the evidence regarding the incidence of weapons and contraband found in the body cavities of women minor offenders, to justify the severity of the governmental intrusion.

Balancing the citizen's right to be free from substantial government intrusions against the mission of law enforcement personnel to ensure a safer society is often a difficult task. While the need to assure jail security is a legitimate and substantial concern, we believe that, on the facts here, the strip searches bore an insubstantial relationship to security needs so that, when balanced against plaintiffs-appellees' privacy interests, the searches cannot be considered ''reasonable.'' The reasonableness standard usually requires, ''at a minimum, that the facts upon which an intrusion is based be capable of measurement against 'an objective standard,' whether this be probable cause or a less stringent test.'' The more intrusive the search, the closer governmental authorities must come to demonstrating probable cause for believing that the search will uncover the objects for which the search is being conducted. *Terry v. Ohio,* 392, U.S.1, 88 S.Ct. 1868, 20 L.Ed.2d 889 (1968). Based on these principles, we agree with the district court that insuring the security needs of the City by strip searching plaintiffs-appellees was unreasonable without a reasonable suspicion by the authorities that either of the twin dangers of concealing weapons or contraband existed. . . .

Accordingly, because the court and jury below could reasonably conclude that the strip search policy of the City as applied in these cases was unreasonable under the fourth amendment, we uphold their determinations on this issue.

[Affirmed.]

CASE DISCUSSION

Four women who were arrested for misdemeanors and strip searched by matrons in lockups while awaiting bail challenged the constitutionality of Chicago's strip search policy. The district court entered judgment in favor of the women on the strip-search issue. The court of appeals held that the strip-search policy violated the Fourth Amendment, and that the jury awards were not excessive, and that plaintiffs were entitled to attorneys' fees.

The jury awarded the plaintiffs $25,000 each, except for Hoffman who received $60,000 because male officers had watched and uttered rude remarks during her search. The City of Chicago claimed that the awards were excessive. Do you agree? How do you assess how much money these intrusions are worth? Why do you suppose the Chicago policy remained unchallenged for so many years?

Sometimes it is said that parolees and probationers have the same rights as other citizens; however, many cases suggest otherwise. Parolees can be arrested and their houses and vehicles searched without either warrants or probable cause. It is not clear whether probationers' Fourth Amendment rights are as diluted as parolees', but clearly, probationers may be searched without either probable cause or warrants. The courts adopt several theories to justify these reduced Fourth Amendment protections. For example, parolees are in constructive custody, that is, still under state control even though they are released. Others say probation and parole are "acts of grace," meaning the state may impose any conditions it wishes on the status of parole or probation. Third, courts say that consent searches and seizures are part of the "contract" of release. Finally, and probably most persuasive, the courts use the balancing approach. Probation and parole are risks taken to help rehabilitate convicted offenders. To protect society from further crimes, reduced Fourth Amendment protections for probationers and parolees are reasonable.[56]

Prison and jail security permits not only shakedowns and searches of prisoners and pretrial detainees but also searches of employees and visitors. The Supreme Court has not decided whether these searches are unreasonable under the Fourth Amendment. In *Kennedy v. Hardiman,* three investigators surrounded Kennedy in the locker room of the Cook County Department of Corrections and subjected him to a strip and body-cavity search. The Court ruled that such searches are reasonable if based on "reasonable suspicion." Also, the Fifth Circuit Court of Appeals addressed the question of strip-searching visitors in the Louisiana prisons in *Thorne v. Maggio.*[57]

CASE

Is strip-searching prisoners' family members reasonable?

Thorne et al. v. Maggio

765 F.2d 1270 (5th Cir. 1985)

[Before Gee, Tate, and Higginbotham, Circuit Judges.]

FACTS

Gee, Circuit Judge:

. . . Peggy and Richard E. Thorne are the parents of Richard J. and Scott Thorne. The younger Thornes are inmates at Louisiana State Penitentiary (LSP), a maximum security facility for prisoners who pose severe security risks. Both brothers have been disciplined while in prison for possession of contraband drugs. LSP permits "contact" visits between inmates and approved friends and family.

Mr. and Mrs. Thorne visited their sons at LSP. Before being allowed to do so, each was required to sign a form that stated, among other things, "I hereby agree to a personal search by security personnel of the [LSP] while on prison grounds.'' A large sign prominently posted just outside the gate of LSP warned, ''Beware Notice If you enter the gates of Angola, you consent to a search of your person and property. . . .''

In November 1981, an LSP inmate told Captain Whistine, an LSP shift commander, that another inmate was receiving contraband in his legal mail and that Scott Thorne was regularly receiving narcotics through the visiting room, probably from his mother. Captain Whistine reported this information to Warden Byargeon. On the Warden's instructions, Captain Whistine ordered a mail watch on the first inmate's legal mail and notified all shifts that Mrs. Thorne was to be asked to submit to a strip search before being allowed to visit Scott Thorne.

Contraband was found in the first inmate's legal mail, lending credence to the informant. When Mrs. Thorne next arrived to visit Scott Thorne, Captain Whistine told her that she would have to be strip searched before seeing him. Mrs. Thorne refused, with some heat, to be searched. Escorted back to the front gates of the prison, she departed. The Warden had her name removed from the list of approved visitors to the prison. Mrs. Thorne was thus unable to visit either of her inmate sons.

Mr. Thorne came to visit Scott Thorne the next day. He, too, was told that a strip search would be required before he could visit his son. Mr. Thorne consented to the search. No contraband was found and the visit took place.

All four Thornes, sensitive to their rights as citizens, obtained counsel and brought actions under 42 U.S.C. § 1983 against the Louisiana Department of Corrections and sundry LSP officials alleging that these doings infringed upon rights secured to them by the Constitution of the United States. Mrs. Thorne and her inmate sons asserted violations of alleged first amendment associational rights; Mr. Thorne alleged violation of his fourth amendment right to be free from unreasonable searches. The actions were consolidated and tried to a jury, which found for all of the Thornes as against some (but not all) of the defendants, awarding damages to each. Defendants (referred to collectively as ''LSP'') moved for judgment notwithstanding the verdict; the trial court denied their motion. From this denial, defendants appeal. We reverse.

OPINION

. . . To justify the strip search of a particular visitor under the reasonable suspicion standard, prison officials must point to specific objective facts and rational inferences that they are entitled to draw from those facts. . . . It was not error for the trial court to look to the particular facts of Mr. Thorne's search to determine its reasonableness.

LSP next argues that the trial court erred in finding Mr. Thorne's search unreasonable under the fourth amendment, either because Mr. Thorne consented to his search or because he waived his fourth amendment rights when he entered the prison. LSP locates this consent or waiver in the visitor form signed by Mr. Thorne and in the warning notices posted at the prison gates. If accepted, this argument would render reasonable a strip search of any such prison visitor; as discussed above, such at-will, random searches are not reasonable under the Fourth Amendment. The argument must therefore fail. . . .

Finally, LSP argues that the search of Mr. Thorne was justified by ''reasonable suspicion,'' and that the trial court erred by holding the search unreasonable under this standard. The argument is untenable. '' '[R]eason-able suspicion' must be specifically directed to the person to be searched. . . . [T]he fourth amendment does not permit any automatic or casual transference of 'suspicion.' '' ''To justify the strip search of a particular visitor under the reasonable suspicion standard, prison officials must point to specific objective facts and rational inferences that they are entitled to draw from those facts in light of their experience. Inchoate, unspecified suspicions fall short of providing reasonable grounds to suspect that a visitor will attempt to smuggle drugs or other contraband into the prison.'' Here, no objective fact pointed to Mr. Thorne as a probable smuggler of drugs into LSP. That an informant pointed to Mrs. Thorne as a likely source of Scott Thorne's contraband does not suffice to justify search of her husband. It is common knowledge that husbands and wives do not concur on all things. LSP offers no other facts on which reasonable suspicion of Mr. Thorne could have been grounded; it is thus clear that the trial court correctly found Mr. Thorne's search to have been without reasonable suspicion, and therefore in violation of the fourth amendment.

. . . LSP contends that the trial court erred in rejecting the individual defendants' defenses of qualified, or ''good faith,'' immunity for liability for money damages.

> Officials 'are shielded from liability for civil damages insofar as their conduct does not violate clearly established statutory or constitutional rights of which a reasonable person would have known.' Whether an official may prevail in his qualified immunity defense depends upon the 'objective reasonableness of [his] conduct as measured by references to clearly established law.' No other 'circumstances' are relevant to the issue of qualified immunity.

LSP must prevail on this issue if it was not clearly established in December 1981 that strip searches of prison visitors conducted without ''reasonable suspicion'' violated the fourth amendment. We conclude that it was not. . . .

The authorities . . . make plain that at the time of the search of Mr. Thorne the law in this area was in a state of uncertainty. Indeed, in our Circuit portions of it became ''clearly established'' only today.

CASE DISCUSSION

Prison inmates and visitors brought an action challenging strip searches. The district court entered judgment for the plaintiffs, and the defendant officers appealed. The court of appeals held that visitors have prior notice that they will be searched, and that such searches are reasonable.

Should visitors to prisons have the right not to be searched? Explain. Did Mr. Thorne waive his right, assuming he has one? Are strip searches of visitors ever ''reasonable''? What interests do they balance? How would you balance the interests involved? Why is LSP entitled to limited immunity? Do you agree with the ''good faith'' standard used to determine qualified immunity? Explain.

Searching Students

Searches of students on educational institution premises are reasonable even when they do not meet the probable cause, warrant, and other standards that the Fourth Amendment requires in typical criminal cases. Sometimes, these searches are based on the **in loco parentis doctrine,** that is, the school stands in the place of parents while students are in school. This doctrine does *not* apply to college and university students who are not minors. Courts have used the balancing approach to support student searches.

Decision Point

A teacher at a New Jersey High School, upon discovering T.L.O., then a 14-year-old freshman, and her companion smoking cigarettes in a school lavatory in violation of a school rule, took them to the Principal's office, where they met with the Assistant Vice Principal. When T.L.O., in response to the Assistant Vice Principal's questioning, denied that she had been smoking and claimed that she did not smoke at all, the Assistant Vice Principal demanded to see her purse. Upon opening the purse, he found a pack of cigarettes and also noticed a package of cigarette rolling papers that are commonly associated with the use of marijuana. He then proceeded to search the purse thoroughly and found some marijuana, a pipe, plastic bags, a fairly substantial amount of money, and two letters that implicated her in marijuana dealing. Thereafter, the State brought delinquency charges against T.L.O. in the Juvenile Court, which, after denying T.L.O.'s motion to suppress the evidence found in her purse, held that the Fourth Amendment applied to searches by school officials but that the search in question was reasonable, and adjudged T.L.O. delinquent.

Does the Fourth Amendment apply to school searches? Was this search reasonable? According to the United States Supreme Court, the answer to both questions is yes. The Court held that the Fourth Amendment's prohibition on unreasonable searches and seizures applies to searches conducted by public school officials and is not limited to searches conducted by law enforcement officers. Nor are school officials exempt from the amendment's dictates by virtue of the special nature of their authority over schoolchildren. In carrying out searches and other functions pursuant to disciplinary policies, school officials cannot claim immunity from the Fourth Amendment. They are not, for these purposes, *in loco parentis*.

Schoolchildren have a legitimate expectation of privacy. But striking a balance between schoolchildren's legitimate expectations of privacy and the school's equally legitimate need to maintain an environment in which learning can take place requires some easing of the restrictions to which searches by public authorities are ordinarily subject. Thus, school officials need not obtain a warrant before searching a student who is under their authority. Moreover, school officials need not be held subject to the requirement that searches be based on probable cause to believe that the subject of the search has violated or is violating the law. Rather, the legality of the search of a student should depend simply on the reasonableness, under all the circumstances, of the search.

Under this standard, the Supreme Court decided that the search of T.L.O. was reasonable.[58]

The Supreme Court has not addressed the problem of the extent to which the Fourth Amendment protects university students in administrative searches. The Fifth Circuit Court of appeals addressed the privacy rights of college students in their dormitory rooms in *Piazzola v. Watkins*.

CASE

Was the room search reasonable?

Piazzola v. Watkins

442 F.2d 284 (5th Cir. 1971)

FACTS

. . . "On the morning of February 28, 1968, the Dean of Men of Troy State University was called to the office of the Chief of Police of Troy, Alabama, to discuss 'the drug problem' at the University. Two State narcotics agents and two student informers from Troy State University were also present. Later on that same day, the Dean of Men was called to the city policy station for another meeting: at this time he was informed by the officers that they had sufficient evidence that marijuana was in the dormitory rooms of certain Troy State students and that they desired the cooperation of University officials in searching these rooms. The police officers were advised by the Dean of Men that they would receive the full cooperation of the University officials in searching for the marijuana. The informers, whose identities have not yet been disclosed, provided the police officers with names of students whose rooms were to be searched. Still later on that same day (which was during the week of final examinations at the University and was to be followed by a week long holiday) the law enforcement officers, accompanied by some of the University officials, searched six or seven dormitory rooms located in two different residence halls. The the rooms of both Piazzola and Marinshaw were searched without their consent. Present during the search of the room occupied by Marinshaw were two State narcotics agents, the University security officer, and a counselor of the residence hall where Marinshaw's room was located. Piazzola's room was searched twice. Present during the first search were two State narcotic agents and a University official; no evidence was found at this time. The second search of Piazzola's room, which disclosed the incriminating evidence, was conducted solely by the State and City police officials.

"At the time of the seizure the University had in effect the following regulation: The college reserves the right to enter rooms for inspection purposes. If the administration deems it necessary, the room may be searched and the occupant required to open his personal baggage and any other personal material which is sealed.

Each of the petitioners was familiar with this regulation. After the search of the petitioners' rooms and the discovery of marijuana, they were arrested, and the State criminal prosecutions and convictions ensued.'' [They were sentenced to five years imprisonment.]

OPINION

. . . The question is whether in light of all the facts and circumstances, including the University regulation, the search which disclosed the marijuana was an unreasonable search. . . .

A student who occupies a college dormitory room enjoys the protection of the Fourth Amendment. True the University retains broad supervisory powers which permit it to adopt the regulation heretofore quoted, provided that regulation is reasonably construed and is limited in its application to further the University's function as an educational institution.[a] The regulation cannot be construed or applied so as to give consent to a search for evidence for the primary purpose of a criminal prosecution. Otherwise, the regulation itself would constitute an unconstitutional attempt to require a student to waive his protection from unreasonable searches and seizures as a condition to his occupancy of a college dormitory room. . . .

The right to privacy is ''no less important than any other right carefully and particularly reserved to the people.'' The results of the search do not prove its reasonableness. This search was an unconstitutional invasion of the privacy both of these appellees and of the students in whose rooms no evidence of marijuana was found. The warrantless search of these students' dormitory rooms cannot be justified. The judgment is therefore

Affirmed.

DISSENT

Clark, Circuit Judge (dissenting).

I respectfully dissent from the Court's opinion as to the defendant, Marinshaw. The college had a direct interest in keeping its dormitories free of the specific criminal activity here involved—the possession of the drug, marijuana. The regulation was a reasonable means of embodying this interest. Marinshaw was found to be familiar with the regulation. When he chose to place the evidence of this criminal conduct in his dormitory room he knowingly exposed this material to inspections by officials of the University. He cannot now reinstate as private an area he had thus agreed was thus accessible. A publicly owned dormitory room is not in my mind the equivalent of a private rooming house. I concur in the result as to the defendant, Piazzola, because I do not believe the regulation can be validly construed to authorize the college to consent to an independent police search.

---

[a]One of the ''Residence Hall Policies'' of this University provides that ''College men are assumed to be mature adults with acceptable and established habits.'' Another adjures students, ''Keep rooms locked at all times.'' The University thus recognized that it cannot exercise that strict control of its students which might be permitted in a boys' school where an ''in loco parentis'' standard would be more appropriate.

CASE DISCUSSION

Piazzola and Marinshaw, following conviction and imprisonment for drug law violations, petitioned the District Court for *habeas corpus*. The district court granted the petitions, and the Government appealed. The court of appeals held that the search for criminal evidence violated the students' Fourth Amendment right against unreasonable searches and seizures.

Did the students consent to this search? Was it reasonable to regulate the rooms to search them? What if the university officials were inspecting for fire hazards, such as hot plates for cooking that violate regulations, and they find drugs? Can they seize them? use them against the students? What arguments can you give to support—or reject—their seizure *and* use in evidence? their seizure but *not* their use in evidence? neither their seizure nor their use in evidence? What interests does each of these alternatives serve?

Illicit Drug Testing

The most recent development in administrative searches is testing employees for the use of illicit drugs. The government directs this type of administrative "search" mainly at employees who may endanger public safety if they are under the influence of illicit drugs. Drug testing reflects the public's recent concern about drug use in general, and the deaths, injuries, and environmental damage stemming from transportation employees' abuse of alcohol. Those accidents receiving the most press attention have been the deaths of students due to a drunk school bus driver, and the Alaska oil spill, stemming in part from the alleged intoxication of the ship's captain. The Supreme Court dealt with the problem of balancing the government's interest in interdicting the importation of illegal drugs and government employees' right to privacy in *National Treasury Employees Union, et al v. Commissioner of the U.S. Customs Service*.

CASE

Was the urine test a reasonable search?

National Treasury Employees Union, et al. v. William Von Raab, Commissioner, United States Customs Service

__ U.S. __, 109 S.Ct. 1384, 103 L.Ed.2d 685 (1989)

[Kennedy, J., delivered the opinion of the Court, in which Rehnquist, C.J., and White, Blackmun, and O'Connor, JJ., joined. Marshall, J., filed a dissenting opinion, in which Brennan, J., joined. Scalia, J., filed a dissenting opinion, in which Stevens, J., joined.]

FACTS

We granted certiorari to decide whether it violates the Fourth Amendment for the United States Customs Service to require a urinalysis test from employees who seek transfer or promotion to certain positions.

The United States Customs Service, a bureau of the Department of the Treasury, is the federal agency responsible for processing persons, carriers, cargo, and mail into the United States, collecting revenue from imports, and enforcing customs and related laws. An important responsibility of the Service is the interdiction and seizure of contraband, including illegal drugs. In 1987 alone, Customs agents seized drugs with a retail value of nearly 9 billion dollars. In the routine discharge of their duties, many Customs employees have direct contact with those who traffic in drugs for profit. Drug import operations, often directed by sophisticated criminal syndicates, United States v. Mendenhall, [see excerpt, chap. 4], may be effected by violence or its threat. As a necessary response, many Customs operatives carry and use firearms in connection with their official duties. In December 1985, respondent, the Commissioner of Customs, established a Drug Screening Task Force to explore the possibility of implementing a drug screening program within the Service. After extensive research and consultation with experts in the field, the Task Force concluded ''that drug screening through urinalysis is technologically reliable, valid and accurate.'' Citing this conclusion, the Commissioner announced his intention to require drug tests of employees who applied for, or occupied, certain positions within the Service. The Commissioner stated his belief that ''Customs is largely drug-free,'' but noted also that ''unfortunately no segment of society is immune from the threat of illegal drug use.'' Interdiction has become the agency's primary enforcement mission, and the Commissioner stressed that ''there is no room in the Customs Service for those who break the laws prohibiting the possession and use of illegal drugs.''

In May 1986, the Commissioner announced implementation of the drug-testing program. Drug tests were made a condition of placement or employment for positions that meet one or more of three criteria. The first is direct involvement in drug interdiction or enforcement of related laws, an activity the Commissioner deemed fraught with obvious dangers to the mission of the agency and the lives of customs agents. The second criterion is a requirement that the incumbent carry firearms, as the Commissioner concluded that ''(p)ublic safety demands that employees who carry deadly arms and are prepared to make instant life or death decisions be drug free.'' The third criterion is a requirement for the incumbent to handle ''classified'' material, which the Commissioner determined might fall into the hands of smugglers if accessible to employees who, by reason of their own illegal drug use, are susceptible to bribery or blackmail. After an employee qualifies for a position covered by the Customs testing program, the Service advises him by letter that his final selection is contingent upon successful completion of drug screening. An independent contractor contacts the employee to fix the time and place for collecting the sample. On reporting for the test, the employee must produce photographic identification and remove any outer garments, such as a coat or a jacket, and personal belongings. The employee may produce the sample behind a partition, or in the privacy of a bathroom stall if he so chooses. To ensure against adulteration of the specimen, or substitution of a sample from another person, a monitor of the same sex as the employee remains close at hand to listen for the normal sounds of urination. Dye is added to the toilet water to prevent the employee from using the water to adulterate the sample.

Upon receiving the specimen, the monitor inspects it to ensure its proper temperature and color, places a tamper-proof custody seal over the container, and affixes an identification label indicating the date and the individual's specimen number. The employee signs a chain-of-custody form, which is initialed by the monitor, and the urine sample is placed in a plastic bag, sealed, and submitted to a laboratory. . . . The laboratory tests the sample for the presence of marijuana, cocaine, opiates, amphetamines, and phencyclidine. . . .

Petitioners, a union of federal employees and a union official, commenced this suit in the United States District Court for the Eastern District of Louisiana on behalf of current Customs Service employees who seek covered positions. Petitioners alleged that the Custom Service drug-testing program violated, the Fourth Amendment. The District Court agreed. The court acknowledged "the legitimate governmental interest in a drug-free work place and work force," but concluded that "the drug testing plan constitutes an overly intrusive policy of searches and seizures without probable cause or reasonable suspicion, in violation of legitimate expectations of privacy." The court enjoined the drug testing program, and ordered the Customs Service not to require drug tests of any applicants for covered positions.

A divided panel of the United States Court of Appeals for the Fifth Circuit vacated the injunction. . . . We granted certiorari. We now affirm so much of the judgment of the court of appeals as upheld the testing of employees directly involved in drug interdiction or required to carry firearms. We vacate the judgment to the extent it upheld the testing of applicants for positions requiring the incumbent to handle classified materials, and remand for further proceedings.

OPINION

In *Skinner v. Railway Labor Executives Assn.*, decided today, we hold that federal regulations requiring employees of private railroads to produce urine samples for chemical testing implicate the Fourth Amendment, as those tests invade reasonable expectations of privacy. Our earlier cases have settled that the Fourth Amendment protects individuals from unreasonable searches conducted by the Government, . . . and, in view of our holding in Railway Labor Executives that urine tests are searches, it follows that the Customs Service's drug testing program must meet the reasonableness requirement of the Fourth Amendment.

While we have often emphasized, and reiterate today, that a search must be supported, as a general matter, by a warrant issued upon probable cause, . . . neither a warrant nor probable cause, nor, indeed, any measure of individualized suspicion, is an indispensable component of reasonableness in every circumstance. . . . [O]ur cases establish that where a Fourth Amendment intrusion serves special governmental needs, beyond the normal need for law enforcement, it is necessary to balance the individual's privacy expectations against the Government's interests to determine whether it is impractical to require a warrant or some level of individualized suspicion in the particular context.

It is clear that the Customs Service's drug testing program is not designed to serve the ordinary needs of law enforcement. Test results may not be used in a criminal prosecution of the employee without the employee's consent. The purposes of the program are to deter drug use among those eligible for promotion to sensitive positions within the Service and to prevent the promotion of drug users to those positions. These substantial interests, no less than the Government's concern for safe rail transportation at issue in Railway Labor Executives, present a special need that may justify departure from the ordinary warrant and probable cause requirements. . . .

The Customs Service is our Nation's first line of defense against one of the greatest problems affecting the health and welfare of our population. We have adverted before to "the veritable national crisis in law enforcement caused by smuggling of illicit narcotics." *United States v. Montoya de Hernandez,* [excerpted in chap. 4.] See also *Florida v. Royer,* [excerpted in chap. 4.[Our cases also reflect the traffickers' seemingly inexhaustible repertoire of deceptive practices and elaborate schemes for importing narcotics, e.g., *United States v. Montoya de Hernandez.* . . . The record in this case confirms that, through the adroit selection of source locations, smuggling routes, and increasingly elaborate methods of concealment, drug traffickers have managed to bring into this country increasingly large quantities of illegal drugs. The record also indicates, and it is well known, that drug smugglers do not hesitate to use violence to protect their lucrative trade and avoid apprehension. Many of the Service's employees are often exposed to this criminal element and to the controlled substances they seek to smuggle into the country. . . .

Where the Government requires its employees to produce urine samples to be analyzed for evidence of illegal drug use, the collection and subsequent chemical analysis of such samples are searches that must meet the reasonableness requirement of the Fourth Amendment. Because the testing program adopted by the Customs Service is not designed to serve the ordinary needs of law enforcement, we have balanced the public interest in the Service's testing program against the privacy concerns implicated by the tests, without reference to our usual presumption in favor of the procedures specified in the Warrant Clause, to assess whether the tests required by Customs are reasonable. We hold that the suspicionless testing of employees who apply for promotion to positions directly involving the interdiction of illegal drugs, or to positions which require the incumbent to carry a firearm, is reasonable. The Government's compelling interests in preventing the promotion of drug users to positions where they might endanger the integrity of our Nation's borders or the life of the citizenry outweigh the privacy interests of those who seek promotion to these positions, who enjoy a diminished expectation of privacy by virtue of the special, and obvious, physical and ethical demands of those positions. We do not decide whether testing those who apply for promotion to positions where they would handle "classified" information is reasonable because we find the record inadequate for this purpose. The judgment of the Court of Appeals for the Fifth Circuit is affirmed in part and vacated in part, and the case is remanded for further proceedings consistent with this opinion. It is so ordered.

DISSENT

Justice Scalia, with whom Justice Stevens joins, dissenting.

The issue in this case is not whether Customs Service employees can constitutionally be denied promotion, or even dismissed, for a single instance of unlawful drug use, at home or at work. They assuredly can. The issue here is what steps can constitutionally be taken to detect such drug use. The Government asserts it can demand that employees perform ''an excretory function traditionally shielded by great privacy,'' ''a monitor of the same sex . . . remains close at hand to listen for the normal sounds,'' and that the excretion thus produced be turned over to the Government for chemical analysis. The Court agrees that this constitutes a search for purposes of the Fourth Amendment—and I think it obvious that it is a type of search particularly destructive of privacy and offensive to personal dignity. Until today this Court had upheld a bodily search separate from arrest and without individualized suspicion of wrongdoing only with respect to prison inmates, relying upon the uniquely dangerous nature of that environment. See Bell v. Wolfish [excerpted earlier]. Today, in *Skinner,* we allow a less intrusive bodily search of railroad employees involved in train accidents. I joined the Court's opinion there because the demonstrated frequency of drug and alcohol use by the targeted class of employees, and the demonstrated connection between such use and grave harm, rendered the search a reasonable means of protecting society. I decline to join the Court's opinion in the present case because neither frequency of use nor connection to harm is demonstrated or even likely. In my view the Customs Service rules are a kind of immolation of privacy and human dignity in symbolic opposition to drug use. . . .

The Court's opinion in the present case will be searched in vain for real evidence of a real problem that will be solved by urine testing of Customs Service employees. . . . The only pertinent points, it seems to me, are supported by nothing but speculation, and not very plausible speculation at that. . . . What is absent in the Government's justifications—notably absent, revealingly absent, and as far as I am concerned dispositively absent—is the recitation of even a single instance in which any of the speculated horribles actually occurred: an instance, that is, in which the cause of bribe-taking, or of poor aim, or of unsympathetic law enforcement, or of compromise of classified information, was drug use. Although the Court points out that several employees have in the past been removed from the Service for accepting bribes and other integrity violations, and that at least nine officers have died in the line of duty since 1974, there is no indication whatever that these incidents were related to drug use by Service employees.

The Court's response to this lack of evidence is that ''(t)here is little reason to believe that American workplaces are immune from (the) pervasive social problem'' of drug abuse. Perhaps such a generalization would suffice if the workplace at issue could produce such catastrophic social harm that no risk whatever is tolerable—the secured areas of a nuclear power plant. But if such a generalization suffices to justify demeaning bodily searches, without particularized suspicion, to guard against the bribing or blackmailing of a law enforcement agent, or the careless use of a firearm, then the Fourth Amendment has become frail protection indeed. In *Skinner,* we took pains to establish the existence of special need for the search or seizure—a need based not upon the existence of a "pervasive social problem" combined with speculation as to the effect of that problem in the field at issue, but rather upon well known or well demonstrated evils in that field, with well known or well demonstrated consequences. In *Skinner,* for example, we pointed to a long history of alcohol abuse in the railroad industry, and noted that in an 8-year period 45 train accidents and incidents had occurred because of alcohol- and drug-impaired railroad employees, killing 34 people, injuring 66, and causing more than $28 million in property damage. In the present case, by contrast, not only is the Customs Service thought to be "largely drug-free," but the connection between whatever drug use may exist and serious social harm is entirely speculative. Except for the fact that the search of a person is much more intrusive than the stop of a car, the present case resembles *Delaware v. Prouse,* 440 U.S. 648, 99 S.Ct. 1391, 59 L.Ed.2d 660 (1979), where we held that the Fourth Amendment prohibited random stops to check drivers' licenses and motor vehicle registration. The contribution of this practice to highway safety, we concluded, was "marginal at best" since the number of licensed drivers that must be stopped in order to find one unlicensed one "will be large indeed." . . .

There is only one apparent basis that sets the testing at issue here apart from all these other situations—but it is not a basis upon which the Court is willing to rely. I do not believe for a minute that the driving force behind these drug-testing rules was any of the feeble justifications put forward by counsel here and accepted by the Court. The only plausible explanation, in my view, is what the Commissioner himself offered in the concluding sentence of his memorandum to Customs Service employees announcing the program: "Implementation of the drug screening program would set an important example in our country's struggle with this most serious threat to our national health and security." Or as respondent's brief to this Court asserted: "if a law enforcement agency and its employees do not take the law seriously, neither will the public on which the agency's effectiveness depends." What better way to show that the Government is serious about its "war on drugs" than to subject its employees on the front line of that war to this invasion of their privacy and affront to their dignity? To be sure, there is only a slight chance that it will prevent some serious public harm resulting from Service employee drug use, but it will show to the world that the Service is "clean," and—most important of all—will demonstrate the determination of the Government to eliminate this scourge of our society! I think it obvious that this justification is unacceptable; that the impairment of individual liberties cannot be the means of making a point; that symbolism, even symbolism for so worthy a cause as the abolition of unlawful drugs, cannot validate an otherwise unreasonable search. There is irony in the Government's citation, in support of its position, of Justice Brandeis's statement in *Olmstead v. United States,* 277 U.S. 438, 485, 48 S.Ct. 564, 575, 72 L.Ed. 944 (1928) that "(f)or good or for ill, (our Government) teaches the whole people by its example." Brandeis was there dissenting from the Court's admission of evidence obtained through an unlawful Government wiretap. He was not praising the Government's example of vigor and enthusiasm in combatting crime, but condemning its example that "the end justifies the means." An even more apt quotation from that famous Brandeis dissent would have been the following:

"(I)t is . . . immaterial that the intrusion was in aid of law enforcement. Experience should teach us to be most on our guard to protect liberty when the Government's purposes are beneficent. Men born to freedom are naturally alert to repel invasion of their liberty by evil-minded rulers. The greatest dangers to liberty lurk in insidious encroachment by men of zeal, well-meaning but without understanding." Id., at 479, 48 S.Ct., at 572.

Those who lose because of the lack of understanding that begot the present exercise in symbolism are not just the Customs Service employees, whose dignity is thus offended, but all of us—who suffer a coarsening of our national manners that ultimately give the Fourth Amendment its content, and who become subject to the administration of federal officials whose respect for our privacy can hardly be greater than the small respect they have been taught to have for their own.

CASE DISCUSSION

The union and union president brought action against United States Customs Service to obtain an injunction and to challenge the constitutionality of a drug-testing program that analyzed urine specimens of employees who applied for promotion to positions involving the interdiction of illegal drugs, the required carrying of firearms, or the handling of classified materials. Customs Service moved to dismiss. The United States District Court denied a motion to dismiss and granted injunctive and declaratory relief. The Customs Service appealed. The Court of Appeals for the Fifth Circuit, vacated the injunction, and *certiorari* was granted. The Supreme Court held that (1) Custom Service's drug-testing program was subject to the reasonableness requirement of Fourth Amendment; (2) Customs Service did not need a warrant to conduct drug-testing program; and (3) suspicionless drug-testing of employees applying for promotion to positions involving interdiction of illegal drugs or the required carrying of firearms was reasonable under Fourth Amendment.

What compelling government interest and what privacy interests did the Court balance in reaching its result in this case? What precise intrusions and deprivations do employees suffer in the Customs drug-testing program? Does Justice Scalia have a point that no evidence established a link between the interest the government seeks to protect in the drug testing and the method used to protect the interest? Should the Court require empirical proof before it accepts plans to further government interests? Does the Court promote the interests of drug control at too high a cost to individual privacy? Or does it balance them properly? Explain your answer.

SUMMARY

The Fourth Amendment protects the "people" against "*un*reasonable searches." Not all intrusions on privacy are searches, and many searches are reasonable. Although nowhere mentioned in the Constitution, the Supreme Court has ruled that the Fourth Amendment protects privacy, specifically, a citizen's reasonable expectation of nonintrusion that society is prepared to recognize. Some invasions on privacy, such as what the unaided senses perceive, are not searches. However, society is not prepared to recognize Fourth Amendment protection for what citizens do in public or take no measures to hide from view or hearing.

The Fourth Amendment balances the citizen's reasonable expectation of privacy against other interests: assuring effective law enforcement, protecting the police, controlling the police, protecting public health and safety, and regulating public institutions such as schools, jails, and prisons.

According to the Fourth Amendment searches must be reasonable. The elements in determining reasonableness include (1) whether agents obtained a warrant based on probable cause and specifically identifying the persons and/or places to be searched and the persons or things to be seized; (2) whether a recognized exception justifies a search without a warrant; (3) whether a search without a warrant requires probable cause to support it or whether something in the absence of probable cause makes the search nonetheless reasonable. The principal recognized exceptions to the warrant requirement include (1) searches incident to lawful arrests; (2) vehicle searches; (3) consent searches; and (4) some regulatory or administrative searches. Searches incident to arrest and consent searches require neither probable cause nor a warrant. Searches incident to lawful arrest are reasonable because of the needs to protect officers and to preserve evidence. Consent searches are reasonable because citizens have voluntarily agreed to the search. Administrative searches, including searching inmates, staff, and visitors in jails and prisons, and students (at least in high school and below), are reasonable without probable cause and warrants if the need to regulate, insure safety, and enforce discipline is reasonable under the particular circumstances of the search.

═══ QUESTIONS FOR REVIEW AND DISCUSSION

1. Describe the trespass doctrine and contrast it with the reasonable expectation of privacy test.
2. What are "constitutionally protected areas" according to the Fourth Amendment search-and-seizure clause?
3. Should the Fourth Amendment protect only searches that involve physical intrusions? Defend your answer.
4. Why did the Supreme Court reject the trespass doctrine?
5. What is the sliding-scale model?
6. Describe the plain view doctrine and explain why it is a misnomer?
7. Should citizens have a reasonable expectation of privacy in their trash? Defend your answer.
8. What is the mere evidence rule?
9. Explain the open fields doctrine. Should a yard enclosed by a privacy fence be excluded from the doctrine. Why? Why not?
10. What is the particularity requirement?
11. Under what circumstances may officers execute a search warrant without announcing their entry?

12. What are the two major purposes of warrantless searches incident to lawful arrests?

13. What two major reasons justify the warrantless searches of vehicles?

14. Under what circumstances should motor homes be considered vehicles? Why?

15. Explain the voluntariness and waiver tests for consent searches. Which test do you think is better? Give reasons for your answer.

16. Under what circumstances should third-party consent be permitted? Explain your answer.

17. What are the elements balanced in declaring airline searches reasonable?

18. Should prisoners, parolees, and probationers have Fourth Amendment rights? Why? Why not?

19. Should students have reduced Fourth Amendment rights against searches and seizures on educational institution premises? Defend your answer.

≡ NOTES

1. *Silverman v. United States,* 365 U.S. 505, 81 S.Ct. 679, 5 L.Ed.2d 734 (1961); Wayne R. LaFave and Jerold H. Israel, *Criminal Procedure,* vol. 1 (St. Paul: West Publishing Co., 1984), 162; Anthony Amsterdam, "Perspectives on the Fourth Amendment," *Minnesota Law Review* 58(1973–1974):356–57.

2. Anthony Amsterdam, "Perspectives on the Fourth Amendment," *Minnesota Law Review* 58 (1974):349–477.

3. *United States v. Billings,* 858 F.2d 617 (10th Cir. 1988).

4. Quoted in Craig M. Bradley, "Two Models of the Fourth Amendment," *Michigan Law Review* 83(1985):1468, 1481.

5. For a useful discussion of the extension of the plain view to other senses, see *U.S. v. Pace* (C.D. Cal.March 3, 1989), reported in 1989 WL 28953.

6. *United States v. Head,* 783 F.2d 1422 (9th Cir. 1986).

7. Ibid., at 1427.

8. See "Note: Fourth Amendment—Further Erosion of the Warrant Requirement for Unreasonable Searches and Seizures: The Warrantless Trash Exception," *Journal of Criminal Law and Criminology* 79(1988):623–46 discusses the *Greenwood* case in depth.

9. *People v. Howard,* 50 N.Y. 2d 583, 430 N.Y.S. 2d 578, 408 N.E.2d 908 (1980); see also discussion in Lafave and Israel, *Criminal Procedure,* 1:176–77.

10. 255 U.S. 298, 41 S.Ct. 261, 65 L.Ed. 647 (1920); Galloway, "The Intruding Eye: A Status Report on the Constitutional Ban Against Paper Searches," *Howard Law Journal* 25(1982):367.

11. 387 U.S. 294, 87 S.Ct. 1642, 18 L.Ed.2d 782 (1967).

12. American Law Institute, *Model Code of Pre-Arraignment Procedure* (Philadelphia: American Law Institute, 1975), 505.

13. Lafave and Israel, *Criminal Procedure,* 1:178–79.

14. *Hester v. United States,* 265 U.S. 57, 44 S.Ct. 445, 68 L.Ed. 898 (1924).

15. *Oliver v. United States,* 466 U.S. 170, 104 S.Ct. 1735, 80 L.Ed.2d 214 (1984).

16. American Law Institute, *Model Code of Pre-Arraignment Procedure* 164; *Oliver v. United States,* 466 U.S. 170 (1984).

17. *California v. Ciraolo,* 476 U.S. 207, 106 S.Ct. 1809, 90 L.Ed.2d 210 (1986); *Dow Chemical Co. v. United States,* 476 U.S. 227, 106 S.Ct. 1819, 90 L.Ed.2d 226 (1986).

18. *Oliver v. United States,* 466 U.S. 170, 104 S.Ct. 1735, 80 L.Ed.2d 214 (1984).

19. *Tomblin v. State,* 128 Ga. App. 823, 198 S.E.2d 366 (1973) (apartment 8-B); *United States v. Busk,* 693 F.2d 28 (3d Cir. 1982); and for many more examples of particularity of place see *Georgetown Law Journal Project: Criminal Procedure* 75(1987):734, n. 134.

20. *United States v. Fawole,* 785 F.2d 1141 (4th Cir. 1986) (address books, etc.); *United States v. Washington,* 782 F.2d 807 (9th Cir. 1986) (items related to prostitution); and for more examples see *Georgetown Law Journal Project: Criminal Procedure* 75(1987):735, notes 137–40.

21. Rule 41(c)(1), Title U.S.C.A. (May 1, 1987).

22. Ibid.; definition of daytime is in Rule 41(h).

23. *United States v. Gervato,* 474 F.2d 40 (3d Cir. 1973); *Payne v. United States,* 508 F.2d 1391 (5th Cir. 1975).

24. *United States v. Micheli,* 487 F.2d 429 (1st Cir. 1973).

25. Ibid.

26. *Harris v. United States,* 331 U.S. 145, 67 S.Ct. 1098, 91 L.Ed. 1399 (1947).

27. American Law Institute, *Model Code of Pre-Arraignment Procedure,* Section 220.3, 130.

28. Ibid.

29. See ibid., reporter's commentary, 513–16; *U.S. v. Tracy,* 835 F.2d 1267 (8th Cir. 1988) (officers need not knock where police saw what they believed were lookouts that led the officers to the reasonable belief that cocaine dealers inside knew the police were coming and would destroy the cocaine in their possession).

30. James B. Haddad, "Well-Delineated Exceptions, Claims of Sham, and Fourfold Probable Cause," *Journal of Criminal Law and Criminology* 68(1977):198–225; Paul Sutton, "The Fourth Amendment in Action: An Empirical View of the Search Warrant Process," *Criminal Law Bulletin* 22(1986):405–29.

31. Craig M. Bradley, "Two Models of the Fourth Amendment," *Michigan Law Review* 83(1985):1468, 1475.

32. Paul Sutton, "The Fourth Amendment in Action," 411.

33. Ibid., 415.

34. Catherine Hancock, "State Court Activism and Searches Incident to Arrest," *Virginia Law Review* 68(1982):1085.

35. *Cupp v. Murphy,* 412 U.S. 291, 93 S.Ct. 2000, 36 L.Ed.2d 900 (1973) (fingernail scraping); *United States v. Edwards,* 415 U.S. 800, 94 S.Ct. 1234, 39 L.Ed.2d 771 (1974).

36. Both reported in *The Criminal Law Reporter,* May 3, 1989, 45:1017.

37. *United States v. Robinson,* 414 U.S. 218 at 234–235, 94 S.Ct. 467 at 476–477, 38 L.Ed.2d 427 (1973).

38. *Zehrung v. State,* 569 P.2d 189 (Alaska 1977).

39. *United States v. Di Re,* 332 U.S. 581, 68 S.Ct. 222, 92 L.Ed. 210 (1948); American Law Institute, *Model Code of Pre-Arraignment Procedure,* 552.

40. American Law Institute, *Model Code of Pre-Arraignment Procedure,* 163.

41. Lloyd Weinreb, "Generalities of the Fourth Amendment," *University of Chicago Law Review* 47(1974):57–58.

42. *United States v. Vasquez,* 858 F.2d 1387 (9th Cir. 1988).

43. *State v. Gonzalez-Valle,* 385 So.2d 681 (Fla. App. 1980) (motive of spite vitiated consent); *Commonwealth v. Martin,* 358 Mass. 282, 264 N.E.2d 366 (1970) (amicable relations not

relevant if they are living together); *United States v. DiPrima* 472 F.2d 550 (1st Cir. 1973) (parent consent for child); also *State v. Kinderman,* 271 Minn. 405, 136 N.W. 577 (1965) (father consented to searching 22-year-old son's room who lived at home in house father owned).

44. *Gillard v. Schmidt,* 579 F.2d 825 (3d Cir. 1978) (psychological profiles in locked desk); *Commonwealth v. Glover,* 266 Pa. Super. 531, 405 A.2d 945 (1979) (search workbench top).

45. *United States v. Matlock,* 415 U.S. 164, 94 S.Ct. 988, 39 L.Ed.2d 242 (1974) (lover consent to search shared bedroom); *United States v. Cataldo,* 433 F.2d 38 (2d Cir. 1970) (roommate consent to search separate bedroom); *Frazier v. Cupp,* 394 U.S. 731, 89 S.Ct. 1420, 22 L.Ed.2d 684 (1969) (shared duffel bag); *New Jersey v. T.L.O.,* 469 U.S. 325, 105 S.Ct. 733, 83 L.Ed.2d 720 (1985) (high school); *Piazzola v. Watkins,* 442 F.2d 284 (5th Cir. 1971) (dormitory rooms in college).

46. American Law Institute, *Model Code of Pre-Arraignment Procedure,* 151; and for discussion of arguments for and against allowing withdrawal of consent, 538.

47. *Smith v. Commonwealth,* 197 Ky. 192, 246 S.W. 449 (1923); *People v. Martinez,* 259 Cal. App. 2d Supp. 943, 65 Cal. Rptr. 920 (1968).

48. 431 U.S. 606, 97 S.Ct. 1972, 52 L.Ed.2d 617 (1977).

49. Lafave and Israel, *Criminal Procedure,* 1:327–28.

50. *United States v. Ramsey et al.,* 431 U.S. 606, 97 S.Ct. 1972, 52 L.Ed.2d 617 (1977).

51. Ibid., 332–333.

52. *United States v. Place,* 462 U.S. 696, 103 S.Ct. 2637, 77 L.Ed.2d 110 (1983).

53. 370 U.S. 139, 82 S.Ct. 1218, 8 L.Ed.2d 384 (1962).

54. *Hudson v. Palmer,* 468 U.S. 517, 104 S.Ct. 3194, 82 L.Ed.2d 393 (1984).

55. *Bell v. Wolfish,* 441 U.S. 520, 99 S.Ct. 1861, 60 L.Ed.2d 447 (1979) (strip search detainees following visits); *Mary Beth G. v. City of Chicago,* 723 F.2d 1263 (7th Cir. 1983) (strip search all women arrested for misdemeanors).

56. Lafave and Israel, *Criminal Procedure,* 1:336–338.

57. *Kennedy v. Hardiman,* 684 F.Supp. 540 (N.D. Ill. 1988).

58. *New Jersey v. T.L.O.,* 469 U.S. 325, 105 S.Ct. 733, 83 L.Ed.2d 720 (1985).

Chapter Seven

Interrogation and Confessions

CHAPTER OUTLINE

CHAPTER MAIN POINTS

1. The intrusions and deprivations comprising interrogation, confessions, and identification procedures are greater than those occurring prior to arrest.

2. The privilege against self- incrimination, the right to counsel, and the due process clause all affect police interrogation.

3. Custodial interrogation is inherently coercive.

4. The *Miranda* warnings are not inherent parts of the Fifth Amendment.

CHAPTER KEY TERMS

accusatory stage when investigation focuses on particular individual

booking entering suspect's name, time of arrival at station, and offense for which arrested in the police log

custodial searches searches conducted after suspects are taken into custody, but before they are put into holding facilities

due process voluntariness doctrine confessions must be voluntary to meet constitutional standards

identification procedures eyewitness identification by means of lineups, showups, and photographs

interrogation questioning suspects and witnesses to crimes

inventory searches officers compile lists of items taken from suspects be-fore they are committed to holding cells

objective test measures conduct by reasonableness

***per se* rules** prescribed rules that police must follow or violate the Constitution

prophylactic rules rules protecting constitutional rights, not inherent to the rights

station-house bail money posted at police station for minor offenses

subjective test measures conduct by intent or belief of individual

totality-of-circumstances test looks at all circumstances surrounding conduct to measure whether constitutional requirements are met

---

≡ THE INTERROGATION SETTING

Police-suspect encounters following arrest take place mainly in the police station, not on the street, in bars, restaurants, homes, or other places familiar to suspects. Police stations appear strange, unfriendly—often hostile—to suspects. Two searches accompany most detentions. Before placing them in lockup, officers conduct **custodial searches** of arrested suspects. Custodial searches are more thorough searches for weapons, other contraband, and evidence than searches incident to arrest. Officers also conduct **inventory searches** to make up lists of all personal property detainees have in their possession. Inventory searches protect detainees' property and custodial institutions from danger and prevent lawsuits for "lost" and damaged property. The police also conduct more-extensive investigation following arrest. This further investigation takes two forms: (1) **interrogation,** or police questioning suspects, discussed in this chapter, and (2) **identification,** or means by which victims and witnesses identify suspects as the perpetrators of crimes, the subject of chapter 8. This stage following arrest is sometimes called the **accusatory stage** of the criminal process.

Intrusions and deprivations intensify during the accusatory stage. Police interrogation in surroundings unfriendly to suspects, lineups, showups, and other identification procedures intrude more deeply into citizens' privacy and subject them to greater deprivations than stops, frisks, arrests, or other seizures and searches discussed in chapters 4 through 6. Hence, balancing the law enforcement need for sufficient power to charge and convict criminals against other interests moves to a stage with higher stakes for both citizens and law enforcement. Determining the proper balance among these interests during custody but prior to the point when prosecutors formally charge suspects has generated tremendous controversy over the years.

The controversy largely surrounds the general question: To what extent, if any, does the Constitution protect arrested citizens in police custody? This general question divides into four specific constitutional questions: (1) Does the Fourteenth Amendment due process clause apply to police interrogations and their principal offshoot, confessions, and to lineups, showups, and other identification procedures? (2) Does the Fifth Amendment privilege against self- incrimination apply to custodial interrogation and identification procedures? (3) Does the Sixth Amendment right to counsel extend to police interrogation and identification procedures? (4) Are lineups, showups, obtaining blood, hair, and voice samples and other identification procedures protected by the Fourth Amendment search-and-seizure clause?

Decision Point

In which of the following hypotheticals are persons *compelled* to be witnesses against themselves?

1. A police officer asks a man he has stopped on the street, "What are you doing out at 1:30 a.m.?" The man replies, "I'm trying to buy some crack, as if it's any of your business."

2. An officer hears screams coming from an apartment. He enters without knocking and asks, "What's going on here?" A woman answers, "I just beat up my baby."

3. An elderly woman was beaten when she would not relinquish her purse to three muggers. She was left on the street and died of exposure. Officers in relays questioned an eighteen-year-old suspect for six hours without a break. Some officers took a belligerent tone, bullying the suspect and telling him he was in "big trouble." They never touched him. One officer befriended him, telling the suspect he knew whoever took the purse didn't mean to kill the woman and that, anyway, it was really her fault for resisting. The suspect finally weakened and confessed.

4. A police officer while interrogating a suspect in the police station, promises the suspect, "If you'll just tell me the truth about raping that college student, I'll see to it that the prosecutor only charges you with misdemeanor assault." The suspect asks, "You can do that?" The officer replies, "Sure, I wouldn't tell you something I couldn't do." The suspect says, "O.K., I did it." He later put the confession in writing.

5. An officer tells a suspect brought to the police station for questioning, "You might as well admit you killed your wife because your neighbor already told us he saw the whole thing." The officer was lying. The suspect replied, "My God, I knew I should have pulled the shades, that nosy bastard is always spying on me."

Interrogation—or questioning suspects and criminal defendants—might take place during several stages in the criminal process. It can occur prior to arrest, in the period immediately following arrest but prior to formal charges, following charge but prior to trial, and then, of course, during the trial itself. Police interrogation, the focus of this section, has provoked more debate over the past twenty years than any other subject in criminal procedure. In fact, perhaps no single procedure is more widely known, for good or ill, than the *Miranda* warnings.

> The word *Miranda* had become a staple of the law enforcement community's vocabulary, and prosecutors and judges alike referred to the station house ritual of giving *Miranda* warnings as "mirandizing." The Hill Street blue read them over national television, and in a nationally syndicated comic strip, Peppermint Patty, on her first assignment as a school safety patrol, read them to a kindergartner who had crossed the street improperly. *Miranda* had become part of the popular culture.[1]

The controversy surrounding police interrogation centers on three questions: (1) How important are confessions in solving crimes and convicting criminals? (2) What kinds of, and how much, pressure can police use to obtain confessions? and (3) How often, and in what ways, do police abuse their power to interrogate? Controversy surrounds these questions both because empirical evidence does not conclusively answer them, and because feelings run strong about how much power the Constitution grants police, and how much restraint the Constitution places on that power during interrogation. One study of confessions showed that confessions are rarely offered in evidence at trials. It did not show how many guilty plea convictions resulted from confessions. Another study demonstrated that the prosecution frequently relies on confessions. It did not, however, show that the government *needed* the confession to convict defendants.[2]

≡ THE IMPORTANCE OF INTERROGATION

Thirty years ago Supreme Court Justice Felix Frankfurter stated the case for interrogation:

> Despite modern advances in the technology of crime detection, offenses frequently occur about which things cannot be made to speak. And where there cannot be found innocent human witnesses to such offenses, nothing remains—if police investigation is not to be balked before it has fairly begun—but to seek out possible guilty witnesses and ask them questions, witnesses, that is, who are suspected of knowing something about the offense precisely because they are suspected of implication in it.[3]

Many agree that Justice Frankfurter's words are equally relevant today. Fred Inbau listed the following three reasons supporting Frankfurter's position.

1. Police can solve many cases, even when the best qualified police departments investigate them, only if guilty persons confess or other suspects provide information that forms the basis of convicting others.
2. Criminals will not admit they committed crimes unless police catch them in the act or question them in private for perhaps a period of hours.
3. "In dealing with criminal offenders, and consequently with criminal suspects who may actually be innocent, the interrogator must employ less refined methods than

are considered appropriate for the transaction of ordinary, every-day affairs by and between law-abiding citizens."[4]

Inbau is a retired but active Northwestern University law professor, author of a leading manual on police interrogation, and

in his younger days . . . the premier lie-detector examiner and just about the craftiest interrogator around. In the course of obtaining hundreds of confessions, he had been known to spill over with such "sympathy" for a murder suspect that he had to "pause and wipe away a tear."[5]

Convincing empirical data do not at this date—perhaps cannot ever—support either the position that convictions require interrogation and confessions or that alternative evidence makes confessions unnecessary to convict criminals.[6]

MEASURING POLICE ABUSE IN INTERROGATING SUSPECTS

Police interrogate suspects privately, privacy generates secrecy, and secrecy makes it difficult, if not impossible, to know what in fact happens during interrogation. The absence of empirical evidence that results from secrecy leads to undue attention to sensational cases that dramatize only the most outrageous police abuse. Critics of police interrogation rely heavily on these sensational cases to support their demands for limits on police interrogation. Those who support interrogation reply that "the examples of police brutality . . . are rare exceptions to the thousands of cases that appear every year in the law reports." The absence of empirical data leads both sides in the controversy to hold different perceptions about what actually takes place in interrogation rooms.[7]

One difficulty in assessing interrogation lies in defining abuse. At one extreme are those who believe that secret interrogation by itself constitutes abuse; hence, all police interrogation is improper. To others, trickery, cajolery, lies, and other interrogation tactics constitute abuse. At the other extreme, some maintain that everything short of beating, whipping, and threats of violence are proper interrogation tactics. Commentators, courts, and advocates differ sharply over where to draw the line. Varying emphases on what interests criminal procedure promotes account for these differences. Those opposed to police interrogation emphasize the potential for wrong decisions, particularly the conviction of the innocent; the primacy of the individual; and controlling police behavior. Those who favor broad police interrogation stress the need to get the facts and convict the guilty, and the need for efficient, speedy criminal justice administration. In other words, the disagreement over defining interrogation reflects differing emphases on the themes of correct result, process, and societal interests.[8]

THE CONSTITUTION, INTERROGATION, AND CONFESSIONS

Although the law of interrogation and confessions has deep historical roots, modern constitutional history of police interrogations and confessions begins in 1936. Since then, the Supreme Court has relied on three independent constitutional doctrines to limit police interrogation and prosecutors' efforts to obtain incriminating statements from criminal defendants: (1) the due process clause of the Fourteenth Amendment; (2) the Fifth Amendment self-incrimination clause; and (3) the Sixth Amendment right to counsel clause. The relevant wording from these amendments is

> No state shall . . . deprive any person of life, liberty, or property without due process of law—Amendment XIV
>
> In all criminal prosecutions, the accused shall . . . have the assistance of counsel for his defense—Amendment VI
>
> No person . . . shall be compelled in any criminal case to be a witness against himself—Amendment V

The doctrines overlap but still follow a roughly chronological line. In 1936, in *Brown v. Mississippi,* the Court ruled that the Fourteenth Amendment due process clause prohibited the admission of forced confessions as evidence in criminal trials. In that case, the police had brutally beaten, tortured, and threatened to kill a black man if he did not confess to killing a white victim. The Court ruled that such a confession could not be trusted. To admit unreliable evidence as proof of guilt would deny defendants of life—as was true in *Brown* because murder was a capital offense— liberty, or property without due process of law. In 1964, in *Escobedo v. Illinois,* the Court turned briefly to the Sixth Amendment right to counsel clause in interrogation and confession cases. The Chicago police refused to allow Escobedo and his lawyer to see each other prior to Escobedo's interrogation. He confessed, but the Supreme Court ruled that the government could not introduce the confession into evidence because Escobedo had confessed without advice of counsel. Two years later in *Miranda v. Arizona,* the Court focused on the incorporation of the Fifth Amendment self-incrimination clause as the primary constitutional doctrine governing interrogation and confessions. The due process, right to counsel, and self-incrimination doctrines do not mutually exclude each other; all are relevant in specific circumstances, but the Court relies mainly on self-incrimination to decide confession cases.[9]

The Meaning of Interrogation

Interrogation obviously includes direct questioning—"Where were you on Friday night?"—but the Supreme Court defines interrogation to encompass more than direct questions. In *Massiah v. United States,* for example, the police arranged for Massiah's co- defendant to discuss their pending trial in a car while Massiah was wired with a radio transmitter hooked up to the police. The Court ruled that Massiah's right to counsel was violated because although officers never directly asked him anything, incriminating words he communicated to his co-defendant "were deliberately elicited from him" by federal agents.

Therefore, interrogation for right to counsel purposes means to elicit incriminating information from suspects intentionally. Eliciting need not mean direct questioning but it probably excludes wholly passive action that generates confessions. For example, planting an electronic listening device is not interrogation because bugging does not "increase the defendant's predisposition toward making an incriminating response." The Supreme Court attempted to define interrogation in *Brewer v. Williams.*[10]

CASE

Was Williams "interrogated"?

Brewer v. Williams

430 U.S. 387, 97 S.Ct. 1232, 51 L.Ed.2d 424 (1977)

[Stewart, J., delivered the opinion of the court, in which Brennan, J., Marshall, Powell, and Stevens, JJ., joined. Marshall, J., Powell, J., and Stevens, J., filed concurring opinions. Burger, C.J., filed a dissenting opinion, White, J., filed a dissenting opinion, in which Blackmun and Rehnquist, JJ., joined. Blackmun, J., filed a dissenting opinion, in which White and Rehnquist, JJ., joined.]

FACTS

On the afternoon of December 24, 1968, a 10-year old girl named Pamela Powers went with her family to the YMCA in Des Moines, Iowa, to watch a wrestling tournament in which her brother was participating. When she failed to return from a trip to the washroom, a search for her began. The search was unsuccessful.

Robert Williams, who had recently escaped from a mental hospital, was a resident of the YMCA. Soon after the girl's disappearance Williams was seen in the YMCA lobby carrying some clothing and a large bundle wrapped in a blanket. He obtained help from a 14-year old boy in opening the street door of the YMCA and the door to his automobile parked outside. When Williams placed the bundle in the front seat of his car the boy "saw two legs in it and they were skinny and white." Before anyone could see what was in the bundle Williams drove away. His abandoned car was found the following day in Davenport, Iowa, roughly 160 miles east of Des Moines. A warrant was then issued in Des Moines for his arrest on a charge of abduction. . . .

In the presence of the Des Moines chief of police and a police detective named Leaming, McKnight [one of William's attorneys] advised Williams that Des Moines police officers would be driving to Davenport to pick him up, that the officers would not interrogate him or mistreat him, and that Williams was not to talk to the officers about Pamela Powers until after consulting with McKnight upon his return to Des Moines. As a result of these conversations, it was agreed between McKnight and the Des Moines police officials that Detective Leaming and a fellow officer would drive to Davenport to pick up Williams, that they would bring him directly back to Des Moines, and that they would not question him during the trip. . . .

Detective Leaming and his fellow officer arrived in Davenport about noon to pick up Williams and return him to Des Moines. Soon after their arrival they met with Williams and Kelly, who, they understood, was acting as Williams' lawyer. Detective Leaming repeated the *Miranda* warnings, and told Williams:

"[W]e both know that you're being represented here by Mr. Kelly and you're being represented by Mr. McKnight in Des Moines, and . . . I want you to remember this because we'll be visiting between here and Des Moines." . . .

The two detectives, with Williams in their charge, then set out on the 160-mile drive. At no time during the trip did Williams express a willingness to be interrogated in the absence of an attorney. Instead, he stated several times that "[w]hen I get to Des Moines and see Mr. McKnight, I am going to tell you the whole story." Detective Leaming knew that Williams was a former mental patient and knew also that he was deeply religious.

The detective and his prisoner soon embarked on a wide-ranged conversation covering a variety of topics, including the subject of religion. Then, not long after leaving Davenport and reaching the interstate highway, Detective Leaming delivered what has been referred to in the briefs and oral arguments as the "Christian burial speech." Addressing Williams as "Reverend," the detective said:

> "I want to give you something to think about while we're traveling down the road. . . . Number one, I want you to observe the weather conditions, its raining, it's sleeting, it's freezing, driving is very treacherous, visibility is poor, it's going to be dark early this evening. They are predicting several inches of snow for tonight, and I feel that you yourself are the only person that knows where this little girl's body is, that you yourself have only been there once, and if you got a snow on top of it you yourself may be unable to find it. And, since we will be going right past the area on the way into Des Moines, I feel that we could stop and locate the body, that the parents of this little girl should be entitled to a Christian burial for the little girl who was snatched away from them on Christmas [E]ve and murdered. And I feel we should stop and locate it on the way rather than waiting until morning and trying to come back out after a snow storm and possibly not being able to find it at all."

Williams asked Detective Leaming why he thought their route to Des Moines would be taking them past the girl's body, and Leaming responded that he knew the body was in the area of Mitchellville—a town they would be passing on the way to Des Moines. Leaming then stated: "I do not want you to answer me. I don't want to discuss it any further. Just think about it as we're riding down the road."

As the car approached Grinnell, a town approximately 100 miles west of Davenport, Williams asked whether the police had found the victim's shoes. When Detective Leaming replied that he was unsure, Williams directed the officers to a service station where he said he had left the shoes; a search proved unsuccessful. As they continued towards Des Moines, Williams asked whether the police had found the blanket, and directed police to the rest area where he said he had disposed of the blanket. Nothing was found. The car continued towards Des Moines, and as it approached Mitchellville, Williams said he would show the officers where the body was. He then directed the police to the body of Pamela Powers.

Williams was indicted for first-degree murder. Before trial, his counsel moved to suppress all evidence relating to or resulting from any statements Williams had made during the automobile ride from Davenport to Des Moines. After an evidentiary hearing the trial judge denied the motion. He found that "an agreement was made between defense counsel and the police officials to the effect that the Defendant was not to be questioned on the return trip to Des Moines,'' and that the evidence in question had been elicited from Williams during ''a critical stage in the proceedings requiring the presence of counsel on his request.'' The judge ruled, however, that Williams had ''waived his right to have an attorney present during the giving of such information.'' . . . [Williams was convicted; the Iowa Supreme Court affirmed his conviction; the federal District Court ordered a new trial on William's habeas corpus petition; the Court of Appeals affirmed.]

OPINION

There can be no serious doubt . . . that Detective Leaming deliberately and designedly set out to elicit information from Williams just as surely as—and perhaps more effectively than—if he had formally interrogated him. Detective Leaming was fully aware before departing for Des Moines that Williams was being represented in Davenport by Kelly and in Des Moines by McKnight. Yet he purposely sought during William's isolation from his lawyers to obtain as much incriminating information as possible. Indeed, Detective Leaming conceded as much when he testified at William's trial:

> ''Q. In fact, Captain, whether he was a mental patient or not, you were trying to get all the information you could before he got to his lawyer, weren't you?
> ''A. I was sure hoping to find out where that little girl was, yes, sir.
> ''Q. Well, I'll put it this way: You was [sic] hoping to get all the information you could before Williams got back to McKnight, weren't you?
> ''A. Yes, sir.''

DISSENT

Mr. Chief Justice Burger, dissenting.

The result in this case ought to be intolerable in any society which purports to call itself an organized society. It continues the Court—by the narrowest margin—on the much criticized course of punishing the public for the mistakes and misdeeds of law enforcement officers, instead of punishing the officer directly, if in fact he is guilty of wrongdoing. It mechanically and blindly keeps reliable evidence from juries whether the claimed constitutional violation involves gross police misconduct or honest human error.

Williams is guilty of the savage murder of a small child; no member of the Court contends he is not. While in custody, and after no fewer than *five* warnings of his rights to silence and to counsel, he led police to the concealed body of his victim. The Court concedes that Williams was not threatened or coerced and that he spoke and acted voluntarily and with full awareness of his constitutional rights. In the face of all this, the Court now holds that because Williams was prompted by the detective's statement—not interrogation but a statement—the jury must not be told how the police found the body.

Today's holding fulfills Judge (late Mr. Justice) Cardozo's grim prophecy that someday some court might carry the exclusionary rule to the absurd extent that its operative effect would exclude evidence relating to the body of a murder victim because of the means by which it was found.[a] In so ruling the Court regresses to playing a grisly game of ''hide and seek,'' once more exalting the sporting theory of criminal justice which has been experiencing a decline in our jurisprudence. . . .

CASE DISCUSSION

Williams was arrested, arraigned, and committed to jail in Davenport, Iowa for abducting a ten-year-old girl. His lawyers advised Williams not to make any statements until he consulted with his lawyer in Des Moines. On the way to Des Moines Williams made incriminating statements to the police. Over his objections, the statements were introduced in evidence against him. He was convicted of murder. The Iowa Supreme Court affirmed, holding that Williams waived his Fifth Amendment rights. Williams petitioned the district court for *habeas corpus,* which held the evidence was wrongfully admitted on the ground that the statements were obtained in violation of his Sixth Amendment right to counsel and decided Williams was entitled to a new trial. The court of appeals affirmed. On write of *certiorari,* the United States Supreme Court affirmed, holding that the incriminating statements were not admissible.

Why does Chief Justice Burger call the result in this case "intolerable"? Do you agree? Why? Why not? How do you define interrogation? According to your definition, did the "Christian burial speech" constitute interrogation? Explain. What interests does the Court promote in its decision? administrative interests? process interests? results? broad social goals? Does Williams go free because of the Court's decision? Should he go free? Explain.

---

[a]"The criminal is to go free because the constable has blundered. . . . A room is searched against the law, and the body of a murdered man is found. . . . The privacy of the home is infringed, and the murderer goes free." *People v. Defore,* 150 N.E. 585, 587, 588 (1926).

The Fifth Amendment, Interrogation, and Confessions

In the controversial *Miranda v. Arizona,* the Supreme Court held, by a close 5–4 majority and a vigorous dissent, that the Fifth Amendment protects suspects during *custodial* police interrogation. (See chap. 2, where *Miranda* is excerpted.) For a brief period prior to *Miranda,* it appeared as if the Court was going to rely on the Sixth Amendment right to counsel as a means to extend the Constitution to police interrogations. Two years prior to *Miranda,* the Court decided *Escobedo v. Illinois.* Danny Escobedo and his lawyer repeatedly tried to meet in a Chicago police station, but the police refused to allow it. The Supreme Court excluded Escobedo's confession because the police had denied him access to his lawyer. However, the Court has largely ignored *Escobedo,* relying instead almost exclusively on the Fifth Amendment self-incrimination clause to govern custodial police interrogation, and applying the Sixth Amendment only after formal institution judicial proceedings have commenced. (See chap. 8.)[11]

Miranda v. Arizona and Self-Incrimination

The Supreme Court addressed the meaning of the word "compelled" in the Fifth Amendment in *Miranda v. Arizona.* (Review excerpt in chap. 2.) The Court held that custodial interrogation is inherently coercive. Suspects are in strange surroundings, not free to go home or call upon relatives and friends for support, and are subjected to relays of skilled police officers using trickery and psychological pressure in incommunicado, secret missions calculated to ''crack'' suspects' will. Such circumstances require strong protection to produce voluntary incriminating statements. The famous *Miranda* warnings were intended to remove *coercion* from police custodial interrogation. However, they were not intended to eliminate all *pressure* on criminal suspects. The distinction between coercion and pressure is difficult to draw in practice.

Decision Point

An interrogator, while still standing in front of the seated suspect and using the case folder as a prop, should state clearly and briefly something along the following lines: ''You're Joe Burns? I'm here to talk to you about the break-in at Jason's Jewelry Store last week.'' As that comment is being made, the interrogator should finger through the case folder to create the impression that it contains material of an incriminating nature about the suspect.

Although the interrogator in this instance has already been insulated from having his own first name used, he has gained a psychological advantage by addressing the suspect by *his* first name. This is particularly so when the suspect is a person with a professional title, or someone of social, political, or business prominence. Such suspects are thereby stripped of the psychological advantage. . . . It is a very disarming tactic. There are exceptions, however. Whenever there is a significant disparity between an interrogator's young age and the older age of a suspect, it may be inappropriate to call the suspect by his first name. Then . . . a psychological gain may accrue to the interrogator by addressing a person of low socio-economic status by his or her *last* name (prefaced in appropriate instances by Mr., Mrs., or Miss).

The direct, positive, confrontation . . . should be ''Joe, the results of our investigation clearly indicate that you broke into Jason's Jewelry Store last week.'' This direct, positive statement should be emphatically expressed in a slow, deliberate, and confident manner. The words ''broke into'' have an unmistakable meaning and, at the same time, avoid the legalistic word ''burglary.'' . . . [T]here is a psychological disadvantage to using words or expressions that conjure up in the suspect's mind the legal consequences of a confession of guilt.)

If ''Joe Burns'' confesses to the burglary, was he coerced? or just pressured? The experienced interrogator and law professor Fred Inbau recommends the above scenario as a legal, effective ''direct, positive confrontation.''[12]

FIGURE 1   DEFENDANT'S RIGHTS*

The Court wishes to advise you of the following matters at this time:

1. You are not required to say anything or submit to questioning. Anything you say may be used against you in this or in any further proceedings;

2. You have a right to an attorney in all further proceedings, including police line-ups and questioning. If you are financially unable to afford an attorney, one will be appointed without cost to you;

3. You have a right to speak with your attorney. A continuance will be granted, if necessary, to enable you to obtain or to speak to an attorney.

4. You have a right to a jury trial.

*Minnesota Rules of Criminal Procedure, Rule 5.01.

The Court intended the *Miranda* warnings, summarized here, and in Figure 7.1, to provide a "bright line" objective, or *per se*, rule for police to follow to prevent coercion but yet allow pressure. A person in custody

1. "must . . . be informed in clear and unequivocal terms that he has the right to remain silent," to enlighten the ignorant and to relieve the pressures of interrogation atmosphere for those who already know their rights;

2. must be told that "anything said can and will be used against the individual in court," so suspects fully understand the consequences of talking to the police;

3. "must be clearly informed that he has the right to consult with a lawyer and to have a lawyer with him during interrogation," because counsel is so important to protecting the privilege;

4. must be told that if he cannot afford a lawyer that a lawyer will be appointed for him because otherwise suspects may think they may have lawyers only if they can afford them;

5. are free to exercise the privilege at any time, and if he "indicate[s] in any manner, at anytime prior to or during questioning" that he wishes "to remain silent, the interrogation must cease"; likewise, if "he states he wants an attorney, the interrogation must cease until an attorney is present."

The rules related to *Miranda* provide the suspect with additional assurances:

1. If the police obtain any statement without an attorney, "a heavy burden rests on the Government to demonstrate that the defendant knowingly and intelligently waived his privilege against self-incrimination and his right to retained or appointed counsel." Waivers may not be presumed either by silence following warnings or from an eventual confession.

2. Statements obtained in violation of the rules may not be admitted into evidence.

3. Exercise of the privilege may not be penalized. Hence, prosecutors may not "use at trial the fact that [the defendant] stood mute or claimed his privilege in the face of accusation."[13]

Decision Point

During interrogation, the suspect asked the police officers interrogating him if he could use the telephone to call his mother to see if she could get him an attorney. One officer asked him whether he was saying he wanted them to stop questioning him until he had an attorney. They continued to question him, and he later confessed. In fact, he even cooperated with the police in the investigation.

Did his request to call his mother constitute a request for an attorney that mandated terminating questioning, according to number five in the *Miranda* warnings? According to the Pennsylvania Supreme Court, the officers' request for clarification of what the defendant meant and the defendant's cooperation did not validate the confession because the defendant had made his wishes clear—he wanted a lawyer.[14]

THE EFFECTS OF *MIRANDA*. *Miranda* provoked intense and immediate controversy. Defense attorneys and civil libertarians hailed it as a new dawn in civilized society. Police, other law enforcement–minded people, and wide segments of the public complained that the decision "hand-cuffed" the police; they feared that law and order would soon break down. Neither the hopes nor fears surrounding *Miranda* ever came to pass. The decision still stands with some—but not much—modification. According to most research, the *Miranda* decision has not significantly affected either law enforcement or crime levels.[15]

The Supreme Court has applied *Miranda*'s ***per se* rules** flexibly. The Court considers them ***prophylactic rules***—not constitutional rights, but a mechanism to guarantee rights. In other words, the warnings are not inherent in the Fifth Amendment privilege against self-incrimination. In the Supreme Court's words, *Miranda*

> recognized that these procedural safeguards were not themselves rights protected by the Constitution but were instead measures to insure that the right against compulsory self-incrimination was protected.[16]

THE MEANING OF "CUSTODY". The Court in *Miranda* required that officers give the warnings "when the individual is first subjected to police interrogation while in custody at the station or otherwise deprived of his freedom of action in any significant way." Police need *not* warn suspects in three situations: (1) "general on-the-scene questioning as to facts surrounding a crime; (2) other general questioning of citizens in the fact- finding process," or (3) "volunteered statements of any kind."

Therefore, if someone walks into a police station and says, "I want to tell you all the gory details of how I murdered my best friend tonight," and a detective says, "Fine, do you mind if I record it?" the incriminating statements that follow do not violate the Fifth Amendment. Citizens who come to police stations of their own accord and freely volunteer statements are not in custody; hence, *Miranda* does not apply. Nor does *Miranda* apply to the brief questioning that occurs during "stops" discussed in chapter 4.[17]

Courts variously determine what constitutes custodial interrogation by analyzing the "totality of the circumstances" surrounding the interrogation. For example, the Fifth Circuit Court of Appeals employs a four-factor test: (1) whether there was probable cause to arrest; (2) whether officers intended to hold suspects; (3) whether suspects believed their freedom was significantly restricted; and (4) whether the investigation had focused on the suspect at the time. The Ninth Circuit uses five factors: (1) officers' language in summoning suspects; (2) the physical surroundings of interrogation; (3) the amount of evidence of guilt officers present to suspects; (4) the duration of detention; and (5) the amount of pressure officers use in detaining suspects. The First, Third, and Fourth Circuits ask whether it was reasonable for suspects to believe they were either in custody or restrained to a degree comparable with arrest.[18]

The Supreme Court has addressed the custody question, an issue that has given the Court considerable problems over the years since *Miranda*. Presence at the station, for example, does not always require the warnings. Where persons appear at the station upon an invitation, they are not in custody. Hence, when police left a note for a suspect saying "I want to discuss something you," the Court ruled that the suspect was not in custody since he voluntarily went to the station and talked to the police, However, a different situation exists when the invitation involves police accompanying suspects to the station. For example, in *Dunaway v. New York,* officers acted on instructions to "pick up" Dunaway and "bring him in." The officers did not tell Dunaway he was arrested, never touched him, and did not book him. Nevertheless, when the police questioned him without telling him he was free to go, the Court ruled that Dunaway was in custody.[19]

In *Miranda,* the Court included questioning outside police stations within the scope of custodial interrogation if suspects are "otherwise deprived of . . . [their] freedom of action in any significant way." The Court used this language intentionally to prevent police from circumventing the *Miranda* requirements by simply questioning suspects somewhere other than a police station. *Miranda* aims at coercive *atmospheres,* not necessarily physical *locations.* Police stations, according to the opinion, are inherently coercive settings. But circumstances outside police stations may also indicate a sufficiently coercive atmosphere to require warnings prior to interrogation. Hence, suspects questioned in squad cars are in custody. Questioning in suspects' homes, on the other hand, ordinarily is not custodial interrogation.

Basically, if questioning takes place in surroundings familiar to the suspect, it is not custodial. On the other hand, in *Orozco v. Texas,* where four police officers entered Orozco's bedroom at 4:00 a.m. to question him about a shooting, the Court ruled it equivalent to station-house interrogation because of its "potentiality for compulsion."[20]

The *Miranda* Court also made clear that

> general on-the-scene questioning as to facts surrounding a crime or other general questioning of citizens in the factfinding process is not affected by our holding. . . .
> In such situations the compelling atmosphere inherent in the process of in-custody interrogation is not necessarily present.[21]

Accordingly, *Miranda* does not apply to the brief questioning that accompanies stops on the street, such as those discussed in chapter 4. Nor does it apply to traffic stops, at least not minor traffic violations or driver's license checks. Therefore, police need not warn citizens they question near the scene of a crime, at traffic accidents, or in public in "suspicious circumstances."[22]

Finally, in determining custody, the courts look at whether the circumstances surrounding interrogation are

> likely to affect substantially the individual's "will to resist and compel him to speak where he would not otherwise do so freely."

Handcuffing, drawing a gun, holding by the arm, or putting in a police car constitute such circumstances. On the other hand, where questioning takes places in the presence of suspects' friends, or where police have not removed suspects from the presence of other third parties so that suspects are not "cut off from the outside world" and "surrounded by antagonistic forces" in a "police dominated atmosphere" and interrogated "without relent," they are not in custody. The Supreme Court addressed interrogation outside police stations in *Minnesota v. Murphy*.[23]

CASE

Was he in "custody"?

Minnesota v. Murphy

465 U.S. 420, 104 S.Ct. 1136, 79 L.Ed.2d 409 (1984)

[White, J., delivered the opinion of the Court, in which Burger, C.J., and Blackmun, Powell, Rehnquist, and O'Connor, JJ., joined. Marshall, J., filed a dissenting opinion in which Stevens, J., joined and in which Brennan, J., joined.]

FACTS

In 1974, Marshall Murphy was twice questioned by Minneapolis police concerning the rape and murder of a teenage girl. No charges were then brought. In 1980, in connection with a prosecution for criminal sexual conduct arising out of an unrelated incident, Murphy pleaded guilty to a reduced charge of false imprisonment. He was sentenced to a prison term of 16 months, which was suspended, and three years' probation. The terms of Murphy's probation required, among other things, that he participate in a treatment program for sexual offenders at Alpha House, report to his probation officer as directed, and be truthful with the probation officer "in all matters." Failure to comply with these conditions, Murphy was informed, could result in his return to the sentencing court for a probation revocation hearing.

Murphy met with his probation officer at her office approximately once a month, and his probation continued without incident until July, 1981, when the officer learned that he had abandoned the treatment program. The probation officer then wrote to Murphy and informed him that failure to set up a meeting would "result in an immediate request for a warrant." . . . At a meeting in late July, the officer agreed not to seek revocation of probation for nonparticipation in the treatment program since Murphy was employed and doing well in other areas.

In September 1981, an Alpha House counselor informed the probation officer that, during the course of treatment, Murphy had admitted to a rape and murder in 1974. After discussions with her superior, the officer determined that the police should have this information. She then wrote to Murphy and asked him to contact her to discuss a treatment plan for the remainder of his probationary period. Although she did not contact the police before the meeting, the probation officer knew in advance that she would report any incriminating statements.

Upon receipt of the letter, Murphy arranged to meet with his probation officer in her office on September 28, 1981. The officer opened the meeting by telling Murphy about the information she had received from the Alpha House counselor and expressing her belief that this information evinced his continued need for treatment. Murphy became angry about what he considered to be a breach of his confidences and stated that he "felt like calling a lawyer." The probation officer replied that Murphy would have to deal with that problem outside the office; for the moment, their primary concern was the relationship between the crimes that Murphy had admitted to the Alpha House counselor and the incident that led to his conviction for false imprisonment.

During the course of the meeting, Murphy denied the false imprisonment charge, admitted that he had committed the rape and murder, and attempted to persuade the probation officer that further treatment was unnecessary because several extenuating circumstances explained the prior crimes. At the conclusion of the meeting, the officer told Murphy that she had a duty to relay the information to the authorities and encouraged him to turn himself in. Murphy then left the office. Two days later, Murphy called his probation officer and told her that he had been advised by counsel not to surrender himself to the police. The officer then procured the issuance of an arrest and detention order from the judge who had sentenced Murphy on the false imprisonment charge. On October 29, 1981, a state grand jury returned an indictment charging Murphy with first-degree murder.

Murphy sought to suppress testimony concerning his confession on the ground that it was obtained in violation of the Fifth and Fourteenth Amendments. The trial court found that he was not "in custody." . . . The Minnesota Supreme Court reversed on federal constitutional grounds. . . .

We granted certiorari to resolve a conflict among state and federal courts concerning whether a statement made by a probationer to his probation officer without prior warnings is admissible in a subsequent criminal proceeding. We now reverse.

OPINION

. . . Even a cursory comparison of custodial interrogation and probation interviews reveals the inaptness of the Minnesota Supreme Court's analogy to *Miranda*. Custodial arrest is said to convey to the suspect a message that he has no choice but to submit to the officers' will and confess. It is unlikely that a probation interview, arranged by appointment at a mutually convenient time, would give rise to a similar impression. Moreover, custodial arrest thrusts an individual into "an unfamiliar atmosphere" or "an interrogation environment . . . created for no purpose other than to subjugate the individual to the will of his examiner." Many of the psychological ploys discussed in *Miranda* capitalize on the suspect's unfamiliarity with the officers and the environment. Murphy's regular meetings with his probation officer should have served to familiarize him with her and her office and to insulate him from psychological intimidation that might overbear his desire to claim the privilege. Finally, the coercion inherent in custodial interrogation derives in large measure from an interrogator's insinuations that the interrogation will continue until a confession is obtained. Since Murphy was not physically restrained and could have left the office, any compulsion he might have felt from the possibility that terminating the meeting would have led to revocation of probation was not comparable to the pressure on a suspect who is painfully aware that he literally cannot escape a persistent custodial interrogator. . . .

DISSENT

. . . In contrast to the inherently adversarial relationship between a suspect and a policeman, the relationship between a probationer and the officer to whom he reports is likely to incorporate elements of confidentiality, even friendship. Indeed, many probation officers deliberately cultivate such bonds with their charges. The point should not be overstated; undoubtedly, few probationers are entirely blind to the fact that their probation officers are "peace officer[s], . . . allied, to a greater or lesser extent with [their] fellow peace officers." On the other hand, many probationers develop "relationship[s] of trust and cooperation" with their fellow officers. Through abuse of that trust, a probation officer can elicit admissions from a probationer that the probationer would be unlikely to make to a hostile police interrogator.

The instant case aptly illustrates the danger. Before she sent her letter to Murphy asking him to make an appointment, the probation officer had decided to try to induce him to confess to the 1974 killing and turn over that information to the police. She was aware that, if she were successful, Murphy would soon be arrested and tried for murder. There was thus no prospect whatsoever that the information she elicited would be used to design a treatment program to be followed by Murphy during the remainder of his probation. Yet, in her letter, she described the purpose of the meeting as that of "discuss[ing] a treatment plan." When Murphy arrived at the meeting, she persisted in the deceit; instead of informing him at once what she intended to do with his anticipated confession to the 1974 murder, she told him that "her main concern was to talk to him about the relationship of the prior case and the one of which he was convicted and about his need for treatment under the circumstances." . . . Only after Murphy had made his confession did the officer inform him of her intent to transmit that information to the police. In short, the environment in which the interview was conducted afforded the probation officer opportunities to reinforce and capitalize on Murphy's ignorance that he had a right to refuse to answer incriminating questions, and the officer deliberately and effectively exploited those opportunities. . . .

The criminal justice system contains safeguards that should minimize the damage done by the Court's decision today. In the future, responsible criminal defense attorneys whose clients are given probation will inform those clients, in their final interviews, that they may disregard probation conditions insofar as those conditions are inconsistent with probationers' Fifth Amendment rights. The attorney will then carefully instruct their clients on the nuances of those rights as we have now explicated them. Armed with this knowledge, few probationers will succumb to the sort of pressure and deceit that overwhelmed Murphy.

CASE DISCUSSION

Murphy pleaded guilty to a sex-related charge in a Minnesota court and was given a suspended prison sentence and placed on probation. During the course of a meeting with his probation officer, he confessed to a rape and murder. After being indicted for first-degree murder, Murphy sought to suppress the confession because it violated the Fifth and Fourteenth Amendments. The Minnesota trial court found that Murphy was not in custody and that the confession was voluntary. The Minnesota Supreme Court reversed, holding that the confession was obtained in violation of the Fifth and Fourteenth Amendments. On writ of *certiorari,* the Supreme Court reversed the Minnesota Supreme Court, holding that the Fifth and Fourteenth Amendments did not prohibit the introduction of the confession into evidence against Murphy.

Was Murphy in "custody"? How does the Court determine this? Do you agree with the dissent that lawyers should advise their probationer clients not to talk to their probation officers? Does this opinion make probation officers' job easier or more difficult? What interests does the Court promote in this decision? Would you decide the case as the majority did? or the dissent? Defend your answer.

THE MEANING OF "INTERROGATION". *Miranda* defined Fifth Amendment interrogation to mean "questioning initiated by law enforcement officers." To *initiate questioning* is a more active method than to *elicit responses,* the standard for triggering the Sixth Amendment right to counsel once judicial proceedings begin. Therefore, confronting a reluctant suspect with an incriminating ballistics report did not constitute interrogation because police did not "question" the suspect. In other words, the ballistics report elicited a response, but it did not initiate questioning. Interrogation, however, does not require a direct question, "punctuated by a question mark." It includes any statement that the "average listener" understands to "call for a response." The Supreme Court has ruled that interrogation encompasses either direct questioning or its "functional equivalent." *Rhode Island v. Innis* addresses this question.[24]

CASE

Did the officers question the suspect?

Rhode Island v. Innis

446 U.S. 291, 100 S.Ct. 1682, 64 L.Ed.2d 297 (1980)

[Stewart, J., delivered the opinion of the court, in which White, Blackmun, Powell, and Rehnquist, JJ., joined. White, J., filed a concurring opinion. Burger, C.J., filed an opinion concurring in the judgment. Marshall, J., filed a dissenting opinion.]

FACTS

. . . Patrolman Lovell . . . arrested the respondent, who was unarmed, and advised him of his so-called *Miranda* rights. While the two men waited in a patrol car for other police officers to arrive, Patrolman Lovell did not converse with the respondent other than to respond to the latter's request for a cigarette.

Within minutes, Sergeant Sears arrived at the scene of the arrest, and he also gave the respondent the *Miranda* warnings. Immediately thereafter, Captain Leyden and other police officers arrived. Captain Leyden advised the respondent of his *Miranda* rights. The respondent stated that he understood those rights and wanted to speak with a lawyer. Captain Leyden then directed that the respondent be placed in a "caged wagon," a four-door police car with a wire screen mesh between the front and rear seats, and be driven to the central police station. Three officers, Patrolmen Gleckman, Williams, and McKenna, were assigned to accompany the respondent to the central station. They placed the respondent in the vehicle and shut the doors. Captain Leyden then instructed the officers not to question the respondent or intimidate or coerce him in any way. The three officers then entered the vehicle, and it departed.

While en route to the central station, Patrolman Gleckman initiated a conversation with Patrolman McKenna concerning the missing shotgun. As Patrolman Gleckman later testified:

> "A. At this point, I was talking back and forth with Patrolman McKenna stating that I frequent this area while on patrol and [that because a school for handicapped children is located nearby,] there's a lot of handicapped children running around in this area, and God forbid one of them might find a weapon with shells and they might hurt themselves."

Patrolman McKenna apparently shared his fellow officer's concern:

> "A. I more or less concurred with him [Gleckman] that it was a safety factor and that we should, you know, continue to search for the weapon and try to find it."

While Patrolman Williams said nothing, he overheard the conversation between the two officers:

> "A. He [Gleckman] said it would be too bad if the little—I believe he said girl—would pick up the the gun, maybe kill herself."

The respondent then interrupted the conversation, stating that the officers should turn the car around so he could show them where the gun was located. At this point, Patrolman McKenna radioed back to Captain Leyden that they were returning to the scene of the arrest, and that the respondent would inform them of the location of the gun. At the time the respondent indicated that the officers should turn back, they had traveled no more than a mile, a trip encompassing only a few minutes.

The police vehicle then returned to the scene of the arrest where a search for the shotgun was in progress. There, Captain Leyden again advised the respondent of his *Miranda* rights. The respondent replied that he understood those rights but that he "wanted to get the gun out of the way because of the kids in the area in the school." The respondent then led the police to a nearby field, where he pointed out the shotgun under some rocks by the side of the road.

On March 20, 1975, a grand jury returned an indictment charging the respondent with the kidnapping, robbery, and murder of John Mulvaney. Before the trial, the respondent moved to suppress the shotgun and the statements he had made to the police regarding it . . . [T]he trial court sustained the admissibility of the shotgun and testimony related to its discovery. That evidence was later introduced at the respondent's trial, and the jury returned a verdict of guilty on all counts. On appeal, the Rhode Island Supreme Court, in a 3–2 decision, set aside the respondent's conviction. . . . We granted certiorari to address for the first time the meaning of "interrogation" under *Miranda v. Arizona*.

OPINION

. . . It is clear . . . that the special procedural safeguards outlined in *Miranda* are required not where a suspect is simply taken into custody, but rather where a suspect in custody is subjected to interrogation. "Interrogation," as conceptualized in the *Miranda* opinion, must reflect a measure of compulsion above and beyond that inherent in custody itself.

We conclude that the *Miranda* safeguards come into play whenever a person in custody is subjected to either express questioning or its functional equivalent. That is to say, the term "interrogation" under *Miranda* refers not only to express questioning, but also to any words or actions on the part of the police . . that the police should know are reasonably likely to elicit an incriminating response from the suspect. . . .

. . . [W]e conclude that the respondent was not "interrogated" within the meaning of *Miranda*. It is undisputed that the first prong of the definition of "interrogation" was not satisfied, for the conversation between Patrolmen Gleckman and McKenna included no express questioning of the respondent. Rather, that conversation was, at least in form, nothing more than a dialogue between the two officers to which no response from the respondent was invited.

Moreover, it cannot be fairly concluded that the respondent was subjected to the "functional equivalent" of questioning. It cannot be said, in short, that Patrolmen Gleckman and McKenna should have known that their conversation was reasonably likely to elicit an incriminating response from the respondent. There is nothing in the record to suggest that the officers were aware that the respondent was peculiarly susceptible to an appeal to his conscience concerning the safety of handicapped children. Nor is there anything in the record to suggest that the police knew that the respondent was unusually disoriented or upset at the time of his arrest.

The case thus boils down to whether, in the context of a brief conversation, the officers should have known that the respondent would suddenly be moved to make a self-incriminating response. Given the fact that the entire conversation appears to have consisted of no more than a few offhand remarks, we cannot say that the officers should have known that it was reasonably likely that Innis would so respond. This is not a case where the police carried on a lengthy harangue in the presence of the suspect. . . .

For the reasons stated, the judgement of the Supreme Court of Rhode Island is vacated, and the case is remanded to that court for further proceedings not inconsistent with this opinion.

It is so ordered.

DISSENT

Mr. Justice Marshall, with whom Mr. Justice Brennan joins, dissenting.

I am utterly at a loss . . . to understand how . . . the facts before us can rationally lead to the conclusion that there was no interrogation. Innis was arrested at 4:30 a.m., handcuffed, searched, advised of his rights, and placed in the back seat of a patrol car. Within a short time he had been twice more advised of his rights and driven away in a four-door sedan with three police officers. . . .

One can scarcely imagine a stronger appeal to the conscience of a suspect—*any* suspect—than the assertion that if the weapon is not found an innocent person will be hurt or killed. And not just any innocent person, but an innocent child—a little girl—a helpless, handicapped little girl on her way to school. The notion that such an appeal could not be expected to have any effect unless the suspect were known to have some special interest in handicapped children verges on the ludicrous. . . .

Gleckman's remarks would obviously constituted interrogation if they had been explicitly directed to respondent, and the result should not be different because they were nominally addressed to McKenna. This is not a case where police officers speaking among themselves are accidentally overhead by a suspect. These officers were "talking back and forth" in close quarters with the handcuffed suspect, traveling past the very place where they believed the weapon was located. . . .

Mr. Justice Stevens, dissenting.

. . . The court's assumption that criminal suspects are not susceptible to appeals to conscience is directly contrary to the teachings of police interrogation manuals, which recommend appealing to a suspect's sense of morality as a standard and often successful interrogation technique. Surely the practical experience embodied in such manuals should not be ignored in a case such as this in which the record is devoid of any evidence—one way or the other—as to the susceptibility of suspects in general or of Innis in particular.

CASE DISCUSSION

A grand jury indicted Innis with kidnapping, robbery, and murder. Before the trial, Innis moved to suppress his incriminating statements and a shotgun as evidence. The trial judge denied his motion. On appeal, the Rhode Island Supreme Court in a 3–2 decision set aside the conviction, holding that the police had unlawfully interrogated Innis. On a writ of *certiorari*, the United States Supreme Court vacated the Rhode Island's Supreme Court and remanded the case for further proceedings consistent with the United States Supreme Court's holding that although he was interrogated, Innis's statements may not have resulted from police "words or actions . . . that they should have known were reasonably likely to elicit an incriminating response."

What do you think the police officers' motives were in discussing the gun's location? Do you agree with the Court that their motives are irrelevant? Do you agree that there was no compulsion in this case? Should the police have known that their words or actions were "likely to elicit an incriminating response" form Brewer? Is the majority more interested in result? Or does it properly balance result and other interests? What other interests?

WAIVER UNDER *MIRANDA.* Despite fears that *Miranda* "hand-cuffs the police," virtually all defendants waive their rights and confess after police give the warnings. Hence, what constitutes a valid waiver and a voluntary confession become crucial in most cases. *Miranda* permits the police to question suspects while in custody if suspects "knowingly and intelligently waived . . . [their] privilege against self-incrimination and . . . [their] right to retained or appointed counsel." However, if "individual[s] indicate in any manner, at any time prior to or during questioning, that [t]he[y] wish to remain silent, the interrogation must cease," because they have "shown that [t]he[y] intend to exercise [their] . . . Fifth Amendment privilege."

Mere silence does not constitute waiver. However, in *North Carolina v. Butler,* a 6–3 decision in which a vigorous dissent argued that the Supreme Court should adopt a "simple prophylactic rule requiring police to obtain an express waiver," the majority nonetheless ruled:

> An express written or oral statement of waiver of the right to remain silent or of the right to counsel is usually strong proof of the validity of that waiver, but is not inevitably either necessary or sufficient to establish waiver. The question is not one of form, but rather whether the defendant in fact knowingly and voluntarily waived the rights delineated in the *Miranda* case. As was unequivocally said in *Miranda,* mere silence is not enough. That does not mean that the defendant's silence, coupled with an understanding of his rights and a course of conduct indicating waiver, may never support a conclusion that a defendant did not waive his rights. The courts must presume that a defendant did not waive his rights; the prosecution's burden is great; but in at least some cases waiver can be clearly inferred from the actions and words of the person interrogated.[25]

In determining whether suspects "knowingly and voluntarily" waive their Fifth Amendment right, the courts consider a variety of factors that make up the totality of circumstances surrounding the alleged waiver. They include age, education, whether suspects gave an explicit waiver, language barriers, whether suspects initiated contact with the police, suspects' prior experience with the criminal justice system, and suspects' physical condition. The Supreme Court dealt with waiver in *Moran v. Burbine.*[26]

CASE

Did he waive his Miranda *rights?*

Moran v. Burbine

475 U.S. 412, 106 S.Ct. 1135, 89 L.Ed.2d 410 (1986)

[O'Connor, J., delivered the opinion of the Court, in which Burger, C.J., and White, Blackmun, Powell, and Rehnquist, JJ., joined. Stevens, J., filed a dissenting opinion, in which Brennan and Marshall, JJ., joined.]

FACTS

On the morning of March 3, 1977, Mary Jo Hickey was found unconscious in a factory parking lot in Providence, Rhode Island. Suffering from injuries to her skull apparently inflicted by a metal pipe found at the scene, she was rushed to a nearby hospital. Three weeks later she died from her wounds.

Several months after her death, the Cranston, Rhode Island police arrested respondent and two others in connection with a local burglary. Shortly before the arrest, Detective Ferranti of the Cranston police force had learned from a confidential informant that the man responsible for Ms. Hickey's death lived at a certain address and went by the name of "Butch." Upon discovering that respondent lived at that address and was known by that name, Detective Ferranti informed respondent of his *Miranda* rights. When respondent refused to execute a written waiver, Detective Ferranti spoke separately with the two other suspects arrested on the breaking and entering charge and obtained statements further implicating respondent in Ms. Hickey's murder. At approximately 6 p.m., Detective Ferranti telephoned the police in Providence to convey the information he had uncovered. An hour later, three officers from that department arrived at the Cranston headquarters for the purpose of questioning respondent about the murder. . . .

At 8:15 p.m., Ms. Munson, [a public defender,] telephoned the Cranston police station and asked that her call be transferred to the detective division. In the words of the Supreme Court of Rhode Island, . . . the conversation proceeded as follows:

> "A male voice responded with the word 'Detectives.' Ms. Munson identified herself and asked if Brian Burbine was being held; the person responded affirmatively. Ms. Munson explained to the person that Burbine was represented by attorney Casparian who was not available; she further stated that she would act as Burbine's legal counsel in the event that the police intended to place him in a lineup or question him. The unidentified person told Ms. Munson that the police would not be questioning Burbine or putting him in a lineup and that they were through with him for the night. Ms. Munson was not informed

that the Providence Police were at the Cranston police station or that Burbine was a suspect in Mary's murder." *State v. Burbine,* 451 A.2d 22, 23–24 (1982).

At all relevant times, respondent was unaware of . . . the fact and contents of Ms. Munson's telephone conversation.

Less than an hour later, the police brought respondent to an interrogation room and conducted the first of a series of interviews concerning the murder. Prior to each session, respondent was informed of his *Miranda* rights, and on three separate occasions he signed a written form acknowledging that he understood his right to the presence of an attorney and explicitly indicating that he ''[did] not want an attorney called or appointed for [him]'' before he gave a statement. Uncontradicted evidence at the suppression hearing indicated that at least twice during the course of the evening, respondent signed three written statements fully admitting to the murder.

Prior to the trial, respondent moved to suppress the statements. The court denied the motion, finding that respondent had received the *Miranda* warnings and had ''knowingly, intelligently, and voluntarily waived his privilege against self-incrimination [and] his right to counsel.'' . . .

The jury found respondent guilty of murder in the first degree, and he appealed to the Supreme Court of Rhode Island. A divided court . . . affirmed the conviction. . . . After unsuccessfully petitioning the United States District Court for the District of Rhode Island for a writ of habeas corpus, respondent appealed to the Court of Appeals for the First Circuit. That court reversed. . . .

We granted certiorari to decide whether a prearraignment confession preceded by an otherwise valid waiver must be suppressed either because the police misinformed an inquiring attorney about their plans concerning the suspect or the attorney's efforts to reach him. We now reverse.

OPINION

. . . *Miranda* holds that ''[t]he defendant may waive effectuation'' of the rights conveyed in the warnings ''provided the waiver is made voluntarily, knowingly, and intelligently.'' The inquiry has two distinct dimensions. First, the relinquishment of the right must have been voluntary in the sense that it was the product of a free and deliberate choice rather than intimidation, coercion, or deception. Second, the waiver must have been made with a full awareness both of the nature of the right being abandoned and the consequences of the decision to abandon it. Only if the ''totality of the circumstances surrounding the interrogation'' reveals both an uncoerced choice and the requisite level of comprehension may a court properly conclude that the *Miranda* rights have been waived.

Under this standard, we have no doubt that respondent validly waived his right to remain silent and to the presence of counsel. The voluntariness of the waiver is not at issue. As the Court of Appeals correctly acknowledged, the record is devoid of any suggestion that police resorted to physical or psychological pressure to elicit the statements. Indeed it appears that it was respondent, and not the police, who spontaneously initiated the conversation that led to the first and most damaging confession. Nor is there any question about respondent's comprehension of the full panoply of rights set out in the *Miranda* warnings and of the potential consequences of a decision to relinquish them. Nonetheless, the Court of Appeals believed that the "[d]eliberate or reckless" conduct of the police, in particular their failure to inform respondent of the telephone call, fatally undermined the validity of the otherwise proper waiver. We find this conclusion untenable as a matter of both logic and precedent. . . .

We hold therefore that the Court of Appeals erred in finding that the Federal Constitution required the exclusion of the three inculpatory statements. Accordingly, we reverse and remand for proceedings consistent with this opinion.

So ordered.

DISSENT

Justice Stevens, with whom Justice Brennan and Justice Marshall join, dissenting.

This case poses fundamental questions about our system of justice. As this Court has long recognized, and reaffirmed only weeks ago, "ours is an accusatorial and not an inquisitorial system." *Miller v. Fenton,* 474 U.S. 104, 110, 106 S.Ct. 445, 449, 88 L.Ed.2d 405 (1985). The Court's opinion today represents a startling departure from that basic insight.

The Court concludes that the police may deceive an attorney by giving her false information about whether her client will be questioned, and that the police may deceive a suspect by failing to inform him of his attorney's communications and efforts to represent him. For the majority, this conclusion, though "distaste[ful]," is not even debatable. The deception of the attorney is irrelevant because the attorney has no right to information, accuracy, honesty, or fairness in the police response to her questions about her client. The deception of the client is acceptable, because, although the information would affect the client's assertion of his rights, the client's actions in ignorance of the availability of his attorney are voluntary, knowing, and intelligent; additionally, society's interest in apprehending, prosecuting, and punishing criminals outweighs the suspect's interest in information regarding his attorney's efforts to communicate with him. Finally, even mendacious police interference in the communications between a suspect and his lawyer does not violate any notion of fundamental fairness because it does not shock the conscience of the majority.

The murder of Mary Jo Hickey was a vicious crime, fully meriting a sense of outrage and a desire to find and prosecute the perpetrator swiftly and effectively. Indeed, by the time Burbine was arrested on an unrelated breaking-and-entering charge, the Hickey murder had been the subject of a local television special. Not surprisingly, Detective Ferranti, the Cranston detective who "broke" the case, was rewarded with a special commendation for his efforts.

The recognition that ours is an accusatorial, and not an inquisitorial system nevertheless requires that the government's actions, even in responding to this brutal crime, respect those liberties and rights that distinguish this society from most others. As Justice Jackson observed shortly after his return from

Nuremberg, cases of this kind present "a real dilemma in a free society . . . for the defendant is shielded by such safeguards as no system of law except the Anglo-American concedes to him." Justice Frankfurter similarly emphasized that it is "a fair summary of history to say that the safeguards of liberty have been forged in controversies involving not very nice people." And, almost a century and a half ago, Macaulay observed that the guilt of Titus Oates could not justify his conviction by improper methods: "That Oats was a bad man is not a sufficient excuse; for the guilty are almost always the first to suffer those hardships which are afterwards used as precedents against the innocent."

The Court's holding focuses on the period after a suspect has been taken into custody and before he has been charged with an offense. The core of the Court's holding is that police interference with an attorney's access to her client during that period is not unconstitutional. The Court reasons that a State has a compelling interest, not simply in custodial interrogation, but in lawyer-free, incommunicado custodial interrogation. Such incommunicado interrogation is so important that a lawyer may be given false information that prevents her presence and representation; it is so important that police may refuse to inform a suspect of his attorney's communications and immediate availability. This conclusion flies in the face of this Court's repeated expressions of deep concern about incommunicado questioning. Until today, incommunicado questioning has been viewed with the strictest scrutiny by this Court; today, incommunicado questioning is embraced as a societal goal of the highest order that justifies police deception of the shabbiest kind. . . .

CASE DISCUSSION

After being informed of his *Miranda* rights, and after a series of written waivers, Burbine confessed to murdering a young woman. Prior to trial, Burbine moved to suppress the confession. The court denied his motion, Burbine was tried and convicted of murder in the first degree. He appealed to the Rhode Island Supreme Court. A divided court rejected Burbine's Fifth and Fourteenth Amendment claims and affirmed. After unsuccessfully petitioning the district court for a writ of *habeas corpus*, Burbine appealed to the court of appeals. The court held that the confession was obtained in violation of the Fifth and Fourteenth Amendments. On writ of *certiorari*, the United States Supreme Court reversed, holding that Burbine's Fifth and Fourteenth Amendment rights were not violated.

Why should there be a problem with Burbine's confession? He received warnings, he signed a waiver, and he confessed without coercion. What interests would the dissent's view of the case promote? Does the crime he committed matter? One homicide detective said recently, "We don't pressure third- degree burglars; we save our efforts for the violent crimes." Should the standard be different for violent crimes? Why?

VOLUNTARINESS AND *MIRANDA*. Until the 1940s, courts excluded coerced confessions because they were not trustworthy, that is, they were probably not true. Due to their lack of trustworthiness, admitting them as evidence undermined the interest in accurate fact-finding; coerced confessions might convict the innocent. Since then, Supreme Court opinions have suggested that protecting two other interests mandate excluding involuntary confessions: controlling offensive police conduct, and excluding evidence simply because coercion produced it. In *Ashcraft v. Tennessee*, for example, the Court excluded a confession secured after thirty-six hours of continual questioning, not only to eliminate untrustworthy evidence from the particular case, but also to condemn police methods that a majority of the Court "conceived as generally dangerous and subject to serious abuse."[27]

Justice Frankfurter summed up the process interests lying behind the voluntariness requirement:

> Our decisions under [the Fourteenth Amendment] have made clear that convictions following the admission . . . of confessions which are involuntary, i.e., the product of coercion, either physical or psychological, cannot stand. This is so not because such confessions are unlikely to be true but because the methods used to extract them offend an underlying principle in the enforcement of our criminal law: that ours is an accusatorial and not an inquisitorial system—a system in which the State must establish guilt by evidence independently and freely secured and may not by coercion prove its charge against an accused out of his own mouth. To be sure, confessions cruelly extorted may be and have been . . . found to be untrustworthy. But the constitutional principle of excluding confessions that are involuntary does not rest on this consideration. Indeed, in many of the cases in which the command of the Due Process clause has compelled us to reverse . . . convictions involving the use of confessions obtained by impermissible methods, independent corroborating evidence left little doubt of the truth of what the defendant had confessed.[28]

Therefore, assuming that police give suspects in custody the required *Miranda* warnings, and that suspects knowingly and voluntarily waive their Fifth and Sixth Amendment rights, the Fourteenth Amendment's due process clause mandates that courts admit only voluntary incriminating statements or confessions of guilt. Hence, administering the *Miranda* warnings and securing effective waivers are necessary, but not sufficient, to satisfy the Fifth Amendment; incriminating statements must also be voluntary. The Court has adopted a totality-of-circumstances test to determine the voluntariness of statements made in custody after effective waivers. Some circumstances the Court found to demonstrate involuntary confessions, include

(1) use or threatened use of force;

(2) stripping off defendant's clothes, keeping him naked for several hours;[29]

(3) informing defendant that the state would cut off aid from her children and take them away from her;[30]

(4) pretending to bring defendant's wife who suffered from arthritis to the station;[31]

(5) removing defendant from jail to a distant and remote place to keep his friends and relatives from securing is release.[32]

Decision Point

On August 18, 1983, Francis Connelly approached a uniformed Denver police officer and began confessing to a murder. Taken aback by these statements, the officer asked Connelly if he had ever undergone therapy for a mental disorder. Connelly responded that he had. The officer gave Connelly the *Miranda* warnings, after which Connelly continued to give details of the murder. After Connelly offered to show the police where the murder took place, the Denver police held him overnight. The next morning Connelly became visibly disoriented, and spoke of voices that ordered him to come to Denver to confess to the murder. At the trial, a state hospital psychiatrist testified that Connelly had been in a psychotic state the day before he confessed and suffered from chronic schizophrenia. Connelly had told the psychiatrist that the "voice of God" told him that he had either to confess or commit suicide.

Was the confession voluntary? Both the trial court and the Colorado Supreme Court said no. In *Colorado v. Connelly*, the United States Supreme Court ruled that the confession was admissible. For the Court majority, Chief Justice Rehnquist held that some form of police coercion is absolutely essential to violate due process on the grounds of an involuntary confession. In other words, although the totality of circumstances surrounding confessions are relevant to determine voluntariness, police coercion stands as a necessary circumstance in a finding of involuntariness.[33]

The Supreme Court recently reaffirmed the totality-of-circumstances test in *Miller v. Fenton*. After reaffirming the test, the Supreme Court remanded the case for application of the test. The excerpt from the court of appeals following the remand applies the totality-of- circumstances test to the case.[34]

CASE

Did Boyce coerce Miller into confessing?

Miller v. Fenton

796 F.2d 598 (3d Cir. 1986)

FACTS

A significant portion of the questioning was in the typical police interrogation mode, developing chronologically Miller's whereabouts on the day in question, confronting him with the identification of his car, asking him point-blank whether he committed the crime, challenging his answers, and attempting to discover the details of the crime. This element of the interrogation is unexceptionable and unchallenged. We shall therefore focus primarily on the features of the interrogation that are at issue.

It is clear that Boyce made no threats and engaged in no physical coercion of Miller. To the contrary, throughout the interview, Detective Boyce assumed a friendly, understanding manner and spoke in a soft tone of voice. He repeatedly assured Miller that he was sympathetic to him and wanted to help him unburden his mind. . . . The Detective's statements of sympathy at times approached the maudlin: Boyce: Now listen to me, Frank. This hurts me more than it hurts you, because I love people. . . .

Boyce: Let it come out, Frank. I'm here, I'm here with you now. I'm on your side, I'm on your side, Frank. I'm your brother, you and I are brothers, Frank. We are brothers and I want to help my brother. . . .

Boyce also gave Miller certain factual information, some of which was untrue. At the beginning of the interrogation, for example, Boyce informed Miller that the victim was still alive; this was false. During the interview, Boyce told Miller that Ms. Margolin had just died, although in fact she had been found dead several hours earlier.

Detective Boyce's major theme throughout the interrogation was that whoever had committed such a heinous crime had mental problems and was desperately in need of psychological treatment. From early in the interview, Detective Boyce led Miller to understand that he believed that Miller had committed the crime and that Miller now needed a friend to whom he could unburden himself. The Detective stated several times that Miller was not a criminal who should be punished, but a sick individual who should receive help. . . .

Boyce: [L]et's forget this incident, [l]et's talk about your problem. This is what, this is what I'm concerned with, Frank, your problem.

Miller: Right.

Boyce: If I had a problem like your problem, I would want you to help me with my problem.

Miller: Uh, huh. . . .

Boyce: You can see it Frank, you can feel it, you can feel it but you are not responsible. This is what I'm trying to tell you, but you've got to come forward and tell me. Don't, don't, don't let it eat you up, don't, don't fight it. You've got to rectify it, Frank. We've got to get together on this thing or I, I mean really, you need help, you need proper help, and you know it, my God, you know, in God's name, you, you, you know it. You are not a criminal, you are not a criminal.

Boyce also appealed to Miller's conscience and described the importance of Miller's purging himself of the memories that must be haunting him. . . .

Boyce: First thing we have to do is let it all come out. Don't fight it because it's worse, Frank, it's worse. It's hurting me because I feel it. I feel it wanting to come out, but it's hurting me, Frank.

When Miller at last confessed, he collapsed in a state of shock. He slid off his chair and onto the floor with a blank stare on his face. The police officers sent for a first aid squad that took him to the hospital. . . .

OPINION

The sole question before this Court is whether Miller's confession was voluntary. . . .

It is well established that an involuntary confession may result from psychological, as well as physical, coercion. . . .

As the Supreme Court has noted, "[t]he line between proper and permissible police conduct and techniques and methods offensive to due process is, at best, a difficult one to draw, particularly in cases such as this where it is necessary to make fine judgments as to the effect of psychologically coercive pressures and inducements on the mind and will of an accused." . . .

To determine the voluntariness of a confession, the court must consider the effect that the totality of the circumstances had upon the will of the defendant. . . .

Factors to be considered include: the youth of the accused; his lack of education or his low intelligence; the lack of any advice to the accused of his constitutional rights; the length of detention; the repeated and prolonged nature of questioning; and the use of physical punishment such as the deprivation of food or sleep. . . .

We emphasize that the test for voluntariness is not a but-for test: we do not ask whether the confession would have been made in the absence of the interrogation. Few criminals feel impelled to confess to the police purely of their own accord, without any questioning at all. . . .

Thus, it can almost always be said that the interrogation caused the confession.

Moreover, it is generally recognized that police may use some psychological tactics in eliciting a statement from a suspect. . . .

A "totality of the circumstances" inquiry defies strictly analytic treatment. We cannot reach a conclusion simply by scrutinizing each circumstance separately, for the concept underlying the phrase "totality of the circumstances" is that the whole is somehow distinct from the sum of the parts. . . . Nevertheless, we can understand the totality only after reviewing the constituent elements of the situation. . . .

1. Miller's Background

Miller is a mature adult, thirty-two years of age. He is of normal intelligence and has some high school education. Such a person is more resistant to interrogation than a person who is very young, uneducated, or weak-minded. . . .

Moreover, Miller had had previous experience with the criminal system; indeed, he had served a jail sentence. Thus, he was aware of the consequences of confessing. In addition to this experience, he received *Miranda* warnings. . . .

2. The Length of the Interrogation

Detective Boyce's interrogation of Miller lasted less than an hour. . . . It is thus distinguishable from the lengthy interrogations during incommunicado detention that have been held to result in involuntary confessions. . . .

3. Boyce's Friendly Approach

Boyce's supportive, encouraging manner was an interrogation tactic aimed at winning Miller's trust and making him feel comfortable about confessing.

Excessive friendliness on the part of an interrogator can be deceptive. In some instances, in combination with other tactics, it might create an atmosphere in which a suspect forgets that his questioner is in an adversarial role, and thereby prompt admissions that the suspect would ordinarily make only to a friend, not to police. . . .

Nevertheless, the "good guy" approach is recognized as a permissible interrogation tactic. . . . Moreover, the Supreme Court has indicated that a sympathetic attitude on the part of the interrogator is not in itself enough to render a confession involuntary. . . . Only if other aspects of the interrogation strengthened the illusion that it was non-adversarial in character could Miller's confession have been involuntary because of psychological coercion.

4. *Boyce's Lie*

While a lie told to the detainee about an important aspect of the case may affect the voluntariness of the confession, the effect of the lie must be analyzed in the context of all the circumstances of the interrogation. . . . We do not believe that the lie about the time of Ms. Margolin's death, by itself, constituted sufficient trickery to overcome Miller's will. . . . We therefore conclude that any pathos or remorse he might have felt was not particularly strong.

5. *Boyce's Promises*

Detective Boyce's statements that Miller was not a criminal, but rather a mentally ill individual not responsible for his actions, and Boyce's promises to help Miller raise a more serious question about the voluntariness of Miller's confession. By telling Miller that he was not responsible for anything he might have done, Boyce may have been understood to be making an implied promise to Miller that Miller would not be prosecuted, or that if he were prosecuted Boyce would aid him in presenting the insanity defense. Similarly, the promises of psychiatric help might have suggested to Miller that he would be treated, rather than prosecuted. If these promises, implicit and explicit, tricked Miller into confessing, his confession may have been involuntary. . . . Miller was questioned less than an hour and was not suffering from lack of sleep or any other physical ailment. The promise of help with his supposed mental problem thus did not have the urgent appeal that a promise of help with acute physical pain would have. Any promise or prosecutorial leniency was made only by implication.

6. *Effect of the Totality of the Circumstances*

In determining whether the circumstances described above indicate that Miller's confession was involuntary, we must consider whether Boyce's tactics were sufficiently manipulative to overbear the will of a person with Miller's characteristics . . . a significant portion of the questioning was in the typical police interrogation mode, developing chronologically Miller's whereabouts on the day in question, confronting him with the identification of his car, asking him point-blank as to whether he committed the crime, challenging his answers, and attempting to discover the details of the crime. This portion of the interrogation would not have an effect upon Miller's will. Moreover, the interrogation did not last very long, and Miller was not suffering from any painful ailment or physical deprivation that would impel him to confess in order to be released from the questioning room. Nor did Miller seek the presence of any other person or, indeed, make any request that was denied. . . . While Boyce's promises of psychiatric help and statements that Miller was "not a criminal," in combination with his friendly manner, may have been a form of psychological trickery, we do not believe that these elements of the interrogation affected the voluntariness of the confession. . . . personal characteristics, . . , support a conclusion that the confession was voluntary, for Miller does not seem to be the type of person whose will would be easily overborne by Boyce's remarks. Miller's age, intelligence, and experience rendered him resistant to the level of persuasiveness that Boyce employed.

Moreover, throughout the interview, Miller made remarks that indicate that he knew that this was an ordinary police interrogation, rather than an encounter with a compassionate friend, and that he was aware that a confession would result in criminal prosecution and possibly in conviction and sentence. Throughout the session, he appears to have retained a suspicious, guarded attitude. At one point, when detective Boyce asked him if he wanted help, Miller replied, "Yes, uh, huh, yes, but yet I'm, I'm not going to admit something that, that I wasn't involved in." In reply to the statement, "I don't think you're a criminal, Frank," Miller said, "No, but you're trying to make me one." . . . Indeed, from the tape of the interrogation, it clearly appears that the precipitating cause of Miller's confession was a desire to make a clean breast of it, rather than a reliance on any promises of leniency or psychiatric help. He expressed the reservation that "this is going to kill my father." Thereupon, Detective Boyce made a speech about the importance of truthfulness both for himself and his family. Miller capitulated immediately thereafter. Apparently, he took Boyce's words to heart and decided that it would be better for all concerned if he told the truth.

The dissent states that we do not make much of Miller's collapse. However, we recognize the possibility that the human psyche, upon being released from the terrible burden of concealing such a heinous crime, might well react just as Miller's did after a confession.

We have little doubt that Detective Boyce's encouraging words, perhaps in combination with the sad announcement that the victim has just died, helped Miller to reach his decision to unburden himself. However, the test for voluntariness is not a but-for test, but a question of whether the confession was a product of free choice. . . .

Detective Boyce's method of interrogation might have overborne the will of another detainee, for example, a young, inexperienced person of lower intelligence than Miller, or a person suffering from a painful physical ailment. It might have overcome the will of Miller himself if the interrogation had been longer or if Miller had been refused food, sleep, or contact with a person he wished to see. Moreover, if Miller had made remarks that indicated that he truly believed that the state would treat him leniently because he was "not responsible" for what he had done or that he believed that he would receive psychiatric help rather than punishment, we might not find the confession voluntary. We hold simply that, under the totality of the circumstances of this case, the confession was voluntarily given. . . .

DISSENT

Gibbons, Circuit Judge, dissenting:

. . . [A]n interrogation that has no investigative purpose and is used only as a means of obtaining a confession, is anything but unexceptional. In this case the interrogation of Miller had no purpose other than obtaining admissions that could be used to charge Miller with felony murder. Such an interrogation requires the closest scrutiny.

For me, . . . the most significant circumstance in this case supporting the conclusion that Miller's admission was obtained in a manner inconsistent with the Constitution is the complete absence of any legitimate investigative purpose for the interrogation. The circumstances of this case provide a classic illustration of the once common practice of obtaining guilty pleas in the back rooms of police stations rather than in open court. . . .

Every word, every nuance of expression, every change in tone of voice, was calculated toward one end, and one end only—obtaining an admission of guilt. From the tone of the majority opinion one might believe that its author actually credits these deceptive expressions of sympathy. . . .

The admissions, which came during the last eleven minutes, were the product of Boyce's factual misstatements about the investigation, misrepresentations about his intentions, and false promises. . . .

. . . [A]pproximately thirty minutes into the second interrogation, Miller made his first incriminating statement. By far the largest part of that thirty minutes is comprised of lies and promises by Boyce. The majority's suggestion that these lies and promises had no effect upon Miller's will is utter speculation.

. . . Incredibly, the only reference in the majority's opinion to Miller's collapse is the cryptic sentence . . . "One hour into the interrogation, Miller confessed to the murder of Deborah Margolin, then passed out." . . . The majority does not even recognize Miller's collapse into a catatonic state and his transportation to a hospital as relevant circumstances in its totality of the circumstances analysis! . . . How can it be honestly represented that he was suffering from no mental or physical illness?

The judges in the majority, determined at any cost to reach the end that no relief will be given to a person they feel to be the perpetrator of a heinous offense, have distorted the record and misstated the law with respect to permissible police methods of interrogation. I share their obvious abhorrence of Mr. Miller's offense. It is well, however, to recall Justice Frankfurter's admonition that "law triumphs when the natural impulses aroused by a shocking crime yield to safeguards which our civilization has evolved for an administration of criminal justice at once rational and effective." . . . The majority has yielded to the natural impulses rather than to the safeguards that the law has imposed to restrain abusive methods of interrogation. I dissent.

CASE DISCUSSION

Miller, convicted of murder, petitioned for a writ of *habeas corpus*. The district court denied the writ and Miller appealed to the circuit court. The court of appeals affirmed. Miller petitioned the United States Supreme Court for a writ of *certiorari*. The Supreme Court reversed and remanded the case.On remand to the court of appeals, the circuit court held that Miller's confession was voluntary.

Exactly what circumstances did the court take into account to determine whether or not Miller's confession was voluntary? Do you agree with the court's conclusion? How does the court define coercion? Would you use the same definition? What interests would you promote in your definition, and how would your decision in this case reflect those interests?

THE PUBLIC SAFETY EXCEPTION TO *MIRANDA*. In at least one circumstance, incriminating statements made during custodial interrogation do not violate the Fifth Amendment, despite police failure to give the *Miranda* warnings and absent suspects' effective waiver. If "a threat to the general public outweighs the need for the prophylactic rule protecting Fifth Amendment privilege against self-incrimination," the police need not give suspects the *Miranda* warnings. The Supreme Court formulated this **public safety exception** in *New York v. Quarles*.

CASE

Did public safety justify not giving the Miranda warnings?

New York v. Quarles

467 U.S. 649, 104 S.Ct. 2626, 81 L.Ed.2d 550 (1984)

[Rehnquist, J., delivered the opinion of the Court, in which Burger, C.J., and White, Blackmun, and Powell, JJ., joined. O'Connor, J., filed an opinion concurring in the judgment in part and dissenting in part, Marshall, J., filed a dissenting opinion in which Brennan and Stevens, JJ., joined.]

FACTS

Respondent Benjamin Quarles was charged in the New York trial court with criminal possession of a weapon. The trial court suppressed the gun in question, and a statement made by respondent, because the statement was obtained by police before they read respondent his "*Miranda* rights." That ruling was affirmed on appeal through the New York Court of Appeals. We granted certiorari, and we now reverse. We conclude that under the circumstances involved in this case, overriding considerations of public safety justify the officer's failure to provide *Miranda* warnings before he asked questions devoted to locating the abandoned weapon.

FACTS

On September 11, 1980, at approximately 12:30 a.m., Officer Frank Kraft and Officer Sal Scarring were on road patrol in Queens, N.Y., when a young woman approached their car. She told them that she had just been raped by a black male, approximately six feet tall, who was wearing a black jacket with the name "Big Ben" printed in yellow letters on the back. She told the officers that the man had just entered an A & P supermarket located nearby and that the man was carrying a gun.

The officers drove the woman to the supermarket, and Officer Kraft entered the store while Officer Scaring radioed for assistance. Officer Kraft quickly spotted respondent, who matched the description given by the woman, approaching a checkout counter. Apparently upon seeing the officer, respondent turned and ran toward the rear of the store, and Officer Kraft pursued him with a drawn gun. When respondent turned the corner at the end of the aisle, Officer Kraft lost sight of him for several seconds, and upon regaining sight of respondent, ordered him to stop and put his hands over his head.

Although more than three other officers had arrived on the scene by that time, Officer Kraft was the first to reach respondent. He frisked him and discovered that he was wearing a shoulder holster which was then empty. After handcuffing him, Officer Kraft asked him where the gun was. Respondent nodded in the direction of some empty cartons and responded, "the gun is over there." Officer Kraft thereafter retrieved a loaded .38- caliber revolver from one of the cartons, formally placed respondent under arrest, and read him his *Miranda* rights from a printed card. Respondent indicated that he would be willing to answer questions without an attorney present. Officer Kraft then asked respondent if he owned the gun and where he had purchased it. Respondent answered that he did own it and that he had purchased it in Miami, Fla.

In the subsequent prosecution of respondent for criminal possession of a weapon, the judge excluded the statement, "the gun is over there," and the gun because the officer had not given respondent the warning required by our decision in *Miranda v. Arizona,* before asking him where the gun was located. . . .

OPINION

We hold . . . that there is a "public safety" exception to the requirement that *Miranda* warning be given before a suspect's answers may be admitted into evidence, and that the availability of that exception does not depend upon the motivation of the individual officers involved. In a kaleidoscopic situation such as the one confronting these officers, where spontaneity rather than adherence to a police manual is necessarily the order of the day, the application of the exception which we recognize today should not be made to depend on *post hoc* findings at a suppression hearing concerning the subjective motivation of the arresting officer. Undoubtedly most police officers, if placed in Officer Kraft's position, would act out of a host of different, instinctive, and largely unverifiable motives—their own safety, the safety of others, and perhaps as well the desire to obtain incriminating evidence from the suspect.

Whatever the motivation of individual officers in such a situation, we do not believe that the doctrinal underpinnings of *Miranda* require that it be applied in all its rigor to a situation in which police officers ask questions reasonably prompted by a concern for public safety. . . .

The police in this case, in the very act of apprehending a suspect, were confronted with the immediate necessity of ascertaining the whereabouts of a gun which they had every reason to believe the suspect had just removed from his empty holster and discarded in the supermarket. So long as the gun was concealed somewhere in the supermarket, with its actual whereabouts unknown, it obviously posed more than one danger to the public safety: an accomplice might make use of it, a customer or employee might later come upon it.

In such a situation, if the police are required to recite the familiar *Miranda* warnings before asking the whereabouts of the gun, suspects in Quarles' position might well be deterred from responding. . . .

We conclude that the need for answers to questions in a situation posing a threat to the public safety outweighs the need for the prophylactic rule protecting the Fifth Amendment's privilege against self-incrimination. We decline to place officers such as Officer Kraft in the untenabale position of having to consider, often in a matter of seconds, whether it best serves society for them to ask the necessary questions without the *Miranda* warnings and render whatever probative evidence they uncover inadmissible, or for them to give the warnings in order to preserve the admissibility of evidence they might uncover but possibly damage or destroy their ability to obtain that evidence and neutralize the volatile situation confronting them.

In recognizing a narrow exception to the *Miranda* rule in this case, we acknowledge that to some degree we lessen the desirable clarity of that rule. . . . The exception will not be difficult for police officers to apply because in each case it will be circumscribed by the exigency which justifies it. We think police officers can and will distinguish almost instinctively between questions necessary to secure their own safety or the safety of the public and questions designed solely to elicit testimonial evidence from a suspect. . . .

We hold that the Court of Appeals in this case erred in excluding the statement, "the gun is over there," and the gun because of the officer's failure to read respondent his *Miranda* rights before attempting to locate the weapon. . . .

DISSENT

Justice Marshall, with whom Justice Brennan and Justice Stevens join, dissenting. . . .

The majority's entire analysis rests on the factual assumption that the public was at risk during Quarles' interrogation. This assumption is completely in conflict with the facts as found by New York's highest court. Before the interrogation began, Quarles had been "reduced to a condition of physical powerlessness." Contrary to the majority's speculations, Quarles was not believed to have, nor did he in fact have an accomplice to come to his rescue. When the questioning began, the arresting officers were sufficiently confident of their own safety to put away their guns. As Officer Kraft acknowledged at the suppression hearing, "the situation was under control." Based on Officer Kraft's own testimony, the New York Court of Appeals found: "Nothing suggests that any of the officers was by that time concerned for his own physical safety." The Court of Appeals also determined that there was no evidence that the interrogation was prompted by the arresting officers' concern for public safety. . . .

[N]o customers or employees were wandering about the store in danger of coming across Quarles' discarded weapon. Although the supermarket was open to the public, Quarles' arrest took place during the middle of the night when the store was apparently deserted except for the clerks at the check-out counter. The police could have easily cordoned off the store and searched for the missing gun. Had they done so, they would have found the gun forthwith. The police were well aware that Quarles had discarded the weapon somewhere near the scene of the arrest. As the State acknowledged before the New York Court of Appeals: "After Officer Kraft had handcuffed and frisked the defendant in the supermarket, *he knew with a high degree of certainty that the defendant's gun was within the immediate vicinity of the encounter.* He undoubtedly would have searched for it in the carton a few feet away without the defendant having looked in that direction and saying that it was there.". .

If after plenary review two appellate courts so fundamentally differ over the threat to public safety presented by the simple and uncontested facts of this case, one must seriously question how law enforcement officers will respond to the majority's new rule in the confusion and haste of the real world.

CASE DISCUSSION

Quarles was charged with illegal possession of a weapon. The trial court suppressed the gun and an incriminating statement by Quarles. The New York Court of Appeals affirmed, and the United States Supreme Court granted *certiorari.* The Supreme Court reversed, holding that Quarles's statements were not obtained in violation of the Fifth and Fourteenth Amendments.

Justice O'Connor predicts that there will now be "a finespun new doctrine on public safety exigencies incident to custodial interrogation, complete with hairsplitting distinctions that currently plague our Fourth Amendment jurisprudence." Do you agree? Does this decision weaken the Fifth Amendment? How? Does it weaken other interests? Which ones? If you favor a public safety exception, does it apply to the facts in this case? Consider the facts the dissent stresses.

≡ SUMMARY

Interrogation usually takes place in the strange and sometimes hostile surroundings of the police station. These station-house procedures are both more extensive and more intimidating than contacts on the street and other public places. The Fifth, Sixth, and

Fourteenth Amendments to the United States Constitution govern the accusatory stage, the period from arrest to formal charge. The Fifth Amendment prohibits custodial interrogation without the *Miranda* warnings or other suitable safeguards. Courts will not admit confessions or other statements without proof that suspects effectively waived their right to remain silent and talked voluntarily. Courts look at the totality of circumstances surrounding interrogation to determine if suspects voluntarily confessed or made statements that the prosecutor wishes to introduce into evidence to prove guilt. The rules governing interrogation balance and promote the interests in accurate fact-finding and effective law enforcement, the process interest in fair proceedings, controlling illegal police practices, and protecting individual dignity and rights.

≡ QUESTIONS FOR REVIEW AND DISCUSSION

1. Explain how the period following arrest differs from that prior to arrest in the criminal process?
2. What major questions surround police interrogation?
3. What main amendments to the Constitution affect police interrogation?
4. At what points in the criminal process do these amendments come into effect?
5. Explain the voluntariness test.
6. What is the difference between objective and subjective tests?
7. What is a *per se* rule?
8. Is the totality of circumstances or a *per se* rule better? Explain your answer.
9. Define custodial interrogation.
10. When are the *Miranda* warnings required? When are they *not* required?

≡ NOTES

1. Liva Baker, *Miranda: Crime, Law and Politics* (New York: Atheneum, 1983), 404.
2. Wayne R. Lafave and Jerold H. Israel, *Criminal Procedure,* vol. 1 (St. Paul: West Publishing Company, 1984), 434–35; Sobel, "The Exclusionary Rules in the Law of Confessions: A Legal Perspective—A Practical Perspective," *New York Law Journal,* November 22, 1965; "Developments in the Law—Confessions," *Harvard Law Review* 79(1966): 938, 943.
3. *Culombe v. Connecticut,* 367 U.S. 568, 81 S.Ct. 1860, 6 L.Ed.2d 1037 (1961).
4. Fred E. Inbau, "Police Interrogation Privileges and Limitations," *The Journal of Criminal Law, Criminology, and Police Science* 52(1961):19.
5. Yale Kamisar, "The Importance of Being Guilty," *The Journal of Criminal Law and Criminology* 68(1977):190.
6. Lafave and Israel, *Criminal Procedure,* 1: 435–36.
7. *Miranda v. Arizona,* 384 U.S. 436, 86 S.Ct. 1602, 16 L.Ed.2d 694 (1966) (dissent).
8. For important discussions of these matters, see Yale Kamisar, "The Importance of Being Guilty," *The Journal of Criminal Law and Criminology* 68(1977):182–97; Steven Schulhofer, "Reconsidering Miranda," *The University of Chicago Law Review* 54(1987):435–61; Stephen J. Schulhofer, "Confessions and the Court," *Michigan Law Review*

79(1981):865–93; Gerald M. Caplan, "Questioning Miranda," *Vanderbilt Law Review* 38(1985):1417–76; Welsh S. White, "Defending Miranda," *Vanderbilt Law Review* 39(1986):1–22.

9. 297 U.S. 278, 56 S.Ct. 461, 80 L.Ed. 682, (1936); 378 U.S. 478, 84 S.Ct. 1758, 12 L.Ed.2d 977 (1964); 384 U.S. 436, 86 S.Ct. 1602, 16 L.Ed.2d 694 (1966).

10. *Massiah v. United States*, 377 U.S. 201, 84 S.Ct. 1199, 12 L.Ed.2d 246 (1964); *United States v. Henry*, 447 U.S. 264, 100 S.Ct. 2183, 65 L.Ed.2d 115 (1980) (passive listening device).

11. *Escobedo v. Illinois*, 378 U.S. 478, 84 S.Ct. 1758, 12 L.Ed.2d 977 (1964).

12. Fred E. Inbau et al., *Criminal Interrogatin and Confessions* (Baltimore: Williams and Wilkins, 1986), 84–85.

13. *Miranda v. Arizona* 384 U.S. 436, 86 S.Ct. 1602, 16 L.Ed.2d 694 (1966); for thorough discussions of *Miranda* and the controversy surrounding the case, see references in notes 1 and 8, supra.

14. *Commonwealth v. Zook*, 553 A.2d 920 (Pa. 1989).

15. Schulhofer, "Reconsidering Miranda," 453–61.

16. *Michigan v. Tucker, 417 U.S. 433, 94 S.Ct. 2357, 41 L.Ed.2d 182 (1974)*.

17. *Miranda v. Arizona*, 384 U.S. 436, 86 S.Ct. 1602, 16 L.Ed.2d 694 (1966).

18. *Georgetown Law Journal*, 75 (1987):827–828.

19. *Oregon v. Mathiason*, 429 U.S. 492, 97 S.Ct. 711, 50 L.Ed.2d 714 (1977) (suspect appeared unacccompanied); *Dunaway v. New York*, 442 U.S. 200, 99 S.Ct. 2248, 60 L.Ed.2d 824 (1979) (police picked suspect up).

20. *United States v. Lee*, 699 F.2d 466 (9th Cir. 1982) (questioning in police car); *Beckwith v. United States*, 425 U.S. 341, 96 S.Ct. 1612, 48 L.Ed.2d 1 (1976) (questioned at home); *Orozco v. Texas*, 394 U.S. 324, 89 S.Ct. 1095, 22 L.Ed.2d 311 (1969) (questioning suspect at 4:00 a.m.).

21. *Miranda v. Arizona*, 384 U.S. 436, 86 S.Ct. 1602, 16 L.Ed.2d 694 (1966).

22. *Laury v. State*, 260 A.2d 907 (Del. 1969) (near crime scene); *State v. Desjardins*, 110 N.H. 511, 272 A.2d 599 (1970) (traffic accident); *State v. Mitchell, 35 Or. App. 809, 583 P.2d 14 (1978)* (suspicious circumstances in public).

23. Lafave and Israel, *Criminal Procedure*, 1: 498.

24. Quotes from Justice Steven's dissent in *Rhode Island v. Innis*, 466 U.S. 291, 100 S.Ct. 1682, 64 L.Ed.2d 297 (1980).

25. 441 U.S. 369, 99 S.Ct. 1755, 60 L.Ed.2d 286 (1979).

26. *Georgetown Law Journal*, 75(1987):831–833 and cases cited therein.

27. *Ashcraft v. Tennessee*, 322 U.S. 143, 64 S.Ct. 921, 88 L.Ed. 1192 (1944); Francis Allen, "The Supreme Court, Federalism, and State Systems of Criminal Justice," *DePaul Law Review* 8(1959):213, 235.

28. *Rogers v. Richmond*, 365 U.S. 534, 81 S.Ct. 735, 5 L.Ed.2d 760 (1961).

29. *Malinski v. New York*, 324 U.S. 401, 65 S.Ct. 781, 89 L.Ed. 1029 (1945).

30. *Lynumn v. Illinois*, 372 U.S. 528, 83 S.Ct. 917, 9 L.Ed.2d 922 (1963).

31. *Rogers v. Richmond*, 365 U.S. 534, 81 S.Ct. 735, 5 L.Ed.2d 760 (1961).

32. *Ward v. Texas*, 316 U.S. 547, 62 S.Ct. 1139, 86 L.Ed. 1663 (1942).

33. 479 U.S. 157, 107 S.Ct. 515, 93 L.Ed.2d 473 (1986); and see Scott A. McCreight, "*Colorado v. Connelly:* Due Process Challenges to Confessions and Evidentiary Reliability Interests," *Iowa Law Review* 73(1987):207.

34. *Miller v. Fenton*, 474 U.S. 104, 106 S.Ct. 445, 88 L.Ed.2d 405 (1985).

Chapter Eight
Identification Procedures

CHAPTER OUTLINE

CHAPTER MAIN POINTS

1. It is easier to prove that a crime has been committed and how, than to identify those who committed the crime.

2. Physiological and psychological factors lead to unreliable eyewitness identification.

3. The principal eyewitness identification procedures are all subject to varying degrees of unreliability.

4. Identification takes place at three points in the criminal process—prior to the initiation of prosecution, following prosecution but prior to trial, and at trial.

5. The Fifth Amendment right against self-incrimination does not protect identification procedures.

6. The Sixth Amendment right to counsel protects identification procedures following the initiation of criminal proceedings.

7. The Fourteenth Amendment due process clause protects all identification procedures.

8. Some states have extended the right to counsel provisions in their state constitutions to identification procedures that take place any time following arrest.

KEY TERMS

adversary proceedings the point when prosecution seriously begins

line-up identification procedure involving several persons from whom witness identifies the suspect

Schmerber **rule** the Fifth Amendment right against self-incrimination protects only *testimonial* evidence

showup the suspect alone is presented to the eyewitness

Stovall **rule** totality of circumstances that demonstrates a confrontation so unnecessarily suggestive and conducive to irreparable mistaken identification that it denies suspect due process of law

---

THE DANGERS OF MISIDENTIFICATION

In most cases, proving that a crime was committed, and how it was committed, is considerably easier than identifying the perpetrator. Fingerprints, voice exemplars, and handwriting analyses sometimes fill the gap, but prosecutors most often rely on eyewitnesses to establish identity. Most criminal cases turn on whether judges or juries believe the eyewitnesses' identifications. At the same time, witness reliability is notoriously low, and police procedures frequently render it less reliable. According to one expert, faulty identifications present the "greatest single threat to the achievement of our ideal that no innocent man shall be punished." The records are full of cases of mistaken identity. In one recent example, seven eyewitnesses swore that Bernard Pagano, a Roman Catholic priest, robbed them with a small, chrome-plated pistol. In the middle of Pagano's trial, Ronald Clouser admitted that he, not Father Pagano, had committed the robberies.[1]

Misidentification occurs for several reasons. The brain does not record exactly what the eye sees. Perceptions vary, hence the phrase "Beauty is in the eye of the beholder." A particularly troubling aspect of misperception is erroneous cross-racial identification. In one famous experiment researchers showed observers a photo of a white man brandishing a razor blade in an altercation with a black man on a subway. When asked immediately afterward to describe what they saw, over *half* the subjects reported that the black man was carrying the knife.

> . . . [C]onsiderable evidence indicates that people are poorer at identifying members of another race than of their own. Some studies have found that, in the United States at least, whites have greater difficulty recognizing blacks than vice versa. Moreover, counterintuitively, the ability to perceive the physical characteristics of a person from another racial group apparently does not improve significantly upon increased contact with other members of that race. Because many crimes are cross-racial, these factors may play an important part in reducing the accuracy of eyewitness perception.[2]

In addition to perceptual difficulties, time distorts initial impressions. Hence, witnesses' memories do not accurately reflect what witnesses saw or heard even minutes earlier and certainly not hours, days, weeks, or months before. Curiously, witnesses' confidence about their recall grows as time passes, while, in fact, actual memory is fading. Finally, distortion occurs in retrieving information from memory. Pure verbal recall, or narrative description without prompting, suffers from incomplete memory. In structured situations, witnesses tend to treat line-ups, showups, and photo arrays as multiple choice questions in which they choose the "best" likeness. Witnesses feel pressure that they might look foolish if they "don't know the answer," or they respond easily to suggestion, particularly in uncomfortable or threatening situations. Suggestions by authority figures, such as the police, aggravate these tendencies.[3]

Traditionally, courts have readily accepted eyewitness identification testimony. For example, during trials prosecutors often ask victims or other witnesses if they see the person who committed the crime in the courtroom. If the testifiers answer yes, which they invariably do, then prosecutors ask them to point to that person, which they also invariably do. Courts also admit evidence of prior identifications, such as those made during line-ups. One court said:

> We think it is evident that an identification of an accused by a witness for the first time in the courtroom may often be of little testimonial force, as the witness may have had opportunities to see the accused and to have heard him referred to by a certain name; whereas a prior identification, considered in connection with the circumstances surrounding its making, serves to aid the court in determining the trustworthiness of the identification made in the courtroom.[4]

The rules governing witness identification primarily promote the interest in accurate fact-finding in particular cases—to convict the guilty and to free the innocent. In addition, the rules that apply to identification promote the process interests and individual rights guaranteed in Fourteenth Amendment. The goal is to provide the government with authority to gather reliable evidence without violating the dignity of individuals or due process of law.

═══ THE CONSTITUTION AND IDENTIFICATION PROCEDURES

The Fifth Amendment, which dominates interrogations and confessions, and the Fourth Amendment, which governs stops, arrests, frisks, searches, and seizures of evidence, do not protect identification procedures. It does not violate defendants' right against self-incrimination to stand in a line-up, to speak words when asked to do so, or to put on items of clothing. Nor is it an unreasonable search and seizure to require suspects to produce blood samples, even when the government intrudes into the body, removes the blood, seizes it, and uses it against the suspect.

According to the Supreme Court, the self-incrimination clause—"no person shall be compelled to be a witness against himself"—refers to *testimonial* evidence. What does this mean? Clearly, it includes spoken and written words. But what about other incriminating evidence that suspects might provide, such as blood, hair, voice samples, or fingerprints? They are incriminating, but if they are provided involuntarily, does the Fifth Amendment protect them? The Supreme Court addressed this problem in *Schmerber v. California.*

CASE

Did the blood-alcohol test compel Schmerber to be a witness against himself?

Schmerber v. California

384 U.S. 757, 86 S.Ct. 1826, 16 L.Ed.2d 908 (1966)

[Mr. Justice Brennan delivered the opinion of the Court.]

FACTS

Petitioner and a companion had been drinking at a tavern and bowling alley. There was evidence showing that petitioner was driving from the bowling alley about midnight November 12, 1964, when the car skidded, crossed the road and struck a tree. Both petitioner and his companion were injured and taken to a hospital for treatment.

Petitioner was convicted in Los Angeles Municipal Court of the criminal offense of driving an automobile while under the influence of intoxicating liquor. He had been arrested at a hospital while receiving treatment for injuries suffered in an accident involving the automobile that he had apparently been driving. At the direction of a police officer, a blood sample was then withdrawn from petitioner's body by a physician at the hospital. The chemical analysis of this sample revealed a percent by weight of alcohol in his blood at the time of the offense which indicated intoxication, and the report of this analysis was admitted in evidence at the trial. Petitioner objected to receipt of this analysis on the ground that the blood had been withdrawn despite his refusal, on the advice of his counsel, to consent to the test. He contended that in that circumstance the withdrawal of the blood and the admission of the analysis in evidence denied him due process of law under the Fourteenth Amendment, as well as specific guarantees of the Bill of Rights secured against the States by that Amendment: his privilege against self- incrimination under the Fifth Amendment; his right to counsel under the Sixth Amendment; and his right not to be subjected to unreasonable searches and seizures in violation of the Fourth Amendment. The Appellate Court rejected these contentions and affirmed the conviction. In view of constitutional decisions since we last considered these issues—we granted certiorari. We affirm.

OPINION

. . . We . . . must . . . decide whether the withdrawal of the blood and admission in evidence of the analysis involved in this case violated petitioner's [Fifth Amendment] privilege [against self-incrimination]. We hold that the privilege protects an accused only from being compelled to testify against himself, or otherwise provide the State with evidence of a testimonial or communicative nature, and that the withdrawal of blood and use of the analysis in question in this case did not involve compulsion to these ends.

It could not be denied that in requiring petitioner to submit to the withdrawal and chemical analysis of his blood the State compelled him to submit to an attempt to discover evidence that might be used to prosecute him for a criminal offense. He submitted only after the police officer rejected his objection and directed the physician to proceed. The officer's direction to the physician to administer the test over petitioner's objection constituted compulsion for the purposes of privilege. The critical question, then, is whether petitioner was thus compelled "to be a witness against himself."

History and a long line of authorities in lower courts have consistently limited its protection to situations in which the State seeks to submerge those values by obtaining the evidence against an accused through "the cruel, simple expedient of compelling it from his own mouth. . . . In sum, the privilege is fulfilled only when the person is guaranteed the right 'to remain silent unless he chooses to speak in the unfettered exercise of his own will.' " . . . [I]t offers no protection against compulsion to submit to fingerprinting, photographing, or measurements, to write or speak for identification, to appear in court, to stand, to assume a stance, to walk, or to make a particular gesture.

DISSENT

[Justice Black, dissenting]
. . . How can it reasonably be doubted that the blood test evidence was not in all respects the actual equivalent of "testimony" taken from petitioner when the result of the test was offered as testimony, was considered by the jury as testimony, and the jury's verdict of guilt rests in part on that testimony? The refined, subtle reasoning and balancing process used here to narrow the scope of the Bill of Rights' safeguard against self-incrimination provides a handy instrument for further narrowing of that constitutional protection, as well as others, in the future. Believing with the Framers that these constitutional safeguards broadly construed by independent tribunals of justice provide our best hope for keeping free from governmental oppression, I deeply regret the Court's holding. . . .

CASE DISCUSSION

Schmerber was subjected to a blood-alcohol test and moved to suppress its results as evidence against him. The trial court denied his motion; Schmerber was convicted of driving while intoxicated. The appellate court affirmed his conviction, holding that the blood-alcohol test did not deny Schmerber due process. On writ of *certiorari*, the United States Supreme Court affirmed, holding that Schmerber's Fifth Amendment rights were not violated.

Does it make sense to restrict the self-incrimination clause to words that come out of defendants' mouths? What interests does such a restriction promote? hinder? Does the dissent's definition make more sense? Explain your answer.

Decision Point

Hudson was arrested and, following a preliminary hearing, was bound over to the grand jury for possible indictment for first-degree murder. While awaiting the hearing, he was detained in custody. Upon a report that Hudson suffered from AIDS, the sheriff took Hudson to county health officials for an examination. Hudson objected on religious grounds to the blood test for the AIDS virus. After an evidentiary hearing, the court ordered a blood sample to be taken. Was the test lawful? The Tennessee Supreme Court ruled that it was. The Court reasoned: "It is apparent that this is not a case of random blood sampling, and the testimony clearly shows that the sheriff and public health officials have reasonable cause to carry out the blood test. If the test is negative, the matter will be at an end. If it is positive, special care and treatment will be required for appellant either in the county jail or at a separate facility. The operation of the jail itself, the safety of the sheriff and his staff, and the safety and welfare of other persons incarcerated in the jail are involved, and any alleged religious belief or conviction of appellant must yield to concerns for the public safety and welfare which are clearly established by the evidence. Further, the appellant's own health, welfare and treatment, both as a prisoner and as a potential patient, justify the blood test which the public health officials propose to conduct."[5]

Thomas was indicted for rape and sodomy in the first degree, sexual abuse in the first degree, and second-degree burglary. The victim was worried that she may have contracted AIDS from the rape and sodomy; the prosecutor moved to have Thomas tested for the AIDS virus because the evidence presented to the grand jury "establishes that defendant forcibly and repeatedly engaged in acts of sexual intercourse and oral sodomy with the victim, and did thereby expose said victim to his body and sexual fluids." Should the court grant the motion? A New York court ordered the test taken:

"[T]his Court holds and determines that the victim has a right to know whether she may have been exposed to the AIDS virus by reason of having been exposed to the body and sexual fluids of the defendant. This Court finds and determines that it has inherent discretionary power to order the defendant to submit to such a blood test simply because it is the intelligent, humane, logical, and proper course of action under the circumstances. The mental anguish suffered by the victim knowing that she was forcibly raped and sodomized by a former inmate of the New York Department of Correctional Services is real and continuing, and the intrusion upon defendant of a routine drawing of a blood sample is very minimal and commonplace.

Hopefully, the result of such a blood test will be negative, thereby relieving the victim of her understandable anxiety. In the unlikely event that the AIDS test of defendant's blood were to prove positive, the defendant could indeed be eventually subjected to a prosecution for depraved indifference murder. However, if the defendant is afflicted with the AIDS virus, he may already be subject to a death sentence which could well claim his life long before he ever serves 7½ years in state prison.

This Court holds and determines that the People's motion should be granted in all respects, and that the defendant will be required to permit the taking of samples of blood from his body in a manner not involving an unreasonable intrusion thereof, or a risk of serious physical injury thereto. The results of such AIDS Antibody Test shall be disclosed not only to the defendant, but also to the victim of the defendant's crimes. In the event that the test for AIDS were positive, the results will also be disclosed to the New York State Department of Correctional Services.''[6]

Brian Barlow was marching at the head of the San Francisco Gay Freedom Day Marching Band and Twirling Corps in a Gay Pride Parade in San Diego. He became involved in a scuffle with police monitoring the event. During the struggle, he bit one of the officers on the right shoulder puncturing the skin and leaving a drop of blood. Barlow bit another officer on the right knuckle breaking the skin and drawing blood. Barlow was arrested. To treat his injuries sustained in the struggle, he was taken to the hospital. There, before any *Miranda* warnings had been given, an officer, concerned for his colleagues' well-being, asked Barlow if he was a homosexual and if he had AIDS. Barlow replied that he was a homosexual and ''You better take it that I do have AIDS for the officers' sake.'' Responsive to that statement, Barlow was taken to the central police station where, without a warrant and over his objection, blood samples for AIDS analysis were taken. Was the blood constitutionally taken? The California Court of Appeal ruled that extracting Barlow's blood violated his Fourth Amendment rights because there was not probable cause to believe that the extraction would prove his intent to kill the officers—the crime with which Barlow was charged.[7]

Two other constitutional provisions govern identification procedures: (1) the Sixth Amendment right to counsel and (2) the Fourteenth Amendment due process clause. Identification arises in three settings: (1) prior to active prosecution; (2) between the initiation of adversary proceedings and trial; and (3) at trial. The right to counsel attaches only after adversary proceedings against the accused begin. (See chapter 8 for a discussion of when adversary proceedings begin.) The due process clause applies to all identification procedures. The Supreme Court addressed the right to counsel following the initiation of the adversary process in *United States v. Wade*.[8]

CASE

Did he have a right to counsel at a line-up?

United States v. Wade

388 U.S. 218, 87 S.Ct. 1926, 18 L.Ed.2d 1149 (1967)

[Mr. Justice Brennan delivered the opinion of the Court.]

FACTS

The federally insured bank in Eustace, Texas, was robbed on September 21, 1964. A man with a small strip of tape on each side of his face entered the bank, pointed a pistol at the female cashier and the vice president, the only persons in the bank at the time, and forced them to fill a pillowcase with the bank's money. The man then drove away with an accomplice who had been waiting in a stolen car outside the bank. On March 23, 1965, an indictment was returned against respondent, Wade, and two others for conspiring to rob the bank, and against Wade and the accomplice for the robbery itself. Wade was arrested on April 2, and counsel was appointed to represent him on April 26. Fifteen days later an FBI agent, without notice to Wade's lawyer, arranged to have the two bank employees observe a line-up made up of Wade and five or six other prisoners and conducted in a courtroom of the local county courthouse. Each person in the line wore strips of tape such as allegedly worn by the robber and upon direction each said something like ''put the money in the bag,'' the words allegedly uttered by the robber. Both bank employees identified Wade in the line-up as the bank robber.

At trial, the two employees, when asked on direct examination if the robber was in the courtroom, pointed to Wade. The prior line-up identification was then elicited from both employees on cross-examination. At the close of the testimony, Wade's counsel moved for a judgement of acquittal or, alternatively, to strike the officials' courtroom identifications on the ground that conduct of the line-up, without notice to and in the absence of his appointed counsel, violated his Fifth Amendment privilege against self-incrimination and his Sixth Amendment right to the assistance of counsel. The motion was denied, and Wade was convicted. The Court of Appeals for the Fifth Circuit reversed the conviction and ordered a new trial at which the in-court identification evidence was to be excluded, holding that, though the line-up did not violate Wade's Fifth Amendment rights, ''the lineup, held as it was, in the absence of counsel, already chosen to represent appellant, was a violation of his Sixth Amendment rights. . . . '' We granted certiorari. . . . We reverse the judgement of the Court of Appeals and remand to that court with direction to enter a new judgement vacating the conviction and remanding the case to the District Court for further proceedings consistent with this opinion. . . .

OPINION

. . . [T]oday's law enforcement machinery involves critical confrontations of the accused by the prosecution at pretrial proceedings where the results might well settle the accused's fate and reduce the trial itself to a mere formality. In recognition of these realities of modern criminal prosecution, our cases have construed the Sixth Amendment guarantee to apply to ''critical'' stages of the proceedings. . . .

[T]he period from arraignment to trial was ''perhaps the most critical period of the proceedings'' . . . during which the accused ''requires the guiding hand of counsel . . . , if the guarantee is not to prove an empty right. . . .

[W]e [must] scrutinize *any* pretrial confrontation of the accused to determine whether the presence of his counsel is necessary to preserve the defendant's basic right to a fair trial as affected by his right meaningfully to cross-examine the witnesses against him and to have effective assistance of counsel at the trial itself. It calls upon us to analyze whether potential substantial prejudice to defendant's rights inheres in the particular confrontation and the ability of counsel to help avoid that prejudice. . . .

The Government characterizes the line-up as a mere preparatory step in the gathering of the prosecution's evidence, not different—for Sixth Amendment purposes—from various other preparatory steps, such as systemized or scientific analyzing of the accused's fingerprints, blood sample, clothing, hair, and the like. . . .

But the confrontation compelled by the State between the accused and the victim or witnesses to a crime to elicit identification evidence is peculiarly riddled with innumerable dangers and variable facts which might seriously, even crucially, derogate from fair trial. The vagaries of eyewitness identification are well-known; the annals of criminal law are rife with instances of mistaken identification. . . .

Moreover, "[i]t is a matter of common experience that, once a witness has picked out the accused at the line-up, he is not likely to go back on his word later on, so that in practice the issue of identity may (in the absence of other relevant evidence) for all practical purposes be determined there and then, before the trial. . . .

The impediments to an objective observation are increased when the victim is the witness. Line-ups are prevalent in rape and robbery prosecutions and present a particular hazard that a victim's understandable outrage may excite vengeful or spiteful motives. In any event, neither witnesses nor line-up participants are apt to be alert for conditions prejudicial to the suspect. . . . Improper influences may go undetected by a suspect, guilty or not, who experiences the emotional tension which we might expect in one being confronted with potential accusers. . . . In short, the accused's inability effectively to reconstruct at trial any unfairness that occurred at the line-up may deprive him of his only opportunity meaningfully to attack the credibility of the witness' courtroom identification. . . .

Since it appears that there is grave potential for prejudice, intentional or not, in the pretrial line-up, which may not be capable of reconstruction at trial, and since presence of counsel itself can often avert prejudice and assure a meaningful confrontation at trial, there can be little doubt that for Wade the postindictment line-up was a critical stage of the prosecution at which he was "as much entitled to such aid [of counsel] . . . as at the trial itself." Thus both Wade and his counsel should have been notified of the impending line-up, and counsel's presence should have been a requisite to conduct of the line-up, absent an "intelligent waiver." . . .

The judgment of the Court of Appeals is vacated and the case is remanded to that court with direction to enter a new judgement vacating the conviction and remanding the case to the District Court for further proceedings consistent with this opinion.

It is so ordered.

DISSENT

Mr. Justice White, whom Mr. Justice Harlan and Mr. Justice Stewart join, dissenting in part and concurring in part.

The Court has again propounded a broad constitutional rule barring use of a wide spectrum of relevant and probative evidence, solely because a step in its ascertainment or discovery occurs outside the presence of defense counsel. This was the approach of the Court in *Miranda* v. *Arizona,* 384 U.S. 436. I objected then to what I thought was an uncritical and doctrinaire approach without satisfactory factual foundation. I have much the same view of the present ruling and therefore dissent from the judgement. . . .

To all intents and purposes, courtroom identifications are barred if pretrial identifications have occurred without counsel being present.

The rule applies to any line-up, to any other techniques employed to produce an identification and *a fortiori* to a face-to-face encounter between the witness and the suspect alone, regardless of when the identification occurs, in time or place, and whether before or after indictment or information. . . .

The premise for the Court's rule is not the general unreliability of eyewitness identifications nor the difficulties inherent in observation, recall, and recognition. The Court assumes a narrower evil as the basis for its rule—improper police suggestion which contributes to erroneous identifications. The Court apparently believes that improper police procedures are so widespread that a broad prophylactic rule must be laid down, requiring the presence of counsel at all pretrial identifications, in order to detect recurring instances of police misconduct. . . .

The Court goes beyond assuming that a great majority of the country's police departments are following improper practices at pretrial identifications. To find the line-up a "critical" stage of the proceeding and to exclude identifications made in the absence of counsel, the Court must also assume that police "suggestion," if it occurs at all, leads to erroneous rather than accurate identifications and that reprehensible police conduct will have an unavoidable and largely undiscoverable impact on the trial. . . .

[R]equiring counsel at pretrial identifications as an invariable rule trenches on other valid state interests. One of them is its concern with the prompt and efficient enforcement of its criminal laws. Identifications frequently take place after arrest but before an indictment is returned or an information is filed. The police may have arrested a suspect on probable cause but may still have the wrong man. Both the suspect and the State have every interest in a prompt identification at that stage, the suspect in order to secure his immediate release and the State because prompt and early identification enhances *accurate* identification and because it must know whether it is on the right investigative track. Unavoidably, however, the absolute rule requiring the presence of counsel will cause significant delay and it may very well result in no pretrial identification at all. . . .

Nor do I think the witnesses themselves can be ignored. They will now be required to be present at the convenience of counsel rather than their own. Many may be much less willing to participate if the identification stage is transformed into an adversary proceeding not under the control of a judge. Others may fear for their own safety if their identity is known at an early date, especially when there is no way of knowing until the line-up occurs whether or not the police really have the right man. . . .

Law enforcement officers have the obligation to convict the guilty and to make sure they do not convict the innocent. They must be dedicated to making the criminal trial a procedure for the ascertainment of the true facts surrounding the commission of the crime. To this extent, our so-called adversary system is not adversary at all; nor should it be. But defense counsel has no comparable obligation to ascertain or present the truth. Our system assigns him a different mission. He must be and is interested in preventing the conviction of the innocent, but, absent a voluntary plea of guilty, we also insist that he defend his client whether he is innocent or guilty. . . .

Whether today's judgement would be an acceptable exercise of supervisory power over federal courts is another question. But as a constitutional matter, the judgement in this case is erroneous. . . .

CASE DISCUSSION

Several weeks after Wade's indictment for robbery, the police put him in a line-up without notifying his lawyer. Two bank employees identified him as the robber. At trial, they identified him again. Urging that the line-up violated his right to counsel, Wade filed a motion for judgment of acquittal or, in the alternative, to strike the courtroom identifications. The trial court denied the motions and Wade was convicted. The court of appeals reversed, holding that the line-up denied Wade his right to counsel. The government appealed on a writ of *certiorari* to the United States Supreme Court, which held that the line-up violated Wade's Sixth Amendment right to counsel.

What reasons did the Court give for holding that Wade had the right to a lawyer at his line-up? What interests does this holding promote? Does it promote process at the expense of result? Does it favor the guilty over the innocent? Why did Justice Black dissent? Do you think that Justice Black's solution improves the efficiency and effectiveness of criminal justice administration? If Wade's constitutional right to a lawyer was violated, what remedy should he get? dismissal? exclusion of the line-up identification? others? Give reasons for your choice.

In *Kirby v. Illinois* the Supreme Court declined to extend the right to counsel to line-ups following arrest but prior to instituting formal proceedings. (See chapter 8 for an excerpt of *Kirby* and a discussion of when formal proceedings begin.) The Court ruled that only after "the institution of judicial proceedings" does the Sixth Amendment right to counsel apply. The due process clause provides adequate protection against unreliable eyewitness testimony derived from unnecessarily and impermissibly suggestive identification procedures.

In this case we are asked to import into a routine police investigation an absolute constitutional guarantee historically and rationally applicable only after the onset of formal prosecutorial proceedings. We decline to do so. . . . What has been said does not suggest that there may not be occasions during the course of a criminal investigation when the police do abuse identification procedures. Such abuses are not beyond the reach of the Constitution. . . . The Due Process Clause of the Fifth and Fourteenth Amendments forbids a lineup that is unnecessarily suggestive and conducive to irreparable mistaken identification.[9]

Hence, the Sixth Amendment applies to line-ups staged after "formal prosecutorial proceedings" commence; the Fourteenth Amendment forbids introducing evidence obtained in identification procedures, *whenever* they take place, if they are "unnecessarily suggestive and conducive to irreparable mistaken identity."

The Sixth Amendment right to counsel applies only to postindictment line-ups. However, some states have interpreted the right to counsel in state constitutions more broadly. The Alaska Supreme Court did so in *Blue v. State*.

CASE

Did he have a right to a lawyer?

Blue v. State

558 P.2d 636 (Alaska 1977)

[Before Boochever, C. J., and Rabinowitz, Connor, Erwin and Burke, JJ. Boochever, Chief Justice.]

FACTS

On April 17, 1975, between 7:30 and 8:00 p.m., the Club Manchu Bar in Fairbanks, Alaska was robbed by two men wearing nylon stockings over their heads. Both men were armed, one with a pistol and the other with a rifle. No one was injured in the robbery, although one of the weapons was discharged, a bullet making a hole in the ceiling over the bar. The men took money from three customers in the bar, amounting to approximately $270.00, as well as about $240.00 from the cash register in the bar which was emptied by the bartender, Frances Nickens.

Shortly after the robbers left the bar, Ms. Nickens telephoned the Fairbanks police emergency number and gave this description of the robbers: two white men, one tall and one a little shorter, both with dark hair down on their necks; nylons over their heads; one had a rifle and one a pistol; one was wearing a blue jacket with patches on it. She couldn't describe the clothing of the other one. Although she thought she recognized one of the men, she told the police that she was too upset at the moment to think too much.

Police officers arrived at the Club Manchu approximately half an hour after the robbery and questioned Frances Nickens and the five customers who were present during the robbery. Ms. Nickens stated that she had recognized one of the men whose first name was Dennis. He was a friend of her ex-husband. She had known him for more than a year and had seen him from eight to twelve times during the preceding year. She did not know his last name. A person who entered the bar shortly after the robbery supplied the last name of Benefield for the man named Dennis after hearing Ms. Nicken's description of him. Six police officers, including one who knew Dennis Benefield, then began a search of several bars which Mr. Benefield was known to frequent.

At approximately 9:30–9:45 p.m., three officers in informal street clothes entered the third bar of their search, the Circle M, where one of the officers recognized Dennis Benefield. A man later identified as Clifton Blue was with Dennis Benefield, and the two were engaged in conversation with a man later identified as Wayne Hyatt. The officers reportedly overheard a conversation in which Hyatt stated to Benefield and Blue that he had heard that they had robbed the Club Manchu. Both men denied this accusation and said that if they were being accused of such a thing then they might as well do it. At this point, three other officers outside the bar were alerted that Dennis Benefield and a man meeting the description of the other robber were inside. They entered the bar, and several officers pulled Benefield and Blue from their bar stools and pushed them against the wall in order to frisk them for weapons. Both men were handcuffed, and both men were given their *Miranda* warnings.

Officer Vogt, who was in charge of the investigation, telephoned Frances Nickens at approximately 10:30 p.m. and asked whether she could come to the Circle M. She arrived approximately 20 minutes later and was shown into the poolroom area of the bar where eight Caucasian men were sitting informally, or playing pool. The eight men were the two defendants, three undercover police officers and three patrons of the bar—all similarly dressed in casual clothing. There were at least three or four tall men. Benefield and Blue were seated at the same table, and there were other people sitting close by. Blue was not wearing handcuffs at the time, by his own admission. While Benefield testified at the preliminary hearing to suppress the results of the line-up that he was handcuffed when Ms. Nickens viewed him, two officers testified that he was not handcuffed during the Circle M line-up.

At the first viewing, Frances Nickens positively identified Dennis Benefield as one of the robbers. She could not identify Blue seated, however, and asked to see the participants standing to help her identify the other suspect. Approximately five minutes later, she was shown a second line-up of all eight men standing against the pool table. At this time she positively identified Blue as the other robber, largely because of the way he moved and his actions. Based on this identification, Blue and Benefield were formally arrested and charged with armed robbery.

A second pre-indictment line-up was held in district court on April 29, 1975, in which the ten participants wore stockings over their heads. Counsel for the defendants were present. At this second line-up, Ms. Nickens was again able to identify Dennis Benefield as one of the robbers but was unable to identify Blue or anyone else. Of the three other eyewitnesses to the robbery who viewed the line-up in district court, no one identified either Blue or Benefield. One of the eyewitnesses, George Haskins, excluded Blue as one of the robbers, although he testified at trial that he was not "100% positive" of this exclusion. Blue and Benefield were subsequently indicted on May 14, 1975.

The defendants were jointly tried in June of 1975. The evidence at trial included the eyewitness identification summarized above. Ms. Nickens identified both Benefield and Blue in court. She based her in-court identification of Blue on her prior identification at the Circle M Bar, as well as her recognition of Blue during a jury view of the Club Manchu on the first morning of trial.

The only physical evidence in the state's case was a blue denim jacket which Blue was wearing on the night he was arrested at the Circle M Bar. Ms. Nickens had described the jacket worn by the taller robber as being blue denim with circular light-colored patches on the chest and one on the right arm near the shoulder. The jacket worn by Blue at the time of his arrest did not have any patches on it. . . .

In addition to eyewitness testimony and the testimony concerning the denim jacket, two police officers testified at trial to the conversations between Hyatt, Blue and Benefield in the Circle M Bar.

OPINION

We first focus our attention on the April 17, 1975 line-up at the Circle M Bar. While police did give the mandatory *Miranda* warnings, they did not inform defendants of the right to have an attorney present at the Circle M line-up. The defendant urges us to hold that failure to provide counsel at this stage in the pre-trial process denies him his constitutional right to counsel as guaranteed by Art. 1, Sec. 11 of the Alaska Constitution.

The United States Supreme Court in *United States* v. *Wade* held that a line-up after an accused has been indicted is a critical stage of a criminal proceeding at which the accused has a sixth amendment right to counsel under the United States Constitution. This right is applicable to the states through the fourteenth amendment. The *Wade* . . . decision created a *per se* exclusionary rule for identifications based on *post-indictment* pre-trial line-ups conducted in the absence of counsel. *Wade* . . . however, arguably left open the question of a defendant's right to an attorney during *pre-indictment* line-up procedures.

The point at which the pre-trial right to counsel attaches under federal law in identification procedures was clarified by the Supreme Court in *Kirby* v. *Illinois*. There the Court, in a plurality opinion, held that the federal constitutional right to counsel does not attach until the accused has been indicted or formally charged with a criminal offense and, hence, does not apply to a pre-indictment line-up. This pre- and post-indictment distinction has been widely applied by federal and state courts. . . .

This court . . . has not yet had the opportunity to discuss the plurality decision in *Kirby* and to determine the issue of an accused's right to counsel under the Alaska Constitution at a pre-indictment line-up. Although a plurality of the United States Supreme Court justices would not recognize a pre-indictment right to counsel, the Alaska Supreme Court is not limited by decisions of the United States Supreme Court or by the United States Constitution when interpreting its state constitution. The Alaska Constitution may have broader safeguards than the minimum federal standards. . . .

The determination whether counsel is required at a pre-indictment line-up involves a difficult balance. On the one hand, the state has a legitimate concern in the "prompt and purposeful investigation of an unsolved crime." Conducting an eyewitness identification procedure as soon as possible and while the memory of the eyewitness is fresh serves a valid purpose. Assuming the line-up complies with due process safeguards, the fresher the memory, the more accurate and trustworthy the identification may be.

On the other hand, we must also view the suspect's legitimate right "to be protected from prejudicial procedures". The interests of a suspect in having counsel present involve the constitutional guarantee of right to counsel, the right to due process during the line-up procedures and the right to confront witnesses which insures effective cross-examination at trial. . . .

In evaluating evidence used at trial from a line-up without counsel, we are not merely concerned with the fundamental fairness of that line-up. We are also concerned with the need for counsel to be present in order to evaluate the circumstances and prepare his argument at trial sufficiently to provide the defendant with his sixth amendment right to confront identifying witnesses. . . .

In balancing the need for prompt investigation against a suspect's right to fair procedures, we hold that a suspect who is in custody is entitled to have counsel present at a pre-indictment line-up unless exigent circumstances exist so that providing counsel would unduly interfere with a prompt and purposeful investigation.

The facts of this case provide an example of both the general rule and exigent circumstances. The police were notified of a crime immediately after it occurred, were on the scene within one half hour, and discovered that an eyewitness thought she knew and could recognize one of the participants; they immediately pursued the suspect. Within two and one half hours, the police had located the suspect and notified the eyewitness who arrived to identify the suspect approximately 20 minutes later. The identification itself was made within three hours of the robbery. Here, the police were making every effort to conduct a line-up while the memory of the witness was fresh. Significantly, the line-up was held at 11:00 p.m., and providing a right to counsel at the late hour of the night might have postponed the line-up until the following day. Under these circumstances, providing counsel could have precluded the state's diligent efforts to obtain an identification while the facts were still fresh in the eyewitness' mind. We cannot find that providing counsel under these circumstances is practical, reasonable or mandated by our constitution.

On the other hand, we would apply the general rule and require that counsel be present under the circumstances of the later district court line-up, even though Blue had not yet been indicted. In contrast to the Circle M line-up, the district court line-up was held several days after the incident, *not* immediately following the crime. There was ample time to notify and have counsel present. Counsel, in fact, was present, and no identification evidence was lost. Under these circumstances, requiring counsel's presence does not substantially interfere with legitimate law enforcement. To the contrary, providing counsel will prevent constitutional errors and increase the likelihood that eyewitness evidence will eventually be admissible at trial.

In summary, absent exigent circumstances, we hold counsel should be provided even though the line-up is before formal charges or indictment, but given the exigencies of this case, we hold that it was not necessary to afford Blue counsel at the Circle M line-up. . . .

The decision of the trial court is therefore reversed, and the case is remanded for a new trial.

CASE DISCUSSION

Blue was convicted before the superior court of armed robbery, and he appealed. The Supreme Court held that absent exigent circumstances, counsel should be provided even though a line-up is held before formal charges or indictment, and that exigent circumstances existed in the pre-indictment line-up.

How does the Alaska Supreme Court's interpretation of its constitution's right to counsel provision differ from that in *Kirby v. Illinois?* What interests does the Alaska court's interpretation favor? What precisely were the "exigent circumstances" that validated the first line-up without Blue's attorney present? What interest does the exigent circumstances exception to the requirement for counsel promote? If Blue is guilty, does it matter whether his lawyer was present at a line-up or not? Why?

PROCEDURES CARRYING THE GREATEST MISIDENTIFICATION THREAT

In a companion case to *Wade v. United States, Stovall v. Denno,* police took Stovall to a hospital room handcuffed to a police officer; the police had arrested Stovall but had not yet indicted him. After the police asked a stabbing victim if Stovall "was the man" who attacked her, she said yes.[10]

The Court did not utilize the Fourth, Fifth, or Sixth Amendments to decide the case. Instead, the Court ruled that if the totality of the circumstances demonstrates that the confrontation "was so unnecessarily suggestive and conducive to irreparable mistaken identification," the procedure denied Stovall due process of law under the Fourteenth Amendment. The test is whether the identification procedure was "so impermissibly suggestive as to give rise to a very substantial likelihood of irreparable misidentification."

The Court established a two-pronged inquiry under *Stovall* to determine whether the procedure denied due process: (1) Is the identification procedure suggestive? (2) Is it "unnecessarily" or "impermissibly" suggestive. In *Stovall,* the Court conceded that showing suspects singly to witnesses is highly suggestive and widely condemned. However, the second prong requires asking whether the procedure was "unnecessarily" or "impermissibly" suggestive. The Court decided that it was not:

> Here was the only person in the world who could possibly exonerate Stovall. Her words, and only her words, "He is not the man" could have resulted in freedom for Stovall. The hospital was not far distant from the courthouse and jail. No one knew how long Mrs. Behrendt might live. Faced with the responsibility of identifying the attacker, with the need for immediate action and with the knowledge that Mrs. Behrendt could not visit the jail, the police followed the only feasible procedure and took Stovall to the hospital room. Under these circumstances, the usual police station line-up, which Stovall now argues he should have had, was out of the question.[11]

Line-ups

The Supreme Court recently reviewed the application of the due process clause to line-ups, the totality-of-circumstances test to measure the application of due process, and the remedies available to defendants whose due process rights the government violates, in *Manson* v. *Braithwaite*.

CASE

Did the "totality of circumstances" validate the line-up?

Manson v. Brathwaite

432 U.S. 98, 97 S.Ct. 2243, 53 L.Ed.2d 140 (1977)

[Blackmun, J., delivered the opinion of the Court, in which Burger, C. J., and Stewart, White, Powell, Rehnquist, and Stevens, JJ., joined. Stevens, J., filed a concurring opinion. Marshall, J., filed a dissenting opinion, in which Brennan, J., joined. . . .]

FACTS

Jimmy D. Glover, a full-time trooper of the Connecticut State Police, in 1970 was assigned to the Narcotics Division in an undercover capacity. On May 5 of that year, about 7:45 p.m., e.d.t., and while there was still daylight, Glover and Henry Alton Brown, an informant, went to an apartment building at 201 Westland, in Hartford, for the purpose of purchasing narcotics from "Dickie Boy" Cicero, a known narcotics dealer. Cicero, it was thought, lived on the third floor of that apartment building. Glover and Brown entered the building, observed by backup Officers D'Onofrio and Gaffey, and proceeded by stairs to the third floor. The area was illuminated by natural light from a window in the third floor hallway. The door was opened 12 to 18 inches in response to the knock. Glover observed a man standing at the door and, behind him, a woman. Brown identified himself. Glover then asked for "two things" of narcotics. The man at the door held out his hand, and Glover gave him two $10 bills. The door closed. Soon the man returned and handed Glover two glassine bags. While the door was open, Glover stood within two feet of the person from whom he made the purchase and observed his face. Five to seven minutes elapsed from the time the door first opened until it closed the second time.

Glover and Brown then left the building. This was about eight minutes after their arrival. Glover drove to headquarters where he described the seller to D'Onofrio and Gaffey. Glover at that time did not know the identity of the seller. He described him as being "a colored man, approximately five eleven inches tall, dark complexion, of heavy build. He was wearing at the time blue pants and a plaid shirt." D'Onofrio, suspecting from this description that respondent might be the seller, obtained a photograph of respondent from the

Records Division of the Hartford Police Department. He left it at Glover's office. D'Onofrio was not acquainted with respondent personally, but did know him by sight and had seen him "[s]everal times" prior to May 5. Glover, when alone, viewed the photograph for the first time upon his return to headquarters on May 7; he identified the person shown as the one from whom he had purchased the narcotics. . . .

Respondent was arrested on July 27 while visiting at the apartment of a Mrs. Ramsey on the third floor of 201 Westland. This was the apartment at which the narcotics sale had taken place on May 5.

Respondent was charged, in a two-count information, with possession and sale of heroin. . . . At his trial in January 1971, the photograph from which Glover had identified respondent was received in evidence without objection on the part of the defense. Glover also testified that, although he had not seen respondent in the eight months that had elapsed since the sale, "there [was] no doubt whatsoever" in his mind that the person shown on the photograph was respondent. Glover also made a positive in-court identification without objection.

No explanation was offered by the prosecution for the failure to utilize a photographic array or to conduct a line-up.

Respondent, who took the stand in his own defense, testified that on May 5, the day in question, he had been ill at his Albany Avenue apartment ("a lot of back pains, muscle spasms . . . a bad heart . . . high blood pressure . . . neuralgia in my face, and sinus"), and that at no time on that particular day had he been at 201 Westland. His wife testified that she recalled, after her husband had refreshed her memory, that he was home all day on May 5. . . .

The jury found respondent guilty on both counts of the information. He received a sentence of not less than six nor more than nine years. His conviction was affirmed *per curiam* by the Supreme Court of Connecticut. . . .

Fourteen months later, respondent filed a petition for habeas corpus in the United States District Court for the District of Connecticut. He alleged that the admission of the identification testimony at his state trial deprived him of due process of law to which he was entitled under the Fourteenth Amendment. The District Court . . . dismissed respondent's petition. On appeal, the United States Court of Appeals for the Second Circuit reversed, with instructions to issue the writ unless the State gave notice of a desire to retry respondent and the new trial occurred within a reasonable time to be fixed by the District Judge. . . .

We granted certiorari. . . .

OPINION

[T]he "sole evidence tying Brathwaite to the possession and sale of the heroin consisted in his identifications by the police undercover agent, Jimmy Glover." . . .

Petitioner at the outset acknowledges that "the procedure in the instant case was suggestive [because only one photograph was used] and unnecessary" [because there was no emergency or exigent circumstance]. . . . Court of Appeals, proposes a *per se* rule of exclusion that he claims is dictated by the demands of the Fourteenth Amendment's guarantee of due process. . . .

Courts of Appeals appear to have developed at least two approaches to such evidence. . . . The first, or *per se* approach, employed by the Second Circuit in the present case, focuses on the procedures employed and requires exclusion of the out-of-court identification evidence, without regard to reliability, whenever it had been obtained through unnecessarily suggested confrontation procedures. The justifications advanced are the elimination of evidence of uncertain reliability, deterrence of the police and prosecutors, and the stated "fair assurance against the awful risks of misidentification." . . .

The second, or more lenient, approach is one that continues to rely on the totality of the circumstances. It permits the admission of the confrontation evidence if, despite the suggestive aspect, the out-of-court identification possesses certain features of reliability. Its adherents feel that the *per se* approach is not mandated by the Due Process Clause of the Fourteenth Amendment. This second approach, in contrast to the other, is ad hoc and serves to limit the societal costs imposed by a sanction that excludes relevant evidence from consideration and evaluation by the trier of fact. . . .

The respondent here stresses . . . the need for deterrence of improper identification practice, a factor he regards as pre-eminent. Photographic identification, it is said, continues to be needlessly employed. . . . He argues that a totality rule cannot be expected to have a significant deterrent impact; only a strict rule of exclusion will have direct and immediate impact on law enforcement agents. Identification evidence is so convincing to the jury that sweeping exclusionary rules are required. Fairness of the trial is threatened by suggestive confrontation evidence, and thus, it is said, an exclusionary rule has an established constitutional predicate.

There are, of course, several interests to be considered and taken into account. The driving force behind *United States* v. *Wade* . . . was the Court's concern with the problems of eyewitness identification. . . .

The second factor is deterrence. Although the *per se* approach has the more significant deterrent effect, the totality approach also has an influence on police behavior. The police will guard against unnecessarily suggestive procedures under the totality rule, as well as the *per se* one, for fear that their actions will lead to the exclusion of identifications as unreliable.

The third factor is the effect on the administration of justice. Here the *per se* approach suffers serious drawbacks since it denies the trier reliable evidence, it may result, on occasion, in the guilty going free. Also, because of its rigidity, the *per se* approach may make error by the trial judge more likely than the totality approach. . . .

[I]nflexible rules of exclusion that may frustrate rather than promote justice have not been viewed recently by this Court with unlimited enthusiasm. . . .

The standard, after all, is that of fairness as required by the Due Process Clause of the Fourteenth Amendment. . . .

We therefore conclude that reliability is the linchpin in determining the admissibility of identification testimony. . . . The factors to be considered are . . . the opportunity of the witness to view the criminal at the time of the crime, the witness' degree of attention, the accuracy of his prior description of the criminal, the level of certainty demonstrated at the confrontation, and the time between the crime and the confrontation. Against these factors is to be weighed the corrupting effect of the suggestive identification itself.

We turn, then, to the facts of this case and apply the analysis:

1. The opportunity to view. Glover testified that for two to three minutes he stood at the apartment door, within two feet of the respondent. The door opened twice, and each time the man stood at the door. The moments passed, the conversation took place, and payment was made. Glover looked directly at his vendor. It was near sunset, to be sure, but the sun had not yet set, so it was not dark or even dusk or twilight. Natural light from outside entered the hallway through a window. There was natural light, as well, from inside the apartment.

2. The degree of attention. Glover was not a casual or passing observer, as is so often the case with eyewitness identification. Trooper Glover was a trained police officer on duty—and specialized and dangerous duty—when he called at the third floor of 201 Westland in Hartford on May 5, 1970. . . .

3. The accuracy of the description. Glover's description was given to D'Onofrio within minutes after the transaction. It included the vendor's race, his height, his build, the color and style of his hair, and the high cheekbone facial feature. It also included clothing the vendor wore. . . .

4. The witness' level of certainty. There is no dispute that the photograph in question was that of respondent. Glover, in response to a question whether the photograph was that of the person from whom he made the purchase, testified: "There is no question whatsoever." . . .

5. The time between the crime and the confrontation. Glover's description of his vendor was given to D'Onofrio within minutes of the crime. The photographic identification took place only two days later. We do not have here the passage of weeks or months between the crime and the viewing of the photograph.

These indicators of Glover's ability to make an accurate identification are hardly outweighed by the corrupting effect of the challenged identification itself. Although identifications arising from single-photograph displays may be viewed in general with suspicion . . . we find in the instant case little pressure on the witness to acquiesce in the suggestion that such a display entails. . . .

Surely, we cannot say that under all circumstances of this case there is "a very substantial likelihood of irreparable misidentification." Short of that point, such evidence is for the jury to weigh. We are content to rely upon the good sense and judgement of American juries for evidence with some element of untrustworthiness is customary grist for the jury mill. Juries are not so susceptible that they cannot measure intelligently the weight of identification testimony that has some questionable feature. . . .

The judgement of the Court of Appeals is reversed.

It is so ordered.

DISSENT

Mr. Justice Marshall, with whom Mr. Justice Brennan joins, dissenting.

Today's decision can come as no surprise to those who have been watching the Court dismantle the protections against mistaken eyewitness testimony erected a decade ago in *United States* v. *Wade.* But it is still distressing to see the Court virtually ignore the teaching of experience embodied in those decisions and blindly uphold the conviction of a defendant who may well be innocent. . . .

[I]n determining the admissibility of the identification in this case, the Court considers two alternatives, a *per se* exclusionary rule and a totality-of-the-circumstances approach. The Court weighs three factors in deciding . . . the totality approach. In my view, the Court wrongly evaluates the impact of these factors.

First, the Court acknowledges that one of the factors, deterrence of police use of unnecessarily suggestive identification procedures, favors the *per se* rule. Indeed, it does so heavily, for such a rule would make it unquestionably clear to the police they must never use a suggestive procedure when a fairer alternative is available. I have no doubt that conduct would quickly conform to the rule.

Second, the Court gives passing consideration to the dangers of eyewitness identification recognized in the *Wade* trilogy. It concludes, however, that the grave risk of error does not justify adoption of the *per se* approach because that would too often result in exclusion of relevant evidence. In my view this conclusion totally ignores the lessons of *Wade*. The dangers of mistaken identification are . . . simply too great to permit unnecessarily suggestive identifications. . . . While the Court is "content to rely on the good sense and judgement of American juries," the impetus for . . . *Wade* was repeated miscarriages of justice resulting from juries' willingness to credit inaccurate eyewitness testimony.

Finally, the Court errs in its assessment of the relative impact of the two approaches on the administration of justice. . . .

First, the *per se* rule here is not "inflexible." Where evidence is suppressed, for example, as the fruit of an unlawful search, it may well be forever lost to the prosecution. Identification evidence, however, can by its very nature be readily and effectively reproduced. . . .

Second, other exclusionary rules have been criticized for preventing jury consideration of relevant and usually reliable evidence in order to serve interests unrelated to guilt or innocence, such as discouraging illegal searches or denial of counsel. Suggestively obtained eyewitness testimony is excluded, in contrast, precisely because of its unreliability and concomitant irrelevance. Its exclusion both protects the integrity of the truth-seeking function of the trial and discourages police use of needlessly inaccurate and ineffective investigatory methods.

Indeed, impermissibly suggestive identifications are not merely worthless law enforcement tools. They pose a grave threat to society at large in a more direct way than most governmental disobedience of the law. . . . For if the police and the public erroneously conclude, on the basis of an unnecessarily suggestive confrontation, that the right man has been caught and convicted, the real outlaw must still remain at large. Law enforcement has failed in its primary function and has left society unprotected from the depredations of an active criminal.

For these reasons, I conclude that adoption of the *per se* rule would enhance, rather than detract from, the effective administration of justice. In my view, the Court's totality test will allow seriously unreliable and misleading evidence to be put before juries. Equally important, it will allow dangerous criminals to remain on the streets while citizens assume that police actions has given them protection. According to my calculus, all three of the factors upon which the Court relies point to acceptance of the *per se* approach.

Even more disturbing than the Court's reliance on the totality test, however, is the analysis it uses, which suggests a reinterpretation of the concept of due process violations in identification procedures may not be measured by whether the government employed procedures violating standards of fundamental fairness. By relying on the probable accuracy of a challenged identification, instead of the necessity for its use, the Court seems to be ascertaining whether the defendant was probably guilty. Until today, I had thought that "Equal justice under law" meant that the existence of constitutional violations did not depend on the race, sex, religion, nationality, or likely guilt of the accused. The Due Process Clause requires adherence to the same high standard of fundamental fairness in dealing with every criminal defendant, whatever his personal characteristics and irrespective of the strength of the State's case against him. Strong evidence that the defendant is guilty should be relevant only to the determination whether an error of constitutional magnitude was nevertheless harmless beyond a reasonable doubt.

CASE DISCUSSION

Brathwaite was charged with, and convicted of, possession and sale of heroin. At his trial, held eight months after the crime, the prosecution introduced Brathwaite's photograph as identification without objection when a witness said he had no doubt was Brathwaite. The Connecticut Supreme Court affirmed the conviction. Brathwaite filed a petition for *habeas corpus* in the federal district court, alleging that the admission of identification testimony denied him due process. The District Court dismissed the petition, but the Court of Appeals reversed. The United States Supreme Court granted *certiorari*. The Supreme Court held that the due process clause did not compel the exclusion of the identification evidence; its reliability depended on the totality of the circumstances that the jury should decide.

What precisely was the "totality of circumstances" taken into account in this case? Do you think it demonstrates "a very substantial likelihood of irreparable misidentification?" Do you agree that Glover had sufficient opportunity to observe Brathwaite? to describe him accurately? to identify the photograph positively? If not, was this "harmless error"? Is the dissent correct that the Court is "dismantling the protections against mistaken eyewitness testimony erected . . . in *United States v. Wade?*" Is it correct in arguing that the Court wrongfully evaluated the impact of the exclusionary rule and the totality of circumstances? Evaluate those arguments. Would you side with the dissent or majority in this case? Has the majority sacrificed accuracy at the expense of finality? at the expense of law enforcement, as the dissent maintains?

Decision Point

Foster was convicted of robbing a Western Union office. The police put Foster, the only one wearing a leather jacket similar to the robber's, in a line-up with two other men who were considerably shorter than Foster. When the manager could not identify the robber, the police permitted a **showup**, or a one-on-one confrontation. The witness manager still made only a tentative identification.

Ten days later, the manager identified Foster, who was the only person from the first line-up to appear in the second. The Supreme Court decided that "the suggestive elements in this identification procedure made it all but inevitable" that the manager would identify Foster, "whether or not he was in fact the man. In effect, the police repeatedly said to the witness, '*This* is the man.' "[12]

Did the line-up deny Foster due process of law? The United States Supreme Court ruled that it did because it was unnecessarily and impermissibly suggestive.

Photograph Identification Procedures

The line-up is the least unreliable, but not the only, identification procedure. Police also frequently use photograph identifications ("mug shots"). However, the fewer the number of photos used, the less reliable the identifications are. Furthermore, photographs in which the suspect stands out are highly suggestive. In addition, police can make remarks such as "Is this the one?" or "The suspect is in this group of photos" that lead to particular conclusions. Despite their unreliability and their potential misuse, as in the specific showings such mentioned here, courts rarely rule that photographic identifications violate the due process clause.[13]

Decision Point

A government informer told authorities that he had discussed a bank robbery with Ash. Acting on this information, an FBI agent showed four witnesses five black-and-white mug shots of black males of generally the same age, height, and weight, one of which was Ash. All four witnesses made uncertain identifications of Ash's picture. Ash, along with a co-defendant Bailey, was indicted for robbery.

Trial was finally set, nearly three years after the crime. In preparing for trial, the prosecutor decided to use a photographic display to determine whether the witnesses he planned to call would be able to make in-court identifications. Shortly before the trial, an FBI agent and the prosecutor showed five color photographs to the four witnesses who had previously tentatively identified the black-and-white photograph of Ash. Three of the witnesses selected the picture of Ash, but one was unable to make any selection. None of the witnesses selected the picture of Bailey that was in the group.

Did this postindictment identification deny Ash his right to counsel? The Supreme Court said no: "Pretrial photographic identifications. . . are hardly unique in offering the possibilities for the actions of the prosecutor to unfairly prejudice the accused. Evidence favorable to the accused may be withheld; testimony of witnesses may be manipulated; the results of laboratory tests may be contrived. In many ways the prosecutor, by accident or design, may improperly subvert the trial. The primary safeguard against abuses of this kind is the ethical responsibility of the prosecutor, who, as so often has been said, may 'strike hard blows' but not 'foul ones.' If that safeguard fails, review remains available under due process standards. These same safeguards apply to misuse of photographs. . . . We are not persuaded that the risks inherent in the use of photographic displays are so pernicious that an extraordinary system of safeguards is required. We hold, then, that the Sixth Amendment does not grant the right to counsel at photographic displays conducted by the Government for the purpose of allowing a witness to attempt identification of the offender."

The dissent argued: "The dangers of mistaken identification . . . are applicable in large measure to photographic as well as corporeal (the body) identification. Indeed, in reality, preservation of the photographs affords little protection to the unrepresented accused. For although retention of the photographs may mitigate the dangers of misidentification due to the suggestiveness of the photographs themselves, it cannot in any sense reveal to the defense counsel the more subtle, and therefore more dangerous, suggestiveness that might derive from the manner in which the photographs were displayed or any accompanying comments or gestures. Finally, and *unlike* the line-up situation, the accused himself is not even present at the photographic identification, thereby reducing the likelihood that irregularities in the procedures will ever come to light."

Showups

The showup is widely regarded as the least reliable identification procedure. One expert called show-ups, "the most grossly suggestive identification procedure now or ever used by the police." The *Stovall* Court conceded that "the practice of showing suspects singly to suspects for the purpose of identification, and not as part of a line-up, has been widely condemned."

Despite these conclusions, courts admit testimony derived from showups in several circumstances. For example, if showups take place within a few hours of the crime, two reasons justify admitting identifications from them: (1) the need for quickly solving the crime; and (2) the desirability of eyewitnesses' fresh, accurate identifications. Furthermore, when witnesses accidentally confront suspects, as in courthouse corridors, courts admit identifications based on them. Other cases in which courts have admitted showup identifications include: when they occur in emergencies, such as when witnesses are hospitalized; when suspects are at large, such when police cruise crime scenes with witnesses; and when external factors "prove" the identification accurate, as when the witness already knows the suspect.[14]

≡ REFUSAL TO COOPERATE IN IDENTIFICATION PROCEDURES

Suspects' refusal to cooperate in identification procedures can have several consequences. Prosecutors might comment on such refusal at trial, urging jurors to read guilt into such refusals since they constitute circumstantial evidence of consciousness of guilt. Furthermore, courts sometimes put suspects who refuse to cooperate in civil or criminal contempt, subjecting them to fines and incarceration. Finally, police may conduct the procedure over suspects' objections, such as they did in *Schmerber v. California*. Officers may even use force to secure compliance so long as they use only the force reasonably necessary to conduct the identification procedure.[15]

≡ SUMMARY

Eyewitnesses are the primary source of suspect identification used in the criminal process; but their identifications are also often unreliable. The Fifth Amendment does not protect identification procedures—blood and other tests, handwriting samples, voice exemplars, line-ups, showups, and photographs. The Sixth Amendment applies to line-ups after formal prosecution begins. The Fourteenth Amendment due process clause prohibits admitting evidence based on identification procedures too suggestive to produce reliable results whenever they take place.

The rules governing identification procedures balance and promote the interests in accurate fact-finding and effective law enforcement, the process interest in fair proceedings, controlling illegal police practices, and protecting individual dignity and rights.

≡ QUESTIONS FOR REVIEW AND DISCUSSION

1. What are the principal sources of witness misidentification?
2. Define the major identification procedures.
3. Why does the Fifth Amendment right against self-incrimination not protect eyewitness identification procedures? Should it? Why? Why not?
4. What provisions in the Constitution protect identification procedures?
5. What are the strengths and weaknesses of line-ups, showups, and photographic identification procedures?
6. At what point in the criminal process do you think suspects should have the right to a lawyer during identification procedures? Why?
7. Should suspects be forced to participate in identification procedures? Explain your answer.

▬ NOTES

1. "Pagano Case Points Finger at Lineups," *National Law Journal* (September 10, 1979), 1.

2. "Notes: Did Your Eyes Deceive You? Expert Psychological Testimony on the Unreliability of Eyewitness Identification," *Stanford Law Review* 29 (1977): 982–83.

3. "Notes: Did Your Eyes Deceive You? Expert Psychological Testimony on the Unreliability of Eyewitness Identification," *Stanford Law Review* 29 (1977): 969; David Bazelon, "Eyewitness News," *Psychology Today,* March 1980, 102–4; Wayne R. Lafave and Jerold H. Israel, *Criminal Procedure,* vol. 1 (St. Paul: West Publishing Company, 1984), 551–53.

4. *Basoff v. State,* 208 Md. 643, 119 A.2d 917 (1956).

5. *Haywood County v. Hudson,* 740 S.W.2d 718 (Tenn. 1987).

6. *People v. Thomas,* 139 Misc. 2d 1072, 529 N.Y.S.2d 429 (1988).

7. *Barlow v. Superior Court,* 190 Cal. App. 3d 1652, 236 Cal.Rptr. 134 (1987).

8. Lafave and Israel, *Criminal Procedure,* 1: 556.

9. 406 U.S. 682, 92 S.Ct. 1877, 32 L.Ed.2d 411 (1972).

10. 388 U.S. 293, 87 S.Ct. 1967, 18 L.Ed.2d 1199 (1967).

11. *Stovall v. Denno,* 388 U.S. 293, 87 S.Ct. 1967, 18 L.Ed.2d 1199 (1967).

12. *Foster v. California,* 394 U.S. 440, 89 S.Ct. 1127, 22 L.Ed.2d 402 (1969).

13. Lafave and Israel, *Criminal Procedure,* 1: 588–60.

14. Lafave and Israel, *Criminal Procedure,* 1: 590–91.

15. Ibid., 557–58.

Chapter Nine

The Decision to Charge and the First Appearance

CHAPTER OUTLINE

CHAPTER MAIN POINTS

1. Formal proceedings begin when prosecutors file complaints in criminal courts.

2. When criminal prosecution begins, defendants have a right to a lawyer to defend them against the power and resources of the state and technicalities of the law.

3. Prosecutors have broad—and largely unreviewable—discretion to charge suspects with crimes.

4. At the initial appearance in court, the magistrate notifies defendants of their rights, sets bail, and assigns lawyers to defendants too poor to afford to hire their own.

5. Defendants do not have the right to a lawyer in *all* criminal cases, and the right does not accrue until after the initial appearance.

6. Pretrial release and detention balances individual rights, community safety, and the expenditure of public resources.

7. Formally, all decisions following the filing of a complaint require judicial approval.

CHAPTER KEY TERMS

arraignment bringing defendant to court to hear criminal charges in court and requiring defendants to plead to the charges

bail schedules lists of bail amounts that do not require court appearances to set

charging instrument the document that gives a court jurisdiction—authority—to hear a criminal case

citation release release by police without arrest or appearance in court

criminal complaint the initial instrument presented to a magistrate charging the defendant with committing a crime coupled with an offer to prove that fact

fair hearing right to representation by counsel, to present evidence, to cross-examine witnesses, and to have findings supported by evidence

first appearance brief judicial proceeding in lower criminal court to read charges against defendants, inform them of their rights, assign attorneys, and set bail

indigent defendants defendants who are too poor to afford their own lawyers

mockery of justice standard standard to determine effectiveness of counsel that asks whether the proceedings were no more than a farce

own recognizance (O.R.) pretrial release in exchange for defendant's promise to appear in court

pro bono to defend a defendant voluntarily and without fees

reasonably competent attorney standard standard to measure effectiveness of counsel that asks whether counsel acted according to usual standards of professional competence

recoupment programs plan by which indigent defendants who later have resources must repay the state for some or all of the cost of appointed counsel and other expenditures

special circumstances rule right to a lawyer only in particular circumstances, not a general right to counsel in all cases

supervised release bail accompanied by requirements to report to third persons or agencies

trial *de novo* a new trial as if the original had not occurred

THE INITIATION OF THE FORMAL CRIMINAL PROCESS

In the brief interval between arrest and initial appearance, both the police and prosecutor make critical decisions. The police decide if, on the basis of their investigation, the case warrants formal judicial action or whether they will release suspects. The police might release suspects outright if they believe suspects are not guilty. Or, police may release suspects with the admonition that the police may "call upon them later.'' In misdemeanors particularly, the police may release suspects on the informal condition that they get "help," such as drug and alcohol treatment or family counseling.

Police take to the prosecutor's office cases that they decide warrant formal criminal charges. Prosecutors make an independent judgment concerning the disposition of cases brought to them. They may decide not to charge and to release suspects outright. On the other hand, they may **divert** the case into a community service, substance abuse, or family violence treatment program. If suspects participate in these programs, prosecutors agree to discontinue the criminal process.

If prosecutors decide to charge, they start the formal judicial proceedings by filing a complaint, information, or indictment. These proceedings test the factual foundation for the decision to charge by having disinterested parties assess the government's quantum of proof. If the government presents the required quantum of proof, defendants must appear to answer the criminal charges against them. (See chap. 10.)

Decision Point

Suppose that a store detective caught three shoplifters at about the same time. The detective reports all the incidents to the prosecutor's office. Which ones should the prosecutor charge with crimes? divert into some program? dismiss?

1. A student took a cassette recorder to record his criminal procedure class because the professor talked too fast. He works part-time to pay for school, and although he could have paid for it, it would have been difficult. He has never been in trouble with the law before, and says he will pay for the recorder.

2. A woman who works only occasionally took a cordless phone for a friend who agreed to pay $35, half the phone's value. The woman has taken compact disks, tape cassettes, and an answering machine from the same store within the past six months.

3. A fifty-year-old woman slipped a pair of stereo earphones in her purse. The woman is wealthy and indignantly denies that she intended to steal the earphones. She tells the detective she put it in her bag because she wanted to pick up some film, batteries, and other small items and simply forgot she had put it there.

Once prosecutors decide to charge them with crimes, suspects make their **first appearance,** which takes place in the lower criminal courts. At the point of charging, suspects formally become criminal defendants. Magistrates perform several duties at the first appearance. They make sure the government has probable cause to detain defendants, if a neutral officer has not already done so. They read the charges against defendants and inform them of their rights as criminal defendants. They determine whether defendants qualify as indigents, and if so, appoint attorneys for them. Finally, they set bail.

The first appearance should not be confused with three other judicial proceedings prior to trial. Grand jury review and preliminary hearings test the government's case against defendants to make sure that probable cause exists to require defendants to answer criminal charges. **Arraignment** brings defendants to court to formally hear the charges and requires defendants to plead to them. The first appearance, on the other hand, mainly serves to prepare defendants for possible further advances into the criminal process.

The decision to initiate judicial criminal proceedings has grave implications, as the Supreme Court has observed:

> The initiation of judicial criminal proceedings is far from a mere formalism. It is the starting point of our whole system of adversary criminal justice. For it is only then that the Government has committed itself to prosecute, and only then that the adverse positions of Government and defendant have solidified. It is then that a defendant finds himself faced with the prosecutorial forces of organized society, and immersed in the intricacies of substantive and procedural criminal law. It is this point, therefore, that marks the commencement of the "criminal prosecutions."[1]

The decision to detain citizens, charge them with crimes, and expend state resources to do so depends first on sufficient and accurate facts. In addition, process, organizational, and societal interests affect these decisions. Decisions regarding bail, conditions of pretrial detention, the appointment and assistance of counsel, and scheduling further proceedings rest on the interests in limiting government power, assuring orderly proceedings, and promoting individual dignity. Assigning counsel to indigent defendants, as well as supervising bail and pretrial detention, reflects both constitutional and societal interests. These actions aim both to reduce discrimination and to protect the poor and the weak from unfair disadvantage—to insure that justice is blind to wealth, class, power, race, and gender. The courts do not always balance these interests to everyone's satisfaction. Some claim that justice favors the strong over the weak. Others maintain that process goals thwart effective criminal law enforcement. Still others believe that the adversary process cannot accurately determine the facts because of time pressures and deficient resources. Finally, some observers assert that adversary proceedings are costly, time-consuming, and inefficient. These observations underline the difficulties in obtaining the correct result while adequately attending to process, organizational, and societal interests.

≡ THE DECISION TO CHARGE

From the time police bring cases to prosecutors' offices, lawyers and judges formally administer the criminal process. The police recede into the background except as lawyers need them for clarification, further investigation, and witness accounts. Nevertheless, police informally influence the charging decision. Police control the cases prosecutors receive. Furthermore, the various forms of police investigation discussed in chapters 4 through 7 determine the amount and quality of evidence available to prosecutors. Finally, prosecutors are likely to take at face value recommendations from officers with reputations for "good" cases. Equally likely, on the other hand, they will discount cases from officers with poor track records. Prosecutors drop some cases without further action or "divert" some suspects into drug or psychological treatment programs, or into restitution plans whereby prosecutors agree not to charge if suspects pay back victims or perform community service.

The numbers of cases prosecutors decide not to pursue ranges from a few in some jurisdictions to nearly half in others. Several interests lie behind the decision to charge. In some cases, prosecutors have insufficient evidence—no witnesses or other evidence—to support prosecution. Available witnesses may be neither reliable nor convincing. Witness problems predominate in violent crimes where victims know their assailants. In over half these cases, witness and victims do not cooperate, either because they are afraid or have a change of heart over prosecuting people they know. Sometimes, prosecutors cannot use evidence because the police seized it illegally. Contrary to the popular belief that many guilty criminals go unpunished due to excluded evidence, less than 2 percent are dismissed for this reason.[2]

Prosecutors transfer some cases to other courts or out of the criminal justice system. Here matters of jurisdiction and the interests of justice affect the decision. Prosecutors may believe that restitution for petty theft serves justice better than criminal prosecution, that wife battering belongs in family court, or that juvenile court better serves some juveniles old enough to face trial as adults.

Decision Point

Defendant was charged with criminal sale and possession of cocaine. By the time he was indicted, the defendant was in an advanced state of AIDS and related complicating illnesses. He had pneumocystis carinii pneumonia, the virus had invaded his brain and his stomach, and peripheral nerve damage caused pain and suffering to the extent that doctors ordered him to limit his physical exercise to sitting in a chair for one hour a day. Doctors' prognosis was death within three to four months. Should the government continue the case against the defendant? The government dropped the case against the defendant because "it does not appear that the interest of justice would be substantially served by the defendant's continued prosecution under this indictment." The court noted that "the uncompromising rampage of the multiple disease processes have condemned this defendant to a painful, imminent death. When the rationale for incarceration becomes unjustifiable because of . . . a deadly disease, it becomes imperative to allow the sufferer to live his last days in the best circumstances possible and with dignity and compassion."[3]

Insufficient resources prevent the prosecution of all cases, even where prosecutors have sufficient convincing evidence. Prosecutors set priorities: petty thefts go to restitution to allow time for armed robbery; violent sex crimes take precedence over prostitution; and a few well-known tax evaders serve as examples to deter tax evasion. According to some, selective prosecution infringes on the legislatures' prerogative to make laws. Others say selectively prosecuting some individuals in a category—like "fat cat" or notorious tax evaders—undermines impartial law enforcement and violates the equal protection clause. Courts have not accepted these arguments.

The prosecutors' charging power gives them, according to former prosecutor and Supreme Court Justice Robert Jackson, "more control over life, liberty, and reputation than any other person in America." The President's Crime Commission concluded that prosecutors are the key administrative officer[s] in the processing of cases. Yet this decision is largely hidden from view because discretion, not formal law, controls prosecutors' charging decisions. Unlike police discretion, which formally anyway, is illegal, prosecutors are lawfully granted broad discretion in the charging process.[4]

For example, a Baltimore Oriole pitcher threw a ball from the bullpen in Fenway Park and hit a Boston Red Sox fan in the head. The fan obtained a complaint against the pitcher, but the district attorney decided not to charge. The fan sought an order compelling the district attorney to prosecute. In denying the request the court said:

. . . A district attorney has wide discretion over whether to prosecute an individual, just as he has wide discretion in determining whether to discontinue a prosecution once commenced. . . . The plaintiff has no constitutional right to direct the conduct of a public prosecutor.[5]

Prosecutors can abuse their discretion; but, they cannot prosecute out of vindictiveness. For example, in *Thigpen v. Roberts,* Roberts lost control of his car, struck a truck, and killed a passenger. He paid fines in a justice of the peace court on a reckless driving citation. When Roberts asserted his right to **trial de novo** (a new trial in a lower criminal court), the prosecutor obtained a felony indictment, charging Rogers with manslaughter. After conviction, the judge sentenced Roberts to twenty years in prison. On appeal, the United States Supreme Court ruled that the prosecutor acted vindictively by using his power to "up the ante" simply because he wanted to discourage misdemeanants from appealing convictions on citations in justice of the peace courts.[6]

Furthermore, prosecutors can select cases to prosecute only according to acceptable criteria. Hence, they cannot prosecute only blacks for murder, only the poor for stealing, or only the young for drug use. That violates the equal protection clause of the Constitution. They need not, however, treat everyone alike. They may, for example, prosecute "big shots" in order to make examples of them. The Seventh Circuit Court of Appeals, in a case involving selecting a public official for prosecution, said:

It makes good sense to prosecute those who will receive the media's attention. Publication of the proceedings may enhance the deterrent effect of the prosecution and maintain public faith in the precept that public officials are not above the law.[7]

Prosecutors may also selectively charge individuals within a large group of violators because the government does not have the resources to prosecute everyone who violates certain laws, such as the tax codes. Recently, the Supreme Court addressed selective prosecution when the federal government prosecuted only a few of many young men who failed to register under the Military Service Act of 1981.

CASE

Were they unfairly chosen for prosecution?

Wayte v. United States

470 U.S. 598, 105 S.Ct. 1524, 84 L.Ed.2d 547 (1985)

[Powell, J., delivered the opinion of the Court, in which Burger, C.J., and White, Blackmun, Rehnquist, Stevens, and O'Connor, JJ., joined. Marshall, J., filed a dissenting opinion in which Brennan, J., joined.]

FACTS

On July 2, 1980, pursuant to his authority under § 3 of the Military Selective Service Act, the President issued Presidential Proclamation No. 4771. . . . This Proclamation directed male citizens and certain male residents born during 1960 to register with the Selective Service System during the week of July 21, 1980. Petitioner fell within that class but did not register. Instead, he wrote several letters to Government officials, including the President, stating that he had not registered and did not intend to do so.[a]

Petitioner's letters were added to a Selective Service file of young men who advised that they had failed to register or who were reported by others as having failed to register. For reasons we discuss, Selective Service adopted a policy of passive enforcement under which it would investigate and prosecute only the cases of nonregistration contained in this file. In furtherance of this policy, Selective Service sent a letter on June 17, 1981, to each reported violator who had not registered and for whom it had an address. The letter explained the duty to register, stated that Selective Service had information that the person was required to register but had not done so, requested that he either comply with the law by filling out an enclosed registration card or explain why he was not subject to registration, and warned that a violation could result in criminal prosecution and specified penalties. Petitioner received a copy of this letter but did not respond.

On July 20, 1981, Selective Service transmitted to the Department of Justice, for investigation and potential prosecution, the names of petitioner and 133 other young men identified under its passive enforcement system—all of whom had not registered in response to the Service's June letter. At two later dates, it referred the names of 152 more young men similarly identified. After screening out the names of those who appeared not to be in the class required to register, the Department of Justice referred the remaining names to the Federal Bureau of Investigation for additional inquiry and to the United

---

[a]On August 4, 1980, for example, petitioner write to both the President and the Selective Service System. In his letter to the President he stated:

"I decided to obey my conscience rather than your law. I did not register for your draft. I will never register for your draft. Nor will I ever cooperate with yours or any other military system, despite the laws I might break or the consequences which may befall me."

In his letter to the Selective Service System, he similarly stated: "I have not registered for the draft. I never plan to register. I realize the possible consequences of my action, and I accept them."

Six months later, the petitioner sent a second letter to Selective Service:

"Last August I wrote to inform you of my intention not to register for the draft. Well, I did not register, and still plan never to do so, but thus far I have received no reply to my letter, much less any news about your much-threatened prosecutions."

"I must interpret your silence as meaning that you are too busy or disorganized to respond to letters or keep track of us draft-age youth. So I will keep you posted of my whereabouts."

He also stated that, although he would "be travelling the nation . . . encouraging resistance and spreading the word about peace and disarmament," he could be reached at his home address in Pasadena, California.

States Attorneys for the districts in which the nonregistrants resided. Petitioner's name was one of those referred.

Pursuant to Department of Justice Policy, those referred were not immediately prosecuted. Instead, the appropriate United States Attorney was required to notify identified nonregistrants by registered mail that, unless they registered in a specified time, prosecution would be considered. In addition, an FBI agent was usually sent to interview the nonregistrant before prosecution was instituted. This effort to persuade nonregistrants to change their minds became known as the "beg" policy. Under it, young men who registered late were not prosecuted, while those who never registered were investigated further by the Government. Pursuant to the "beg" policy, the United States Attorney for the Central District of California sent petitioner a letter on October 15, 1981, urging him to register or face possible prosecution. Again petitioner failed to respond.

On December 9, 1981, the Department of Justice instructed all United States Attorneys not to begin seeking indictments against nonregistrants until further notice. On January 7, 1982, the President announced a grace period to afford nonregistrants a further opportunity to register without penalty. This grace period extended until February 28, 1982. Petitioner still did not register.

Over the next few months, the Department decided to begin prosecuting those young men who, despite the grace period and "beg" policy, continued to refuse to register. It recognized that under the passive enforcement system those prosecuted were "liable to be vocal proponents of nonregistration" or persons "with religious or moral objections." It also recognized that prosecutions would "undoubtedly result in allegations that the [case was] brought in retribution for the nonregistrant's exercise of his first amendment rights." The Department was advised, however, that Selective Service could not develop a more "active" enforcement system for quite some time. Because of this, the Department decided to begin seeking indictments under the passive system without further delay. On May 21, 1982, United States Attorneys were notified to begin prosecution of nonregistrants. On June 28, 1982, FBI agents interviewed petitioner, and he continued to refuse to register. Accordingly on July 22, 1982, an indictment was returned against him for knowingly and willfully failing to register with the Selective Service. This was one of the first indictments returned against any individual under the passive policy.

Petitioner moved to dismiss the indictment on the grounds of selective prosecution. He contended that he and the other nonregistrants[a] were "vocal opponents of the registration program who had been impermissibly targeted (out of an estimated 674,000 nonregistrants)[b] for prosecution on the basis of their exercise of First Amendment Rights.

On November 15, 1982, the District Court dismissed the indictment. . . .

The Court of Appeals reversed. . . .

[a]The record indicates that only 13 of the 286 young men Selective Service referred to the Department of Justice had been indicted at the time the District Court considered this case. As of March 31, 1984, three more men had been indicted. The approximately 270 not indicted either registered, were found not to be subject to registration requirements, could not be found, or were under continuing investigation. The record does not indicate how many fell into each category.
[b]On July 28, 1982, Selective Service stated that 8,365,000 young men had registered out of the estimated 9,039,000 who were required to do so. This amounted to a nonregistration rate of approximately 7.5 percent.

OPINION

... It is appropriate to judge selective prosecution claims according to ordinary equal protection standards. These standards require petitioner to show both that the passive enforcement system had a discriminatory effect and that it was motivated by a discriminatory purpose. ... All petitioner has shown here is that those eventually prosecuted, along with many not prosecuted, reported themselves as having violated the law. He has not shown that the enforcement policy selected nonregistrants for prosecution on the basis of their speech. ... It did not subject vocal nonregistrants to any special burden. Indeed, those prosecuted in effect selected themselves for prosecution by refusing to register after being reported and warned by the Government.

Even if the passive policy had a discriminatory effect, petitioner has not shown the Government intended such a result. The evidence he presented demonstrated only that the Government was aware that the passive enforcement policy would result in prosecution of vocal objectors and that they would probably make selective prosecution claims. As we have noted, however: " 'Discriminatory purpose' . . . implies more than . . . intent as awareness of consequences. It implies that the decisionmaker . . . selected or reaffirmed a particular course of action at least in part 'because of,' not merely 'in spite of,' its adverse effects upon an identifiable group." In the present case, petitioner has not shown that the government prosecuted him *because* of his protest activities. Absent such a showing, his claim of selective prosecution fails. ...

[Affirmed.]

DISSENT

[Marshall, J., dissenting, Brennan, J., joins.]

The claim here is . . . that the system by which the Department defined the class of possible prosecutees—the "passive" enforcement system—was designed to discriminate against those who had exercised their First Amendment rights. Such governmental action cannot stand if undertaken with discriminatory intent. ... If the Government intentionally discriminated in defining the pool of potential prosecutees, it cannot immunize itself from liability merely by showing that it used permissible methods in choosing whom to prosecute from this previously tainted pool.

Under the Court's flawed approach, there would have been no equal protection violation in *Yick Wo v. Hopkins,* 118 U.S. 356 (1886), this Court's seminal selective prosecution decision. In *Yick Wo,* the Court reversed a conviction under a municipal ordinance that prohibited the construction of wooden laundries without a license. The Court held that such a conviction could not stand because the municipal licensors had discriminatorily denied licenses to individuals of Chinese origin. If the Court then had focused only on the prosecutions themselves, as it does now, it would have found no discrimination in the choice, among violators of the ordinance, of the individuals to be prosecuted. Indeed, all but one of these violators were of Chinese origin. Instead, the Court properly focused on the official action that led to those prosecutions. In *Yick Wo,* that prior action was the discriminatory denial of licenses, which affected the definition of the class from which prosecutees were chosen. In this case, the referrals made by Selective Service to the Justice Department for investigation and possible prosecution played a similar role and may also have been discriminatory. It is to that issue that the Court should have directed its attention. . . .

CASE DISCUSSION

The Department of Justice obtained an indictment of Wayte for knowingly and willfully failing to register with the Selective Service. Wayte moved to dismiss the indictment on the grounds of selective prosecution. The district court dismissed the indictment, and the court of appeals reversed the district court's dismissal. On writ of *certiorari,* the United States Supreme Court affirmed the court of appeals.

What arguments did Wayte advance in favor of his claim that the prosecution used improper means to decide to prosecute him? Do you believe that the government intentionally discriminated against Wayte? How could he prove that the government did discriminate against him? What is the dissent's point concerning *Yick Wo v. Hopkins?* Do you think this case is similar to *Yick Wo?* Explain. What should the test be for determining improper selectivity in prosecution? Should the government prosecute *all* defendants? What criteria ought to determine who not to prosecute? results? process? organizational interests? societal interests? What interests did the Court promote by upholding Wayte's conviction?

THE FIRST APPEARANCE

The **first appearance** is a brief proceeding in which defendants appear before a judicial officer in a lower criminal court. Magistrates make sure that the defendants in court are in fact those the prosecutor has decided to charge. The magistrates also inform defendants of their rights, assign attorneys to their cases, and set bail. For defendants not in custody the first appearance may take place several days after charging. Furthermore, some defendants, notably white-collar defendants, never have a first appearance. White-collar crime entails intricate, involved, and long-range investigation that frequently results in indictment prior to arrest; hence, white-collar defendants first appear at arraignment following indictment. (See chap. 10.)[8]

Defendants held in custody without arrest warrants, that is, without judicial determination that probable cause supports their detention, present an urgent situation. Nearly all suspects detained without warrants and prior to the filing of formal charges against them are suspected of "street crime"—robbery, burglary, and theft, or personal crimes of violence, such as rape, assault, and murder. All states have rules requiring that criminal justice officials promptly present suspects held in custody without warrants before a judge. Sometimes, the rules specify a time, such as twenty-four or thirty-six hours; others simply say, "without unnecessary delay."

The basic idea behind these rules is that independent magistrates assess the accuracy and sufficiency of the facts supporting the detention of citizens under the intrusive conditions outlined in chapter 7. This determination of probable cause to detain, occurring either at or sometime near, the first appearance should not be confused with the determination made at preliminary hearings and grand jury review. At these latter proceedings, the determination consists of whether or not evidence exists to require defendants to answer charges and proceed to trial. The probable cause to detain requires less quantum of proof than that required to proceed to trial, although no prescribed number of facts establishes either. The Supreme Court addressed the issue of judicial probable cause determinations for pretrial detentions following arrest in *Gerstein v. Pugh.*

CASE

Did he have a right to a probable cause "hearing"?

Gerstein v. Pugh

420 U.S. 103, 95 S.Ct. 854, 43 L.Ed.2d 54 (1975)

[Mr. Justice Powell delivered the opinion of the Court.]

FACTS

In March 1971 respondents Pugh and Henderson were arrested in Dade County, Fla. Each was charged with several offenses under a prosecutor's information.[a] Pugh was denied bail because one of the charges against him carried a potential life sentence, and Henderson remained in custody because he was unable to post a $4,500 bond.

In Florida, indictments are required only for prosecution of capital offenses. Prosecutors may charge all other crimes by information, without a prior preliminary hearing and without obtaining leave of court. At the time respondents were arrested, a Florida rule seemed to authorize adversary preliminary hearings to test probable cause for detention in all cases. But the Florida courts had held that the filing of an information foreclosed the suspect's right to a preliminary hearing. They had also held that habeas corpus could not be used, except perhaps in exceptional circumstances, to test the probable cause for detention under an information. The only possible methods for obtaining a judicial determination of probable cause were a special statute allowing a preliminary hearing after 30 days, and arraignment, which the District Court found was often delayed a month or more after arrest. As a

---

[a]Respondent Pugh was arrested on March 3, 1971. On March 16 an information was filed charging him with robbery, carrying a concealed weapon, and possession of a firearm during commission of a felony. Respondent Henderson was arrested on March 2, and charged by information on March 19 with the offenses of breaking and entering and assault and battery. The record does not indicate whether there was an arrest warrant in either case.

result, a person charged by information could be detained for a substantial period solely on the decision of a prosecutor. Respondents Pugh and Henderson filed a class action against Dade County officials in the Federal District Court, claiming a constitutional right to a judicial hearing on the issue of probable cause and requesting declaratory and injunctive relief. Respondents Turner and Faulk, also in custody under informations, subsequently intervened.[a] Petitioner Gerstein, the State Attorney for Dade County, was one of several defendants. . . .

[T]he District Court . . . ordered the Dade County defendants to give the named plaintiffs an immediate preliminary hearing to determine probable cause for further detention. It also ordered them to submit a plan providing preliminary hearings in all cases instituted by information. . . . The Court of Appeals for the Fifth Circuit stayed the District Court's order pending appeal, but while the case was awaiting decision, the Dade County judiciary voluntarily adopted a similar procedure of its own. . . . Under the amended rules every arrested person must be taken before a judicial officer within 24 hours. This 'first appearance' is similar to the 'first appearance hearing' ordered by the District Court in all respects but the crucial one: the magistrate does not make a determination of probable cause. The rule amendments also changed the procedure for preliminary hearings, restricting them to felony charges and codifying the rule that no hearings are available to persons charged by information or indictment. In a supplemental opinion the District Court held that the amended rules had not answered the basic constitutional objection, since a defendant charged by information still could be detained pending trial without a judicial determination of probable cause. Reaffirming its original ruling, the District Court declared that the continuation of this practice was unconstitutional. The Court of Appeals affirmed, modifying the District Court's decree in minor particulars and suggesting that the form of preliminary hearing provided by the amended Florida rules would be acceptable, as long as it was provided to all defendants in custody pending trial. State Attorney Gerstein petitioned for review, and we granted certiorari because of the importance of the issue. We affirm in part and reverse in part. . . .

OPINION

Both the standards and procedures for arrest and detention have been derived from the Fourth Amendment and its common-law antecedents. The standard for arrest is probable cause, defined in terms of facts and circumstances 'sufficient to warrant a prudent man in believing that the (suspect) had committed or was committing an offense.' This standard, like those for searches and seizures, represents a necessary accommodation between the individual's right to liberty and the State's duty to control crime.

These long-prevailing standards seek to safeguard citizens from rash and unreasonable interferences with privacy and from unfounded charges of crime. They also seek to give fair leeway for enforcing the law in the community's protection. Because many situations which confront officers in

---

[a]Turner was being held on a charge of auto theft, following arrest on March 11, 1971. Faulk was arrested on March 19 on charges of soliciting a ride and possession of marihuana.

the course of executing their duties are more or less ambiguous, room must be allowed for some mistakes on their part. But the mistakes must be those of reasonable men, acting on facts leading sensibly to their conclusions of probability. The rule of probable cause is a practical, nontechnical conception affording the best compromise that has been found for accommodating these often opposing interests. Requiring more would unduly hamper law enforcement. To allow less would be to leave law-abiding citizens at the mercy of the officers' whim or caprice.'

To implement the Fourth Amendment's protection against unfounded invasions of liberty and privacy, the Court has required that the existence of probable cause be decided by a neutral and detached magistrate whenever possible. . . .

'The point of the Fourth Amendment, which often is not grasped by zealous officers, is not that it denies law enforcement the support of the usual inferences which reasonable men draw from evidence. Its protection consists in requiring that those inferences be drawn by a neutral and detached magistrate instead of being judged by the officer engaged in the often competitive enterprise of ferreting out crime.' . . . Maximum protection of individual rights could be assured by requiring a magistrate's review of the factual justification prior to any arrest, but such a requirement would constitute an intolerable handicap for legitimate law enforcement. Thus, while the Court has expressed a preference for the use of arrest warrants when feasible, it has never invalidated an arrest supported by probable cause solely because the officers failed to secure a warrant. . . .

Under this practical compromise, a policeman's on-the-scene assessment of probable cause provides legal justification for arresting a person suspected of crime, and for a brief period of detention to take the administrative steps incident to arrest. Once the suspect is in custody, however, the reasons that justify dispensing with the magistrate's neutral judgment evaporate. There no longer is any danger that the suspect will escape or commit further crimes while the police submit their evidence to a magistrate. And, while the State's reasons for taking summary action subside, the suspect's need for a neutral determination of probable cause increases significantly. The consequences of prolonged detention may be more serious than the interference occasioned by arrest. . . .

Under the Florida procedures challenged here, a person arrested without a warrant and charged by information may be jailed or subjected to other restraints pending trial without any opportunity for a probable cause determination. Petitioner defends this practice on the ground that the prosecutor's decision to file an information is itself a determination of probable cause that furnishes sufficient reason to detain a defendant pending trial. Although a conscientious decision that the evidence warrants prosecution affords a measure of protection against unfounded detention, we do not think prosecutorial judgment standing alone meets the requirements of the Fourth Amendment. . . . [P]robable cause for the issuance of an arrest warrant must be determined by someone independent of police and prosecution. . . .

'A democratic society, in which respect for the dignity of all men is central, naturally guards against the misuse of the law enforcement process. Zeal in tracking down crime is not in itself an assurance of soberness of judgment.

Disinterestedness in law enforcement does not alone prevent disregard of cherished liberties. Experience has therefore counseled that safeguards must be provided against the dangers of the overzealous as well as the despotic. The awful instruments of the criminal law cannot be entrusted to a single functionary. The complicated process of criminal justice is therefore divided into different parts, responsibility for which is separately vested in the various participants upon whom the criminal law relies for its vindication.' . . .

Both the District Court and the Court of Appeals held that the determination of probable cause must be accompanied by the full panoply of adversary safeguards—counsel, confrontation, cross-examination, and compulsory process for witnesses. A full preliminary hearing of this sort is modeled after the procedure used in many States to determine whether the evidence justifies going to trial under an information or presenting the case to a grand jury. . . .

These adversary safeguards are not essential for the probable cause determination required by the Fourth Amendment. The sole issue is whether there is probable cause for detaining the arrested person pending further proceedings. This issue can be determined without an adversary hearing. The standard is the same as that for arrest. That standard—probable cause to believe the suspect has committed a crime—traditionally has been decided by a magistrate in a nonadversary proceeding on hearsay and written testimony, and the Court has approved these informal modes of proof. . . .

Because of its limited function and its nonadversary character, the probable cause determination is not a 'critical stage' in the prosecution that would require appointed counsel. . . .

We agree with the Court of Appeals that the Fourth Amendment requires a timely judicial determination of probable cause as a prerequisite to detention, and we accordingly affirm that much of the judgment. As we do not agree that the Fourth Amendment requires the adversary hearing outlined in the District Court's decree, we reverse in part and remand to the Court of Appeals for further proceedings consistent with this opinion.

It is so ordered.

Affirmed in part, reversed in part, and remanded.

CASE DISCUSSION

Florida prisoners brought a class action suit under the Civil Rights Act against various officials, claiming a constitutional right to a judicial hearing on the issue of probable cause for pretrial detention and requesting injunctive and declaratory relief. The district court granted the relief, ordering an adversary hearing in the particular case and further ordering the judicial officers to draw up a plan for future probable cause hearings. The court of appeals affirmed. The Supreme Court affirmed the requirement for judicial probable cause determination but denied the requirement that the determination must be made in an adversary proceeding.

Why is the probable cause standard higher for detention than arrest? Should it be? What interests do different standards promote? What reasons did the court give for denying the petitioners the right to an adversary hearing? Do you agree? Explain.

The **criminal complaint,** or **charging instrument,** grants magistrates the jurisdiction to preside over the first appearance. Although in a few jurisdictions police file complaints directly with courts, in most large urban districts, prosecutors must sign complaints *before* judges review them for probable cause. Ordinarily, complaints state the crime with which suspects are charged. Attached to the complaint are police incident reports, confessions, results of identification procedures, affidavits of witnesses, informants, and other products of police investigation.

When suspects appear in court at the first appearance, the magistrate informs them of the charges against them. Defendants charged with felonies do not plead at this time; they await arraignment following preliminary hearings and grand jury review, discussed in chapter 10. However, if charged with misdemeanors, particularly ones punishable by small fines, they will probably plead (usually guilty) at the initial appearance. Once magistrates inform felony suspects of the charges (often read by clerks)—or in misdemeanor cases where suspects plead not guilty—magistrates make three additional decisions at the initial appearance: they (1) notify suspects of their constitutional rights; (2) determine whether suspects are indigent and, if so, assign attorneys to them; and (3) determine whether to release suspects on bail and, if so, what, if any, conditions to affix to suspects' release, or determine instead to detain suspects.

Informing Suspects of Their Rights

When suspects (now defendants) first appear in court, magistrates advise them of the nature of the charges against them, although in felonies and gross misdemeanors they are not called upon to plead since they have not had time to consult with lawyers. If defendants do not already have them, the court provides them with copies of the complaint and supporting affidavits and other documents. Typically, court rules provide:

> The judge, judicial officer, or other duly appointed personnel shall advise the defendant substantially as follows:
> (a) That he is not required to say anything or submit to interrogation and that anything he says may be used against him in this or in any subsequent proceedings;
> (b) That he has a right to counsel in all subsequent proceedings, including police line-ups and interrogations, and if he appears without counsel and is financially unable to afford counsel, that counsel will forthwith be appointed without cost to him if he is charged with an offense punishable upon conviction by incarceration;
> (c) That he has a right to communicate with his counsel and that a continuance will be granted if necessary to enable defendant to obtain or speak to counsel;
> (d) That he has a right to jury trial or a trial to the court;
> (e) That if the offense is a misdemeanor, he may either plead guilty or not guilty, or demand a complaint prior to entering a plea.
> The judge, judicial officer, or other duly authorized personnel may advise a number of defendants at once of these rights, but each defendant shall be asked individually before he is arraigned whether he heard and understood these rights as explained earlier.[9]

The Supreme Court has not decided exactly what constitutes appearance before a magistrate without unnecessary delay, and it has further declined to prescribe in precise hours or days what may amount to too long a period between detention following arrest and first appearance. However, the Federal District Court for the Southern District Court of Texas closely examined and ruled on the Houston Police Department's procedures regarding postarrest detention procedures prior to first appearance.

CASE

Were they taken before a magistrate without unnecessary delay?

Sanders et al. v. City of Houston

543 F.Supp. 694 (S.D. Tex. 1982)

FACTS

I. Introduction

. . . Jackie Sanders, Bernie Stevenson, and Lanita Moore, initiated this action on their own behalf and on behalf of all others similarly situated. . . .

Plaintiffs contend generally that the current policy of the Houston Police Department which authorizes the police to detain arrestees on ''investigative hold'' violates the Fourth and Fourteenth Amendments to the United States Constitution, Article 1, Section 11 of the Texas Constitution. . . .

II. Findings of Fact

[1] . . . Plaintiff Sanders was booked into the city jail at 10:10 p.m. on March 15, 1979, and charged with assault and misdemeanor theft. She was then placed on ''investigative hold.'' Such hold was not released until this suit was filed some nineteen (19) hours later. Plaintiff was interrogated during this time, and the bond which has been set was tendered but refused. Plaintiff Sanders was not presented before a magistrate until over forty-three (43) hours after the time of her arrest.

[2] Plaintiff Stevenson was booked into the city jail at 3:14 a.m. on July 4, 1979, and charged with criminal trespass, a class C misdemeanor. At the time he was booked, bond was set. Yet, he was placed on ''hold'' by the narcotics division. Thirteen and one-half (13½) hours later, plaintiff Stevenson filed suit, and he was thereafter released on the charge of possession of a controlled substance. Plaintiff Stevenson did not see a magistrate until more than forty-three (43) hours after his arrest.

[3] Plaintiff Moore was arrested at 2:15 a.m. on September 26, 1979, and charged with misdemeanor assault, a class C misdemeanor. She was placed on ''hold'' by the homicide division during which time she was interrogated and, was not eligible for bond. At the time the present suit was filed, plaintiff

Moore had been on "hold" for almost sixty (60) hours and was thereafter released with the charge of credit card abuse, a felony. Plaintiff Moore did not see a magistrate until more than five (5) days after her arrest. . . .

[4] Persons in the custody of the Houston Police Department who are on hold are usually not taken before a magistrate, nor are they permitted to be released on bond while they are on hold. . . .

[5] There is an unwritten rule in the Houston Police Department that a suspect may be detained on investigative hold for as long as seventy-two (72) hours without charging the person or presenting him or her to a magistrate.

[6] The procedures employed in processing an arrestee at the Houston Police Station are as follows. When the arresting officer and the suspect arrive at the police station, the officer fills out the police report and then takes the suspect to the jail complaint officer for booking.

[7] The booking process includes typing the police blotter (or information form), conducting a thorough search of the suspect, inventorying his property, and providing any necessary medical treatment. During this period, the Identification Division participates in processing the prisoner by taking his fingerprints and photograph and by checking for any criminal history. Laboratory tests, especially in narcotics cases, are conducted to properly identify any evidence confiscated by the arresting officer. . . .

[8] It is accepted as efficient police procedure to wrap up the loose ends of an investigation after the arrest but before a probable cause hearing. This may include such things as checking for outstanding warrants or other pertinent information in the departments records; ascertaining whether the records reveal a similar description in another but similar type crime; verifying background information obtained from another area if the suspect is not of this locale; and interrogating the suspect. . . .

[9] Part of the reason given by the defendant for the lengthy holds is the Intake Division of the Harris County District Attorney's Office, the agency with the responsibility for determining whether charges should be filed, demands a greater quantum of evidence than just probable cause in order to file charges. The Intake Division requires, first, that there was probable cause for the arrest and, second, that there is sufficient evidence to obtain a conviction which will withstand scrutiny on appeal.

[10] The Intake Division requires reasonable certainty of the identity of the suspect, and this necessitates scheduling line-ups to have the witnesses or complainant view the suspects. . . .

[11] A survey was conducted by the Houston Police Department from March 3, 1980, through March 24, 1980, which revealed that 5,602 prisoners were processed through the city's detention centers. The arrests were categorized according to the degree of the crime, and for the category of "county and district charges," which includes felonies, class A misdemeanors, and class B misdemeanors, there were 1503 arrests. Of the 178 prisoners from this category who were ultimately released without charges having been filed, 29% or 52 persons were held more than twenty-four (24) hours.

[12] For the remainder of persons in the category of "county and district charges" who were charged with a crime and released on bond, the average time of detention, that being the time from arrival at the station until the posting of the bond, was thirteen and one-half (13½) hours.

[13] In the City of Houston during 1981, there were over 96,000 prisoners processed through the detention centers. There are approximately one thousand (1000) robberies per month in Houston. Additionally, there are up to two hundred fifty (250) burglaries per day in Houston. Homicides are numerous, and there is tremendous backlog in outstanding warrants in the Homicide Division.

[14] In arriving at the above Findings of Fact, the Court has weighed carefully the credibility of the witnesses who have testified and finds that in instances wherein significant factual conflicts exist, the plaintiffs' witnesses are more persuasive.

OPINION

. . . After an arrest based on a policeman's on-the-scene assessment of probable cause, a suspect may be held in custody for a brief period of detention to take the administrative steps incident to arrest. However, the Fourth Amendment requires a judicial determination of probable cause as a prerequisite to extend restraint of liberty following arrest. *Gerstein v. Pugh*, 420 U.S. 103, 95 S.Ct. 854, 43 L.Ed.2d 54 (1974).

Plaintiffs assert that the "administrative steps" allowed by *Gernstein*, include only transportation to the station, booking into the jail, and filing charges. Rule 5(a) of Federal Rules of Criminal Procedure requires that a person who has been arrested shall be brought before the nearest available federal magistrate "without unnecessary delay." . . .

This Court concludes that "administrative steps" as used in *Gerstein* include more than transportation, booking, and filing charges. The rights of a suspect are subject to limitations arising out of society's interest in police activity undertaken to aid in the identification of the culprit and to obtain evidence which would aid in apprehending and convicting criminals. . . .

There is a delicate balance to be struck between the interests of the State in its duty to protect society and the interests of the individual in his freedom of movement. This Court is not unaware of the high crime rate in the City of Houston, and assuredly the given environment must be taken into account when considering limitations upon enforcement procedures. Yet, *Gerstein* teaches that once a suspect is in custody, his need for a neutral determination of probable cause increases significantly. Unfounded interference with liberty can take a disastrous toll on one's life.

Hence, it is the conclusion of this Court that when a person has been arrested on a policeman's assessment of probable cause, the person arrested must be brought before a judicial officer as soon as possible, but in any event not longer than twenty-four (24) hours after the arrest. This limitation will apply as well on a weekend or holiday, and the appropriate magistrates or other judicial officers will make the necessary arrangements to be available to perform such duties on weekends and holidays so that this ruling is strictly observed and enforced.

Consequently, the Court concludes that within the City of Houston Police Department, there is the established practice of unlawfully detaining arrestees which is tantamount to significant pretrial restraint of liberty. This is evidenced by the fact that the Houston Police Department permits an investigative hold to remain in effect for as long as seventy-two (72) hours without an explanation therefor. Additionally, the average time for investigative holds in the Robbery Division is twenty-six (26) hours if no charges are filed and thirty-five (35) hours if charges are filed. This does not even account for all of those persons who are held far beyond the average time. This policy is in violation of the suspects' rights guaranteed under the Fourth Amendment.

Similarly, the constitutional rights of the three named plaintiffs were violated by the extended detention to which they were subjected without being presented to a magistrate for a determination of probable cause. Plaintiff Sanders was held for more than forty-three (43) hours before seeing a magistrate. Plaintiff Stevenson was detained also for over forty-three (43) hours. And Plaintiff Moore did not see a magistrate for a probable cause determination until more than five (5) days after her arrest. It is abundantly clear to the Court that these persons were wrongfully detained. . . .

Permanent Injunction

In accordance with the conclusions set forth above, it is hereby ordered that defendant City of Houston, its agents and employees, shall be enjoined from detaining persons arrested for probable cause longer than twenty-four (24) hours without bringing the persons before a judicial officer for a neutral determination of probable cause. In addition to determining whether there exists probable cause for detaining arrestee, the judicial officer shall inform the person of his constitutional rights. If from the information the magistrate or other judicial officer determines that there was probable cause for the arrest, the prisoner shall be admitted to bail as allowed by law, or, if he is unable to secure bail, be committed to custody. Otherwise, if the magistrate finds that there was no probable cause for arrest, the prisoner must be released.

CASE DISCUSSION

Arrested persons, including Sanders, brought an action against the city of Houston and others challenging the police department's policy authorizing the police to detain arrested persons on investigative hold. The district court held that arrested persons detained for between forty-three hours and five days without a first appearance violated their Fourth Amendment rights. The court further enjoined the city from detaining persons for more than twenty-four hours without appearing before a judicial officer for a probable cause determination. In addition to determining probable cause for detaining arrested persons, judicial officers were ordered to inform the detained persons of their rights.

What factors did the court take into account in determining what amounts to reasonable delay in bringing suspects before a magistrate? What actions can police take before they present their cases to prosecutors? Do you favor the *per se* twenty-four-hour rule the court prescribes? What should the remedy be for failing to comply with the rule? Do you agree with the court's resolution of the problem? What interests was the court promoting in its decision? Do you think that the court favors results over process? or process over results? Does the court take adequate account of the administrative problems that the police face in dealing with detained suspects? Explain.

Determination of Probable Cause

Where police have arrested suspects without warrants, magistrates must review the documents attached to the complaint to determine whether there is probable cause to go forward with the case, or more immediately, whether there are grounds to detain suspects. An order for detention may be issued, provided that

> the judge or judicial officer determines from the facts set forth separately in writing in or with the complaint and any supporting affidavits or supplemental sworn testimony that there is probable cause to believe that an offense has been committed and that defendant committed it. Otherwise, the defendants shall be discharged, the complaint and any supporting papers shall not be filed, and no record made of the proceedings.[10]

Appointment of Counsel

The Sixth Amendment to the United States provides:

> In all criminal prosecutions, the accused shall enjoy the right . . . to have the assistance of counsel for his defense.

The Fifth and Fourteenth Amendment provide that

> no person shall be deprived of life, liberty, or property, without due process of law.

These amendments govern the appointment of counsel.

Throughout American history, courts have made clear that the Sixth Amendment guarantees the right to have a lawyer in criminal cases, provided that defendants can afford them or someone is willing to provide counsel **pro bono,** that is, without fees. Not so clearly accepted, however, was the state's obligation to provide counsel for **indigent defendants,** or those too poor to afford a lawyer.

It was not until 1932, in *Powell v. Alabama,* the famous "Scotsboro 7" case, that the United States Supreme Court ruled that "fundamental fairness" under the Fourteenth Amendment due process clause requires that courts appoint lawyers for indigent defendants who otherwise cannot get a **fair hearing,** a crucial element in due process of law. (See excerpt in chap. 2.) In the Scotsboro case, indigent black youths were charged with raping two white women in the South in 1930. Without a lawyer to help them through the intricacies and technicalities of the criminal law and its processes, the Court ruled, they were denied due process of law. If due process means anything, the Court reasoned, it means getting a fair hearing in court. Justice Sutherland wrote:

> [I]n a capital case, where the defendant is unable to employ counsel, and is incapable adequately of making his own defense because of ignorance, feeble-mindedness, illiteracy, or the like, it is the duty of the court, whether requested or not, to assign counsel for him as a necessary requisite of due process of law; and that duty is not discharged by an assignment at such a time or under such circumstances as to preclude the giving of effective aid in the preparation of the trial of the case.[11]

In 1938, the Supreme Court moved from the due process underpinnings to the Sixth Amendment. In *Johnson v. Zerbst,* the Court ruled that the Sixth Amendment conferred the right to appointed counsel for indigent defendants. But *Johnson* provided that right only to defendants in *federal* cases. Furthermore, in *Betts v. Brady,* the Court adopted a **special circumstances rule** that only in cases involving the death penalty, ignorant defendants, and other circumstances such as those in *Powell v. Alabama* does the Sixth Amendment guarantee appointed counsel to indigent defendants. Not until 1963, in *Gideon v. Wainright,* did the Supreme Court both reject the special circumstances rule and extend the right to counsel to defendants in *state* proceedings. The Court in *Gideon* ruled that due process required the appointment of counsel for indigent defendants in *all* criminal prosecutions.[12] (See chap. 2 for excerpt of *Gideon*.)

Several important questions arise out of indigent defendants' right to appointed counsel in criminal prosecutions: (1) At what stage in the proceedings does the right go into effect? That is, what does *prosecution* mean under the Sixth Amendment? (2) What is a *criminal* prosecution? Is a traffic offense a *criminal* prosecution? (3) Does the right to counsel mean the right to *effective* counsel? (4) How poor must defendants be to be considered indigent?

WHEN PROSECUTION BEGINS. Clearly persons on trial are prosecuted. Just as clearly citizens questioned briefly on the street are not prosecuted. Suspects in custody are not prosecuted either but they may have the right to an attorney for a different reason: Custodial interrogation is so coercive that it violates the Fifth Amendment privilege against self-incrimination without, *inter alia,* the right to a lawyer. (See chap. 5.) Indicted defendants are prosecuted, according to court rulings; defendants making their first appearance are not prosecuted. In *Kirby v. Illinois* the Supreme Court addressed the issues of when does the right to an attorney come into effect, and what criteria determine for Sixth Amendment purposes when prosecution commences.

CASE

Did the hearing begin prosecution?

Kirby v. Illinois

406 U.S. 682, 92 S.Ct. 1877, 32 L.Ed.2d 411 (1972)

[Stewart, J., announced the Court's judgement and delivered an opinion in which Burger, C.J., and Blackmun and Rehnquist, JJ., joined. Burger, C.J., filed a concurring statement. Powell, J., filed a statement concurring in the result, Brennan, J., filed a dissenting opinion, in which Douglas and Marshall, JJ., joined. White, J., filed a dissenting statement.]

FACTS

On February 21, 1968, a man named Willie Shard reported to the Chicago police that the previous day two men had robbed him on a Chicago street of a wallet containing, among other things, traveller's checks and a Social Security card. On February 22, two police officers stopped the petitioner and a companion, Ralph Bean, on West Madison Street in Chicago.[a] When asked for identification, the petitioner produced a wallet that contained three traveller's checks and a Social Security card, all bearing the name of Willie Shard. Papers with Shard's name on them were also found in Bean's possession. When asked to explain his possession of Shard's property, the petitioner first said that the traveller's checks were "play money," and then told the officers that he had won them in a crap game. The officers then arrested the petitioner and Bean and took them to a police station.

Only after arriving at the police station, and checking the records there, did the arresting officers learn of the Shard robbery. A police car was then dispatched to Shard's place of employment, where it picked up Shard and brought him to the police station. Immediately upon entering the room in the police station where the petitioner and Bean were seated at a table, Shard positively identified them as the men who had robbed him two days earlier. No lawyer was present in the room, and neither the petitioner nor Bean had asked for legal assistance, or been advised of any right to the presence of counsel.

More than six weeks later, the petitioner and Bean were indicted for the robbery of Willie Shard. Upon arraignment, counsel was appointed to represent them, and they pleaded not guilty. A pretrial motion to suppress Shard's identification testimony was denied, and at the trial Shard testified as a witness for the prosecution. In his testimony he described his identification of the two men at the police station on February 22, and identified them again in the courtroom as the men who had robbed him on February 20. He was cross-examined at length regarding the circumstances of his identification of the two defendants. The jury found both defendants guilty, and the petitioner's conviction was affirmed on appeal. The Illinois appellate court held that the admission of Shard's testimony was not error. We granted certiorari.

OPINION

In a line of constitutional cases in this Court stemming back to the Court's landmark opinion in *Powell v. Alabama,* 287 U.S. 45, 53 S.Ct. 55, 77 L.Ed. 158, it has been firmly established that a person's Sixth and Fourteenth Amendment right to counsel attaches only at or after the time that adversary judicial proceedings have been initiated against him.

This is not to say that a defendant in a criminal case has a constitutional right to counsel only at the trial itself. The *Powell* case makes clear that the right attaches at the time of arraignment,[b] and the Court has recently held that it exists also at the time of a preliminary hearing. *Coleman v. Alabama,* [399 U.S. 1, 90 S.Ct. 1999, 26 L.Ed.2d 387]. But the point is that, where members of the Court have differed as to existence of the right to counsel in the contexts of some of the above cases, *all* of those cases have involved

---

[a]The officers stopped the petitioner and his companion because they thought the petitioner was a man named Hampton, who was "wanted" in connection with an unrelated criminal offense. The legitimacy of this stop and the subsequent arrest is not before us.

[b]"[D]uring perhaps the most critical period of the proceedings against these defendants, that is to say, from the time of their arraignment until the beginning of their trial, when consultation, thoroughgoing investigation and preparation were vitally important, the defendants did not have aid of counsel in any real sense, although they were as much entitled to such aid during that period as at the trial itself." *Powell v. Alabama,* 287 U.S. 45, 57, 53 S.Ct. 55, 59, 77 L.Ed. 158.

points of time at or after the initiation of adversary judicial criminal proceedings—whether by way of formal charge, preliminary hearing, indictment, information, or arraignment.

The only seeming deviation from this long line of constitutional decisions was *Escobedo v. Illinois,* 378 U.S. 478, 84 S.Ct. 1758, 12 L.Ed.2d 977. But *Escobedo* is not apposite here for two distinct reasons. First, the Court in retrospect perceived that the "prime purpose" of *Escobedo* was not to vindicate the constitutional right to counsel as such, but, like *Miranda,* "to guarantee full effectuation of the privilege against self-incrimination. . . .

The initiation of judicial criminal proceedings is far from a mere formalism. It is the starting point of our whole system of adversary criminal justice. For it is only then that the government has committed itself to prosecute, and only then that the adverse positions of government and defendant have solidified. It is then that a defendant finds himself faced with the prosecutorial forces of organized society, and immersed in the intricacies of substantive and procedural criminal law. It is this point, therefore, that marks the commencement of the "criminal prosecutions" to which alone the explicit guarantees of the Sixth Amendment are applicable.

In this case we are asked to import into a routine police investigation an absolute constitutional guarantee historically and rationally applicable only after the onset of formal prosecutorial proceedings. We decline [to] impos[e] a *per se* exclusionary rule upon testimony concerning an identification that took place long before the commencement of any prosecution whatever.

DISSENT

Mr. Justice Brennan, with whom Mr. Justice Douglas and Mr. Justice Marshall join, dissenting.

. . . *Powell v. Alabama* . . . requires that we scrutinize *any* pretrial confrontation of the accused to determine whether the presence of his counsel is necessary to preserve the defendant's basic right to a fair trial as affected by his right meaningfully to cross-examine the witnesses against him and to have effective assistance of counsel at the trial itself. . . .

[T]he presence of counsel at pretrial confrontations for identification purposes . . . is required . . . because "the dangers inherent in eyewitness identification and the suggestibility inherent in the context of the pretrial identification," mean that protection must be afforded to the "most basic right [of] a criminal defendant—his right to a fair trial at which the witnesses against him might be meaningfully cross-examined." . . .

Hence, "the initiation of adversary judicial criminal proceedings," is completely irrelevant to whether counsel is necessary at a pretrial confrontation for identification in order to safeguard the accused's constitutional rights to confrontation and the effective assistance of counsel at his trial. . . .

The plurality offers no reason, and I can think of none, for concluding that a post-arrest confrontation for identification, unlike a post-charge confrontation, is not among those "critical confrontations of the accused by the prosecution at pretrial proceedings while the results might well settle the accused's fate and reduce the trial itself to a mere formality."

The highly suggestive form of confrontation employed in this case underscores the point. This showup was particularly fraught with the peril of mistaken identification. In the setting of a police station squad room where all present except petitioner and Bean were police officers, the danger was quite real that Shard's understandable resentment might lead him too readily to agree with the police that the pair under arrest, and the only persons exhibited to him, were indeed the robbers. "It is hard to imagine a situation more conveying the suggestion to the witness that the one presented is believed guilty by the police." The State had no case without Shard's identification testimony, and safeguards against that consequence were therefore of critical importance. Shard's testimony itself demonstrates the necessity for such safeguards. On direct examination, Shard identified petitioner and Bean not as the alleged robbers on trial in the courtroom, but as the pair he saw at the police station. His testimony thus lends strong support to the observation, quoted by the Court in *Wade*, 388 U.S., at 229, 87 S.Ct. at 1933, 18 L.Ed.2d 1149, that "[i]t is a matter of common experience that, once the witness has picked out the accused at the line-up, he is not likely to go back on his word later on, so that in practice the issue of identity may (in the absence of other relevant evidence) for all practical purposes to be determined there and then, before the trial." Williams and Hammelmann, Identification Parades, Part I, [1963] Crim. L. Rev. 479, 482.

CASE DISCUSSION

Kirby and his partner were indicted for robbery. They pleaded not guilty. The judge denied a pretrial motion to suppress identification testimony, holding that a lineup *prior* to indictment did not violate Kirby's right to counsel guarantee. The jury found both defendants guilty and the appeals court affirmed. The United States granted *certiorari* and affirmed.

According to the Court, what determines when formal adversary proceedings begin? Why is it important to know when they begin? Review *United States v. Wade,* discussed in chapter 8 under identification procedures. There the Supreme Court ruled that defendants have a right to a lawyer *after* the government indicts them. Why should defendants have different rights regarding lineups before and after indictment? Review the discussion of identification procedures in chapter 8. Is the indictment a magic dividing line that makes so great a difference that defendants need lawyers in lineups taking place after indictments but not before them? What interests does such a rule promote? process or results? Why does the dissent argue that lineups without attorneys deny defendants a fair trial? Do you Agree? Explain.

THE MEANING OF CRIMINAL PROSECUTION. Beginning with *Powell v. Alabama,* the Court applied the right to appointed counsel to capital cases. In *Gideon v. Wainright* the Court expanded the right to counsel to include felonies against property. Then, in *Argersinger v. Hamlin,* the Court extended the protection to misdemeanors punishable by jail terms. Argersinger, a Florida indigent, was convicted of carrying a concealed weapon, a misdemeanor punishable by up to six months' imprisonment, a $1,000 fine, or both. A Florida rule limited assigned counsel to "non-petty offenses punishable by more than six months imprisonment." The Court struck down the rule, holding that

> absent a knowing and intelligent waiver, no person may be imprisoned for any offense, whether classified as petty, misdemeanor, or felony unless he was represented by counsel.[13]

Argersinger did not decide if indigents had the right to assigned counsel in *all* criminal cases. The Court in *Argersinger* had noted a practical problem in applying the right to counsel—insufficient resources to provide everyone with a lawyer. Although, of course, budgetary considerations cannot determine constitutional right in the abstract, available resources naturally affect their implementation. This intermix of practice and theory surfaced again in *Scott v. Illinois*. The Court specifically addressed the question whether the right to assigned counsel extends to offenses that do not actually result in prison sentences.

CASE

Do indigents have a right to assigned counsel for shoplifting?

Scott v. Illinois

440 U.S. 367, 99 S.Ct. 1158, 59 L.Ed.2d 383 (1979)

[Rehnquist, J., delivered the opinion of the Court, in which Burger, C.J., and Stewart, White, and Powell, JJ., joined. Powell, J., filed a concurring opinion, Brennan, J., filed a dissenting opinion, in which Marshall and Stevens, JJ., joined. Blackmun, J., filed a dissenting opinion.]

FACTS

. . . Petitioner Scott was convicted of theft and fined $50 after a bench trial in the Circuit Court of Cook County, Ill. His conviction was affirmed by the state intermediate appellate court and then by the Supreme Court of Illinois, over Scott's contention that the Sixth and Fourteenth Amendments to the United States Constitution required that Illinois provide trial counsel to him at its expense.

Petitioner Scott was convicted of shoplifting merchandise valued at less than $150. The applicable Illinois statute set the maximum penalty for such an offense at a $500 fine or one year in jail, or both. . . .

We granted certiorari in this case to resolve a conflict among state and lower federal courts regarding the proper application of our decision in *Argersinger v. Hamlin,* 407 U.S. 25, 92 S.Ct. 2006, 32 L.Ed.2d 530 (1972). . . .

OPINION

There is considerable doubt that the Sixth Amendment itself, as originally drafted by the Framers of the Bill of Rights, contemplated any guarantee other than the right of an accused in a criminal prosecution in a federal court to employ a lawyer to assist in his defense. . . .

We believe that the central premise of *Argersinger*—that actual imprisonment is a penalty different in kind from fines or the mere threat of imprisonment—is eminently sound and warrants adoption of actual imprisonment as the line defining the constitutional right to appointment of counsel. *Argersinger* has proved reasonably workable, whereas any extension would create confusion and impose unpredictable, but necessarily substantial, costs on 50 quite diverse States. We therefore hold that the Sixth and Fourteenth Amendments to the United States Constitution require only that no indigent criminal defendant be sentenced to a term of imprisonment unless the State has afforded him the right to assistance of appointed counsel in his defense. The judgement of the Supreme Court of Illinois is accordingly
Affirmed.

DISSENT

. . . Mr. Justice Brennan, with whom Mr. Justice Marshall and Mr. Justice Stevens join, dissenting.

The Sixth Amendment provides: "In all *criminal,* prosecutions, the accused shall enjoy the right . . . to have the Assistance of Counsel for his defence." (Emphasis supplied.). . . .

The offense of "theft" with which Scott was charged is certainly not a "petty" one. It is punishable by a sentence of up to one year in jail. Unlike many traffic or other "regulatory" offenses, it carries the moral stigma associated with common-law crimes traditionally recognized as indicative of moral depravity. The State indicated at oral argument that the services of a professional prosecutor were considered essential to the prosecution of this offense. Likewise, nonindigent defendants charged with this offense would be well advised to hire the "best lawyers they can get." . . .

[T]he "authorized imprisonment" standard more faithfully implements the principles of the Sixth Amendment. The procedural rules established by the state statutes are geared to the nature of the potential penalty for an offense, not to the actual penalty imposed in particular cases. The authorized penalty is also a better predictor of the stigma and other collateral consequences that attach to conviction of an offense. With the exception of *Argersinger,* authorized penalties have been used consistently by this Court as the true measures of the seriousness of offenses. . . .

In any event, the extent of the alleged burden on the States is, as the Court admits, speculative. Although more persons are charged with misdemeanors punishable by incarceration than are charged with felonies, a smaller percentage of persons charged with misdemeanors qualify as indigent, andmisdemeanor cases as a rule require far less attorney time. . . .

The apparent reason for the Court's adoption of the "actual imprisonment" standard for all misdemeanors is concern for the economic burden that an "authorized imprisonment" standard might place on the States. But, with all respect, that concern is both irrelevant and speculative.

This Court's role in enforcing constitutional guarantees for criminal defendants cannot be made dependent on the budgetary decisions of state governments.

Mr. Justice Blackmun, dissenting. . . .

. . . I would hold that an indigent defendant in a state criminal case must be afforded appointed counsel whenever the defendant is prosecuted for a nonpetty criminal offense, that is, one punishable by more than six months' imprisonment, *or* whenever the defendant is convicted of an offense and is actually subjected to a term of imprisonment, *Argersinger v. Hamlin,* 407 U.S. 25, 92 S.Ct. 2006, 32 L.Ed.2d 530 (1972). This resolution, I feel, would provide the "bright line" that defendants, prosecutors, and trial and appellate courts all deserve. . . .

CASE DISCUSSION

Scott was convicted of theft and fined $50 in a trial without a jury. Both the Illinois intermediate appellate court and the Illinois Supreme Court affirmed Scott's conviction over his objection that the trial denied him Sixth Amendment right to counsel under the due process clause of the Fourteenth Amendment. The United States Supreme Court granted *certiorari* to resolve a conflict between state and lower federal courts regarding the right to counsel. The Supreme Court affirmed the Illinois Supreme Court, holding that defendants do not have a right to counsel in cases involving a "mere threat of imprisonment."

Should every defendant who cannot afford a lawyer have one in *all* criminal cases at state expense? Would such an interpretation of the right to counsel promote the public interest in result over process? or would it promote both? Would it serve the societal interest in aiding the poor and weak in our society? Should it do so? Should economic considerations be taken into account in deciding who should have constitutional rights? What interests does taking them into account promote? sacrifice? Is Justice Blackmun's recommendation for a "bright line" rule a good one?

THE STANDARD OF INDIGENCE. The Supreme Court has never defined indigence. However, federal appellate courts have established some general guidelines: (1) indigence does not mean total destitution; (2) only defendant's earnings and assets can be considered, not the help their friends and relatives might provide; (3) actual, not potential, earnings are the measure; (4) the state may tap future earnings, however, by establishing **recoupment programs,** or programs designed to collect in the future the costs of counsel, transcripts, and other defense expenditures.

Some jurisdictions have established specific standards for determining indigence. Minnesota's rules for judges' assessment of indigence at defendants' first appearance are typical:

Rule 5.02 Appointment of Counsel

Subd. 1. **Felonies and Gross Misdemeanors.** If the defendant is not represented by counsel and is financially unable to afford counsel, the judge or judicial officer shall appoint counsel for him.

Subd. 2. **Misdemeanors.** Unless the defendant charged with a misdemeanor punishable upon conviction by incarceration voluntarily waives counsel in writing or on the record, the court shall appoint counsel for him if he appears without counsel and is financially unable to afford counsel. . . .

Subd. 3. **Standard of Indigence.** A defendant is financially unable to obtain counsel if he is financially unable to obtain adequate representation without substantial hardship for himself or his family.

(1) A defendant will be presumed to be financially unable to afford counsel if:

   (a) his cash assets are less than $300.00 when entitled to only a court trial; or

   (b) his current weekly net income does not exceed $500.00 when entitled to a jury trial; and

   (c) his current weekly net income does not exceed forty times the federal minimum hourly wage . . . if he is unmarried and without dependents; or,

   (d) his current weekly net income and that of his spouse do not exceed sixty times the federal minimum hourly wage . . . if he is married and without dependents. In determining the amounts under either section (c) or section (d), for each dependent the amount shall be increased by $25.00 per week.

(2) A defendant who has cash assets or income exceeding the amounts in paragraph (1) shall not be presumed to be financially able to obtain counsel. The determination shall be made by the court as a practical matter, taking into account such other factors as the defendant's length of employment or unemployment, prior income, the value and nature of his assets, number of children and other family responsibilities, number and nature of debts arising from any source, the amount customarily charged by members of the practicing bar for representation of the type in question, and any other relevant factor.

(3) In determining whether a defendant is financially able to obtain adequate representation without substantial hardship to himself or his family:

   (a) cash assets include those assets which may be readily converted to cash . . . without jeopardizing the defendant's ability to maintain his home or employment. A single family automobile shall not be considered an asset.

   (b) the fact that defendant has posted or can bail is irrelevant. . . .

   (c) the fact that the defendant is employable but unemployed shall not be in itself proof that he is financially able to obtain counsel without substantial hardship to himself or his family.

   (d) the fact that parents or other relatives of the defendant have the financial ability to obtain counsel for the defendant is irrelevant, except under the following circumstances:

      (i) where the defendant is unemancipated, under the age of 21 years, living with his parents or other relatives, and such parents or other relatives have the clear ability to obtain counsel; or

      (ii) where the parents or other relatives of the defendant have the financial ability to obtain counsel for the defendant but are unwilling to do so only because of the relatively minor nature of the charge.

Under part (1) . . . a defendant will be presumed financially unable to retain his own attorney and counsel shall be appointed for him . . . [P]art (1) provides a presumption of indigence and is not to be taken as indicating that a defendant with a higher income and assets must obtain his own attorney. A defendant with a higher income or assets should still be appointed counsel if his is unable . . . to obtain adequate representation without substantial hardship to himself or his family. . .

Subd. 4. **Financial Inquiry.** An inquiry to determine financial eligibility of a defendant for the appointment of counsel shall be made whenever possible prior to the court appearance and by such persons as the court may direct.

Subd. 5. **Partial Eligibility and Reimbursement.** The ability to pay part of the cost of adequate representation at any time while the charges are pending against a defendant shall not preclude the appointment of counsel for the defendant. The court may require a defendant, to the extent of his ability, to compensate the governmental unit charged with paying the expense of appointed counsel.[14]

THE RIGHT TO *EFFECTIVE* COUNSEL. The Sixth Amendment, according to *Powell v. Alabama,* requires *effective* representation, but until recently, the Supreme Court did not clearly define it. In the absence of Supreme Court guidance, both federal and state lower courts adopted the **mockery of justice standard.** Under this standard, only circumstances so shocking that they reduced the trial to a farce satisfied defendants' claims of ineffective representation by counsel. One judge put it this way:

> ineffective assistance existed only when the trial was a farce, or a mockery of justice, or was shocking to the conscience of the reviewing court, or the purported representation was only perfunctory, in bad faith, a sham, [or] a pretense.[15]

Even lawyers who appear in court drunk did not violate this standard.[16]

Courts and commentators have criticized the mockery of justice standard as too subjective, vague, and narrow. The standard's focus on the trial excludes many serious errors that might occur in preparing for trial. Furthermore, in the overwhelming majority of cases that result in guilty pleas, the standard is totally irrelevant. Judge Bazelon, an experienced and respected federal judge, said that the test requires "such a minimal level of performance from counsel that it is itself a mockery of the Sixth Amendment." He continued,

> I have often been told that if my court were to reverse in every case in which there was inadequate counsel, we would have to send back half the convictions in my jurisdiction.[17]

Courts hesitate to get involved in the ineffectiveness question. Close scrutiny by trial judges of defense attorneys' performance may well lead to a degree of interference intolerable both to the adversary system and to the professional independence of defense attorneys. Furthermore, judges who criticize lawyers' performance are, in a sense, criticizing themselves since they, too, are members of the same profession. Hence, trial judges hesitate to criticize too quickly the lawyers who practice before their courts.[18]

Most jurisdictions have abandoned the mockery of justice standard, replacing it with the **reasonably competent attorney standard.** According to this standard, judges measure lawyers' performance against the "customary skills and diligence that a reasonably competent attorney would perform under similar circumstances." Attorneys must be more diligent under the reasonably competent attorney standard than was required under the mockery of justice standard. However, both the mockery of justice and the reasonably competent attorney standards are "vague to some appreciable degree and . . . susceptible to greatly varying subjective impressions." The Supreme Court has declined to rule that the Constitution mandates either standard.[19]

Recently the Court has taken a more active role in reviewing ineffective representation claims. In 1984, the Court examined the question in *Strickland v. Washington.*

CASE

Did his lawyer effectively *represent him?*

Strickland v. Washington

466 U.S. 668, 104 S.Ct. 2052, 80 L.Ed.2d 674 (1984)

[O'Connor, J., delivered the opinion of the Court, in which Burger, C.J., and White, Blackmun, Powell, Rehnquist, and Stevens, JJ., joined. Brennan, J., filed an opinion concurring in part and dissenting in part. Marshall, J., filed a dissenting opinion.]

FACTS

During a 10-day period in September 1976, respondent planned and committed three groups of crimes, which included three brutal stabbing murders, torture, kidnapping, severe assaults, attempted murders, attempted extortion, and theft. After his two accomplices were arrested, respondent surrendered to police and voluntarily gave a lengthy statement confessing to the third of the criminal episodes. The State of Florida indicted respondent for kidnapping and murder and appointed an experienced criminal lawyer to represent him.

Counsel actively pursued pretrial motions and discovery. He cut his efforts short, however, and he experienced a sense of hopelessness about the case, when he learned that, against his specific advice, respondent had also confessed to the first two murders. By the date set for trial, respondent was subject to indictment for three counts of first-degree murder and multiple counts of robbery, kidnapping for ransom, breaking and entering and assault, attempted murder, and conspiracy to commit robbery. Respondent waived his right to a jury trial, again acting against counsel's advice, and pleaded guilty to all charges, including the three capital murder charges.

In the plea colloquy, respondent told that trial judge that, although he had committed a string of burglaries, he had no significant prior criminal record and that at the time of his criminal spree he was under extreme stress caused by his inability to support his family. He also stated, however, that he accepted responsibility for the crimes. The trial judge told respondent that he had "a great deal of respect for people who are willing to step forward and admit their responsibility" but that he was making no statement at all about his likely sentencing decision.

Counsel advised respondent to invoke his right under Florida law to an advisory jury at his capital sentencing hearing. Respondent rejected the advice and waived the right. He chose instead to be sentenced by the trial judge without a jury recommendation.

In preparing for the sentencing hearing, counsel spoke to respondent about his background. He also spoke on the telephone with respondent's wife and mother, though he did not follow up on the one successful effort to meet with them. He did not otherwise seek out character witnesses for respondent. Nor did he request a psychiatric examination, since his conversations with his client gave no indication that respondent had psychological problems.

Counsel decided not to present and hence not to look further for evidence concerning respondent's character and emotional state. That decision reflected trial counsel's sense of hopelessness about overcoming the evidentiary effect of respondent's confessions to the gruesome crimes. It also reflected the judgment that it was advisable to rely on the plea of colloquy for evidence about respondent's background and about his claim of emotional stress: the plea colloquy communicated sufficient information about these subjects, and by foregoing the opportunity to present new evidence on these subjects, counsel prevented the State from cross-examining respondent on his claim and from putting on psychiatric evidence of his own.

Counsel also excluded from the sentencing hearing other evidence he thought was potentially damaging. He successfully moved to exclude respondent's "rap sheet." Because he judged that a presentence report might prove more detrimental than helpful, as it would have included respondent's criminal history and thereby would have undermined the claim of no significant history of criminal activity, he did not request that one be prepared.

At the sentencing hearing, counsel's strategy was based primarily on the trial judge's remarks at the plea colloquy as well as on his reputation as a sentencing judge who thought it important for a convicted defendant to own up to his crime. Counsel argued that respondent's remorse and acceptance of responsibility justified sparing him from the death penalty. Counsel also argued that respondent had no history of criminal activity and that respondent committed the crimes under extreme mental or emotional disturbance, thus coming within the statutory list of mitigating circumstances. He further argued that respondent should be spared death because he had surrendered, confessed, and offered to testify against a codefendant and because respondent was fundamentally a good person who had briefly gone badly wrong in extremely stressful circumstances. The State put on evidence and witnesses largely for the purpose of describing the details of the crimes. Counsel did not cross-examine the medical experts who testified about the manner of death of respondent's victims. . . .

In short, the trial judge found numerous aggravating circumstances and no (or a single comparatively significant) mitigating circumstance. With respect to each of the three convictions for capital murder, the trial judge concluded: "A careful consideration of all matters presented to the court impels the conclusion that there are insufficient mitigating circumstances . . . to outweigh the aggravating circumstances." He therefore sentenced respondent to death on each of the three counts of murder and to prison terms for other crimes. The Florida Supreme Court upheld the convictions and sentences on direct appeal.

Respondent subsequently sought collateral relief in state court on numerous grounds, among them that counsel had rendered ineffective assistance at the sentencing proceeding. Respondent challenged counsel's assistance in six respects. He asserted that counsel was ineffective because he failed to move for a continuance to prepare for sentencing, to request a psychiatric report, to investigate and present character witnesses, to seek a presentence investigation report, to present meaningful arguments to the sentencing judge, and to investigate the medical examiner's reports or cross-examine the medical experts. . . .

The trial court denied relief without an evidentiary hearing, finding that the record evidence conclusively showed that the ineffectiveness claim was meritless. . . . The court specifically found: "[As] a matter of law, the record affirmatively demonstrates beyond any doubt that even if [counsel] had done each of the . . . things [that respondent alleged counsel had failed to do] at the time of sentencing, there is not even the remotest chance that the outcome would have been any different. The plain fact is that the aggravating circumstances proved in this case were completely *overwhelming*. . . ."

The Florida Supreme Court affirmed the denial of relief.
[Washington filed a habeas corpus petition in U.S. District Court, and the District Court denied the petition. He appealed to the U.S. Court of Appeals. Florida filed petition for writ of certiorari to the U.S. Supreme Court.]

OPINION

. . . [W]e granted certiorari to consider the standards by which to judge a contention that the Constitution required that a criminal judgement be overturned because of the actual ineffective assistance of counsel. . . .

The same principle applies to a capital sentencing proceeding such as that provided by Florida law. . . . A capital sentencing proceeding like the one involved in this case, is sufficiently like a trial in its adversarial format and in the existence of standards for decision, that counsel's role in the proceeding is comparable to counsel's role at trial—to ensure that the adversarial testing process works to produce a just result under the standards governing decision. For purposes of describing counsel's duties, therefore, Florida's capital sentencing proceeding need not be distinguished from an ordinary trial.

A convicted defendant's claim that counsel's assistance was so defective as to require reversal of a conviction of death sentence has two components. First, defendant must show that counsel's performance was deficient. This requires showing that counsel made errors so serious that counsel was not functioning as the "counsel" guaranteed the defendant by the Sixth Amendment. Second, the defendant must show that the deficient performance prejudiced the defense. This requires showing that counsel's errors were so serious as to deprive the defendant of a fair trial, a trial whose result is reliable. Unless a defendant makes both showings, it cannot be said that the conviction or death sentence resulted from a breakdown in the adversary process that renders the result unreliable.

As all the Federal Courts of Appeals have now held, the proper standard for attorney performance is that of reasonably effective assistance. . . .

Application of the governing principle is not hard in this case. The facts as described above, make clear that the conduct of respondent's counsel at and before respondent's sentencing proceeding cannot be found unreasonable. They also make clear that, even assuming the challenged conduct of counsel was unreasonable, respondent suffered insufficient prejudice to warrant setting aside his death sentence.

With respect to the performance component, the record shows that respondent's counsel made a strategic choice to argue for the extreme emotional distress mitigating circumstance and to rely as fully as possible on respondent's acceptance of responsibility for his crimes. Although counsel understandably felt hopeless about respondent's prospects, nothing in the record indicates that counsel's sense of hopelessness distorted his professional judgement. Counsel's strategy choice was well within the range of professionally reasonable judgments, and the decision not to seek more character or psychological evidence than was already in hand was likewise reasonable.

The trial judge's views on the importance of owning up to one's crimes were well known to counsel. The aggravating circumstances were utterly overwhelming. Trial counsel could reasonably surmise from his conversations with respondent that character and psychological evidence would be of little help. Respondent had already been able to mention at the plea colloquy the substance of what there was to know about his financial and emotional troubles. Restricting testimony on respondent's character to what had come in at the plea colloquy ensured that contrary character and psychological evidence and respondent's criminal history, which counsel had successfully moved to exclude, would not come in. On these facts, there can be little question, even without application of the presumption of adequate performance, that trial counsel's defense, though unsuccessful, was the result of reasonable professional judgment.

With respect to the prejudice component, the lack of merit of respondent's claim is even more stark. The evidence that respondent says his trial counsel should have offered at the sentencing hearing would barely have altered the sentencing profile offered to the sentencing judge. As the state courts and District Court found, at most this evidence shows that numerous people who knew respondent thought he was generally a good person and that a psychiatrist and a psychologist believed he was under considerable emotional stress that did not rise to the level of extreme disturbance. Given the overwhelming aggravating factors, there is no reasonable probability that the omitted evidence would have changed the conclusion that the aggravating circumstances outweighed the mitigating circumstances and, hence, the sentence imposed. Indeed, admission of the evidence respondent now offers might even have been harmful to his case: his "rap sheet" would probably have been admitted into evidence, and the psychological reports would have directly contradicted respondent's claim that the mitigating circumstance of extreme emotional disturbance applied to his case.

We conclude, therefore, that the District Court properly declined to issue a writ of habeas corpus. The judgement of the Court of Appeals is accordingly *Reversed*.

DISSENT

Justice Marshall, dissenting.

. . . My objection to the performance standard adopted by the Court is that it is so malleable that, in practice, it will either have no grip at all or will yield excessive variation in the manner in which the Sixth Amendment is interpreted and applied by different courts. To tell lawyers and the lower courts that counsel for a criminal defendant must behave "reasonably" and must act like "a reasonably competent attorney," is to tell them almost nothing. In essence, the majority has instructed judges called upon to assess claims of ineffective assistance of counsel to advert to their own intuitions regarding what constitutes "professional" representation, and has discouraged them from trying to develop more detailed standards governing the performance of defense counsel. In my view, the Court has thereby not only abdicated its own responsibility to interpret the Constitution, but also impaired the ability of the lower courts to exercise theirs.

The debilitating ambiguity of an "objective standard of reasonableness" in this context is illustrated by the majority's failure to address important issues concerning the quality of representation mandated by the Constitution. It is an unfortunate but undeniable fact that a person of means, by selecting a lawyer and paying him enough to ensure he prepares thoroughly, usually can obtain better representation than that available to an indigent defendant, who must rely on appointed counsel, who, in turn, has limited time and resources to devote to a given case. Is a "reasonably competent attorney" a reasonably competent adequately paid retained lawyer or a reasonably competent appointed attorney? It is also a fact that the quality of representation available to ordinary defendants in different parts of the country varies significantly. Should the standard of performance mandated by the Sixth Amendment vary by locale? The majority offers no clues as to the proper responses to these questions. . . .

Second and more fundamentally, the assumption on which the Court's holding rests is that the only purpose of the constitutional guarantee of effective assistance of counsel is to reduce the chance that innocent persons will be convicted. In my view, the guarantee also functions to ensure that convictions are obtained only through fundamentally fair procedures. The majority contends that the Sixth Amendment is not violated when a manifestly guilty defendant is convicted after a trial in which he was represented by a manifestly ineffective attorney. I cannot agree. Every defendant is entitled to a trial in which his interests are vigorously and conscientiously advocated by an able lawyer. A proceeding in which the defendant does not receive meaningful assistance in meeting the forces of the State does not, in my opinion, constitute due process. . . .

CASE DISCUSSION

Strickland pleaded guilty to three capital murder charges. Finding numerous aggravating circumstances and no mitigating circumstance, the trial judge sentenced respondent to death on each of the murder counts. The Florida Supreme Court affirmed, and respondent then sought collateral relief in state court on the ground, inter alia, that counsel had rendered ineffective assistance at the sentencing proceeding. The trial court denied relief, and the Florida Supreme Court affirmed. Respondent then filed a habeas corpus petition in federal district court advancing the claim of ineffective assistance of counsel. After an evidentiary hearing, the district court denied relief. The court of appeals ultimately reversed, stating that the Sixth Amendment accorded criminal defendants a right to counsel rendering "reasonably effective assistance given the totality of the circumstances." After outlining standards for judging whether a defense counsel fulfilled the duty to investigate nonstatutory mitigating circumstances and whether counsel's errors were sufficiently prejudicial to justify reversal, the court of appeals remanded the case for application of the standards. The United States Supreme Court reversed, holding that Strickland was not denied the effective representation of counsel, and that assuming counsel's conduct was unreasonable, respondent suffered insufficient prejudice to warrant setting aside his death sentence.

What were the totality of circumstances that led the Court to conclude that Strickland received "reasonably effective" assistance of counsel? Why did the Court conclude that even if Strickland did not receive effective assistance, the sentence would have been the same anyway? What reasons did the dissent give for not joining the majority? Do you think the Court promoted the interest in finality at the expense of obtaining the correct result? Do you think the Court responded to societal interest in crime control? If so, did it do so at the expense of procedural regularity? Explain.

Release on Bail and Pretrial Detention

Authorities release most defendants charged with crimes at some point before trial; in some jurisdictions the number released exceeds 90 percent. Despite these high numbers of released defendants, pretrial detention remains a serious problem: detaining even 10 percent of defendants contributes to jail overcrowding. The principal reason for detention is defendants' inability to post bail.[20]

Defendants' detention can last for considerable time periods: one-third for more than thirty days and 20 percent for more than ninety days. Finally, detention prior to trial places a heavy burden on local jurisdictions. Housing an individual detainee prior to trial costs about $30 a day, on the average.

Courts rely on a variety of release mechanisms. About 20 percent of defendants secure release without appearing before judges. They obtain **citation release,** or a summons to appear in minor cases similar to that used in traffic offenses. Or, they post bond according to **bail schedules** that list amounts required for various offenses. Defendants can obtain release any time by posting the amount in the schedule.[21]

Judges attach a variety of conditions to release of defendants who appear in court. They release some defendants on **O.R.** (own recognizance) or release on defendants' promise to appear in court. Some judges release defendants on the relatively nonrestrictive condition that they either report periodically to a pretrial release program, or promise to reside in the community until trial. Sometimes, judges attach more restrictive conditions in a **supervised release,** in which defendants must report to drug, alcohol, or mental illness treatment, or to employment programs, or to third persons such as relatives.[22]

Money bond takes a variety of forms. The least restrictive unsecured bond requires defendants to pay only if they fail to appear. The court-administered deposit bond requires defendants to post 10 percent of the bond's amount; if they appear, the court returns the deposit. Under privately administered bail bonds, bail bondsmen (most are men) charge 10 percent of the amount of bond they advance. Defendants forfeit this 10 percent fee even if they appear.[23]

Following the first appearance, courts may reconsider the initial pretrial release decision and the conditions attached to it. As many as half of all defendants who do not initially obtain release may do so as a result of this bail review after the initial appearance. However, since up to thirty days may pass before bail review, the critical release decision occurs at the first appearance.[24]

A typical state provision to guide judges in making the bail decision at the first appearance reads:

[T]he court, judge or judicial officer shall impose the first of the following conditions of release which will reasonably assure the appearance of the person for trial or hearing, or when otherwise required, or, if no single condition gives that assurance, any combination of the following conditions:

    (a) Place the person in the care and supervision of a designated person or organization agreeing to supervise him;

    (b) Place restrictions on travel, association, or place of abode during his period of release;

    (c) Require the execution of an appearance bond in an amount set by the court with sufficient solvent sureties, or the deposit of cash or other sufficient security in lieu thereof; or

    (d) Impose any other condition deemed reasonably necessary to assure appearance as required, including a condition requiring that the person return to custody after specified hours.

In any event, the court shall also fix the amount of money bail without other conditions upon which the defendant may obtain his release.[25]

Decision Point

I. Earl Ball was incarcerated while awaiting trial on charges of rape, robbery, and sodomy because he could not raise the $5,000 bail that the trial court imposed. The trial court had set the $5,000 bail because the court determined "that no other conditions of release available . . . would reasonably assure appellant's appearance for trial." Ball's lawyer proposed the following conditions of release in lieu of the $5,000 bond.

"Appellant shall be released on his personal recognizance on the following conditions:

"A. Initially, he shall be released from the jail from 9 to 5 to report to the offices of the Offender Rehabilitation Project, 711 - 14th Street, N.W., Room 810, to obtain aid in seeking employment, and to make and keep job interviews. On each subsequent day he shall be released from jail only between the hours of 9 to 5, until his attorney notifies the Chief Judge of the District Court that he has in fact obtained regular employment.

"Upon the representation of counsel that appellant Ball has obtained regular employment, he shall be released from jail on a full-time basis on the following conditions:

(1) He shall appear in the District Court when required to do so and not depart the jurisdiction of the District Court without leave of court.

(2) He shall reside with his family at 3339 - 17th Street, N.W., Washington, D.C., and notify the Court of any change of address.

(3) He shall be a party to the following arrangements among him, Mr. Douglas Lindsey, Roving Leader, Department of Recreation, and the court:

    (a) He shall report once a week to Mr. Douglas Lindsey, 3149 - 16th Street, N.W.

    (b) Mr. Lindsey will check regularly by phone call or visit on defendant-appellant's employer to assure that he is maintaining his employment satisfactorily.

    (c) Mr. Lindsey shall report any failure of appellant to report regularly to him, any failure to maintain employment, and any arrests of appellant of which he learns, to Mr. William Collins, Assistant United States Attorney, ST 3–5700, to Barbara A. Bowman, counsel for appellant, ST 3–5700, Extension 391, and to the Criminal Clerk's Office of the United States District Court, ST 3–5700, Extension 521.

(4) Every pay-period, defendant-appellant shall deposit with his counsel 10% of his net earnings, until this sum reaches $250.00. At that time defendant-appellant, with the aid of his counsel, shall deposit this sum in the Registry of the Court as security for his appearance, to be returned in full when appellant appears for trial, to be forfeited in whole or part, as directed by the trial court, should he fail to appear.

(5) Appellant shall, with his counsel, make a monthly appearance in Assignment Court, at a time to be arranged by his counsel with the Assistant United States Attorney, and counsel shall, after consultation with Mr. Lindsey, Offender Rehabilitation Project, and appellant, represent to the court that appellant is maintaining the conditions of his release as set forth herein. The aforesaid personal recognizance shall be executed in the United States District Court for the District of Columbia.

"I have read the conditions of release as stated above and agree to comply, with the understanding that a failure to do so may result in my being arrested. I understand that a violation of these conditions will subject me to the contempt powers of this court and that I may receive a $500.00 fine, six months in jail, or both, and that the penalties for failure to appear at trial are five years imprisonment, $5,000.00, or both.

—————————Earl E. Ball, Jr.''

Are the proposed conditions appropriate and lawful? According to the District of Columbia United States Court of Appeals, they are.[26]

II. On April 3, 1987, defendant was charged with first-degree rape and second-degree burglary. After arraignment in the local criminal court, the court set bail at $10,000 and added as a condition of release that the defendant "undergo a blood test to confirm to the court that [defendant] is not a carrier or infected with the VIRUS associated with ACQUIRED IMMUNE DEFICIENCY SYNDROME, more commonly known as 'AIDS.' '' After a bail hearing on April 6, 1987, the court reduced the bail

> amount to $2,500 but continued the condition of the negative AIDS test. Was the condition lawful? The New York Court of Appeals found that "it was improper and an abuse of discretion . . . to impose a condition of a negative AIDS test prior to release on bail."[27]

BALANCING INDIVIDUAL DEPRIVATIONS AND PUBLIC SAFETY. Pretrial detention imposes a severe deprivation on defendants. Incarceration, loss of wages, or even employment, separation from family and friends, restrictions on aiding in their defense, and loss of reputation may all result. Furthermore, these deprivations occur prior to conviction. Defendants may be incarcerated on probable cause before the state proves beyond a reasonable doubt that they have committed crimes. On the other hand, pretrial release incurs costs for society. Defendants may not appear for trial, released defendants may commit further crimes, and the community may experience anxiety over the threats to public safety released defendants may pose. The decision whether to release or detain defendants prior to trial, then, requires balancing the rights of individuals to be free until they are proven guilty and the need of the community to feel safe from crime and its interest in bringing criminals to justice.

The basic question that bail and pretrial detention raises is: Do the purposes of bail and detention and the foundation upon which they rest warrant the deprivations they produce? That basic question breaks down into two more specific questions: (1) What constitutional rights do defendants have in connection with bail and pretrial detention? (2) What proper purposes do bail and pretrial detention serve?

THE CONSTITUTION, BAIL, AND PRETRIAL DETENTION. The Constitution does not guarantee defendants an absolute right to bail despite the severe deprivations pretrial detention entails. It does, however, place restrictions on the state's power to deny bail and it imposes standards on the conditions of pretrial detention. The two amendments to the United States Constitution relevant to pre-trial release and detention are:

> Excessive bail shall not be required . . . nor cruel and unusual punishments inflicted. Amendment VIII
> . . . No state shall . . . deprive any person of life, liberty, or property, without due process of law; nor deny to any person within its jurisdiction equal protection of the laws. Amendment XIV

EXCESSIVE BAIL. In a leading Supreme Court bail case, *Stack v. Boyle,* Chief Justice Vinson wrote for the Court:

> From the passage of the Judiciary Act of 1789, to the present . . . federal law has unequivocally provided that a person arrested for a non-capital offense *shall* be admitted to bail. This traditional right to freedom permits the unhampered preparation of a defense, and serves to prevent the infliction of punishment prior to conviction. . . . Unless this right to bail before trial is preserved, the presumption of innocence, secured only after centuries of struggle, would lose its meaning.[28]

In *Stack v. Boyle,* twelve people were charged with conspiring to violate the Smith Act, which made it a crime to advocate the violent overthrow of the government. The case arose at the height of the cold war when anticommunism and fear of radicalism gripped the nation. The trial court fixed bail at $50,000. The Supreme Court ruled that amounts exceeding those necessary to secure the petitioners' appearance at trial violated the Eighth Amendment. The Court held that magistrates must calculate how much money to attach to release to minimize the risk that defendants will not appear.

The amount necessary to secure defendants' appearance at trial, of course, varies according to a number of circumstances. Judges typically take the following conditions into account:

1. seriousness of the offense charged;
2. weight of the evidence against the defendant;
3. defendants' family ties, employment, financial resources, character, and mental condition;
4. length of defendants' residence in the community;
5. defendants' prior criminal record;
6. prior record of appearing or "jumping" bail.

Generally, judges do not take defendants' word for the answers to the above factors. Most large urban jurisdictions provide for prerelease investigations, administered either by the probation department or a special pretrial release agency.

No amount of bail may be high enough to secure their wealthy defendants' appearance. For example, in *United States v. Abrahams,* Abrahams had three previous convictions, was an escaped prisoner from another state, had given false information at a prior bail hearing, had failed to appear on a former bail of $100,000, had failed to appear on a previous charge in California from which he was a fugitive, had several aliases, and had recently transferred $1.5 million to Burmuda! The First Circuit Court of Appeals upheld the district court's finding that no condition "or any combination . . . will reasonably assure the appearance of defendant for trial if admitted to bail." According to former Attorney General William French Smith, this problem is particularly acute among major drug dealers who can post bail of as high as a million dollars with no difficulty. "Some of these people net $250,000 to $500,000 a month from their drug sales. Paying bail of $100,000 is like getting rid of pocket money to these people," Smith said.[29]

At the other extreme—and much more common—any amount may be too much for indigents to pay. Professor Caleb Foote, a noted bail scholar, believes our bail system violates the Constitution in several ways by denying indigent defendants:

1. due process because detention adversely affects the outcome of their cases due to their inability to help with their defense;
2. equal protection of the law because they are detained solely due to their poverty;
3. Eighth Amendment right against excessive bail because they cannot raise any amount the court requires.[30]

The Fifth Circuit Court of Appeals dealt with the problem of indigent defendants' bail in *Pugh v. Rainwater.* Florida's bail system provided for a range of conditions for release. However, the system did not establish a presumption in favor of release on recognizance nor did it establish a priority for nonfinancial conditions. The Court ruled:

> Because it gives the judge essentially unreviewable discretion to impose money bail, the rule [is] . . . discriminatory . . . : When a judge decides to set money bail, the

indigent will be forced to remain in jail. We hold that equal protection standards are not satisfied unless the judge is required to consider less financially onerous forms of release before he imposes money bail. Requiring a presumption in favor of non-money bail accommodates the State's interest in assuring the defendant's appearance at trial as well as the defendant's right to be free pending trial, regardless of his financial status.[31]

Hence, as the Court put it later on rehearing,

an indigent, whose appearance at trial could reasonably be assured by one of the alternative forms of release, pretrial confinement for inability to post money bail would constitute imposition of an excessive restraint.[32]

Lower courts set bail in almost all cases. Occasionally defendants appeal the bail determination. The Texas intermediate appellate court reviewed a bail decision in a murder case in *Ex parte Walton*.

Interfering with the Preparation of a Defense

Pretrial detention clearly impedes defendants' ability to prepare their best defense. They cannot help locate either witnesses or physical evidence more accessible to them than to outside investigators. Cramped jail quarters and restricted visiting hours inhibit conferences with attorneys. Pretrial detention affects defendants' appearance and demeanor in the courtroom—rumpled clothes, pallid complexion, and other results of confinement are difficult to conceal. Released defendants, on the other hand, can both help in their own defense and demonstrate to the court that they are working and maintaining their responsibilities to themselves and, if present, to their families.[33]

PREVENTIVE DETENTION. Commentators, lawyers, courts, and criminal justice personnel have hotly debated whether the only legitimate purpose for bail and pretrial detention is to secure defendants' appearance at trial. Might courts detain ''dangerous'' defendants—those who pose a threat to community safety and specific individuals—to prevent them from doing or threatening further harm while they await trial? Troubling reports exist that defendants released on bail commit crimes or intimidate, hurt, and terrorize victims and potential witnesses.

Congress enacted the Bail Reform Act of 1984 that authorizes federal courts to detain arrested individuals when a judge determines, after a hearing, that no condition of release would ''reasonably'' assure the appearance of the individual and ''the safety of . . . the community.'' Defendants have a right to testify at the hearing, to present evidence, to counsel, and to cross-examine witnesses. To detain defendants the court must have ''clear and convincing evidence''—more than probable cause but less than proof beyond a reasonable doubt. (See chap. 5 for a full discussion of probable cause and chap. 12 for a full treatment of proof beyond a reasonable doubt.)

Several empirical—and constitutional—questions surround preventive detention. The major empirical question is whether probable cause to believe a person has committed a crime predicts future dangerous or criminal behavior. Most available research suggests this is difficult to answer, both because dangerous is a vague term and because human behavior, particularly violent behavior, cannot easily be foreseen. The constitutional question is whether preventive detention violates the Eighth Amendment prohibition against cruel and unusual punishment and the due process clause requiring a fair trial because detention presumes guilt and punishes prior to conviction beyond a reasonable doubt.[34]

The Supreme Court has recently addressed **preventive detention,** or detaining "dangerous" defendants prior to trial, in *United States v. Salerno.*

CASE

Were their pretrial detentions "punishment"?

United States v. Salerno

481 U.S. 739, 107 S.Ct. 2095, 95 L.Ed.2d 697 (1987)

[Rehnquist, C.J., delivered the opinion of the Court, in which White, Blackmun, Powell, O'Connor, and Scalia, JJ., joined. Marshall, J., filed a dissenting opinion, in which Brennan, J., joined. Stevens, J., filed a dissenting opinion.]

FACTS

Respondents Anthony Salerno and Vincent Cafaro were arrested on March 21, 1986, after being charged in a 29-count indictment alleging various Racketeer Influenced and Corrupt Organizations Act (RICO) violations, mail and wire fraud offenses, extortion, and various criminal gambling violations. The RICO counts alleged 35 acts of racketeering activity, including fraud, extortion, gambling, and conspiracy to commit murder. At respondent's arraignment, the Government moved to have Salerno and Cafaro detained pursuant to § 3142(e), on the ground that no condition of release would assure the safety of the community or any person. The District Court held a hearing at which the Government made a detailed proffer of evidence. The Government's case showed that Salerno was the "boss" of the Genovese Crime Family of La Cosa Nostra and that Cafaro was a "captain" in the Genovese Family. According to the Government's proffer, based in large part on conversations intercepted by a court-ordered wiretap, the two respondents had participated in wide-ranging conspiracies to aid their illegitimate enterprises through violent means. The Government also offered the testimony of two of its trial witnesses, who would assert that Salerno personally participated in two murder conspiracies. Salerno opposed the motion for detention, challenging the credibility of the Government's witnesses. He offered the testimony of several character witnesses as well as a letter from his doctor stating that he was suffering from a serious medical condition. Cafaro presented no evidence at the hearing, but instead characterized the wiretap conversations as merely "tough talk."

OPINION

The Bail Reform Act of 1984 allows a federal court to detain an arrestee pending trial if the government demonstrates by clear and convincing evidence after an adversary hearing that no release conditions "will reasonably assure . . . the safety of any other person and the community." The United States Court of Appeals for the Second Circuit struck down this provision of the Act as facially unconstitutional, because, in that court's words, this type of pretrial detention violates "substantive due process." We granted certiorari because of a conflict among the Courts of Appeals regarding the validity of the Act. We hold that, as against the facial attack mounted by these respondents, the Act fully comports with constitutional requirements. We therefore reverse.

Responding to "the alarming problems of crimes committed by persons on release," Congress formulated the Bail Reform Act of 1984. . . .

To this end, § 3141(a) of the Act requires a judicial officer to determine whether an arrestee shall be detained. Section 3142(e) provides that "[i]f, after a hearing pursuant to the provisions of subsection (f), the judicial officer finds that no condition or combination of conditions will reasonably assure the appearance of the person as required and the safety of any other person and the community, he shall order the detention of the person prior to trial." . . .

The judicial officer is not given unbridled discretion in making the detention determination. Congress has specified the considerations relevant to that decision. These factors include the nature and seriousness of the charges, the substantiality of the government's evidence against the arrestee, the arrestee's background and characteristics, and the nature and seriousness of the danger posed by the suspect's release. Should a judicial officer order detention, the detainee is entitled to expedited appellate review of the detention order. . . .

Respondents present two grounds for invalidating the Bail Reform Act's provisions permitting pretrial detention on the basis of future dangerousness. First, they rely upon the Court of Appeals' conclusion that the Act exceeds the limitations placed upon the Federal Government by the Due Process Clause of the Fifth Amendment. Second, they contend that the Act contravenes the Eighth Amendment's proscription against excessive bail. We treat those contentions in turn. . . .

Respondents first argue that the Act violates substantive due process because the pretrial detention it authorizes constitutes impermissible punishment before trial. The Government, however, has never argued that pretrial detention could be upheld if it were "punishment." . . . [P]retrial detention under the Bail Reform Act is regulatory, not penal. . . .

The government's interest in preventing crime by arrestees is both legitimate and compelling. . . . On the other side of the scale, of course, is the individual's strong interest in liberty. We do not minimize the importance and fundamental nature of this right. But, as our cases hold, this right may, in circumstances where the government's interest is sufficiently weighty, be subordinated to the greater needs of society. . . .

Respondents also contend that the Bail Reform Act violates the Excessive Bail Clause of the Eighth Amendment. . . . We think that the Act survives a challenge founded upon the Eighth Amendment. . . . While we agree that a primary function of bail is to safeguard the courts' role in adjudicating the guilt or innocence of defendants, we reject the proposition that the Eighth Amendment categorically prohibits the government from pursuing other admittedly compelling interests through regulation of pretrial release. . . . Nothing in the text of the Bail Clause limits permissible government considerations solely to questions of flight. . . .

We believe that when Congress has mandated detention on the basis of a compelling interest other than prevention of flight, as it has here, the Eighth Amendment does not require release on bail.

In our society liberty is the norm, and detention prior to trial or without trial is the carefully limited exception. We hold that the provisions for pretrial detention in the Bail Reform Act of 1984 fall within that carefully limited exception. The Act authorizes the detention prior to trial of arrestees charged with serious felonies who are found after an adversary hearing to pose a threat to the safety of individuals or to the community which no condition of release can dispel. . . . We are unwilling to say that this congressional determination, based as it is upon that primary concern of every government—a concern for the safety and indeed the lives of its citizens—on its face violates either the Due Process Clause of the Fifth Amendment or the Excessive Bail Clause of the Eighth Amendment.

The judgement of the Court of Appeals is therefore
Reversed.

DISSENT

Justice Marshall, with whom Justice Brennan joins, dissenting.

This case brings before the Court for the first time a statute in which Congress declares that a person innocent of any crime may be jailed indefinitely, pending the trial of allegations which are legally presumed to be untrue, if the Government shows to the satisfaction of a judge that the accused is likely to commit crimes, unrelated to the pending charges, at any time in the future. Such statutes, consistent with the usages of tyranny and the excesses of what bitter experience teaches us to call the police state, have long been thought incompatible with the fundamental human rights protected by our Constitution. Today a majority of this Court holds otherwise. Its decision disregards basic principles of justice established centuries ago and enshrined beyond the reach of governmental interference in the Bill of Rights. . . .

The majority finds that "Congress did not formulate the pretrial detention provisions as punishment for dangerous individuals," but instead was pursuing the "legitimate regulatory goal" of "preventing danger to the community." Concluding that pretrial detention is not an excessive solution to the problem of preventing danger to the community, the majority thus finds that no substantive element of the guarantee of due process invalidates the statute. . . .

The absurdity of this conclusion arises, of course, from the majority's cramped concept of substantive due process. The majority proceeds as though the only substantive right protected by the Due Process Clause is a right to be free from punishment before conviction. The majority's technique for infringing this right is simple: merely redefine any measure which is claimed to be punishment as "regulation," and, magically, the Constitution no longer prohibits its imposition. . . .

"The principle that there is a presumption of innocence in favor of the accused is the undoubted law, axiomatic and elementary, and its enforcement lies at the foundation of the administration of our criminal law.'' Our society's belief, reinforced over the centuries, that all are innocent until the state has proved them to be guilty, like the companion principle that guilt must be proved beyond a reasonable doubt, is ''implicit in the concept of ordered liberty.''

The statute now before us declares that persons who have been indicted may be detained if a judicial officer finds clear and convincing evidence that they pose a danger to individuals or to the community. . . . The conclusion is inescapable that the indictment has been turned into evidence, if not that the defendant is guilty of the crime charged, then that left to his own devices he will soon be guilty of something else. '' 'If it suffices to accuse, what will become of the innocent?' '' . . .

''It is a fair summary of history to say that the safeguards of liberty have frequently been forged in controversies involving not very nice people.'' *United States v. Rabinowitz,* 339 U.S. 56, 69, 70 S.Ct. 430, 436, 94 L.Ed. 653 (1950) (Frankfurter, J., dissenting). Honoring the presumption of innocence is often difficult; sometimes we must pay substantial social costs as a result of our commitment to the values we espouse. But at the end of the day the presumption of innocence protects the innocent; the shortcuts we take with those whom we believe to be guilty injure only those wrongfully accused and, ultimately, ourselves.

Throughout the world today there are men, women, and children interned indefinitely, awaiting trials which may never come or which may be a mockery of the word, because their governments believe them to be ''dangerous.'' Our Constitution, whose construction began two centuries ago, can shelter us forever from the evils of such unchecked power. Over two hundred years it has slowly, through our efforts, grown more durable, more expansive, and more just. But it cannot protect us if we lack the courage, and the self-restraint, to protect ourselves. Today a majority of the Court applies itself to an ominous exercise in demolition. Theirs is truly a decision which will go forth without authority, and come back without respect.

I dissent.

CASE DISCUSSION

Salerno and Cafaro were committed for pretrial detention pursuant to the Bail Reform Act by the United States District Court. The court of appeals vacated the commitment and remanded. On writ of *certiorari,* the United States Supreme Court reversed, holding that pretrial preventive detention does not violate the constitutional rights of those detained and that the due process does not categorically prohibit pretrial detention as a regulatory measure.

Is pretrial detention punishment or a ''regulatory device''? What criteria do you use to answer this question? What does Justice Marshall mean when he says, ''If it suffices to accuse, what will become of the innocent?'' Does pretrial detention undermine the presumption of innocence? What, in your opinion, is (are) the proper purposes of bail? Defend your answer.

CONDITIONS OF PRETRIAL CONFINEMENT. Detention prior to trial, whether to secure defendants' appearance or to protect public safety, is nonetheless confinement. Jailed defendants are not free to leave: they live in cells, subject to jail discipline and routine, and they must conform to rules intended to preserve safety and order within the detention facility. But jailed defendants are legally innocent; they do not forfeit their constitutional rights simply because of their incarceration. A number of years ago someone asked one jail administrator if surveillance of jailed defendants in cells through two-way mirrors of which inmates were unaware violated defendants' right to privacy. The administrator replied "They have no rights," but that is untrue. Jailed defendants do have rights but they are "diminished" because of confinement. The United States Supreme Court addressed the questions What rights? and How diminished? in *Bell v. Wolfish.*

CASE

Were the defendants' "punished"?

Bell v. Wolfish

441 U.S. 520, 99 S.Ct. 1861, 60 L.Ed.2d 447 (1979)

[Rehnquist, J., delivered the opinion of the Court, in which Burger, C.J., and Stewart, White, and Blackmun, JJ., joined. Powell, J., filing an opinion concurring in part and dissenting in part. Marshall, J., filed a dissenting opinion. Stevens, J., filed a dissenting opinion, in which Brennan, J., joined.]

FACTS

The MCC (Metropolitan Correctional Center) differs markedly from the familiar image of a jail; there are no barred cells, dank, colorless corridors, or clanging steel gates. It was intended to include the most advanced and innovative features of modern design of detention facilities. "[I]t represented the architectural embodiment of the best and most progressive penological planning." The key design element of the 12-story structure is the "modular" or "unit" concept, whereby each floor designed to house inmates has one or two largely self-contained residential units that replace the traditional cell-block jail construction. Each unit in turn has several clusters or corridors of private rooms or dormitories radiating from a central 2-story "multipurpose" or common room, to which each inmate has free access approximately 16 hours a day. Because our analysis does not turn on the particulars of the MCC concept or design, we need not discuss them further.

When the MCC opened in August 1975, the planned capacity was 449 inmates, an increase of 50% over the former West Street facility. Despite some dormitory accommodations, the MCC was designed primarily to house these inmates in 389 rooms, which originally were intended for single occupancy. While the MCC was under construction, however, the number of persons committed to pretrial detention began to rise at an ''unprecedented'' rate. The Bureau of Prisons took several steps to accommodate this unexpected flow of persons assigned to the facility, but despite these efforts, the inmate population at the MCC rose above its planned capacity within a short time after its opening. To provide sleeping space for this increased population, the MCC replaced the single bunks in many of the individual rooms and dormitories with double bunks. Also, each week some newly arrived inmates had to sleep in cots in the common areas until they could be transferred to residential rooms as space became available.

On November 28, 1975, less than four months after the MCC had opened, the named respondents initiated this action by filing in the District Court a petition for a writ of habeas corpus. . . . The petition served up a variable potpourri of complaints that implicated virtually every facet of the institution's conditions and practices. Respondents charged, *inter alia,* that they had been deprived of their statutory and constitutional rights because of overcrowded conditions, undue length of confinement, improper searches, inadequate recreational, educational, and employment opportunities, insufficient staff, and objectionable restrictions on the purchase and receipt of personal items and books. The District Court, in the words of the Court of Appeals for the Second Circuit, ''intervened broadly into almost every facet of the institution'' and enjoined no fewer than 20 MCC practices on constitutional and statutory grounds. The Court of Appeals largely affirmed the District Court's constitutional rulings and in the process held that under the Due Process Clause of the Fifth Amendment, pretrial detainees may ''be subjected to only those 'restrictions and privations' which 'inhere in their confinement itself or which are justified by compelling necessities of jail administration.' '' We granted certiorari to consider the important constitutional questions raised by these decisions and to resolve an apparent conflict among the Circuits. We now reverse.

OPINION

. . . Not every disability imposed during pretrial detention amounts to ''punishment'' in the constitutional sense. . . . Once the Government has exercised its conceded authority to detain a person pending trial, it obviously is entitled to employ devices that are calculated to effectuate this detention. Traditionally, this has meant confinement in a facility which, no matter how modern or antiquated, results in restricting the movement of a detainee in a manner in which he would not be restricted if he simply were free to walk the streets pending trial. Whether it be called a jail, a prison, or a custodial center, the purpose of the facility is to detain. Loss of freedom of choice and privacy are inherent incidents of confinement in such a facility. And the fact that such detention interferes with the detainee's understandable desire to live as comfortably as possible and with as little restraint as possible during confinement does not convert the conditions or restrictions of detention into ''punishment.'' . . .

Judged by this analysis, respondents' claim that ''double-bunking'' vio-. lated their due process rights fails. . . . On this record, we are convinced as a matter of law that "double-bunking" as practiced at the MCC did not amount to punishment and did not, therefore, violate respondents' rights under the Due Process Clause of the Fifth Amendment.

Each of the rooms at the MCC that house pretrial detainees has a total floor space of approximately 75 square feet. Each of them designated for "double-bunking," contains a double bunkbed, certain other items of furniture, a wash basin, and an uncovered toilet. Inmates are generally locked into their rooms from 11 p.m. to 6:30 a.m. and for brief periods during the afternoon and evening head counts. During the rest of the day, they may move about freely between their rooms and the common areas. . . .

We disagree with both the District Court and the Court of Appeals that there is some sort of "one man, one cell" principle lurking in the Due Process Clause of the Fifth Amendment. While confining a given number of people in a given amount of space in such a manner as to cause them to endure genuine privations and hardships over an extended period of time might raise serious questions under the Due Process Clause as to whether those conditions amounted to punishment, nothing even approaching such hardship is shown by this record.

Detainees are required to spend only seven or eight hours each day in their rooms, during most or all of which they presumably are sleeping. During the remainder of the time, the detainees are free to move between their rooms and the common area. While "double-bunking" may have taxed some of the equipment or particular facilities in certain of the common areas, this does not mean that the conditions at the MCC failed to meet the standards required by the Constitution. Our conclusion in this regard is further buttressed by the detainees' length of stay at the MCC. Nearly all of the detainees are released within 60 days. We simply do not believe that requiring a detainee to share toilet facilities and this admittedly small sleeping space with another person for generally a maximum period of 60 days violates the Constitution. . . .

[M]aintaining institutional security and preserving internal order and discipline are essential goals that may require limitation or retraction of the retained constitutional rights of both convicted prisoners and pretrial detainees. "[C]entral to all other corrections goals is the institutional consideration of internal security within the corrections facilities themselves." . . .

Finally . . . the problems that arise in the day-to-day operations of the corrections facility are not susceptible of easy solutions. Prison administrators therefore should be accorded wide-ranging deference in the adoption and execution of policies and practices that in their judgment are needed to preserve internal order and discipline and to maintain institutional security. . . .

Inmates at all Bureau of Prisons facilities, including the MCC, are required to expose their body cavities for visual inspection as part of a strip search conducted after every contact visit with a person from outside the institution. Corrections officials testified that visual cavity searches were necessary not only to discover but also to deter the smuggling of weapons, drugs, and other contraband into the institution. The District Court upheld the strip-search procedure but prohibited the body-cavity searches, absent probable cause to believe that the inmate is concealing contraband. Because petitioners proved only one instance in the MCC's short history where contraband was found during a body-cavity search, the Court of Appeals affirmed. In its view, the "gross violation of personal privacy inherent in such a search cannot be outweighed by the government's security interest in maintaining a practice of so little actual utility."

Admittedly, this practice instinctively gives us the most pause. However, assuming for present purposes that inmates, both convicted prisoners and pretrial detainees, retain some Fourth Amendment rights upon commitment to a corrections facility, we nonetheless conclude that these searches do not violate that Amendment. The Fourth Amendment prohibits only unreasonable searches, and under the circumstances, we do not believe that these searches are unreasonable. . . .

A detention facility is a unique place fraught with serious security dangers. Smuggling of money, drugs, weapons, and other contraband is all too common in occurrence. And inmate attempts to secrete these items into the facility by concealing them in body cavities is documented in this record. That there has been only one instance where an MCC inmate was discovered attempting to smuggle contraband into the institution on his person may be more a testament to the effectiveness of this search technique as a deterrent than to any lack of interest on the part of the inmates to secrete and import such items when the opportunity arises. . . .

There was a time not too long ago when the federal judiciary took a completely "hands-off" approach to the problem of prison administration. In recent years, however, these courts largely have discarded this "hands-off" attitude and have waded into this complex arena. . . . But many of these same courts have, in the name of the Constitution, become increasingly enmeshed in the minutiae of prison operations. Judges, after all, are human. They, no less than others in our society, have a natural tendency to believe that their individual solutions to often intractable problems are better and more workable than those of the persons who are actually charged with and trained in the running of the particular institution under examination. But under the Constitution, the first question to be answered is not whose plan is best, but in what branch of the Government is lodged the authority to initially devise the plan. . . . The wide range of "judgment calls" that meet constitutional and statutory requirements are confided to officials outside of the Judicial Branch of Government.

DISSENT

Mr. Justice Stevens, with whom Mr. Justice Brennan joins, dissenting.

This is not an equal protection case. An empirical judgment that most persons formally accused of criminal conduct are probably guilty would provide a rational basis for a set of rules that treat them like convicts until they establish their innocence. No matter how rational such an approach might be—no matter how acceptable in a community where equality of status is the dominant goal—it is obnoxious to the concept of individual freedom protected by the Due Process Clause. If ever accepted in this country, it would work a fundamental change in the character of our free society.

Nor is this an Eighth Amendment case. That provision of the Constitution protects individuals convicted of crimes from punishment that is cruel and unusual. The pretrial detainees whose rights are at stake in this case, however, are innocent men and women who have been convicted of no crimes. Their claim is not that they have been subjected to cruel and unusual punishment in violation of the Eighth Amendment, but that to subject them to any form of punishment at all is an unconstitutional deprivation of their liberty.

This is a due process case. The most significant—and I venture to suggest the most enduring—part of the Court's opinion today is its recognition of this initial constitutional premise. The Court squarely holds that "under the Due Process Clause, a detainee may not be punished prior to an adjudication of guilt in accordance with due process of law." . . .

Prior to conviction every individual is entitled to the benefit of a presumption both that he is innocent of prior criminal conduct and that he has no present intention to commit any offense in the immediate future. . . .

It is not always easy to determine whether a particular restraint serves the legitimate, regulatory goal of ensuring a detainee's presence at trial and his safety and security in the meantime, or the unlawful end of punishment. . . . [Discussion of double-bunking, searches of mail, and cells is omitted.]

The body-cavity search—clearly the greatest personal indignity—may be the least justifiable measure of all. After every contact visit a body-cavity search is mandated by the rule. The District Court's finding that searches have failed in practice to produce any demonstrable improvement in security, is hardly surprising. Detainees and their visitors are in full view during all visits, and are fully clad. To insert contraband into one's private body cavities during such a visit would indeed be "an imposing challenge to nerves and agility." There is no reason to expect, and the petitioners have established none, that many pretrial detainees would attempt, let alone succeed, in surmounting this challenge absent the challenged rule. Moreover, as the District Court explicitly found, less severe alternatives are available to ensure that contraband is not transferred during visits. Weapons and other dangerous instruments, the items of greatest legitimate concern, may be discovered by the use of metal detecting devices or other equipment commonly used for airline security. In addition, inmates are required, even apart from the body-cavity searches, to disrobe, to have their clothing inspected, and to present open hands and arms to reveal the absence of any concealed objects. These alternative procedures, "amply satisf[y]" the demands of security. In my judgment, there is no basis in this record to disagree.

It may well be, as the Court finds, that the rules at issue here were not adopted by administrators eager to punish those detained at MCC. The rules can all be explained as the easiest way for administrators to ensure security in the jail. But the easiest course for jail officials is not always one that our Constitution allows them to take. If fundamental rights are withdrawn and severe harms are indiscriminately inflicted on detainees merely to secure minimal savings in time and effort for administrators, the guarantee of due process is violated.

CASE DISCUSSION

Inmates brought a class action in federal district court challenging the constitutionality of numerous conditions of confinement and practices in the

Metropolitan Correctional Center, a federally operated, short-term custodial facility for pretrial detainees in New York City. The district court, on several constitutional grounds, enjoined various practices in the facility. The Court of Appeals affirmed the District Court's rulings. On writ of *certiorari,* the United States Supreme Court reversed, holding that the conditions and practices in the detention center did not violate pretrial detainees' constitutional rights.

How can you distinguish between detention and punishment? One critic said of this case that was all well and good for Supreme Court justices to say this was detention, not punishment, but it probably would be little comfort for the detainees to know that. Does it matter that most pretrial detainees are subject to confinement because they cannot afford bail? What interests are at stake in the case? How would you balance them?

☰ SUMMARY

Shortly after arrest, the police forward some cases to prosecutors. Prosecutors decide whether to dismiss the cases, to divert those arrested into social and community service programs or civil courts, or to file formal charges against defendants. Prosecutors possess enormous discretion in deciding whether to charge, and what specific charges to bring against criminal suspects. While prosecutors wield wide power, they do not have unlimited discretion in charging criminal suspects. Constitutional rules against discriminatory prosecution, the formal rules of evidence, and the satisfaction of justice, organizational, and societal interests restrain prosecutors' decisions to charge.

The first appearance takes place shortly after the decision to charge, particularly for defendants detained without warrants or prior judicial determination of probable cause to detain them. The first appearance is a brief proceeding before magistrates or other judicial officers in the lower criminal courts. Judicial officers perform several functions at the first appearance, including (1) determining probable cause to detain if such determination has not already taken place; (2) reading the charges against defendants; (3) informing defendants of their constitutional rights; (4) determining indigency and assigning attorneys for defendants qualifying as indigent; and (5) setting bail. The criminal complaint acts as the charging instrument at the first appearance. The Supreme Court has not ruled that the first appearance constitutes adversary proceedings for purposes of the Sixth Amendment right to counsel.

The right to counsel did exist in criminal cases at the common law. At the time of its adoption and for a considerable period following, the Sixth Amendment right to counsel meant only that defendants who could afford them had the right to have lawyers represent them at criminal trials. The Supreme Court and the state courts have expanded the scope of the right since the early years following the adoption of the United States Constitution. It now extends to pretrial proceedings, such as the right to an attorney during custodial interrogation, at lineups after indictment, and at all stages following the inception of judicial proceedings. Furthermore, defendants who cannot afford attorneys have a constitutional right to appointed counsel, except for petty offenses. Finally, indigent defendants have a right to *effective* counsel under the Sixth Amendment.

The Eighth Amendment prohibits excessive bail. Most defendants are released during determination of the charges against them. The Constitution permits setting bail, either by money, bond, or other conditions sufficient to secure defendants' appearance at trial. Furthermore, the Constitution allows preventive detention, that is, detaining defendants whose dangerousness—likelihood of committing other offenses or endangering the community or specific individuals such as victims and witnesses— justifies detaining them during the determination of the charges against them. The Supreme Court has ruled that preventive detention is a regulatory device; it does not constitute cruel and unusual punishment, nor does it deny preventively detained defendants due process of law.

≡ QUESTIONS FOR REVIEW AND DISCUSSION

1. Distinguish between the stage in the criminal process discussed in chapters 4 through 7 and that discussed in this chapter.
2. What are the acceptable and unacceptable criteria upon which prosecutors can decide to charge?
3. What decisions must prosecutors make when police bring them cases for further action?
4. Describe the major functions magistrates perform at the initial appearance.
5. How does the initial appearance differ from arraignment? preliminary hearings? grand jury review?
6. Should defendants have a right to a lawyer in *every* criminal case? Defend your answer.
7. At what point should defendants have the right to a lawyer in a criminal proceeding? Do they need one at the first appearance? Defend your answer.
8. What is "effective" counsel, according to the Constitution? Do you agree? Explain.
9. Should there be an absolute right to bail? Explain.
10. What, in your opinion, is a good definition of indigent?
11. What are the arguments in favor of and against preventive detention? Which do you think are most persuasive?
12. Can you identify all the result, process, organizational, and broad social interests that are balanced and promoted in the decisions to charge, assign counsel to indigent defendants, and release or detain defendants prior to trial? How would you balance these interests?

≡ NOTES

1. *Kirby v. Illinois,* 406 U.S. 682, 92 S.Ct. 1877, 32 L.Ed.2d 411 (1972).
2. Barbara Boland et al., *The Prosecution of Felony Arrests, 1982* (Washington, D.C.: National Institute of Justice, May 1988); Thomas Y. Davies, "A Hard Look at What We Know (and Still Need to Learn) About the 'Costs' of the Exclusionary Rule: The NIJ Study and Other Studies of 'Lost' Arrests," *American Bar Foundation Research Journal* 1983

(Summer):611–89; Peter F. Nardulli, ''The Societal Cost of the Exclusionary Rule: An Empirical Assessment,'' *American Bar Foundation Research Journal* 1983(Summer):585–609.

3. *People v. Camargo,* 135 Misc. 2d 987, 516 N.Y.S.2d 1004 (1986).

4. *Journal of the American Judicature Society* 34(1940):18–19; President's Commission on Law Enforcement and the Administration of Justice, *The Challenge of Crime in a Free Society* (Washington, D.C.: Government Printing Office, 1967), 10; Wayne R. LaFave, ''The Prosecutor's Discretion in the United States,'' *American Journal of Comparative Law* 18(1970):533–35.

5. *Manning v. Municipal Court,* 372 Mass. 315, 361 N.E.2d 1274 (1977).

6. *Thigpen v. Roberts,* 468 U.S. 27, 104 S.Ct. 2916, 82 L.Ed.2d 23 (1984).

7. *United States v. Peskin,* 527 F.2d 71 (7th Cir.1975).

8. Kenneth Mann, *Defending White Collar Crime* (New Haven: Yale University Press, 1985), 3–30.

9. *Minnesota Rules of Court: State and Federal,* Rules of Criminal Procedure (St. Paul: West Publishing, 1987), Rule 5.01, 112.

10. *Minnesota Rules of Court: State and Federal,* Rules of Criminal Procedure, Rule 4.02, Subd. 5(2), 110.

11. 287 U.S. 45, 53 S.Ct. 55, 77 L.Ed. 158 (1932).

12. *Johnson v. Zerbst,* 304 U.S. 458, 58 S.Ct. 1019, 82 L.Ed. 1461 (1938); *Betts v. Brady,* 316 U.S. 455, 62 S.Ct. 1252, 86 L.Ed. 1595 (1942); *Gideon v. Wainright,* 372 U.S. 335, 83 S.Ct. 792, 9 L.Ed.2d 799 (1963).

13. *Powell v. Alabama,* 287 U.S. 45, 53 S.Ct. 55, 77 L.Ed. 158 (1932); *Gideon v. Wainright,* 372 U.S. 335, 83 S.Ct. 792, 9 L.Ed.2d 799 (1963); *Argersinger v. Hamlin,* 407 U.S. 25, 92 S.Ct. 2006, 32 L.Ed.2d 530 (1972).

14. *Minnesota Rules of Court: State and Federal,* Rules of Criminal Procedure, Rule 5, 112, 114–115.

15. *Williams v. Beto,* 354 F.2d 698 (5th Cir. 1965).

16. Finer, ''Ineffective Assistance of Counsel,'' *Cornell Law Review* 58 (1973):1077.

17. Smithburn and Springman, ''Effective Assistance of Counsel: In Quest of a Uniform Standard.'' *Wake Forest Law Review* 17(1980):497; Erickson, ''Standards of Competency for Defense Counsel in a Criminal Case,'' *American Criminal Law Review* 17(1979):233; Bazelon, ''The Defective Assistance of Counsel,'' *University of Cincinnati Law Review* 42(1973):22.

18. Waltz, ''Inadequacy of Trial Defense Representation as a Ground for Post-Conviction Relief in Criminal Cases,'' *Northwestern University Law Review* 59(1964):289.

19. Wayne R. Lafave and Jerold H. Israel, *Criminal Procedure,* vol. 2 (St. Paul: West Publishing Company, 1984), 99–102.

20. Mary A. Toborg, *Pretrial Release: A National Evaluation of Practices and Outcomes,* (Washington, D.C.: National Institute of Justice, 1981).

21. Ibid.

22. Ibid.

23. Malcolm M. Feeley, *The Process Is the Punishment: Handling Cases in a Lower Criminal Court* (New York: Russell Sage Foundation, 1979), especially chap. 4.

24. Ibid.

25. *Minnesota Rules of Court: State and Federal,* ''Rules of Criminal Procedure,'' Rule 6.02, Subd. 1, 118–19.

26. *Ball v. United States,* 402 F.2d 206 (D.C.Cir. 1968).

27. *People v. McGreevy,* 134 Misc. 2d 1085, 514 N.Y.S.2d 622 (1987).

28. 342 U.S. 1, 72 S.Ct. 1, 96 L.Ed. 3 (1951).

29. 575 F.2d 3 (1st Cir. 1978), certiorari denied 439 U.S. 821 99 S.Ct. 85, 58 L.Ed.2d 112 (1978); quoted in *The Pretrial Reporter* 5(June, 1981).

30. Caleb Foote, "The Coming Constitutional Crisis in Bail," *University of Pennsylvania Law Review* 113(1965):959–1185.

31. 557 F.2d 1189 (5th Cir. 1977).

32. 572 F.2d 1053 (5th Cir. 1978).

33. "The Unconstitutional Administration of Bail: *Bellamy v. the Judges of New York City,*" *Criminal Law Bulletin* 8(1972):459–506.

34. For the empirical dimension to the problem, see Mark H. Moore et al., *Dangerous Offenders: The Elusive Target of Justice* (Cambridge, Mass.: Harvard University Press, 1984).

Chapter Ten

Pretrial Proceedings: Preliminary Hearing and Grand Jury Review

CHAPTER OUTLINE

CHAPTER MAIN POINTS

1. The government must test the evidentiary basis of its decision to charge before either disinterested judges in preliminary hearings or citizens in grand jury review.

2. A judge's bindover or a grand jury's indictment requires defendants to appear in court to hear and answer criminal charges—arraignment.

3. Probable cause that a crime was committed and that the defendant committed it constitutes the quantum of proof required to bind over.

4. The probable cause to indict or bind over requires a greater quantum of proof than probable cause to arrest.

5. Preliminary hearings are public adversary proceedings that defendants and their attorneys attend where judges decide the evidentiary sufficiency to bind over.

6. Grand jury review is secret, *ex parte,* and members of the community decide the sufficiency of the evidence with prosecutors' advice and aid.

7. Preliminary hearings emphasize the fact-finding benefits associated with adversary open proceedings, as well as the rights of criminal defendants to face their accusers.

8. Grand jury review stresses the importance of community participation in criminal justice administration.

9. The remedies adopted for improper proceedings in pretrial screening depend on the result and process interests promoted in appellate review of criminal proceedings.

CHAPTER KEY TERMS

affirmative defense defense, such as self-defense or insanity, that requires defendants to present facts in addition to denying the charge

arraignment bringing defendants to court to hear and answer (plead) to criminal charges

binding over decision in preliminary hearing to send a criminal case on for trial

charging the grand jury judges' address to grand jury prior to their review and deliberations

confrontation requirement the Sixth Amendment right of defendants' to confront the accusers and witnesses against them

discovery government providing evidence in its possession to the defense and *vice versa*

ex parte proceedings defendant not present or represented

grand jury targets grand jury witnesses who are themselves under investigation

hand up an indictment grand jury's delivering an indictment to a judge after their deliberations

harmless error an irregularity in proceedings that does not affect the outcome of the case

hearsay rule cannot introduce out-of-court statements to prove the truth of those out of court statements

impeach showing that a witness's testimony is not credible

indictment formal charging instrument issued by the grand jury that requires the defendant to answer charges

information formal charging instrument drawn up by the prosecutor

no-bill grand jury finding insufficient evidence to indict a criminal suspect

plea the defendant's answer to the government's criminal charge

prima facie **case** enough evidence to convict unless rebutted

quantum of proof the amount of evidence or factual foundation to authorize a government deprivation or intrusion

prior testimony exception testimony given under oath prior to trial is admissible at trial

purging the grand jury eliminating prospective grand jurors who have compelling reasons not to serve

true bill record of the number of grand jurors voting for indictment

---

TESTING THE GOVERNMENT'S CASE

The decision to charge indicates the government's commitment to criminal prosecution. The first appearance readies defendants for the consequences of this decision. However, before the government can require defendants to answer the charges against them, prosecutors must test the factual foundation for the government's case before disinterested parties. There is good reason for this test. Pursuing the criminal process beyond arrest and charge subjects defendants to further intrusions and deprivations. These include continued confinement for detained defendants and, for released defendants, the conditions imposed on bail. For all defendants, further proceedings require additional appearances in court and time, money, and energy devoted to preparing a defense. Other intrusions and deprivations, although indirect, are no less consequential. These entail separation from family and friends, loss of wages and employment, and in some instances loss of reputation and emotional well-being. One court observed:

> [W]hile in theory a trial provides a defendant with a full opportunity to contest and disprove charges against him, in practice, the handing up of an indictment will often have a devastating personal and professional impact that a later dismissal or acquittal can never undo.[1]

There are costs to society as well as to defendants. Taxpayers pay prosecutors, judges, and public defenders. Indirectly, defendants and their families often become burdens on society for at least the period of the criminal proceedings, and sometimes for a considerable period following. In 1983, it cost more than $25 for each day the government detained one person in a local jail. The cost has obviously risen greatly since then.[2]

Two principal mechanisms test the government's case against defendants: (1) grand jury review and (2) preliminary hearings. These proceedings also satisfy other goals in the criminal process, including (1) that rules govern the conduct of the proceedings; (2) that the proceedings do not unduly infringe on individual dignity; and (3) that the proceedings further, or at least do not thwart, broader social goals, such as public confidence in criminal justice, equality and impartiality in conducting public business, and community participation in—or at least awareness of—criminal proceedings. Hence, the pretrial proceedings balance society's interest in criminal law enforcement, accurate fact-finding, individual rights, the rule of law, and broad social goals in a free and democratic society.

When prosecutors seek an indictment, they test the government's case by presenting it to a grand jury. When they draw up an **information**—a formal accusation outlining the charges—they test the case at a preliminary hearing before a judge. If the government establishes the required quantum of proof in grand jury review, the grand jury returns the indictment as a **true bill.** If the government satisfies the evidentiary standard in the preliminary hearing, the judge **binds over** the defendant for trial. In either case, the true bill and the bindover require defendants to answer the criminal charges, that is, they constitute the formal charging instruments that can bring defendants before a court. The formal answer to these charges—the **plea**—takes place at the **arraignment,** a proceeding that brings a defendant to court to hear and to plead to, or formally answer, criminal charges.

Formally, the preliminary hearing and grand jury review determine the quantum of evidence, that is, whether probable cause exists to try defendants and, hence, proceed further in the criminal process. Pretrial screening also facilitates organizational interests, particularly the informal negotiation that takes place outside the restrictions that adversary proceedings impose. Preliminary hearings, for example, affect both pleas and plea bargaining. If the prosecution has a strong case, these proceedings are ''educational experiences'' for defendants, persuading them to plead guilty, or at least to plea bargain. This pressure to negotiate guilty pleas rather than determine guilt by adversary proceedings is always high. (See chap. 12.) Moreover, the preliminary hearing assists defense counsel in preparing tactics and strategy by offering counsel the opportunity to learn more about the prosecution's case. Although not formally visible, these underlying considerations nonetheless have a potent, if informal, affect on preliminary hearings.

The Fifth Amendment requires grand jury indictment for all serious crimes. The original states included similar provisions in their own constitutions. In the middle of the nineteenth century, some of the newer states adopted the information and preliminary hearing alternative to grand jury indictment. In recent years, the older states have also adopted the use of information and preliminary hearing. The twenty states that still require indictment permit defendants to waive the right to grand jury review and substitute information and preliminary hearing. The remaining states permit prosecutors to choose between indictment and information. (See Table 10.2.)

⬛ DIFFERENCES BETWEEN PRELIMINARY HEARING AND GRAND JURY REVIEW

Both grand jury review and preliminary hearings test the government's case for the quantum of proof required to go to trial. They differ, however, in several important respects. The preliminary hearing is an adversary proceeding in which the defense can challenge the prosecution's case. The grand jury hears only the prosecution's case without the defense's participation. Grand jury proceedings are *ex parte,* that is, they take place outside the presence of defendants and their counsel. Defendants and their lawyers attend preliminary hearings. Grand jury proceedings are secret; preliminary hearings are public. Judges preside over preliminary hearings; prosecutors manage grand jury proceedings without judicial participation. Finally, grand jury review relies on lay determination of the facts: grand jurors are not lawyers, they are citizens selected to serve a term as grand jurors. In preliminary hearings, magistrates determine the sufficiency of the evidence.

TABLE 10.1   Differences between Preliminary Hearing and Grand Jury Review

Preliminary Hearing	Grand Jury Review
Public hearing	Secret proceeding
Adversary proceeding	Only government's case presented
Judge presides	Citizens manage
Judge determines facts	Citizens (grand jurors) determine facts
Defendant present and represented	*Ex parte,* defendant not present or represented

The differences between preliminary hearings and grand jury proceedings illustrate varying emphases on interests in the criminal process. The preliminary hearing stresses adversarial, open, accusatory values and represents control by experts. Grand jury review, on the other hand, underscores the value of the democratic dimension to the criminal process—lay participation in criminal proceedings. Both, however, determine whether sufficient evidence exists to proceed further into the criminal process.

▬ PRELIMINARY HEARING

The preliminary hearing, sometimes called the preliminary examination, is a judicial hearing held sometime after the first appearance discussed in chapter 9. The time lapse between the first appearance and the preliminary hearing varies among jurisdictions, and even within jurisdictions, according to whether defendants are in custody or released on bail. For example, the Federal Rules of Criminal Procedure, which many states follow in rough outline, provide:

> If the defendant does not waive the preliminary examination, the magistrate shall schedule a preliminary examination. Such examination shall be held within a reasonable time but in any event not later than 10 days following the initial appearance if the defendant is in custody and no later than 20 days if he is not in custody. . . .[3]

A magistrate, justice of the peace, municipal court judge, or other member of the lower court judiciary usually presides over the preliminary hearing. However, statutes in most jurisdictions authorize all judges to conduct preliminary hearings.

The Right to a Preliminary Hearing

The United States Constitution does not grant defendants the right to a preliminary hearing. In *Lem Woon v. Oregon,* a unanimous Supreme Court held that eliminating all pretrial screening did not violate the due process clause of the Fourteenth Amendment. If states do provide for preliminary hearings, however, the Sixth Amendment guarantees defendants a right to counsel at the hearing. Preliminary hearings, according to *Coleman v. Alabama,* are critical stages in the criminal process. To have a fair trial, at the preliminary hearing defendants need the expertise of counsel "meaningfully to cross-examine the witnesses against" themselves.[4]

The Court listed the functions counsel could perform at the preliminary hearing:

> First, the lawyer's skilled examination and cross-examination of witnesses may expose fatal weaknesses in the State's case that may lead the magistrate to refuse to bind the accused over. Second, in any event, the skilled interrogation of witnesses by an experienced lawyer can fashion a vital impeachment tool for use in cross-examination of the State's witnesses at the trial, or to preserve testimony favorable to the accused of a witness who does not appear at the trial. Third, trained counsel can more effectively discover the case of a proper defense to meet that case at the trial. Fourth, counsel can also be influential at the preliminary hearing in making effective arguments for the accused on such matters as the necessity for an early psychiatric examination or bail.[5]

Rule 5(c) of the Federal Rules of Criminal Procedure provides for preliminary hearings in all cases with three exceptions: (1) petty offenses; (2) waiver by defendants; (3) indictment or information filed (charging defendants with crimes on the prosecutor's own authority) prior to the scheduled time for the preliminary hearing.[6]

Federal prosecutors commonly manipulate Rule 5(c) to suit their purposes. Sometimes, with judges' cooperation, prosecutors schedule indictments to avoid preliminary hearings. In some jurisdictions, for example, United States Attorneys arrange for their districts to have no more than one preliminary hearing for every hundred felonies. They can even stop a preliminary hearing in progress. If preliminary hearings are not proceeding well for the government, prosecutors may obtain a continuance, meanwhile obtaining an indictment that eliminates the need for the preliminary hearing.[7]

Although one court acknowledged

> sympathy with the notion that the government ought not to be allowed to freely abandon its prosecution in a preliminary examination the moment that an unfavorable ruling is made or an adverse result is imminent, [the court nonetheless ruled that] consistent with the strong weight of authority . . . no substantive rights of the defendant have been lost.[8]

Thirty states mandate preliminary hearings. Prosecutors initiate prosecution in these states by an instrument called an information, a charge brought on the prosecutor's sole authority. The preliminary hearing provides the opportunity to review judicially the evidence supporting the information. Twenty states have provisions similar to the Fifth Amendment to the United States Constitution that guarantees grand jury review in cases of serious crimes. Preliminary hearings are not ordinarily required in these jurisdictions. However, these states, called **indictment states,** allow prosecutors to choose between grand jury review and information followed by preliminary hearings as the means to test the quantum of proof and to compel defendants to answer the charges against them. In some jurisdictions, prosecutors routinely choose information for misdemeanors and indictment for felonies.

TABLE 10.2   States Adopting Information and Indictment as of 1984

Information States	Indictment for Capital Punishment and Life Imprisonment States	Indictment States
Arizona	Connecticut	Alabama
Arkansas	Florida	Alaska
California	Louisiana	Delaware
Colorado	Minnesota	Georgia
Hawaii	Rhode Island	Kentucky
Idaho		Maine
Illinois		Massachusetts
Indiana		Mississippi
Iowa		New Hampshire
Kansas		New Jersey
Maryland		New York
Michigan		North Carolina
Missouri		Ohio
Montana		Pennsylvania
Nebraska		South Carolina
Nevada		Tennessee
New Mexico		Texas
North Dakota		Virginia
Oklahoma		West Virginia
Oregon		
South Dakota		
Utah		

Vermont
Washington
Wisconsin
Wyoming

Prosecutors frequently choose information and preliminary hearing rather than grand jury review in indictment states. Unlike federal prosecutors, state prosecutors rarely seek prior indictments to avoid preliminary hearings for practical reasons. Grand juries, particularly in large cities, have heavy caseloads whose schedules prosecutors cannot easily control. In addition, prosecutors find preliminary hearings useful for the reasons already mentioned in the section on the preliminary hearing's functions.[9]

In the rare instances when prosecutors avoid preliminary hearings, the reasons for doing so include (1) saving time where many witnesses and exhibits must be presented, or where numerous defendants require separate hearings; (2) avoiding defense discovery, particularly to protect informants who are key witnesses; (3) limiting the number of times complainants, especially victims of sex offenses, will have to testify in public. Critics maintain that one reason not often mentioned for avoiding preliminary hearings is that it enables prosecutors to push weak cases through a "pliable" grand jury where they would fail to win a preliminary bind over.[10]

A few states have interpreted their state constitutions to require preliminary hearings even where grand jury review has taken place. The California Supreme Court, for example, ruled that the state's equal protection clause guaranteed preliminary hearings to criminal defendants, even though the Fourteenth Amendment to the United States Constitution does not require that states provide defendants with them.[11]

Differences between Preliminary Hearing and Trial

Preliminary hearings are adversary proceedings. Hence, they are open, public proceedings; prosecution, defense counsel, and defendant are present; the prosecution presents evidence; the defense can challenge the prosecution's evidence and present its own evidence. But preliminary hearings are not full-blown trials. Ordinarily, the prosecution presents only sufficient evidence to satisfy the bind-over standard. Usually this means that one or two prosecution witnesses appear and perhaps the prosecutor introduces some physical evidence. Typically, the defense introduces no witnesses, and often no evidence at all, restricting its role instead to challenging the prosecution's evidence by cross-examination.

Significantly, preliminary hearings do not follow the rigid rules of evidence adhered to at trial. Once again, the idea of deprivations and intrusions explains this, as the *Schramm* case clearly demonstrates. Defendants suffer less serious consequences from binding over, than they do upon conviction. Courts vary greatly in the degree to which they relax the rules of evidence in preliminary hearings. Some jurisdictions require that only evidence admissible at trial can be presented at preliminary hearings. Others apply the rules of evidence "generally" to preliminary hearings, permitting magistrates to consider some evidence that would be inadmissible at trial. Sometimes, court rules or statutes make explicit what types of evidence magistrates can accept in preliminary hearings. In other jurisdictions, appellate courts adopt general guidelines, such as that the rules at preliminary hearings need not be applied "as rigidly as in trials." In a few jurisdictions, magistrates have complete discretion to disregard the rules of evidence.[12]

THE QUANTUM OF PROOF FOR BINDING OVER. The quantum of proof adopted by most courts for binding over is probable cause that a crime has been committed and that the defendant committed it. However, courts vary in interpreting probable cause in the context of the preliminary hearing. Some hold that probable cause to bind over constitutes the same quantum of proof as probable cause to arrest. Other courts hold that probable cause to bind over requires a higher evidentiary standard than arrest because graver consequences follow binding over. Binding over leads to longer detention, and to the ordeals of criminal prosecution, conviction, and punishment. Furthermore, even if they are not convicted, defendants must pay attorney's fees, suffer stigma from the prosecution, and subject their families to hardships as well. The state must expend scarce resources to prove guilt, thereby draining such resources from other services. The bind-over standard reflects the idea that the greater the intrusion and deprivation, the higher the factual foundation required to authorize them.

Just how many facts satisfy the bind-over standard cannot be stated precisely. Some courts have adopted a *prima facie* **case** requirement. According to this standard, the judge can bind the defendant over if the prosecution presents evidence that could convict if the defense did not rebut it at trial. Others have adopted a directed verdict standard:

> Since the examining magistrate's determination of the minimum quantum of evidence required to find probable cause to bind over is somewhat analogous in function to the court's ruling on a motion for a directed verdict at trial as to whether there is sufficient evidence to warrant submission of the case to the jury, we have decided to adopt a "directed verdict" rule in defining the minimum quantum of credible evidence necessary to support a bind-over determination. The examining magistrate should view the case as if it were a trial and he were required to rule on whether there is enough credible evidence to send the case to the jury. Thus, the magistrate should dismiss the complaint when, on the evidence produced, a trial court would be bound to acquit as a matter of law. The minimum quantum of evidence required by this bind-over standard is more than that for probable cause for arrest but less than would "prove the defendant's guilt beyond a reasonable doubt."[13]

Determining whether prosecutors have established the quantum of evidence required to bind over falls mainly to trial courts. A challenge to the trial court's decision to bind over, when it occurs, ordinarily gets resolved in the state intermediate appellate courts, whose principal business is reviewing the sufficiency of evidence to support the findings of trial courts. The Delaware intermediate appellate court performed that function in reviewing the bind-over decision in *Schramm v. State*. Although intermediate appeals courts around the country, or even in Delaware, may have resolved the case differently, most courts would have followed the Delaware court's procedure and would perform the same function.[14]

CASE

Was there a factual foundation to bind over?

Schramm v. State

366 A.2d 1185 (Del. 1976)

FACTS

At approximately 2:00 p.m., a state police officer attached to a special investigative drug unit, received a telephone call from an unnamed individual whom the officer had known personally for several years. The officer also knew that the caller was a drug-trafficker presently awaiting trial on drug charges. The caller informed the officer that Barton Schramm, the defendant, had told him earlier in the day that he was going to Philadelphia to buy a large quantity of drugs, and would be transporting them back to Delaware. The informant stated he believed that Schramm would be returning "anytime soon" via I-95 because he had been with him previously on a similar mission when they had taken that route. He further informed the officer that defendant, a thin, white male with a mustache, would be riding in a dark brown 1974 Mustang II with a light tan top and Pennsylvania license; that the destination would either be defendant's home in Woodside Apartments, Newark, or the Presidential Towers (apartments) near the Naamans Road exit off of I-95.

The officer, who had heard from other informants that Schramm was involved in drug trafficking, picked up the informant in the area of I-95, and at approximately 2:45 p.m. the Mustang II was sighted. The informant pointed out Schramm riding in the passenger seat.

Pursuit was undertaken via I-95 to the Naamans Road exit, and Presidential Towers, which the officer knew to be the residence of Wallace, another drug dealer, whom he had previously arrested and who the informant stated was involved in the traffic with Schramm. The car was stopped, defendant was arrested, and a search was conducted revealing a large quantity of drugs which were seized and admitted as evidence at trial.

At the preliminary hearing the arresting officer described the events, including the informant's statements, and defendant was held for trial in Superior Court. He was subsequently indicted, and following a suppression hearing, was tried and convicted. . . .

OPINION

Defendant contends that it was error for the Justice of the Peace at the preliminary hearing to admit the hearsay statements of an informant, probative of the question of intent to deliver drugs, absent a preliminary showing of the informant's credibility. A preliminary hearing is not a trial where strict rules of evidence must apply and where the concern is guilt beyond a reasonable doubt. The purpose of the hearing is simply to have a neutral and detached person hear the evidence, to determine therefrom if "there is probable cause to believe that an offense has been committed and that the defendant committed it," and if so, to bind defendant over for trial in the appropriate court. The difference between the two proceedings is clear:

> "Trials are necessarily surrounded with evidentiary rules 'developed to safeguard men from dubious and unjust convictions.' [citation omitted] But before the trial we deal only with probabilities that 'are not technical; they are the factual and practical considerations of everyday life on which reasonable and prudent men, not legal technicians, act.' "

For this reason, probable cause does not demand the quantity and quality of evidence of each element of the offense charged as would be needed to support a conviction. Nowhere is this more evident than in the present case. Defendant was arrested for possession of a substantial quantity of drugs, and charged with intent to deliver. At trial, mere possession and quantity is insufficient to prove beyond a reasonable doubt defendant intended to deliver the drugs; on the other hand, "factual and practical considerations of everyday life" as well as his own common sense, could lead a reasonable man to believe the defendant probably intended to deliver drugs when he is found in possession of a large quantity. In sum, probable cause is a common sense determination.

To this end, while the hearing magistrate must remain neutral and detached, he only need hear enough evidence to satisfy himself that probable cause exists, subject to defendant's right to cross-examine and produce evidence in his own behalf. He should consider the evidence presented without regard to whether that evidence may or may not be admissible if and when the case reaches the trial stage. For this reason, hearsay is admissible in a preliminary hearing with no requirement that the Justice of the Peace first determine if that hearsay is reliable, unless, of course, the Justice of the Peace in his discretion believes an inquiry into credibility of witnesses or reliability of the information is necessary to satisfy himself that probable cause exists. . . .
Affirmed.

CASE DISCUSSION

Schramm was convicted of a drug offense. Schramm objects that the judicial officer who presided at the preliminary hearing had insufficient evidence to bind him over, that is, to require him to answer the charges against him. The intermediate appeals court held that it was within the discretion of the judicial officer who conducted the preliminary hearing to decide whether or not to admit the hearsay.

What facts did the judge have in making the bind-over decision? Do you agree that judicial officers have the discretion to admit or exclude hearsay evidence at preliminary hearings? What guidelines would you prescribe for the introduction of evidence at preliminary hearings? If you were deciding this case, would you think there were sufficient facts to bind Schramm over to answer the charges? Which facts convince you? Would you permit this evidence at the preliminary hearing? Why? Why not? To what extent does the court's ruling on admitting evidence promote the interest in efficiency and economy? fact-finding? process values? Does it promote—or sacrifice—or have no effect on societal interests in criminal procedure?

HEARSAY TESTIMONY. The government can introduce neither hearsay nor illegally seized evidence at trial. Judges largely disregard these prohibitions in preliminary hearings. In federal courts, bind-over decisions may be based on hearsay in whole or in part. Many states follow the federal rule, but frequently with limitations. Colorado, for example, prohibits hearsay evidence at preliminary hearings if better evidence is available, such as when the victim is in court and can testify.[15]

There are arguments both for and against admitting hearsay evidence at preliminary hearings. Supporters of its admission argue that (1) hearsay can often be reliable; (2) magistrates who are often not lawyers cannot apply the hearsay rule competently; (3) it places too heavy a burden on witnesses to require them to appear both at preliminary hearing and trials; (4) testimony is not in dispute and need not be given directly; (5) grand juries can indict on hearsay; and (6) magistrates can issue warrants on hearsay and the standard for preliminary hearing should be the same.[16]

The arguments against admitting hearsay include (1) it protects defendants from the ordeal of going to trial on insufficient evidence to convict; (2) it conflicts with the right of defense to challenge the prosecution's case and cross-examine witnesses; (3) applying the hearsay rule should present no difficulties since lawyers are there to interpret them; (4) appearing at preliminary hearings does not excessively burden witnesses. The Supreme Court of Utah addressed the problem of admitting hearsay evidence at preliminary hearings in *State v. Anderson.*[17]

CASE

Should the hearsay be admitted?

State v. Anderson

612 P.2d 778 (Utah 1980)

FACTS

The defendants,· Anderson and Brackenbury, entered the J & M Saloon, located in Soldier's Summit, Utah, to investigate suspected illegal sale of alcohol. At the time of the incident in question, Anderson was the Chief of Police of Soldier's Summit and Brackenbury was the Justice of the Peace. In the saloon a confrontation ensued between Anderson and the manager of the saloon, James Garner, hereinafter "Garner." During the confrontation a patron of the saloon, Ray Applegate, hereinafter "Applegate," came to the aid of Garner, who referred to him as his bouncer. However, Applegate testified at trial that upon being informed Anderson was the Chief of Police he returned to his original place at the other end of the bar.

The escalating confrontation ended when Garner struck Anderson in the face. Anderson announced that Garner was under arrest and, although emotionally distraught, left the saloon to enjoin the aid of the police officer then on duty before taking Garner into custody. Once out of the saloon Brackenbury left Anderson and returned to his trailer. Upon enlisting the aid of officer Butch Curtis, hereinafter "Curtis," Anderson, who was still quite excited from the earlier controversy, reentered the saloon and forcibly detained Garner. In the ensuing scuffle Garner was thrown to the floor, handcuffed and removed from the saloon.

Curtis assumed custody of Garner and proceeded to the Utah County Jail to incarcerate him, while Anderson returned to the saloon in search of the "bouncer" Applegate. After finding Applegate there, Anderson escorted him across the highway to Brackenbury's trailer, which was also used as the Justice Court of Soldier's Summit.

Once inside the trailer, Anderson declared Applegate was under arrest for interfering with an officer in the course of his duty, and Brackenbury proclaimed the Justice Court to be in session. According to the testimony of Applegate, Anderson then proceeded to physically intimidate him into signing false statements[a] concerning the prior activities in the bar. The first two statements concerned Garner striking Anderson and Applegate's purchase from Garner of liquor, "over the bar," in the J & M Saloon. The third statement recounted the details of the earlier incident in the bar and the arrest of Garner. Applegate testified he signed the false statements because he was scared of possible further violence.[b]

Applegate's account of the incident in the trailer was corroborated by the testimony of Curtis. Curtis testified that upon returning to Soldier's Summit, after delivering Garner, he initiated a conversation with Anderson in which the former explained how he had procured a sworn statement from Applegate concerning the sale of liquor "over the bar" by Garner. When Curtis asked Anderson if the statement was made voluntarily Anderson replied, "Well, I had to rough him (Applegate) up a little bit, but I got the statement."[c] Subsequently, the defendants were arrested for the crime of tampering with a witness. . . . The defendants appeared at their arraignment and requested a preliminary hearing. . . .

---

[a] Applegate explained:
"A. He (Anderson) grabbed me by my shirt and he said, 'Yes, you did it. You seen him strike me,' and picked me up and he tore my shirt across, like that. (Indicating)
Q. What do you mean he picked you up?
A. Picked me up by my shirt, raised me up out of the chair.
Q. All right, when he picked you up did he say anything to you?
A. He said, 'Let me show you some judo, or something or another; and he put his leg out and he pushed me over his leg backwards.'
Q. What happened to you?
A. I hit the floor on my back.
Q. And while you were lying on the floor what happened?
A. He picked me back up.
Q. How?
A. The same way, with my shirt.
Q. Did he say anything to you while he was doing that?
A. He called me a cotton picking dink.
Q. Did he call you anything else?
A. When he picked me up he called me a—he said that—he said, 'I could kill you with my bare hands, you fat—and—.' "
[b] When asked why he did not defend himself from Anderson's attack, Applegate explained:
"Because I was scared; He had identified himself in the bar as the Chief of Police, and it was in a court of law, and I couldn't see fighting back in a court of law. Didn't seem like the right thing to do."
[c] Curtis also testified that Brackenbury, who was present at the conversation between Anderson and Curtis, stated that Anderson had roughed Applegate up "pretty good."

At the preliminary hearing Garner and Curtis were presented as witnesses for the prosecution. However, instead of presenting Applegate at the preliminary examination, the prosecution moved to introduce Applegate's sworn affidavit relating the essence of his testimony. The prosecution explained Applegate would be present at the trial to testify, but they reasoned the inconvenience of bringing him from his home in Muskogee, Oklahoma, to Utah rendered his absence at the preliminary examination permissible and the admission of his sworn affidavit justified. . . . The judge agreed with the prosecution's contentions and allowed, over the objection of the defendant, the introduction of the affidavit into evidence. The judge found the evidence presented at the preliminary examination sufficient to bind the matter over to the District Court for trial. At the subsequent trial, the defendants were convicted by a jury of the crime as charged.

OPINION

. . . Preliminary examinations in Utah are adversarial proceedings in which the prosecution must present evidence sufficient to establish: (a) that a public offense has been committed, and (b) sufficient cause to believe the defendant guilty thereof.

The probable cause showing necessary in the preliminary examination differs from that required for an arrest warrant. In the latter, the facts presented must be sufficient to establish that an offense has been committed and a reasonable belief the defendant committed it. The facts presented, however, do not have to establish a prima facie case against the defendant.

Conversely the probable cause showing at the preliminary examination must establish a prima facie case against which the trier of fact could conclude the defendant was guilty of the offense as charged.

The prosecution is not required to introduce enough evidence to establish the defendant's guilt beyond a reasonable doubt, but must present a quantum of evidence sufficient to warrant submission of the case to the trier of fact.[a] Also, the determination of sufficient cause to bind the accused over for trial must be based on facts which are proved at the examination and may not depend on the information, complaint or depositions taken before the issuance of the arrest warrant.

While the burden falls upon the prosecution to establish sufficient cause to believe the accused guilty of the crime charged, the adversarial qualities of the examination allow the defendant an opportunity to attack the prosecution's evidence and to present any affirmative defenses. Although the hearing is not a trial per se, it is not an ex parte proceeding nor one-sided determination of probable cause, and the accused is granted a statutory right to cross-examine the witnesses against him, and the right to subpoena and present witnesses in his defense. Thus, the preliminary examination is an adversarial proceeding in which certain procedural safeguards are recognized as necessary to guarantee the accused's substantive right to a fair hearing. . . .

---

[a]Thus, the minimum quantum of evidence is more than required to establish probable cause for arrest but less than would prove the defendant guilty beyond a reasonable doubt.

The adversarial nature of the preliminary hearing is conducive to the imposition of these procedural safeguards. The application of the right of cross-examination, and the exclusion of certain out of court statements at this stage of the criminal prosecution insures essential protection of the defendant's substantive rights.

Specifically, the cross-examination of witnesses presenting testimony against the accused at the hearing provides a means of attacking their credibility and thus the substance of their testimony. In a proceeding such as the preliminary examination, where the credibility of the witnesses is an important element in the determination of probable cause, the recognition of a procedural right of cross-examination is essential to the preservation of a fair hearing. . . .

If the preliminary examination is to retain any meaningful significance in the criminal prosecution and provide an effective means of weeding out improvident prosecutions, the protections attendant the defendant's right to present an affirmative defense cannot be circumvented by allowing the prosecution to base its showing of probable cause on hearsay evidence. Therefore, the trial court's interpretation of 77–15–19, which allowed the prosecution to present the testimony of a material witness via an extra judicium affidavit, cannot be accepted. . . .

We must turn now to determine the effect of this holding in the present case. Although the judge's interpretation of the statute and his acceptance of the hearsay evidence constitute error, that error was not prejudicial to the defendants. Rather, in this case, the error was rendered harmless by the testimony of the other witnesses at the hearing. Their testimony, when in conjunction with the copies of the false statements signed by Applegate which were presented at the hearing, was sufficient to surmount the prosecution's burden and establish sufficient cause to bind the matter over to trial. The introduction of the sworn affidavit of Applegate was in actuality favorable to the defendants because it provided additional discovery and possible impeachment evidence. Thus, the character of the error and the defendants' failure to prove any significant prejudice denies a reversal of the present conviction based upon it. . . .

CASE DISCUSSION

Anderson was convicted of tampering with a witness. Anderson requested a preliminary hearing. Instead of direct testimony, the prosecution moved to introduce a sworn affidavit relating the essence of a material witness's testimony. Over the defendant's objections, the judge admitted the affidavit. The judge found the evidence presented at the preliminary hearing sufficient to bind the defendant over for trial. The defendant appealed that decision on the ground that the introduction of the affidavit violated his right to confrontation of his accusers guaranteed by the Sixth Amendment. The Supreme Court held that the defendant's right to confrontation was violated, but that it constituted harmless error because other witnesses corroborated the hearsay.

Do you agree with the court's ruling on hearsay at preliminary hearings? Is the court turning the hearing into a "mini-trial"? Does the decision impair the interest in timeliness and efficiency? Does it promote accuracy in result?

Should the court have reversed the conviction? to promote what interest(s)? Does the court's decision that the error was harmless make sense? Does it promote result over process? Should the conviction be overturned simply because the defendant's constitutional right was violated, or should the conviction stand as long as the result was correct? Explain.

ILLEGALLY OBTAINED EVIDENCE. The states are divided over admitting illegally seized evidence at preliminary hearings: most states admit it; several exclude it. Two arguments support admitting illegally obtained evidence at preliminary hearings. First, the function of the hearings is to determine probable cause; excluding relevant evidence hampers that determination. Second, to permit challenges to evidence at the preliminary hearing interferes with the efficient and economical administration of justice because the question whether the police obtained evidence illegally then has to be answered twice—first at preliminary hearing and then again later, either at a special suppression, or other pretrial, hearing or during the trial itself.[18]

THE RIGHT TO CROSS-EXAMINE. The Sixth Amendment confrontation clause does not guarantee the defense the right to cross-examine the prosecution's witnesses at the preliminary hearing. Nevertheless, all jurisdictions permit such cross-examination. But the right to cross-examine at the preliminary hearing is not so extensive as the right to cross-examine at trial. For example, most jurisdictions do not permit cross-examination for the sole purpose of discovering the prosecution's case.[19]

Courts are divided on whether to terminate cross-examination aimed at developing affirmative defenses—defenses such as self-defense and entrapment—that acknowledge that a crime was committed but rely on a justification that relieves the defendant of criminal responsibility for it. In *State v. Altman,* the Arizona Supreme Court upheld the magistrate's refusal to permit cross-examination on entrapment on the ground that

full and complete exploration of all facts of the case is reserved for trial and is not the function of a preliminary examination.[20]

In *Jennings v. Superior Court,* on the other hand, the California Supreme Court declared:

The purpose of the preliminary hearing is to weed out groundless or unsupported charges of grave offense, and to relieve the accused of the degradation and expense of a criminal trial. . . . To effectuate this constitutional and statutory purpose the defendant must be permitted, if he chooses, to elicit testimony or introduce evidence tending to overcome the prosecution's case or establish an affirmative defense.[21]

Ancillary Functions of the Preliminary Hearing

The preliminary hearing serves primarily to screen cases that the government has seriously committed itself to pursue. In addition to testing the government's case, the preliminary hearing performs several secondary but useful functions.

DISCOVERY. Preliminary hearings provide an opportunity for defense attorneys to learn more about the prosecution's case. Despite the prevailing view that the preliminary hearing is not a vehicle for discovery, ''in practice this hearing may provide the defense with the most valuable technique available.'' **Discovery** means providing notice of specific evidence that the other side in a lawsuit will introduce at trial. It modifies the pure adversary nature of proceedings in criminal cases by informing the accused in advance of the fact mustered against him or her; but it facilitates the adversary process by ensuring that the accused can prepare an adequate defense. It facilitates a fair and equal fight between a very powerful state and defendants with limited resources. In practice, discovery principally benefits defendants because at preliminary hearings prosecutors, not the defense, must present evidence to justify sending defendants to trial.[22]

In addition to hearing (and occasionally seeing) the prosecution's evidence, defense counsel can cross-examine prosecution witnesses and subpoena potential trial witnesses. The extent of discovery depends on several factors. If the prosecution relies on hearsay, then, of course, the defense cannot cross-examine the source of this evidence. Furthermore, some states restrict cross-examination to direct rebuttal, thereby preventing defense from broad inquiry into the prosecution's case. Moreover, prosecutors frequently call only the minimum number of witnesses, which also sharply limits discovery.[23]

Court-prescribed or statutory discovery rules provide opportunities for discovery outside the preliminary hearing. Such rules, for example, make arresting officers' reports available to defendants. If defendants can discover the prosecution's case in these other ways, they may choose not to utilize the preliminary hearing for that purpose because the tactical costs may be too high. The experienced defense lawyer Anthony Amsterdam writes about these tactical considerations:

> Frequently counsel may find that s/he is working at cross-purposes in seeking to discover and lay a foundation for impeachment simultaneously. S/he will obviously have to accommodate these objectives in particular situations with an eye to which objective is more important in dealing with an individual prosecution witness. If counsel vigorously cross-examines a witness, in an effort to get a contradiction or concession on record, the witness will normally dig in and give a minimum of information in an effort to save his or her testimonial position; and, more than likely, s/he will be uncooperative if counsel thereafter attempts to interview the witness prior to trial. On the other hand, if counsel engages the witness in routine examination, amiable and ranging, counsel may be able to pick up many clues for investigation and for planning of the defense. Of course, some witnesses resent any form of cross-examination. If counsel thinks that this type of witness is lying or confused, counsel may wish to pin the witness down. Under no circumstances, however, should counsel educate the witness about the weakness of his or her testimony.[24]

These tactical considerations curtail the use of the preliminary hearing for discovery purposes. Professor Samuel Dash refers to this shortcoming in federal court preliminary hearings. According to Professor Dash, discovery is

> not the discovery to prepare his defense for trial, but it is the kind of discovery in which he is confronted with his accuser and informed of what he is charged with, and given some indication as to the strength of the Government's case. This is the kind of discovery that allows him to make decisions as to his plea, not as to how he will present evidence, and how he will combat the Government's case.[25]

Arizona's practice regarding cross-examination in preliminary hearing proceedings reveals the variety of ways magistrates interpret the discovery function. Some argue that the state's liberal discovery rules reduce the need for extensive cross-examination.

Arizona cases support this view. In *State v. Canaday,* the court ruled that defense opportunity to cross-examine witnesses during preliminary hearings is "a limited one."

In *State v. Williams,* the Arizona Supreme Court held that due process does not require "limitless cross-examination" at the preliminary hearing for discovery purposes. Nevertheless, individual magistrates construe defense capacity to cross-examine broadly. One justice of the peace, for example, permits cross-examination if it (1) is relevant; (2) relates to an **affirmative defense,** a defense such as self-defense that requires the defense to do more than merely denying the facts in the complaint; or (3) tests the credibility of the witness. This particular justice of the peace grants defendants wide latitude in cross-examination, "believing that such latitude is in conformity with the generally broad discovery rules in Arizona." "Otherwise," he said, "cases might as well go to the grand jury."[26]

In states where law and practice provide for little alternative pretrial discovery, or where the discovery is not available until the critical time for plea bargaining passes, defense counsel may not have any choice but to rely on the preliminary hearing for discovery.[27]

FUTURE IMPEACHMENT. Cross-examining prosecution witnesses might aid the defense even if it produces little in the way of discovery. The Supreme Court recognized this advantage in *Coleman v. Alabama,* a leading case on the preliminary hearing. Justice Brennan, writing for the Court, noted that

> the skilled interrogation of witnesses by an experienced lawyer can fashion a vital impeachment tool for use in cross-examination of the State's witnesses at the trial. . . .[28]

The preliminary hearing provides several opportunities to **impeach** witnesses, that is, show witnesses are not credible. For example, witnesses frequently make damaging statements at preliminary hearings because prosecutors have not prepared them as well as they do for trial. Furthermore, the more witnesses say at the preliminary hearing, the greater the chances they will contradict themselves at the trial. These contradictions are more damaging than those made to police because at preliminary hearings witnesses make them under oath.

Too much cross-examination, however, has pitfalls for the defense. Professor Amsterdam's quote on tactical considerations indicates some of these. Too much focus on witnesses' weaknesses educates them about those weaknesses and provides them with the opportunity to correct them. Witnesses may "rehabilitate" themselves "for the trial and state at the hearing" that they were "confused, but that everything is now clear in" their "mind." If witnesses might otherwise "soften" their view of the facts with passing time, lessening their "emotional involvement," extensive cross-examination might "harden" their position and make them less likely to "retreat to a more friendly position." Witnesses may also recant, or change their mind about, their testimony. Finally, if witnesses are not available later at the trial, defense counsel may discover that they have presented damaging testimony that they prefer not to appear at trial.[29]

PERPETUATING TESTIMONY. A frequent problem in criminal trials is that witnesses cannot testify—they die, fall ill, disappear, or are otherwise not available. If they have testified at the preliminary hearing their testimony may be used at trial under certain conditions. Although an advantage technically accessible to both prosecution and defense, in practice perpetuating testimony helps the prosecution most because the defense calls witnesses at preliminary hearings only infrequently. Despite the Supreme Court's statement that preliminary hearings provide the opportunity to "preserve testimony favorable to the accused of a witness who does not appear at the trial," defense attorneys generally consider perpetuation a *dis*advantage of preliminary hearings.[30]

The **hearsay rule** prohibits the introducing of a statement from someone not in court as evidence to prove the truth of the matter stated. For example, I cannot as a witness testify that Jeff murdered Colleen because Sharon told me he did. I cannot give testimony to prove the truth of Sharon's out-of-court statement. However, if Sharon's statement had been tested for its credibility prior to trial, then it falls under the **prior testimony exception.** The prior testimony exception admits testimony taken under oath prior to trial, if witnesses are not available to testify at the trial. Testimony at preliminary hearings, if competently tested, falls within the exception.

Despite the exception, prosecutors cannot introduce prior testimony unless they comply with the Sixth Amendment's **confrontation requirement,** which provides:

> In all criminal prosecutions, the accused shall enjoy the right . . . to be confronted with the witnesses against him. . . .

The Supreme Court addressed the confrontation question in relation to testimony from preliminary hearings introduced at trial in *California v. Green.* Green was charged with furnishing marijuana to Porter, a minor. Porter testified at the preliminary hearing but when the prosecution called him to testify at Green's trial, he was evasive and uncooperative, claiming that he could not remember matters about which the prosecution examined him.

The prosecution introduced Porter's testimony from the preliminary hearing "to prove the truth of the matter asserted in his statements." The defense objected, claiming that mere lapse of memory did not render Porter "unavailable." The state court held the preliminary testimony inadmissible because it violated Green's Sixth Amendment right to confrontation; the Supreme Court reversed. The Court held that if the defense had the opportunity to fully cross-examine Porter at the preliminary hearing, then Green had "confronted" Porter, and the Sixth Amendment requirement was satisfied.[31]

Decision Point

The defense cross-examined only one eyewitness to a murder at the preliminary hearing. The preliminary hearing was held on short notice, but the defense brought out numerous facts relating to the witness's morals and capacity for observation. The defense did not have access to the ballistic reports and autopsy reports because they were not available at the time of the preliminary hearing. The witness was not available at the trial. Should the witness's testimony be admitted at the trial?

The Fifth Circuit Court of Appeals held that the testimony was admissible because the cross-examination was extensive enough to bring out all the information the witness could supply. Furthermore, there was no suggestion that the ballistics and autopsy reports would have led to any pertinent facts not covered at the preliminary hearing.[32]

The functions of the preliminary hearing vary from jurisdiction to jurisdiction. Some jurisdictions utilize the preliminary hearing in conjunction with grand jury review. Others depend solely upon the preliminary hearing. Jurisdictions also differ in how they conduct preliminary hearings, how extensively they review the evidence, and what functions they serve other than screening. Whatever the differences among the jurisdictions, however, preliminary hearings screen cases by requiring defendants to answer criminal charges made against them to determine if sufficient facts exist to continue the criminal process.

═══ GRAND JURY REVIEW

The grand jury has an ancient heritage. Originating in medieval England as a council of local residents that aided the king in looking into matters of royal concern—crime, revenues, and official misconduct—the grand jury was an investigating body. By the time of the American Revolution, the grand jury assumed another fundamental function: it screened criminal cases to protect citizens from malicious and unfounded prosecution. Hence, the grand jury acquired dual functions—to act as a sword to root out crime and corruption and as a shield to protect innocent citizens from unwarranted state intrusion.

The shield function particularly attracted the colonists because it protected them from prosecution for antiroyalist sentiments. For that reason, the Fifth Amendment to the United States Constitution provides that

> No person shall be held to answer for a capital, or otherwise infamous crime, unless on a presentment or indictment by a Grand Jury. . . .

Most state constitutions have similar provisions.

In 1859, Michigan became the first state to provide for an alternative to grand jury screening by adopting the **information,** a formal charging instrument drawn by the prosecutor without the grand jury. Several states followed suit. In 1884, the United States Supreme Court ruled that grand jury screening is not essential to preserving "fundamental principles of liberty and justice" under the Fourteenth Amendment due process clause. Hence, the Fifth Amendment grand jury clause does not apply to the states.[33]

Today, twenty-six states permit prosecutors to choose between information (usually with a requirement that preliminary hearing bind over support it) or indictment. Since prosecutors nearly always select information and preliminary hearing, these states are called information states. Five states require indictments only in capital cases (including life imprisonment). The remaining nineteen states—called indictment states—require grand jury screening. The official charging instrument in these states must be an indictment. Prosecutors have absolute discretion to choose between information and indictment in information states. Reasons for choosing the grand jury include prosecutors' (1) wish to avoid a preliminary hearing; (2) effort to erect a buffer against negative public opinion in politically sensitive cases; and (3) desire to share responsibility in difficult cases. In most indictment jurisdictions, defendants can waive their right to such screening, although some prohibit waiver in capital cases. Most waivers occur as part of a plea bargaining arrangement in which defendants plead guilty.[34]

COMPOSITION AND SELECTION. Grand juries in individual jurisdictions differ greatly both in composition and screening procedures. Hence, generalizations about grand jury operation do not describe any particular jurisdiction's grand jury operation. This section outlines the operation of the federal grand jury in the Southern District of New York, a jurisdiction that includes Manhattan, the Bronx, and several New York counties as far north as Albany.[35]

Federal grand juries consist of not less than sixteen or more than twenty-three jurors. To qualify, prospective grand jurors must (1) be United States citizens; (2) be over eighteen; (3) reside in the jurisdiction; (4) have no felony convictions; (5) speak, write, and read English; (6) suffer no physical impairments that might hamper their participation, such as insufficient hearing or vision.

The jurisdiction sometimes summons nearly two hundred citizens for jury service—many more than the sixteen to twenty-three citizens needed to meet these requirements. The process of narrowing down the number of potential jurors and selecting the final sixteen to twenty-three is called **purging the grand jury.** The process eliminates prospective grand jurors with compelling reasons not to serve—business, family, and health obligations—but it often impairs the grand jury's representative nature. Federal grand juries overrepresent retired persons or those not burdened with other obligations.

Every grand jury has a foreperson who acts as an administrator for the grand jury. The principal duties of foreperson include (1) signing indictments; (2) swearing in witnesses who appear before the grand jury; (3) arranging grand juror absences; (4) giving directions to witnesses; (5) maintaining order and decorum in the grand jury room. Judges appoint forepersons to the duty not often sought by grand jurors. Some judges ask for volunteers; if no one offers to serve, judges turn to other selection methods. Other judges simply pick the first juror they see. Some choose members who admit to previous jury experience.

In some jurisdictions, grand jury forepersons do not represent a fair cross-section of the community. For example, in the Eastern District of North Carolina between 1974 to 1981 not a single black or female was selected to serve as foreperson. This selection pattern led to claims that it violated the Constitution. The United States Supreme Court rejected these claims. The Court concluded that grand jury forepersons were just there to "mind the store." Chief Justice Burger wrote:

> Unlike the grand jury itself, the office of grand jury foreman was originally instituted by statute for the convenience of the court. . . . The responsibilities of the grand jury foreman are essentially clerical in nature. . . . [T]he ministerial trappings of the post carry with them no special powers or duties that meaningfully affect the rights of persons that the grand jury charges with a crime. . . . Even the foreman's duty to sign the indictment is a formality, for the absence of the foreman's signature is a mere technical irregularity that is not necessarily fatal to the indictment. . . . Simply stated, the role of the foreman of a federal grand jury is not so significant to the administration of justice that discrimination in the appointment of that office impugns the fundamental fairness of the process itself so as to undermine the integrity of the indictment.[36]

Proceedings

After swearing in the grand jurors, judges **charge the grand jury,** a speech that varies somewhat according to individual judges' preference. Sometimes, the charges constitute calls to action against specific dangers. Others resemble stump speeches for law and order or constitutional rights. Almost all include a history and outline of grand jury duties and responsibilities, warnings about the secrecy of grand jury proceedings, and admonitions to protect the innocent and condemn the guilty. Following the charge, judges turn grand jurors over to prosecutors to conduct grand jury proceedings. Unlike preliminary hearings, grand jury proceedings do not require a judge's participation.

Grand jury secrecy severely restricts those who may legally attend proceedings. In addition to the grand jurors themselves, only the prosecutor, witnesses called to testify, and stenographers appear in the grand jury room. Defendants do not appear; nor do witnesses' attorneys, even though these witnesses are often themselves **grand jury targets,** that is, people who are under suspicion and investigation. However, witnesses may, and frequently do, bring their lawyers to the courthouse for consultation outside the grand jury room.

Jurors may question witnesses. In some jurisdictions they do so only through the prosecutor; in others they do so directly. In some jurisdictions, prosecutors inform the grand jurors that if witnesses exercise their Fifth Amendment right to remain silent, jurors should not infer guilt from such silence. Prosecutors may also inform grand jurors that they can order witnesses to appear to support hearsay evidence. After some questioning, prosecutors may temporarily excuse witnesses so that grand jurors may question prosecutors. If jurors want to question witnesses or have prosecutors do so, recesses provide them with the opportunity to discuss questions with prosecutors. If prosecutors think it unwise to ask the questions, jurors rarely oppose them. Either stenographers or electronic devices record all testimony given before grand juries.

After all witnesses have testified and prosecutors have introduced any other evidence, prosecutors draw up an indictment and present it to the grand jury for consideration. Prosecutors then sum up the reasons why the evidence constitutes a crime and leave during grand jury deliberations, ordinarily only a few minutes. Grand juries rarely disagree with prosecutors' recommendations. Forepersons sign both the indictment and another document called a **true bill,** recording the number of jurors who voted to indict. Federal grand jury proceedings require twelve jurors' concurrence to indict.

The entire grand jury, accompanied by the prosecutor, then proceeds to a designated courtroom to **hand up the indictment,** an action that constitutes the formal filing of charges, requiring defendants to answer in court. After judges check to make sure all documents are in order, they accept the indictment, which becomes a matter of public record. They also accept the true bill, but it does not become a public record. The judges' acceptance initiates the criminal prosecution by indictment.

The Debate over the Grand Jury

Since the sixteenth century, observers have found much to criticize about the grand jury. The Elizabethan Justice of the Peace William Lambarde's charges to the Kent grand juries have preserved these early criticisms. Justice Lambarde lauded the grand juries *capacity* to aid in law enforcement but scorned their *conduct* in carrying out their responsibilities. Mainly, Lambarde attacked their sword function, maintaining that they were too timid in rooting out wrongdoing, but he also found them wanting in screening cases.[37]

In modern times, the debate has shifted to the grand jury's screening function. From the early twentieth century, the confidence that many reformers had in science and experts led them to call for eliminating lay participation in criminal justice. Nowhere was their condemnation more forceful than when they considered the jury. They wanted both grand and petty juries abolished. In their place, trained experts would more effectively weigh the evidence. Two prestigious presidential commissions, the Wickersham Commission appointed by President Hoover, and the National Advisory Commission appointed by President Nixon, urged the abolition of mandatory grand jury review. In the last decade, most legal commentary has condemned the grand jury.[38]

ARGUMENTS FOR ABOLITION OF GRAND JURY REVIEW. Critics make several arguments against grand jury screening. They maintain that grand juries are prosecutors' rubber stamp. One former prosecutor said, a prosecutor "can indict anybody, at any time, for almost anything before a grand jury." Statistics bear these critics out, at least on the surface. In only a small percentage of cases do grand juries issue **no-bills** (refusals to indict). Even the no-bills do not necessarily demonstrate grand jury independence. In sensitive or controversial cases, prosecutors choose grand jury review over preliminary hearing to put the burden for deciding whether or not to charge on the grand jury.[39]

Critics also condemn the nonadversary nature of grand jury review, which prevents it from either effectively screening cases or adequately protecting citizens against unwarranted prosecutions. Moreover, the secrecy of grand jury proceedings creates doubts and suspicion. That defendants and their lawyers cannot attend grand jury sessions provides further ammunition for critics. It is both unfair and results in inadequate screening by excluding defendants and their lawyers from the process. In addition, critics maintain that grand jury review is inefficient, expensive, and time-consuming.

> Empaneling and servicing grand jury is costly in terms of space, manpower, and money. The members must be selected, notified, sworn, housed, fed, and provided with a multitude of services.

Finally, grand juries screen cases more slowly than magistrates. The law surrounding grand jury proceedings is complex and technical, giving rise to delay in proceedings and in later successful challenges to grand jury proceedings.

> Use of a grand jury may result in prosecutions failing for reasons unrelated to innocence. In several jurisdictions, the intricacies and complexities of empaneling a grand jury guarantee attack by a skilled defense attorney and frequently result in dismissal of charges for minor discrepancies in the empaneling procedure.[40]

ARGUMENTS IN FAVOR OF GRAND JURY REVIEW. Supporters make several arguments to defend grand jury review. First, they maintain, grand jury costs no more than preliminary hearings. Preliminary hearings have become elaborate affairs to which lawyers, judges, other court personnel, and witnesses devote a great deal of court time. Furthermore, the number of requests defense attorneys make for continuances leads to greater delay in, and higher chances of successful challenges to, preliminary hearings than in grand jury proceedings.

Grand jury supporters also reject the contention that the grand jury does not effectively screen cases. They cite prosecutors who believe grand juries constitute valuable sounding boards, and that grand jurors definitely have minds of their own. The high percentage of indictments that grand juries return is not the important figure, according to supporters. Rather, the percentage of convictions—as high as 98 percent—based on indictments demonstrates that grand jury effectively screen out cases that should not go to trial.[41]

Finally, perhaps grand jury review represents democracy at work. Supporters maintain that what grand jury review loses in its secret and nonadversary proceedings, it more than recaptures in community participation in screening criminal cases. Citizen participation enhances public confidence in the criminal justice system. In a system where most cases do not go to trial, grand jury proceedings provide private citizens with their only opportunity to participate actively on the "front lines" of the criminal process. In fact, grand jurors are not nearly so representative of the community as trial jurors, who are not wholly representative either. Grand jury duty spans a long period of time, usually a year, and requires service at least two or three days a week. Only citizens with considerable free time can devote such extended—if valuable—service in the criminal process.[42]

Remedies for Irregular Grand Jury Proceedings

Irregularities in grand jury proceedings, and challenges to indictments, stem from several sources. Grand jury composition that either discriminates or does not reflect a representative community cross-section is one source. Also, grand jurors' personal and individual biases might taint indictments. The evidence submitted—or withheld—also affects the review. For example, some jurisdictions allow prosecutors to present to grand juries only evidence admissible at trial. Some require that prosecutors provide grand jurors with **exculpatory evidence,** that is, evidence that shows the defendant did not commit the crime. Finally, the defense might challenge indictments for prosecutorial misconduct.

The principal question that tainted indictments raise is what remedies should redress tainted grand jury proceedings.[43]

The remedy depends on the interests jurisdictions choose to promote. Jurisdictions committed to accurate fact-finding may conclude that despite irregular proceedings, if a proper trial produced a conviction, then the tainted indictment should not affect the conviction. According to one court:

> [E]rrors before the grand jury, such as perjured testimony, normally can be corrected at trial, where evidentiary and procedural rules safeguard the accused's constitutional rights.[44]

Jurisdictions committed to broad social goals such as community participation in law enforcement or ending racial and gender discrimination might dismiss the indictment and reverse a conviction based upon it. The rationale behind these decisions is

> that the court should strive to preserve societal values—deterrence of official misconduct and preservation of the appearance of fairness—regardless of whether the misconduct results in prejudice to the defendant.[45]

Before dismissing an indictment for prosecutors' misconduct, some courts require defendants to prove two things: (1) that "prosecutorial misconduct is a long-standing or common problem in grand jury proceedings. . . ."; and (2) that the grand jury was prejudiced by the prosecutor's actions. That is, defendants must prove that the misconduct affected the outcome of the case and was not simply **harmless error,** an error that did not affect the outcome of the case. The Supreme Court has largely left it to individual jurisdictions to fashion remedies for irregular grand jury proceedings. The federal District Court for the Eastern District of Louisiana addressed the remedy for prosecutorial misconduct in *United States v. McKenzie.*

CASE

Should McKenzie's conviction be reversed?

United States v. McKenzie

524 F. Supp. 186 (E.D. La. 1981)

FACTS

On November 9, 1980, while on duty, New Orleans Police Patrolman Gregory Neupert was shot to death. His body was found next to his police car parked near a public housing project in the Algiers area of New Orleans. There followed immediately an intensive investigation by the New Orleans Police Department to learn the identity of his murderers. On November 13, while police officers were engaged in an attempt to arrest three suspects, gun battles ensued, resulting in the death of the suspects. Three concurrent investigations into all of the circumstances were begun almost immediately, one by the New Orleans Police Department Internal Affairs Division, a second by the United States Department of Justice, Civil Rights Division and the New Orleans United States' Attorney's office, with a federal grand jury, and a third by the District Attorney for the Parish of Orleans, with a local grand jury. These investigations concerned not only the events surrounding Neupert's murder and the subsequent killing of the three suspects, but also public allegations of police brutality allegedly occurring in the course of their efforts to apprehend whoever was responsible for Neupert's murder. On July 9, 1981, the federal grand jury returned an indictment containing numerous counts, all relating to the alleged deprivation of the civil rights of various persons questioned by police following Neupert's murder. No indictment was returned related to the killing of the three suspects.

All seven defendants filed a motion to dismiss the indictment because of circumstances involved in the grand jury proceedings. . . .

OPINION

The court dismisses this indictment both on constitutional grounds and under its duty to exercise supervisory power over grand jury proceedings. We are convinced that the defendants have been denied their constitutional right not to be brought to trial except after a valid indictment. We are equally convinced that the integrity of the grand jury process must be protected from prosecutorial activity such as has occurred here. To refuse to dismiss this indictment would invite the repetition of such activity in future grand jury proceedings by signifying the court's approval thereof. . . .

At the outset of the penultimate day of the grand jury proceedings the prosecutor engaged in repeated references to press reports and to suspected leaks to the press reports and to suspected leaks to the press of confidential grand jury information. Moreover, the government attorneys made the grand jury a virtual battlefield in the war between themselves and the Orleans Parish District Attorney's office, a war in which the grand jurors were conscripted on the federal side, through repeated use by federal prosecutors of grand jury subpoenas and constant innuendo concerning the local district attorney. . . .

On numerous occasions during the grand jury's final two days, several government attorneys repeatedly expressed to the grand jury their personal opinions as to the credibility of various witnesses and as to the weight and effect of the evidence which the grand jury had heard. A trial tactic uniformly condemned by courts and warranting reversal of a guilty verdict occurs when a prosecutor expresses to a jury his personal opinion on the merits of the case or the credibility of a witness. . . .

Just before formal deliberation began, . . . the local Assistant United States Attorney, not only added his own personal appeal but also that of the U.S. Attorney himself, Mr. Volz.

> The indictment is signed John Volz, Stephen P. Clark, Michael D. Johnson and Morris W. Reed. And, . . . he would not have signed the indictment without a careful examination of all the evidence . . . and would not have signed the indictment had he not thought that the evidence . . . satisfied the elements of the statute. . . .
>
> That goes for me, also. . . .

At this point, the prosecutor permitted his zeal to overcome his obligation not to appeal to prejudice:

> I would like to briefly say that everyone would like to think that our police officers are performing their duties and performing their duties according to the law. We certainly hate to see any police officers outside of the law. However, a police officer, because he dons a police badge and gun and night stick and blackjack and mace and has the authority to make arrests and use that force to take custody and have that individual bound over by the Court for trial, he does not have the authority that places him above the law. . . .
>
> So, I just wanted to say that by Mr. Volz signing this indictment and also by my signing this indictment, this indicates that we think . . . that it has certainly satisfied the statutes and all the elements as dictated by the law. We are satisfied by the evidence that's been presented to the Jury, and it's up to you Ladies and Gentlemen to make your decision during your deliberations. . . .

Another serious instance of objectionable activity on the part of the prosecutors occurred after a period of grand jury deliberation outside the presence of government attorneys. . . . The grand jurors advised the prosecutors that they had "concluded [their] work." . . .

> A JUROR:
> We have a discussion going that—well, being in the final analysis of all the things that we had in the past, you know, that everyone had the chance to cast their ballot according to what they believed, and that it came out ten-ten. And, that's the way it stands. Do we go before the Federal Magistrate with this?

The juror's question is answered in the court's charge recommended by the Judicial Conference of the United States: "If less than 12 members of the Grand Jury vote in favor of an indictment which has been submitted to you for your consideration, the foreperson will endorse the indictment 'Not a True Bill' and return it to the court, and the court will impound it.'' The grand jury had been given similar advice by one of the prosecutors before its deliberation. The prosecutors' actions following the announcement of the 10–10 vote are astonishing. The government attorneys improperly participated in the grand jury deliberations and exerted undue pressure to secure an indictment.

At the outset the grand jury was misled as to the effect of fewer than 12 votes for an indictment after full deliberation. The government attorneys should have advised the jury that it was obliged to follow the court's charge set forth above. Considering his earlier correct advice to the jury as to the effect of fewer than 12 votes for an indictment, the response of the government attorney to the juror's question, ''Do we go before the Federal Magistrate with this?'' is incredible:

> We have just encountered a point of law that I have never encountered before which is less than twelve Grand Jury votes. . . .

[T]he prosecutors repeatedly and persistently probed into the jurors' thought process after the vote was announced, refusing to accept the repeated statements by the jurors, of which the following is an example:

> You asked for a decision. We have voted. We have voted on written ballots. There is no chance that the court was not correct. It's Over. That's it. Over. Finished.

Urged on by prosecutors, the jury again deliberated privately and voted to reconsider and indictment as to ''the beatings'' only. The prosecutors did not accept that decision by the jury. Instead, they engaged in lengthy deliberations concerning what they considered unlawful detention. . . .

Undue pressure was put upon the members of the grand jury to return some kind of indictment. In effect, the prosecutive team refused to accept any other result.

After the other prosecutor's misleading statement about the effect of the deadlock vote, the local Assistant United States Attorney . . . invoked the stature of the United States Attorney himself: ''Let me check with Mr. Volz *and see what he wants*. . . .'' (Underscoring added). Apparently he did just that, for the U.S. Attorney came in later with his chief assistant (there were then five prosecutors with the grand jury) and told the jury ''what he wants.'' ''I don't see why you don't do it tomorrow.''

. . . The court's decision [to dismiss the indictment] should not be construed as an open invitation to invade grand jury secrecy in every case, nor as a limitation upon the right of a prosecutor fairly to summarize evidence and law prior to submission to an indictment to the grand jury for deliberation and decision. Neither does this decision imply that every error by a prosecutor in his conduct before a grand jury will result in an invalid indictment. Rather it is a signal to prosecutors that there are limits beyond which they cannot go in their relationship with grand juries. Even though they act in good faith and out of commendable motives in seeking an indictment, prosecutors can no more violate constitutional rights of others. It is a mark of the majesty of the United States Constitution that it applies alike to the murderers of officer Gregory Neupert, to those who would seek to shield these murderers, and to the policemen who seek to apprehend them.

All who violate the law should be brought to justice, but only through lawful, constitutional efforts.

CASE DISCUSSION

The defendant filed a pretrial motion to dismiss an indictment because of prosecutorial misconduct during grand jury review. The district court granted the motion on the ground that the prosecutorial misconduct violated the defendant's constitutional right to grand jury review in federal courts under the Fifth Amendment. (The indictment requirement does not apply to the states under the Fourteenth Amendment incorporation doctrine discussed in chap. 2.) The court held that the proper remedy for the constitutional violation was to dismiss the indictment.

Of just exactly what did the prosecutorial misconduct consist in this case? How did the prosecutor's remarks interfere with the grand jury's determination? Should the district court automatically dismiss the indictment if there is prosecutorial misconduct? Why? to control the government and deter future prosecutorial wrongful action? to protect the defendant? What if the facts support the grand jury's conclusions? Should the court still dismiss the indictment? Is the cost too high in result? or in process? or efficiency? to dismiss the indictment? Did this prosecutor's behavior interfere with the democratic interest in community participation in criminal justice administration? If so, how?

SUMMARY

Following the decision to prosecute, and the initial appearance that prepares the defense for that prosecution, the government must test its decision to prosecute before disinterested parties. Preliminary hearings and grand jury review represent the two mechanisms to test the factual sufficiency of the government's case against defendants. In order to require defendants to answer criminal charges, the government must satisfy either a judge in a preliminary hearing, or a grand jury in a grand jury review, by presenting facts sufficient to demonstrate probable cause that a crime was committed and that the defendant committed it. Neither the Supreme Court nor any other body has ever prescribed the *number* of facts that satisfy this quantum of proof. However, probable cause to bring defendants to trial requires more facts than probable cause to arrest or to detain following arrest until preliminary hearing. In other words, it takes more facts to arraign defendants than to arrest them.

Important contrasts between preliminary hearing and grand jury review include: (1) Preliminary hearings are public hearings; grand jury review takes place in secret. (2) Judges preside over preliminary hearings; citizens predominate in grand jury deliberations. (3) Defendants are present and are represented in preliminary hearings; grand jury review is *ex parte*. (4) Preliminary hearings are adversary proceedings in which defense and prosecution argue; only the government presents its case to the grand jury.

The preliminary hearing and grand jury review proceedings vary among jurisdictions. However, both constitute a decision point that can result either in greater expenditures of public resources and greater deprivations to defendants and their families, or in terminating the criminal process. In arriving at these decisions, balancing the legal interests in result and process weighs heavily, but it does not solely determine the decision. Informally, the interests in efficiency, economy, human dignity, and community participation in criminal justice also play their part.

Specifically, the informal process of plea bargaining proceeds alongside and is intimately related to the formal decision making in preliminary hearings and grand jury review. The amount and quality of evidence against the defendant and the hardship of further criminal proceedings affect both formal testing of the government's case and informal plea negotiations. It is no coincidence that guilty pleas take place near in time to these formal proceedings. Frequently the arraignment reflects the influence of informal plea bargaining more than it does formal fact-finding in preliminary hearings and grand jury review. (See chap. 12).

═══ QUESTIONS FOR DISCUSSION AND REVIEW

1. What are the main differences between grand jury review and preliminary hearings?
2. Describe the principal functions of the preliminary hearing. Which one, or ones, is most important? Explain.
3. Distinguish between the quantum of proof required to arrest, and that required to bind over or indict.
4. Is there a *right* to a preliminary hearing? Explain.
5. What rules of evidence apply to preliminary hearings?
6. What is the root of the criticism that preliminary hearings are becoming "mini-trials"?
7. What interests do preliminary hearings further? Which do they minimize?
8. What interests do grand jury reviews emphasize? Which does it reduce?
9. Should grand jury review be abolished? Give reasons for and against.
10. What are the remedies for improper grand jury proceedings?

═══ NOTES

1. *United States v. Udziela,* 671 F.2d 995, 1001 (7th Cir. 1982).
2. Bureau of Justice Statistics, *Report to the Nation on Crime and Justice,* 2nd ed. (Washington, D.C.: Bureau of Justice Statistics, 1988).
3. *Federal Rules of Criminal Procedure,* 1987 edition (St. Paul: West, 1987), Rule 5(c).
4. *Lem Woon v. Oregon,* 229 U.S. 586, 33 S.Ct. 783, 57 L. Ed. 1340 (1913); *Gerstein v. Pugh,* 420 U.S. 103, 95 S.Ct. 854, 43 L. Ed. 2d 54 (1975).
5. *Coleman v. Alabama,* 399 U.S. 1, 90 S.Ct. 1999, 26 L. Ed. 2d 387 (1970).
6. Rule 5(c).
7. Wayne R. Lafave and Jerold H. Israel, *Criminal Procedure,* vol. 2 (St. Paul: West Publishing Company, 1984), 247–48.
8. *United States v. Quinn,* 357 F.Supp. 1348 (N.D.Ga. 1973).

9. Lafave and Israel, *Criminal Procedure,* 2: 249.

10. Ibid., 250–51.

11. *Hawkins v. Superior Court,* 22 Cal. 3d 584, 150 Cal. Rptr. 435, 586 P.2d 916 (1978).

12. Lafave and Israel, *Criminal Procedure,* 2: 263–64.

13. *Myers v. Commonwealth,* 363 Mass. 843, 298 N.E.2d 819 at 824 (Mass. 1973).

14. Thomas Y. Davies, ''Affirmed: A Study of Criminal Appeals and Decision-Making Norms in a California Court of Appeal,'' *American Bar Foundation Research Journal* 1982:548–52.

15. *McDonald v. District Court,* 195 Colo. 159, 576 P.2d 169 (1978).

16. Lafave and Israel, *Criminal Procedure,* 2: 265.

17. Ibid., 266.

18. *Federal Rules of Criminal Procedure* (St. Paul: West Publishing Company, 1987), 21.

19. *Goldsby v. United States,* 160 U.S. 70, 16 S.Ct. 216, 40 L. Ed. 343 (1895).

20. 107 Ariz. 93, 482 P.2d 460 (1971).

21. 66 Col. 2d 867, 59 Cal. Rptr. 440, 428 P.2d 304 (1967).

22. Lafave and Israel, *Criminal Procedure,* 2:434, 239–40.

23. Ibid., 240–41.

24. Anthony Amsterdam, *Trial Manual for the Defense of Criminal Cases,* 4th ed. (Philadelphia: American Law Institute, 1984), 1:152–53.

25. *Hearings on Federal Magistrates Act Before Subcommittee on Improvements in Judicial Machinery of Senate Committee on Judiciary,* 89th Congress, 2d Sess., 90th Congress, 1st Sess. (1966–1967), 133.

26. 574 P.2d 60 (App. 1977); 554 P.2d 646 (Ariz. 1976); and see generally, Nancy L. Ames, *The Role of the Grand Jury and the Preliminary Hearing in Pretrial Screening* (Washington, D.C.: National Institute of Justice, May 1984), 58–59.

27. Lafave and Israel, *Criminal Procedure,* 2:241.

28. *Coleman v. Alabama,* 399 U.S. 1 at 9, 90 S.Ct. 1999 at 2003, 26 L. Ed.2d 387 (1970).

29. Lafave and Israel, *Criminal Procedure,* 2:241–42.

30. *Coleman v. Alabama,* 399 U.S. 1, 90 S.Ct. 1999, 26 L.Ed.2d 387 (1970).

31. *California v. Green,* 399 U.S. 149, 90 S.Ct. 1930, 26 L.Ed.2d 489 (1970).

32. *Mechler v. Procunier,* 754 F.2d 1294 (5th Cir. 1985).

33. *Hurtado v. California,* 110 U.S. 516, 4 S.Ct. 111, 28 L. Ed. 232 (1884), excerpted in chap. 2 and discussed there.

34. Lafave and Israel, *Criminal Procedure,* 2:280–81.

35. This description is based on *Federal Rules of Criminal Procedure,* (St. Paul: West Publishing Company, 1987), Rule 6, and Marvin E. Frankel and Gary F. Naftalis, *The Grand Jury: An Institution on Trial* (New York: Hill and Wang, 1977), chap. 4.

36. *Hobby v. United States,* 468 U.S. 339 at 344–345, 104 S.Ct. 3093 at 3096–3097, 82 L. Ed. 2d 260 (1984).

37. Conyers Read, ed., *William Lambarde and Local Government* (Ithaca, N.Y.: Cornell University Press, 1962).

38. Conclusions about the early years of the twentieth century rest on the author's own research in early twentieth-century criminal justice, not yet published. There is abundant support for these conclusions. For a few references, see Maurice Parmelee, *Anthropology and Sociology in Relation to Criminal Procedure* (New York: Macmillan, 1911); National Commission on Law Observance and Law Enforcement (Wickersham Commission), *Report on Prosecution*

(Washington, D.C.: Government Printing Office, 1931); National Advisory Commission on Criminal Justice Standards and Goals, *Courts* (Washington, D.C.: Government Printing Office, 1973); Note, *Southern Illinois Law Review* (1981): 281, 284.

39. Lafave and Israel, *Criminal Procedure,* 2: 282–83.

40. National Advisory Commission on Criminal Justice Standards and Goals, *Courts* (Washington, D.C.: Law Enforcement Assistance Administration, 1973), 75.

41. New York Temporary Commission on the Constitutional Convention, *Individual Liberties* (1967), 117–42; R. Younger, *The People's Panel* (1967).

42. Kenneth Graham and Leon Letwin, ''The Preliminary Hearing in Los Angeles: Some Field Findings and Legal-Policy Questions,'' 18 *U.C.L.A. Law Review* 636 (1971), 681.

43. *United States v. Vetere,* 663 F.Supp. 381, 386 (S.D.N.Y. 1987).

44. *United States v. Udziela,* 671 F.2d 995, 1001 (7th Cir. 1982).

45. *United States v. Griffith,* 756 F.2d 1244, 1249 (6th Cir. 1985).

Chapter Eleven

Pretrial Motions

CHAPTER OUTLINE

CHAPTER MAIN POINTS

1. Result, due process, and organizational interests predominate in pretrial motions and hearings.

2. Double jeopardy gives the state "one fair shot" at conviction, preventing a powerful state from taking undue advantage of citizens charged with crimes.

3. Speedy trial promotes the interest in timeliness, the organizational interest in economy, and the social interest in equality.

4. Change of venue balances the defendant's right to a fair trial, the community's interest in criminal justice administration, and the organizational interest in economy and efficiency.

5. Judicial bias does not deny defendants a fair trial; personal bias does.

6. The suppression hearing primarily aims at controlling government.

CHAPTER KEY TERMS

actual prejudice proof that defendant cannot get a fair trial

autrefois convict a plea in bar that the defendant has already been indicted, tried, and convicted of the crime charged

bench trial trial before a judge without a jury

change of venue moving the location of the trial to a place more likely to insure a fair trial

demand-waiver rule delay in trial measured from point defendant demands speedy trial

dismissal without prejudice case terminated but can be reprosecuted

hung jury jury unable to reach a verdict

interlocutory appeal provisional appeals taken before judgment

judicial bias favoring a particular legal principle

lesser included offense crime composed of some, but not all, of the elements of a more serious crime

manifest necessity doctrine circumstances that require terminating proceedings

nolo contendere plea not to contest the indictment

orthodox rule courts, not juries, decide whether evidence is admissible

prior restraint restraint on statements before publication

reasonable likelihood of prejudice test circumstances may prevent fair trial

statute of limitations time permitted to lapse between commission of a crime and initiating prosecution

venue place where a trial is held

voir dire examining prospective jurors

writ of mandamus an order from a superior court to a municipality, any of its officers, or to a trial court ordering that the object of the writ take some action

BALANCING INTERESTS IN PRETRIAL MOTIONS

Following the grand jury or preliminary hearing, the criminal process enters a period when the interests of finality, timeliness, and other due process interests increasingly affect formal court decisions. The filing, hearing, and determination of pretrial motions focus on these interests. Organizational interests in negotiating the charges, settling disputes, and avoiding the conflict and uncertainty of adversary proceedings also become prominent. Most plea negotiations take place, and plea bargains are struck, sometime during the period between grand jury screening, preliminary hearings, hearings on pretrial motions, and trial. The time, energy, and resources devoted to filing, arguing, and resolving the issues raised by pretrial motions create anxiety and impose costs. If decisions go against defendants, pretrial motions lead to costly, time-consuming trials and, ultimately, to the great deprivation—criminal punishment.

THE ORIGINS OF PRETRIAL MOTIONS

Pretrial motions grew out of the ancient common-law pleadings, a highly stylized method of deciding cases in English law. The pleader for the Crown entered the first pleading—the indictment that initiated the criminal process. The indictment formed the legal basis for the arraignment that required defendants to appear in court to hear the charges and to answer—"plead"—to them. Defendants could answer the indictment—or plead—only according to rigidly prescribed rules. The most common pleas were either not guilty or guilty, but there were others. The plea to jurisdiction challenged the court's authority to hear the case; the plea in abatement challenged the technical sufficiency of the indictment due to defects in the grand jury process. The motion to quash challenged the form and substance of the indictment: the demurrer claimed that the indictment failed to state an offense. The plea in bar raised claims prohibiting action, such as double jeopardy and statute of limitations.

The indictment, along with the information, remains the only pleading that initiates criminal proceedings. Except for the guilty, not guilty, *nolo contendere,* and insanity pleas, the pretrial motions have replaced the other common-law pleadings available to the defense to answer the state's charges. The Federal Rules of Criminal Procedure, for example, provide:

> Rule 12(a) **Pleadings and Motions.** Pleadings in criminal proceedings shall be the indictment and the information, and the pleas of not guilty, guilty, and nolo contendere. All other pleas, and demurrers and motions to quash are abolished, and defenses and objections raised before trial which heretofore could have been raised by one or more of them shall be raised only by motion to dismiss or grant appropriate relief, as provided in these rules.

> Rule 12(b) **Pretrial Motions.** Any defense, objection, or request which is capable of determination without the trial of the general issue may be raised before trial by motion. Motions may be written or oral at the discretion of the judge. The following must be raised prior to trial:
> (1) Defenses and objections based on defects in the institution of prosecution; or
> (2) Defenses and objections based on defects in the indictment or information (other than that it fails to show jurisdiction in the court or to charge an offense which objections shall be noticed by the court at any time during the pendency of the proceedings); or
> (3) Motion to suppress evidence; . . .

This chapter analyzes and discusses issues surrounding the following pretrial motions: (1) double jeopardy; (2) dismissal for lack of speedy trial; (3) request for change of venue; (4) request for change of judge; (4) request to suppress evidence.

DOUBLE JEOPARDY MOTIONS

Double Jeopardy and the Constitution

The Fifth Amendment to the United States Constitution provides in part: "No person . . . shall . . . be subject for the same offence to be twice put in jeopardy of life or limb. . . ." Although the words "life or limb" strictly defined apply only to crimes punishable by death or corporal punishment, the courts interpret double jeopardy to include all crimes, including decisions in juvenile proceedings. In 1937, in *Palko v. Connecticut,* the Supreme Court held that the double jeopardy clause did not apply to the states through the due process clause of the Fourteenth Amendment. (See chap. 2.) Connecticut tried Palko for first-degree murder; the jury convicted him of a **lesser included offense,** the offense of second-degree murder that is part of the more serious crime of first-degree murder. The state retried Palko for first-degree murder over his objection that the second trial violated the double jeopardy clause. Justice Cardozo, writing for a divided court, asked:

> Is that kind of double jeopardy to which the statute has subjected him a hardship so acute and shocking that our polity will not endure it? Does it violate those "fundamental principles of liberty and justice" which lie at the base of all our civil and political institutions? The answer surely must be "no."[1]

During the "due process revolution" of the 1960s the Supreme Court reconsidered the double jeopardy clause and held that it applied to the states through the Fourteenth Amendment.

The Interests Double Jeopardy Protects

The prohibition against double jeopardy protects several interests both of the state and of the individual defendants. It allows the government "one fair shot" to serve the public interest in convicting criminals. At the same time, it limits the government from utilizing its disproportionate share of power and resources to subject citizens accused of crime to repeated attempts to convict them. Furthermore, it protects individuals from the embarrassment, expense, and ordeal—and the anxiety and insecurity—that repeated prosecutions generate. Defendants also have an interest in completing their trials under one tribunal and jury. In addition, both the state and defendants have an interest in the finality and integrity of judgments, that is, judgments not susceptible to repeated reconsideration. Finally, the prohibition against double jeopardy reduces costs both to defendants and to the state. Retrials consume time that impedes the efficient and economical disposition of other cases on crowded criminal court calendars.

Attachment of Jeopardy

The Fifth Amendment prohibition against double jeopardy attaches as soon as the state "put[s defendants] to trial." In jury trials, this occurs upon the empaneling and swearing in of the jury. In bench trials, that is, trials without juries where judges find the facts, jeopardy attaches when the court begins to hear evidence. Jeopardy attaches at this point in the proceedings because until the state begins to hear evidence, the trial has not started. In trials without juries, defendants have a "valued right to have . . . [their] trial[s] completed by a particular tribunal." The Supreme Court referred to the history of this definition of jury trials when it struck down Montana's rule that despite swearing in the jury, jeopardy did not attach until the first witness commenced to testify.

> The reason for holding that jeopardy attaches when the jury is empaneled and sworn lies in the need to protect the interest of an accused in retaining a chosen jury. . . . It is an interest with roots deep in the historic development of trial by jury in the

Anglo-American system of criminal justice. Throughout that history there ran a strong tradition that once banded together a jury should not be discharged until it had completed its solemn tasks of announcing a verdict.[2]

Reprosecution Barred by Double Jeopardy

The attachment of jeopardy has been called the linchpin of the double jeopardy inquiry; however, the Fifth Amendment prohibits *double* jeopardy. Hence, the attachment of jeopardy is the first, but not the only, inquiry. The double jeopardy clause bars only some reprosecutions. Reprosecution might occur (1) prior to conviction or acquittal, as in mistrials and dismissals; (2) after acquittal; and (3) following conviction.

Where jeopardy has attached but proceedings terminate prior to conviction or acquittal, the double jeopardy clause does not prevent reprosecution for the same offense in two types of cases. If the defendant moves to dismiss the case, or asks for or acquiesces in a **mistrial,** and the judge rules in the defendant's favor, the prosecution may reprosecute after the dismissal without offending the double jeopardy clause. Furthermore, even where defendants object to dismissal or mistrial, the government may reprosecute for the same offense if the judge dismissed the case or ordered a mistrial due to **manifest necessity,** or circumstance that requires termination to serve the ends of justice. The classic example of manifest necessity is the **hung jury,** or jury unable to reach a verdict. The Supreme Court ruled that reprosecution following a hung jury did not violate the double jeopardy clause.

> We think, [wrote the Court,] that in cases of this nature, the law has invested Courts of justice with the authority to discharge a jury from giving any verdict, whenever, in their opinion, taking all the circumstances into consideration, there is a manifest necessity for the act, or the ends of public justice would otherwise be defeated. They are to exercise a sound discretion on the subject; and it is impossible to define all the circumstances, which would render it proper to interfere. To be sure, the power ought to be used with the greatest of caution, under urgent circumstances.[3]

The manifest necessity doctrine is not limited to hung juries. It also applies to a range of situations where the prosecution is in a no-win situation. For example, where the court declared a mistrial over the defendant's objection because of a defect in the indictment that would have provided a basis for overturning any conviction if the trial proceeded, the Supreme Court ruled that reprosecution did not violate the double jeopardy clause. The Court balanced two interests in reaching its decision: "a defendant's valued right to have his trial completed by a particular tribunal must in some instances be subordinated to the public's interests in fair trials designed to end in just judgments."

> A trial judge properly exercises his discretion to declare a mistrial . . . if a verdict of conviction could be reached but would have to be reversed on appeal due to an obvious procedural error in the trial. If an error would make reversal on appeal a certainty, it would not serve "the ends of public justice" to require that the Government proceed with its proof, when, if it succeeded before the jury, it would automatically be stripped of that success by an appellate court.[4]

Reprosecution does not violate the double jeopardy clause if *defendants* appeal convictions; reprosecution for the same offense following acquittal, on the other hand, does put the defendant in double jeopardy. The **dual sovereignty doctrine**—that the same acts that constitute crimes in two jurisdictions may be prosecuted in both— appears to contradict the rule that prevents reprosecution following conviction.

However, the Court's definition of "same offense" in the clause explains the apparent contradiction. Same does not mean identical, according to the United States Supreme Court. Ordinarily, this situation arises when the same conduct constitutes a crime under both state and *federal* law. In *Heath v. Alabama,* the Supreme Court addressed this unusual situation: If one state convicts a defendant under its laws, does the double jeopardy clause bar a second *state* from reprosecuting the defendant for a like offense under the second state's laws?

CASE

Were they subjected to double jeopardy?

Heath v. Alabama

474 U.S. 82, 106 S.Ct. 433, 88 L.Ed.2d 387 (1985)

[O'Connor, J., delivered the opinion of the Court, in which Burger, C.J., and White, Blackmun, Powell, Rehnquist, and Stevens, JJ., joined. Brennan, J., filed a dissenting opinion, in which Marshall, J., joined. Marshall, J., filed a dissenting opinion, in which Brennan, J., joined.]

FACTS

In August 1981, petitioner, Larry Gene Heath, hired Charles Owens and Gregory Lumpkin to kill his wife, Rebecca Heath, who was then nine months pregnant, for a sum of $2,000. On the morning of August 31, 1981, petitioner left the Heath residence in Russell County, Alabama, to meet with Owens and Lumpkin in Georgia, just over the Alabama border from the Heath home. Petitioner led them back to the Heath residence, gave them the keys to the Heaths' car and house, and left the premises in his girlfriend's truck. Owens and Lumpkin then kidnaped Rebecca Heath from her home. The Heath car, with Rebecca Heath's body inside, was later found on the side of a road in Troup County, Georgia. The cause of death was a gunshot wound in the head. The estimated time of death and the distance from the Heath residence to the spot where Rebecca Heath's body was found are consistent with the theory that the murder took place in Georgia, and respondent does not contend otherwise.

Georgia and Alabama authorities pursued dual investigations in which they cooperated to some extent. On September 4, 1981, petitioner was arrested by Georgia authorities. Petitioner waived his Miranda rights and gave a full confession admitting that he had arranged his wife's kidnaping and murder. In November 1981, the grand jury of Troup County, Georgia indicted petitioner for the offense of "malice" murder. . . . Georgia then served petitioner with notice of its intention to seek the death penalty, citing as the aggravating circumstance the fact that the murder was "caused and directed" by petitioner. On February 10, 1982, petitioner pleaded guilty to the Georgia murder charge in exchange for a sentence of life imprisonment, which he understood could involve his serving as few as seven years in prison.

On May 5, 1982, the grand jury of Russell County, Alabama, returned an indictment against petitioner for the capital offense of murder during a kidnaping. Before trial on this indictment, petitioner entered pleas of autrefois convict [a plea in bar that the defendant has already been indicted, tried, and convicted] and former jeopardy under the Alabama and United States Constitutions, arguing that his conviction and sentence in Georgia barred his prosecution in Alabama for the same conduct.

After a hearing, the trial court rejected petitioner's double jeopardy claims. . . .

OPINION

The States power to undertake criminal prosecutions derive from separate and independent sources of power and authority originally belonging to them before admission to the Union and preserved to them by the Tenth Amendment. The States are equal to each other "in power, dignity and authority, each competent to exert that residuum of sovereignty not delegated to the United States by the Constitution itself." Thus, "[e]ach has the power, inherent in any sovereign, independently to determine what shall be an offense against its authority and to punish such offenses, and in doing so each 'is exercising its own sovereignty, not that of the other.' "

This Court has plainly and repeatedly stated that two identical offenses are not the "same offence" within the meaning of the Double Jeopardy Clause if they are prosecuted by different sovereigns. If the States are separate sovereigns, as they must be under the definition of sovereignty which the Court consistently has employed, the circumstances of the case are irrelevant.

The Court's express rationale for the dual sovereignty doctrine is not simply a fiction that can be disregarded in difficult cases. It finds weighty support in the historical understanding and political realities of the States' role in the federal system and in the words of the Double Jeopardy Clause itself, "nor shall any person be subject for the same offense to be twice put in jeopardy of life or limb."

To deny a State its power to enforce its criminal laws because another State has won the race to the courthouse "would be a shocking and untoward deprivation of the historic right and obligation of the States to maintain peace and order within their confines."

Such a deprivation of a State's sovereign powers cannot be justified by the assertion that under "interest analysis" the State's legitimate penal interests will be satisfied through a prosecution conducted by another State. A State's interest in vindicating its sovereign authority through enforcement of its laws by definition can never be satisfied by another State's enforcement of its own laws. The Court has always understood the words of the Double Jeopardy Clause to reflect this fundamental principle, and we see no reason why we should reconsider that understanding today.

The judgment of the Supreme Court of Alabama is affirmed.

It is so ordered.

DISSENT

Justice Marshall, with whom Justice Brennan joins, dissenting.

Seizing upon the suggestion in past cases that every "independent" sovereign government may prosecute violations of its laws even when the defendant has already been tried for the same crime in another jurisdiction, the court today gives short shrift to the policies underlying those precedents. The "dual sovereignty" doctrine, heretofore used to permit federal and state prosecutions for the same offense, was born of the need to accommodate complementary state and federal concerns within our system of concurrent territorial jurisdictions. It cannot justify successive prosecutions by different States. Moreover, even were the dual sovereignty doctrine to support successive state prosecutions as a general matter, it simply could not legitimate the collusion between Georgia and Alabama in this case to ensure that petitioner is executed for his crime.

Had the Georgia authorities suddenly become dissatisfied with the life sentence petitioner received in their courts and reindicted petitioner in order to seek the death penalty once again, that indictment would without question be barred by the Double Jeopardy Clause of the Fifth Amendment, as applied to the States by the Fourteenth Amendment. Whether the second indictment repeated the charge of malice murder or instead charged murder in the course of a kidnaping, it would surely, under any reasonable constitutional standard, offend the bar to successive prosecutions for the same offense.

The only difference between this case and such a hypothetical volte-face by Georgia is that here Alabama, not Georgia, was offended by the notion that petitioner might not forfeit his life in punishment for his crime. The only reason the Court gives for permitting Alabama to go forward is that Georgia and Alabama are separate sovereigns.

The dual sovereignty theory posits that where the same act offends the laws of two sovereigns, "it cannot be truly averred that the offender has been twice punished for the same offence; but only that by one act he has committed two offenses, for each of which he is justly punishable." No evidence has ever been adduced to indicate that the Framers intended the word "offense" to have so restrictive a meaning.

CASE DISCUSSION

Heath was convicted in the Alabama Circuit Court of murder during a kidnaping in the first degree and was sentenced to death. Both the Alabama Circuit Court of Appeals and the Alabama Supreme Court affirmed the conviction. On writ of *certiorari,* the United States Supreme Court affirmed, holding that successive prosecutions by two states for the same offense does not constitute double jeopardy.

Why would it be "shocking," as the Court says, to deny both states the authority to try Heath? Should the dual sovereignty doctrine be limited to federal-state cases, as the dissent argues? Why? Does this decision give the state more than "one fair shot" at convicting Heath? Should the state have more than "one shot" in this case? Explain.

Prosecuting a defendant in a series of trials for separate offenses arising out of the same incident does not subject the defendant to double jeopardy, although it might violate the due process clause. The Supreme Court addressed this issue in *Ciucci v. Illinois*.

CASE

Were they subjected to double jeopardy?

Ciucci v. Illinois

356 U.S. 571, 78 S.Ct. 839, 2 L.Ed.2d 983 (1958)

[Per Curiam.]

FACTS

Petitioner was charged in four separate indictments with murdering his wife and three children, all of whom, with bullet wounds in their heads, were found dead in a burning building during the early hours of December 5, 1953. In three successive trials, petitioner was found guilty of the first degree murder of his wife and two of his children. At each of the trials the prosecution introduced into evidence details of all four deaths. Under Illinois law the jury is charged with the responsibility of fixing the penalty for first degree murder from 14 years' imprisonment to death. At the first two trials, involving the death of the wife and one of the children, the jury fixed the penalty at 20 and 45 years' imprisonment respectively. At the third trial, involving the death of a second child, the penalty was fixed at death. On appeal the Supreme Court of Illinois affirmed the conviction, and we granted certiorari to consider petitioner's claim that this third trial violated the Due Process Clause of the Fourteenth Amendment to the Constitution of the United States.

OPINION

It is conceded that under Illinois law each of the murders, although apparently taking place at the same time, constituted a separate crime and it is undisputed that evidence of the entire occurrence was relevant in each of the three prosecutions. . . .

The five members of the Court who join in this opinion are in agreement that upon the record as it stands no violation of due process has been shown. The State was constitutionally entitled to prosecute these individual offenses singly at separate trials, and to utilize therein all relevant evidence, in the absence of proof establishing that such a course of action entailed fundamental unfairness. Mr. Justice Frankfurter and Mr. Justice Harlan, although believing that the matters set forth in the aforementioned newspaper articles might, if established, require a ruling that fundamental unfairness existed here, concur in the affirmance of the judgment because this material, not being part of the record, and not having been considered by the state courts, may not be considered here.

Accordingly, the judgment of the Supreme Court of Illinois is affirmed, with leave to petitioner to institute such further proceedings as may be available to him for the purpose of substantiating the claim that he was deprived of due process.

It is so ordered.

DISSENT

Mr. Justice Douglas, with whom the Chief Justice and Mr. Justice Brennan concur, dissenting.

This case presents an instance of the prosecution being allowed to harass the accused with repeated trials and convictions on the same evidence, until it achieves its desired result of a capital verdict.

Petitioner's wife and three children were found dead in a burning building. It was later established that death was due both to the fire and to bullet wounds each had received in the head. Petitioner was first tried on an indictment charging that he had murdered his wife. At that trial the evidence was not limited to the wife's death. The deaths of the three children were also introduced, and testimony as to the cause of death of all of the victims was received. This trial was in effect a trial for the murder of all four victims for the gruesome details of each of the four deaths were introduced into evidence. Petitioner was found guilty. Under Illinois law the jury determines the sentence in a murder case between a minimum of 14 years' imprisonment and a maximum of death. At that first trial the jury fixed the penalty at 20 years' imprisonment.

The prosecutor demanded another trial. Accordingly petitioner was next tried on a charge of murdering one of his daughters.

At the second trial the same evidence was introduced as in the first trial. Evidence concerning the four deaths once more was used. Once more all the gruesome details of the four crimes were presented to the jury. Once more the accused was tried in form for one murder, in substance for four. This time a different jury again found petitioner guilty and sentenced him to 45 years' imprisonment.

The prosecutor was still not satisfied with the result. And so a third trial was held, the one involved here.

In this third trial, petitioner was charged with murdering his son. This time petitioner objected before trial that he was being subjected to double jeopardy. He also moved to exclude testimony concerning the other deaths and after verdict he protested that he had been denied a fair trial guaranteed by the Due Process Clause of the Fourteenth Amendment. The trial court overruled those objections. At the trial complete evidence of all of the deaths and their causes was again introduced. Once more the gruesome details of four murders were presented to a jury—the gathering of the family in their home, the fire at 2 a.m., the .22 caliber bullets in the bodies of the four victims, the borrowing by the accused of a .22 rifle, the arrival of the firemen, the autopsies at the morgue. This time a third jury sentenced petitioner to death.

In my view the Due Process Clause of the Fourteenth Amendment prevents this effort by a State to obtain the death penalty. This is an unseemly and oppressive use of a criminal trial that violates the concept of due process contained in the Fourteenth Amendment, whatever its ultimate scope is taken to be.

Mr. Justice Black concurs in this dissent on the ground that the Fourteenth Amendment bars a State from placing a defendant twice in jeopardy for the same offense.

CASE DISCUSSION

In an Illinois State Court, Ciucci was charged in four separate indictments with killing his wife and three children. In three successive trials, he was convicted of first-degree murder of his wife and two of his children. In each trial, the prosecution introduced details of all four deaths. At the third trial, Ciucci was sentenced to death. The Illinois Supreme Court affirmed. The United States Supreme Court, on writ of *certiorari* affirmed, with leave to Ciucci to institute further proceedings to test whether the trials denied him due process of law under the fundamental fairness doctrine. (See chap. 2.)

Did the state "harass" Ciucci, as the dissent argues? How? Do you agree with the plurality's conclusion that there was no due process violation? Does this decision demonstrate that result was promoted over process? Explain. Did the prosecution get more than "one fair shot"?

═══ SPEEDY TRIAL MOTIONS

The Sixth Amendment provides that "[i]n all criminal trials, the accused shall enjoy the right to a speedy . . . trial." However, the notion that defendants are entitled to have their cases timely decided is much older than the Bill of Rights. In 1187, King Henry II provided for "speedy justice" in the Assizes of Clarendon. King John promised in the Magna Carta in 1215 that " . . . every subject of this realme . . . may . . . have justice . . . speedily without delay." In Coke's *Institutes*—according to Thomas Jefferson "the universal elementary book of law students"—Lord Coke wrote that the English itinerant justices in 1600 "have not suffered the prisoner to be long detained, but at their next coming have given the prisoner full and speedy justice . . . without detaining him long in prison." The Virginia Declaration of Rights in 1776, the state bills of rights, and the speedy trial clause of the Sixth Amendment quoted at this paragraph's outset reflect this history. Even though the state constitutions guarantee speedy trial, the Supreme Court has extended the Sixth Amendment federal speedy trial protection to the states.[5]

Interests Protected by the Speedy Trial Clause

The speedy trial clause promotes and balances several interests. For the accused, it prevents prolonged detention prior to trial; reduces the anxiety and uncertainty surrounding criminal prosecution; and guards against weakening the defense's case through loss of alibi witnesses and other evidence. Hence, the decision to go to trial quickly affects the intrusions and deprivations defendants suffer in criminal prosecutions. The speedy trial provision also promotes the interest in arriving at the correct result in individual cases. Delay means lost evidence, lost witnesses—or at least loss of memory—not only for the defense but also for the prosecution. The clause also promotes process goals, particularly that decisions should be made in a timely fashion.

Organizational interests are also at stake. Failure to provide prompt trials contributes to large case backlogs, particularly in urban areas. Furthermore, long pretrial detention is costly: maintaining prisoners in jails costs on average about $25 a day. In addition, of course, lost wages and greater welfare burdens result from incarceration. Finally, since the majority of detained defendants are poor, both the process interest in equal protection of the laws and the societal interest in protecting the poor and less powerful are at stake in speedy trial decisions.[6]

Attachment of the Right to Speedy Trial

According to the Supreme Court, the Sixth Amendment does not protect against delay prior to formal accusation because the speedy trial clause specifically refers to the ''accused.'' Therefore, time begins to measure delay for purposes of the Sixth Amendment speedy trial clause as soon as citizens are arrested or otherwise formally charged.

Defendants are not without relief due to delays prior to charge. The **statutes of limitations**—the lengths of time permitted between commission of a crime and initiation of prosecution—and the due process clause provide relief from precharge delays. Hence, where the Court rejected a speedy trial violation in a delay of three years between the commission of the crime and an indictment, the Supreme Court wrote:

> the due process clause of the Fifth Amendment would require dismissal of the indictment if it were shown at trial that the pre-indictment delay . . . caused substantial prejudice to appellants' rights to a fair trial and that the delay was an intentional device to gain tactical advantage over the accused.[7]

Furthermore, some states have extended their state constitution speedy trial clauses to the pre-accusation stage. The Alaska Supreme Court, for example, recognizes speedy trial rights even before the state initiates formal charges.[8]

Assessing Speedy Trial Claims

The speedy trial clause bans only *undue* delays. Three possible approaches determine what constitutes undue delay: (1) a bright line rule prescribing a specific number of days until trial; (2) a **demand-waiver rule** that measures delay only from the time defendants demand a speedy trial; (3) a balancing test that weighs what courts determine are relevant considerations. According to the Supreme Court, flexibility governs the determination of whether delays violate the speedy trial clause; hence, the Court has adopted the balancing test. The four elements that determine whether delay prejudices the defendant are (1) length of delay; (2) reason for delay; (3) defendants' assertion of their right to speedy trial; and (4) the prejudice that delay causes to defendants' case. The Court balanced these elements in *Barker v. Wingo*.

CASE

Did he receive a speedy trial?

Barker v. Wingo

407 U.S. 514, 92 S.Ct. 2182, 33 L.Ed.2d 101 (1972)

[Powell, J., delivered the opinion for a unanimous court. White, J., filed a concurring opinion, in which Brennan, J., joined.]

FACTS

Mr. Justice Powell delivered the opinion of the Court.

On July 20, 1958, in Christian County, Kentucky, an elderly couple was beaten to death by intruders wielding an iron tire tool. Two suspects, Silas Manning and Willie Barker, the petitioner, were arrested shortly thereafter. The grand jury indicted them on September 15. Counsel was appointed on September 17, and Barker's trial was set for October 21. The Commonwealth had a stronger case against Manning, and it believed that Barker could not be convicted unless Manning testified against him. Manning was naturally unwilling to incriminate himself. Accordingly, on October 23, the day Silas Manning was brought to trial, the Commonwealth sought and obtained the first of what was to be a series of 16 continuances of Barker's trial. Barker made no objection. By first convicting Manning, the Commonwealth would remove possible problems of self-incrimination and would be able to assure his testimony against Barker.

The Commonwealth encountered more than a few difficulties in its prosecution of Manning. The first trial ended in a hung jury. A second trial resulted in a conviction, but the Kentucky Court of Appeals reversed because of the admission of evidence obtained by an illegal search. At his third trial, Manning was again convicted, and the Court of Appeals again reversed because the trial court had not granted a change of venue. A fourth trial resulted in a hung jury. Finally, after five trials, Manning was convicted, in March 1962, of murdering one victim, and after a sixth trial, in December 1962, he was convicted of murdering the other.

The Christian County Circuit Court holds three terms each year—in February, June, and September. Barker's initial trial was to take place in the September term of 1958. The first continuance postponed it until the February 1959 term. The second continuance was granted for one month only. Every term thereafter for as long as the Manning prosecutions were in process, the Commonwealth routinely moved to continue Barker's case to the next term. When the case was continued from the June 1959 term until the following September, Barker, having spent 10 months in jail, obtained his release by posting a $5,000 bond. He thereafter remained free in the community until his trial. Barker made no objection, through his counsel, to the first 11 continuances.

When on February 12, 1962, the Commonwealth moved for the twelfth time to continue the case until the following term, Barker's counsel filed a motion to dismiss the indictment. The motion to dismiss was denied two weeks later, and the Commonwealth's motion for a continuance was granted. The Commonwealth was granted further continuances in June 1962 and September 1962, to which Barker did not object.

In February 1963, the first term of court following Manning's final conviction, the Commonwealth moved to set Barker's trial for March 19. But on the day scheduled for trial, it again moved for a continuance until the June term. It gave as its reason the illness of the ex-sheriff who was the chief investigating officer in the case. To this continuance, Barker objected unsuccessfully.

The witness was still unable to testify in June, and the trial, which had been set for June 19, was continued again until the September term over Barker's objection. This time the court announced that the case would be dismissed for lack of prosecution if it were not tried during the next term. The final trial date was set for October 9, 1963. On that date, Barker again moved to dismiss the indictment, and this time specified that his right to a speedy trial had been violated. The motion was denied; the trial commenced with Manning as the chief prosecution witness; Barker was convicted and given a life sentence.

Barker appealed his conviction to the Kentucky Court of Appeals, relying in part on his speedy trial claim. The court affirmed. In February 1970 Barker petitioned for habeas corpus in the United States District Court for the Western District of Kentucky. The District Court rejected the petition without holding a hearing. On appeal, the Court of Appeals for the Sixth Circuit affirmed the District Court. We granted Barker's petition for certiorari.

OPINION

The right to a speedy trial is generically different from any of the other rights enshrined in the Constitution for the protection of the accused. In addition to the general concern that all accused persons be treated according to decent and fair procedures, there is a societal interest in providing a speedy trial which exists separate from, and at times in opposition to, the interests of the accused. The inability of courts to provide a prompt trial has contributed to a large backlog of cases in urban courts which, among other things, enables defendants to negotiate more effectively for pleas of guilty to lesser offenses and otherwise manipulate the system. In addition, persons released on bond for lengthy periods awaiting trial have an opportunity to commit other crimes. It must be of little comfort to the residents of Christian County, Kentucky, to know that Barker was at large on bail for over four years while accused of a vicious and brutal murder of which he was ultimately convicted. Moreover, the longer an accused is free awaiting trial, the more tempting becomes his opportunity to jump bail and escape. Finally, delay between arrest and punishment may have a detrimental effect on rehabilitation.

If an accused cannot make bail, he is generally confined, as was Barker for 10 months, in a local jail. This contributes to the overcrowding and generally deplorable state of those institutions. Finally, lengthy pretrial detention is costly. The cost of maintaining a prisoner in jail varies from $3 to $9 per day, and this amounts to millions across the Nation. In addition, society loses wages which might have been earned, and it must often support families of incarcerated breadwinners.

A second difference between the right to speedy trial and the accused's other constitutional right is that deprivation of the right may work to the accused's advantage. Delay is not an uncommon defense tactic. As the time between the commission of the crime and trial lengthens, witnesses may become unavailable or their memories may fade. If the witnesses support the prosecution, its case will be weakened, sometimes seriously so. And it is the prosecution which carries the burden of proof.

Finally, and perhaps most importantly, the right to speedy trial is a more vague concept than other procedural rights. It is, for example, impossible to determine with precision when the right has been denied. We cannot definitely say how long is too long in a system where justice is supposed to be swift but deliberate.

Perhaps because the speedy trial right is so slippery, two rigid approaches are urged upon us as ways of eliminating some of the uncertainty which courts experience in protecting the right. The first suggestion is that we hold that the Constitution requires a criminal defendant to be offered a trial within a specified time period. The result of such a ruling would have the virtue of clarifying when the right is infringed and of simplifying courts' application of it.

But such a result would require this Court to engage in legislative or rulemaking activity, rather than in the adjudicative process to which we should confine our efforts. We find no constitutional basis for holding that the speedy trial right can be quantified into a specified number of days or months.

The second suggested alternative would restrict consideration of the right to those cases in which the accused has demanded a speedy trial. Most States have recognized what is loosely referred to as the "demand rule." It is not clear, however, precisely what is meant by that term.

The demand-waiver doctrine provides that a defendant waives any consideration of his right to speedy trial for any period prior to which he has not demanded a trial. Under this rigid approach, a prior demand is a necessary condition to the consideration of the speedy trial right.

Such an approach, by presuming waiver of a fundamental right from inaction, is inconsistent with this Court's pronouncements on waiver of constitutional rights. The Court has defined waiver as "an intentional relinquishment or abandonment of a known right or privilege."

The nature of the speedy trial right does make it impossible to pinpoint a precise time in the process when the right must be asserted or waived, but that fact does not argue for placing the burden of protecting the right solely on defendants.

We reject, therefore, the rule that a defendant who fails to demand a speedy trial forever waives his right. This does not mean, however, that the defendant has no responsibility to assert his right. We think the better rule is that the defendant's assertion of or failure to assert his right to a speedy trial is one of the factors to be considered in an inquiry into the deprivation of the right.

The approach we accept is a balancing test, in which the conduct of both the prosecution and the defendant are weighted.

A balancing test necessarily compels courts to approach speedy trial cases on an ad hoc basis. We can do little more than identify some of the factors which courts should assess in determining whether a particular defendant has been deprived of his right. Though some might express them in different ways, we identify four such factors: Length of delay, the reason for the delay, the defendant's assertion of his right, and prejudice to the defendant.

The length of the delay is to some extent a triggering mechanism.

Closely related to length of delay is the reason the government assigns to justify the delay. A deliberate attempt to delay the trial in order to hamper the defense should be weighted heavily against the government. A more neutral reason such as negligence or overcrowded courts should be weighted less heavily but nevertheless should be considered since the ultimate responsibility for such circumstances must rest with the government rather than with the defendant. Finally, a valid reason, such as a missing witness, should serve to justify appropriate delay.

Whether and how a defendant asserts his right is closely related to the other factors we have mentioned. The strength of his efforts will be affected by the length of the delay, to some extent by the reason for the delay, and most particularly by the personal prejudice, which is not always readily identifiable, that he experiences.

A fourth factor is prejudice to the defendant. Prejudice, of course, should be assessed in the light of the interests of defendants which the speedy trial right was designed to protect. This Court has identified three such interests: (i) to prevent oppressive pretrial incarceration; (ii) to minimize anxiety and concern of the accused; and (iii) to limit the possibility that the defense will be impaired.

We have discussed previously the societal disadvantages of lengthy pretrial incarceration, but obviously the disadvantages for the accused who cannot obtain his release are even more serious.

We regard none of the four factors identified above as either a necessary or sufficient condition to the finding of a deprivation of the right of speedy trial. Rather, they are related factors and must be considered together with such other circumstances as may be relevant. In sum, these factors have no talismanic qualities; courts must still engage in a difficult and sensitive balancing process.

The difficulty of the task of balancing these factors is illustrated by this case, which we consider to be close. It is clear that the length of delay between arrest and trial—well over five years—was extraordinary.

Two counterbalancing factors, however, outweigh these deficiencies. The first is that prejudice was minimal. Of course, Barker was prejudiced to some extent by living for over four years under a cloud of suspicion and anxiety. But there is no claim that any of Barker's witnesses died or otherwise became unavailable owing to the delay.

More important than the absence of serious prejudice, is the fact that Barker did not want a speedy trial.

The probable reason for Barker's attitude was that he was gambling on Manning's acquittal. The evidence was not very strong against Manning, as the reversals and hung juries suggest, and Barker undoubtedly thought that if Manning was acquitted, he would never be tried.

We hold, therefore, that Barker was not deprived of his due process right to a speedy trial.

The judgment of the Court of Appeals is
Affirmed.

CASE DISCUSSION

Barker was tried for murder more than five years after his arrest, during which time the prosecution secured numerous continuances. Barker did not object to the continuances until three-and-a-half years after his arrest. In a *habeas corpus* proceeding, the Circuit Court of Appeals held that Barker had waived his right to speedy trial and affirmed the district court's conviction. On writ of *certiorari*, the United States Supreme Court affirmed, holding that the right to speedy trial cannot be established by any inflexible rule but only by means of an *ad hoc* balancing that weighs the conduct of both the government and defense.

Would a demand-waiver rule solve the problem of this case better than the balancing test? What were the critical facts that the Court balanced? What are the interests the Court balanced in deciding the case? To what extent was the delay in this case due to the defendant? to the state? Was anybody really "at fault" for the delay? Explain.

Remedies for Violations of Speedy Trial Guarantees

The Supreme Court has ruled that only **dismissal,** either **without prejudice** or the more drastic **dismissal with prejudice**—barring prosecution for the same offense—can remedy a violation of the speedy trial clause. According to a unanimous Supreme Court, even though sufficient evidence to convict exists, undue delay subjects defendants to "emotional stress" that requires dismissal as "the only possible remedy." The Court's ruling has raised strong objections on the ground that such a drastic remedy as dismissal will make courts "extremely hesitant" to find speedy trial violations. Hence, the remedy will lead to further abuses.[9]

Speedy Trial Legislation

Although the Sixth Amendment does not require it, several states have enacted statutes or court rules that set time limits for bringing cases to trial. These limits vary widely among the states. The federal Speedy Trial Act of 1974 provides definite time periods for bringing defendants to trial. The government must initiate prosecution within thirty days following arrest (sixty days if no grand jury is in session); arraign defendants within ten days after filing indictments or information; and bring defendants to trial within sixty days following arraignment. Some delays do not count in computing days under the act: (1) time to determine defendant's competency to stand trial; (2) delays due to other trials of the defendant; (3) delays due to hearings on pretrial motions; (4) delays because of **interlocutory appeals**—provisional appeals that interrupt the proceedings, such as an appeal from a ruling on a pretrial motion. Section

3161(h)(1)(F), for example, excludes certain delays occasioned by filing pretrial motions from the seventy days allowed to bring defendants to trial:

> (h) The following periods of delay shall be excluded in computing the time within which an information or an indictment must be filed, or in computing the time within which the trial of any such offense must commence:
>
> (1) Any period of delay resulting from other proceedings concerning the defendant, including but not limited to—
>
> (F) delay resulting from any pretrial motion, from the filing of the motion through the conclusion of the hearing on, or other prompt disposition of, such motion.

In *Henderson v. United States,* the defendant asked the Supreme Court to interpret this section to limit the exclusion to "*reasonably necessary* delays." The Court declined, arguing that the words of the statute, "*any* period of delay," did not permit the broader meaning.

> There is no requirement that the hearing be held promptly, and the reason for the delay is irrelevant. Regardless whether a hearing is postponed due to a stipulated continuance, the sudden illness of counsel, or the trial judge's decision to play golf, until the hearing is concluded, the 70-day clock remains at a standstill. Moreover, if at the conclusion of the hearing the trial judge determines that more information would be helpful to his resolution of the motion, or if the prosecutor simply announces his intention to file supplemental papers, the period of excludable delay continues indefinitely until the court receives all of the papers it reasonably expects.[10]

In some instances, the government can unilaterally exclude time under the act. For example, if prosecutors ask for dismissals with leave to reprosecute, the time following dismissal does not count; delays due to court congestion are not excludable.[11]

If the government exceeds the timetable, the statute prescribes dismissal either with *or* without prejudice. Some states, such as Alaska and Washington, require courts to dismiss with prejudice.[12]

CHANGE OF VENUE AND CONTINUANCE MOTIONS

The Sixth Amendment provides that

> In all criminal prosecutions, the accused shall enjoy the right to a . . . public trial, by an impartial jury of the State and district wherein the crime shall have been committed.

A defendant's pretrial motion to change **venue**—the place where trial is held—waives the Sixth Amendment right to have a trial in the state and district where the crime was committed. Only defendants not the prosecution, may move to change venue, and changes of venue are not automatic. According to Rule 21(a) of the Federal Rules of Criminal Procedure:

> The court upon motion of the defendant shall transfer the proceeding as to that defendant to another district . . . if the court is satisfied that there exists in the district where the prosecution is pending so great a prejudice against the defendant that the defendant cannot obtain a fair and impartial trial at any placed fixed for holding court in that district.[13]

Interests at Stake in Change of Venue

Defendants waive their right to trial in the place where the crime was committed because they believe they cannot get an impartial public trial in that location. When courts rule on the motion, they balance the right to a public trial in the place where the crime was committed against the right to an impartial trial. In that respect, changing venue reflects the interest in obtaining a proper result in the individual case—prejudiced jurors cannot find the truth. Process values are also at stake: the integrity of the judicial process requires a calm, dignified, reflective atmosphere; due process demands unbiased fact-finding; the equal protection clause prohibits trying defendants who are the object of public outrage differently from other defendants.

Change of venue impedes organizational interests. Moving proceedings to jurisdictions farther away, providing for witnesses to appear, and working in unfamiliar court surroundings prevent the smooth, efficient, economical resolution of criminal cases. Furthermore, there is a strong societal interest in maintaining public confidence in the criminal justice system, and providing an outlet for community reaction to crime. Citizens resent moving trials both because they wish to follow the proceedings and because they feel affronted that their own jurisdiction cannot insure a fair trial.

Assessing Change of Venue Motions

In *Sheppard v. Maxwell,* the United States Supreme Court held that

> where there is a reasonable likelihood that the prejudicial news prior to trial will prevent a fair trial, the judge should continue the case until the threat abates, or transfer it to another county not so permeated with publicity.[14]

Ohio tried Dr. Sam Sheppard for the bludgeoning murder of his pregnant wife, Marilyn, a Cleveland socialite. The case attracted enormous press coverage both prior to, and during, the trial. Lurid headlines and long stories appeared regularly, detailing the brutality of the murder, and Sheppard's failure to cooperate with authorities. The editorials accused Sheppard of the murder. One on the front page charged that "somebody is getting away with murder," alleging that Sheppard's wealth and prominent social position protected him from strong police investigation. Finally, the papers printed detailed analyses of evidence that came to light during the investigation, editorializing about its credibility, relevance, and materiality to the case.

The trial itself attracted enormous publicity. The press, public, and other observers filled the courtroom. One local radio station set up broadcasting facilities on the third floor of the courthouse. Television and newsreel cameras awaiting outside on the courthouse steps filmed jurors, lawyers, witnesses, and other participants in the trial. All the jurors were exposed to the heavy publicity prior to the trial. Referring to the "carnival atmosphere" at the trial, the Supreme Court concluded that Sheppard was entitled to a new trial without showing actual prejudice—reasonable likelihood of prejudice was sufficient.

In determining the reasonable likelihood of prejudice test, courts balance four elements: (1) the nature and extent of publicity that evidences community bias and poses a danger to fair trial; (2) the size of the community from which jury panels are selected; (3) the nature and gravity of the offense; (4) the status of the victim and the accused. These elements may vary in intensity and, in fact, not all need to be present in each case; rather, they are guidelines by which judges measure the likelihood the accused will receive fair trial. California applied the reasonable likelihood of prejudice test in *Martinez v. Superior Court of Placer County.*

CASE

Could he get a fair trial?

Martinez v. Superior Court of Placer County

29 Cal. 3d 574, 174 Cal.Rpt. 701, 629 P.2d 502 (1981)

[Tobriner, Justice.]
Petitioner Martinez is charged by information with one count of murder, three counts of robbery and one count of attempted robbery.

FACTS

On September 23, 1979, petitioner moved for change of venue for his trial, then scheduled for November 13, 1979, on grounds that, because of pretrial publicity concerning the charges against him, he could not obtain a fair and impartial trial in Placer County. After denial of the motion, Martinez filed a petition for writ of mandate seeking to compel the trial court to grant a change of venue. An alternative writ was issued and trial has been stayed pending resolution of this matter.

OPINION

"A Motion for change of venue or continuance shall be granted whenever it is determined that because of the dissemination of potentially prejudicial material, there is a reasonable likelihood that in the absence of such relief, a fair trial cannot be had. A showing of actual prejudice shall not be required." The phrase "reasonable likelihood" denotes a lesser standard of proof than "more probable than not." Further, when the issue is raised before trial, any doubt as to the necessity of removal to another county should be resolved in favor of a venue change.

With these general principles in mind, we examine the record in this case and attempt to isolate the factors which have been considered criteria of the potential for prejudice from pretrial publicity. Factors to be considered include the extent and kind of the publicity as well as the size of the community in which the crime occurred. The nature and gravity of the crime serves as an important factor. We also consider the standing of the victim and the accused in the community. . . .

1. The nature and extent of publicity evidences community bias and poses a danger to a fair trial.

The charges against petitioner stem from an attempted robbery of the Owl Club Bar in Roseville on the evening of July 14, 1978, and the robbery of the Onyx Club also in Roseville, on the morning of July 15, 1978. During the Onyx Club robbery, George Robert Alves was shot.

For more than a year before petitioner moved to change venue, three local newspapers (the Auburn Journal, Press-Tribune, and Sacramento Bee) covered petitioner's pending trial. Commencing with front page pictures of petitioner and Davis in chains shortly after their arrest, the press followed the legal maneuverings that attend capital cases and, in almost daily articles, followed the testimony and developments in the trial of codefendant Davis.

Petitioner submits 97 newspaper articles to support his motion for change of venue. The press gave substantial coverage to the fact that the accused forced the patrons to lie face down on the floor during the robbery and shot the victim at close range in the back, reportedly because the killer mistook him for a police officer.

One headline, in the Auburn Journal, proclaimed "Death penalty OK in Onyx killing," arguably implying that the law approves imposition of that penalty on the person who killed Alves. . . .

"The goal of a fair trial in the locality of the crime is practically unattainable when the jury panel has been bathed in streams of circumstantial incrimination flowing from the news media." In this case, not only did the alleged crime partners point the finger at petitioner, but presumably knowledgeable officials also made statements indicating their belief in petitioner's guilt. We conclude, therefore, that the nature and extent of the publicity is a factor which in this case weighs in favor of a change of venue.

2. Although not alone determinative, the size of the population of Placer County weighs in favor of a change of venue.

In a small town, in contrast to a large metropolitan area, a major crime is likely to be embedded in the public consciousness with greater effect and for a longer time.

While size of community does not in itself resolve the venue issue, it clearly composes an important factor which in the present case weighs toward the necessity of a change of venue.

3. The nature and gravity of the offense, capital murder, is a primary consideration in requiring a change of venue.

The peculiar facts or aspects of a crime which make it sensational, or otherwise bring it to the consciousness of the community, define its "nature"; the term "gravity" of a crime refers to its seriousness in the law and to the possible consequences to an accused in the event of a guilty verdict. The Attorney General contends this case does not qualify for either category; he characterizes petitioner as a person "of no particular status," accused of murder in a "nondescript" Roseville bar holdup. This characterization ignores publicity given to the fact that the victim was shot in the back, while lying on the floor, because the killer mistakenly thought him to be a police officer. Indeed, one newspaper article referred to the tavern as the "scene of a cold-blooded killing."

The seriousness of the charged crime stands out clearly. Murder is a crime of utmost gravity; inasmuch as the state is seeking the death penalty, it is a crime of the gravest consequences to petitioner. Because it carries such grave consequences, a death penalty case inherently attracts press coverage; in such a case the factor of gravity must weigh heavily in a determination regarding the change of venue.

4. The status of the victim and the accused in the community are significant but not controlling factors in assessing the necessity for change of venue.

Although the trial court correctly stated that the victim was "no public figure," his status nonetheless appears to be significant. At the time of the murder, he was employed as a brakeman for the largest single employer in Roseville, Southern Pacific Railroad; virtually every newspaper article described him as a Southern Pacific brakeman. The victim's prominence in the public eye thus derives from the status of his employer, and that factor undoubtedly engendered community sympathy.

On the other hand, the press described petitioner in terms unlikely to evoke the sympathy or concern of the community. The newspapers repeatedly referred to the fact that when arrested petitioner had been confined in the state rehabilitation center for drug abuse because of parole violation. The district attorney's opening statement in the Davis trial, which was widely reported, claimed that a conspiracy to obtain funds for buying heroin set the scene for the robbery and murder. A witness testifying for the prosecution under immunity reportedly also stated that defendants had planned the robbery in order to obtain money to buy heroin. Petitioner, a member of a minority group and an alleged heroin addict, "friendless in the community," represents exactly the type of defendant whom pretrial publicity can most effectively prejudice.

5. Conclusion.

Based upon the record and our evaluation of it in terms of the factors outlined above, we conclude that there is a reasonable likelihood that petitioner will not receive a fair and impartial trial in Placer County. No one factor controls our determination that a change of venue is appropriate here; rather we weigh all of the factors and, mindful of our duty, resolve all doubts in favor of petitioner.

Bird, C.J., and Jewman, Rattigan and Pauline David Hanson, JJ., concur.

DISSENT

Richardson, Justice, dissenting.

I respectfully dissent, believing that Placer County can afford a fair trial to petitioner.

The charged homicide was, allegedly, a drug-related shooting incident to a robbery at a bar. Although murder is a crime of the utmost gravity, this particular offense was neither sensational in nature nor did it arouse the same sense of community shock or indignation generally associated with cases in which change of venue has been granted.

Secondly, Placer County is neither so small nor unsophisticated as to render unlikely the selection of an unprejudiced jury from its populace. Connected by California's major freeways, this highly mobile community stretches from the Sacramento metropolitan area (population approaching 1 million) to the Nevada state line. It is served by numerous television and radio stations, and several newspapers. With a population in excess of 109,000, Placer County is the home of industry, agriculture, and popular resort areas.

There are no particular facets of either the defendant or victim which are likely to generate community antipathy towards the defendant or sympathy towards the victim. The defendant's status as a Mexican-American does not make him the object of any community hatred nor is he a member of any unpopular subculture. Placer County is a community of many ethnic groups, including Japanese, Chinese, blacks, American Indians, and Filipinos. I find significance in the fact that petitioner's codefendant, who was acquitted by a panel of Placer County jurors, was of Indian and Mexican descent, and in the absence of any showing of anti-Hispanic prejudice, there is no reason to believe that petitioner's minority status would prohibit his receiving a fair trial in Placer County.

The victim, on the other hand, was a stranger, a nonresident transient worker with no particular prominence in Placer County. His fate drew no particular expressions of broad public sympathy or community antipathy towards petitioner. . . . I also find significance in the fact that nearly three years have passed since the offense, and it is reasonable to believe that any pretrial publicity will have subsided by the time of petitioner's trial.

CASE DISCUSSION

Martinez was charged with murder and several counts of robbery. On a **writ of mandamus,** an order from a superior court to an inferior court, a municipality, or any of its officers, to do something, in this case seeking to compel the trial court to grant a **change of venue,** to change the location of the trial. The Supreme Court held that writ issue and that the location of the trial be changed.

How would you assess the factors determining the "reasonable likelihood" that Martinez could not get a fair trial in the county? Is this court promoting result, process, organizational, or social interests in the criteria it adopts for determining the change of venue question? Were they balanced properly in your judgment? Explain.

Despite this **reasonable likelihood of prejudice test,** most courts do not grant changes of venue even if defendants show that trial in the jurisdiction where the crime took place will produce a reasonable likelihood of such prejudice. Instead, they adopt an **actual prejudice** test to determine whether to change the venue or take less drastic measures to eliminate prejudice due to pretrial publicity. Unless the government concedes prejudice, defendants must show that adverse publicity actually negatively affected—prejudiced—their case. Practically speaking, this means proving that the adverse publicity prior to trial reached prospective jurors. Hence, most pretrial motions for change of venue are not resolved until after the **voir dire**—examining prospective trial jurors.

In the actual prejudice test, the courts consider such factors as the number of jurors who have opinions that the defendant is guilty, the number exposed to pretrial publicity, the jurors' knowledge of the details of the crime, and the information introduced at *voir dire.* Courts do not often find that defendants have adequately shown that the jury is partial. For example, in *Swindler v. State,* Swindler showed both that three jurors had read and heard about the case, and over 80 percent of prospective jurors were excused for cause. Despite this showing, the Arkansas Supreme Court upheld Swindler's death sentence, rejecting Swindler's claim that the trial court's refusal to grant his motion for change of venue denied him a fair trial.[15]

Several reasons explain why so few defendants prevail in demonstrating actual prejudice. Trials at distant locations burden witnesses; communities have a substantial interest in the trial taking place where the crime was committed; change of prosecutors might disrupt the government's case. Perhaps equally important, under the actual prejudice test, the court cannot decide the partiality question until the jury has been empaneled. After the considerable resources courts invest in the *voir dire*, they transfer cases only reluctantly. For the most part, these decisions do not reach the United States Supreme Court. If they go beyond the trial court, ordinarily intermediate state appellate courts resolve the issues. The Alaska Supreme Court resolved a problem under the actual prejudice test in *Mallott v. State*.[16]

CASE

Were the jurors actually prejudiced?

Mallott v. State

608 P.2d 737 (Alaska 1980)

[Matthews, Justice.]

Jay B. Mallott was convicted by a jury of the rape of a three year old girl. He contends that his rights, a fair trial, have been violated.

Mallott initially moved for a change of venue on July 15, 1976. He advised the court at that time, however, that he wished to have a ruling deferred until some two weeks prior to trial because he hoped to obtain a fair trial in Anchorage. Subsequently Mallott was granted a continuance and trial was rescheduled for October 21. The motion was finally heard on the merits and denied on October 4, at which time the court indicated its belief that voir dire would be a far superior barometer of prejudice.

FACTS

. . . In the instant case, the pre-trial publicity in July, 1976, approached an inflammatory level. At that time, however, Mallott's attorney indicated that a fair trial might yet be possible in Anchorage, and if such were the case, venue in Anchorage would be desirable. A ruling on the motion was therefore deferred, and, as a result of a continuance granted by the trial court, was not made until October 4. By that time media coverage of this case was minimal and not inflammatory, and, with only one exception, the few articles that appeared in August and September were concerned with bail procedures generally rather than with the facts of this case. We therefore find that the trial court neither abused its discretion nor violated Mallott's right to an impartial jury in choosing to proceed with voir dire to determine the impact of the July publicity.

The voir dire conducted in this case was exceptionally thorough. Thirty-six jurors were examined individually over a period of four days, producing testimony filling more than seven hundred pages of transcript. Counsel, with encouragement from the court, probed extensively for juror exposure to and prejudice from the pre-trial publicity.

The ultimate burden imposed on a defendant by the Supreme Court with respect to transfer of venue has been to demonstrate that pre-trial publicity actually resulted in "a partiality that could not be laid aside" in those jurors finally seated to adjudicate guilt or innocence. Under such a standard Mallott's claim would most certainly fail, since he cannot and does not maintain that the voir dire examinations of his jury panel revealed even a shred of evidence that any of the impaneled jurors were predisposed to convict him.

Of the thirty-six persons examined, more than one-fourth had heard or read nothing about the alleged crime and another third had heard no more than the bare allegation, which in any event was read to the venire prior to voir dire. Of the remaining thirteen venirepersons, only six can even arguably be said to have been exposed in any depth to the pre-trial publicity, and only one potential juror had any inkling that Mallott had made incriminating statements. Of the persons selected to serve on the jury, including the alternate juror, only two had even heard of the bail controversy. Finally, five or six venirepersons confessed to varying degrees of emotional reaction upon learning of the crime, but the voir dire examinations indicated that, for more of these persons, the same response might as easily have occurred upon learning of the nature of crime from the trial judge rather than the media. Given the minimal degree to which the venire was exposed to pre-trial publicity, the non-incriminating nature of the information to which the vast majority were exposed, and the lack of prejudicial attitudes revealed by the venire generally, we find the likelihood that Mallott's panel harbored unrevealed prejudices as a result of the publicity to be very slight. The trial court's decision to retain venue in Anchorage is therefore affirmed.

Affirmed.

Rabinowitz, C. J., concurs and dissents.

Burke, J., did not participate.

DISSENT

Rabinowitz, Chief Justice, concurring and dissenting.

Although the trial jury was not shown to reflect any partiality as a result of pre-trial prejudicial publicity, I conclude that Mallott's motion for a change of venue should have been granted on October 4. I think inflammatory pre-trial publicity was so great by October 4 that it was sufficient to warrant a change of venue. . . .

The publicity given this case was clearly inflammatory. Although the initial incident received little or no media coverage, the case did in fact begin to garner extensive media coverage starting with a July 3, 1976, Anchorage Times front page article under a bold face headline reading "Alleged Rapist Can Go Fishing."

. . . The ensuing atmosphere of hostility towards Mallott's release in all probability chilled Mallott's ability to have the facts of his case dispassionately evaluated by an Anchorage trial jury. . . .

For example, letters to the editor in the Anchorage Times, July 10, 1976, included the following statements:

When a three-year-old is raped and her life maybe ruined, why should the man charged with the crime be allowed reduced bail so he can go fishing.

We have just read of Judge Moody's bail reduction. At first, we encountered a feeling of unbelievable horror. My God! We have a two-year-old daughter. Shall we lock her in her room until the trial.

What is wrong with this judge and the court system? Can they be responsible for the safety of every little girl?

A letter to the editor in the Anchorage Times on July 11, 1976, stated:

It really makes me do a slow burn reading the big headline in the July 3 issue of the Times, "Alleged Rapist Can Go Fishing," and I imagine lots more folks who have baby girls are feeling the same as I.

What do the little brothers feel after watching the episode that took place in front of their eyes, not to mention what the baby went through, and no doubt will leave a mental scar on her for life.

CASE DISCUSSION

Mallott was convicted in the Superior Court of raping a three-year-old girl and appealed to the Alaska Supreme Court. The supreme court affirmed, holding that the jury was not prejudiced by pretrial publicity.

Do you favor the "actual prejudice test" the court adopts? Do you agree that if the court waits until after jury selection to rule on change of venue, it will have invested too much time and effort to the case to grant the motion? What interests prevailed in this case? Would the result have been different if the court had adopted the "reasonable likelihood of prejudice" test? Review *Martinez v. Superior Court* excerpted earlier. Explain.

Fair Trial and Free Press

In *Sheppard v. Maxwell,* the Supreme Court said "the trial court might well have proscribed extra-judicial statements by any lawyer, party, witness, or court official." The Court has never ruled on the constitutionality of orders to these persons; however, it has declared that "gag orders" directed at the press violate the First Amendment free press guarantee. In *Nebraska Press Association v. Stuart,* the Court ruled that barring the press from reporting what transpired at a public preliminary hearing constituted **prior restraint.** A fundamental First Amendment principle prohibits imposing a restraint on statements before they are published, except when such publications constitute a "clear and present danger" to the country, invade privacy, or are obscene.[17]

The right to a public trial is a personal right that only defendants may invoke. However, the press and the public have a right of access to criminal trials. The right of access promotes the public interest in "ensuring that the individual citizen can effectively participate in and contribute to our republican system of government." The keys to defining the right of access are the long tradition of openness and the contribution public access makes to the criminal justice system's functioning. Under these guiding principles the right of access extends not only to trials but also to pretrial proceedings—first appearances, preliminary hearings, hearings on pretrial motions, and *voir dire* examinations. The press has no right of access either to the secret grand jury proceedings or to trial jury deliberations.[18]

The First Amendment right to free press, linked to the community's interest in law enforcement, and the defendant's right to a public trial, associated with the individual's interest in governmental accountability, must be balanced against the due process guarantee that defendants receive fair trials. Hence, the press's right of access to all public proceedings and its freedom to report those proceedings is not absolute; the defendant's right to a fair trial may restrict both access and reporting. Judges may close proceedings "necessitated by a compelling government interest, and [which are] . . . narrowly tailored to serve that interest." The Supreme Court held that a compelling government interest protected minor victims of sex crimes "from further" trauma that press coverage would generate.[19]

≡ CHANGE OF JUDGE MOTIONS

The right to a fair trial includes not only the rights to an impartial jury and an atmosphere not poisoned by prejudice, but also the right to an unbiased judge. According to the Supreme Court:

> [I]t certainly violates the Fourteenth Amendment and deprives a defendant in a criminal case of due process of law to subject his liberty or property to the judgment of a court, the judge of which has a direct, personal, substantial pecuniary interest in reaching a conclusion against him in his case.[20]

Hence, where a mayor who also acted as a justice of the peace received fees and costs he levied on violators, the personal interest disqualified the judge from hearing such cases.

Personal prejudice is not limited to pecuniary interests. Judges cannot hear cases in which they have a personal interest. A relationship to any of the parties in a case or an involvement in any affairs related to a case might influence the judge and affect judicial impartiality. Judges cannot conduct contempt proceedings following trials over which they have presided and in which defendants have personally insulted or otherwise vilified judges; another judge must decide the contempt issue. However, judges can try cases in which they conducted preliminary proceedings, such as determining probable cause to issue warrants, presiding over preliminary hearings, and resolving pretrial motions.

> Judges repeatedly issue arrest warrants on the basis that there is probable cause to believe that a crime has been committed and that the person named in the warrant committed it. Judges also preside at preliminary hearings where they must decide whether the evidence is sufficient to hold a defendant for trial. Neither of these pretrial involvements has been thought to raise any constitutional barrier against the judge presiding over the criminal trial and, if the trial is without a jury, against making the necessary determination of guilt or innocence.[21]

Personal bias denies defendants a fair trial; **judicial bias** does not. Judicial bias means favoring a particular legal principle. Hence, judges who oppose the death penalty have a judicial bias, but that does not disqualify them from presiding over capital murder trials. In other words, while judicial philosophy unquestionably leads to judicial bias, there is an assumed confidence that judges can put their judicial biases aside and decide cases fairly.

Jurisdictions have different grounds for disqualifying judges depending upon the interests disqualification promotes. Several interests govern disqualification standards: (1) the organizational interest in cost of justice; (2) the process interests in fairness and timeliness of judicial proceedings; (3) the result interest in correct decisions; (4) the societal interest in maintaining public confidence in the judicial process; and (5) the professional and personal interests of judges in their own capacity to maintain neutrality. These competing interests have led some states to adopt "easy" disqualification standards while others employ "hard" ones. New Mexico is an easy disqualification state:

> Our legislature in effect has said that a judge, even though blessed with all of the virtues any judge ever possessed, shall not be permitted to exercise judicial power to determine the fact of his own disqualifications, not because the judge in doing so would attempt to act otherwise than conscientiously, but because in their legislative judgment it is not fitting for him to make such an attempt, and it is better that the courts shall maintain the confidence of the people than that the rights of judge and litigant in a particular case be served.[22]

Pennsylvania, a "hard" disqualification state, contends:

> Due consideration should be given by him [the judge] to the fact that the administration of justice should be beyond the appearance of unfairness. But while the mediation of courts is based upon the principle of judicial impartiality, disinterestedness, and fairness pervading the whole system of judicature, so that courts may as near as possible be above suspicion, there is, on the other side, an important issue at stake; that is, that causes may not be unfairly prejudiced, unduly delayed, or discontent created through unfounded charges or prejudice or unfairness made against the judge in the trial of a cause.[23]

The Fifth Circuit Court of Appeals addressed recusal in *United States v. Harrelson*, in which the defendant argued that then Judge Sessions, now FBI director, should have recused himself because of his ties to the victim of the crime in the trial over which Judge Sessions presided.

CASE

Should Judge Sessions have recused himself? ·

United States v. Harrelson

754 F.2d 1153 (5th Cir. 1985)

[Before Gee, Reavley and Davis, Circuit Judges.]

FACTS

Gee, Circuit Judge:

In late May of 1979, Judge Wood was instantly killed by a dumdum [hollow point] bullet fired into his back from a six millimeter rifle capable of extremely high velocity. He was shot while entering his automobile at his townhouse residence in north San Antonio, preparatory to driving to work at the courthouse downtown. Witnesses placed appellant Charles Harrelson at the townhouse complex that morning; further investigation indicated that Judge Wood's murder by Harrelson was arranged by appellant Jamiel Chagra, a gambler and narcotics dealer under indictment for drug offenses, who was to be tried before Judge Wood and who feared his reputation for imposing severe sentences in drug cases.

Charles Harrelson, Chagra and his brother Joseph were charged with conspiring to murder Judge Wood on account of the performance of his duties. Harrelson and Jamiel Chagra were charged with the murder itself. Elizabeth Chagra and the Harrelsons were tried together and convicted on all charges. This is their appeal from those convictions.

We affirm all convictions on the instant appeal save that of Elizabeth Chagra for conspiracy to murder which we reverse for reasons to be assigned.

OPINION

Appellants were tried before Judge William S. Sessions, a federal judge of the Western District of Texas, on charges arising from the murder of John H. Wood, Jr., also a federal judge of that district. Judge Sessions had known and worked with Judge Wood for eight or nine years at the time of the latter's death and admired him. The appellants contend that these facts are sufficient to render the trial court's denial of their motion for recusal reversible error.

Appellants moved for recusal of the trial court pursuant to 28 U.S.C. paragraph 455(a), which provides, ''Any justice, judge, magistrate or referee in bankruptcy of the United States shall disqualify himself in any proceeding in which his impartiality might reasonably be questioned.'' A motion for recusal is committed to the sound discretion of the district judge; denial of such a motion will not be reversed on appeal unless the judge has abused his discretion. Whether an abuse of discretion has occurred is determined ''on the basis of conduct which shows bias or lack of impartiality.'' The alleged biased or prejudiced conduct must, as a general rule, be personal to mandate disqualification. The conduct complained of must, in addition, be such as would cause a reasonable person, knowing all the circumstances, to harbor doubts about the court's impartiality.

We have carefully examined this record; nowhere in it is to be found any remark by Judge Sessions smacking of impropriety in the faintest degree.

Whatever the relationship between the two judges was, it can at most have served to create a degree of hostility toward the actual killers. As such, it is entirely consistent both with a desire that those not guilty be acquitted and with one that the guilty be convicted.

Judge Sessions' conduct advanced by appellants as a basis for his recusal demonstrates only such behavior as one might expect of a civilized and honorable man upon the death of a colleague—and that whether or not he harbored any particular affection for him. As such, it falls far short of casting his impartiality in doubt to reasonable people.

CASE DISCUSSION

Harrelson and others were convicted before Judge William S. Sessions of conspiracy to murder a federal judge, and conspiracy to obstruct justice. One defendant was convicted of murder and conspiring to possess large quantities of marijuana. Defendants appealed. The court of appeals held that the trial judge was not required to recuse himself, even though the murdered judge was his colleague.

Was Judge Sessions personally biased? Was he judicially biased? What facts answer these questions? Can personal and judicial bias be separated in this case? Explain. If you were deciding the case, would you grant Harrelson a different judge? Why? Why not?

MOTIONS TO SUPPRESS CONFESSIONS AND OTHER EVIDENCE

The principal subjects of the motion to suppress are confessions and evidence seized during searches. Most jurisdictions follow the **orthodox rule** that courts, not juries, determine whether evidence is admissible. Many jurisdictions require that courts decide the question of admissibility *prior* to trial. Some states permit the jury to reconsider the admissibility question at trial.

Interests Protected in the Suppression Hearing

The motion to suppress primarily promotes the interest in controlling government misconduct. Controlling the government requires pretrial determination of the admissibility question. If the jury hears or sees the evidence, it may influence their decision. To effectively control government misconduct, convictions must not rest on evidence "tainted" by government misconduct. In suppression, therefore, the interest in insuring that the police act lawfully in obtaining evidence outweighs the interest in obtaining the right result in particular cases. Justice White wrote in *Lego v. Twomey:*

> . . . [T]here may be a relationship between the involuntariness of a confession and its unreliability. But our decision was not based in the slightest on the fear that juries might misjudge the accuracy of confessions and arrive at erroneous determinations of guilt or innocence. That case was not aimed at the possibility of convicting innocent men.
>
> Quite the contrary, we feared that the reliability and truthfulness of even coerced confessions could impermissibly influence a jury's judgment as to voluntariness. The use of coerced confessions, whether true or false, is forbidden because the method used to extract them offends constitutional principles.[24]

The pretrial motion to suppress also promotes the process interests in timeliness and finality, as well as the organizational interest in efficiency and economy. Deciding the admissibility question prior to trial enables the trial to proceed smoothly, without interruptions and delay caused when jurors must leave the room while judges decide whether to admit questionable evidence. The court in *State v. Broxton* considered the advantages and disadvantages of pretrial determination of admissibility.

> There are obvious advantages and disadvantages in a separate hearing either before or at trial. . . . It may be well for the state and defense to know before trial whether the confessions will come in. . . . But on the other hand, when the issue is tried outside the presence of the jury, the issue must then be retried before the jury both under the orthodox and the Massachusetts rules. A replay is rarely as satisfactory, for there is absent the freshness of the first cross-examination. Moreover, the burden upon all concerned, principal and witnesses, is substantial, to say nothing of the burden on the judicial process which already moves at a snail's pace in criminal matters. . . .[25]

Procedures in the Suppression Hearing

According to the United States Supreme Court, the Constitution does not require the state to prove beyond a reasonable doubt that confessions are voluntary—a preponderance of the evidence suffices. A majority of jurisdictions follow this rule; a minority have adopted the proof beyond a reasonable doubt standard. Most jurisdictions require defendants to bear the burden of proof in suppressing evidence seized pursuant to searches. In consent searches, however, the state must prove that defendants voluntarily consented. Defendants also bear the burden of proof in eyewitness identification cases. Defendants must prove that the state illegally denied counsel or conducted an unreasonably suggestive confrontation, such as those discussed in chapter 7.[26]

Pretrial suppression hearings determine not only whether sufficient evidence supports the motion and who bears the burden of presenting it, but also how much weight to give the evidence. One difficult question is whether defendants can challenge affidavits supporting search warrants in pretrial proceedings. The Supreme Court dealt with that question in *Franks v. Delaware*.

CASE

Did the affidavit support probable cause?

Franks v. Delaware

438 U.S. 154, 98 S.Ct. 2674, 57 L.Ed.2d 667 (1978)

[Blackmun, J., delivered the opinion of the Court, in which Brennan, Stewart, White, Marshall, Powell, and Stevens, JJ., joined, Rehnquist, J., filed a dissenting opinion, in which Burger, C. J., joined.]

FACTS

On Friday, March 5, 1976, Mrs. Cynthia Bailey told police in Dover, Del., that she had been confronted in her home earlier that morning by a man with a knife, and that he had sexually assaulted her. She described her assailant's age, race, height, build, and facial hair, and gave a detailed description of his clothing as consisting of a white thermal undershirt, black pants with a silver or gold buckle, a brown leather three-quarter length coat, and a dark knit cap that he wore pulled down around his eyes.

That same day, petitioner Franks coincidentally was taken into custody for an assault involving a 15-year-old girl, Brenda B._____, six days earlier. After his formal arrest, and while awaiting a bail hearing in Family Court, petitioner allegedly stated to Robert McClements, the youth officer accompanying him, that he was surprised the bail hearing was "about Brenda B._____. I know her. I thought you said Bailey. I don't know her." At the time of this statement, the police allegedly had not yet recited to petitioner his rights under Miranda v. Arizona.

On the following Monday, March 8, Officer McClements happened to mention the courthouse incident to a detective, Ronald R. Brooks, who was working on the Bailey case. On March 9, Detective Brooks and Detective Larry D. Gray submitted a sworn affidavit to a Justice of the Peace in Dover, in support of a warrant to search petitioner's apartment. In paragraph 8 of the affidavit's "probable cause page" mention was made of petitioner's statement to McClements. In paragraph 10, it was noted that the description of the assailant given to the police by Mrs. Bailey included the above-mentioned clothing. Finally, the affidavit also described the attempt made by police to confirm that petitioner's typical outfit matched that of the assailant. Paragraph 15 recited: "On Tuesday, 3/9/76, your affiant contacted Mr. James Williams and Mr. Wesley Lucas of the Delaware Youth Center where Jerome Franks is employed and did have personal conversation with both these people." Paragraphs 16 and 17 respectively stated: "Mr. James Williams revealed to your affiant that the normal dress of Jerome Franks does consist of a white knit thermal undershirt and a brown leather jacket," and "Mr. Wesley Lucas revealed to your affiant that in addition to the thermal undershirt and jacket, Jerome Franks often wears a dark green knit hat."

The warrant was issued on the basis of this affidavit. Pursuant to the warrant, police searched petitioner's apartment and found a white thermal undershirt, a knit hat, dark pants, and a leather jacket, and, on petitioner's kitchen table, a single-blade knife. All these ultimately were introduced in evidence at trial.

Prior to the trial, however, petitioner's counsel filed a written motion to suppress the clothing and the knife found in the search; this motion alleged that the warrant on its face did not show probable cause and that the search and seizure were in violation of the Fourth and Fourteenth Amendments. At the hearing on the motion to suppress, defense counsel orally amended the challenge to include an attack on the veracity of the warrant affidavit; he also specifically requested the right to call as witnesses Detective Brooks, Wesley Lucas of the Youth Center, and James D. Morrison, formerly of the Youth Center. Counsel asserted that Lucas and Morrison would testify that neither had been personally interviewed by the warrant affiants, and that, although they might have talked to another police officer, any information given by them to that officer was "somewhat different" from what was recited in the affidavit. Defense counsel charged that the misstatements were included in the affidavit not inadvertently, but in "bad faith."

In rebuttal, the State's attorney argued in detail, (a) that Del. Code Ann., Tit. 11, paragraphs 2306, 2307 (1974), contemplated that any challenge to a search warrant was to be limited to questions of sufficiency based on the face of the affidavit. . . .

The trial court sustained the State's objection to petitioner's proposed evidence. The motion to suppress was denied, and the clothing and knife were admitted as evidence at the ensuing trial. Petitioner was convicted.

On appeal, the Supreme Court of Delaware affirmed. We reverse.

OPINION

Whether the Fourth and Fourteenth Amendments, and the derivative exclusionary rule made applicable to the States . . . ever mandate that a defendant be permitted to attack the veracity of a warrant affidavit after the warrant has been issued and executed, is a question that encounters conflicting values.

Because it is the magistrate who must determine independently whether there is probable cause, it would be an unthinkable imposition upon his authority if a warrant affidavit, revealed after the fact to contain a deliberately or recklessly false statement, were to stand beyond impeachment.

In saying this, however, one must give cognizance to competing values that lead us to impose limitations. They perhaps can best be addressed by noting the arguments of respondent and others against allowing veracity challenges. The arguments are several:

First, respondent argues that the exclusionary rule created is not a personal constitutional right, but only a judicially created remedy extended where its benefit as a deterrent promises to outweigh the societal costs of its use.

Second, respondent argues that a citizen's privacy interests are adequately protected by a requirement that applicants for a warrant submit a sworn affidavit and by the magistrate's independent determination of sufficiency based on the face of the affidavit.

Third, it is argued that the magistrate already is equipped to conduct a fairly vigorous inquiry into the accuracy of the factual affidavit supporting a warrant application. He may question the affiant, or summon other persons to give testimony at the warrant proceeding. The incremental gain from a post-search adversary proceeding, it is said, would not be great.

Fourth, it is argued that it would unwisely diminish the solemnity and moment of the magistrate's proceeding to make his inquiry into probable cause reviewable in regard to veracity. The less final, and less deference paid to, the magistrate's determination of veracity, the less initiative will he use in that task.

Fifth, it is argued that permitting a post-search evidentiary hearing on issues of veracity would confuse the pressing issue of guilt or innocence with the collateral question as to whether there had been official misconduct in the drafting of the affidavit. The weight of criminal dockets, and the need to prevent diversion of attention from the main issue of guilt or innocence, militate against such an added burden on the trial courts.

Sixth and finally, it is argued that a post-search veracity challenge is inappropriate because the accuracy of an affidavit in large part is beyond the control of the affiant. An affidavit may properly be based on hearsay, on fleeting observations, and on tips received from unnamed informants whose identity often will be properly protected from revelation.

None of these considerations is trivial. Indeed, because of them, the rule announced today has a limited scope, both in regard to when exclusion of the seized evidence is mandated, and when a hearing on allegations of misstatements must be accorded. But neither do the considerations cited by respondent and others have a fully controlling weight; we conclude that they are insufficient to justify an absolute ban on post-search impeachment of veracity. On this side of the balance, also, there are pressing considerations:

First, a flat ban on impeachment of veracity could denude the probable-cause requirement of all real meaning.

Second, the hearing before the magistrate not always will suffice to discourage lawless or reckless misconduct. The magistrate has no acquaintance with the information that may contradict the good faith and reasonable basis of the affiant's allegations. The pre-search proceeding will frequently be marked by haste, because of the understandable desire to act before the evidence disappears; this urgency will not always permit the magistrate to make an extended independent examination of the affiant or other witnesses.

Third, the alternative sanctions of a perjury prosecution, administrative discipline, contempt, or a civil suit are not likely to fill the gap. " 'Self-scrutiny is a lofty ideal, but its exaltation reaches new heights if we expect a District Attorney to prosecute himself or his associates for well-meaning violations of the search and seizure clause during a raid the District Attorney or his associates have ordered.' "

Fourth, allowing an evidentiary hearing, after a suitable preliminary proffer of material falsity, would not diminish the importance and solemnity of the warrant-issuing process.

Fifth, the claim that a post-search hearing will confuse the issue of the defendant's guilt with the issue of the State's possible misbehavior is footless. The hearing will not be in the presence of the jury. An issue extraneous to guilt already is examined in any probable-cause determination or review of probable cause.

Sixth and finally, as to the argument that the exclusionary rule should not be extended to a "new" area, we cannot regard any such extension really to be at issue here. Despite the deep skepticism of members of this Court as to the wisdom of extending the exclusionary rule to collateral areas, such as civil or grand jury proceedings, the Court has not questioned, in the absence of a more efficacious sanction, the continued application of the rule to suppress evidence from the State's case where a Fourth Amendment violation has been substantial and deliberate.

There is, of course, a presumption of validity with respect to the affidavit supporting the search warrant. To mandate an evidentiary hearing, the challenger's attack must be more than conclusory and must be supported by more than a mere desire to cross-examine. There must be allegations of deliberate falsehood or of reckless disregard for the truth, and those allegations must be accompanied by an offer of proof. They should point out specifically the portion of the warrant affidavit that is claimed to be false; and they should be accompanied by a statement of supporting reasons. Affidavits or sworn or otherwise reliable statements of witnesses should be furnished, or their absence satisfactorily explained. Allegations of negligence or innocent mistake are insufficient. The deliberate falsity or reckless disregard whose impeachment is permitted today is only that of the affiant, not of any nongovernmental informant. Finally, if these requirements are met, and if, when material that is the subject of the alleged falsity or reckless disregard is set to one side, there remains sufficient content in the warrant affidavit to support a finding of probable cause, no hearing is required. On the other hand, if the remaining content is insufficient, the defendant is entitled, under the Fourth and Fourteenth Amendments, to his hearing. Whether he will prevail at that hearing is, of course, another issue.

The judgment of the Supreme Court of Delaware is reversed, and the case is remanded for further proceedings not inconsistent with this opinion.

It is so ordered.

DISSENT

[Mr. Justice Rehnquist, with whom the Chief Justice joins, dissenting.]

The Court's opinion in this case carefully identifies the factors which militate against the result which it reaches, and emphasizes their weight in attempting to limit the circumstances under which an affidavit supporting a search warrant may be impeached. I am not ultimately persuaded, however, that the Court is correct as a matter of constitutional law that the impeachment of such an affidavit must be permitted under the circumstances described by the Court, and I am thoroughly persuaded that the barriers which the Court believes that it is erecting against misuse of the impeachment process are frail indeed.

CASE DISCUSSION

Prior to Frank's Delaware state trial on rape and related charges in connection with his motion to suppress on Fourth Amendment grounds items of clothing and a knife found in a search of his apartment, he challenged the truthfulness of certain factual statements made in the police affidavit supporting the warrant to search his apartment. He sought to call witnesses to disprove the misstatements in the affidavit. The trial court sustained the government's objections to such proposed testimony and denied the motion to suppress. The clothing and knife were admitted at the trial, and Franks was convicted. The Delaware Supreme Court affirmed, holding that a defendant under *no* circumstances may challenge the veracity of a sworn statement used by the police to obtain a search warrant. On *certiorari,* the United States Supreme Court reversed and remanded.

What are the competing values that the Court balanced to reach its decision? Would you balance the way the Court did? Explain. Does the Court sacrifice efficiency, timeliness, and finality to individual rights and the search for truth? Or, is the Court attempting to ''control the police''?

≡ SUMMARY

Following the preliminary hearing or grand jury review, formal proceedings increasingly focus on procedural regularity and the search for truth through the adversarial process. At the same time, the informal negotiating process continues, furthering the organizational interests in efficiency, harmony, and predictability. Most felony defendants plead guilty, or strike plea bargains, during this stage in the criminal process. The decisions to proceed to trial, to file pretrial motions, and to enter into plea negotiations all draw upon public resources and result in greater expense to defendants of means, continued deprivations of liberty to poorer defendants, and increasing anxiety to all defendants and their families.

The pretrial motions grew out of the ancient common law pleadings that severely restricted defendants to pleas of guilty or not guilty, pleas to the court's jurisdiction, to the technical sufficiency of the indictment, double jeopardy, and the statute of limitations. Indictments and informations that form the legal basis for arraignment remain the only government pleadings. Defendants can plead guilty, not guilty, *nolo contendere,* or insanity. The pretrial motions have replaced other criminal defendants' pleadings.

The principal pretrial motions discussed in this chapter have mainly to do with (1) double jeopardy; (2) speedy trial; (3) change of venue; (4) change of judge; (5) suppression of evidence. The essence of double jeopardy procedural law is that government should have "one fair shot" at convicting defendants. To allow more threatens interests in finality and timeliness, causes defendants undue anxiety, and subjects both the government and individual defendants to unwarranted expense and other burdens. The right to speedy trial has ancient roots: in 1187 King Henry II promised his subjects "speedy trials." Speedy trial promotes interests in timeliness and finality and prevents the government from subjecting individual defendants to undue anxiety, expense, and loss of liberty. The motions to change venue and judge mainly relate to balancing the interest in obtaining the correct result by reducing prejudice that might corrupt the truth-finding function against the community interest in trying defendants in the place where they committed their crimes. Finally, the motion to suppress balances the legal interests in obtaining the correct result and procedural regularity and the societal interests in sanctioning abuse of government power and controlling crime.

Once the parties have resolved the issues raised by pretrial motions, either in formal hearings or informally by plea bargaining, the decision to release defendants or to proceed to the final decision point—determining innocence or guilt—occurs. The determination of guilt can take place either formally in trial or by guilty pleas, the subjects of chapter 12.

≡ QUESTIONS FOR REVIEW AND DISCUSSION

1. What predominant interests do pretrial motions promote?
2. Define double jeopardy and explain its primary purpose.
3. When does time start to elapse for speedy trial purposes?
4. What factors are taken into account in determining whether to grant a motion to change venue?

5. What is the difference between personal and judicial bias? Which is used to determine whether to grant a change of judge?

6. What is the orthodox rule in deciding the admissibility of evidence?

7. What interest does suppression primarily promote?

≡ NOTES

1. *Palko v. Connecticut,* 302 U.S. 319, 58 S.Ct. 149, 82 L.Ed. 288 (1937).

2. *Crist v. Bretz,* 437 U.S. 28, 98 S.Ct. 2156, 57 L.Ed.2d 24 (1978).

3. *United States v. Perez,* 22 U.S. (9 Wheat.) 579, 6 L.Ed. 165 (1824).

4. *Illinois v. Somerville,* 410 U.S. 458, 93 S.Ct. 1066, 35 L.Ed.2d 425 (1973); *Wade v. Hunter,* 336 U.S. 684 (1949).

5. *Klopfer v. North Carolina,* 386 U.S. 213, 87 S.Ct. 988, 18 L.Ed.2d 1 (1967) (speedy trial clause applies to states).

6. *Report to the Nation on Crime and Justice,* 2nd ed. (Washington D.C.: Bureau of Justice Statistics, 1988), 123.

7. *United States v. Marion,* 404 U.S. 307, 92 S.Ct. 455, 30 L.Ed.2d 468 (1971).

8. *United States v. Marion,* 404 U.S. 307, 92 S.Ct. 455, 30 L.Ed.2d 468 (1971) (attaches at arrest); *Dixon v. State,* 605 P.2d 882 (Alaska 1980) (Alaska speedy trial provision extends to period prior to charge).

9. *Strunk v. United States,* 412 U.S. 434, 93 S.Ct. 2260, 37 L.Ed.2d 56 (1973); Anthony Amsterdam, "Speedy Criminal Trial: Rights and Remedies," *Stanford Law Review* 27(1975):525.

10. *Henderson v. United States,* 476 U.S. 321, 106 S.Ct. 1871, 90 L.Ed.2d 299 (1986).

11. *United States v. May,* 771 F.2d 980 (6th Cir. 1985); *United States v. Gallardo,* 773 F.2d 1496 (9th Cir. 1985).

12. 18 U.S.C.A. § 3162(a)(1)(2); Alaska Crim. R. 45(g); Washington Sup.Ct.Rule 33(1).

13. *Federal Criminal Code and Rules,* (St. Paul: West Publishing Company, 1988), 89, rule 21(a).

14. 384 U.S. 333 at 363, 86 S.Ct. 1507 at 1552, 16 L.Ed.2d 600 (1966).

15. *Swindler v. State,* 267 Ark. 418, 592 S.W.2d 91 (1979).

16. *Mallott v. State,* 608 P.2d 737 (Alaska 1980).

17. *Sheppard v. Maxwell,* 384 U.S. 333, 86 S.Ct. 1507, 16 L.Ed.2d 600 (1966); *Schenck v. United States,* 249 U.S. 47, 39 S.Ct. 247, 63 L.Ed. 470 (1919) (clear and present danger).

18. *Gannett Co., Inc. v. DePasquale* 443 U.S. 368, 99 S.Ct. 2898, 61 L.Ed.2d 608 (1979) (public trial personal right of defendant); *Richmond Newspapers, Inc. v. Virginia,* 448 U.S. 555, 100 S.Ct. 2814, 65 L.Ed.2d 973 (1980) (public's right of access to criminal trial).

19. *Globe Newspaper Company v. Superior Court,* 457 U.S. 596, 102 S.Ct. 2613, 73 L.Ed.2d 248 (1982).

20. *Tumey v. Ohio,* 273 U.S. 510, 47 S.Ct. 437, 71 L.Ed. 749 (1927).

21. *Mayberry v. Pennsylvania,* 400 U.S. 455, 91 S.Ct. 499, 27 L.Ed.2d 532 (1971) (defendant repeatedly insulted and vilified trial judge and at conclusion of trial was pronounced guilty of 11 contempts and sentenced to 11 to 22 years, judgment of contempt vacated).

22. Quoted in Frank, "Disqualification of Judges," *Yale Law Journal* 56(1947):605.

23. Ibid.

24. 404 U.S. 477, 92 S.Ct. 619, 30 L.Ed.2d 618 (1972).

25. 49 N.J. 373, 230 A.2d 489 (1967).

26. James B. Haddad, et al., *Criminal Procedure,* 3d ed. (St. Paul: West Publishing Company, 1987), 970.

Chapter Twelve

Conviction by Trial and Guilty Plea

CHAPTER OUTLINE

CHAPTER MAIN POINTS

1. Most convictions result from guilty pleas, not trial.

2. Conviction by trial promotes interests in fact-finding by the adversary process, procedural regularity, and community participation in criminal justice administration.

3. Conviction by guilty plea promotes fact-finding, efficiency, harmony, and predictability.

4. The right to jury trial does *not* include the right to trial by jury in *all* criminal cases, to trial by a *twelve*-member jury, or to conviction by a *unanimous* guilty verdict.

5. The presentation of evidence is the high point in the adversary criminal process.

6. Trials promote the search for truth and procedural regularity over efficiency, harmony, and economy.

7. The empirical evidence does not necessarily support the conclusion that conviction by guilty plea promotes organizational interests at the expense of obtaining the correct result.

8. Defendants forfeit their rights against self-incrimination, to trial by jury, and to confront their accusers and witnesses when they plead guilty.

9. Guilty pleas do not violate the Constitution if defendants plead guilty *knowingly* and *voluntarily*.

CHAPTER KEY TERMS

Allen **charge** judges encouraging dead-locked juries to reach a verdict

challenge for cause removal of prospective juror upon showing impartiality

hearsay testimony testimony introduced as truth by a witness not present in court

hung jury unable to reach a verdict after protracted deliberations

judgment the final outcome of the case

jury instructions judge's explanation of law to the jury

jury nullification jury's authority to reach a not guilty verdict despite proof of guilt

jury challenges removal of prospective jurors

missing witness instruction jurors can draw negative inference from prosecution witnesses' failure to testify

moral seriousness standard Sixth Amendment right to jury trial extends to morally serious misdemeanors

negotiated plea guilty plea entered in return for concessions from the state

pattern instructions published, standard jury instructions

peremptory challenges jurors removed without showing cause

res gestae witnesses eyewitnesses

sequester the jury put jury in room to deliberate without outside interference

stipulation fact not contested

straight plea guilty plea without negotiation

voir dire examination of prospective jurors

☰ CONTRASTS BETWEEN CONVICTION BY GUILTY PLEA AND TRIAL

Conviction results in the greatest deprivations in the criminal process—loss of property, liberty, privacy, and perhaps even life itself. Hence, the factual foundation or quantum of proof required to convict is the highest—proof beyond a reasonable doubt—and the procedures to determine it are the most elaborate in the formal criminal process. Guilty pleas determine conviction in the vast majority of cases. Some of these guilty pleas result from negotiations, but many are "straight" pleas, or pleas of guilty without negotiation. Trials, on the other hand, result from pleas of not guilty and account for only about 10 to 15 percent of the convictions in criminal cases. The process of conviction promotes the same interests as decisions at other stages in the criminal process. The trial promotes fact-finding by the adversary process, procedural regularity, and public participation in criminal proceedings. The guilty plea promotes efficiency, economy, harmony, and speed. Plea negotiations also promote fact-finding, utilizing informal discussion and the give and take that occur in reaching an agreement over the plea.

≡ CONVICTION BY TRIAL

Article III, § 2, of the United States Constitution commands:

> The Trial of all Crimes, except in Cases of Impeachment, shall be by Jury; and such Trial shall be held in the State where the Crimes shall have been committed.

The Fifth Amendment guarantees:

> No person shall be . . . compelled in any criminal case to be a witness against himself. . . .

The Sixth Amendment mandates:

> In all criminal prosecutions, the accused shall enjoy the right to a speedy and public trial, by an impartial jury of the State and District wherein the crime shall have been committed . . . to be confronted with the witnesses against him, . . . and to have the assistance of Counsel for his defense.

Conviction by trial operates within this constitutional framework. Of course, defendants can waive their right to conviction by trial, as they obviously do when they plead guilty.

Jury Trial

Jury trial has an ancient history, with roots in the societies of the Teutonic tribes in Germany and the Normans before their conquest of England. Certainly, the Assizes of Clarendon in 1187 and, more directly, the Magna Carta in 1215 reveal traces of its origins. Jury trial appeared in the English Bill of Rights in 1689; it came to America with the English colonists. From the start, the colonists resented royal interference with the right to jury trial. Complaints regarding that interference appear in the Stamp Act Congress's resolutions, the First Continental Congress's resolves, and the Declaration of Independence. Article III, § 2 of the United States Constitution reflects that history, and the Sixth Amendment reveals that the drafters of the Bill of Rights believed that the right needed even stronger assurances. Every state has adopted a right to trial by jury provision in its constitution, and the Supreme Court has extended its protection to the states through the due process clause of the Fourteenth Amendment.[1]

Jury trial promotes several interests. It checks and balances government power by interposing an independent body between the state with all its resources and a single individual. Furthermore, it balances official power with citizen participation in criminal law enforcement. In addition, it guarantees that accused citizens who prefer that other citizens decide their innocence or guilt shall have that preference honored. In extending the Sixth Amendment's jury trial right to the states, Justice White wrote:

> The guarantees of jury trial . . . reflect a profound judgment about the way in which law should be enforced and justice administered. . . . Providing an accused with the right to be tried by a jury of his peers gave him an inestimable safeguard against the corrupt or overzealous prosecutor and against the compliant, biased, or eccentric judge. . . . Beyond this, the jury trial . . . reflect a fundamental exercise about the exercise of official power—a reluctance to entrust plenary powers over the life and liberty of the citizen to one judge or to a group of judges. Fear of unchecked power, so typical of our State and Federal Governments in other respects, found expression in the criminal law in this insistence upon community participation in the determination of guilt or innocence.[2]

Despite this long history, and the several clauses in the Constitution commanding trial by jury, the courts have not taken literally the words "all crimes" from Article III, § 2, and "all criminal prosecutions" in the Sixth Amendment. The Supreme Court has ruled that the right to jury trial excludes "petty offenses" from its scope. The Court based its conclusion on the historical reality of the common law that did not protect petty offenses by jury trial.[3]

In the absence of specific legislation drawing a line, the Court has used a potential six months' imprisonment to divide serious from petty crimes. However, the "moral quality" of some offenses might take them outside the petty offense category even if the penalty is less than six months' imprisonment. Under the **moral seriousness test,** courts have held that defendants have a right to jury trial in conspiring to deceive immigration officials, driving while intoxicated, and shoplifting cases despite the minor penalties ordinarily attached to them.[4]

JURY SIZE. The Supreme Court at one time ruled that the right to jury trial included the right to the historical twelve jurors; it has since retreated from that position. In upholding Florida's six-member jury, Justice White concluded that although the Court could "not pretend" to know the Framers' intent, and that the number twelve was a historical accident, based on superstition about the number itself—twelve apostles, twelve tribes or Israel, twelve stones—these are not sufficient reasons to maintain the twelve-member jury in the twentieth century. Rather, the Court ruled that numbers sufficient to achieve the goals of the jury—protecting the innocent from unfounded prosecution, providing checks and balances, arriving at the truth, enabling community representation in law enforcement—satisfied the right to jury trial requirement. Furthermore, according to the Court, twelve-member juries give the defendant neither an advantage in finding individuals more likely to acquit, nor a significantly better chance of obtaining a whole jury representative of the whole community.

> . . . [T]hat the jury at common law was composed of precisely 12 is a historical accident, unnecessary to effect the purposes of the jury system and wholly without significance "except to mystics." To read the Sixth Amendment as forever codifying a feature so incidental to the real purpose of the Amendment is to ascribe a blind formalism to the Framers which would require considerably more evidence than we have been able to discover in the history and language of the Constitution or in the reasoning of our past decisions.[5]

The twelve-member jury has strong supporters, despite the Court's dismissal of it as superstitious, supported only by mystics. Justice Harlan called the Court's argument "much too thin." If the number twelve was merely an accident, it was one that "has recurred without interruption since the 14th century." Furthermore, Justice Harlan argued, if "12 jurors are not essential, why are six?"

> Can it be doubted that a unanimous jury of 12 provides a greater safeguard than a majority vote of six? The uncertainty that will henceforth plague the meaning of trial by jury is itself a further reason for not hoisting the anchor of history.

Finally, Justice Harlan contended,

> The [Court's] circumvention of history is compounded by the cavalier disregard of numerous pronouncements of this Court that reflect the understanding of the jury as one of twelve members and have fixed expectations accordingly.[6]

Support for the twelve-member jury comes not only from judges but also from scholars. Social scientists have found that juries with twelve members both obtain more reliable verdicts and represent more of the community than do members with fewer than twelve members.

Suppose that in a given community, 90 percent of the people share one viewpoint and the remaining 10 percent have a different viewpoint. Suppose further that we draw 100 twelve-member and 100 six-member juries. Using standard statistical methods, it can be predicted that approximately 72 of the twelve-member juries will contain a representative of the 10 percent minority, as compared to only 47 juries composed of six persons. This difference is by no means negligible.[7]

The Supreme Court addressed the twelve-member jury in *Ballew v. Georgia*.

CASE

Does a five-member jury guarantee a jury trial?

Ballew v. Georgia

435 U.S. 223, 98 S.Ct. 1029, 55 L.Ed.2d 234 (1978)

[Blackmun, J., announced the Court's judgment and delivered an opinion, in which Stevens, J., joined. Stevens, J., filed a concurring statement. White, J., filed a statement concurring in the judgment. Powell, J., filed an opinion concurring in the judgment, in which Burger, C. J., and Rehnquist, J., joined. Brennan, J., filed a separate opinion, in which Stewart and Marshall, JJ., joined.]

FACTS

In November 1973 petitioner Claude Davis Ballew was the manager of the Paris Adult Theatre at 320 Peachtree Street, Atlanta, Ga. On November 9 two investigators from the Fulton County Solicitor General's office viewed at the theater a motion picture film entitled "Behind the Green Door."

On September 14, 1974, petitioner was charged in a two-count misdemeanor accusation with "distributing obscene materials in violation of the Georgia Code in that the said accused did, knowing the obscene nature thereof, exhibit a motion picture film entitled 'Behind the Green Door' that contained obscene and indecent scenes."

Petitioner was brought to trial in the Criminal Court of Fulton County. After a jury of 5 persons had been selected and sworn, petitioner moved that the court impanel a jury of 12 persons. That court, however, tried its misdemeanor cases before juries of five persons pursuant to Ga. Const., Art. 6. paragraph 16, § 1. Petitioner contended that for an obscenity trial, a jury of only five was constitutionally inadequate to assess the contemporary standards of the community. He also argued that the Sixth and Fourteenth Amendments required a jury of at least six members in criminal cases.

The motion for a 12-person jury was overruled, and the trial went on to its conclusion before the 5-person jury that had been impaneled. At the conclusion of the trial, the jury deliberated for 38 minutes and returned a verdict of guilty on both counts of the accusation. The court imposed a sentence of one year and a $1,000 fine on each count, the periods of incarceration to run concurrently and to be suspended upon payment of the fines.

The Supreme Court of Georgia denied certiorari. We granted certiorari.

OPINION

The Fourteenth Amendment guarantees the right of trial by jury in all state nonpetty criminal cases.

The purpose of the jury trial, is to prevent oppression by the Government. This purpose is attained by the participation of the community in determinations of guilt and by the application of the common sense of laymen who, as jurors, consider the case.

Rather than requiring 12 members, then, the Sixth Amendment mandated a jury only of sufficient size to promote group deliberation, to insulate members from outside intimidation, and to provide a representative cross-section of the community.

When the Court in *Williams* permitted the reduction in jury size—or, to put it another way, when it held that a jury of six was not unconstitutional—it expressly reserved ruling on the issue whether a number smaller than six passed constitutional scrutiny. The Court refused to speculate when this so-called "slippery slope" would become too steep. We face now, however, the two-fold question whether a further reduction in the size of the state criminal trial jury does make the grade too dangerous, that is, whether it inhibits the functioning of the jury as an institution to a significant degree, and, if so, whether any state interest counterbalances and justifies the disruption so as to preserve its constitutionality.

First, recent empirical data suggest that progressively smaller juries are less likely to foster effective group deliberation. At some point, this decline leads to inaccurate fact-finding and incorrect application of the common sense of the community to the facts. The smaller the group, the less likely are members to make critical contributions necessary for the solution of a given problem. As juries decrease in size, then, they are less likely to have members who remember each of the important pieces of evidence or argument. Furthermore, the smaller the group, the less likely it is to overcome the biases of its members to obtain an accurate result. When individual and group decision-making were compared, it was seen that groups performed better because prejudices of individuals were frequently counterbalanced, and objectivity resulted.

Second, the data now raise doubts about the accuracy of the results achieved by smaller and smaller panels. Statistical studies suggest that the risk of convicting an innocent person rises as the size of the jury diminishes.

Third, the data suggest that the verdicts of jury deliberation in criminal cases will vary as juries become smaller, and that the variance amounts to an imbalance to the detriment of one side, the defense.

Fourth, as juries decrease in size foretells problems not only for jury decisionmaking, but also for the representation of minority groups in the community. The Court repeatedly has held that meaningful community participation cannot be attained with the exclusion of minorities or other identifiable groups from jury service.

While we adhere to, and reaffirm our holding in *Williams v. Florida,* these studies, most of which have been made since *Williams* was decided in 1970, lead us to conclude that the purpose and functioning of the jury in a criminal trial is seriously impaired, and to a constitutional degree, by a reduction in size to below six members.

With the reduction in the number of jurors below six creating a substantial threat to Sixth and Fourteenth Amendment guarantees, we must consider whether any interest of the State justifies the reduction. We find no significant state advantage in reducing the number of jurors from six to five.

The States utilize juries of less than 12 primarily for administrative reasons. Savings in court time and in financial costs are claimed to justify the reductions. A reduction in size from six to five or four or even three would save the States little. They could reduce slightly the daily allowances, but with a reduction from six to five the saving would be minimal.

The judgment of the Court of Appeals is reversed, and the case is remanded for further proceedings not inconsistent with this opinion.

It is so ordered.

CASE DISCUSSION

Ballew, charged with a misdemeanor was tried before a five-member jury pursuant to Georgia law, and convicted. On writ of *certiorari,* the Supreme Court reversed the judgment, holding that the five-member jury violated Ballew's right to jury trial. The Court remanded the case for proceedings consistent with its decision. Why does a six-member jury satisfy the Constitution but not a five-member jury, according to the Court? How does the Court arrive at its conclusion? Does social science research provide a better guide to how many jurors should constitute a jury than history? Explain your answer.

VERDICTS. The Supreme Court has followed a pattern in ruling on unanimity similar to that in its ruling on numbers of jurors. In an early case, the Court held that the Sixth Amendment guaranteed conviction by unanimous jury verdicts. In 1972 in *Apodaca v. Oregon,* the Court decided that verdicts of 11-1 and 10-2 did not violate two convicted felons' right to jury trail.

A requirement of unanimity, . . . does not materially contribute to . . . [the jury's] commonsense judgment. . . . [A] jury will come to such a verdict as long as it consists of a group of laymen representative of a cross section of the community who have the duty and the opportunity to deliberate, free from outside attempts at intimidation, on the question of a defendant's guilt. In terms of this function we perceive no difference between juries required to act unanimously and those permitted to convict or acquit by votes of 10 to two or 11 to one. Requiring unanimity would obviously produce hung juries in some situations where nonunanimous juries will convict or acquit. But in either case, the interest of the defendant in having the judgment of his peers interposed between himself and the officers of the state who prosecute and judge him is equally well served.[8]

The Court also rejected the argument that proof beyond a reasonable doubt required unanimous verdicts. In a companion case to *Apodaca*, *Johnson v. Louisiana*, the Court upheld a 9-3 majority–jury guilty verdict in a robbery case. Justice White wrote for the Supreme Court majority (5-4):

nine jurors—a substantial majority of the jury—were convinced by the evidence. Disagreement of the three jurors does not alone establish reasonable doubt, particularly when such a heavy majority of the jury, after having considered the dissenters' views, remains convinced of guilt.[9]

The *Apodaca* and *Johnson* decisions have received harsh criticism from some quarters. Critics maintain that unanimous verdicts instill confidence in the criminal justice process, guarantee that the jury carefully reviews the evidence, insure hearing and considering minority viewpoints, prevent government oppression, support the principle that convicting innocent defendants is worse than freeing guilty ones, and fulfill the proof beyond a reasonable doubt requirement.[10]

The Court has not answered the question how many votes short of unanimity satisfy the Sixth Amendment. However, it did address the problem of what happens when there are neither twelve members nor unanimity. A unanimous Court struck down a Louisiana provision that misdemeanors punishable by more than six months "shall be tried before a jury of six persons, five of whom must concur to render a verdict."

The Court reasoned that to preserve the right to jury trial, they needed to draw a line at verdicts of six-member juries, noting that only two states permitted such verdicts; hence, the "near-uniform judgment of the nation" provided a useful guide to draw the line on the other side of the Louisiana provision.[11]

JURY NULLIFICATION. The jury's function—except in a few states—is to decide the facts and apply them to the law. Despite the jury's duty to apply the facts to the law, juries have the power to acquit even when the facts clearly point to conviction. Jury acquittals are final; the prosecution cannot appeal them. Juries usually acquit despite proof beyond a reasonable doubt when they sympathize with defendants or when the state prosecutes defendants for violating unpopular laws. Acquittals in mercy killings—technically, first-degree murder—represent one obvious example of **jury nullification,** the practice of acquitting in the face of sufficient proof to convict.

Jury nullification has an ancient lineage. The

pages of history shine on instances of the jury's exercise of its prerogative to disregard uncontradicted evidence and instructions of the judge.[12]

In the famous Peter Zenger case, the jury flouted the facts and the judge's instructions, to acquit Zenger of the charge of sedition. The Supreme Court has not confronted the question directly, but its language supports the conclusion that the Sixth Amendment encompasses jury nullification.

If a jury may rightfully disregard the direction of the court in matters of law, and determine for themselves what the law is in the particular case before them, it is difficult to perceive any legal ground upon which a verdict of conviction can be set aside by the court as being against law.[13]

Nullification promotes, as perhaps no other doctrine in criminal procedure, the interest in community participation in criminal law enforcement. Juries become safety valves for exceptional cases, and act not only on the law strictly defined in judges' instructions but also on "informal communication from the total culture."[14]

Decision Point

Oliver North was charged with several crimes arising out of the sale of arms to Iran and the transfer of funds to the Nicaraguan "contras." He was tried in the Federal District Court for the District of Columbia on twelve counts, including lying to Congress, shredding documents, and diverting government funds to his private use. His defense was that he was following the orders of his superiors. Judge Gerhard Gesell specifically instructed the jury that it was no defense to commit a crime at the order or wish of a superior. No one can legally order another person to commit a crime; no responsible person can comply with such an order and hope to escape criminal liability.

The jury deliberated for twelve days, returning verdicts of not guilty on nine of the twelve counts on the ground that Oliver North was only following the orders of his superiors. This verdict directly contradicted Judge Gesell's instructions concerning the superior orders defense. Repeatedly in interviews following the verdict, jurors indicated that they saw North as a scapegoat who was unfairly blamed for following the instructions of his superiors, and that is why, they readily revealed, they had acquitted him on the nine counts. The jurors voted to convict on only those crimes—shredding documents, diverting government funds to his personal use, and accepting a home security system—that they believed North decided on his own to commit.

North's attorney intends to appeal the convictions on several grounds. The government cannot appeal the acquittals, despite the jury's clear nullification of the law that does not permit the defense of superior orders in this case. Initial surveys indicate that the jury's nullification reflects widespread public agreement that North should not pay for doing what his superiors wanted him to do.[15]

JURY SELECTION. The equal protection clause of the Fourteenth Amendment prohibits juries that systematically exclude members of the defendant's racial, gender, ethnic, religious, or other group. The right to an impartial jury also requires that juries represent a fair cross-section of the community. To meet these constitutional mandates, the Federal Jury Selection and Service Act requires that juries be

selected at random from a fair cross-section of the community in the district or division wherein the court convenes, and further that

> [n]o citizen shall be excluded from service as a grand or petit juror in the district courts of the United States on account of race, color, religion, sex, national origin, or economic status.[16]

Most states adopt similar provisions. To implement them, jurisdictions select jurors at random from the local census, tax rolls, city directories, telephone books, and drivers' license lists. Some states, mainly in New England and the South, use the "key-man" system in which civic and political leaders recommend people they know. Understandably, the "key-man" system undergoes repeated challenges that it does not represent a fair cross-section of the community and that it discriminates against various segments in the community.[17]

Most prospective jurors ask to be excused. Courts rarely refuse their requests; they find "it easier, administratively and financially, to excuse unwilling people. . . ." Common excuses include economic hardship, advanced age, illness, need to care for small children, and distance between home and the courthouse. Jurisdictions frequently disqualify some groups from jury service: persons below voting age, convicted felons, persons not able to write and read English. Some categories also receive exemptions because of their occupations: doctors, pharmacists, teachers, clergy, lawyers, judges, criminal justice professionals, and some other public employees.[18]

IMPARTIAL JURY. From the panel of prospective jurors, the attorneys for the government and the defendant select the jurors who will actually serve. The principal method for assuring the trial jury's impartiality is the **voir dire**—literally, "to speak the truth"—in which defense and prosecution examine prospective jurors. Attorneys for both sides can have prospective jurors they find unacceptable removed by means of **jury challenges.** Attorneys for both sides have **peremptory challenges,** or the power to remove jurors without showing cause why. The number of challenges depends on the jurisdiction. At common law, prosecutors had an unlimited number of peremptory challenges in felony cases; the defendant had thirty-five. Today the numbers vary depending on the jurisdiction. In the federal system each side has twenty peremptories in capital offenses, three in misdemeanors. In felony cases, the defendant has ten and the government six. Lawyers use peremptory challenges to eliminate prospective jurors who appear either sympathetic to the other side, or at least not sympathetic to their side.

The government and defense also have an unlimited number of **challenges for cause,** challenges based on showing that particular prospective jurors would deny defendants an impartial jury trial. Attorneys use challenges for cause only in those instances where they can demonstrate juror bias to the judge's satisfaction. Neither the government nor the defense exercises the challenge for cause frequently—ordinarily from one to three to assemble a jury of twelve.[19]

The voir dire provides the opportunity for lawyers to decide whether to accept prospective jurors; hence, their freedom to question prospective jurors bears heavily on their making sound decisions about jurors' impartiality. Trial judges have considerable discretion to determine the scope of voir dire questioning; appellate courts rarely reverse on the grounds that the trial judge refused to permit certain questions. *Ham v. South Carolina* was one of the few instances in which the defendant achieved reversal for a judge's refusal to permit his counsel to ask a question. Ham was a bearded, black civil rights activist convicted of marijuana possession. His counsel tried to elicit prospective jurors' opinions about their prejudice about either Ham's race or his beard. The trial court prohibited the questioning. The Supreme Court ruled in the defendant's favor regarding the trial judge's refusal to inquire about race prejudice, but not for his refusal to question the prospective jurors about Ham's beard.

> While we cannot say that prejudice against people with beards might not have been harbored by one or more of the potential jurors in this case, this is the beginning and not the end of the inquiry as to whether the Fourteenth Amendment required the trial judge to interrogate the prospective jurors about such possible prejudice. Given the traditionally broad discretion accorded to the trial judge in conducting voir dire, and or inability to constitutionally distinguish possible prejudice against beards from a host of other possible similar prejudices, we do not believe the petitioners' constitutional rights were violated when the trial judge refused to put this question.[20]

The courts have narrowly applied the ruling on questioning race prejudice. In *Dukes v. Waitkevitch,* for example, the First Circuit Court of Appeals ruled that the trial court did not commit constitutional error when it refused to inquire into race prejudice in a case where the black defendant participated in a gang rape of white women. In capital cases, however, the Supreme Court has ruled otherwise.

> The risk of racial prejudice infecting capital sentencing proceedings is especially serious in light of the complete finality of the death sentence. . . . We hold that a capital defendant accused of an interracial crime is entitled to have prospective jurors informed of the race of the victim and questioned on the issue of racial bias.[21]

Balanced against the interest in obtaining impartial juries to assure accurate results as well as promote the societal interests in community participation in law enforcement, prejudice-free proceedings, and public confidence in criminal justice, are the organizational interests in efficiency, economy, and dispatch.

> It is of course true that any examination on the voir dire is a clumsy and imperfect way of detecting suppressed emotional commitments to which all of us are to some extent subject, unconsciously or subconsciously. It is of the nature of our deepest antipathies that often we do not admit them even to ourselves; but when that is so, nothing but an examination, utterly impracticable in a courtroom, will disclose them, an examination extending even at times for months, and even then unsuccessful. No such examination is required; indeed, it was exactly the purpose of Criminal Rule 24(a), which allows the judge to frame questions on the *voir dire* if he thinks best, to avoid interminable examinations sometimes extending for weeks on end that had frequently resulted from the former method. If trial by jury is not to break down by its own weight, it is not feasible to prove more than the upper levels of a juror's mind.[22]

The United States Supreme Court dealt with the issue of the death-qualified jury in *Lockhart v. McCree.*

CASE

Are 'death-qualified" juries impartial?

Lockhart v. McCree

476 U.S. 162, 106 S.Ct 1758, 90 L.Ed.2d 137 (1986)

[Rehnquist, J., delivered the opinion of the Court, in which Burger, C.J., and White, Powell, and O'Connor, JJ., joined. Blackmun, J., concurred in the result. Marshall, J., filed a dissenting opinion, in which Brennan and Stevens, JJ., joined.]

FACTS

In the case we address the question. Does the Constitution prohibit the removal for cause, prior to the guilt phase of a bifurcated capital trial, of prospective jurors whose opposition to the death penalty is so strong that it would prevent or substantially impair the performance of their duties as jurors at the sentencing phase of the trial? We hold that it does not.

On the morning of February 14, 1978, a gift shop and service station in Camden, Arkansas, was robbed, and Evelyn Boughton, the owner, was shot and killed. That afternoon, Ardia McCree was arrested in Hot Springs, Arkansas, after a police officer saw him driving a maroon and white Lincoln Continental matching an eye-witness' description of the getaway car used by Boughton's killer. The next evening, McCree admitted to police that he had been at Boughton's shop at the time of the murder. He claimed, however, that a tall black stranger wearing an overcoat first asked him for a ride, then took McCree's rifle out of the back of the car and used it to kill Boughton. McCree also claimed that, after the murder, the stranger rode with McCree to a nearby dirt road, got out of the car, and walked away with the rifle. McCree's story was contradicted by two eyewitnesses who saw McCree's car between the time of the murder and the time when McCree said the stranger got out and walked away, and who stated that they saw only one person in the car. The police found McCree's rifle and a bank bag from Boughton's shop alongside the dirt road. Based on ballistics tests, an F.B.I. officer testified that the bullet that killed Boughton had been fired from McCree's rifle.

McCree was charged with capital felony murder. In accordance with Arkansas law, the trial judge at voir dire removed for cause, over McCree's objections, those prospective jurors who stated that they could not under any circumstances vote for the imposition of the death penalty. Eight prospective jurors were excluded for this reason. The jury convicted McCree of capital felony murder, but rejected the State's request for the death penalty, instead setting McCree's punishment at life imprisonment without parole.

The District Court held a hearing on the "death qualification" issue in July 1981, receiving in evidence numerous social science studies concerning the attitudes and beliefs of *"Witherspoon-*excludables," [jurors opposed to the death penalty] along with the potential effects of excluding them from the jury prior to the guilt phase of a bifurcated capital trial. In August 1983, the court concluded, based on the social science evidence, that "death qualification" produced juries that "were more prone to convict" capital defendants than "non-death-qualified" juries.

The Eighth Circuit found "substantial evidentiary support" for the District Court's conclusion and affirmed the grant of habeas relief on the ground that such removal for cause violated McCree's constitutional right to a jury selected from a fair cross-section of the community.

OPINION

Of the six studies introduced by McCree that at least purported to deal with the central issue in this case, namely, the potential effects on the determination of guilt or innocence of excluding "Witherspoon excludables" from the jury, three were also before this Court when it decided *Witherspoon*. There, this Court reviewed the studies and concluded:

"The data adduced by the petitioner . . . are too tentative and fragmentary to establish that jurors not opposed to the death penalty tend to favor the prosecution in the determination of guilt. We simply cannot conclude, either on the basis of the record now before us or as a matter of judicial notice, that the exclusion of jurors opposed to capital punishment results in an unrepresentative jury on the issue of guilt or substantially increases the risk of conviction. In light of the presently available information, we are not prepared to announce a per se constitutional rule requiring the reversal of every conviction returned by a jury selected as this one was."

It goes almost without saying that if these studies were "too tentative and fragmentary" to make out a claim of constitutional error in 1968, the same studies, unchanged but for having aged some eighteen years, are still insufficient to make out such a claim in this case.

Nor do the three post-*Witherspoon* studies introduced by McCree on the "death qualification" issue provide substantial support for the "per se constitutional rule" McCree asks this Court to adopt. All three of the "new" studies were based on the responses of individuals randomly selected from some segment of the population, but who were not actual jurors sworn under oath to apply the law to the facts of an actual case involving the fate of an actual capital defendant. We have serious doubts about the value of these studies in predicting the behavior of actual jurors.

In addition, two of the three "new" studies did not even attempt to simulate the process of jury deliberation, and none of the "new" studies was able to predict to what extent, if any, the presence of one or more "*Witherspoon*-excludables" on a guilt-phase jury would have altered the outcome of the guilt determination.

Finally, and most importantly, only one of the six "death qualification" studies introduced by McCree even attempted to identify and account for the presence of so-called "nullifiers," or individuals who, because of their deep-seated opposition to the death penalty, would be unable to decide a capital defendant's guilt or innocence fairly and impartially.

Having identified some of the more serious problems with McCree's studies, however, we will assume for purposes of this opinion that the studies are both methodologically valid and adequate to establish that "death qualification" in fact produces juries somewhat more "conviction-prone" than "non-death-qualified" juries. We hold, nonetheless, that the Constitution does not prohibit the States from "death qualifying" juries in capital cases.

We have never invoked the fair cross-section principle to invalidate the use of either for-cause or peremptory challenges to prospective jurors, or to require petit juries, as opposed to jury panels or venires, to reflect the composition of the community at large.

We remain convinced that an extension of the fair cross-section requirement to petit juries would be unworkable and unsound, and we decline McCree's invitation to adopt such an extension.

The essence of a "fair cross-section" claim is the systematic exclusion of "a 'distinctive' group in the community." In our view, groups defined solely in terms of shared attitudes that would prevent or substantially impair members of the group from performing one of their duties as jurors, such as the "*Witherspoon*-excludables" at issue here, are not "distinctive groups" for fair cross-section purposes.

Our prior jury-representativeness cases, have involved such groups as blacks, women, and Mexican-Americans. The wholesale exclusion of these large groups from jury service clearly contravened the fair cross-section requirement. The exclusion from jury service of large groups of individuals not on the basis of their inability to serve as jurors, but on the basis of some immutable characteristic such as race, gender, or ethnic background, undeniably gave rise to an "appearance of unfairness."

The group of "*Witherspoon*-excludables" involved in the case at bar differs significantly from the groups we have previously recognized as "distinctive." "Death qualification," unlike the wholesale exclusion of blacks, women, or Mexican-Americans from jury service, is carefully designed to serve the State's concededly legitimate interest in obtaining a single jury that can properly and impartially apply the law to the facts of the case at both the guilt and sentencing phases of a capital trial.

Furthermore, unlike blacks, women, and Mexican-Americans, "*Witherspoon*-excludables" are singled out for exclusion in capital cases on the basis of an attribute that is within the individual's control. It is important to remember that not all who oppose the death penalty are subject to removal for cause in capital cases; those who firmly believe that the death penalty is unjust may nevertheless serve as jurors in capital cases so long as they state clearly that they are willing to temporarily set aside their own beliefs in deference to the rule of law.

McCree argues that, even if we reject the Eighth Circuit's fair cross-section holding, we should affirm the judgment below on the alternative ground, adopted by the District Court, that "death qualification" violated his constitutional right to an impartial jury.

We do not agree. According to McCree, when the State "tips the scales" by excluding prospective jurors with a particular viewpoint, an impermissibly partial jury results. We have consistently rejected this view of jury impartiality, including as recently as last Term when we squarely held that an impartial jury consists of nothing more than "jurors who will conscientiously apply the law and find the facts."

DISSENT

Justice Marshall, with whom Justice Brennan and Justice Stevens join, dissenting.

The data strongly suggest that death qualification excludes a significantly large subset—at least 11% to 17%—of potential jurors who could be impartial during the guilt phase of trial. Among the members of this excludable class are a disproportionate number of blacks and women.

The perspectives on the criminal justice system of jurors who survive death qualification are systematically different from those of the excluded jurors. Death-qualified jurors are, for example, more likely to believe that a defendant's failure to testify is indicative of his guilt, more hostile to the insanity defense, more distrustful of defense attorneys, and less concerned about the danger of erroneous convictions. This pro-prosecution bias is reflected in the greater readiness of death-qualified jurors to convict or to convict on more serious charges. And, finally, the very process of death qualification—which focuses attention on the death penalty before the trial has even begun—has been found to predispose the jurors that survive it to believe that the defendant is guilty.

The evidence thus confirms, and is itself corroborated by, the more intuitive judgments of scholars and of so many of the participants in capital trials—judges, defense attorneys, and prosecutors.

The chief strength of respondent's evidence lies in the essential unanimity of the results obtained by researchers using diverse subjects and varied methodologies. Even the Court's haphazard jabs cannot obscure the power of the array.

Faced with the near unanimity of authority supporting respondent's claim that death qualification gives the prosecution a particular advantage in the guilt phase of capital trials, the majority here makes but a weak effort to contest that proposition.

CASE DISCUSSION

After his conviction for capital felony-murder was affirmed on direct appeal, Lockhart filed a habeas corpus petition. The United States District Court for the Eastern District Court of Arkansas granted relief, and the Circuit Court for the Eighth Circuit affirmed. On writ of *certiorari,* the United States Supreme Court reversed. The Supreme Court held that the Constitution allows removal for cause of prospective jurors who oppose the death penalty, and death qualification does not violate fair cross-section requirements under the Sixth Amendment nor the right to an impartial jury.

Do "death qualified juries" deny defendants fair trials? Is the majority or the dissent "right" in interpreting the statistics? Should juries represent a fair cross-section of attitudes in the community? Why? Why not? Why are attitudes different from race, ethnicity, and gender, according to the Court? Should they be? Explain. How would you have decided this case? Defend your decision.

The Right to a Public Trial

Both the Sixth Amendment right to confrontation and the due process clause of the Fifth and Fourteenth Amendments guarantee defendants' right to a public trial. The right encompasses two dimensions: (1) access of the public in general to attend proceedings; and (2) defendants' right to attend. The right extends to "every stage of the trial,'' including jury selection, communications between judge and jury, jury instructions, and in-chamber conversations between judge and jurors. It does not include brief conferences at the bench outside the defendant's hearing or other brief conferences involving only questions of law.

ACCESS OF THE GENERAL PUBLIC. Public trials support defendants' interest in avoiding persecution through secret proceedings, enhance community participation in law enforcement, and aid in the search for truth by encouraging witnesses to come forth who otherwise might not. These interests are not absolute. Courtroom size limits public access. Furthermore, the need to protect threatened witnesses justifies closing the courtroom. Also, shy and introverted witnesses may not come forward. Moreover, protecting undercover agents authorizes exclusion during their testimony. Finally, judges might restrict access during sensitive proceedings. For example,

> exclusion of spectators during the testimony of an alleged rape victim ''is a frequent and accepted practice when the lurid details of such a crime must be related by a young lady.'' . . . Primary justification for this practice lies in protection of the personal feelings of the complaining witness. . . . Rape constitutes an intrusion upon areas of the victim's life, both physical and psychological, to which our society attaches the deepest sense of privacy. Shame and loss of dignity, however unjustified from a moral standpoint, are natural byproducts of an attempt to recount details of a rape before a curious . . . audience. The ordeal of describing an unwanted sexual encounter before persons with no more than a prurient interest in it aggravates the original injury. Mitigation of the ordeal is a justifiable concern of the public and of the trial court.[23]

THE PRESENCE OF THE DEFENDANT. Defendants do not possess an absolute right to attend their own trials; they forfeit their right to attend by disruptive behavior. For example, Allen who was on trial for armed robbery, repeatedly interrupted the judge in a ''most abusive and disrespectful manner'' and threatened him—''When I go out for lunchtime, you're going to be a corpse here.'' When the judge warned Allen that he could attend only so long as he behaved himself, Allen answered, ''There is going to be no proceeding. I'm going to start talking all through the trial. There's not going to be no trial like this.'' The judge, according to the Supreme Court, properly removed Allen from the court room.

> It is essential to the proper administration of criminal justice that dignity, order, and decorum be the hallmarks of all court proceedings in our country. The flagrant disregard in the courtroom of elementary standards of proper conduct should not and cannot be tolerated. We believe that trial judges confronted with disruptive, contumacious, stubbornly defiant defendants must be given sufficient discretion to meet the circumstances of each case. We think there are at least three constitutionally permissible ways for a trial judge to handle an obstreperous defendant like Allen: (1) bind and gag him, thereby keeping him present; (2) cite him for contempt; (3) take him out of the courtroom until he promises to conduct himself properly.[24]

Judges may also exclude defendants from some questioning of child witnesses in sex abuse cases. For example, Stincer was on trial for sodomizing two children, aged eight and seven. The trial court conducted an in-chambers hearing to determine whether the children could remember certain details and whether they understood the significance of telling the truth in court. The judge permitted Stincer's lawyer to attend but refused

Stincer's request to do so. The Supreme Court upheld the judge's ruling because Stincer had an adequate opportunity to "confront" the children during the trial.

Courts can also require dangerous defendants to appear only under sufficient guard to protect the public, witnesses, and court officials from harm and to prevent defendants' escape. Under ordinary circumstances, however, defendants have the right to attend trial in a way that will not prejudice their cases. The government cannot bring defendants to court in jail dress, nor can it require that their witnesses appear in shackles. Such apparel prejudices the jury, furthers no state policy, and acts mainly against poor defendants.[25]

Presenting the Evidence

The adversary process reaches its high point in presenting evidence. Each side follows strict, technical rules in presenting its case to the fact-finders, whether they be jurors or the judge in a bench trial. Since the consequences are the most severe in the criminal process, the state must prove the defendant guilty beyond a reasonable doubt, the highest standard of proof in the law. The main stages in presenting the evidence include (1) opening statements, the prosecution first followed by the defense; (2) presenting the state's case, including cross-examination by defense counsel; (3) presenting the defendant's case, including cross-examination by the prosecution; (4) closing arguments; (5) instructions to the jury; (6) jury deliberations; (7) jury verdict; (8) judgment of the court.

The defense need not present any evidence in fact, or speak at all. The burden of proof rests solely upon the government to prove defendants' guilt beyond a reasonable doubt. Defendants need not either "prove their innocence" or raise a reasonable doubt about the government's case. Furthermore, the right against self-incrimination permits defendants to remain silent throughout the trial. Hence, trials may proceed, and some do, in which neither defendants nor their lawyers present a case for the defense. Not only does the Constitution permit it; strategy and tactics may dictate that the defense not present a case.

The presentation of evidence promotes and balances the interest in arriving at the truth against the process values of controlling government officials, the societal interest in community participation in criminal justice administration, and maintaining public confidence in a fair and just legal system and process. In the presentation of evidence, promoting organizational interests plays a lesser role; criminal trials are perhaps the least efficient and harmonious, as well as the most expensive, stage of the criminal process. Even in the trial, however, decorum and proper exchanges between defense and prosecution receive attention, if not paramount concern.

PROOF BEYOND A REASONABLE DOUBT. The Supreme Court has ruled *In re Winship* that due process requires that both federal and state prosecutors prove every fact necessary to constitute a crime beyond a reasonable doubt. The **reasonable doubt standard** is

> bottomed on a fundamental value determination of our society that it is far worse to convict an innocent man than to let a guilty man go free. [Two propositions cannot be disputed:] First, in a judicial proceeding in which there is a dispute about the facts of some earlier event, the factfinder cannot acquire unassailably accurate knowledge of what happened. Instead, all the factfinder can acquire is a belief of what *probably* happened. The intensity of this belief—the degree to which a factfinder is convinced

that a given act actually occurred—can, of course, vary. In this regard, a standard of proof represents an attempt to instruct the factfinder concerning the degree of confidence our society thinks he should have in the correctness of factual conclusions for a particular type of adjudication. Although the phrases "preponderance of the evidence" and "proof beyond a reasonable doubt" are quantitatively imprecise, they do communicate to the finder of fact different notions concerning the degree of confidence he is expected to have in the correctness of his factual conclusions.

A second proposition, which is really nothing more than a corollary of the first, is that the trier of fact will sometimes, despite his best efforts, be wrong in his factual conclusions. [This can lead to one of two results. On the one hand] would be the conviction of an innocent man. On the other hand, an erroneous factual determination can result . . . in the acquittal of a guilty man.[26]

Despite the constitutional command, courts struggle to define the reasonable doubt standard. Courts have used various language, often leading to more confusion than clarity. Some common definitions from the cases include (1) a doubt that would cause prudent men to hesitate before acting in a matter of importance to themselves; (2) a doubt based on reason and common sense; (3) not frivolous or fanciful doubt nor one that can be easily explained away; (4) substantial doubt; (5) persuasion to a reasonable or moral certainty. A few definitions brought about reversal: (1) beyond a reasonable doubt is about "7½ on a scale of 10"; (2) reasonable doubt standard is met when the scales of justice are substantially out of equipoise. Some courts prohibit trial judges from defining reasonable doubt, leaving juries to decide it for themselves.[27]

Decision Point

At Werbrouck's trial for violating the federal gambling laws, the government proved: (1) Werbrouck owned and operated the Holiday Inn Motel and the adjoining Lincoln Highway Inn Restaurant in South Bend, Indiana; (2) Werbrouck moved out of his personal room at the Holiday Inn to allow a gambling casino to move in; (3) he permitted certain motel rooms to be physically altered for gambling purposes, including the building of partition walls and the installation of a steel door, cameras, monitors, and electronically controlled door locks; (4) Werbrouck charged no rent for the motel casino rooms and regularly provided customers free food and drinks from his adjoining restaurant; (5) he held keys to the electronically controlled doors and at times admitted persons to the rooms; and (6) Werbrouck was observed in the gambling casino.

Werbrouck claimed that this was insufficient evidence to prove beyond a reasonable doubt and establish his involvement with the gambling business either as a principal or aider and abettor. Did the above constitute proof beyond a reasonable doubt? The federal court of appeals held that the "jury and trial court could plainly have concluded that the defendant was guilty beyond a reasonable doubt."[28]

OPENING STATEMENTS. Prosecutors and defense counsel may address the jury before they present their evidence. Prosecutors make their opening statements first;

defense counsel address the jury either immediately after the prosecutor's opening statement or, in a few jurisdictions, following the presentation of the state's case. The opening statements have a narrow scope—to outline the case the two sides hope to prove, not to prove the case. Proving the case falls to the presentation of evidence phase of the criminal trial. In fact, it is unprofessional for either side to refer to any evidence in which the attorneys do not have a good faith belief is both competent and admissible in court. It is rare for them to do so, but appeals courts have occasionally reversed when prosecutors have referred to points they intend to prove with evidence they know is either inadmissible or incompetent or both.[29]

THE PROSECUTION'S CASE-IN-CHIEF. The prosecution carries the burden of proof in criminal prosecution; the defense need only raise a reasonable doubt about the proof in order to gain an acquittal. Hence, the prosecution presents its case-in-chief first. In presenting its case, the rules of evidence restrict what evidence the state may use, mainly excluding illegally obtained testimony and physical evidence and most hearsay. The prosecution must prove every element in the case, but the defense frequently **stipulates** (agrees not to contest) to some material facts, particularly those which might prejudice the defendant's case—detailed photographs and descriptions of a brutally murdered victim, for example. The prosecution can decline a stipulation. Most courts do not compel them to accept stipulations because to do so might weaken the force, persuasiveness, and coherence of the prosecution's case.[30]

The state ordinarily presents all the available eyewitnesses to the crime (the *res gestae* witnesses). In some instances, if the prosecution does not call a material witness (particularly a victim), the defense can ask for a **missing witness instruction,** an instruction to the effect that jurors can infer that the witness's testimony would have been unfavorable to the prosecution. The prosecution can ask the court to inform the jury that a key witness is unavailable and not to draw negative inferences from the failure to testify. Prosecutors may decide not to call witnesses such as spouses, priests, and doctors who they know will claim a valid privilege; doing so may result in reversible error.[31]

DEFENDANT'S RIGHT TO CROSS-EXAMINE. The Sixth Amendment confrontation clause includes the right to cross-examine the prosecution's witnesses. In *Smith v. Illinois,* the prosecution's key witness, an informant, testified that he bought heroin from Smith; the trial court allowed the informant to conceal his real name and address and to use an alias. The Supreme Court ruled that this violated Smith's right to confrontation:

> when the credibility of a witness is at issue, the very starting point in "exposing falsehood and bringing out the truth" through cross-examination must necessarily be to ask the witness who he is and where he lives. The witness' name and address open countless avenues of in-court examination and out-of-doors investigation. . . . It is of the essence of a fair trial that reasonable latitude be given to the cross-examiner, even though he is unable to state to the court what facts a reasonable cross-examination might develop. . . . To say that prejudice can be established only by showing that the cross-examination, if pursued, would necessarily have brought out facts tending to discredit testimony in chief, is to deny a substantial right and withdraw one of the safeguards essential to a fair trial.[32]

Only compelling reasons can limit the defendant's right to cross-examine witnesses.[33]

THE PROSECUTION'S USE OF HEARSAY. The confrontation clause also restricts the prosecution's use of **hearsay**—out-of-court statements offered to prove the truth of the statements. Hearsay violates the confrontation clause because defendants cannot ferret out the truth through the adversary process unless the defense can cross-examine the witnesses against them. The jury, therefore, cannot have an adequate basis for fact-finding.

The confrontation clause does not absolutely bar hearsay testimony. The prosecution can introduce hearsay if it meets two tests: (1) demonstrate witness's unavailability and, hence, the necessity to use out-of-court statements; (2) show that the state obtained the evidence under circumstances that clearly establish its reliability. In *Ohio v. Roberts*, the majority found that the state satisfied the tests under these circumstances: the witness's mother said her daughter left home, saying she was going to Tucson, two years ago; shortly thereafter a San Francisco social worker contacted her mother concerning a welfare claim her daughter filed there; the mother was able to reach her daughter once, by phone; when her daughter called a few months ago, she told her mother she was travelling but did not reveal her whereabouts. The dissent argued that relying solely on the parents was not sufficient; the prosecution had the burden to go out and find the witness.[34]

DEFENDANT'S RIGHT TO COMPULSORY PROCESS. The Sixth Amendment guarantees defendant's right "to have compulsory process for obtaining witnesses in [their] . . . favor. . . ." This means defendants can compel witnesses to come to court to testify for them. Most states provide indigent defendants with process without charge. Some states permit prescribed numbers of such process without showing cause. Others require that defendants demonstrate that witnesses have material, relevant, and useful evidence. Most states do not provide compulsory process without charge for evidence that merely corroborates or adds to evidence already available. Furthermore, most states require that defendants state in detail precisely why they need the evidence.

DEFENDANT'S TESTIMONY. The Fifth Amendment provides that "no person . . . shall be compelled in any criminal case to be a witness against himself. . . ." This means that the state cannot call defendants to the witness stand in criminal trials. It also prohibits the prosecution from commenting on defendants' refusal to testify; it even entitles defendants to ask judges to instruct juries not to infer guilt from defendants' silence. However, if defendants decide to take the stand in order to tell "their side of the story," the prosecution can cross-examine defendants as they would any other witness.

DEFENDANT'S CASE. The defense need not present a case; cross-examining the prosecution's witnesses alone may raise a reasonable doubt about the proof against the defendant. Or, defendants may call their own witnesses to rebut the prosecution's witnesses or raise a reasonable doubt about their guilt: establishing alibis, for example. Defendants may also have affirmative defenses that negate their criminal liability: self-defense, insanity, duress, and entrapment. They may have evidence that reduces the grade of the offense, such as provocation to reduce murder to manslaughter; diminished capacity to reduce first-degree murder to second-degree murder. The prosecution, of course, has the right to cross-examine defense witnesses and to otherwise challenge the defense's defendants raise.

CLOSING ARGUMENTS. Prosecutors close first; the defense follows; then the prosecution rebuts. Prosecutors cannot waive their right to make a closing argument and save their remarks for rebuttal. Waiving the right to make a closing argument automatically bars prosecution rebuttal. Furthermore, prosecutors cannot raise ''new'' matters in rebuttal: they must restrict rebuttal to matters introduced in either theirs or the defense's closing argument. Fairness dictates this procedure; the defense should hear all the arguments in favor of conviction before responding to them.

Formally, prosecutors have the duty not only to convict criminals but also to seek justice; the latter restricts the advocacy proper in the closing argument. The American Bar Association Standard for Criminal Justice includes the following guidelines for prosecutors: It is improper to (1) intentionally misstate the evidence or mislead the jury; (2) refer to evidence excluded, or not introduced, at trial; (3) express personal belief or opinion about the truth or falsity of the evidence or defendant's guilt; (4) engage in argument that diverts jurors' attention by injecting issues beyond the case or predicting consequences of the jury's verdict; (5) make arguments calculated to inflame jurors' passions and prejudices.[35]

Violating these standards rarely results in reversal.

> If every remark made by counsel outside of the testimony were grounds for a reversal, comparatively few verdicts would stand, since in the ardor of advocacy, and in the excitement of the trial, even the most experienced counsel are occasionally carried away by this temptation.[36]

When determining whether to reverse convictions based on improper closing arguments, appellate courts consider: (1) whether defense counsel invited or provoked the remarks; (2) whether defense counsel made timely objection to the remarks; (3) whether the trial judge took corrective action, such as instructing the jury to disregard the remarks; (4) whether the comments were brief and isolated in an otherwise proper argument; (5) whether there were other errors during the trial; and (6) whether the evidence of guilt was overwhelming.[37]

Appellate courts, although rarely reversing convictions for them, frequently express their displeasure with prosecutors' improper remarks during closing arguments. Recently in Minnesota, the state's intermediate appeals court warned that if prosecutors persisted in ignoring the standards for proper arguments, the court was prepared to reverse convictions to control their excesses.[38]

Decision Point

Bowen was convicted of raping and murdering a twelve-year-old girl. The prosecutor, in the course of the closing statement, made the following comment:

"And now we come up here with this idea that a man . . . is subject to be rehabilitated and released back into society. Yeah, I guess he can be rehabilitated. Hitler could have been. I believe in about six or eight months if I'd had him chained to a wall and talked to him and beat him on one side of the head for a while with a stick telling him you believe this don't you then beat him on the other side with a stick telling him you believe that don't you I believe I could have rehabilitated Hitler." The prosecutor went on to call Bowen ''a product of the devil,'' a ''liar,'' who was ''no better than a beast.'' And, ''You know for a criminal to go without proper punishment is a disgrace to the society we live in and it's shown to us every day by the fruits that we reap from day to day in our society when we have the bloody deeds such as this occur.''

Were the prosecutor's remarks improper? Should Bowen's conviction be vacated? The Circuit Court of Appeals affirmed the conviction. It conceded that the remarks were improper but found ''no reasonable probability that, absent the improper statements of opinion, Bowen would not have been sentenced to death.''

The American Bar Association places on defense counsel restraints similar to those imposed on prosecutors in closing arguments. Defense closing statements, however, do not raise concerns because appellate review rarely occurs. If juries acquit defendants, the state cannot appeal because it would put defendants in double jeopardy under the Fifth and Fourteenth Amendments; if the defense appeals, then only prosecution errors are at issue. Of course, defense closing arguments may neutralize otherwise improper prosection remarks during closing, if the defense invited or provoked the prosecution's remarks.

The Supreme Court addressed the question whether the improper comments the prosecutor makes during closing arguments violate the due process clause, and also the remedy for making such comments, in *Donnelly v. DeChristoforo.*

CASE

Did the prosecutor's statement violate due process?

Donnelly v. DeChristoforo

416 U.S. 637, 94 S.Ct. 1868, 40 L.Ed.2d 431 (1974)

[Rehnquist, J. delivered the opinion of the Court, in which Burger, C.J., and Stewart, White, Blackmun, and Powell, J.J. joined. Stewart, J., filed a concurring opinion, in which White J., joined. Douglas, J. filed a dissenting opinion, in which Brennan and Marshall, J.J, joined.]

FACTS

Respondent and two companions were indicted for the first-degree murder of Joseph Lanzi, a passenger in a car in which the defendants were riding. Police had stopped the car at approximately 4 a.m. on April 18, 1967, and had discovered Lanzi's dead body along with two firearms, one of which had been fired. A second gun, also recently fired, was found a short distance away.

Respondent and one companion avoided apprehension at that time, but the third defendant was taken into custody. He later pleaded guilty to second-degree murder.

Respondent and the other defendant, Gagliardi, were finally captured and tried jointly. The prosecutor made little claim that respondent fired any shots but argued that he willingly assisted in the killing. Respondent, on the other hand, maintained that he was an innocent passenger. At the close of the evidence but before final argument, Gagliardi elected to plead guilty to a charge of second-degree murder. The court advised the jury that Gagliardi had pleaded guilty and that respondent's trial would continue. Respondent did not seek an instruction that the jury was to draw no inference from the plea, and no such instruction was given.

Respondent's claims of constitutional error focus on two remarks made by the prosecutor during the course of his rather lengthy closing argument to the jury. The first involved the expression of a personal opinion as to guilt,[1] perhaps offered to rebut a somewhat personalized argument by respondent's counsel. The majority of the Court of Appeals agreed with the Supreme Judicial Court of Massachusetts that the remark was improper, but declined to rest its holding of a violation of due process on that remark. It turned to a second remark that it deemed "more serious."

The prosecutor's second challenged comment was directed at respondent's motives in standing trial: "They [the respondent and his counsel] said they hope that you find him not guilty. I quite frankly think that they hope you find him guilty of something less than first-degree murder." Respondent's counsel objected immediately to the statement and later sought an instruction that the remark was improper and should be disregarded. The court then gave the following instruction:

> "Closing arguments are not evidence for your consideration. . . .
> "Now in his closing, the District Attorney, I noted, made a statement: 'I don't know what they want you to do by way of a verdict. They said that they hope you find him not guilty. I quite frankly think that they hope you find him guilty of something a little less than first-degree murder.' There is no evidence whatsoever, of course, you are instructed to disregard that statement made by the District Attorney.
> "Consider the case as though no such statement was made."

The Supreme Judicial Court of Massachusetts, though again not disputing that the remark was improper, held that it was not so prejudicial as to require a mistrial and further stated that the trial judge's instruction "was sufficient to safeguard the defendant's rights." Despite this decision and the District Court's denial of a writ of habeas corpus, the Court of Appeals found that the comment was potentially so misleading and prejudicial that it deprived respondent of a constitutionally fair trial.

OPINION

The Court of Appeals in this case noted, as petitioner urged, that its review was "the narrow one of due process, and not the broad exercise of supervisory

---

[1]The challenged remark was: "I honestly and sincerely believe that there is no doubt in this case, none whatsoever."

power that [it] would possess in regard to [its] own trial court." We regard this observation as important for not every trial error or infirmity which might call for application of supervisory powers correspondingly constitutes a "failure to observe that fundamental fairness essential to the very concept of justice." . . .

This is not a case in which the State has denied a defendant the benefit of a specific provision in the Bill of Rights, . . . [such as the right to counsel or the privilege against self-incrimination.] But here the claim is only that a prosecutor's remark about respondent's expectations at trial by itself so infected the trial with unfairness as to make the resulting conviction a denial of due process. We do not believe that examination of the entire proceedings in this case supports that contention.

. . . [I]t is by no means clear that the jury did engage in the hypothetical analysis [that the prosecutor's remark invited the jury to infer that respondent had offered to plead guilty and was looking for a conviction of second-degree murder] . . . or even probable that it would seize such a comment out of context and attach this particular meaning to it. . . .

In addition, the trial court took special pains to correct any impression that the jury could consider the prosecutor's statements as evidence in the case. . . . Although some occurrences at trial may be too clearly prejudicial for such a curative instruction to mitigate their effect, the comment in this case is hardly of such character . . . [T]he prosecutor's remark . . . was but one moment in an extended trial and was followed by specific disapproving instructions. Although the process of constitutional line drawing in this regard is necessarily imprecise, we simply do not believe that this incident made respondent's trial so fundamentally unfair as to deny him due process. . . . [W]e reverse the judgment of the Court of Appeals. It is so ordered.

DISSENT

Mr. Justice Douglas, dissenting:

The function of the prosecutor under the Federal Constitution is not to tack as many skins of victims as possible to the wall. His function is to vindicate the right of people as expressed in the laws and give those accused of crime a fair trial. . . . We have here a state case, not a federal one; and the prosecutor is a state official. But we deal with an aspect of a fair trial which is implicit in the Due Process Clause of the Fourteenth Amendment by which the States are bound. . . .

[The prosecutor's] statements in the setting of the case and in light of the fact that the jury knew the codefendant had pleaded guilty to second-degree murder, are a subtle equivalent of a statement by the prosecutor that the respondent sought a lesser penalty. Counsel for respondent immediately objected but the court at the time did not admonish the prosecutor or tell the jury to disregard the statement, although it did cover the matter later in its general instructions. . . .

As a matter of procedural due process the Confrontation Clause of the Sixth Amendment, applicable to the States by reason of the Fourteenth Amendment would bar a person from testifying that the defendant had sought a guilty plea unless the right of cross-examination of the witness was afforded. That requirement of procedural due process should be sedulously enforced . . . lest the theory that the end justifies the means gains further foothold here. The prosecutor is not a witness; and he should not be permitted to add to the record either by subtle or gross improprieties. Those who have experienced the full thrust of the power of government when leveled against them know that the only protection the citizen has is in the requirement of a fair trial. The assurance of the Court that we make no retreat from constitutional government by today's decision has therefore a hollow ring.

Activist judges have brought federal habeas corpus into disrepute at the present time. It is guaranteed by the Constitution. It is built-in restraint on judges—both state and federal; and it is also a restraint on prosecutors who are officers of the court. Our activist tendencies should promote not law and order, but *constitutional* law and order. Judges, too, can be tyrants and often have been. Prosecutors are often eager to take almost any shortcut to win, yet as I have said they represent not an ordinary party but We the People. As I have noted, their duty is as much to "refrain from improper methods as it is to use every legitimate means to bring about a just one."

It is, I submit, quite "improper" for a prosecutor to insinuate to the jury the existence of evidence not in the record and which could not be introduced without the privilege of cross-examination.

CASE DISCUSSION

DeChristoforo and a companion were indicted, tried, and convicted for first-degree murder. DeChristoforo appealed after the trial judge denied his motion for mistrial based on improper remarks made by the prosecutor during the closing arguments. The Massachusetts Supreme Judicial Court affirmed. The United States District Court denied *habeas corpus* relief, and the court of appeals reversed. On writ of *certiorari*, the United States Supreme Court reversed, holding that the remarks, although improper, did not violate due process of law.

Why were the prosecutors remarks improper? If they were, why did the Supreme Court not reverse the decision and vacate the conviction? Did the Supreme Court sacrifice the search for truth in order to promote crime control, as the dissent suggests? What should the remedy for the improper remarks be? Is it more important to control the prosecutor than to convict DeChristoforo? Is that what the Supreme Court is saying? Do you agree with the dissent?

Jury Instructions

Before they begin their deliberations, judges "instruct" the jury about the law and how jurors should apply it. The principal matters in the instructions include (1) the respective roles of judge to decide the law and jury to decide the facts; (2) that defendants are presumed innocent until proven guilty; (3) that the state bears the burden of proving guilt beyond a reasonable doubt; (4) the definition of all the elements of the crime with which the defendant is charged; (5) jury room procedures. Both prosecution and defense submit requested instructions to the judge prior to jury instruction; they may object to the judge's refusal to give the requested instruction and frequently base appeals on such failure.

Some jurisdictions have adopted **pattern instructions,** published standard instructions for a matters relevant to most cases. Supporters praise pattern instructions' clarity, accuracy, impartiality, and efficiency; critics call them too abstract to aid jurors. Studies indicate that jurors understand only about half the content of judges' instructions to them, whether pattern or individually crafted.[39]

Jury Deliberations

The judge **sequesters** the jury—orders them to retire to a separate room under supervision and without interruption to deliberate together until they reach a verdict. The jurors take the instructions, any exhibits received in evidence, and a list of the charges against the defendant with them to the jury room. During the course of their deliberations, they may request the court for further instruction or information concerning the evidence or any other matter. The court can discharge **hung juries**— juries unable to reach a verdict after protracted deliberations.

Until recently, both federal and state judges encouraged reluctant juries to reach verdicts by giving them the *Allen* **charge,** or "dynamite charge" to "blast loose the deadlocked jury." For example, after the jury sent the court a note that read, "Our discussion is six guilty, six not guilty," the judge called them into the courtroom and charged them as follows:

> Members of the jury, it is now not quite 9:00 o'clock. You have been at work since 4:30 this afternoon, omitting the dinner hour. The note you have sent in a moment ago indicates that your number stands at six for one side and six for the other.
>
> It is my duty to urge you to reach a decision on this case. This case has to be tried either now or later. It is unlikely that this case will ever be tried by any jury more competent and more representative of the community than yourselves. It is unlikely that the evidence would be any different before any later trial than it was before this one and so it is important that the matter be resolved. Those of you who stand on one side of the question should give respectful attention and consideration to the views of those opposed. And vice-versa.
>
> None of this, however, should be construed by you as suggesting that I believe that you should not vote any other way than your own conscience based upon the evidence and the instructions in this case. None of us expects you to do anything other than that. But I am sure that you realize along with me that this case should be decided. It ought not to be decided unless it is decided by the appropriate number ten to two and it ought not to be decided unless those ten of you who concur, if you do, reach your decision honestly base [sic] upon the evidence and the law and your own view of the matter; so nothing I say should be taken as meaning that I want any of you to vote other than what your own good judgment dictates. But for the reasons I have mentioned I urge you to go back and deliberate further and see if you can reach a verdict. You may now be excused to the jury room.[40]

In recent years both federal and state courts have stopped using the *Allen* charge. They criticize it for several reasons: it is coercive; it defeats the unanimity rule; it threatens jury impartiality; and it brings extraneous factors—pressure to reach a decision to end the case—into jury deliberations.[41]

Verdict and Judgment

In most cases the jury returns one of three verdicts: guilty, not guilty, and special verdicts, mainly related to insanity or capital punishment. If the jury acquits (the not guilty verdict), defendants' ordeal with the criminal process ends immediately; they are free to go. If the jury convicts, the case continues to **judgment**—the only authentic decision that determines the final outcome of the case. Juries cannot pass judgment on defendants; only the court has the authority to render judgment. Following the court's judgment of guilty or acquittal, the criminal trial ends.

≡ CONVICTION BY GUILTY PLEA

There are two types of guilty pleas: straight and negotiated. Straight guilty pleas are ordinarily made in "dead bang" cases, those in which proof of guilt is overwhelming. **Negotiated pleas,** or those in which the state makes concessions in return for a guilty plea, appear mainly in large urban courts. They arise when the state has problems with witnesses who are not reliable or the case is otherwise weak, and defendants have a strong defense or can gain the jury's sympathy. Until twenty years ago, the negotiated plea, although common, did not receive formal recognition by the courts. Since *Brady v. United States,* decided in 1970, the Supreme Court has recognized and approved its legality.[42]

Defendants plead guilty in exchange for the government taking one of three actions: (1) dismiss other charges; (2) recommend a particular sentence or refrain from making a recommendation; (3) agree to a specific sentence.

Conviction by guilty plea, whether negotiated or straight, promotes several interests, but according to the United States Supreme Court "the chief virtues of the plea system [are] speed, economy, and finality."

> Whatever might be the situation in an ideal world, the fact is that the guilty plea and the often concomitant plea bargain are important components of this country's criminal justice system. Properly administered, they can benefit all concerned. The defendant avoids extended pretrial incarceration and the anxieties and uncertainties of a trial; he gains a speedy disposition of his case, the chance to acknowledge his guilt, and a prompt start in realizing whatever potential there may be for rehabilitation. Judges and prosecutors conserve vital and scarce resources. The public is protected from the risks posed by those charged with criminal offense who are at large on bail while awaiting completion of criminal proceedings.[43]

The arguments for and against conviction by plea are heated, complex, and by no means empirically resolved. Some say that negotiation better serves the search for truth and factual accuracy; others argue that the adversary process best serves the ends of justice. Some maintain that guilty pleas save time; others contend that plea negotiations more than make up for time saved in trials. Some urge that the criminal justice system would collapse under its own weight if only a few of the now-vast majority of defendants who plead guilty asserted their right to trial; others contend that jurisdictions that prohibit plea bargaining find it makes little difference. Some maintain that the guilty plea intimidates the innocent and emboldens the guilty; others say that outcomes between convictions by plea and those by trial do not materially differ. The public and police officers oppose plea bargaining because they believe that it "lets criminals off." The available empirical data do not resolve these questions. Nevertheless, most of the cases studied adopt the view outlined in the earlier Supreme Court quote: conviction by plea serves the organizational interest in economy, speed, and finality.[44]

The Guilty Plea and the Constitution

The social scientists and the policy makers have not resolved the empirical and policy issues surrounding conviction by plea; the Supreme Court *has* settled the question of its legality and constitutionality. The guilty plea, whether or not negotiated, waives three constitutional rights. By pleading guilty, defendants stand as witnesses against themselves, hence putting aside the Fifth Amendment's protection against self-incrimination. Defendants who plead guilty also forego both the right to trial and the right to confront the witnesses against them that the Sixth Amendment guarantees. Hence, in order to satisfy the Constitution, defendants who plead guilty must waive their Fifth and Sixth Amendment rights—they must plead guilty voluntarily, know-ingly, and intelligently. There is a

> minimum requirement that his plea be the voluntary expression of his own choice. But the plea is more than an admission of past conduct; it is the defendant's consent that judgment of conviction may be entered without a trial—a waiver of his right to trial before a jury or a judge. Waivers of constitutional rights not only must be voluntary but must be knowing, intelligent acts done with sufficient awareness of the relevant circumstances and likely consequences.[45]

Trial judges have a duty to insure that defendants plead voluntarily, intelligently, and knowingly. The Supreme Court has established the following standard for trial judges' inquiry:

> A plea of guilty entered by one fully aware of the direct consequences, including the actual value of any commitments made to him by the court, prosecutor, or his own counsel, must stand unless induced by threats (or promises to discontinue improper harassment), misrepresentation (including unfulfilled or unfulfillable promises), or perhaps by promises that they are by their nature improper as having no prior relationship to the prosecutor's business (e.g. bribes).[46]

The Court has held that a trial judge's failure to ask a defendant questions concerning his plea constituted reversible error because the trial court accepted the plea "without an affirmative showing that it was intelligent and voluntary." A court cannot presume that defendants waive the three fundamental rights by pleading guilty "from a silent record." All jurisdictions now require that judges inform defendants that by pleading guilty they waive their rights to trial, to confrontation, and not to incriminate themselves.[47]

Furthermore, the Court has ruled that to plead voluntarily, defendants must know "the true nature of the charge[s]" against them. Therefore, when one defendant pleaded guilty to second-degree murder without knowing the elements of the crime and neither defense counsel nor the trial judge explained to him that second-degree murder required an intent to kill, that defendant's version of what he did negated intent, and the court ruled that the record did not establish a knowing plea. Most jurisdictions now require that judges determine that the pleas rests upon a "factual basis." To determine the factual basis judges might ask defendants to describe the conduct that led to the charges, ask prosecutor and defense attorneys similar questions, and consult presen-tence reports.[48]

Negotiated Pleas and the Constitution

Brady v. United States established that negotiated pleas were not *per se* involuntary; it did not address the variety of situations in which plea negotiations occur and under which they may be voluntary. One problem arises when defendants plead guilty following threats during negotiations that the prosecutor will seek indictment for more serious charges if defendants do not accept the bargain. The Supreme Court addressed the problem of prosecutorial threats as "bargain chips" in *Bordenkircher v. Hayes.*

CASE

Is the threat to bring more serious charges legal?

Bordenkircher v. Hayes

434 U.S. 357, 98 S.Ct. 663, 54 L. Ed. 2d 604 (1978)

[Stewart, J., delivered the opinion of the Court, in which Burger, C. J., and White, Rehnquist, and Stevens, JJ., joined. Blackmun, J., filed a dissenting opinion, in which Brennan and Marshall, JJ., joined. Powell, J., filed a dissenting opinion.]

FACTS

The respondent, Paul Lewis Hayes, was indicted by a grand jury on a charge of uttering a forged instrument in the amount of $88.30, an offense then punishable by a term of 2 to 10 years in prison. After arraignment, Hayes, his retained counsel, and the Commonwealth's Attorney met in the presence of the Clerk of the Court to discuss a possible plea agreement. During these conferences the prosecutor offered to recommend a sentence of five years in prison if Hayes would plead guilty to the indictment. He also said that if Hayes did not plead guilty and "save the court the inconvenience and necessity of a trial," he would return to the grand jury to seek an indictment under the Kentucky Habitual Criminal Act, which would subject Hayes to a mandatory sentence of life imprisonment by reason of his two prior felony convictions. Hayes chose not to plead guilty, and the prosecutor did obtain an indictment charging him under the Habitual Criminal Act.

A jury found Hayes guilty on the principal charge of uttering a forged instrument and, in a separate proceeding, further found that he had twice before been convicted of felonies. As required by the habitual offender statute, he was sentenced to a life term in the penitentiary. The Kentucky Court of Appeals rejected Hayes' constitutional objections to the enhanced sentence, holding that the prosecutor's decision to indict him as a habitual offender was a legitimate use of available leverage in the plea-bargaining process.

On Hayes' petition for a federal writ of habeas corpus, the United States District Court for the Eastern District of Kentucky agreed that there had been no constitutional violation. The Court of Appeals for the Sixth Circuit reversed the District Court's judgment.

OPINION

While the prosecutor did not actually obtain the recidivist indictment until after the plea conferences had ended, his intention to do so was clearly expressed at the outset of the plea negotiations. Hayes was thus fully informed of the true terms of the offer when he made his decision to plead not guilty.

To punish a person because he has done what the law plainly allows him to do is a due process violation of the most basic sort, and for an agent of the State to pursue a course of action whose objective is to penalize a person's reliance on his legal rights is "patently unconstitutional." But in the "give-and-take" of plea bargaining, there is no such element of punishment or retaliation so long as the accused is free to accept or reject the prosecution's offer.

Plea bargaining flows from "the mutuality of advantage" to defendants and prosecutors, each with his own reasons for wanting to avoid trial. Indeed, acceptance of the basic legitimacy of plea bargaining necessarily implies rejection of any notion that a guilty plea is involuntary in a constitutional sense simply because it is the end result of the bargaining process.

While confronting a defendant with the risk of more severe punishment clearly may have a "discouraging effect on the defendant's assertion of his trial rights, the imposition of these difficult choices [is] an inevitable"—and permissible—"attribute of any legitimate system which tolerates and encourages the negotiation of pleas." It follows that, by tolerating and encouraging the negotiation of pleas, this Court has necessarily accepted as constitutionally legitimate the simple reality that the prosecutor's interest at the bargaining table is to persuade the defendant to forgo his right to plead not guilty.

There is no doubt that the breadth of discretion that our country's legal system vests in prosecuting attorneys carries with it the potential for both individual and institutional abuse. We hold only that the course of conduct engaged in by the prosecutor in this case, which no more than openly presented the defendant with the unpleasant alternatives of forgoing trial or facing charges on which he was plainly subject to prosecution, did not violate the Due Process Clause of the Fourteenth Amendment.

Accordingly, the judgment of the Court of Appeals is Reversed.

DISSENT

Mr. Justice Powell, dissenting.

I am not satisfied that the result in this case is just or that the conduct of the plea bargaining met the requirements of due process.

Respondent was charged with the uttering of a single forged check in the amount of $88.30. Under Kentucky law, this offense was punishable by a prison term of from 2 to 10 years, apparently without regard to the amount of the forgery. During the course of plea bargaining, the prosecutor offered respondent a sentence of five years in consideration of a guilty plea. I observe, at this point, that five years in prison for the offense charged hardly could be characterized as a generous offer. Apparently respondent viewed the offer in this light and declined to accept it; he protested that he was innocent and insisted on going to trial.

Respondent was 17 years old when he committed his first offense. He was charged with rape but pleaded guilty to the lesser included offense of "detaining a female." Respondent's second offense was robbery. This time he was found guilty by a jury and was sentenced to five years in prison. The addition of a conviction on a charge involving $88.30 subjected respondent to a mandatory sentence of imprisonment for life. Persons convicted of rape and murder often are not punished so severely.

The plea-bargaining process, as recognized by this Court, is essential to the functioning of the criminal-justice system. It normally affords genuine benefits to defendants as well as to society. Only in the most exceptional case should a court conclude that the scales of the bargaining are so unevenly balanced as to arouse suspicion. In this case, the prosecutor's actions denied respondent due process because their admitted purpose was to discourage and then to penalize with unique severity his exercise of constitutional rights. Implementation of a strategy calculated solely to deter the exercise of constitutional rights is not a consitutionally permissible exercise of discretion.

CASE DISCUSSION

Hayes was indicted for uttering a forged check. After arraignment, plea negotiations opened. The prosecutor threatened Hayes with reindictment on more serious charges if he did not plead guilty. Hayes chose not to plead guilty and was reindicted on more serious charges. The Kentucky Court of Appeals affirmed. The federal district court denied a petition for *habeas corpus*. The court of appeals reversed the district court's judgment. The United States Supreme Court reversed the court of appeals, holding that the threat made during negotiations did not violate due process of law.

Was the threat to bring more serious charges part of the bargaining? Does it give the state an unfair advantage? Explain. Did the defendant's plea represent a forfeiture of rights that was unconstitutional, as the dissent maintains? Does the case demonstrate commitment to result or organizational interests? Explain.

A second problem arises when prosecutors or defendants break the bargains they make. For example, after New York indicted Santabello on two felony counts, he pleaded guilty to one lesser included offense in exchange for the prosecutor's agreement not to make a sentence recommendation. At the sentencing hearing, the prosecutor broke his part of the bargain, and asked for a maximum sentence. When defense counsel objected that the prosecutor had broken the state's bargain, the judge said:

Mr. Aronstein [defense counsel], I am not at all influenced by what the District Attorney says . . . It doesn't make a particle of difference what the District Attorney says he will do, or what he doesn't do.

I have here, . . . a probation report. I have here a history of a long, serious criminal record. I have a picture of the life history of this man. . .

He is unamenable to supervision in the community. He is a "professional criminal." . . . just putting him away is the only means of halting his antisocial activities, and protecting you, your family, me, my family, protecting society. . . . Plain language, put him behind bars.

Under the plea, I can only send him to the New York Correctional Institution for men for one year, which I am hereby doing.

Santobello appealed. The Supreme Court ruled:

This phase of the process of criminal justice and the adjudicative element inherent in accepting a plea of guilty, must be attended by safeguards to insure the defendant what is reasonably due in the circumstances. Those circumstances will vary, but a constant factor is that when the plea rests in any significant degree on a promise or agreement of the prosecutor, so that it can be said to be part of the inducement or consideration, such promise must be fulfilled.[49]

The Supreme Court has ruled that prosecutors can repudiate agreements if defendants do not fulfill their promises under them. Therefore, when a defendant promised to testify against co-defendants as part of a plea bargain and reneged on his promise, the Court held that the prosecutor acted legally in invalidating the agreement and initiating prosecution on the original charge. If *courts* reject bargains, defendants may withdraw their guilty pleas unless courts inform defendants before they plead that the court may not accept the plea.[50]

Sometimes defendants plead guilty but maintain their innocence. Usually, the reason for their plea is that the prosecution has a strong case against them. They have pleaded guilty in exchange for a lesser charge, a recommendation for less severe sentence, or an agreed sentence because they believe going to trial will result in conviction and more severe sentence even though they are innocent. In other words, they are what the law calls *factually* innocent, that is, they did not commit the crime, but they are *legally* guilty, that is, enough evidence exists to convict them. The Supreme Court addressed this problem in *North Carolina v. Alford*.

CASE

Was his plea voluntary?

North Carolina v. Alford

400 U.S. 25, 91 S.Ct. 160, 27 L.Ed.2d 162 (1970)

[White, J., delivered the opinion of the Court, in which Burger, C.J., and Harlan, Stewart, and Blackmun, JJ., joined. Black, J., filed a statement concurring in the judgment. Brennan, J., filed a dissenting opinion, in which Douglas and Marshall, JJ., joined.]

FACTS

Mr. Justice White delivered the opinion of the Court.

On December 2, 1963, Alford was indicted for first-degree murder, a capital offense under North Carolina law. The court appointed an attorney to represent him, and this attorney questioned all but one of the various witnesses who appellee said would substantiate his claim of innocence. The witnesses, however, did not support Alford's story but gave statements that strongly indicated his guilt. Faced with strong evidence of guilt and no substantial·evidentiary support for the claim of innocence, Alford's attorney recommended that he plead guilty, but left the ultimate decision to Alford himself. The prosecutor agreed to accept a plea of guilty to a charge of second-degree murder, and on December 10, 1963, Alford pleaded guilty to the reduced charge.

Before the plea was finally accepted by the trial court, the court heard the sworn testimony of a police officer who summarized the State's case. Two other witnesses besides Alford were also heard. Although there was no eyewitness to the crime, the testimony indicated that shortly before the killing Alford took his gun from his house, stated his intention to kill the victim and returned home with the declaration that he had carried out the killing. After the summary presentation of the State's case, Alford took the stand and testified that he had not committed the murder but that he was pleading guilty because he faced the threat of the death penalty if he did not do so. In response to the questions of his counsel, he acknowledged that his counsel had informed him of the difference between second- and first-degree murder and of his rights in case he chose to go to trial. The trial court then asked appellee if, in light of his denial of guilt, he still desired to plead guilty to second-degree murder and appellee answered, "Yes, sir. I plead guilty on—from the circumstances that he [Alford's attorney] told me." After eliciting information about Alford's prior criminal record, which was a long one, the trial court sentenced him to 30 years' imprisonment, the maximum penalty for second-degree murder.

After giving his version of the events of the night of the murder, Alford stated:

"I pleaded guilty on second degree murder because they said there is too much evidence, but I ain't shot no man, but I take the fault for the other man. We never had an argument in our life and I just pleaded guilty because they said if I didn't they would gas me for it, and that is all."

In response to questions from his attorney, Alford affirmed that he had consulted several times with his attorney and with members of his family and had been informed of his rights if he chose to plead not guilty. Alford then reaffirmed his decision to plead guilty to second-degree murder:

"Q [by Alford's attorney]. And you authorized me to tender a plea of guilty to second degree murder before the court?

"A. Yes, sir.

"Q. And in doing that, that you have again affirmed your decision on that point?

"A. Well, I'm still pleading that you all got me to plead guilty. I plead the other way, circumstantial evidence; that the jury will prosecute me on—on the second. You told me to plead guilty, right. I don't—I'm not guilty but I plead guilty."

On appeal, a divided panel of the Court of Appeals for the Fourth Circuit reversed on the ground that Alford's guilty plea was made involuntarily.

OPINION

The standard [for determining the validity of a quality plea is] whether the plea represents a voluntary and intelligent choice among the alternative courses of action open to the defendant. Ordinarily, a judgment of conviction resting on a plea of guilty is justified by the defendant's admission that he committed the crime charged against him and his consent that judgment be entered without a trial of any kind. The plea usually subsumes both elements, and justifiably so, even though there is no separate, express admission by the defendant that he committed the particular acts claimed to constitute the crime charged in the indictment. Here Alford entered his plea but accompanied it with the statement that he had not shot the victim.

State and lower federal courts are divided upon whether a guilty plea can be accepted when it is accompanied by protestations of innocence and hence contains only a waiver of trial but no admission of guilt. Some courts, giving expression to the principle that "[o]ur law only authorizes a conviction where guilt is shown," require that trial judges reject such pleas. But others have concluded that they should not "force any defense on a defendant in a criminal case," particularly when advancement of the defense might "end in disaster."

While most pleas of guilty consist of both a waiver of trial and an express admission of guilt, the latter element is not a constitutional requisite to the imposition of criminal penalty. An individual accused of crime may voluntarily, knowingly, and understandably consent to the imposition of a prison sentence even if he is unwilling or unable to admit his participation in the acts constituting the crime.

Nor can we perceive any material difference between a plea that refuses to admit commission of the criminal act and a plea containing a protestation of innocence when, as in the instant case, a defendant intelligently concludes that his interests require entry of a guilty plea and the record before the judge contains strong evidence of actual guilt. Here the State had a strong case of first-degree murder against Alford. Whether he realized or disbelieved his guilt, he insisted on his plea because in his view he had absolutely nothing to gain by a trial and much to gain by pleading. Because of the overwhelming evidence against him, a trial was precisely what neither Alford nor his attorney desired. Confronted with the choice between a trial for first-degree murder, on the one hand, and a plea of guilty to second-degree murder, on the other, Alford quite reasonably chose the latter and thereby limited the maximum penalty to a 30-year term. When his plea is viewed in light of the evidence against him, which substantially negated his claim of innocence and which further provided a means by which the judge could test whether the plea was being intelligently entered, its validity cannot be seriously questioned. In view of the strong factual basis for the plea demonstrated by the State and Alford's clearly expressed desire to enter it despite his professed belief in his innocence, we hold that the trial judge did not commit constitutional error in accepting it.

Alford now argues in effect that the State should not have allowed him this choice but should have insisted on proving him guilty of murder in the first degree. The States in their wisdom may take this course by statute or otherwise and may prohibit the practice of accepting pleas to lesser included offenses under any circumstances. But this is not the mandate of the Fourteenth Amendment and the Bill of Rights. The prohibitions against involuntary or unintelligent pleas should not be relaxed, but neither should an exercise in arid logic render those constitutional guarantees counterproductive and put in jeopardy the very human values they were meant to preserve.

The Court of Appeals judgment directing the issuance of the writ of habeas corpus is vacated and the case is remanded to the Court of Appeals for further proceedings consistent with this opinion.

It is so ordered.

DISSENT

Mr. Justice Brennan, with whom Mr. Justice Douglas and Mr. Justice Marshall join, dissenting.

The facts set out in the majority opinion demonstrate that Alford was ''so gripped by fear of the death penalty'' that his decision to plead guilty was not voluntary but was ''the product of duress as much so as choice reflecting physical constraint.''

CASE DISCUSSION

Alford was indicted for the capital offense of first-degree murder. North Carolina law provided for the penalty of life imprisonment when a plea of guilty was accepted to a first-degree murder charge; for the death penalty following a jury verdict of guilty, unless the jury recommended life imprisonment, and for a term of from two to thirty years' imprisonment for second-degree murder. Alford's attorney recommended that Alford plead guilty to second-degree murder, which the prosecutor accepted. Alford pleaded guilty and was sentenced to thirty years in prison. On writ of habeas corpus, the Court of Appeals found Alford's plea involuntary. On writ of *certiorari*, the Supreme Court reversed, holding that the trial judge did not commit constitutional error by accepting the guilty plea.

Did Alford knowingly and voluntarily plead guilty? Consider the dissent's comment that Alford was ''so gripped by fear of the death penalty'' that his decision was ''the product of duress.'' Can defendants ever plead guilty, if they believe they are innocent? Why? Why not?

SUMMARY

Conviction leads to the greatest expenditures of public money and time and to the greatest deprivations to crimial defendants—loss of property, liberty, and occasionally life. Even acquittal does not represent total vindication, and it certainly follows considerable deprivations, as the preceding chapters clearly demonstrate. Conviction or acquittal may follow the formal public trial that emphasizes adversary fact-finding, procedural regularity, and community participation. Conviction may also ensue from informal plea negotiation or straight guilty pleas. Negotiated pleas can reflect the search for truth through informal fact-gathering, efficiency, predictability, and organizational harmony.

The trial adheres to formal and strictly prescribed procedures to present evidence, challenge it, and assess its truth. Judges preside over trials, and lawyers present the physical evidence and examine the witnesses. Judges decide the law in the case, and also the facts in bench trials. Juries decide the facts in jury trials. The jury's guilty or not guilty verdict embodies its decision regarding the truth or falsity of the facts. Jury selection aims to enpanel an impartial cross-section of the community, although not necessarily a mirror reflection. Juries are biased in favor of older, estalished elements in the population.

Most convictions do not result from trials. Some defendants enter straight guilty pleas, either because they want to admit their guilt, or because the government's case leaves them no alternative. Others plead guilty following plea negotiations. In negotiations, both the government and defendants concede something. Negotiations sometimes arise out of the desire to maintain harmonious relations within the courtroom work group. Sometimes, the weakness of the government's case encourages negotiated pleas. In addition, the pressures of heavy caseloads contribute to by-passing formal proceedings in the name of efficiency and managing scarce resources. Finally, negotiations are more predictable than trials.

The guilty plea depends on defendants giving up their rights to trial, to confront the witnesses against them, and against self-incrimination. Nevertheless, the Supreme Court has held plea bargaining constitutional on the ground that defendants can waive their constitutional rights. The Court has also recognized it as a necessity in modern criminal justice in dealing with heavy caseloads.

The trial and guilty plea bring together all the major themes and represent the last decision point in criminal procedure. They constitute the greatest expenditures of public resources, and the greatest deprivations to individual defendants. The highest quantum of proof—proof beyond a reasonable doubt—must support the decision to convict. Conviction proceeds along both formal and informal lines. The trial, the negotiated plea, and the straight guilty plea promote the legal interests in obtaining the correct result and procedural regularity and the organizational interest in harmony, efficiency, economy, and predictability. They also reflect the societal interests in controlling both government and crime. Finally, the criminal trial jury represents *par excellence* the democratic interest in community participation in criminal justice administration.

═══ QUESTIONS FOR REVIEW AND DISCUSSION

1. Compare and contrast the interests promoted by conviction by plea and trial.
2. What are the arguments against extending the right to jury trial to *all* criminal cases?
3. What are the arguments for and against twelve-member juries? six-member juries; fewer than six-member juries?

4. What are the arguments for and against unanimous jury verdicts?

5. Define jury nullification. What are the reasons for and against it?

6. Why is the presentation of evidence the high point in the criminal process?

7. What are the main issues concerning the advantages and disadvantages of guilty pleas?

8. Distinguish between straight and negotiated guilty pleas.

9. Why do defendants enter straight guilty pleas?

10. What rights to defendants forfeit when they plead guilty?

11. Can defendants voluntarily plead guilty if they believe they are innocent? Explain.

≡ NOTES

1. *Duncan v. Louisiana*, 391 U.S. 145, 88 S.Ct. 1444, 20 L.Ed.2d 491 (1968).

2. *Duncan v. Louisiana*, 391 U.S. 145, 88 S.Ct. 1444, 20 L.Ed.2d 491 (1968).

3. Ibid.

4. *Baldwin v. New York*, 399 U.S. 66, 90 S.Ct. 1886, 26 L.Ed.2d 437 (1970) (offenses punishable by less than six months imprisonment are petty offenses); *United States v. Sanchez-Meza*, 547 F.2d 461 (9th Cir. 1976) (conspiring to deceive immigration officials); *United States v. Craner*, 652 F.2d 23 (9th Cir. 1981) (driving while intoxicated); *State v. Superior Court*, 121 Ariz. 174, 589 P.2d 48 (1978) (shoplifting).

5. *Thompson v. Utah*, 170 U.S. 343, 18 S.Ct. 620, 42 L.Ed. 1061 (1898) (12 member jury required); *Williams v. Florida*, 399 U.S. 78, 90 S.Ct. 1893, 26 L.Ed.2d 446 (1970) (upholding Florida's six-member jury in criminal traials).

6. *Williams v. Florida*, 399 U.S. 78, 90 S.Ct. 1893, 26 L.Ed.2d 446 (1970).

7. For references to several social science studies that support the twelve-member jury, see Wayne R. Lafave and Jerold Israel, *Criminal Procedure*, vol. 2 (St. Paul: West Publishing Company, 1984), 695–97; Zeisel quote in note 57, paeg 696.

8. *Maxwell v. Dow,* 176 U.S. 581, 20 S.Ct. 448, 44 L.Ed. 597 (1900) (unanimous verdict required); *Apodaca v. Oregon,* 406 U.S. 404, 92 S.Ct. 1628, 32 L.Ed.2d 184 (1972) (unanimous verdict not constitutionally required, quote from that opinion).

9. 406 U.S. 356, 92 S.Ct. 1620, 32 L.Ed.2d 152 (1972).

10. Lafave and Israel, *Criminal Procedure*, 2:698.

11. *Burch v. Louisiana*, 441 U.S. 130, 99 S.Ct. 1623, 60 L.Ed.2d 96 (1979).

12. Quoted in Lafave and Israel, *Criminal Procedure*, 2:700.

13. *Sparf and Hansen v. United States*, 156 U.S. 51, 15 S.Ct. 273, 39 L.Ed. 343 (1895).

14. *United States v. Dougherty*, 473 F.2d 1113 (D.C.Cir. 1972).

15. David E. Rosenbaum, "North Jurors See Him as a Scapegoat for Superiors," *New York Times*, May 6, 1989, and Stephen Engleberg, "The North Verdict," *New York Times*, May 7, 1989.

16. 28 U.S.C.A. §§ 1861, 1862.

17. Lafave and Israel, *Criminal Procedure*, 2:708.

18. Ibid., 708–9.

19. J. Van Dyke, *Jury Selection Procedures* (1977), 140.

20. *Ham v. South Carolina*, 409 U.S. 524, 93 S.Ct. 848, 35 L.Ed.2d 46 (1973).

21. *Dukes v. Waitkevitch,* 536 F.2d 469 (1st Cir. 1976), cert. denied 429 U.S. 932, 97 S.Ct. 340, 50 L.Ed.2d 302 (1976); *Turner v. Murray,* 106 S.Ct. 1683 (1986) (questioning about racial bias in capital cases involving black defendants and white victims).

22. *United States v. Dennis,* 183 F.2d 201 (2d Cir. 1950), affirmed 341 U.S. 494, 71 S.Ct. 857, 95 L.Ed. 1137 (1951).

23. *United States ex. rel. Latimore v. Sielaff,* 561 F.2d 691 (7th Cir. 1977), cert. denied 434 U.S. 1076, 98 S.Ct. 1266, 55 L.Ed.2d 782 (1978).

24. *Illinois v. Allen,* 397 U.S. 337, 90 S.Ct. 1057, 25 L.Ed.2d 353 (1970).

25. *Holbrook v. Flynn,* 475 U.S. 560, 106 S.Ct. 1340, 89 L.Ed.2d 525 (1986) (defendant brought to trial under guard); *Estelle v. Williams,* 425 U.S. 501, 96 S.Ct. 1691, 48 L.Ed.2d 126 (1976) (appearing in prison garb prejudiced defendant).

26. *In re Winship,* 397 U.S. 358, 90 S.Ct. 1068, 25 L.Ed.2d 368 (1970).

27. Cases follow in order of definitions: *United States v. Jones,* 663 F.2d 567 (5th Cir. 1981); *United States v. DeVincent,* 632 F.2d 147 (1st Cir. 1980); *Tsoumas v. New Hampshire,* 611 F.2d 412 (1st Cir. 1980); *State v. Butler,* 277 S.C. 452, 290 S.E.2d 1 (1982); *Commonwealth v. Conceicao,* 388 Mass. 255, 446 N.E.2d 383 (1983); reversals, *State v. Moss,* 189 Conn. 364, 456 A.2d 274 (1983); *United States v. Regilio,* 669 F.2d 1169 (7th Cir. 1981).

28. *United States v. Werbrouck,* 589 F.2d 273 (7th Cir. 1978).

29. Lafave and Israel, *Criminal Procedure,* 3:12.

30. *People v. McClellan,* 71 Cal.2d 793, 80 Cal. Rptr. 31, 457 P.2d 871 (1969).

31. *Bowles v. United States,* 439 F.2d 536 (D.C.Cir. 1970) (unavailable witness).

32. 390 U.S. 129, 88 S.Ct. 748, 19 L.Ed.2d 956 (1968).

33. Lafave and Israel, *Criminal Procedure,* 3:15.

34. 448 U.S. 56, 100 S.Ct. 2531, 65 L.Ed.2d 597 (1980).

35. American Bar Association, *Standards for Criminal Justice,* § 3.5 (2d ed. 1980).

36. *Dunlop v. United States,* 165 U.S. 486, 17 S.Ct. 375, 41 L.Ed. 799 (1897).

37. Lafave and Israel, *Criminal Procedure,* 3:35.

38. Recent radio news story on Minnesota Public Radio; also see LaFave and Israel, *Criminal Procedure,* 3:36, same effect.

39. Lafave and Israel, *Criminal Procedure,* 3:39–40.

40. *Allen v. United States,* 164 U.S. 492, 17 S.Ct. 154, 41 L.Ed. 528 (1896) (origin of the *Allen* charge); *State v. Marsh,* 260 Or. 416, 490 P.2d 491 (1971) (modern *Allen* charge).

41. *State v. Marsh,* ibid., surveys these and many other arguments against the *Allen* charge and includes several variations on it. In its decision, the Oregon Supreme Court prohibited its further use on the ground that it created more problems than it solved.

42. 397 U.S. 742, 90 S.Ct. 1463, 25 L.Ed.2d 747 (1970).

43. *Blackledge v. Allison,* 431 U.S. 63, 71, 97 S.Ct. 1621, *1627,* 52 L.Ed.2d 136 (1977).

44. The guilty plea literature is vast. *Law and Society Review* 13, no. 2 (1979), a special issue devoted entirely to some of the plea bargaining issues contains some of the best social science research and public policy debate surrounding it.

45. *Brady v. United States,* 397 U.S. 742, 748, 90 S.Ct. 1463, 1469, 25 L.Ed.2d 747 (1970).

46. *Brady v. United States,* 397 U.S. 742, 90 S.Ct. 1463, 25 L.Ed.2d 747 (1970).

47. *Boykin v. Alabama,* 395 U.S. 238, 89 S.Ct. 1709, 23 L.Ed.2d 274 (1969).

48. *North Carolina v. Alford,* 400 U.S. 25, 91 S.Ct. 160, 27 L.Ed.2d 162 (1970); *Federal Criminal Code and Rules,* 1988 Edition, (St. Paul: West Publishing Co., 1988), Rule 11(f) and Commentary, p. 45.

49. *Santobello v. New York,* 404 U.S. 257, 92 S.Ct. 495, 30 L.Ed.2d 427 (1971).

50. *Ricketts v. Adamson,* 483 U.S. 1, 107 S.Ct. 2680, 97 L.Ed.2d (1987) (defendant's broken promise).

Index

Blind
Country
Rules.

Kill.